W
201

M
464

M
88

9

21

5

20

76

M
372

19

M
88

8

Mariana Is.

Marshall Is.

Caroline Is.

19

20

28

21

6

80

9

4

6

2

10

16

Communist Bloc	W World Powers
Anti - Communist Bloc	M Other Major States
Neutralist Group	Other Independent States have dot shading only
Trusteeships , Mandates	Population figures in millions 1954 U.N. Demographic Yearbook
Colonies, Dependencies, Protectorates	

World Politics
in Transition

World Politics in Transition

Lennox A. Mills

UNIVERSITY OF MINNESOTA

Charles H. McLaughlin

UNIVERSITY OF MINNESOTA

Henry Holt and Company

NEW YORK

Behold, my son, with how little
wisdom the world is governed.

Count Axel Oxenstjerna, 1583–1654
CHIEF MINISTER TO KING GUSTAVUS ADOLPHUS OF SWEDEN

PREFACE

This book is intended as a text for introductory courses in international relations, and it has been consciously planned with reference to their needs. It is directed toward two classes of students: those who want to understand contemporary world politics but will take no further courses; and those who wish to take a basic course for further specialization in the subject. One principal problem in writing an introductory text is that international relations require an understanding of so many fields of knowledge that it is not easy to steer a course between simplification and unnatural oversimplification. The authors have many memories of beginning students who have been so confused by a meticulously worked out exposition of a topic that they have been unable to distinguish between essentials and lesser details. Yet it is equally possible to "make a complicated subject simpler than God ever intended it to be," as was said of a clever yet unsuccessful general of World War I.

As far as possible, minor details have not been emphasized, in the belief that if a beginning text is made too encyclopedic it militates against the student's acquiring an understanding of the main outlines. We believe that this is adequate for those who want a better understanding of events as they occur, and that it provides the necessary foundation for the students who intend to go further into the subject and will deepen their knowledge as they take more advanced courses. For this reason the usual scholarly apparatus of footnotes has been omitted. Additional readings have been reduced to a number and type such as beginning students might be expected to use. This explains the omission of authors whose works would be essential for advanced students, but which are unsuitable for an elementary course since they presuppose a fair knowledge of the field. Sometimes the views of these writers are mentioned in the text without referring explicitly to them, following the general principle of the book that source references should be avoided. Although we have expressed our opinions about the topics treated, our principal concern has been to open a path into the various fields contributing to the study of international relations rather than to present a philosophical position with regard to the subject. We feel that the authors of an introductory text book should try to explain and clarify and not to urge a point of view. We have therefore attempted to give the student the basic facts which will help him to draw his own conclusions, rather than press our own opinions upon him. We have also tried, consistently with accuracy and thoroughness, to make the book readable and interesting.

Grateful acknowledgments are due to the colleagues in Political Science, History, Economics, and Geography who generously gave their time to read and criticize the manuscript, and to Miss Barbara Fenton of the Department of Geography of the University of Minnesota who drew many of the maps. At this point it is customary to thank the authors' wives because without their encouragement the book would never have been written. A professor in the throes of composition however does not require encouragement: to quote Churchill his book is first a mistress, then a master, then a tyrant, and then just as he has learned how to live with it he finds that he has slain the monster. So we wish to thank our wives for the patience with which they listened to endless discussions of the manuscript, for the shrewdness of their comments, and for the unsparing zeal with which they pointed out obscurities where the authors had fondly believed their writing was perfectly clear.

By permission of *Foreign Affairs* the chapter on Russian policy includes a quotation from an article by Peter Wiles on the Soviet economy that appeared in the issue for July, 1953, and another quotation from an article by Sir Arthur Salter in the issue for January, 1950, is given in the chapter on contemporary economic problems. The *Round Table* quarterly permitted the use of excerpts from an article on Communist tactics of infiltration in the issue of September, 1954. The quotation from Sir Eyre Crowe's Memorandum on the British balance of power policy is taken from *British Documents on the Origin of the War 1898–1914,* Vol. III, edited by G. P. Gooch and H. Temperley, by permission of the Controller of Her Britannic Majesty's Stationery Office. The University of Minnesota allowed the republication of part of a paper on the situation in Southeast Asia which was written for the inter-university conference held at Allerton House, Illinois, in 1954, and the use of materials on the domestic jurisdiction of the United Nations Charter prepared for the Institute on United Nations Charter Review conducted in 1954 by the University's World Affairs Center and Center for Continuation Study. To the Minnesota *Law Review* we are indebted for permission to reproduce in slightly altered form materials on collective security in an article on "Legislative Neutrality in the United States" (April, 1938). The tabulation of international administrative unions before World War I, given in Chapter 15, was taken from Leonard Woolf's pioneer study, *International Government* (1916), with the consent of Coward-McCann, Inc., New York. Permission to use the striking quotation in Chapter 4 from George Bernard Shaw's *The Man of Destiny* (in *Four Plays: Pleasant and Unpleasant . . . the Second Volume, Containing the Four Unpleasant Plays* [1905]) was granted by the Public Trustee and the Society of Authors, London, England.

L.A.M.
C.H.M.

MINNEAPOLIS, MINN.
March 1, 1956

CONTENTS

The Rise and Fall of Fascism

The Growth of Communism

PART 5: MAJOR PROBLEMS OF INTERNATIONAL
         RELATIONS

APPENDIX

INDEX   735

PART 1

THE A B C
OF INTERNATIONAL
RELATIONS

CHAPTER 1

INTERNATIONAL RELATIONS

The lama in Kipling's *Kim* remarked that "Education is excellent if it is the right sort: otherwise it is no earthly use."

It is a fair question to ask under which heading a study of international relations comes. As good an answer as any can be got by examining how the modern word "idiot" acquired its meaning. It is derived from the classical Greek *idiotes*, which originally meant a private person who attended to his own affairs and did not interest himself in any thing else. The Greeks disapproved of one who was so completely wrapped up in himself; it seemed to them so unnatural that they concluded that no man of normal intelligence could behave in such fashion. So *idiotes* came to mean mentally deficient. The events of the last forty years have shown that it is neither wise nor practicable to live the world forgetting, by the world forgot.

It is not possible to escape from the impact of international affairs. One cannot get away from them even at the North Pole: in 1954 the Soviet army announced that some of its parachute troops practiced jumping on the ice floes there. In an age which debates whether the next war will be fought with atom bombs and the one after that with stone clubs, there is a certain melancholy satisfaction in understanding why the world is in such a state, rather than looking upon it as the dispensations of an inscrutable Providence.

Altogether apart from such general speculations, foreign affairs have intruded themselves into domestic politics, and the voter has to have an opinion about them. Should there be a preventive war with Russia? Would a naval blockade of China do any good? Should Quemoy and the Matsus be given up? Was France justified in opposing the re-creation of a German army? Should the United States lower its tariffs to increase international trade? Knowledge is essential if one is to weigh the merits of conflicting courses of action, and in a democracy the citizen ought to have an informed opinion before he supports this policy or that. If he does not, all the talk about democratic control of foreign policy will end in nothing. An ignorant electorate cannot give a wise decision: it will be at the mercy of propaganda or of waves of popular emotion, and both are bad guides in foreign policy. Since World War I far more information has been available than ever before; yet Churchill considered that the best name for World War II was "the unnecessary war." Part of the responsibility for it lay with the peoples of the democratic states who clamored for a policy that played into Hitler's hands.

A first acquaintance with international affairs may well give the impression that they are a Mad Hatter's paradise, without rhyme or reason. The Russian friend and ally of 1945 became the menace of 1948, while the Japanese and German enemies were sought after as allies. Nehru striving for freedom from British rule was an object of sympathy, but Nehru as the prime minister of the Indian republic is a cause of irritation. In reality these changes are perfectly reasonable, if one has the key to them. To a minor extent there is the element of pure chance: the wartime agreements with Russia, which helped her to win control over the European satellite states, were made in part because President Roosevelt badly misread the character and intentions of Stalin. But in general events rarely happen by accident: they are produced by causes operating in the background, and these can be dissected and understood. To do so is not easy; but it is worth while.

The principal source of information for day to day events is the foreign news columns in a reliable newspaper. One can follow them with far more understanding if one has studied the underlying causes, and applies them to the items one reads. Like everything else the ability to do this grows with practice. One purpose of this book is to help the reader to understand his newspaper better. In time too he will be able to prophesy coming events, at least as accurately as the average radio commentator or columnist. This does not mean that he can peer years into the future. In a far more settled age when events moved more slowly, Bismarck said that it was possible to look ahead ten years. The foreseeable future today is much shorter than that, and one cannot expect to be able to foretell the exact date when some event will take place. Even a minister for foreign affairs, with all his sources of information, is frequently unable to do this. It is possible, however, to be sure in a general way that causes known to be operating will sooner or later produce certain results.

FACTORS IN FOREIGN AFFAIRS

The basic factors affecting international relations are not mysterious, though they are complicated. The starting point of the study must be the sovereign state. International relations are the relations between sovereign states, and it is necessary to have a clear idea of their nature and powers. There is no outside authority which has the legal right to limit their freedom of action, except insofar as they voluntarily accept obligations to other states, e.g., by treaties or membership in the United Nations. If the sovereign state chooses to flout its obligations and encroach on the rights of other states, there is no way of checking it unless it is opposed by states stronger than itself. Throughout history the sovereign state has tended strongly to be a law unto itself, and the principal restraints upon it have been sometimes a self-imposed moderation in striving for its own interests, and more often a fear that other states would take action against it. This tendency of the sovereign state to think only of its own interests has been strengthened by the growth of nationalism—the strongest force in the world today. It influences profoundly the policy of every state, and it is impossible to understand international affairs unless one remembers that nationalism is a modern religion, and that national interests come ahead of all others—first, last, and most of the time. Nationalism has two phases, political and economic, and one is as important as the other. On the political side are such aspects as the defense of independence, and the cult of patriotism. Economic nationalism includes the whole process of trying to increase national power and prosperity through increased production. It involves problems such as free trade versus protection, convertibility of currencies, and the desirability of foreign markets. It is impossible to understand international relations without a background knowledge of economics, especially in matters of production and foreign trade. In the long run the question of whether capitalism or communism will win the cold war will depend in large degree on whether the West can maintain its superiority in rate of economic growth. If the Soviet bloc should be able to surpass the West in material power and a higher standard of living, capitalism would lose through its inability to compete.

As long as the world is made up of sovereign states, power will continue to be essential to their existence. An aggressor must be powerful in order to compel other states to give in to its demands, and nations which only wish to be let alone (often called peace-loving or satiated states) must be strong enough to defend themselves against an aggressor. If ever there is an effective world government, it too will need power in order to maintain its authority. The United Nations (U.N.) could not have saved South Korea from conquest unless its members had lent it the military strength needed for this purpose. There is a very real sense in which international relations are power politics. Undoubtedly it is an outstanding factor, and the contemporary world cannot be understood unless one comprehends its importance. The most obvious element of power is the armed forces of the state, and war is the supreme example of its exercise. There is no need to labor this point on a continent which is building a chain of radar stations inside the Arctic Circle 3000 miles across Alaska and northern Canada at a cost of $1,000,000,000. This leads to the topic of the attempts to limit or forbid recourse to war as an instrument of national power and includes an examination of the disarmament conferences held during the past half century plus the reasons for their failure. Such in-

quiry should help in evaluating the probable effectiveness of the attempt
which the United Nations is still making to control atomic and other weapons. Another element of power is alliances, such as those of the Soviet bloc
and the North Atlantic Treaty Organization. There is also the technique
known as the balance of power policy. This has been used again and again
in the history of the Western world to curb the power of a strong aggressor
by forming an alliance of the states which feel themselves threatened. Political warfare is a weapon of national power which has been used increasingly
since World War I. Its employment is not confined to any one state, but its
best known and most successful practitioner has been Soviet Russia. Political
warfare uses all the methods short of armed force which have been employed during the period of the cold war. Amongst them are propaganda,
fifth columns, sabotage and espionage.

Geography has an important influence: whether a nation can be a great
power today was largely determined in past geologic ages when mineral deposits were formed. One basic reason why the United States and Russia are
superpowers is that both have developed steel manufacturing on a very large
scale, using their resources of coal and iron, which are greater than those of
any other state. Steel plants are potential war plants, and the ability to equip
large armed forces is a basic element in national strength. Geography too is
very influential in determining the policies which each state tries to follow.
During the nineteenth century isolation was the obvious American policy,
since the country was protected from invasion by an ocean on each side, and
the national interest was to concentrate on the development of natural resources. Demography cannot be neglected: to give an illustration, if the
population of Asia continues to increase faster than its food supply, as it
threatens to do, this may help the Communists in the cold war. Asians want
to raise their low standard of living; but if more and more people have to
eat less and less food, their discontent may lead them to follow Communist
leaders who assure them that Russia has solved all economic problems. Imperialism is not dead: it has merely migrated from the traditional colonial
powers to Russia and perhaps China. Nehru's policy toward Kashmir makes
one suspect that Pakistan may be right when it talks of "Hindu imperialism." A very important legacy of European imperialism is the revolt of Asia
against Western control, and the way in which this is being exploited by Russia and China in the global struggle for power.

Ideology cannot be ignored in an age when virtually every people
on earth except the Eskimos include a number of Communists. Part of the
reason why the imperialism of Soviet Russia is a greater menace than was that
of Nazi Germany is that the first has an international appeal while the second
did not. Hitler was the incarnation of nationalism: he preached the superiority of the German people and their right to rule over other nations. In this

way he was able to obtain the cooperation of Germans living abroad, but his fifth columns contained few foreign nationals except those who had been bribed to support him. The Communist fifth columns are composed of nationals of the state in which they operate. With a few exceptions, like Tito of Yugoslavia, they have acquired what one might call a Russian patriotism, and are ready to sacrifice the interests of their own country to those of Russia. Most of them have not been bribed or blackmailed into turning traitor. Some do it from motives of ambition, hoping that when Russia wins the global war they will become the rulers of their country. A large number, however, work for the triumph of Moscow because they are convinced that its success means a better and happier world for the mass of the population. Consider the number of eminent physicists who have believed that in betraying their countries' atomic secrets they were working for the best interests of humanity. When one turns to the underdeveloped countries of Asia, one finds that communism has an economic as well as an ideological appeal. In a generation Russia has changed from an underdeveloped agricultural state to an industrialized great power. To Asians who want to raise their standard of living quickly, communism seems to offer a short cut to greater prosperity. Before one can comprehend the nature of the cold war one must understand the Communist creed, and why it appeals to Westerners and Asians alike.

Nazism and fascism were also ideologies, and they cannot be written off as ancient history that ended in 1945. There are neo-Nazi and neofascist parties in Germany and Italy today, and one of the present uncertainties is whether they will grow stronger or will be defeated by democracy. Totalitarianism as a principle of government is older than democracy, and one tends to forget that the large majority of the states of the world are dictatorships. Nazism and fascism were merely recent forms of a governmental system which is as old as history. They were as hostile to democracy as to communism, and their ideas had influence outside Germany and Italy. Franco Spain shows that it is possible to be fascist without being Italian.

The cold war is in part a struggle for the minds of men. Since thought leads to action, it is of vital importance what belief they adopt. The ideological weapon of the West is democracy, and it is necessary to understand its meaning, its strength, and its weakness. Why is it for instance that the Communist attacker has a fiery zeal that is often lacking in the democratic defender? Is it the old story that the new doctrine, communism, has the psychological advantage that it must attack to win, and that this gives its supporters a crusading fanaticism that is lacking in the democrats who have the comfortable feeling that their battle was won over a century ago? Why is it again that the Communist dictatorship does not repel many Asians as it does Americans?

Diplomacy includes how a government formulates its policies, the influence of public opinion upon it, and the methods by which it tries to carry them out through negotiations with foreign governments. The same technique is often used for the settlement of disputes, and many wars have been avoided by successful diplomacy. International law has also played quite an important part in peacefully settling quarrels between states. Like diplomacy it has its limitations, however, and neither is a panacea for all the world's troubles.

Internationalism is a potent factor in foreign affairs. In the past its supporters were unduly optimistic and underestimated the strength of opposing forces, particularly nationalism. They were defeated by the hard facts of international life, and this reaction from unjustified hopes has created a tendency to minimize the importance of internationalism. The truth lies somewhere between the claim that it is a panacea for the world's troubles and the cynicism that it is merely words. Internationalism and nationalism alike have increased in strength, and to date the latter has grown faster than the former. Exceedingly few people feel a loyalty to the whole human race, as they do to their own nation. At the same time the older and wiser states, especially in the West, realize that unbridled nationalism can ruin civilization owing to the vast power that man has acquired through scientific invention. So national policy becomes a blend of national interests and internationalism. One of the problems of the future is to arrange a workable compromise between the two forces. Both are needed, and neither can afford to ignore the other within the foreseeable future. Here one is not concerned with what the situation may be a century from now: it is impossible to look so far ahead. One must take the short view, and part of this book will be concerned with what practicable compromise can be worked out between national interests and international solidarity.

The factors in international affairs already referred to have been global in their character. Every state is influenced by political and economic nationalism, for instance, and at one time or another a good many nations have had imperialistic ambitions. In addition to these general factors, the policies of the great powers are of the highest importance. All of them are distinguished from the lesser states, such as Belgium or Peru, by their far greater material strength. This is evident in any important crisis: the lesser powers can talk about what should be done, but if effective action is to be taken, it has to be the great powers which do most of the work. To a very considerable degree the trend of international affairs is molded by the policies of the great powers, their conflicts, and their friendships. Each of them has its own policies, and they embody the national interests of the state, as interpreted by its government and people. Often they are older than nationalism, the effect of which has been greatly to strengthen the support which the policies are given by the people of the country. American policy is the expression of the American form of nationalism, German policy of German nationalism, and so on. With every country the national interests usually take precedence over considerations of internationalism.

The student who decides to explore more widely the subject of international affairs has a wide range of choice. If his interest lies on the legal and organizational side, he can study international law and organization. The latter deals with such topics as the League of Nations and the United Nations and their agencies, arbitration tribunals, and the World Court. There are courses on American foreign policy, how it is formulated and carried out. Comparative government should not be overlooked: a study of the forms of government and political parties in the democracies and the dictatorships throws light on one fundamental cause of the cleavage between East and West. Underlying all the complicated machinery of legislatures and executives is a basic difference of opinion as to the proper relation between the government and the people. This opens up a wide field of speculation known as political theory. Americans take it for granted that government by the people is the norm, but many Asians and Europeans are sincerely convinced that autocracy is better. It is a good idea to examine the broad principles of government, and arrive at an informed opinion of exactly why one is preferable to another. Then there is imperialism: whatever one thinks of it, there is no denying that it has played and is playing an important role in the world. There is a whole series of more specialized phases of international affairs— South America, the Middle East, South and Southeast Asia, the Far East, and the British Empire. They are all making their contribution to the world of today, and none can be written off as negligible.

The weakness in many books on contemporary events is the lack of background. The writer diligently describes what he observes, but he often misses its real significance because he does not know that it is merely the contemporary phase of something rooted in the past. After all, for nearly two centuries the American view of Britain and the British Empire has been powerfully affected by the ghost of George III. Work in history is an indispensable adjunct to an understanding of the present day. It disabuses the mind of any notion that the past is buried and can be safely ignored. Work in diplomatic, American, European, and Far Eastern history is strongly recommended. Geography cannot be forgotten: it is a most important element in molding the attitude and the policies of a nation. Consider the influence of the frontier on the development of the American character. Marx was wrong when he explained everything in heaven and earth in terms of economics, but no one can understand international relations without a knowledge of production and foreign trade. Cultural anthropology, sociology, and social psychology in recent years have begun to examine the basic motivations and the factors which condition human conduct in many relationships, including foreign affairs—why, for example, the youth of Germany were receptive to Hitlerism, or what are the roots of American isolationism. Much basic research needs to be done in these fields before we can be sure of our ground in analyzing political behavior. Journalism should not be overlooked. It offers courses on international communications, particularly mass communications techniques and the control of them, the foreign press, and public opinion and propaganda. A study of propaganda is a very useful vaccine in a world which is increasingly saturated with it. To sum it all up, an expert is often defined as a man who knows more and more about less and less. This does not apply to international relations: before he can call himself a specialist, the student needs to acquire a firm knowledge of selected phases of Political Science, History, Geography, and Economics, with excursions into Journalism, Sociology, and Anthropology. By that time he will have graduated from a university, and whatever his profession in life, he will have an interest that will keep him more than busy for the rest of his days. One advantage of a college education is to help a student to choose a hobby. There is nothing wrong with say golf or fishing, except that they are seasonal and one may become a monumental bore to one's acquaintances. International affairs does have the advantage that it is everlasting and one never runs out of material.

READINGS ON INTERNATIONAL AFFAIRS

The reader of this book should have a knowledge of the factors which underlie events in the international field. They might be called the keys to the understanding of world politics. It is to be hoped too that the student will have a knowledge of what is happening in the world as of the date at which he takes a course on the subject. Events move so fast, however, that if he stops at that point, in six months he will be absolutely prehistoric. World politics is like an endless carpet where the pattern is always changing and the weaving is never finished. To keep up to date, the student must educate himself. The best way to do it is to read the daily reports of foreign affairs in a reliable newspaper and decide what are the causes that underlie them. A weekly magazine that gives good coverage of international affairs is useful. Publications such as the *Bulletin* of the Foreign Policy Association give impartial and factual accounts of important developments. Longer and more detailed analyses are found in such magazines as *Foreign Affairs*. If a student wishes to go more deeply into any topic, he will find a short list of selected readings following each chapter in this book. Many of the books cited contain bibliographies, and these can be used to obtain a still further knowledge. If it be objected that this is a grim program, the only answer is that there is no short cut to a sound understanding of international affairs.

THE KOREAN CRISIS

Anyone who reads the foregoing may perhaps fear that the connection between these underlying factors and daily news reports is remote, and that world politics should be classed with higher mathematics and archaeology as abstruse subjects which normal people had better avoid. For this reason a case study is given to show how a knowledge of the basic factors can be used to obtain a fuller understanding of international affairs. The Korean war was chosen because it was one of the most important events since World War II. This state of decidedly secondary importance cost the United States 142,091 casualties, of whom 33,629 were killed.

Korea was an ancient but rather weak kingdom. A border state lying between two more powerful neighbors (China and Japan), it was unable to maintain real independence. For centuries it had to some degree been a Chinese dependency, but in 1910 it was annexed by Japan. The state of Chosen, as it was called by the Japanese, occupied a position of considerable strategic importance since it could be a base for the invasion of either Japan or China, and both countries had used it for this purpose. It lay along the road of invasion from Japan to Manchuria, industrially the most developed Chinese province. Finally, it was only 100 miles from the Russian naval base at Vladivostok, and so after World War II it was to the interest of the Soviet Union as well as to Communist China that Korea be brought under Communist control.

The Japanese had developed and exploited the country for their own benefit and made it a valuable prize well worth taking. They had developed important industries in the northern part of Korea, while the southern portion remained predominantly agricultural. Strategically and economically the country was a unit, and any attempt permanently to divide it was artificial. Furthermore the Koreans were strongly nationalistic and very much opposed to the division of their country. By a wartime agreement Russia occupied Korea north of the 38th parallel and the United States the territory to the south of it to disarm the Japanese garrison. This was intended to be a temporary arrangement and was to be followed in due course by the reunion of the whole country under a democratic Korean government. American attempts to carry out the agreement failed, and the military line of demarcation hardened into a political frontier. The Russians organized a government and army controlled by Communists and rejected the U.N. recommendation that free elections be held throughout Korea so that the country could be united under a single government. In 1948 elections were held in South Korea, and the U.N. recognized the result as the national government of the republic of Korea with Syngman Rhee as president. Russia refused recognition and sponsored the "Democratic People's Republic" in North

Korea, which was proclaimed in 1948. In that year the Russian troops withdrew, and the American army left in 1949, with the exception of a military mission which remained to train a South Korean army.

Frequent clashes occurred during 1949 near the 38th parallel between the troops of the two republics, and early in 1950 Syngman Rhee's government warned the U.N. that aggressive plans by North Korea were maturing. The North Korean army was much larger and better armed than that of South Korea. At 4 A.M. on Sunday, June 25, 1950, the northern army attacked in great strength and the outnumbered South Koreans were forced to retreat. It soon became clear that the country would be conquered unless help was sent promptly. Moscow has always charged that the South Koreans were the attackers and that the North Koreans were merely resisting the invasion of "imperialist warmongering American aggressors." Against this can be set the evidence of the U.N. Commission of Observation in South Korea. It reported that the South Korean army was organized for defense and did not have the tanks, aircraft, and heavy artillery necessary for an invasion. The North Korean army was much better equipped, and undertook a well-planned, concerted, and full-scale invasion. The commission also reported that for two years the North Korean regime had been conducting a campaign designed to weaken and destroy Syngman Rhee's government and unite the whole peninsula under its control. The attempt to overthrow the government from within failed, and in 1950 South Korea "improved in economic and political stability." Then came the attempt to conquer the republic by open invasion.

There can be no reasonable doubt that this was a variant of the technique of the "inside job" described in the chapter on Russian foreign policy. There it is explained how Communist dictatorships were created in the present European satellite states by undermining the anticommunist governments through the action of the local Communist parties. As a rule the Russian army did not intervene actively, and the whole maneuver was represented as the spontaneous act of the democratic forces of the country. In Korea the technique was carried a stage further by armed invasion: but here again the Russian army did not move and the attack could be represented as a civil war. Korea was sufficiently important both strategically and economically to make its acquisition by the Communist bloc desirable. Then too, as is pointed out below, the successful conquest of South Korea would have global repercussions and would be a damaging blow to America's position of leadership in the Western world. The exact role of Moscow and Peking is unknown, but it is obvious that they must have been privy to the plans of the North Korean government. It is inconceivable that a second-rate state would have attacked the especial protégé of the United States and flouted the U.N. unless it was assured of the support of the Soviet bloc. It seems quite possible that Moscow did not anticipate armed intervention and expected merely diplomatic protests. American troops had been withdrawn in 1949, and it was known that the army was opposed to any defensive commitments in South Korea. Looking back, it is evident that Russia blundered badly. It provoked the first partially successful attempt to apply collective security, and the revelation of the military weakness of the Western powers frightened them into adopting a policy of intensive rearmament.

The news of the invasion reached Washington on Saturday night, June 24, at 9.26 P.M. President Truman held a hasty conference with his advisers, and at 3 A.M. on Sunday, June 25, he requested an immediate meeting of the U.N. Security Council. It met at 2 P.M. that same day, and by a vote of 9 to 0 adopted an American resolution that called for an immediate withdrawal of the North Korean army to the frontier, and requested all members of the U.N. to give every assistance in carrying out this resolution and to refrain from helping the North Korean government. President Truman had international approval for his announcement of June 26 that he had authorized General MacArthur, the American commander in the Far East, to give South Korea military supplies and assistance. The North Korean army ignored the U.N. resolution and continued its advance, and the U.N. commission in South Korea warned that Syngman Rhee's weak army was in serious danger of being knocked out and the country conquered. On June 27 President Truman announced that he was sending air and sea forces to Korea. The same day the U.N. Council met again and adopted an American resolution requesting all members to assist South Korea. Fifty-three of the fifty-nine U.N. members promised moral support, and a smaller number agreed to give actual assistance. On July 7 the Security Council created a unified command under the U.N. flag and requested the United States to select the commander of the international army. President Truman appointed General MacArthur to the post.

The U.N. Council can take action on a substantive matter (i.e., a matter of special importance or likely to involve member states in collective security actions) only if the majority includes the five great powers. This raises the question why Malik, the Soviet delegate, did not use Russia's veto power and paralyze the Council. The answer is that he was absent, for Russia had been boycotting meetings of the Council since January because it had rejected her resolution to unseat the representative of Nationalist China (Chiang Kai-shek's government on Formosa) and substitute that of the Peking Communist regime. Only Malik's absence made it possible for the U.N. Council to take the action just described. On August 1 he returned to the Council and effectively blocked any further attempts to deal with the Korean question. Moscow also protested that the Council's resolutions were illegal, since the U.N. Council required the concurrence of the five great powers on all substantive proposals. In other words, it claimed that Malik's absence from a meeting had the same effect as a veto. The precedent had already been established, however, that when the representative of a great power was present at a Council meeting but abstained from voting, his abstention did not constitute a veto and so make illegal the Council's action. The U.N. now decided that the absence of the Soviet delegate was equivalent to his abstention from voting and that the Council's resolutions were legal.

The speed with which the Council acted in June when Malik was absent and its inability to do anything after his return illustrated vividly the effect of the cold war on the international organization. The U.N. is not a super-state, but a means for cooperating when the members feel like cooperating. It is a machine which can operate successfully when the members—and especially the great power members—work together. But if they are in downright opposition to one another, as is the case with the Soviet and the Western blocs, their conflict shows itself in the U.N. as in every other phase of international affairs. The Council can then do nothing.

It was fortunate for the future of the United Nations that the Council took prompt action to counter the invasion of South Korea. Russia's earlier use of the veto to prevent action had seriously damaged U.N. prestige in the eyes of the world. If the Council had been unable to proclaim a U.N. war against the aggressor in 1950, the U.N. would have collapsed as the League of Nations did after the Ethiopian fiasco of 1935–1936. It was equally fortunate that the response of the members to the recommendation that they assist South Korea was fairly good. In the Korean war seventeen nations sent troops to the U.N. army, and five more gave medical assistance. This cannot be described as overwhelming support when fifty-three of the fifty-nine U.N. members endorsed the Council's resolutions. Compared with the Ethiopian affair, however, when no effective help whatever was given, it did show that the non-Communist world was willing to go considerably further in support of collective security than it had been fifteen years earlier. To put it bluntly, the nations which sent troops had no vital interests in South Korea which were immediately and directly threatened any more than they had had in Ethiopia in 1935. They gave help partly because they had a genuine desire to support the U.N., and in part because of enlightened self-interest. If aggression succeeded in Korea, the Communists might follow the same policy elsewhere, and it was therefore advisable to show them that such tactics would not succeed. By contrast in the Ethiopian affair the League members failed to realize that if they did not stop Mussolini's invasion, he and Hitler would be encouraged to commit further acts of aggression.

Inevitably the United States provided the large majority of the armed forces. Not only was it by far the most powerful of the Western nations, but since 1945 the other powers had virtually withdrawn from the Far East, leaving to the United States almost a monopoly in the determination of policy. The policy toward Japan after her surrender, the support of Chiang Kai-shek, and the opposition toward the Chinese Communists had largely been made in America, and the other Western powers had had only a minor share in determining them. Traditionally, too, it was Americans who had sympathized with Korea's aspirations for independence, and it was they who had built up the South Korean Republic after its liberation from Japan. The Far East was regarded as primarily an American field of action, and South Korea was everywhere looked upon as an American creation. The North Korean invasion not only menaced America's protégé: it also threatened her position as the leader of the free world against communism. There were lingering doubts how far she would carry her opposition to Russia, remembering the strong American traditions of isolationism and aversion to war. If the United States would not fight for South Korea, it was even less likely to defend the states of Europe and Asia against Communist aggression. There were very many Europeans and Asians in 1950 who wanted to be independent, but who wondered whether resistance to communism would merely make them marked men if the Communists seized control. The temptation was strong to play for safety by joining what they feared would be the winning side. Consequently, they were watching American policy very closely. If the Truman administration had merely protested against the North Korean invasion, the will to resist communism would have been dangerously weakened. In the end this would have had grave consequences for the security of the United States as well as of the other nations. President Truman's firm stand was a serious check to Russian ambitions and notably strengthened American leadership.

The two major powers which assisted the United States were Great Britain and France; but, as already indicated, neither was deeply concerned with the Far East. Britain's vital interests stopped at Singapore about 2700 miles to the south, and in the Far East she had only her colony of Hong Kong and a moderate amount of trade and investment. France's economic stake was far smaller, and neither had ever shown any interest in what happened to Korea. The greater part of the British army was needed for the defense of Germany and the Suez Canal Zone, and the bulk of the remainder was fighting the Chinese Communist revolt in Malaya or protecting Hong Kong, which might have been attacked by China after it entered the war. Subtracting the contingent sent to Korea, the strategic reserve remaining in Great Britain for service anywhere in the world was no more than one single brigade. Nearly half the French long-service professional soldiers were fighting in Indochina, and most of the rest of the troops were needed at home for the defense of France and Western Europe.

The other participants like Australia were minor powers which did not have many soldiers to send. Their limited contingents showed that the lesser states can only make a small contribution to collective security: most of the burden must fall on the major powers. Moreover, the Far East was of marginal concern to most of these minor powers, e.g., Holland or Turkey. The exceptions were Australia, New Zealand, Thailand, and the Philippines, which owing to their geographic proximity had not forgotten the Japanese invasion during World War II and feared lest some time they might again be attacked from the Far East. The only Asian states which did contribute troops were the Philippines, an American ally, and Turkey and Thailand, which fear Communist attack and have given their foreign policy a Western orientation. India and the other states of South Asia and the Middle East approved the U.N.'s support of South Korea, but their active help was limited to a field ambulance. They had limited armed forces; they wished to remain neutral in the cold war; they feared that the West including the United States had imperialistic motives, while at the same time they did not regard Russia as imperialistic; and they had some sympathy for the Chinese as brother Asians. Their attitude is more fully explained in the chapters on the British Commonwealth and on power vacuums.

The North Koreans almost succeeded in occupying the whole peninsula, but in a successful counterattack General MacArthur forced them back to the 38th parallel. This posed the problem for the United Nations whether the army should invade North Korea and reunite the country. The United States pressed for a decision to this effect, but was opposed by India, which feared that China would enter the war if the advance were made. The U.N. Assembly passed a resolution by a large majority which implied approval of crossing the frontier, and the U.N. army continued to advance until it approached the Manchurian border. In November, 1950, China launched a full-scale offensive, and the U.N. army was driven back with heavy losses below the 38th parallel. It fought its way back approximately to the South Korean frontier, but by early 1951 a virtual stalemate had developed. China probably intervened in Korea because of mixed motives. The Communist government looked upon the United States as its most dangerous enemy; it feared that an American base might be established in Korea from which an attack could be made on China; and Chinese imperialism may have welcomed the chance of re-establishing its traditional control over Korea.

Meanwhile twelve Asian-Arab states headed by India tried to arrange a cease fire, but without success. The United States pressed for the U.N. condemnation of China as an aggressor, and on February 1, 1951, the Assembly passed a resolution to this effect by a vote of 44 to 7 with 9 abstentions. India and Burma voted with the Soviet bloc against the resolution, and the rest of the Arab-Asian group abstained from voting. Despite the large majority the vote had disturbing implications. The majority was almost entirely made up of the Western members of the U.N., very few Asian states supporting it.

In other words, a dangerous cleavage was revealed, with the Soviet bloc and the Arab-Asian neutrality group opposing the condemnation of China and the Western states supporting it. This was disquieting since one of the most important contests of the cold war has been the attempts of the West and the Communist powers to win the support of South Asia and the Middle East. In May the Assembly voted in favor of an embargo on the shipment of strategic raw materials to China and North Korea, but the Soviet bloc and some Asian states refused to adhere to it.

Discussions for a cease fire and an armistice began in July, 1951. They dragged on interminably while hostilities continued, but finally a truce was signed on July 27, 1953, at Panmunjom. It was agreed that a final settlement should be arranged at a future conference, but the attempt to achieve this in 1954 failed. So the fighting ended without a definitive treaty of peace. The result of the war was a compromise: neither side attained its full objectives. The United States and the U.N. achieved their original aim: they prevented the Communist conquest of South Korea and showed that it was possible to use the policy of collective security to prevent aggression. On the other hand, the West failed to overthrow the Communist dictatorship of North Korea and unify the whole country. The information available indicates that North Korea is becoming a Chinese satellite. In violation of the truce terms the North Korean air force and army have been strengthened, thereby altering the balance of power between the two halves of the country. Periodically Washington has had to restrain President Syngman Rhee, who has threatened to renew the war. He would have to fight China as well as North Korea, and since the Western powers could not afford to allow South Korea to be defeated, they would have to intervene. A renewal of the Korean war could have incalculable consequences. The blunt truth is that short of a renewal of hostilities the Western powers can do nothing to prevent breaches of the truce agreement, or honor the promise to Syngman Rhee to work toward reunification of the peninsula. Moreover, it seems evident that Asian opinion believes that China prevented the West in general, and the United States in particular, from conquering North Korea and that this has raised Chinese prestige. This is an asset to China in the campaign that the Communists are now waging for the control of South and Southeast Asia.

The Korean armistice of 1953 is linked with the disaster at Dien Bien Phu in Vietnam in 1954, when the whole of a large French garrison was captured by the Vietminh army of the Communist Ho Chi-minh. This defeat was the final blow in an interminable and unsuccessful war which led Mendès-France, the French premier, to make peace with Ho Chi-minh in 1954. The connection between Dien Bien Phu and Korea lies in the matter of armaments. China has limited facilities for their manufacture, and throughout the Korean war her aircraft, tanks, artillery, and trucks were supplied by the states of the Soviet bloc. As long as the fighting continued most of this was needed in Korea, and Chinese assistance to Ho Chi-minh was limited. With the signing of the Korean armistice it was possible to divert to him more and better equipment. One reason for the capture of Dien Bien Phu was that the besiegers used much more powerful artillery than they had previously employed. The French commander in chief had assumed that the equipment of the Vietminh army would be the same as in earlier engagements. Therefore, he placed a French garrison in a position which was untenable if heavily bombarded, and which was at the same time so inaccessible that the siege could not be raised by the main French army. The gamble failed owing to the Korean armistice, and the result was the collapse of French resistance in northern Vietnam.

This analysis of the Korean war is a typical example of how to study international affairs. The factors involved were complex, but they could be sorted out and the parts they played in influencing events identified. Geography explained the economic and strategic reasons why Korea was important to several states. Ideology came in, as a partial explanation of the actions of China and Russia. The part played by the U.N. showed both what it might become in international affairs and the severe limitations upon its effectiveness as long as East and West were deadlocked in the cold war. One outstanding feature was the great importance of the policies and national interests of the different states, Western, Communist, and neutral, in determining their attitude. The whole episode gave a practical illustration of what was said earlier in this chapter about the sovereign state as the basic element in international affairs, and particularly of the observation that if it chose to break its international obligations it could not be restrained except by a combination of states stronger than itself. Putting it another way, the war showed that the role of force was an inescapable factor in international affairs.

CHAPTER 2

THE SOVEREIGN STATE IN THE INTERNATIONAL COMMUNITY

THE FOCUS OF INTERNATIONAL RELATIONS

The study of modern international relations has traditionally been the study of relations among national states. Why should this be so? Is it not obvious that men are themselves the primary units of activity and that as individuals they can enter into relationships with other men, whatever their race, language, or residence, always assuming that facilities for communication exist? There is, indeed, a sense in which one might study international relations without much attention to the political-social units which we call states, concentrating upon personal relationships. International trade might be examined in this way, with emphasis upon business organization, contracts of sale, and transportation of goods. Foreign travel, or exploration, or emigration, or missionary activity might be considered mainly in personal terms.

In earlier days the freedom of individuals to move about and enter into individual international relationships was even greater. As late as 1914 one could still wander over all of Europe without a passport, freely crossing frontiers. With very little formality one could go to another country for permanent residence. The movement of commerce, sharply controlled in eighteenth-century mercantilism, was relatively free in the nineteenth century, although of course subject to tariffs, mainly for revenue purposes. Even during the Napoleonic wars the British fed goods into the continent through English ports, using the revenue to finance the war. However, one would have to go back to a period before the development of modern national states to find complete freedom to carry goods into another country and there to sell and buy without restriction. At a still earlier date, when feudal conditions prevailed and there was little central governmental control, even the field of warfare was not closed to individuals, and private wars among dukes, earls, or barons were common. Legal treatises of that day drew a distinction between public and private war, and deduced a number of legal consequences from it. There was even a day when standards of gentility appeared to require that one should sally forth as a knight errant, weighted down with buckler, lance, and sword, to pick a fight with any other irresponsible warrior who could be found.

To recall these things is enough to emphasize in what a different age we now live. Certain fields, such as warfare and diplomacy, are wholly closed to individual enterprise. Thus the Logan Act of 1799 made it a criminal offense for a private citizen of the United States to undertake without authorization to negotiate with a foreign government. States invariably have professional diplomatic services for this purpose. And it has long been a requirement of international law that states shall restrain their more impulsive nationals from organizing filibustering, i.e., private military expeditions against other states or their nationals. In the field of foreign trade many states encourage private enterprise, but only within a framework of legal control and regulation by the state, which regularly includes tariffs, export and import quotas, exchange controls, licensing arrangements, subsidies, and may extend on occasion to embargo or boycott—the whole regulatory system being designed to direct private enterprise into those areas considered to be consistent with the public policy of the state.

Private travel is now subject in most countries to close scrutiny. Some individuals find that they cannot obtain exit permits because their political opinions are thought to be subversive and their connections with unfriendly countries dangerous. Passports and visas are almost always required. Resident aliens may be required to report at intervals to government officers. Many states place sharp restrictions upon the right of aliens to enter for permanent residence or to acquire nationality by naturalization. And almost without exception large states not only reserve the right of warfare to governmental decision, but put themselves into a posture of defense (or aggression) by maintaining military forces, producing weapons, stockpiling strategic materials, and securing alliances. In doing so they greatly affect the private lives of their citizens: some are drafted for military service; all are taxed heavily to support the military establishment, pay for weapons research and production, buy needed supplies, and send economic and military aid to allies. The whole national economy is attuned to military production.

Even in the United States, where great importance is attached to individual liberty and free enterprise, it is clear that the area of governmental control has greatly expanded because the conditions of international relations today place more and more pressure upon free enterprise states to regulate production and control private activity in order to assure the security of the state. But we have also to take account of the fact that there is a growing bloc of states in which free enterprise is not even regarded as a significant social value. Communist states closely control industrial production and make efforts of varying intensity to collectivize agricultural production. Their foreign trade is conducted by public bureaus or trading corporations and usually consists in governmental bartering of exports for commodities more essential to whatever type of production their governments choose to emphasize. Their nationals rarely go abroad unless in official capacities or as refugees, and they are wholly prohibited from expatriating themselves or acquiring a foreign nationality. Nor are aliens freely admitted to Communist states or permitted to travel there. Even diplomats are commonly confined to the national capitals. Finally, we should bear in mind that great areas which have for several centuries been colonial possessions of European states have recently attained their independence. This has often meant an immediate increase of governmental control of private activities and invariably a whole new set of public international relationships.

Considering these facts, one can only conclude that the focus of international relationships has not for a long time been primarily, and in recent years has been less and less, at the private level. Such private international activity as is permitted is shaped by state regulation to consistency with state policy. And the scope of private activities as a whole has diminished in the face of state enterprise, both domestic and external.

But does it follow that because individual activity is not the focus of international relations that state activity must be? Is it not true that there has also been an immense growth of activity by international organizations? It is true, and no study of international relations which failed to give attention to this activity could be complete. Dozens of international organizations exist. Some, like the United Nations or the Universal Postal Union, have general memberships; others, like the Organization of American States or the Arab League, are regional associations. Some have multiple functions, including political consultation and collective security; others perform a single function, usually in the field of economic or social regulation. All together encompass a very broad range of international services which a hundred years ago either were not available at all or had to be specially arranged through diplomatic negotiations. Why can we not say, then, that the true focus of international relations lies at the international level, in the work of these international organizations?

We cannot say it for the very reason that they are truly "inter-national." They function not above but between or among states. Although they possess what is called international legal personality, they were created by international agreement among states as instruments of collective state action. Just as an individual state may create a government corporation (e.g., the Tennessee Valley Authority) and endow it with legal personality so that it may perform a particular governmental function, so a group of states may by treaty create such a corporate entity as the United Nations to perform a set of functions which are of value to the whole group. It too is given a separate legal personality, but it does not become a state. Since it was created by an agreement of states, it could be discontinued by them, or any one of them could withdraw from the association. What is perhaps even more important, it has no independent means of action; its policy decisions are simply the decisions reached in common by the representatives of its member states. It may with much truth be said that a modern international organization is just a permanently organized diplomatic round table, with a secretariat to do its preparatory work and carry out some of its decisions. In most cases it cannot act at all, but can only recommend action to the member states, which may follow the recommendation or not in their own discretion.

It may be urged that although international organizations are created as state instrumentalities, the fact that they possess a distinct legal personality and are not subject to direct control by any single state will lead them inevitably to consolidate their position and increase their powers until, with the support or sufferance of individuals throughout the world, they do become an independent layer of government superimposed upon states and not responsible to them. Perhaps—but at present international organizations of that type exist only in the dreams of World Federalists. As this book is concerned with the realities of the present and the probabilities of the foreseeable future, it must deal with international organizations as it finds them —not the masters but the creatures of state policy, often enough rendered nearly impotent by the unwillingness of states to collaborate.

It is then the national state which for good or ill must be the focus of international relations study. To say this is not at all to exclude other factors from consideration. For what is a national state but a political community of individuals associated by such cultural ties as race, language and literature, history, religion, and the like, who inhabit a particular area having special geographic, economic, and strategic characteristics, and who are subject to a government of which the internal organization and external demeanor may reflect all these and perhaps other factors? To discuss the relations of modern states in any terms likely to illuminate their conduct is therefore to discuss all these factors, a thing which might not have been necessary before the French Revolution, when states were still governed by dynastic policy and the sense of national union among the populace was weaker. But let us begin our discussion with some peculiar characteristics of statehood itself.

THE RISE OF MODERN STATES

The term "state" is a modern one, having entered political literature with Machiavelli's use of it in *The Prince* (1523). As the "national state" has been the characteristic type throughout the post-Renaissance era the adjective is almost redundant, although sanctioned by common usage. What we now call the city state of the Greeks and early Romans was by the Greeks termed simply *polis,* or city. The Latin word *civitas* had at first the same connotation, although when states came to include one or more cities and surrounding territory the term *urbs* was used for city. Later Roman usage favored the term *respublica* (from which our word "republic"), the sense of which might be nearly conveyed by "commonwealth." It was from the phrase *status rei publicae* (the public domain) that "state" was derived.

We have no occasion to review the history of the city as a form of polity. No doubt emphasis upon it by the ancient Greeks merely reflected a particularism imposed by the conditions of Hellenic geography, for large territorial states were common in the Middle East in that era. Later, Rome passed through every stage from a city state to a vast empire. Nor need we give attention to the peculiar political institution of feudalism which prevailed in Europe from about the ninth to the thirteenth century, except to note certain legacies it bequeathed to the modern state. There was never, as has often been said, a feudal system; feudalism was rather the common factor in an infinite variety of local institutions. Its essential feature was the use of land tenures as a basis for political obligation. The tenant held his land of the lord not upon payment of money rent, although this was not unknown, but for services to and defense of the lord. And the lord in turn, if of low degree, say a knight, held under a baron to whom he owed service, and the baron of the earl, and the earl of the duke, and the duke of the king. Thus a hierarchy of rights was founded upon tenure in the land, but no one in the succession "owned" the land in the modern sense of that term. If the king or a lesser lord engaged in war he formed his forces by feudal levy, i.e., he simply called upon his tenants who owed military service as an obligation of tenure and they in turn called upon their tenants. This indeed is an oversimplification, for feudalism also involved personal relationships which might give rise to obligations. Certain obligations, however, adhered to the land itself as servitudes upon it; if the Lord did not obtain performance of them from his tenants, he would himself be obligated, for the tenement itself was burdened with these services. It was even possible for a tenant who held lands from two or more lords to find he owed military service to lords at war with each other. In time the system gave rise also to a conception of territorial jurisdiction, in that the lord undertook to do justice among tenants of the land. Obligations of personal loyalty of vassal to lord became grafted upon the tenure system with some resulting confusion of the basis of political obligation. Yet there was no absolute authority, and no state. The king and the intermediate lords possessed *dominium* (dominion), i.e., they shared in a hierarchy of interests in the same land, none having a complete interest. The king's right was not different in character from the lord's; his position was superior only in that he was at the top of the proprietary heap, without obligation to an overlord, and that his proprietary rights ran to fiefs throughout the kingdom. As a feudal lord he was superior but not absolute, for his rights were only those arising from his tenures.

When modern states emerged, the transition from the system of feudal tenures was accomplished by elimination of intermediate tenants. Thus in England after the statute *Quia Emptores* (Stat. Westminster III [18 Edw. I. c. 1; A.D. 1290]) subinfeudation (i.e., the granting of part or all of a feudal estate to a subtenant) was prohibited, for a conveyance of land was made to result in the grantee's holding of the grantor's lord. In time the politico-proprietary interests came to be concentrated in the king, the lords no longer possessed *dominium* but only property, and tenants either owned their land or paid money rent without political services. Thus political authority moved upward to the king, property rights downward to the tenants. For the first time there was a single situs of political authority in the crown, i.e., the state. The tenure system of feudalism was destroyed, but the habitual sense of personal loyalty and obligation to the lord continued and, with the elimination of intermediate lords, was transferred exclusively to the crown. Henceforth, even though freeholders, men were subjects of the crown and owed allegiance thereto. On the other hand, the feudal tradition of a political authority limited by law was not lost but reappeared in the theory of limited sovereignty.

The political counterpart of these legal changes was the long and ultimately successful struggle of the kings with the feudal nobility, which is not to be understood merely as the personal victory of strong leaders. Kings eventually won the baronial wars because they represented the principle of central government while the baronage represented feudal disintegration. The conditions of the period required stronger government than feudal lords could supply. The restraining influence of a universal church was no longer effective and the church itself was divided, the growth of trade and development of private property required more effective administration of justice, better transport and communications. Opening of new worlds demanded governmental initiative and support. As central governments increasingly provided better governmental services than feudal lords could offer, the affections of the populace shifted to them, a shift coincident with growing homogeneity and sense of nationality.

In terms of international relations the strong states posed difficulties.

Feudalism had been in some sense a universal, albeit sadly ineffective, system of public law. Its legal tenets discountenanced arbitrary political power, and as a political institution it produced such actual diffusion of power that excesses were improbable. In the background were the universal systems of Roman law, the Germanic Holy Roman Empire, and the Church, to which appeal could be made. But the national state emerged at a time when the universality of Christendom was crumbling before the forces of the Reformation, and notions of universal law based upon natural law were giving way to the positivism of national legal systems. What was to restrain the strong national sovereign from arbitrary and irresponsible conduct toward neighboring states? This was the problem which perplexed Grotius, shocked by the barbarous excesses of the Thirty Years War at the beginning of the seventeenth century. His answer was an effort to construct a new system of international law capable of regulating the conduct of states. It must be said, however, that at no time since has the world been wholly free from disturbances by irresponsible governments, and despite some progress the problem is with us still.

GENERAL CHARACTER OF THE STATE

In modern usage the term "state" is so loosely and variously employed, frequently as synonymous with "country," "nation," "society," "government," or collective action generally as distinguished from individual action, that it is necessary to clarify the sense in which it is used here—which is the usage of political science, international relations, and international law. In these disciplines the term "state" signifies the institutional form for political purposes of a society territorially delimited. Any society will develop within itself many types of institutions—churches, business associations, labor organizations, cultural or educational groups—which perform particular functions for a part of the society. The state is also an institution but must be distinguished from all other institutions in that it includes the whole population and has the capacity to regulate all other institutions. The extent to which it in fact does so will depend upon its ideology: communist and other "totalitarian" states, for example, have attempted a maximum absorption of social functions and a corresponding elimination or curtailment of other institutions.

As an institution the state is a concept, i.e., a set of legal and political relationships not visible to the eye. However, it has physical attributes which are perfectly visible, and it is therefore usual to define the state in terms of these attributes. Thus it can be said that a state is a political entity which possesses (a) permanent population, (b) defined territory, (c) a government capable of enforcing its regulations. For purposes of international law or relations we are more narrowly concerned with those states which have

(d) capacity to enter into relations with other states. Perhaps none of these attributes can be stated in terms quite so absolute without excluding from statehood communities which are in common usage regarded as states. To this point we shall return presently.

Certain distinctions should be emphasized. A nation is not the same thing as a state although the terms are confused in popular usage. There is reason for this, since the original notion of a nation as an ethnic group, based upon racial or linguistic homogeneity, will no longer (if it ever did) suffice. The peoples of the United States, or Switzerland, or Belgium in each case constitute a nation. The United States is a hotchpotch in terms of ethnic origins, although language minorities seem not very durable. In Switzerland there are several races and several languages; in Belgium Flemish and Walloons speak dialects of Low German and French respectively. Yet they are nations because the peoples occupying these defined territories do think and feel, despite local differences, as single peoples. These feelings arise from a complex of factors including common cultural and political experiences. In some cases ethnically and linguistically diverse stocks living together in a given area achieve this cultural and spiritual affinity; in other cases they do not. Probably the Austro-Hungarian Empire as it existed before World War I, although clearly a state, could not be called a single nation, for its numerous peoples retained strong separatist feelings and had not developed sufficient homogeneity to wish to live together as one people. Today, partly as a result of the emergence of new states formed upon the principle of national self-determination, and partly as a result of assimilation of national minorities, the boundaries of state and nation often nearly coincide. Yet there are many instances in which this is not true, and minorities included within one state feel greater affinity for the people of another, or desire a separate national state of their own. Attention will be given to these problems in the next chapter.

The state must be distinguished from the government. The latter is simply a mechanism to formulate and carry out the purposes of the state. It is an organization of men to whom the conduct of political affairs is entrusted (or who seize control), who are formed into legislative, executive, administrative, judicial, or electoral bodies for this purpose. If one wishes to deal with the state, he must do so through government, but a particular government seldom embodies all the powers and capacities of the state. Local functions are sure to be delegated to local governments either by the central government or by constitutional provision. Federal states, which are a composite of states which have united themselves under one central government, also retain provincial governments of the member states for certain functions. However, these do not greatly complicate international relations today, for the conduct of foreign affairs is usually vested in the central government. It is the federal state which is the state for international purposes. Federal states sometimes do have special problems in carrying out international undertakings because their central governments may not be able to commit their provincial governments to carry out these undertakings locally. Historically it would be important to distinguish several gradations of unification of states according to the importance of the powers given to the central government, as follows:

a. Treaties or alliances of states which retain their independence, but agree to act or refrain from acting in a specified manner. No central government is created.

b. Personal unions, i.e., independent states which have a personal sovereign in common. Thus, Queen Elizabeth II is the formal sovereign of each member of the British Commonwealth of Nations, but each is quite independent of the others.

c. Real unions, in which powers are transferred from member states to a central government. These may be:

(1) *Confederations,* in which only minor functions and powers are given to the central government so that it lacks capacity to function independently even in external relations. Such unions are often unstable, as was the case with the German Bund (1815–1867) and the American government under the Articles of Confederation and Perpetual Union (1781–1789). International organizations generally are confederations. While confederations may have limited international personality, they are not states; the members of the confederations are states. Names cannot be trusted: the Swiss Confederation is actually a federation.

(2) *Federations,* in which important functions and powers are delegated to the central government, almost invariably including external relations, military affairs, interstate and foreign commerce, with independent taxing power and control of citizens: the federation is itself a state; the members cannot for international purposes be deemed states, although they may continue to be called such, as in the United States. The United States, Canada, the Federal Republic of Germany, and the U.S.S.R., are examples of federation, although the last-named is a kind of pseudofederation in which political direction is highly centralized.

d. Unitary states, in which all legal powers have passed to the central government, and local governments are agents of the national government with delegated and therefore revocable authority. Examples are the United Kingdom, France, and Italy. Empires may be regarded as unitary structures; although they could be founded by either a federal or a unitary state, the relationship of the colony to the mother country is a unitary one.

STATE AND SOVEREIGNTY

The modern territorial state, with its concentration of political power in a central government, at first generally in the hands of a king, has produced a new theory of absolute and irresponsible sovereignty. Its formulation has been ascribed to the French publicist, Jean Bodin (1530–1596), who analyzed sovereignty systematically in his *Les Six Livres de la République* (1576), but this does him less than justice. Bodin, it is true, spoke of sovereignty in absolute terms ("Sovereignty is the absolute and perpetual power of a Republic"), and he certainly believed that feudal and religious wars could be terminated only by strong central government, which in turn required that final authority to make and enforce law should be vested in a single sovereign person or body. He also said that the sovereign, since he made the laws, could not be subject to them. Nevertheless, he did not argue that the sovereign should be irresponsible. Today it may seem to us a contradiction in terms to speak of a sovereign who is absolute yet not irresponsible, but Bodin spoke in the spirit of the medieval view that there is a fundamental law which binds all men, even kings. As the state exists to serve certain ends, so the scope of sovereignty is limited to these objects. The sovereign is free of the laws only in the sense of the positive laws which he enacts; he is not free of the fundamental laws. He is "absolute" only within the limited sphere of his sovereignty.

In Bodin's system the fundamental law included (a) natural law, i.e., rules of conduct which men know through their faculty of distinguishing right and wrong, and which medieval men would certainly have considered divinely ordained; (b) the *leges imperii,* or constitutional law defining the royal office, which in France comprised the so-called Salic Law and the law prohibiting the alienation of the royal domain or the royal authority; and (c) certain laws considered fundamental to the structure of a particular society, which to Bodin meant the sanctity of private property and of the family. Perhaps this is sufficient to show that Bodinian sovereignty did stress the completeness of state authority over subjects within a sphere consistent with the ends of the state but did not interpose any obstacle to the subjection of the state itself to a larger framework of law. It was not a theory that might makes right and was quite consistent with the view that a sovereign state can be subject to international law.

In contrast with Bodinian sovereignty we have the theory of Thomas Hobbes (1588–1679), which in the nineteenth century was given careful juristic expression by John Austin. This is clearly an assertion that sovereignty is not merely absolute and indivisible but irresponsible. Hobbes lived in England in the period of the civil wars and was a strong monarchist. His views are in some sense a rationalization of these preferences and a reflection of the lawless struggle for power in his day. However, they are stated in terms

of a general political theory. In his great work, *Leviathan* (1651), Hobbes
begins with an analysis of the character of man in a state of nature. He makes
man to be purely selfish and predatory, with "a perpetuall and restless desire
of Power after power, that ceaseth only in Death. And the cause of this, is
. . . because he cannot assure the power and means to live well, which he hath
present, without the acquisition of more." In a state of nature men of this
stamp are either at each other's throats or warily regarding each other in an
uneasy peace. Neither industry, nor agriculture, nor transport, nor building,
much less the arts and letters, can be pursued, "and the life of man, solitary,
poor, nasty, brutish, and short . . . To this warre of every man against every
man, this also is consequent: that nothing can be Unjust. The notions of Right
and Wrong, Justice and Injustice, have there no place. Where there is no common Power, there is no Law: where no Law, no Injustice."

From this sorry condition Hobbes proceeds to rescue men by having them
invent the peculiar Hobbesian social contract, in which to secure peace and
protection they agree among themselves to create Leviathan, the sovereign
state, endowing it with all the powers they possess. Nor can they thereafter
recover their liberties and revert to the jungle; the state which they have
created has been given absolute power of government and law irrevocably, and
the contracting parties are its subjects. For them the mandate of the sovereign
is law. They cannot even allege breach of contract by the sovereign if he acts
irresponsibly, for the sovereign was not a party to the contract. We need not
pursue here the logical inconsistencies of Hobbes' explanations, for it is his
final scheme of things which is important. This amounts to an assertion that
sovereignty is final, absolute, and irresponsible power which can compel obedience by all others. Whatever person or body of persons has this power is
sovereign, and his mandate is law. Might makes right; or as his contemporary,
Cleaveland, put it:

> Then come, Bring a Sum, *Law* is dumb,
> And submits to our wits:
> For it's *Policy* guides a *State*.

It follows, in the Hobbesian analysis, that sovereignty may be vested in only
one authority. A division between two, as between the civil power of the
state and the "ghostly authority" of the church, would be a contradiction in
terms and in principle. "If two men ride upon a horse, one must ride in
front."

Since Hobbes asserted that individuals sought protection and peace by
surrendering themselves to the sovereign state, he might very reasonably have
argued that states, which he described as in a kind of international Hobbesian state of nature ("in continual jealousies and in the state and posture of
gladiators, having their weapons pointing, and their eyes fixed, on one an-

other; which is a posture of war")—that states, too, should seek peace through submission to an international legal order. But Hobbes does not carry us far along this road. Although he speaks of a law of nature in the relations of states, which he calls *ius gentium* (law of nations), he cannot have anticipated that it could be effective in the absence of a supranational power capable of coercing states. "Covenants without the sword are but words," he said, and further argued that engagements need not be kept unless some benefit was obtained from the other parties. Such views would be destructive of any law based upon international treaty—an early expression of the view that a treaty is just "a scrap of paper." Nor did Hobbes put natural law in the same category as law by mandate of the sovereign—to him the only true law.

Following Hobbes, the English jurist, John Austin (1790–1859), founder of the analytical school of jurisprudence, based his whole system of analysis (*The Province of Jurisprudence Determined* [1832]; later incorporated into *Lectures on Jurisprudence, or the Philosophy of Positive Law*) upon a set of postulates precisely conforming to the Hobbesian state—i.e., a territorial state in which the population renders habitual obedience to a determinate person or persons (the sovereign) who render no habitual obedience to any others. It is only the law of such a state which is to him "law properly so called," and this law consists in "a command relating to the general conduct of the subjects, to which command such sovereign authority has given legal obligation by annexing a sanction or penalty in case of neglect." Whether the habitual obedience is rendered because of the sanction or for other reasons, Austin does not inquire. Given such postulates, he, of course, cannot include international law within the body of "law properly so called" and concludes to call it "positive international morality." Given his premises it is pointless to criticize this conclusion; on the other hand, one may with some reason question whether a set of postulates which would exclude primitive law, the law of democratic states (for want of a determinate sovereign), and international law, is likely to provide an analytical method of high value. Unfortunately the Austinian system has been given a more general application by uncritical persons than by its author, with the result that they deny the possibility of international law because of state sovereignty, whereas Austin seems not to have intended that international law was the less binding by reason of not being "law properly so called." It was merely not law in the sense of a sovereign mandate, a proposition obvious from the outset.

It should perhaps be noted that the sovereignty of Hobbes and Austin does not require any particular type of sovereign, except that Austin's rather irrelevant specification of a "determinate" person or persons would make it difficult to locate the sovereign in a system like that of the United States. He finally decided that to avoid admitting the divisibility of sovereignty there he must locate it in the body of electors or legislators who could amend the constitution—a most absurd distortion of the usual understanding of sovereignty. But Hobbesian sovereignty is certainly applicable to monarchy, oligarchy, a representative parliament, or even popular sovereignty. Popular sovereignty, indeed, if conceived as an unrestrained power of the majority (or the controlling minority) is perhaps more likely to be irresponsible, less likely to respect fundamental law, than sovereignty in a smaller group or an individual.

These two basic approaches to the nature of sovereignty—the Bodinian conception of it as an authority unlimited within its sphere but that sphere legally defined and the Hobbesian-Austinian conception of it as absolute, final, and irresponsible authority based upon physical power—have the most serious implications for international relationships. Physical power is in fact concentrated today in national states—and indeed in a quite small number of large states. If the Hobbesian view were generally accepted, it would provide a rationalization of imperialism and aggression in terms of national mission, for it argues that there is no law above the state, only moral compulsion. Imperialists and aggressors generally have a set of moral values convenient to their purposes. To take an obvious example, the moral values of Hitler's Nazi government justified German expansion. And it is the essence of communist virtue to destroy free enterprise systems. Unless there are legal restraints which are respected and enforced, such conflicting moral standards can lead only to power conflicts.

We must, of course, face the question whether such uninhibited power struggles are not in fact typical of relations among states, however much we may deplore them. It is certainly rather easy to reach such a conclusion in the twentieth century, which has seen a succession of wars and rumors of wars. But we should make the same mistake which Hobbes made in generalizing his personal experience if we concluded that there are no forces in the world but physical forces. There have been other periods of revolution followed by widespread cleavages in value systems and international conflict, yet forces of order and law have in the end restored harmony in the community of states. We do less than justice to men's responsiveness to international values such as orderly commercial intercourse, peaceful adjustment of disputes, and international justice, if we assume that there is no support for law and organization in the international community.

Men are in fact torn betwen national and international appeals, and the concensus which controls action seems to veer sometimes in one direction, sometimes in another. The difficulty is accentuated by the fact that egalitarian tendencies since the French Revolution have subjected all government, even in dictatorships, to the necessity of taking account of public opinion, either by giving effect to a spontaneous concensus or by deliberately shaping a desired one. At times the people may be, as Hamilton remarked, "a great beast." Popular concensus will introduce a capricious element into policy unless the popular sovereign also learns subjection to legal limitations—a lesson which peoples may have read more effectively to monarchs than they can to themselves. In such a situation it certainly appears essential to think of sovereignty in Bodinian terms, which allow full scope for the state yet place it within a framework of international rights and duties. This conception of limited sovereignty has been a powerful force in achieving government under constitutional limitations within the state. It is also the basis upon which an international community of sovereign states regulated by law is possible.

THE COMMUNITY OF STATES

From juristic theory has come the notion that states are equal, co-ordinate entities in a society of states. Equal, that is, in the sense that we say that men, although obviously unequal in physical strength, mental powers, or worldly goods, are yet "equal before the law," or equally entitled to have their rights protected by law. But if states are equal before the law and equally entitled to the protection of international law, it must be understood that this is not the same thing as saying states have equal substantive rights (e.g., as to control of territory or jurisdiction over persons). They have only equality in the procedural right to have the protection of law for their unequal substantive rights. We shall form a very incorrect and formalistic picture of the community of states or of legal and political relationships among states if we conceive of them as units either physically, politically, or legally equal, in any other sense.

Certainly they are not alike in physical attributes, unless in the fact that they possess the minimal attributes required for statehood. Even these are not sharply defined. When statehood is said to presuppose permanent population, defined territory, and a government capable of internal control and external relations, we can at once ask: How much population? To what extent may it be migratory or nomadic? How much territory? How demarcated? Must the government rest upon the acquiescence of the governed? If so, how can this be determined? Must it meet any standards of efficiency or political morality? What if it is independent as to certain functions, say internal government, but subject to another state as to other functions, i.e., foreign relations? As soon as we begin to examine the seventy-five or more territorial states which now comprise the community of states, we discover them to be an extremely ill-assorted and heterogeneous lot. The disparities are indeed so great as to raise doubts whether some are states at all; they are simply admitted to have international legal personality for special or limited purposes.

In fact the occasions upon which governments have to decide whether another political community is or is not a state seldom present the issue neatly and directly. The actual question may be whether the government of another state is entitled to sovereign immunity from suit in a state's courts, or whether the acts of another government within its own territory should be recognized as effective, e.g., an expropriation of private property. In such cases the inquiry may be a somewhat technical juristic one, relatively free from policy overtones. And an affirmative answer may be given on the basis of demonstrated "internal sovereignty," even though the community is not independent in external relations. But what if the question is whether to extend recognition to a new state which has broken away from another and established its independence? Here the recognizing state will certainly inquire as to population, territory, effective government, and capacity to enter into foreign relations, but in many cases it may also regard the question as one of political policy, since recognition normally leads to regular diplomatic relations. In fact there are different views of the force of recognition. It may be argued that statehood is a physical fact which exists independently of recognition by other states and that recognition merely determines diplomatic relations. But some states assume that the international legal capacity of a state depends upon recognition by other states and that there is a duty to recognize states which qualify. Given such different viewpoints, states often reach opposite decisions upon the same facts. The principles involved will be considered in more detail in Chapter 14. Still another type of decision is the question whether a particular community shall be admitted to an international organization which is restricted to states. Here too the basic physical attributes of statehood may be examined, but the decision as to these is likely to be obscured by other criteria of membership and by the political attitudes of the members in voting. This can be seen in the admission of members to the United Nations, discussed in Chapter 15.

It is, therefore, hardly possible to answer the questions posed except in a relative way, but even so the disparities among states are clear. What of population and territory? At one end of the scale are the U.S.S.R. with an area of over 8 million square miles and population of over 200 millions, China with more than 4 million square miles and nearly 500 million people, India with more than a million square miles and about 370 million people. In contrast with these huge and populous states are such Lilliputian "states" as Andorra (180 square miles, 5000 population), the Bahrein Islands (213 square miles, 110,000 population), the Principality of Liechtenstein (62 square miles, 13,500 population), the Grand Duchy of Luxembourg (998 square miles, 300,000 population), the Principality of Monaco (368 acres, 20,000 population), San Marino (38 square miles, 12,000 population), and the Vatican City State (108.7 acres, 1000 population, many of whom must be nationals of other states). Some of these have significance in the international community: Bahrein for its oil, Luxembourg as a member of the customs union known as Benelux, and the Vatican for the far-reaching religious and political influence of the Holy See, especially in Roman Catholic countries. The others have little independent capacity. The applications of Liechtenstein, Monaco, and San Marino for membership in the League of Nations were rejected "on account of their small size." Of those mentioned, only Luxembourg is a member of the United Nations. There are some established states which do not even have well-defined boundaries, as the Sultanate of Muscat and Oman, which extends inland to the "Empty Quarter" of the Great Desert of Arabia. In the isolated states of the Great Himalaya the real boundaries are occupational: for the Tibetan herdsman the end of the grasslands and the 50-inch rainfall contour beyond which there is no salt; for the Bhutanese the upland tree-lowland tree line dividing pine forest from hardwood. The boundaries of Israel are not wholly determined, a situation which the United States delegate to the U.N. Security Council argued was not a barrier to statehood, as shown by the unsettled state of United States boundaries long after independence was generally recognized. There are also states which have partly nomadic populations, as the Bedouins of North Africa and Arabia, and the herdsmen of Mongolia. It is unlikely that they are close respecters of boundaries or appear regularly for the census.

But these difficulties are as nothing to the confusion encountered in trying to determine the degree of independence of political entities. The neutrality of Switzerland has been guaranteed by other powers since 1815, which effectively limits its rights in time of war and has been taken by it to be inconsistent with membership in the United Nations. It joined the League of Nations under reservation that it could not assist in military sanctions. Belgium and Luxembourg were formerly neutralized but have abandoned that status. Other states are protectorates, a relationship defined in each instance by treaty but generally involving the complete management of external relations by the protecting state, and often some control of internal administration. Andorra is under the joint suzerainty of the bishop of Urghel and the president of France, San Marino is a protectorate of Italy, Monaco of France. The sheikdoms of Kuwait, the Trucial States, Qatar, and Bahrein are under protection of Great Britain, as are the states of the Malay Federation.

A special type of protection is the trusteeship system of the United Nations, as was the mandate system of the League of Nations which preceded it. Here the unique feature is a specification of legal relationships in an agreement between the protecting state and the United Nations, followed by continuing United Nations supervision of the trustee state's administration in the trust area. The extent of internal administration by the trustee state is adjusted to the capacity of inhabitants of the area for autonomy, and designed to carry them toward independence if that appears feasible. Sometimes special provisions affecting international status are found in treaties, as in the "Platt Amendment," which the United States inserted into the Treaty of Havana (1903), whereby Cuba agreed not to enter into any arrangements with other

suggested by universal state jurisdiction without regard to nationality in piracy and war crimes. A step in that direction was taken by the "international military tribunals" of Nuremberg and Tokyo. The theory that international claims are claims by a state against a state even though occasioned by an injury to an individual national by a foreign national or company has led to many legal incongruities. There are those who urge international tribunals in which individuals can directly prosecute their claims against foreign states. These may be straws in the wind, but they have not blown far. The problem will be examined more fully in Chapter 14.

SELECTED READING

AUSTIN, JOHN, *Lectures on Jurisprudence, or the Philosophy of Positive Law* (5th ed., by Robert Campbell). London: John Murray, 1885. Lectures I, V, and VI.

BODIN, JEAN, *Les Six Livres de la République*. Paris, 1576; 5th ed., Frankfurt, 1609. English trans. by R. Knolles, London, 1606.

BRIERLY, J. L., *The Law of Nations: An Introduction to the International Law of Peace* (5th ed.). Oxford: The Clarendon Press, 1955. Chs. I–IV.

DICKINSON, EDWIN D., *Cases and Materials on International Law*. Brooklyn: The Foundation Press, 1950. Ch. 1, Section 2.

———, *The Equality of States in International Law*. Cambridge: Harvard University Press, 1920.

GARNER, JAMES WILFORD, *Political Science and Government*. New York: American Book Company, 1928. Chs. 4, 5, 6, 8, 9.

HOBBES, THOMAS, *Leviathan, or the Matter, Form, and Power of a Commonwealth, Ecclesiastical and Civil* (1651), Reprint edition, Oxford: Clarendon Press, 1909. Other modern editions by Morley (3d ed., 1887), Waller (Cambridge English Classics, 1904), A. D. Lindsay (Everyman's Library, 1914).

JESSUP, PHILIP C., *A Modern Law of Nations*. New York: The Macmillan Company, 1948. Chs. 1, 2.

MAC IVER, R. M., *The Modern State*. Oxford: Clarendon Press, 1926. Esp., Introduction and Part Two.

MC ILWAIN, CHARLES HOWARD, *Constitutionalism and the Changing World*. New York: The Macmillan Company, 1939. Chs. II–IV.

———, *The Growth of Political Thought in the West*. New York: The Macmillan Company, 1932. Chs. V–VII.

SOLTAU, ROGER H., *An Introduction to Politics*. London: Longmans, Green and Company, 1951. Chs. I–VII.

The Statesman's Yearbook. London: Macmillan and Company, Ltd., annually (for current data concerning attributes of states).

PART 2

BASIC FACTORS
OF INTERNATIONAL
RELATIONS

CHAPTER 3

POLITICAL NATIONALISM

Political nationalism is the most pervasive and powerful force, partly for good and partly for evil, which exists in world politics today. Every politically conscious citizen is aware of it, most participate in it, some lose themselves in it with religious intensity. It "has become for the European of our age," said Norman Angell in 1932, "the most important thing in the world, more important than civilization, humanity, decency, kindness, piety; more important than life itself." He would no doubt agree that the observation must now be extended to the peoples of every continent, and that the greatest surge of nationalism today is not in Europe, but among the peoples of Asia and Africa. A whole library of books and innumerable articles have been devoted to analysis of its historical development and its social basis. Yet it remains difficult to say precisely what nationalism is, to estimate the proportionate influence of the factors which contribute to it, or to predict what directions it will take. The reason is that we are confronted with a problem of multiple correlation, and the factors which enter into the equation vary from country to country.

We may say in a tentative way that nationalism is an attitude held by a group of people who think of themselves as a nation and on that account want to be a separate state (whether or not they now are) and whose political reactions and policy inclinations with respect to relations among states are mainly governed by this desire. This is in many respects an unsatisfactory statement, but it provides a starting point. If the group, or part of the group, is not yet a state but exists as a minority within one or more states, the effect of the attitude is to produce pressure for separation from those states and creation of a new state or union with a different state toward which the group does have this feeling of political affinity. If the group is already a state the result may be a feeling of exclusiveness as against other states, a desire to defend the integrity of the state against outside forces, a wish to reclaim irredentist parts of the group which may exist in other states, or in some cases a feeling of self-appreciation, of national mission, of manifest destiny, which will support efforts to dominate other peoples. However, it is improper to generalize very much, for the strength and direction of nationalism vary from state to state, and within any given state from one period to another, as the resultant of many factors.

Probably the only way of approaching the matter which promises to throw light upon it is to inquire how far each of a number of factors which have at times been advanced as the basis of nationalism can really be held responsible. This will at least enable us to clear away certain false impressions about it and to concentrate upon the relevant factors in a more sophisticated manner.

FACTORS CONTRIBUTING TO NATIONALISM

Spiritual Factors

Volksgeist; national mission. The German writer Herder (1744–1803) developed an idea which had been expressed by others and gave it great impetus in the eighteenth and nineteenth centuries. He considered that every civilization has a natural life cycle of emergence, flowering, and decay, and that each is in itself unique and perfect. The goal of all social development is humanity, and in seeking it all nations should function harmoniously in a cosmopolitan spirit. Nevertheless, each has its own individuality, determined by environmental influence and by the folkspirit (*Volksgeist*) which is a natural attribute of any people. Each nation must therefore seek the common humanity according to its own lights, and its institutions—state, law, economy, religion, literature, etc.—are all shaped by the compulsions of these natural forces. Thus he advanced an organic, even a genetic, theory of nation and state, which assumed that a unique historical position and mission for each was implicit in its nature, and nationalism was only the inevitable and therefore good expression of its *Volksgeist*. Influential philosophies of nationalism, such as those of Fichte and Görres in Germany, Guizot and Michelet in France, Bluntschli in Switzerland, stem from Herder. The notion of natural, organic laws determining the course of political development also fits well with the pseudo-scientific explanations of the state as a product of social contract which we find in Hobbes, Locke, and Rousseau, and which dominated political thought until David Hume brought them all crashing down with a few puffs of historical evidence.

The difficulty with Herder's approach, apart from the fact that it has no scientific foundation, lies in the ease with which it can be subverted by those who lack liberal cosmopolitan impulses. One may take the teleological element of such a theory and divorce it from natural law with distressing results. Thus Hegel and Treitschke accepted the view of a German historical mission and a national ethic without admitting natural law, and Treitschke emerged with *Machtpolitik* (power politics) as the basis of the state. Ernest Renan also conceived of nationalism in terms of a spiritual principle, which he found in identification of a people with a continuous national tradition and heritage. "To have common glories in the past, a common will at present, to have achieved great things together, to intend to achieve more of them in the future"—this is the spiritual principle of the nation. He denied the force of environmental factors and was a religious skeptic, yet he concludes with what is a mystical or metaphysical view of the national soul emerging from historical tradition. In one form or another many people have felt that their nation had special virtues and that a kind of spiritual determinism defined its historic mission. The fact that without exception they have never conceived of this mission as a mean or insignificant one may indeed arouse suspicion of the objectivity of their thought, but the prevalence of such attitudes is nevertheless a factor to be reckoned with.

Religion. The question whether religion is a factor in nationalism is of a different order. The rise of Protestantism cannot be regarded as prompted by nationalism, although sometimes convenient to the purpose of rulers who had personal difficulties with the Catholic Church (e.g., Henry VIII of England and Frederick III, elector of Saxony and protector of Martin Luther). It may also have had consequences which promoted the sense of national consciousness. The translation of the Bible into national languages everywhere stimulated the vernacular literatures. In some cases national churches were created. Although not thought of as national in a doctrinal sense, they were in an institutional sense, and probably added to feelings of national unity. However, most churches now transcend national lines. They appear not to be institutions which any longer possess the power of drawing men into universal communities as medieval Christianity did. Certainly a common religion does not prevent two or more states from having very divergent national policies. This was apparent in French support of protestant states against the Catholic empire throughout the European balance of power struggle. When Turkey joined the Central Powers in World War I, Arab nationalism moved to the British camp despite religious affinity. Latin American states are almost uniformly Roman Catholic, but their relations have been marked by numerous wars over what seem rather petty boundary disputes.

It appears then that nationalism is seldom coextensive with religion and must generally be explained in terms of factors other than religion. Nevertheless, there are situations in which religious differences when coupled with political differences may do much to enforce nationalistic feeling. Mohammedan states have many differences among themselves, but as against European states, which they regard as economic exploiters of their resources, they react with feeling which is probably accentuated by religious exclusiveness. This may indeed be a factor artificially used to drum up support for govern-

RELIGIONS

Legend:

- Christian – Catholicism
- Christian – Protestant
- Christian – Eastern Rites
- Christian – Sect not distinguished
- Islam – Sunni
- Islam – Shiah
- Buddhism – Northern
- Buddhism – Southern
- Hinduism
- Japanese Religion (Shinto & Buddhism)
- Chinese Religion (Confucianism, Taoism, Buddhism)
- Tribal Religions
- Undifferentiated

Modified from map of Religions — Department of State
1943

ment policy, as in Premier Mohammed Mossadegh's fanatical rousing of the masses at the time of Iran's nationalization of the Anglo-Iranian Oil Company properties.

In general it can be said that in countries in which the dominant religion enjoys a majority of 80 percent or more, religion is not a sensitive element in politics. There are also many countries in which the division is narrower, but the historical development of toleration has removed religion from sharp controversy. In Europe there is little relationship between national boundaries and the delimitation of the zones of Roman Catholic, Protestant, and Eastern Orthodox dominance. Protestantism dominates in the northwest part, Roman Catholicism in the west and south, the Orthodox Church in the Balkans and Russia. These shade into each other in mixed zones. But there are few areas in which religion is a political issue capable of dividing a nation. The German Protestants in Memel, which was awarded to Lithuania by the League of Nations but later seized by Hitler, were such a problem. In Rumania are several minority religious groups—Roman Catholic Magyars, Orthodox Russians in Bessarabia, German Protestants in Transylvania. Before Rumania passed behind the Communist iron curtain these minorities were a source of disturbance in which religion probably supported nationalistic irredentism. Yugoslavia contains Orthodox Serbs, formerly the politically dominant group, Roman Catholic Croats and Slovenes, dominant in the Communist regime, Mohammedan Albanians and Macedonians, and a sprinkling of Protestant and Uniate elements. Religious differences coupled with distinct political and cultural traditions create several potential irredentist minorities and a serious cleavage between major groups. These differences are at present under wraps due to Communist control methods. Attitudes with respect to Jews in Germany and Poland are not primarily a matter of religion. The Cromwellian settlement of Scotch Protestants in Ulster injected religious antagonism into relations between the Catholics of South Ireland (now Eire) and the Ulster Protestants. It was not a simple religious issue, however, for the Catholic Irish lost their lands and were subjected to absentee English landlords through the eighteenth and nineteenth centuries.

The Islamic faith predominates among the Arabs of North Africa and the Near East, Turkestan, the Malay islands and Malay Peninsula, and in parts of India and China. There are two divisions, the Shias, found in Iran and Iraq and in the Indian province of Oudh, and the Sunnis, found in Turkey, Arabia, North Africa, Pakistan, and India. Despite the separation of Pakistan from India, many Muslims remain in northern India, and clashes between them and the dominant Hindus have been frequent. To some extent this may be attributed to unresolved territorial claims, but the policy of India toward the Mohammedan minority, while officially correct, has tolerated local measures of repression. Hindu-Muslim hostility results from a complica-

tion of religious, historical, economic, and political factors. Differences between Islamic sects are unlikely to present problems except perhaps in Iraq,
where the Shiite majority is not heavy. To date, the sense of national consciousness seems to have outweighed such differences. Syria is a mixture of
50 percent Sunnite Moslems, 25 percent Shiite, 25 percent assorted Christians
—Greek Orthodox, Armenian Orthodox, Maronite, Melkite, Roman Catholic
—and some Jews. There is persistent quarreling among these groups and
need for strong state control. The problem in Palestine, although involving
warfare between Jew and Muslim, is not one concerned with religious issues
but with political control of the area and the relative economic status of Arab
and Jew. However, the religious differences serve to accentuate hostility, and
Zionism is a genuine motivation in Jewish support of the new state of Israel.

In Africa the transition zone between Muslims and the central African
natives, whose religion is nature worship somewhat penetrated by Christian
and Islamic missionary endeavor, occurs in Nigeria and the Guinea coast on
the west and Ethiopia and Somaliland on the east. Coptic Christianity is
dominant in Ethiopia. Elsewhere the Muslim and Negro religions have not
presented much of a problem but do create political difficulties as autonomous
governments are organized. Nevertheless, sentiment for nationality seems the
stronger force.

In Southeast Asia there is a mingling of religions. Burmese, Thais, and
the peoples of Indochina are mainly Buddhist; Indonesians and Malays, Muslims; Filipinos, Roman Catholic. Religious differences are one of many factors
preventing regional integration, and they contribute to political disturbances
within some states. Thus, in Burma the fact that the debt-laden peasantry are
Buddhist and the creditors Hindu *Chettyars* has helped to accent the agricultural revolution. A similar situation exists in Malaya and Indonesia except
that the peasantry are Muslims and the moneylenders Chinese Buddhists. The
nearly equal strength of Chinese and Malays in Malaya prevents a unified
nationalism, but religion is not the sole cause of division.

In most of the situations mentioned it seems clear that religious differences, while continuing in one degree or another to pose political problems
within countries, have been subordinated to nationalism, for these countries
are today centers of some of the strongest nationalist movements.

In states which have moved toward rationalism and secularism, as in
much of Europe and the Western Hemisphere, nationalism tends to sup-
plant religion and itself to become a kind of secular religion. As Carlton
J. H. Hayes pointed out in his *Essays on Nationalism,* it has a marked tendency to take on the characteristic trappings of religion—national holidays for
holy days; national heroes for saints; pilgrimages to historic buildings, tombs
of statesmen, and the national capital; symbols such as the flag and the national
anthem; sacred scriptures such as the Declaration of Independence and the

Constitution; oaths, creeds, and ceremonies. He quotes also Albert Mathiez's description of the reception by the French Assembly in 1791 of the constitution embodying the Declaration of the Rights of Man: "twelve old men went in procession to seek the Book of the Constitution. They came back, having at their head the archivist Camus, who holding up the Book with his two hands and resting it on his breast, carried with slow and measured tread the new Blessed Sacrament of the French. All the deputies stood up and bared their heads. Camus, with meditative mien, kept his eyes lowered."

Societal Factors

It has often been suggested that common racial origin is a primary ingredient of nationalism, which is merely the urge to draw the racial or tribal group together into a political group. The strongest advocates of this view have been men who had no knowledge of modern anthropology, but followed some popular notion of "race" having no scientific validity. Anthropologists attempt no more than a classification of types according to physical characteristics—cephalic index, stature, pigmentation, hair texture, shape of nose, and the like—and are well aware that all nations are such an intermingling of racial strains that basic types (Alpine, Nordic, Mediterranean, Dinaric, etc.) are found in all Western countries. Furthermore each individual has become such a mixture of gene and chromosome structures that he may bear within himself dozens of races, for the genes do not blend but simply mix in an infinite number of combinations. Who then is to say what is his race? There is no British, or French, or German race—even less an American race. Nor would it have any significance for nationalism if there were, for nationalism is an attitude, whereas race is a set of biological characteristics which have no known connection with attitudes. Children of one racial group, if removed at a tender age and reared in another country and racial group, do not retain attitudes characteristic of their people but fit easily into the new pattern. Actually we can say nothing from the standpoint of biological science about attitudes. Nor can psychologists tell us the structure of an attitude.

Although the race theory must be accounted completely unscientific and invalid, it cannot on that account be dismissed, for it has attracted a host of irrational followers even to the present day. Of particular note in the development of this view was Count Joseph Arthur de Gobineau (1816–1882), a French aristocrat and diplomat. In his *Essai sur l'inégalité des races humaines* (1855) he observed that there are three great racial groups, black, yellow, and white, created in that order and marking stages in the improvement of the Creator's experimental technique. Thus the white race is a superior product in physical beauty, mental capacity, spiritual force, and the urge to conquest. Civilization is entirely the product of the Aryan race, and the rise and decay of particular civilizations can be traced to migration and conquest

by Aryans followed by racial intermingling with inferior stocks and consequent deterioration. Gobineau's view of the future was gloomy; only in
Germanic peoples, the "last bud upon the Aryan stem," did he find reasonably pure white stock, and even there he perceived the beginnings of deterioration. He was no nationalist; on the contrary, nations seemed to him
the product of the racial mingling he deplored, and he saw in democracy
the sign that the natural dictatorship of the Aryan had disintegrated.

Gobineau obtained little following in France, as might have been expected in view of the wretched deterioration of stock he detected there, but
among the remaining "noble Aryans" of Germany his work enjoyed a great
success. It was taken up by the expatriate Englishman, Houston Stewart
Chamberlain (1855-1927), son-in-law of Richard Wagner, who grasped the
Gobineau thesis of the superiority of the Aryans and the purity of the master
race in Germanic countries and went on from there undeterred by any considerations of fact. In his *Die Grundlagen des 19. Jahrhunderts* (1899; translation, *Foundations of the Nineteenth Century*, 1913) he abandoned the notion of universal deterioration of the white race and applied instead an idea
of evolution of races by splitting off of groups so that the Germanic peoples
were conceived not as a last Aryan outpost but as the final flower of racial
development. European history is for him a contest between inferior Ro-
manic peoples and a materialistic Catholic Church on the one hand, and the
northern Aryans whose spiritual flowering appears in Protestantism. His extreme distaste for the Jews led him to conclude that Christ came from
Germanic stocks which had settled in Galilee. The Kaiser patronized the work
and according to von Bülow was given to reading long excerpts to the ladies
of the court until they fell asleep. It was widely circulated and read throughout Germany and all too obviously had its practical consequences in the Nazi
doctrine of racial supremacy and the terrible massacres of European Jewry.
This is not to say that other motives were not important in Nazi policy,
but the mystical race ideology of Chamberlain provided the conceptual framework. It can be found in all its hysterical and irrational force in the pages of
Hitler and Rosenberg and in the propaganda materials of Goebbels and
Streicher.

Apart from this sort of doctrine there has been a good deal of speculation upon the possibility that the nation and nationalism are products of
gregarious instincts of men or of impulses to fighting, conquest, and aggrandizement of power. It seems a sufficient comment to say that institutions
in general must indeed result from the social tendencies of man, but that little
evidence exists to suggest that any particular forms of social or political community are inevitable. There is nothing in such ideas which helps us to
understand why the nation emerged as a basic unit. One might equally well
argue that feudalism was a product of man's impulses toward separatism

and individualism, or the Holy Roman Empire of his drives toward universalism. Why at a particular stage of history the nation and nationalism dominate must be explained upon some other basis. If there is a predestined sequence of institutional forms, this has still to be demonstrated scientifically. The same consideration applies to fighting impulses. In other eras men have fought just as vigorously for other values as they do now for the nation state. As Gibbon remarked, bitter street fighting in ancient Alexandria occurred when one religious faction chanted, "Glory be to the Father, and to the Son, and to the Holy Ghost," and another replied, "Glory be to the Father, *in* the Son, and *by* the Holy Ghost." There is scarcely any human value for which some men will not fight, and a considerable number seem to find the pleasure of fighting a sufficient value in itself.

Geography and Economy

Are nations and therefore nationalism perhaps the result of soil, climate and other physical conditions within an area having natural frontiers, so that a people extends itself to these frontiers and thereafter becomes a homogeneous group conditioned by the environment? Probably one could have spoken with some justice of natural frontiers in a day of primitive transport when oceans and great mountain ranges and deserts imposed barriers not easily surmounted. Rivers and oceans were never barriers but highways. Why one geographic feature more than another should be the obvious frontier is often difficult to comprehend. Where is the northern "natural" frontier of the United States west of the Lake of the Woods? Renan properly remarked: "There is not the mouth of a river from Biarritz to Tornea which has, more than one of the other rivers, the character of a boundary. Had history willed it, the Loire, the Seine, the Meuse, the Oder, as well as the Rhine would have taken the character of natural frontiers. . . ." After the battle of Leipzig (1813) the Allies offered Napoleon the "natural frontiers" of France, including the Rhine. Not nature but force of circumstance prompted the offer (which was rejected), and the area west of the Rhine has been a bone of contention ever since. As another sample of "natural frontier" thinking, Napoleon demanded Holland because it is merely an alluvial deposit of French rivers.

Even given a set of frontiers which one might elect to call natural we obtain little help in explaining the growth of national consciousness within them. Unfortunately for the theory many highly nationalistic states are so large and geographically diversified that the influence of climate and physical features can only be to produce great diversification of types. One has only to think of the large number of variant types in the United States or the U.S.S.R. to appreciate this. The rural New Englander, the Pennsylvania miner, the Tennessee mountain farmer, the Texas cattleman, vary consider-

ably and are capable of not caring greatly for each other, but they all participate in United States nationalism.

It seems equally impossible to derive nationalism from a community of
economic interest in any country which has a diversified economy, for it seems
just as prevalent and strong there as in a country with a simple economy and
a homogeneous occupational pattern.

No doubt there is a feeling of love of home which must be accounted
significant in the national consciousness. Certainly literature is filled with
expressions of such sentiment which awake a chord in the hearts of the
authors' compatriots:

> Oh, to be in England
> Now that April's there,
> And whoever wakes in England
> Sees, some morning, unaware,
> That the lowest boughs and the brush-wood sheaf
> Round the elm-tree bole are in tiny leaf,
> While the chaffinch sings on the orchard bough
> In England—now!
> > (*Robert Browning*)

> So it's home again, and home again, America for me!
> My heart is turning home again, and there I long to be,
> In the land of youth and freedom beyond the ocean bars,
> Where the air is full of sunlight and the flag is full of stars.
> > (*Henry Van Dyke*)

Yet nostalgia is not quite the same sentiment as nationality. It fixes
itself more particularly upon familiar haunts wherever they may be, and
only by association upon the nation. There are many instances in which
love of home has been at cross purposes with national consciousness, notably
when population transfers are effected and people must decide to migrate
to the country of the national group or to remain at home as a minority group
without special rights. Wherever such options are given a considerable proportion prefers home to nation, as in the case of the Greco-Bulgarian exchange
of 1919 and of the Germans of the southern Tyrol in 1940. Great difficulty
was experienced in inducing German landlords of the Baltic countries to re-
settle in Germany.

Cultural Factors

The proposition that language, literature, art, music, and other cultural
patterns contribute to nationalism can be accepted with some reservations.
Since several languages are often found within one nation, and even more
often many distinct nations within one language area, it is pretty clear that an

exclusive language is not essential to the formation of a nation or to nationalistic feeling. It is, however, extremely helpful in developing national consciousness to be able to communicate freely in a single idiom, since the connotations and cultural nuances in a language are never perfectly translatable into another. Retention of a minority language within a nation is generally associated with a certain amount of cultural or political exclusiveness, even if it does not rise to the level of a separate nationalism.

Certainly language alone is not the key to nationalism. The United States and the older British dominions speak English, but in each case a separate national consciousness arose and they became independent states. The United States and Great Britain have been waggishly described as "two nations separated by a common language." Eire developed such hatred of England after the days of Cromwell, despite a common language, that after obtaining independence she artificially revived Gaelic. A similar re-emphasis of local languages has occurred in India. In both English continues to be used by educated people, and in India may be more widely available as a common language than Hindi. French has been systematically taught in Alsace-Lorraine since World War I and is displacing German. Czech nationalism did not subside although all educated Czechs had come to speak and write German, and the native language was revived as a part of the independence movement. In these cases the native language stands as a symbol of national unity and integrity rather than a cause of it. There have been cases of European plebiscites in which the result did not follow the language division among the voters, e.g., the decision of Marienwerder and Allenstein, East Prussia (predominantly Polish speaking, but Protestant), to go to Germany and of Klagenfurt (the southern part of which is Slovenian) to go to Austria.

With respect to literature, art, and music, it can of course be said that the best of them have universal appeal which transcends boundaries, and that great writers and artists, however much they deal with the particular and the local, express through it the universal. There is nothing less important about Hamlet, Prince of Denmark, than the fact of his Danish nationality. What is really meant by associating nationalism with culture is the popular or folk culture. For example, the work of the brothers Grimm in gathering up and popularizing German folk tales; the heroic literature of various countries such as the *Song of Roland* or the *Tale of the Cid* or the Volsunga Saga; popular histories emphasizing the heroic element; folk music and songs associated with national history (*La Marseillaise, Rule Britannia, Yankee Doodle*); these have undoubtedly had power to increase social cohesion and sentimental national feelings. Eighteenth- and nineteenth-century nationalism very often began with intellectual movements centered in the aristocracy and spread through characteristic literary or artistic products until national consciousness had been awakened.

We are told with some reason in the constitution of UNESCO that "wars begin in the minds of men"; they do in the sense that prejudices, misconceptions, ethnocentrism, and xenophobia may be cultivated there by the biases of a national cultural pattern. These biases are often imbedded in the educational system of a country. Some attention has been given in the last quarter century to the nationalistic tone, inaccuracies, and biases which pervade history textbooks for public school use. These often fall below the standards of historical scholarship even of the country where they are used. The War of 1812 was a political blunder and in large part a series of military fiascoes. The Mexican War was an unfortunate consequence of expansionist sentiment and tactless policy in the United States, met by bull-headed incompetency and self-esteem in the Mexican government. The Spanish-American War, fought from a mixture of humanitarian and materialistic motives, was in its Cuban phase an exhibition of military ineptitude and administrative incompetency which could not have been afforded against a major power. Yet the average American school child gains only the impression that all three wars were heroic steps in the progress of democracy. As Delaisi said, "apart from a handful of scholars, people are interested in the past only in so far as it is a justification of the present." One of the strongest impulses in nationalism is the individual's association through education and popular culture with a national tradition, which is certain to be an idealized version of the nation's achievements and virtues. Genuinely cosmopolitan attitudes are not often found among persons of meager education, and public opinion polls in the United States have shown a markedly higher incidence of bellicose, jingoistic, militaristic, imperialistic, racially prejudiced, and isolationist attitudes among adults having only grade school training than among high school and college graduates.

Historical Influences

It must not be forgotten that nationalism is a modern phenomenon which has accompanied the growth of the national state and has become accentuated only in the period since the French Revolution. Feudalism was the negation of nationalism, and the early rise of strong monarchies in England and France had long to contend with divisive forces within and with the influence of medieval universalism. Early wars, such as the Hundred Years War between France and England, were of great importance in unifying these states but were actually fought by feudal rather than national armies. They were important, however, in that they created a national tradition in which loyalty to the king and patriotic sacrifice for his cause came to be identified with a feeling for country. The point is all too clear in the stirring words which Shakespeare put into the mouth of the king before the Battle of Agincourt—but the significance lies in their power to stir the national pride of men at the end of

the sixteenth century and later, for Shakespeare correctly showed the king
as exhorting a small feudal array—"we few, we happy few":

> He that outlives this day, and comes safe home,
> Will stand a tip-toe when this day is name'd,
> And rouse him at the name of Crispian,
> He that shall live this day, and see old age,
> Will yearly on the vigil feast his neighbours,
> And say "Tomorrow is Saint Crispian":
> Then will he strip his slieve and show his scars,
> And say "These wounds I had on Crispin's day."
> Old men forget; yet all shall be forgot,
> But he'll remember with advantages
> What feats he did that day. Then shall our names,
> Familiar in his mouth as household words,
> Harry the king, Bedford and Exeter,
> Warwick and Talbot, Salisbury and Gloucester,
> Be in their flowing cups freshly remember'd.
> This story shall the good man teach his son;
> And Crispin Crispian shall ne'er go by,
> From this day to the ending of the world,
> But we in it shall be remembered;
> We few, we happy few, we band of brothers;
> For he today that sheds his blood with me
> Shall be my brother; be he ne'er so vile
> This day shall gentle his condition:
> And gentlemen in England now a-bed
> Shall think themselves accurs'd they were not here,
> And hold their manhoods cheap while any speaks
> That fought with us upon Saint Crispin's day.
> (*Henry V,* Act IV, Scene III)

After the Reformation the emphasis was wholly upon national development, but there was little popular participation and foreign relations were
a matter of dynastic politics. It is doubtful that the monarchs and aristocracy
had much feeling of nationalism, even though involved in balance of power
politics. Frederick the Great, although he sought the aggrandizement of
Prussia persistently and skillfully, was in his cultural preferences more French
than German and spoke and wrote French better than German. Monarchs
commanded the loyalty of subjects and sometimes, as in the case of Elizabeth of England, Louis XIV of France, Maria Theresa of Austria, did a great
deal to stimulate national consciousness. But armies were still composed of
mercenaries, diplomacy was aristocratic, and in general national consciousness was not much projected into international relations.

Indeed, a case can be made for the proposition that nationalism did not lead to the formation of the first national states but rather was a product of them. As late as the sixteenth and seventeenth centuries national consciousness was so little developed that peoples were malleable and could be transferred from one sovereignty to another without sharp political reactions. "The cause of the statue," said René Johannet (*Le Principe des Nationalités*), "is not the marble but the artist. In the case of nationality, it is primarily the dynasty." Dynastic politics united England and Scotland, and although a few Scottish nationalists try to publicize their attitudes by stealing the Stone of Scone from Westminster Abbey, no one doubts the existence today of a strong British nationalism. France at an earlier date was sharply divided, and antagonism between north and south continued through the middle ages. Unification was achieved by the piecemeal acquisition of territories through five centuries, first by the Capetians, then by Valois and Bourbon rulers. This dynastic success was eventually followed by national consciousness. In Spain Castile was united with Aragon and Catalonia by the marriage of Ferdinand and Isabella. Portugal, under the rule of the Braganzas, went its own way. The Spanish provinces had long had distinct traditions and were held together more by the strong national policy of Charles V and Philip II than by a natural affinity. It was the rise of the Hohenzollern dynasty in Prussia which largely determined the conditions upon which Germany would later be unified.

But with the French Revolution and the Napoleonic wars there came a major historical change, the consequences of which are still being felt. The Revolution marked the overturn not so much of monarchy as of the privileged aristocratic class and the rise to political participation and power of the bourgeoisie, or middle class—i.e., not the peasantry or laborers, but the business and professional people. For the first time a broad popular basis for policy was provided, and for the first time the people could feel that national policy was in some sense their policy. The result was an explosive outburst that united the French in a wave of enthusiasm which infected all Europe. Although the dynastic state had made nationalism possible, nationalism now captured the state and made it its instrument. Class privileges were eliminated; royal, local, and provincial administration was swept away and replaced by administrative units of the revolutionary government; the new symbolism of the flag, the anthem, the Declaration of the Rights of Man, was invoked; and the *levée en masse* for the first time showed the irresistible force of a nation in arms. The French overnight became a dedicated people, determined to defend the position gained and to encourage subject peoples throughout Europe to join the banner of bourgeois revolution.

French armies repelled the invading forces of alarmed dynastic rulers with ease and then swept across Europe under the guiding genius of Napoleon. The effect was partly to stimulate nationalistic movements of revolt and

partly to stimulate resistance movements which also tended to become nationalistic. The Balkans, Italy, and Poland became centers of independence
movements. Napoleon found it convenient to stimulate the last two by creating the "Kingdom of Italy" and the Grand Duchy of Warsaw. Nationalism
as a reaction against French conquest, which soon took on the color of imperialism, was strongest in Spain, Germany, and Russia. The great national
effort by the Allies which was required to defeat Napoleon at Waterloo
marked the end of the old type of dynastic wars and the consolidation of the
position of nationalism as a force in nearly every country of Europe. However,
the Congress of Vienna did not give effect to demands for national self-
determination but sought to impose a conservative peace and to restore the
position of dynasties. The Italian states which Napoleon had united were
parceled out to various princes; Venetia and Lombardy were incorporated
into Austria; Norway was taken from Denmark and given to Sweden; most
of the Grand Duchy of Warsaw went to Russia; Holland and Belgium were
joined; two fifths of Saxony was awarded to Prussia; divided Poland remained divided.

NATIONAL SELF-DETERMINATION IN EUROPE

This resurgence of dynastic interest proved to be futile. The century from
1815 to 1914 was marked by movements for national self-determination that
liberated the Spanish colonies, separated Belgium from Holland, unified
Italy and Germany as strong national states, freed the Balkans from Turkish
rule, and undermined the polyglot Hapsburg Empire. Nevertheless, in the
period after 1848 great efforts were made by four states of eastern Europe
(Russia, Germany, Austria-Hungary, and Turkey) to hold the line against
movements of national self-determination. The German Empire after 1871
included Danes in Schleswig, French in Alsace-Lorraine, and Poles in
Posen. The other three states were conglomerates which could not exist if
self-determination became effective. The Austro-Hungarian Empire contained Czechs, Slovaks, Poles, Ruthenians, Serbs, Croats, Slovenians. In the
Ottoman Empire a minority of Turks ruled Arabs, Armenians, Greeks, and
Kurds. Russia had many distinct nations within it, such as the Finns, Estoni-
ans, Letts, Lithuanians, Georgians, and Ukrainians. The effort of these states
to control independence movements led to many repressive measures which
only served to heighten the nationalistic feelings already aroused. World
War I marked the end of this struggle and the culmination of the national
self-determination movement in Europe, for it broke up the Austro-Hungarian
Empire and reduced Germany, Turkey, and Russia, creating the succession
states of Austria, Hungary, Yugoslavia, Czechoslovakia, and Poland in central Europe, the Baltic States of Estonia, Latvia, and Lithuania, the republic

of Finland, and the Arab states of the Near East. A nationalist movement in
Turkey after the war overthrew the Ottoman dynasty. Alsace-Lorraine was
returned to France, Schleswig to Denmark, Transylvania and Bukovina to
Rumania.

Not only did the Paris Peace Conference make these major concessions to
the demand for national self-determination by subject peoples, but it also
sought to rectify boundaries so as to permit national minority pockets to select
one state or another. Nine plebiscites for this purpose were authorized. The
idea of the plebiscite was not novel, for it had been used by Napoleon III before the annexation of Nice and Savoy, in the Italian revolution of 1848, in the
union of Moldavia and Wallachia after the Crimean War, in the separation
of Norway and Sweden in 1905, and upon other occasions. When conducted in
a wholly impartial manner by an international administration or third state,
with assurance of secret ballot, the plebiscite may be a proper device, but it
is difficult to obtain such conditions and nearly impossible to exclude bribes,
irresponsible promises, and intensive propaganda. Two of the plebiscites,
Marienwerder-Allenstein and Klagenfurt, have been mentioned. The others
were in Schleswig (between Denmark and Germany), Upper Silesia (Poland
and Germany), Eupen and Malmédy (Belgium and Germany), Burgenland
(Austria and Hungary), and the Saar (France and Germany). In the case
of Eupen and Malmédy Belgium was in control of the area, and those who
wished a transfer to German sovereignty could sign an open register. Only 271
out of 63,000 cared to vote in this manner, a pretty clear indication they
feared reprisals. In Schleswig voting was limited to those domiciled there
before 1900, in Upper Silesia before 1919. It is said that many Germans
formerly domiciled there returned for the election. Both plebiscites resulted
in a division of the contested territory. In Upper Silesia this meant splitting
a unified industrial area, which afterwards produced serious conflicts between Germany and Poland over minorities. The Saar plebiscite was deferred
for fifteen years, during which the League of Nations conducted a model
administration of the territory in the capacity of a trustee. In 1935 the plebiscite
was held. Hitler's government had made a great effort to persuade the predominantly German population and won a decisive victory.

Exchange of minorities is a device which has been used by some states
to rid themselves of the nuisance and danger of continuing to harbor an intransigent irredentist minority. Voluntary exchange is in principle considerate
of the rights of minorities and of self-determination, but fully voluntary
transfers have seldom been effective because the natural inertia of the members of the minority prevents a sufficient response even from families which
could be resettled without hardship. This might be overcome by resettling
all who did not positively elect to remain, with the understanding that such

option meant loss of all group minority rights as to language, schools, political status, etc., that is, assimilation to the status of individual resident aliens.

After World War I there were two notable exchanges of minorities, between Bulgaria and Greece on the one hand and Greece and Turkey on the other. The Bulgarian-Greek exchange was authorized by the Treaty of Neuilly in terms of a right of voluntary emigration, but without any prohibition against governmental pressures to emigrate. In fact, so few registered voluntarily for emigration that both governments began in 1923 to exert substantial pressures. Under the provisions of the treaty 30,000 Greeks were repatriated, and 53,000 Bulgarians; of 70,000 Bulgarians who had emigrated before the convention, 39,000 took advantage of its arrangements to liquidate their property in Greece. Nevertheless, the results were only unilaterally effective. Only 10,000 Greeks remained in Bulgaria, but there were still 82,000 Bulgarians in Greece, concentrated in western and central Macedonia, where they have continued to be a source of friction between the two countries. Although an international commission was set up to supervise the exchange and to provide arrangements for liquidation of realty, there was a good deal of personal hardship. Land had to be sold at less than normal value and inflation reduced the value of negotiable bonds in which the emigrants were paid. Great difficulties were experienced by both governments in resettlement, complicated in Greece by the addition of a million Greek refugees from Turkey. Refugee settlement loans and relief operations had to be undertaken by the League of Nations.

The Greek-Turkish exchange was in no sense voluntary, although authorized by the Treaty of Lausanne. In fact, the rout of the Greek army in Turkish Asia Minor by the forces of Mustapha Kemal had led to the flight of thousands of Greek refugees from Turkey to Greece. The treaty in effect denied these refugees the right to return to Turkey. As there was not enough arable land in Greece to support a million refugees, the government asked that the Turks in Greek Macedonia be transferred to Turkey, and to this compulsory resettlement Turkey agreed. In Greece resettlement was especially difficult not only because of shortage of agricultural land, but also from inability of the industrial economy to support the many skilled artisans, tradesmen, and professional people who returned from Turkey. This was accomplished with the help of the League of Nations Refugee Settlement Commission and large loans, ultimately to the economic benefit of Greece, for nearly a million acres of land were reclaimed for agricultural use and a skilled, enterprising population was added. The Turkish government, since it had ample land for the farmers moved from Macedonia, undertook resettlement without outside aid but was unable to give much financial assistance to the settlers.

Another aspect of the great concern at Paris for subject peoples was the effort to protect linguistic minorities from repression of civil and religious liberties, denial of political rights, or suppression of native-language education. For this purpose a network of minorities treaties between the Principal Allied and Associated Powers of the War and ten European states was concluded. These were placed under supervision of the League of Nations, and other states upon entering the League accepted similar responsibilities. Although the treaties were not very successful the fact of their being used suggests that it was recognized there must be some limits to self-determination. This should indeed have been obvious from the fact that nearly 17 million Germans, Magyars, Bulgarians, Yugoslavs, Ruthenians, and Poles constituted minorities within east European states after the treaties. After World War II some effort was made to utilize treaty guaranties as a means of protecting the position of minorities, but the obligations accepted by central European states were usually couched in terms of protection of human rights generally rather than of any group minority status. The possibility of making such guaranties effective in the face of opposition or indifference within the state concerned appears no greater than in the case of the more specific guaranties of minority rights after World War I. Hungary, Rumania, and Bulgaria have already refused to submit to procedures stipulated in the peace treaties for inquiry into violations. The United Nations has also attempted to state universal standards of human rights, but has been less successful in finding international devices for giving effect to them. Problems of minorities have been taken up as individual political issues. Even when it felt a very direct responsibility for the result, as in the status of the Arab minority in Israel, the United Nations did not find it possible to penetrate national controls.

Self-determination in forming national states may eliminate certain types of difficulties, but it creates others. If a state is to remain economically viable, it may be impossible to amputate every minority area. The difficulties experienced by Austria after the breakup of the Austro-Hungarian Empire are a case in point. Vienna had been the industrial, financial, and distributing center for a large empire. It found itself with only the small Austrian hinterland, cut off by tariff barriers from its former markets. It is probable, too, that excessive disintegration into small states, however happy a solution in a cultural sense, may effectively block large-scale capital investment and industrial development necessary to the support of heavily populated areas. If one could conceive of political boundaries which did not also constitute artificial economic boundaries, the situation might be different, but experience has shown that political nationalism often produces economic nationalism. The latter will be discussed in Chapter 7. The Polish Corridor to the sea separating East Prussia from the rest of Germany, which was instituted by the Treaty of Versailles, was also an instance in which self-determination (by

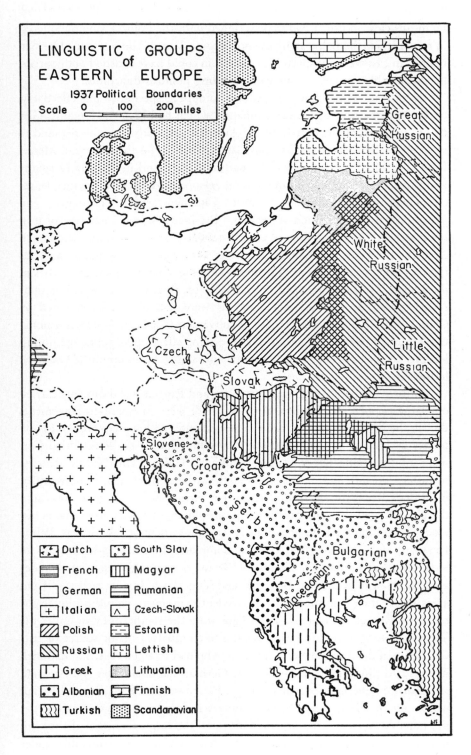

LINGUISTIC GROUPS
of
EASTERN EUROPE

1937 Political Boundaries

Scale 0   100   200 miles

Great
Russian

White
Russian

Czech

Little
Russian

Slovak

Slovenes

Croat

Serb

Bulgarian

Macedonian

Dutch		South Slav	
French		Magyar	
German		Rumanian	
Italian		Czech-Slovak	
Polish		Estonian	
Russian		Lettish	
Greek		Lithuanian	
Albanian		Finnish	
Turkish		Scandanavian	

no means clear in itself) had to be weighed with the Polish economic interest in free access to the Baltic along the north-south Vistula route and the German interest in east-west transport. No conclusion could have satisfied both parties, but the corridor proved a source of unending political difficulties.

In the end Hitler found it possible to appeal, speciously but effectively, to the very principle of self-determination which had been used against Germany. It served as the argument for Austrian *Anschluss,* for the demand to separate the Sudeten Germans from Czechoslovakia, for the seizure of Memel from Lithuania, and finally for the partition of Poland in 1939 by Germany and Russia. Here we have a kind of *reductio ad absurdum* of the principle, yet one which was rather difficult to meet on its own terms after the great emphasis on self-determination at Paris and President Wilson's assertion of it in the Fourteen Points as a kind of ethical standard for international settlement. Actually, the Sudeten Germans had never been a part of Germany, nor was there any doubt they were well treated—far better than German minorities in the Italian Tyrol or in Poland, infinitely better than the Nazis treated their Jewish minority. The German demands were not, of course, accepted by Chamberlain and Daladier because of conviction that Hitler's self-determination argument was sound, but it did have some effect upon public opinion in leading people to believe that "appeasement" might be accomplished on such terms.

During the period 1939–1945 the Nazi and Russian Governments carried out large population transfers. Some of these were pursuant to agreements during the period of the German-Russian entente. Although expressed as voluntary exchanges, it is apparent that the willingness of the long-settled Germans of the Baltic republics, the Wolhynia, Galicia, and Narew districts of eastern Poland, and of Bessarabia and northern Bukovina, to be resettled in Hitler's Reich sprang from a sense that incorporation of these areas into the U.S.S.R. and the consequent extension to them of Soviet economic policy made emigration the lesser evil. The reverse movement of Ukrainians, White Russians, and Russians from German-dominated Polish provinces seems to have been less substantial. Groups of Germans were also repatriated under agreements with Rumania, Bulgaria, and Yugoslavia, but in each case from areas where their continuance as an irredentist minority would no longer be tolerated. Evacuation of 100,000 Germans from the southern Tyrol under the Treaty of October 21, 1939, was essential to eliminate a major source of friction between the Axis partners. For those who had retained Austrian nationality and had thus automatically become German nationals after the Austrian *Anschluss,* resettlement was mandatory. For those who had acquired Italian nationality, it was supposed to be voluntary but this was only formally true; the Italian government unofficially cultivated the impression that if they did not go to Germany they would be resettled (which was permissible under the treaty) in poor areas of Italy or of Ethiopia. After the fall of 1943 the precarious position of German forces in Russia led to the evacuation of large German populations in the Caucasus, southern Ukraine, Soviet East Wolhynia, and Transnistria. Germans of the Banat and Voivodina in Yugoslavia could not be evacuated in time and were deported by the Russians for forced labor. Some 400,000 Germans long established as a German province in the Volga region were transplanted to Siberia. Other important resettlements were the movement of Finns from Karelia into southern Finland; substantial transfers of Poles from Lithuania, White Russia, and the Ukraine to Poland; and exchange of Rumanians and Hungarians in Transylvania.

These and other movements of population probably resulted in the resettlement of more than 3,000,000 persons in eastern Europe during World War II. It may certainly be expected that some long-standing sources of political difficulty have been removed by these procedures, although no estimate of this is possible in the conditions of iron curtain control which have existed. It must be added that great personal hardship was imposed upon many of those who were resettled. The most somber fact is that the Germans, not far short of a million, who were reclaimed by Hitler, were resettled principally in the Polish provinces which had been incorporated into Germany and some in the area of Poland organized by the German occupation government as the Government General, generous land grants being made available for them by ruthlessly driving out the Poles and by wholesale decimation of Jews and Poles.

The post-World War II settlement remains incomplete, but what has been done to date suggests substantially less emphasis upon self-determination than after World War I. Temporary boundary adjustments were simply dictated. Apart from some minor transfers to the Netherlands, German boundaries were not disturbed. France took temporary control of the Saar and proceeded to tie it into a customs union. The Saar has continued a sore point in relations between the two countries. An agreement was reached in 1954 during negotiations for the European Defense Community, but on October 23, 1955, the Saarlanders rejected by a decisive vote a draft statute to place the area under administration of the Western European Union. As Premier Hoffman, widely regarded as the protégé of the French, supported the statute the vote may probably be interpreted as basically an expression of anti-French sentiment and of desire to be reunited with Germany. This was confirmed by the sweeping victory of pro-German parties in the election of December 18, 1955. Eastern European boundaries remain to be legally adjusted, but for all practical purposes Poland, Czechoslovakia, Hungary, Bulgaria, and Rumania have lost all power of self-determination under Communist party control, and the Baltic republics have been absorbed again into Russia. Communists would probably explain that the proletarian revolution

is designed to eliminate all classes, and that in the classless society the state
will wither away leaving no place for nationalism or self-determination in
national terms. Nevertheless, nationalism remains very strong in Eastern
Europe and national self-determination has led to Yugoslavia's breach with
the U.S.S.R. We may assume that the last chapter in this story is yet to be
written.

NATIONALISM AND IMPERIALISM

When we consider the course of European nationalism and self-determination, it is apparent that its early form was liberal and cosmopolitan, concerned with personal liberty and designed to give political expression to popular movements within a cultural group. Associated as it was with bourgeois
values, it was conceived as a movement of liberation and social justice in the
spirit of Herder and Mazzini. There was nothing in it which appeared to
threaten like benefits for other peoples.

But the forces set in motion proved too strong to be constrained by
their original goals. Having achieved national unification and strong nation-
states, the states turned the energies released into aggrandizement at the
expense of others. That is to say, nationalism became one of the impulses
to imperialism. In the case of Great Britain, France, the Netherlands, Spain,
and Portugal early national unification had made possible a drive for colonies after the sixteenth century which was less a response to popular nationalism than to economic motives and dynastic initiative. But the energies released
in Europe after the French Revolution produced a new scramble in Africa
and the Far East for control of remaining areas. In this the Germans and
Italians, having achieved unification and strong central government late in
the century, were far behind and reduced to accepting the left-overs. German imperialism, although it pushed very hard both in Africa and the Far
East, remained unsatisfied. Italy obtained relatively barren areas in North
Africa and revived its efforts in East Africa under Mussolini, who complained that he did not wish to be a collector of deserts.

There were two results which concern nationalism. In the non-Euro-
pean colonies the powers placed themselves in the position of denying those
rights of national self-determination which were in Europe a major political
goal. They tempered this inconsistency by social and educational programs
designed to improve the personal status of colonials and to prepare them for
political participation. It was inevitable that the day would soon come when
groups of educated natives would put themselves at the head of movements
of national liberation and confront European states with their own value
systems as ground for self-determination. The tremendous dislocations of
World War II made this possible as a general movement throughout Asia

and Africa. Nevertheless, it was not a movement quite parallel to the bourgeois nationalism of Europe, for the new states of South and Southeast Asia lack a substantial middle class. The goals which have set their nationalism into motion include desire for political participation and replacement of Europeans by educated natives in higher government posts, coupled with hostility to Western economic development, which is considered exploitation. Their low standard of living is attributed by them to a systematic bleeding of the country by Europeans and to a failure of European administration to save them from money lenders and extortionate landlords. Native nationalist movements have profited from these feelings by promising that the expulsion of colonial government will lead to agrarian reform, lower taxes, debt commutation, and higher prices. Thus Asian nationalism becomes associated with anticolonialism.

The second result was that the latecomers at the colonial table, Germany and Italy, unable to satisfy themselves overseas, turned their aggressive nationalism upon their neighbors. German nationalism from Herder to Hitler is a complete *volte face* from beneficent expression of the national spirit to the ruthless crushing of the national spirit of others who stand in the way of expansion. This is evident from the systematic efforts made to dismember the national state and root out the national consciousness of conquered peoples. The professional class and civil service is destroyed, propaganda substituted for education, churches persecuted, national symbols prohibited, industrial workers deported and industries dismantled, dissident elements eliminated by mass starvation or murder in concentration camps or by a slower attrition in slave labor camps. These techniques, perfected (if that word be appropriate) in Nazi Germany and used also by Communist Russia, aim at the complete disintegration of the elements of the national state beyond hope of recovery. Communists in theory have rejected nationalism even as the basis of their own political organization and demanded reconstruction upon the basis of a larger social community, conceived as the international proletariat represented by the Communist party, which is supposed to give way to the classless communistic society in which the state will have withered away. Nevertheless, Russian nationalism has attempted a rigid control and domination of areas brought within the Communist bloc. In the case of the Nazis a biological group, the Master Race, was conceived as the one group entitled to carve its own boundaries, but this is merely a form of racial nationalism. Thus Hitler, as reported by Rauschning (*Hitler Speaks* [1939]):

Nations are the outward and visible forms of our history. So I have to fuse these nations into a higher order if I want to get rid of the chaos of an historic past that has become an absurdity. . . . Just as the conception of the nation was a revolutionary change from the purely dynastic feudal states, and just as it introduced a biological conception, that of the people, so our own revolution is a further step, or, rather, the final step in the rejection of the historic order and the recognition of purely biological values.

This can be fully appreciated only with the knowledge that Houston Stewart Chamberlain's *Foundations of the Nineteenth Century* was one of the few books Hitler is known to have read. The Nazi imperialism is fortunately dead, but the Russian brand continues.

These things have immediate bearing upon the world crisis today. The nationalism of Asia has brought into being a group of populous, economically underdeveloped, and politically weak and disorganized states—India, Pakistan, Burma, Indonesia, Indochina (the political structure of which is not yet determined), and the Philippines. In the Near East and Africa some Arab states have attained independence, others have it almost within their grasp. Less advanced Negro colonies are pressing for autonomy. Reversing the European sequence, the nationalism of these areas has called into being the states and has done so in many instances without a sufficient middle class to support effective government. Yet these governments must satisfy the universal demand for improvement in living standards or play into the hands of the communists, who are quite prepared to promise what they cannot deliver. In its perhaps premature escape from the older imperialism Asian nationalism is thus subject to the far greater hazards of the totalitarian imperialism of Russian. This danger is less immediate in Africa, but its future will depend upon the fate of Asia.

Since World War I the Russians have made a particular effort to exploit the propaganda possibilities of nationalism in neighboring states. They seem at first to have supposed that there would be spontaneous risings to establish communist governments. In 1919 the Congress of the Peoples of Baku was summoned and the 1,200 delegates, many of whom were not Communists, were urged to go home and proclaim freedom in the name of international communism. A few short-lived revolts followed, especially in Iran, but the results were negligible. Thereafter Communist leaders developed a less naive technique. Recognizing the strength of nationalism in Asia, they adopted the strategy of forming temporary alliances with nationalists—not the nationalists in control of governments but minority nationalists. This policy has continued. After World War II the Russians attempted to stir up national minorities in Greece, Turkey, and Iran.

In Iran the province of Azerbaijan, where the greater part of the population speaks Turkish, had been divided by the Treaty of Turkmanchai (1829), whereby Iran was obliged to cede the northern part to Russia. During the Russian occupation after 1941 a propaganda campaign for unification of Azerbaijan was conducted, of course with the thought that this unification would be in the form of an Azerbaijani S.S.R. within the Soviet Union. With respect to Turkey the national minorities selected were the Kurds and the Armenians. This could be tied in with a plan at the Paris Peace Conference after World War I to dismember Turkey and set up Kurdish and Armenian republics in the eastern part. However, Turkey refused to accept the Treaty of Sèvres and under Mustapha Kemal Pasha fought its way to a bargaining position which enabled it to retain Anatolia. The disappointed Kurds and Armenians, therefore, were considered ripe for nationalist movements. A Kurdish national state was proclaimed under sponsorship of the Russians when in Iran, which claimed not only Kurdish Iran but a great area in eastern Turkey and Syria. Again the Russian assumption apparently was that Kurdish nationalism would take the bait of unification with the small number of Kurds in the U.S.S.R. as a Kurdish S.S.R. With respect to the Armenians there was in fact little physical basis for a movement, for most of the Armenians in Turkey had been butchered by the Turks in 1916–1917. However, Russia had excellent propaganda material in President Wilson's plan for an Armenian state which, on the theory of economic viability, would include such large areas that the Turks would outnumber the Armenians. This plan was dusted off by the Russians and used to stimulate a new Armenian nationalist movement, which for a short time made some stir in Washington. However, Russia was disappointed in its hopes in all three cases, for the nationalist leaders soon became convinced that the Communists had no genuine interest in promoting independent states of Azerbaijan, Kurdistan, and Armenia, but merely wished to attract these areas into the U.S.S.R.

In Greece the Communist party members played the same game, trying to build up a minority movement group which was advertised as antiroyalist Macedonian nationalism. A movement for Macedonian self-determination is certainly highly artificial, but the antiroyalist propaganda proved quite effective for several years and enabled Greek Communists to marshal sympathy in the United States which they did not deserve. It seems probable that these incidents have now served to disclose the true character of Russian overtures to nationalist groups, and that they will in future not find it easy to make much political capital in this way, at least in the Middle East.

PAN-NATIONALISM

There have been many movements and organizations devoted to cultural or political collaboration among peoples of a national group dispersed in several states or even more among peoples of a "race." Writing in 1925, Raymond Leslie Buell enumerated no less than ten such movements, but only a few have had continuing political significance. The Norden movement among Scandinavian peoples has been concerned with cultural and economic relations and does not seriously project political unity. Much the same may be said of such Pan-Angle groups as the English-Speaking Union, although it may add some support to the project of Atlantic Union. However the latter is not confined to countries of English origin. The Pan-African movement has mainly centered in irresponsible leaders among American Negroes, who had no real ties with African Negroes. Pan-Latinism and Pan-Hispanism have failed to create any enthusiasm for closer ties with Spain and have become chiefly a countermovement to Pan-Americanism by those who fear the dominance of the United States. Nevertheless, the Pan-American movement has progressed to a regional security organization—the Organization of American States—while Latin American regionalism has made few gains. Steps toward Central American political and economic collaboration are, however, under consideration.

Pan-Germanism was a genuine political force in the unification of Germany and in the German imperialism of the present century. Its final perversion under the Nazis has been noted. However, it cannot be expected that we have heard the last of it, for the present divided condition of Germany and the separation of Austria have recreated the conditions for such a movement. With the establishment of the independent Federal Republic of Germany in the west it is clear that a fundamental goal of its policy will be reunification with East Germany. Whether a renewed Pan-Germanism of larger scope can be expected is not clear, and may depend upon the effectiveness of European regional controls.

Pan-Slavism is an old movement which began among Balkan Slavs and was cultivated solicitously by Russia. It derived some strength from fear among East European Slavs of German expansion. But the emergence of Czechoslovakia and Yugoslavia after World War I, coupled with the Bolshevist revolution in Russia, for some time interrupted Russian leadership of other Slavic states. This was forcibly re-established after World War II, when these states became satellites under Communist party control and the iron curtain descended. Russia then found it very convenient to dust off Pan-Slavism and to use it as a propaganda tag, dwelling upon the equal status of the various Slav states within this happy family. After the breach with Yugoslavia the party line shifted to the paternal leadership of Russia, the model upon which other communist states should pattern themselves. However, there have been some signs lately of a reversion to the former line. Pan-Slavism in this sense cannot be taken seriously as a movement of national collaboration; it is simply a propaganda cloak for Soviet Communist imperialism.

Among Muslims there have been a number of movements. The older Pan-Islam movement begun about 1876 by Abdul Hamid was intended to improve the sultan's control over the Arabs and to increase unity among Mohammedans everywhere. It was not successful and the dissolution of the

Ottoman Empire broke Turkish control of the Muslim world, a fact signaled by the abolition of the caliphate in 1924. Some ineffective efforts were made in Turkey toward a Pan-Turanian movement, but the possibility of any sort of union of the widely separated Finno-Ugrian peoples of Turkey, Hungary, and central Asia seems remote. In the Arab world Great Britain organized a revolt against the Ottoman Empire in World War I and thus stimulated a movement for national self-determination of Arab states. Since World War II many have coalesced in the Arab League, which sought to present a united front in the struggle to prevent the creation of the state of Israel. However, the effectiveness of the League as an instrument for national movements toward Pan-Arab unity for any more general purposes seems slight. This is due to the serious differences of policy among the Arabs and to the fact that the League is mainly a conference of rulers of states, in many of which the social structure is still semifeudal.

On the whole it cannot be said that pan-national movements are today very effective. Probably the reason is that they appeal to racial, religious, or cultural ties which transcend national feelings while overlooking divisive forces, and thus mistake the effective basis of nationalism.

SELECTED READING

CARR, EDWARD H., *Nationalism and After.* London: Macmillan and Company, Ltd., 1945.

CLAUDE, INIS, *National Minorities, An International Problem.* Cambridge: Harvard University Press, 1955.

COBBAN, ALFRED, *National Self-Determination.* Chicago: University of Chicago Press, 1944.

DELAISI, FRANCIS, *Political Myths and Economic Realities.* New York: Viking Press, 1927.

DEUTSCH, KARL W., *Nationalism and Social Communication: An Inquiry into the Foundations of Nationality.* New York: Technology Press of the Massachusetts Institute of Technology and John Wiley and Sons, 1953.

EARLE, EDWARD MEADE (ed.), *Nationalism and Internationalism, Essays Inscribed to Carlton J. H. Hayes.* New York: Columbia University Press, 1950.

FRIEDMANN, W., *The Crisis of the National State.* London: Macmillan and Company, Ltd., 1943.

HAYES, CARLTON J. H., *Essays on Nationalism.* New York: The Macmillan Company, 1926.

——, *The Historical Evolution of Modern Nationalism.* New York: Richard R. Smith, 1931.

HERTZ, FREDERICK, *Nationality in History and Politics: A Study of the Psychology and Sociology of National Sentiment and Character.* New York: Oxford University Press, 1944.

KOHN, HANS, *The Idea of Nationalism: A Study in Its Origins and Background.* New York: The Macmillan Company, 1948.

Nationalism: A Report by a Study Group of Members of the Royal Institute of International Affairs. London: Oxford University Press, 1939.

SCHECHTMAN, JOSEPH B., *European Population Transfers, 1939–1945.* New York: Oxford University Press, 1946.

SHAFER, BOYD, *Nationalism: Myth and Reality.* New York: Harcourt, Brace and Company, 1955.

SULZBACH, WALTER, *National Consciousness.* Washington: American Council on Public Affairs, 1943.

ZNANIECKI, FLORJAN, *Modern Nationalism: A Sociological Study.* Urbana: University of Illinois Press, 1952.

CHAPTER 4

NATIONAL CHARACTER
AND IDEOLOGY

WHAT IS NATIONAL CHARACTER?

What has been said of nationality suggests the importance of being able to assess correctly any peculiarities in the cultural pattern of a people which help to explain its international attitudes. This has become more important as the popular element in government has increased and public opinion has become dominant. Even in dictatorships account must be taken of public opinion, not to follow it but to adjust it by propaganda or education to government action. A correct estimate of what may be expected from another government must therefore go beyond study of the government itself to inquire what policy it will feel compelled to follow in view of the character and attitudes of its people.

If such an inquiry is to be valid or useful, it should be as scientifically conducted as possible. However, governments have been obliged, in the absence of any better indications, to rely upon the conclusions of careful and experienced observers. Such observers may, indeed, appreciate very accurately the character and attitudes of a people with which they have long been familiar and in occasional flashes of insight may sometimes illuminate its deeper motivations. Yet the procedure is impressionistic, much like that of a literary man who evokes an image of a society at some time and place. Any one who reads the diplomat J. J. Morier's well-known novel, *The Adventures of Hajji Baba of Ispahan,* will recognize that it is an acute and subtle picture of the Persian national character of that day. Yet it is not free from caricature, and its merit lies more in facile delineation of character than in systematic analysis of the ingredients and motivations in the Persian cultural pattern.

In the hands of less competent persons surface observation may become wholly caricature. A certain tendency toward stereotyping may be found even in the comments of so experienced a writer as Harold Nicolson when

69

he compares the diplomacy and diplomatic services of different countries (*Diplomacy* [2d ed., 1950] ch. vi). Certainly we are all influenced by stereotyped caricatures of other peoples which have obtained currency. These are not the result of our own direct observations at all, but are what Lippmann called pictures in our heads, which reflect our own ignorance and bias. Thus, the Englishman is a man impatient of philosophy, with a genius for muddling through. He is dull in conversation, lacking in humor, socially unbending; his food is also tasteless. He has an instinct for fair play, developed on the playing fields of Eton; his conduct is upright and idealistic, but practical. He is devoted to his church, his club, his garden, and phlegmatically transplants them unchanged to Kenya or Borneo. He does not deceive his wife, although she is likely to be rather tasteless, too. The German is seemingly a schizophrenic. On the one hand he is full of sentiment for family and home, he enjoys beer and *Gemütlichkeit,* music and philosophical speculation (but only at the level of metaphysics), and devotes himself to scholarly pursuits. On the other hand he has the social philosophy of the bee, and is happy only when regimented. He works with methodical industry and marked precision, but without imagination, and rushes forth from the factory to drill with equal vigor under the grim eye of a Prussian officer. He is convinced it is his destiny to rule Europe, yet he has feelings of inferiority in the presence of French culture, like a Spartan about to conquer Athens. The Frenchman is an extreme individualist; he is highly rationalistic and materialistic, a religious skeptic though a Roman Catholic; lucid and persuasive in speech but without instinct for public or private order. In politics he is impractical, intensely debating theoretical positions while the state goes to ruin. He drinks wine excessively, is gay, witty, gallant with the ladies, and sexually uninhibited in a dispassionate sort of way. He regards his personal interest more highly than the national interest and does not pay his income tax. Let us draw the curtain of charity over the stereotypes of the American and the Russian.

However ludicrous such notions are, they at least indicate that nearly everyone recognizes there are national differences which go beyond speech and dress and affect outlook, ideals, and patterns of conduct. There is a sense in which anthropologists and sociologists also appear to admit the concept of national character. They deny that any unique, permanent character traits spring from race, and find only a few biological differences, such as maturational sequences, hand-eye co-ordination, or capacity for symbolic behavior, which might affect culture. For the most part culture must therefore be taken, in Margaret Mead's words, as "historically developed, shared, learned behavior of members of a society." Traditional patterns evolved with reference to environmental factors are presumably transmitted through child training and other contacts from generation to generation. In an isolated society change may be very slow, so that some primitive tribes carry their culture patterns into the modern world with little modification. But most cultures are subject to outside influence by invasion or cultural contacts, and therefore undergo continuous change. National character may therefore be conceived as a composite of those uniform character traits found within a national society which result from the shared experience within the nation and the characteristic institutions it produces—linguistic, educational, political, legal, economic, etc.

NATIONAL CHARACTER AS A FACTOR IN INTERNATIONAL RELATIONS

Considered in this way the understanding of national character is of the first importance for international politics. Every nation is in considerable degree culture bound, moving within its own set of dominant ideas and values. It can be understood only in its own terms. Even ideas which are the common property of many nations are seen upon examination to mean different things in different societies. As Ernest Barker put it, "most of them suffer a sea-change as soon as they cross a frontier." "Democracy" is everywhere esteemed, but it means quite different things in the United States, Great Britain, Argentina, Russia. The Russian idea of democracy is not esteemed in the United States, and *vice versa*. Even between the United States and Great Britain, which speak the same language, share many political ideals, and realize their dependency upon each other, there are frequent misunderstandings which could be reduced by a better appreciation of the international attitudes of the two countries.

In his admirable study of comparative psychology, *Englishmen, Frenchmen, Spaniards,* Salvador de Madariaga makes the interesting observation that the sets of characteristic subconscious impulses of the three peoples which he labels—for the Englishman, *fair play,* for the Frenchman, *le droit,* for the Spaniard, *el honor*—are not even translatable into the other languages. Neither *law* nor *derecho* conveys in English or Spanish what *le droit* means to a Frenchman. *Honor* in English has connotations of extravagant idealism without practical value which are not present in *el honor.* The difficulty is that each language subtly reflects the value patterns of a people. When an American speaks of *failure,* or *theory,* or *leisure,* or *foreigners,* or *communism,* these words all take on a connotation of moral disapproval reflecting the success ethic basic to American attitudes. It is assumed that if one works hard, he will succeed. This can be done by plain horse sense better than by philosophic speculation. It is frustrated by foreign systems but encouraged by the American system, in which energy and drive have their just rewards in Cadillacs and television sets. Some appreciation of foreign value systems is therefore a prerequisite even for effective communication among peoples.

It is not very useful to speak of democracy to an Indochinese peasant as if it were a goal to which all good men naturally aspire. For him it has no such associations but more probably invokes the idea of French colonialism.

The reliability of any appreciation of national character is affected by the rapidity of change, and this varies from country to country. Perhaps Professor Barker is right in supposing that as with the iceberg "the great mass of national character rides as it were underseas, with a steady permanence." Still one cannot help suspecting that his conclusion reflects British experience. The national character of the United States, under the impact of the cosmopolitan composition of its population, the rapid change in its economic and social structure from rural to urban industrial society, and its abrupt shift from isolation to international involvement, seems to be more fluid. The same may be true in many Asiatic states which have moved abruptly into fundamental political and social revolutions. However, one must reserve judgment until the pendulum of these movements swings back and it becomes apparent how deep the inroad into tradition has been.

TRADITIONAL APPROACHES TO THE STUDY OF NATIONAL CHARACTER

Granted the importance of a correct delineation of the national character of peoples with whom we deal, how is it to be obtained? Most of the materials have in the past been supplied by travelers, writers, diplomats, journalists, historians, and political scientists. Many of them have been inadequate because merely descriptive and impressionistic, or limited in scope. One cannot on that account dismiss such approaches as useless or invalid; on the contrary, they have provided interpretations of national character of greater sophistication and depth than the more recent "scientific" approaches have yet produced, and have also furnished psychologists, sociologists, and anthropologists with a fund of data to which their analytical methods can be applied. Yet it is certainly true that one must use their comments upon the psychological traits of a people with some reserve, realizing that they may reflect the writer's character quite as much as that of the subject. Thus Carlyle's view of the French people, or Dickens's opinion of Americans, or Mark Twain's of Europeans, would have to be heavily discounted. The more analytical estimates of Alexis de Tocqueville, or André Siegfried, or Salvador de Madariaga would need to be taken for what they are—conclusions of brilliant, incisive, minds well-acquainted with the peoples described, and therefore entitled to respect, but still conclusions not based upon any scientific technique of analysis or upon data carefully selected and controlled. One cannot but feel that their insights are often profoundly true or suggestive, but they ought nevertheless to be verified—all the more so in that they have been presented with such persuasive literary power. Historians seeking to explain the popular forces or cultural trends of a particular people at some stage, political scientists trying to estimate the influence of popular traits and individual or group leadership upon political processes, diplomats trying to predict reactions of a people to particular international situations or policies, have all an advantage in a sharper focus of inquiry and more consciously selected data. Yet their evidence as to national character may be quite circumscribed in terms of time and circumstance.

Some effort has been made to overcome these difficulties. Although one man's observations of the national character of a people may easily be askew this is much less probable when many observers agree. Historians (e.g., Henry Steele Commager, Allan Nevins) have made collections of comments by foreign observers and have found a considerable degree of concensus about some American characteristics. This has been done for one or two other countries, but a great deal of material remains for such classification and comparison. A beginning has also been made in studies at the New School for Social Research to determine how far the national predispositions of writers of various nationalities have influenced their impressions of the American people.

THE PSYCHO-CULTURAL ANALYSIS OF NATIONAL CHARACTER

In recent years, indeed primarily during and since World War II, a number of new methods of examining national character have been used by social scientists. The most ambitious of these has been the application by cultural anthropologists of techniques developed in the study of primitive cultures to analysis of national character in complex modern cultures. They seem to feel that the trained ethnologist can readily determine by testing and interviewing a small number of representatives of a particular culture what are the characteristic features of the culture which differentiate it from others. These they often find in patterns of child training and parental relationships with children. The methods of testing rely heavily upon Freudian psychology and psychoanalysis. Projective tests are commonly used, that is tests which lead the subject to project his own attitudes, preoccupations, and general cultural conditioning into his responses. In the Rorschach Test, developed by a Swiss psychiatrist, the subject tells what he sees in ink blots of the irregular sort made by pressing or folding a sheet of paper over a drop of ink. In the Thematic Apperception Test pictures are used, which the subject interprets or builds stories upon. Manipulation of paints, clay, or dolls according to the subject's fancy may also be used. An elaborate technique of Freudian analysis is then applied to the interpretation of the results. Working with these data and with interviews designed to provide the necessary controls by determining whether the individuals are typical products of the culture or have been subjected to outside influences, the anthropologist proceeds to develop their personality characteristics and to extrapolate these to the society of which they are members.

These methods have been criticized by social psychologists and sociologists upon several grounds. The anthropologists frequently make a rather non-Freudian application of Freudian conceptions. Freud concluded that overstimulation or frustration of erogenous zones in infants by practices in feeding and toilet training would in later life be reflected in fixed reactions, frustrations, or sublimations affecting the character or personality. Thus his theory is essentially a biological one. What the cultural anthropologist is interested in, on the contrary, is not the libidinous reactions of infants as a key to adult reactions but their relations with parents during training periods, which are supposed to fix attitudes with respect to authority, dependence, confidence, instability, and the like, which are important for social conduct. How far such attitudes can really be referred to childhood training is a point upon which there is little agreement. Some critics are also disturbed by the assumption that a small sampling can be sufficiently well controlled by interviewing to be sure that it is a general social pattern which emerges and not an eccentric one reflecting local or family peculiarities. They suggest that success with such methods in a homogeneous primitive society is no proof it can be used in complex heterogeneous societies. How far the patterns developed are characteristic of a whole national group must therefore be determined by a representative sampling.

It must be admitted that the principal studies of national character thus far published by anthropologists are not such as to disarm criticism. Among others, Margaret Mead (*And Keep Your Powder Dry*) and Geoffrey Gorer (*The American People*) have attempted explications of American character which will serve to illustrate. Miss Mead finds that American parents bestow affection or withhold it on the basis of the child's achievement; hence in adult life he comes to regard success, or more specifically the approbation of others, as almost a moral value. The result is an immense competitive drive and a craving for the esteem of others. Further, the immigrant origins of most American families have led children to reject the cultural pattern of parents in favor of that in the new environment, which results in a general weakening of their respect for authority, and by depriving them of traditional cultural ruts in which they can move with a feeling of emotional security forces them to take up transitory standards or fads, moving from one to another in unstable manner. The American is also put down as an optimist with great confidence in improvisation, the direct personal approach, good will, and effort. If these fail, his optimism is confounded and his spirits wilt; hence he is likely to fluctuate impatiently between moods of optimism and depression—he is not one for the long uphill pull against steady odds.

Gorer makes the American even more antiauthoritarian than Mead but does give some weight to revolutionary tradition and frontier environment in his analysis. He also develops the "mother-land" thesis, according to which training of children by the female element of society induces a soft, idealistic tendency; thereafter children are thrust into the competitive, materialistic business world of the male and forced to adopt a new set of standards. The result is that they vacillate between the routine of money-making competition and outbursts of benevolence and generosity. These suggestions are interesting and, if true, might explain certain characteristic international conduct of Americans, such as the persistent confidence of our statesmen that adjustments of international issues will be possible if only the heads of state can be gathered round a table for direct exchanges, or the more general tendency to drive a hard bargain in international trade and then hand over the profits in foreign economic aid, or the apparent discomfort of Americans when foreigners fail to praise their conduct or exhibit suspicion of their motives. However, the argument is a little too naive to be accepted without verification.

Ruth Benedict advanced a hypothesis, developed more extensively with respect to the Great Russians by Geoffrey Gorer and John Rickman (*The People of Great Russia* [1949]), that practices in the swaddling of infants may affect later personality characteristics. Miss Benedict suggested that the unusually tight and prolonged swaddling of Russian infants produces a reaction of personal isolation connected with the "personal inviolability Russians maintain in adulthood." She even associated Russian references to the eyes as the mirrors of the soul (which is surely not a very unique expression) with the fact that a tightly swaddled infant must communicate mainly with its eyes! Gorer connected the "orgiastic nature of adult Russian gratifications" with the fact that babies were unswaddled for nursing. He also considered that tight swaddling might provoke undirected fear and frustration resulting later in vague guilt feelings, and speculated that Russians might in consequence have a tendency to confess when charged with crimes. A somewhat simpler explanation of Russian political trials certainly seems possible.

Gregory Bateson has suggested that analysis of personality might provide a clue to an armaments race: in the United States and England building up to the opponent's strength will be considered fair play; in Germany the stronger will be expected to take advantage of his position, the weaker to submit; in Russia it is considered essential to attain your full strength although not necessarily to exceed others. Hence, the values motivating armament will be differently assessed in different states, and so presumably would be an effort to agree upon disarmament.

INTERDISCIPLINARY STUDY OF NATIONAL CHARACTER

It would be unfair to give the impression that cultural anthropologists feel the psycho-cultural approach to be a shorthand substitute for study of history, economics, geography, language and literature, or religion, as elements in shaping national character. Most of them are very ready to combine their work with the methods of other disciplines and consider this necessary to obtain a definitive picture. Thus Gorer denies that the group makes any claim, overt or implied, ". . . that studies of national character were meant to describe all the phenomena of a nation's life; as far as the studies I have made are concerned, all that is attempted is the isolation and description of the main motives of the majority of the population over and above those rational ones which are gratified by the operation of the institutions which historical accident and technological development have produced at a given time."

In interdisciplinary approaches to national character there does indeed appear to be more promise. The effort of Miss Benedict during World War II to delineate Japanese character as an aid to occupation forces (*The Chrysanthemum and the Sword* [1946]) was based of necessity upon content analysis of historical and literary records, motion pictures, novels, social data, and interviews with Japanese in the United States. Although there is a good deal of psycho-cultural hypothesis there is also an effort to correlate all these data and to determine from them the Japanese assumptions about the conduct of their lives. Miss Benedict's conclusions attach great weight to the structuring of society in Japan, which retains feudal hierarchical notions of personal obligation and of the appropriate place of each person in society. A possibly related orderliness in the arrangement of the individual's own life into separate spheres or orders of activity is noted. Although several critics have pointed out inadequacies or errors in the data used for particular points, the results as a whole are rather impressive.

Erik Erikson's study of "Hitler's Imagery and German Youth" assumes that the crossroads position of Germany and consequent frequency of military and cultural invasions of it have produced two types of German, the overly cosmopolitan and the overly nationalistic. The former held control during the Weimar Republic but was unable to solve immediate economic and social problems. The German people then reacted toward the nationalist, race-conscious Hitler, and his promises of expansion and unification. Erich Fromm (*Escape from Freedom* [1941]) is also concerned with the appeal of Nazism to Germans, which he considers in the light of historical, geographic, and economic forces. He finds conflicting tendencies toward free expression and isolation in the influences of Lutheranism and capitalism and describes German social structure as "authoritarian" and "sado-masochistic," with class hierarchies in which each group obeys superiors and demands obedience from inferiors. But superiors had failed in the war and in avoiding the depression and inflation following it. Disillusioned and confused, the bourgeois elements made no resistance to Hitler. The lower middle class, on the other hand, actively espoused his cause, for they demanded strong authority and responded sympathetically to the resentful, nationalistic attitudes he expressed. Many other factors enter into Fromm's analysis. Whether it is correct or incorrect is not clear, for we have no data to verify the extent of the attitudes described, but the study is certainly suggestive of a possible method of relating psychoanalysis of personality traits to historical-social situations which serve to stimulate or set off certain tendencies. Whether the method would have much predictive value is doubtful; it is a good deal easier to apply to explanation of what has already occurred.

Efforts to describe the composition and perspective of groups important in the shaping and control of foreign policy have been aided a good deal by public opinion polls and the techniques of interviewing and testing. Although polls have frequently been undertaken for the primary purpose of predicting voting behavior, the data collected often indicate reactions to international issues and foreign policy. It is also possible in most cases to differentiate the reactions of several classes of persons according to sex, education, occupation, geographical area, economic status, and the like. Careful reworking of the materials collected may reveal a good deal about correlations between one or another type of personal status and attitude toward or knowledge of international problems, although it is probable that the available data will need to be supplemented largely by polls more specifically designed for that purpose. The few studies which have utilized available polls (e.g., Thomas A. Bailey's *The Man in the Street* [1948], Hadley Cantril's *Public Opinion, 1935-1946* [1951] and Buchanan and Cantril's *How Nations See Each Other* [1953], Gabriel Almond's *The American People and Foreign Policy* [1950], Jerome Bruner's *Mandate from the People* [1944]) have at least demonstrated the usefulness of this approach.

Since the control of foreign policy within most countries is rather narrowly held the importance of special studies of elite groups which exercise an influence disproportionate to their numbers is apparent. Older studies of the diplomatic elite were usually biographical or autobiographical. These tended to be impressionistic, but often threw much light upon the motivations and conditioning of individual statesmen or diplomats. They were less successful in defining the role of policy makers as a class in the decision-making process. Studies of editorial opinion and content analysis of news stories gave some conception of the role of mass communications media. More recent studies have sought to apply objective opinion and attitude analysis to the policy makers and thus to reach generalizations about decision making in various governments, an effort which must of course depend upon the willingness of the policy makers to collaborate. Extensive use of depth interviews of important policy makers has been made in several countries by Lloyd Free and Hadley Cantril in studies conducted by the Public Opinion Center of Princeton University; by Harold Isaacs, Daniel Lerner, and others for the Research Program in International Communications at the Massachusetts Institute of Technology; and by Nathan Leites, Margaret Mead, Gabriel Almond, and others for the Rand Corporation. In connection with the studies of Soviet culture undertaken by the Rand Corporation, Leites has attempted to formulate what he terms the operational code of the Politburo, i.e., a statement of the assumptions about objectives, methods, and strategies upon which that group acts (*Study of Bolshevism* [1953], *The Operational Code of the Politburo* [1951]). In a similar vein is the collection of studies bearing upon the characteristics of Soviet international behavior in Raymond Dennett and Joseph E. Johnson's *Negotiating with the Russians* (1951). Other approaches to elite analysis may be found in Stanford University's Hoover Institute Studies of elites and ideological symbols and the UNESCO studies of international tensions. It is perhaps too early to evaluate these attempts. Clearly they make large demands upon the political behavior analyst, for not only must he understand the testing and interviewing techniques which can be employed to obtain data about attitudes or opinion, but he must be intimately acquainted with the nature of the political problem or decision-making context he is investigating and with the national and individual peculiarities of the persons selected for study. For this reason such studies need often to be planned through collaboration of representatives of several disciplines—polling experts, psychoanalysts, historians, political scientists, economists, sociologists, anthropologists. These difficulties do not mean that the method is impractical, and progress has in fact been encouraging.

SOME CONTRIBUTIONS OF SOCIAL PSYCHOLOGY AND SOCIOLOGY

Some light may eventually be thrown upon the group behavior of nations by the research of social psychologists in group dynamics. The experiments have to date been confined to small groups which can be readily controlled, so that no immediate applications can be made to problems of such a complex group, with myriad overlapping subgroups, as the nation. Perhaps this will prove in the end to be too complex a social structure for effective group dynamics study, but there is no reason at this stage to dismiss the possibility that as empirical data from small group research accumulate, it may become feasible to make applications to group situations of ever increasing complexity.

Among the problems upon which research has been undertaken are a number connected with group pressures and group standards. For example Muzafer Sherif and Solomon E. Asch have attempted to determine how far individual members of a group are dependent upon group judgments or tend to conform to group norms in a variety of situations. Sherif concluded that in a situation in which the individual cannot tell whether his answer is right or wrong he depends almost completely upon group judgments. Asch presented a simple test of perceptual relations to a group, asking them to match the length of a given line with one of three unequal lines, then instructed all members of the group but one to give an agreed but incorrect answer to see what effect this would have upon the uninstructed member. In many cases he abandoned the evidence of his own senses to conform to group opinion, and even those individuals (about 25 percent) who completely maintained their independence of judgment did so hesitantly, uncomfortably, or apologetically. Further inquiry has been made into the reasons for differences in individual reactions under such circumstances. This may of course depend greatly upon individual personality, but the experiments of Leon Festinger, Stanley Schacter, and others, suggest that his attitudes toward the group, whether favorable, neutral, or unfavorable, and the cohesiveness of the group in terms of tradition, values, or objectives, may greatly affect the tendency to conform.

Still another factor of great significance is group leadership. The older assumption that leaders emerged because they possessed certain special traits has undergone some modification, although the need for at least minimal qualifications may be assumed and the compulsive desire of some individuals for power or attention is certainly a factor. Nevertheless group aims are now seen to control the choice in many cases, and a sense of responsibility to the group or a feeling that the group regards one's contribution as important may provide incentives to accept leadership. An effort has also been made by Ralph White and Ronald Lippitt to determine what effect the use of three different types of leadership—authoritarian, democratic, and laissez-faire— has upon group attitudes. In general, they concluded that laissez-faire leadership led to irresponsibility and inefficiency; autocratic leadership to somewhat greater work output while the leader was present but to discontent, hostility, aggressive behavior to scapegoats, and "release" behavior on transfer to a different type of leadership; democratic leadership to greater individuality, better work motivation, and friendlier, group-minded attitudes.

There is a temptation which must be resisted to suppose that conclusions from these studies of small groups can be directly applied to such problems as the basis of political conformity under democracy, fascism, and communism, or the attitude toward dictators in authoritarian states, or the basis of concensus in different types of societies. It must be emphasized that the field of inquiry is a new one, that the experimental data are suggestive but often not conclusive, and that political groups are far more complex structures than those investigated. For the present group dynamics is probably important to international relations mainly in providing a fund of hypotheses which can be used in considering the situations presented there. As yet little progress has been made in this direction.

The interest of sociologists in studying different types of social structure, the structuring and operation of elite groups, the interaction of persons within a society, and social conflicts, may also prove valuable for an eventual science of international relations. These inquiries are not so much focused upon individual personality in its relation to national character as upon the institutional framework of relationships within which individuals and groups interact or which are products of such interactions. The effort to move from a consideration of intergovernmental relations to a broader inquiry into the interaction of groups and individuals within a state which determines each government's actions must rest upon clarification of these relationships. The sociologist's approach greatly but necessarily complicates the study of international relations and has not as yet given as much attention to problems at that level as to interaction of and within smaller groups. It may eventually contribute greater knowledge of the conditions of group assimilation, as in federation or international organization, of the basis of international conflict, and of the formation of opinion, concensus, values, and ideology at national and international levels.

IDEOLOGY

National character is a direct reflection of the development and transmission of a culture. It must be distinguished from ideology, which may indeed spring from a culture but which is developed as an abstract, organized system of ideas, beliefs, or values and can be artificially disseminated through propaganda or education. Indeed, ideologies are not characteristically transmitted to infants or unconsciously acquired through cultural contacts, but are rational, integrated systems consciously taught. Far from being culture-bound, they frequently migrate and take root more firmly in other cultures than in the one in which they originate. They may sometimes be traceable to dominant personalities who are far from typical of the cultures in which they move. Religious ideologies such as Christianity, Buddhism, Mohammedanism and politico-economic ideologies such as communism, fascism, or laissez-faire capitalism, have shown power to spread to quite alien cultures. Christianity originated among the Jewish people but was not received by them. Communism was developed by the German intellectuals Marx and Engels with primary reference to English economic data and was assumed by its founders to apply most immediately to industrial societies; yet its

success to date has been mainly in east European and Asiatic agrarian economies. The ideology may of course become institutionalized, after which it
usually takes on some coloration from the institutions and exhibits individual
differences in different places. Christianity acquired a number of different
institutional forms (Roman Catholic, Eastern Orthodox, Coptic, etc.) which
reflected and themselves produced ideological deviations as they developed.
Communism was greatly modified by the practical requirements of its do-
mestication in Russia, as a result of which Leninism, Trotskyism, Stalinism,
must be distinguished as ideological deviations from Marxism. No doubt it
will develop other ideological variants in countries to which it has subsequently moved.

These facts suggest that there is an interplay between cultural-institutional
traditions and ideologies, or we may say for simplicity between ideology and
national character, which makes it unwise to jump to conclusions about
national action on the basis of ideology alone. Such action is a resultant of
a complex of such forces as ideology, national character, the effect of both
upon specific groups and individuals and the interaction of these individuals
and groups in the political process, the system of controls within the state,
the strength of political leadership, etc. To think of the U.S.S.R. as steadily
pursuing a fixed ideological goal, subject only to tactical retreats when necessary, is to ignore several plain facts: (a) many of the goals of the U.S.S.R.,
such as territorial aggrandizement, are historic goals of Russia which have
been pursued for centuries; (b) Russian leaders have found it expedient to
issue the official reinterpretations of the ideology already mentioned; (c) many
Russians have other ideologies, not wholly compatible with communism,
which have exhibited marked staying powers: thus the attack upon traditional religion was only partially successful and a compromise was struck,
the early elimination of money and wages was a failure and had to be abandoned, the collectivization of farms has apparently broken down personal
incentives to produce and may have to be modified; (d) the ideology is itself
vigorously espoused only within a relatively small group, the Communist
party, comprising less than 5 percent of the population; (e) the government
of the U.S.S.R. is an oligarchy which hardly responds to the ideological
standard of dictatorship of the proletariat, or even dictatorship of the Communist party, which is itself a serious modification of Marxist ideology. It
would be foolish to minimize the power of communist ideology in view of
the driving force it has shown, or to underestimate the extent of the commitment of doctrinaire communists to it, but it would be equally foolish to
suppose that it negates history, geography, economics, national character, or
even expediency.

This raises a very difficult question: What part does ideology play in
controlling political conduct? No careful study of this appears to have been

made, and it may well be that national variations would be too great to permit general conclusions if all the data were assembled. There is strong professional opinion among experts on Japanese politics that the ideology of the Shinto state religion, posing the divine descent of the emperor and the familial relationship of all Japanese to the emperor, has been a central factor in Japanese nationalism and the highly centralized state control. American occupation authorities considered the disestablishment of the Shinto religion necessary primarily because it was a useful ideological weapon for Japanese militarists. Yet it might be difficult to demonstrate that modern Japanese really accept the myth of imperial divinity in any other sense than a myth, or that the apparent reverence for the emperor is different in kind from the deep respect of the British for their ruler. It seems at least possible that such habits of deference may have become imbedded as institutional attitudes in the traditional culture even though they are no longer believed as a formal ideology. In the previous chapter attention was drawn to the Nazi use of an ideology of racial nationalism. There was certainly some degree of acceptance of the Aryan supremacy myth long before Hitler, but there must also have been millions of Germans who rejected it as irrational and supported the Nazis, as Erikson and Fromm argued, upon grounds of frustration, disillusionment, and dissatisfaction. Unfortunately there is no way of determining how far this extraordinary ideology may have been influential. Americans consider themselves deeply committed to democracy and laissez-faire capitalism, but it is perfectly clear that these terms subsume very wide differences of opinion as to government ownership and regulation, as to representation, even as to restrictions upon freedom of opinion and political affiliation. Can it be that their ideology has become a political mythology and symbology with about the same relationship to political conviction and action as the Apostles' Creed bears to the convictions and actions of the average churchgoer? Is it a fixed symbol with variable content? To ask such questions is at present much easier than to give answers, for the basic research upon the problem remains to be done. Perhaps the most logical hypothesis in the present state of knowledge would be that the force of ideologies as such is greatest in their initial stages of militant and evangelical expansion, but that as they are accepted and obtain institutional vehicles they become enmeshed with the cultural patterns involved in national character and become less and less consistent philosophical positions and more and more the catch words and shibboleths of a more complicated and qualified social system.

There has been a tendency stemming from the sociologist, Karl Mannheim, to regard ideology as pretext or disguise for actions which are really motivated by interests. Mannheim used the term "particular ideology" (as distinguished from "total ideology") in situations where the ideas or representations of an opponent arouse skepticism. "They are regarded as more or less conscious disguises of the real nature of a situation, the true recognition of which would not be in accord with his interests. These distortions range all the way from conscious lies to half-conscious and unwitting disguises; from calculated attempts to dupe others to self-deception." By "total ideology" he meant the whole structure of mind of "a concrete historico-social group," e.g., the ideology of the medieval church or of British mercantilists. The assumption that a particular ideology is either deliberate deception or self-deception and that interest motivates policy has been developed by several writers, notably Edward H. Carr and Hans J. Morgenthau. Unfortunately, neither has really pressed the concept of "national interest" far enough to demonstrate that it can thus be separated from ideology.

We are here in an area in which psychology does not yet afford the assistance required, but it seems hardly demonstrable that people (or governments) act solely in terms of a set of observable interests. If we say that they can deceive themselves as to ideology, can they not equally deceive themselves as to interest? Interests such as food and shelter are obvious enough but this is of no value for analysis of national interest. If one begins with an assumption that security and prosperity are national interests, he can only go on to consider a number of alternative methods of securing these interests, the choice among which is seldom obvious. Why does he conclude that security can best be obtained by military strength, or by alliances, or by reliance upon collective security? Presumably because action is not determined simply by interest, but by a combination of interest, knowledge (or ignorance), and value judgments. If so, it would seem that conclusions about national interest are inextricably bound up with ideologies.

There is no policy which is absolutely and demonstrably in the national interest. There are only opinions about securing the national interest. Perhaps there will be a concensus of opinions, but only history can test the wisdom of the concensus, and history itself may be just a later opinion. Who can say, for example, whether the entry of the United States into the two world wars was in the national interest? We all have convictions upon the subject, but they arise from our sense of values rather than from any absolute standard at our disposal. In this sense it appears a somewhat meaningless exercise to separate ideology and interest when our view of interest is necessarily colored by ideology.

On the other hand it can certainly be admitted that a government which has one conception of interest and of appropriate action to secure it could deliberately use for propaganda purposes an ideology which was not involved in its decisions. But it is far from clear how far this happens. We are prone to assume Macchiavellian conduct by other governments and to credit our own with transparent sincerity. Both conclusions may need qualification. In *The Man of Destiny* George Bernard Shaw put into the mouth of Napoleon some comments upon the British which illustrate the tendency. Napoleon remarks that the Englishman is born with a remarkable capacity to translate all his actions into terms of high moral purpose:

> . . . He is never at a loss for an effective moral attitude. As the great champion of freedom and national independence, he conquers and annexes half the world, and calls it Colonization. When he wants a new market for his adulterated Manchester goods, he sends a missionary to teach the natives the gospel of peace. The natives kill the missionary: he flies to arms in defense of Christianity; fights for it; conquers for it; and takes the market as a reward from heaven. In defense of his island shores, he puts a chaplain on board his ship; nails a flag with a cross on it to his top-gallant mast; and sails to the ends of the earth, sinking, burning and destroying all who dispute the empire of the seas with him. He boasts that a slave is free the moment that his foot touches British soil; and he sells the children of his poor at six years of age to work under the lash in his factories for sixteen hours a day. He makes two revolutions, and then declares war on our one in the name of law and order. There is nothing so bad or so good that you will not find the Englishmen doing it; but you will never find an Englishman in the wrong. He does everything on principle. He fights you on patriotic principles; he robs you on business principles; he enslaves you on imperial principles; he bullies you on manly principles; he supports his king on loyal principles, and cuts off his king's head on republican principles. His watchword is always duty; and he never forgets that the nation which lets its duty get on the opposite side to its interest is lost.

Only an Irishman could have written this, but Napoleon would no doubt have enjoyed speaking it, for he might have recalled that he overran all of Europe upon the principle of liberty, equality, and fraternity.

Most governments attempt to explain themselves in terms of value objectives, but it seems probable that the choice of propaganda more often reflects genuine ideological positions which affected their choice of policy than deliberate falsifications of their motives. Imperialism may be presented as "manifest destiny" or the "white man's burden" or the mission of a superior people, but these are quite as likely to be genuine convictions as the equally debatable assumptions that imperialism always pays or the possession of colonies always increases national power. We are in some danger in criticizing ideological representations as false that we are judging them in terms of other ideological suppositions we arbitrarily assume to be true. In any case we are left with ideological conflicts which must be admitted to have an influence in international relations, whether or not they can be shown to be the dominant determinants of action. Ideologies connected with sovereignty, international community, nationalism, and self-determination have been referred to already. Others involving imperialism, autarchy, collective security, international justice, international order, will require consideration in later chapters. Because of their central position in recent international controversy it seems desirable here to outline briefly the doctrinal content of the ideologies we call communism, fascism, and democracy.

Socialism and Communism

"Communism" is a particular form of "socialism." Socialism in general is a protest against "capitalism." Capitalism is an economic system in which private persons are permitted with a minimum of government regulation to own and operate productive enterprises, finding the necessary capital and employing the labor needed to do this, marketing the finished products, and retaining any profits which may remain after the costs of production and marketing have been met. It is assumed that the incentive to profit will lead individuals to risk capital, and that to minimize this risk they must maximize the efficiency of production so as to be able to keep prices of finished articles low enough to compete with those of other producers. Inefficient producers will thus be eliminated, and the economy as a whole will be stimulated to maximum output. However, completely unregulated or laissez-faire capitalism is likely to lead to serious abuses because of the entrepreneur's disposition to minimize his costs and maximize his profits. Labor is likely to be secured at minimal wages and to be laid off seasonally or in periods of economic dislocation. Prices will sometimes be determined in relation not to costs or the needs of the community but to what the market will bear. The laborer will have little incentive or pride of workmanship, and may find himself in distress in old age. Some improvement in conditions can of course be expected from the operation of natural forces. Artificially high prices will be driven down by entry of other producers into the field or by hope of increasing total profits by larger sales at lower unit price. Wages and social security provisions for labor can be improved by labor organization and collective bargaining. A modification of complete laissez faire by government regulations which give legal status to collective bargaining, or affect price structures, or compel employers and employees to contribute to social security funds, or even assume ownership and operation of certain public utilities, is common. This has been the pattern in the United States. But the socialist would argue that serious inequities will persist despite such regulations, and that the general interest can be served best by collective ownership and control of the instruments of production and exchange, coupled with careful public planning.

However, there is little agreement among socialists as to how these general objectives should be realized. They differ as to the type of collective organization which should assume control of the instruments of production, some arguing for workers guilds or cooperatives, others for the state. More importantly, they differ as to whether the process of transformation can be evolutionary, through normal constitutional methods, or requires revolution.

In several states of Western Europe (Great Britain, the Scandinavian countries) there has been a substantial socializing trend in the taking over by the state of important enterprises and the provision of comprehensive "cradle to grave" social security through wholly democratic processes.

Contrasted with this are the socialists who insist that the new order they desire can be secured only by revolution and violence. Of these the most important group are the communists. In terms of ideology they stem from the theoretical writings of Karl Marx and Friedrich Engels. Marx's principal exposition of the position is given in his massive treatise *Capital* (1867–1894), but the essentials may be found in striking form in the famous *Communist Manifesto* (1848). In terms of a movement communism began with the First International, an organization of individuals founded in 1864 by Marx, which broke up in 1872 because of disagreement between anarchist and socialist members. Social democrats then founded in 1889 the Second International, members of which are social democratic parties of various countries. A Third, or Communist International, was formed in 1919 by Lenin, and functioned almost as an arm of the Russian Government for international communist activity. As its propagandistic and subversive activities had been widely criticized, it was formally dissolved in 1941 as a gesture toward Russia's allies in World War II. However, in 1947, the Cominform, a federation of Communist parties in iron curtain countries and France and Italy, took up the tasks of the International. There is also a Fourth International, of little practical political significance, formed by the followers of Trotsky after his break with Lenin and expulsion from Russia. Each of these groups espouses a different version of socialist ideology.

Marx postulated the inevitable decay of capitalism from inner corruption. His theory of society is based upon historical (or dialectical) materialism, in which exploitation of labor in capitalist societies is seen as creating a class struggle. Related to this are two doctrines, the labor theory of value and the theory of surplus value. Labor is assumed to be the source of all value in commodities. It is assumed that the amount paid for labor is always far less than the value it contributes to the finished product. The surplus value accrues to the capitalist, who is thus enriched by the exploitation of labor. Capitalism, in its greed for profit, overexpands until it wrecks the market, then unduly contracts by laying off workers, and so creates erratic cycles of prosperity and depression. Unsuccessful capitalists drop into the proletariat, leaving a greater concentration of capital in fewer hands. Thus the middle class is gradually destroyed and class conflict becomes sharper between workers and capitalists, until the workers are driven to despair by their deteriorating position and revolution occurs. To consolidate their position the triumphant workers must then impose "the dictatorship of the proletariat." In fact the workers will be unable to control the situation and must temporarily accept the leadership of the communist party. For a time the role of the state under the dominant proletariat will be intensified until all capitalists are eliminated or become workers, when classes will no longer exist, the need for state protection of the new order will disappear, and the state will "wither away."

It is probably pointless to observe that there are serious fallacies in Marxism as an economic theory. Arthur Koestler is even quite correct in saying that the nineteenth-century posing of capitalism or socialism as alternatives has lost most of its meaning, for great flexibility has been shown by capitalism in adjusting to the demand for improved labor conditions or even unifying capital and labor, and continues to avoid its supposedly inevitable demise as a victim of the class struggle. The classless society might even be thought closer at hand in America than in Russia. These rational considerations may come in time to have their effect, but for the present communism continues as a powerful force because it became attached to a revolution in which it was the ideology and the article of faith. It continues as a position of great propagandistic value to an aggressive dictatorship, and has been adjusted by Lenin and Stalin as circumstances required. Leninism is an exposition of Marxism applied to the period of revolution in the age of capitalistic imperialism. Stalinism is a further adjustment of doctrine for the period of dictatorship of the Communist party supposed to follow the revolution. Although either one can properly be denounced as a fraudulent misrepresentation of the political purposes of dictators in any communistic country, they may be taken as a statement of ideals or objectives which constitute the dedicated communist's credo—perhaps his religion. For the doctrinaire communist submission to a harsh dictatorship, suppression of all individualism, and acceptance of a grinding poverty and occupational regimentation, are the sacrifices which must be made to assure the eventual attainment of the classless society and the Marxist millenium. How long the millenium can be deferred without shaking his convictions is not clear, but postponement is aided by the relatively more comfortable position enjoyed by the party man in his own society. "All are equal, but some are more equal than others." The masses, of course, submit not from conviction but from necessity.

Fascism

One element sometimes found in fascism is a conception of race supremacy, which has been discussed in connection with German nationalism. It is associated also with Japanese fascism, but it has not been an element of much importance in the Italian, Spanish, or Argentinian varieties. As an ideology, fascism incorporates a number of doctrines which may be mixed in somewhat different proportions. They include the totalitarian state, the leadership principle, rule by an elite class, power as the basis of authority, subordination of the individual to the ends of the state in the belief that he achieves self-realization (whatever that means) only in this way.

The state is conceived as a living, spiritual, organic being composed of individuals who have no independence or individual value except as units within it. It has a predestined end and hence a moral value in itself to which individual interests must be completely subordinated. Individualism as a value is wholly rejected. The state does not exist to serve individuals but to realize its destiny through them. To that end it must seek and use power, and must control every activity within it, political, economic, or moral. In that sense it is totalitarian. Without its permission there cannot be political parties, industrial organization, trade unions, publications, education, even religious institutions; all are subject to control and regulation in its interest. Army, police, elite corps, concentration camps, centralized administration, schools, mass communications, a state-controlled economy are the instruments of its regimentation.

According to Mussolini, fascism repudiates pacifism, socialism, democracy, and individualism. The state is born through struggle and advances through war. Peace is not regarded as an end in itself, and internationalism is rejected as weakness. "War is to man what maternity is to woman." The totalitarian state is indeed a form of collectivism, but it has little in common with socialism in its objectives. However, fascism has characteristically accepted the traditional institutions of family and private property, perhaps upon the assumption that this encourages the production of more individuals for the service of the state. Frequent maternity was extolled by both Mussolini and Hitler and state bounties provided for exceptional productivity. These tendencies have led socialists to condemn fascism as a final perversion of capitalism created in the effort to fend off its dissolution.

A characteristic element is the leadership principle and the elite. Society is conceived in terms of a natural hierarchy with all authority emanating from the top and various layers of lesser leaders, each of which dictates to those below. Every person in a position of authority, e.g., a factory foreman, is for that purpose a dictator. The leader or Führer of the state is also conceived as having emerged as a matter of historical destiny or divine mission; he is the personal embodiment of the mission of the state. No rational considerations such as ability, training, or legitimacy affect his position. There is a deal of mystical nonsense about his charismatic character which obscures the strong-arm methods of the military clique which brought him to power. Usually he surrounds himself with symbols to convey the sense of his identification with the destiny of the state—the mystical symbol of the swastika in Nazi Germany, the power symbol of the fasces in Fascist Italy. But he is even more careful to surround himself with the elite corps of bullies who assure his control of army, police, industry, and such political exercises as the state may permit.

Democracy

Democracy is a form of government or political process which is founded upon belief in the value of individual personality and designed to permit individuals, directly or through representatives, to govern themselves in accordance with the concensus of free opinion. Generally this is conceived in terms of majority rule, but such a definition may be unduly restrictive as placing too much emphasis upon the form rather than the substance. Fascism and communism are notorious for their ability to produce tremendous supporting majorities. States generally regarded as democratic do not always have very broad electorates, or complete political participation, so that the deciding votes are often only a minority. One must look a little beyond these formal processes for the essence of democracy, which seems to lie in a social structure which permits independent opinion and expression, a free market of ideas, a tolerant willingness to hear and weigh all points of view before deciding, and a political process designed generally to give effect to the prevailing view which emerges.

In a negative sense the political freedom essential to democracy is only the absence of any greater restraint than is needed to assure a like freedom to others. This requires the rule of law and a system of protection of human rights. In a positive sense it is recognized that democracy requires an alert, informed, citizenry; individuals are not able to bring their individual personalities and judgments to bear in influencing the consensus unless they have sufficient education to express themselves, sufficient economic resources to be freed from dependency upon others, and free sources of information to obtain facts. Consequently democratic states endeavor to provide public education, to raise living standards, and to prevent a monopoly of mass communication media in the hands of one class. Economic and social democracy are handmaidens of political democracy. These are all difficult problems which have not been fully solved in any democratic state. But democracy as an ideology poses such objectives.

There is no necessary inconsistency between democracy and socialism, since the latter may be brought into existence with popular assent. There is inconsistency with communism insofar as that dogma demands change by revolution and a temporary period of dictatorship. And fascism, with its studied disregard for the individual and individual values, must be accounted the antithesis of democracy. World politics cannot indeed be reduced into terms so simple as a clash of these three ideologies, but they are points of view and ways of life which affect many problems in international relations.

SELECTED READING

BARKER, SIR ERNEST, *National Character and the Factors in Its Formation,* 4th ed., rev. London: Methuen and Company, Ltd., 1948.

BATESON, GREGORY, "The Pattern of an Armaments Race: An Anthropological Approach—Part I," in *Bulletin of the Atomic Scientists,* 2 (5–6): 10–11, 26–28 (1946).

BENEDICT, RUTH, *The Chrysanthemum and the Sword.* Boston: Houghton Mifflin Company, 1946.

BUCHANAN, WILLIAM and CANTRIL, HADLEY. *How Nations See Each Other.* Urbana, Ill.: University of Illinois Press, 1953.

CARTWRIGHT, DORWIN, and ZANDER, ALVIN (eds.), *Group Dynamics: Research and Theory.* Evanston: Row, Peterson and Company, 1953.

COMMAGER, H. S., *America in Perspective: the United States through Foreign Eyes.* New York: Random House, 1947.

ERIKSON, E. H., "Hitler's Imagery and German Youth," in *Psychiatry,* 5: 475–493 (1942).

FROMM, ERICH, *Escape from Freedom.* New York: Farrar and Rinehart, 1941.

GORER, GEOFFREY, *The American People.* New York: W. W. Norton and Company, 1948.

———, and RICKMAN, JOHN, *The People of Great Russia: A Psychological Study.* London: The Cresset Press, 1949.

KLINEBERG, OTTO, *Tensions Affecting International Understanding.* New York: Social Science Research Council, 1950 (Bulletin 62).

LEITES, NATHAN, *A Study of Bolshevism.* Glencoe, Ill.: Free Press, 1953.

LERNER, MAX, *Ideas are Weapons.* New York: The Viking Press, 1939.

LLOYD, CHRISTOPHER, *Democracy and Its Rivals: An Introduction to Modern Political Theories,* 2d ed. London: Longmans, Green and Company, 1946.

MADARIAGA, SALVADOR DE, *Englishmen, Frenchmen, Spaniards: An Essay in Comparative Psychology.* London: Humphrey Milford (Oxford University Press), 1928.

MANNHEIM, KARL, *Ideology and Utopia.* New York: Harcourt, Brace and Company, 1936.

MEAD, MARGARET, *And Keep Your Powder Dry.* New York: William Morrow and Company, 1942.

———, *Soviet Attitudes toward Authority.* New York: McGraw-Hill Book Company, 1951.

SNYDER, RICHARD C. and WILSON, H. HUBERT, *Roots of Political Behavior.* New York: American Book Company, 1949. Chs. 10–12.

SOLTAU, ROGER H., *An Introduction to Politics.* London: Longmans, Green and Company, 1951. Ch. XIV.

CHAPTER 5

FORCE AND POWER POLITICS

"Force rules the world: has ruled it: shall rule it." Like most generalizations the old Viking proverb was too sweeping, but there was a great deal of truth in it. A state without power is a contradiction in terms, and with too little is like a house built upon sand. Power of one kind or another is the inescapable means by which the state carries out its policies, and this is as true in the domestic as in the foreign field.

THE OVERMIGHTY SUBJECT

Law and order in internal affairs are so firmly established that they are taken for granted, and few stop to consider that they are maintained not only by custom and morality but when necessary by force. A judge who had to depend on moral suasion would not get much cooperation from a gangster with an automatic. The men of the middle ages had a clearer perception of the facts of life. The curse of fifteenth-century England, for instance, was the "overmighty subject," the rich baron who could afford to pay his private army of professional soldiers. He took his weaker neighbor's property with a high hand, he intimidated judges and juries, and he flouted the king and his government. The rise of the modern state with its machinery of army, police, and administration gradually established the reign of law, so firmly that from the late sixteenth century onwards the ordinary citizen ceased to carry a dagger or a stout cudgel when he went abroad.

In the international field there is no superstate which can discharge the functions performed by the government within the boundaries of each individual nation. This is the inevitable result of a world that is made up of sovereign states. They may voluntarily limit their powers to some degree, e.g., by signing treaties which obligate them to submit certain types of disputes to arbitration. The only compulsion to carry out their promises is the good faith of the signatories, or the power of a stronger state to enforce obedience to treaty obligations. Some states have on the whole a good reputation for keeping their word, while others have not. As regards coercion, a great power can usually make a weaker one live up to its promises (unless it is supported by another great power), but the only way to compel a great power to do so is by force. The great powers are like the overmighty subjects of fifteenth-century England. The sovereign state refuses to create an authority superior to itself, endowed with the material power to compel obedience to its orders. There are times when legal or moral authority is no substitute for a big stick. The League of Nations discovered that justice divorced from strength is ineffectual. The decisions of the United Nations have been defied by North Korea, South Africa, and Albania. There is nothing new in this situation: it has existed wherever and whenever there have been independent states. The only modern change is that the attempt to create an international authority by agreement has been made more difficult than before by the rise of nationalism during the past century and a half. It has developed a more intense loyalty to the state than was known in earlier centuries.

Each state has certain vital interests which it strives to attain, and quite often they conflict with those of other nations. This is as true of small states as of the great powers. Self-interest is the guiding motive of every state, though governments may show greater or lesser restraint in pursuing it. But none can afford to sacrifice state interests altogether, and it can be argued that they have no right to do so, being trustees for the welfare of the state. Sometimes the conflict of interests is settled with reason and justice on both sides, and again it is not.

Bismarck made a useful distinction between satiated and unsatiated states, the former being those which were content with their position in international society and the latter being dissatisfied. A satiated state wants no change in the established international order or status quo and desires peace. An unsatiated state seeks more territory, wealth and power and wants to change the status quo. This cannot be done by persuasion since no nation will willingly give up what it possesses, so the unsatiated state follows an aggressive foreign policy if it dares to do so. The aggressor state is almost as old as recorded history: the title deeds of most nations to their territories are founded upon the conquest of earlier possessors. Power is of the first importance in such a system, for conquest and survival alike. An aggressor obviously needs power if it is to strip its neighbors of their territory. This is equally true of a genuinely peace-loving state, the only aim of which is to increase the welfare and liberty of its own people. It must watch closely any other state which shows signs of predatory ambition. It neglects at its peril the maintenance of sufficient power to defend the position it has established for itself. Self-preservation and self defense are the first law of nature for any sovereign state, and power is essential if it is to survive.

Power may be defined as the capacity of a state to impose its will on others by reliance on effective pressure in case of noncompliance. Its essence is the ability to use compelling pressure irrespective of its reasonableness. The ultimate form of pressure is war. This was summed up in the old proverb "War is the final argument of kings." Inseparable from it is economic power, for modern war cannot be waged successfully without it. Less extreme forms of pressure can be exercised through, e.g., tariff wars and the control of loans and transportation. The influencing of public opinion abroad through propaganda is a manifestation of power with which the cold war has made the world familiar. Diplomacy cannot be divorced from power, for the effectiveness of a state's diplomacy depends in considerable measure upon it. Beyond this, however, the caliber of a state's foreign ministers and ambassadors has sometimes given it an influence out of proportion to its actual power. The consummate skill of Talleyrand at the Congress of Vienna enabled his defeated country, France, to come out of the peace conference with far less losses than its conquerors had originally intended.

POWER POLITICS

Power politics was already an old story when Lugalzaggisi, King of Umma, carved out a considerable kingdom for himself in Iraq and Syria nearly 5000 years ago, apparently because he discovered that archers who could shoot from a distance were more effective soldiers than spearmen, who could only fight at close quarters. From that day to this, power politics has been an unavoidable element of international affairs. The relations between states are based upon power; and to ignore or condemn it is about as helpful as to inveigh against death or taxes. It could not be ended even if a world government were set up to enforce peace and justice, for the superstate would have to have an army to compel obedience to its orders. So irresistible power would have to be created to end conflicts of power. Until that day arrives, the world must get on as best it can. No better illustration can be found of the inevitability of power politics than the contemporary policy of the United States. It has time and again condemned power politics and hoped that it had abolished it. That it has practiced it by rearming and forming NATO and its other post-1945 alliances merely illustrates that power politics is an inseparable part of international affairs. As Schwarzenberger points out in his *Power Politics*, "the tone is not so much set by States with a record for self-restraint and law-abidingness, but by States which are powerful enough to threaten the existing international status quo, and from which the worst must be expected. The law of the lowest level operates within such a society."

ELEMENTS OF NATIONAL POWER

The most obvious element of state power is the size and efficiency of the armed forces. They are essential for defense or attack, and if they are inadequate, the war will be lost, as happened to Russia in 1917. The wrong kind of equipment or the wrong use of it is equally disastrous, as witness the defeat of the French army in 1940. The weapons of modern war are so complex and the consumption of ammunition so astronomical, that paramount importance attaches to the extent and variety of industrial plants, and the adequacy of the system of transportation from the factory to the armies in the field. A rough but useful indication of a nation's military potential is given by its output of steel, since heavy industry can be converted to war production. The cost of war is so colossal that only the richest nations can stand the strain, and therefore the national wealth becomes a very important element of power. Technology is essential, as is scientific research. A good illustration of the latter is the story of the invention of the atom bomb. The scientists of the Western powers and the Axis were both working on the problem, and one of the anxieties of the American and British governments was that the Germans might discover the secret first.

Factories are useless without fuel and military raw materials, and so geography becomes an element of power. A state must either have within its own territories ample resources of coal, oil, and minerals, or else it must have assured access to them. The adequacy of the national agriculture is highly important: one weakness of Great Britain is that it could be starved into surrender in a few months if imports of food could be cut off. Size has become of very great importance: contemporary war covers a vast extent of territory, and a small state like Holland may be overrun in the opening stages of a campaign. Wide dispersal of war plants and other strategic objectives is vital in an age of long-range aircraft and guided missiles. One reason why the United States and Russia are super powers is that they are uniquely favored in all these geographic factors. Size of population is not as important as it was in old-fashioned war, when battles were decided in hand-to-hand combat and, as Napoleon said, "God is on the side of the big battalions." In World War I the Germans defeated very much bigger Russian armies because of the almost unbelievable shortage of matériel (equipment of all kinds) in the tsarist forces. Large armies however are still needed in modern war, and great numbers of men and women must work in the factories and on the farms.

The imponderables of morale and leadership are as important as they are difficult to measure. Morale cannot work miracles; but surprisingly often it produces a fairly good approximation to them. One reason why raw French levies defeated veteran European armies in the 1790's was the do or die spirit that the Revolution of 1789 had aroused. On the civilian side, morale will make men and women sacrifice more and work longer hours and so produce more food and equipment. The more one reads about 1940, the more one feels that morale was one reason for the contrasting fates of France and Great Britain. French morale had deteriorated woefully from what it had been in 1914. Too many civilians and part of the army had lost the determination to win no matter what the cost with which they met the earlier German invasion. The British situation after the fall of France appeared so desperate that General Weygand, the French commander in chief, predicted that "In six weeks England will have her neck wrung like a chicken." The only observable effect on the British was to make them work as they had never done before to replace the equipment lost at Dunkirk: spend their spare time drilling with shot guns and spears to defend their homes when the German army landed: and endure a bombing of their cities to which they could make no effective reply. What kept them going was that something above and beyond the call of duty that is called morale.

Inept leadership can be the cause of diplomatic and military defeat. Contrariwise exceptional leadership cannot only produce success, but also tends to heighten morale. Once more the events of 1940 give examples. When the French army was defeated, most of the leaders despaired of victory: they rejected the proposal to go to North Africa and continue the war from there, and voted to surrender. With morale and leadership both at a low ebb the defeat of the army was decisive, and few in 1940 agreed with General de Gaulle that "France has lost a battle; she has not lost the war." Churchill in the 'thirties was almost universally distrusted as a warmonger who demanded intensive rearmament and opposed appeasement. When his prophecies came true, he was practically the only leader who had not been discredited by his prewar blunders. On top of that, he had first-class ability, unflinching determination, driving energy, a genius for oratory, and an instinctive understanding of his own people which enabled him to bring out the best that was in them. The leader and the morale both were there: and the one inspired and intensified the other. On his eightieth birthday Churchill gave an appreciation of his own services. "I have never accepted what many people have kindly said, namely that I inspired the nation. Their will was resolute and remorseless and it proved unconquerable. It fell to me to express it, and if I found the right word you must remember that I have always earned my living by my pen, and by my tongue. It was the nation and the race dwelling all round the globe that had the lion's heart. I had the luck to be called upon to give the roar. I also hope that I sometimes suggested to the Lion the right place to use his claws."

The elements of national power are interdependent. The armed forces will run short of equipment if the factories fail to turn out a flood of supplies or if the transportation system breaks down. If scientific invention lags, or if there are not enough technologists to apply the discoveries to large-scale production, the enemy may win by improved weapons and more of them. The factories are useless unless they can get fuel and raw materials and unless the workmen will go all out in production. The mere possession of natural resources by itself is not power: Russia in World War I had the same supplies of raw materials as in World War II, but they were undeveloped. If part of the raw materials and equipment must be bought abroad, there must be foreign exchange to pay for them. Population by itself is not power: 400 million Chinese were unable to defeat the Japanese army in 1937–1945. People are helpless without weapons, training, and leadership. Technology can do nothing without raw materials, factories, and workmen. Morale is almost useless without the other elements of power, just as they are ineffective without the determination to use them. Leadership by itself is futile, but without it the result can be disaster. Unless all the elements of power are present, a state cannot be strong.

FLUCTUATIONS OF POWER

National power is relative: it is not something that exists in a vacuum. It is always measured against the power of some other state with which the first may come into conflict. At the present time speculation about the strength of the United States does not concern itself with say Tibet, a country so remote from American interests that war with it is inconceivable. American is measured against Russian power. The consequence of this relativity is that if one state becomes stronger, the other is automatically weaker. If Russia were to increase her strength, America would become relatively weaker to the extent that Russian power had been strengthened. This is an important and perennial principle of international relations.

The power of a state is never static: it is continually increasing or decreasing. The French army in 1939 was better equipped than in World War I yet it was far weaker because its leaders did not realize that military tactics had changed radically. A basic reason why the German army was victorious against tsarist Russia and was defeated when it invaded Soviet Russia was that in the meantime Stalin had transformed his country into an industrial great power. New industrial processes or weapons may suddenly enhance the importance of a raw material and so affect the power position of a country which has large deposits of it, e.g., the uranium mines of Canada and the Belgian Congo. The increased importance of size since World War II is fundamental in the lessening of the power of the states of Western Europe as compared with the United States and Russia. Financial strength may increase or decrease: the contemporary weakness of Great Britain can be partially attributed to the fact that two world wars changed it from a creditor to a debtor nation. Morale may rise and fall, and no infallible recipe exists for producing first-class leadership whenever it is vitally needed. France in 1917 was in grave danger of collapse from war weariness and very heavy casualties, but Premier Clemenceau pulled her together and kept her in the fight. There was nobody of his caliber in 1940. Again, the strength of a state may depend partly on its alliances, and the one certain thing about alliances is that they are uncertain. One reason France was able to turn back the German invasion in 1914 was that the tsar's army deliberately sacrificed itself in a premature attack to divert some of the German pressure from the West. The next time the Germans entered France, Russia was aiding the invader.

The effect upon international relations of the eternal waxing and waning of national strength is very important. Power ratios are never constant: they are always in a state of flux. France and her allies had the hegemony of Europe for about a decade and a half after World War I, and then within a few years every one of them had been conquered by Germany. The shrewdest calculations of strength may be falsified in a few years by variations in any of the diverse factors which together constitute power. No remedy exists for this problem, for no way has been found to prevent a state from growing or decaying. An added complication is that it is impossible to assess the power of the different states with mathematical accuracy. Many of the elements cannot be measured exactly; and the difficulty is enhanced because states may try to conceal their true measure of strength. All that a government can achieve is an approximate estimate of the power of its own and of foreign states.

WAR AND NATIONAL POLICY

The statement that "War settles nothing" is very inaccurate: it determines which combatant shall have the chance to write the peace treaty. World War I showed that it is possible to win the war and lose the peace. This was not the fault of the generals: the blame lay with the civilian leaders who misused their opportunity. Because of its decisive character war is the supreme exercise of power. It has persisted down the ages because situations arise in which no substitute for it exists. Hitler expected to establish an empire which would last a thousand years, and war was the only means by which he could impose German rule upon the states of Europe. Looking at it from their point of view, war was the only means by which they might avoid German control. This second example illustrates an important point. States have been willing to renounce war as an instrument of national policy, e.g., in the Kellogg-Briand Pact, but they have always made the exception that they are entitled to go to war in self-defense. Furthermore, peoples have fought when this was the only way to end a situation which was regarded as intolerable, e.g., the American Revolution and Civil War.

Broadly speaking, states go to war in pursuit of what they consider their vital national interests. This covers both wars of aggression and of genuine self-defense. When the attempt is made to define vital national interests, the complexity of the causes of war is revealed. Volumes have been published on the subject, and one authority listed over 250 causes. Usually a war comes about not because of one single reason, but from a variety of motives. During earlier centuries religion was an important cause, e.g., the wars between Protestants and Roman Catholics in the sixteenth century. In a changed form this cause is operative today, to the degree that Soviet foreign policy is motivated by a crusading zeal to impose Marxist doctrines on the noncommunist states. One factor which won German support for Hitler was the widespread belief in Nordic superiority and the mission of the German people to impose their rule on inferior races. Fear has its place among the causes of war. Armaments are necessary for security, but they can arouse suspicion and fear, which increase the risk of war. Some wars have been strategic in their origin. The real reason why Britain occupied Egypt in 1882 was that it was the base from which to control the Suez Canal.

Vital national interests have often been political. Under this heading come the wars of nationalism of the nineteenth and twentieth centuries. The liberation of the Balkan states from Turkish rule and the unification of Italy and Germany were brought about by war. In the twentieth century nationalistic wars have been transferred from Europe to Asia, and in recent years there have been the revolts in Indonesia and Vietnam against European control. Sometimes a government has provoked a war to allay domestic discontent, e.g., Mussolini's conquest of Ethiopia. Both the world wars were primarily political, having as their stake the domination of Europe and perhaps of the world. Victory of course would bring economic advantages; but these were by products and not the main purpose. The desire for power is one of the strongest of motives, and it has played a prominent part in the history of war. The Marxist theory that wars are the result of economic causes does not square with the facts. With the partial exception of the Boer War of 1899, no war of the last century between major powers has been fought exclusively or even predominantly for economic reasons. More often than not financiers, merchants, and manufacturers as a class, apart from individual capitalists, have opposed imperialistic ambitions and war. Their attitude has been based on the hard-headed conviction that war did not pay, and that peace was more profitable for business as a whole.

PRE-MODERN WAR

Until a little more than a century ago war was an exclusive and professional affair, and often a very profitable enterprise. A man joined the army as a lifelong occupation as he might have entered any other trade or profession. The troops in a single theater of hostilities did not exceed 40,000, since this was the largest number which could be fed and supplied in one place. If the army was larger than this—Louis XIV had the prodigious number of 100,000—it would unite for battle but at other times operate in different parts of the country. The muzzle-loading musket had an effective range of 100 yards, and the best results were obtained if the opposing armies closed to within forty feet before firing. The rate of fire was about one shot per minute. An army's range of action was limited to a few miles on each side of its line of march, owing to the poor roads and the reliance upon horses for transportation. Within this radius civilians endured miseries that they were not to experience again until the wars of the twentieth century arrived. Usually soldiers lived off the country, and in addition to food they helped themselves to "souvenirs."

The bulk of the civilians, however, were not in the track of the army and were little affected by a war. It even helped to solve social problems by giving jailbirds the choice of serving their sentences or volunteering to die for their country. Gradually, too, laws of war were evolved which sharply distinguished between combatants and civilian noncombatants. The latter were protected from attack and spoliation, and it became illegal to bombard undefended towns. During the nineteenth century wars between Western nations were humanely conducted, compared with what occurred before and afterward. The cost of old-fashioned war was moderate, owing to the limited number of troops who had to be paid and outfitted. The manufacture of the equipment did not call for special machinery: carpenters and iron workers made it with their hand tools. It was financially possible to require the defeated state to pay the victor's cost of operations. In addition, the latter often annexed territory, and made a handsome profit on the whole transaction.

MODERN WAR

The change began about a century ago and revolutionized the character of war. The salient characteristics of modern war are its dependence on scientific discovery, industrialization and mass participation, and its enormously increased cost. The inventor evolved weapons of vastly greater range, accuracy and rapidity of fire. The Franco-Prussian War showed that the cavalry charge had become obsolete, for a horseman armed with a saber did not have a chance against an infantryman with an early type of modern rifle. At present the Garand semiautomatic rifle can fire 100 aimed rounds a minute, or ten times more than the fastest rifle of 1914. A machine gun can fire 1000 rounds a minute. In 1850 the point-blank range of a nine-pounder muzzle-loading cannon was 300 yards, while today the radius of a fully loaded bombing plane (which is really flying artillery) capable of returning to its base is 2000 miles. The maximum range of an aircraft is 10,000 miles, and provided it carries a light load of bombs and is not required to return to its base, there are few places on earth which it cannot reach. For comparison it is only about 4700 miles from New York to Moscow by the most direct route, and the distance between any major American and Russian city and the other country's territory is not much more than 6000 miles. Fifty years ago a shell would gut a house but leave the walls standing. By World War I it could demolish an entire house, and by 1945 a single block-buster bomb could destroy most of a city block. The atom bomb dropped on Hiroshima demolished a square mile of the city. The hydrogen bomb exploded in 1954 could have devastated an area eight miles in diameter and contaminated 7000 square miles so that survival would depend on evacuation or taking shelter.

The weapons of modern war are very intricate in their construction, and their parts must be made with the most meticulous accuracy. The craftsman with his hand tools has been replaced by a machine as complicated and expensive as the weapon it produces. Moreover, the immense increase in rapidity of fire requires enormous quantities of ammunition. The variety and quantity of the matériel are so colossal that it is impossible to accumulate adequate stocks prior to the outbreak of war. It is equally impossible to supply the demand with the output of factories built specifically for war purposes. The whole range of national industry becomes the essential basis of military power. A factory that makes typewriters, for instance, can be used to manufacture machine guns with some alterations to its machinery. Practically every variety of factory must be converted from peace to war production. This cannot be improvised after war breaks out: the most careful and detailed plans for economic mobilization must be prepared long in advance so that the change can take place as quickly and efficiently as possible. Industry becomes part of the war potential of the state. This term means its degree of military strength when the mobilization for war purposes has been completed of all its resources, industrial, agricultural, financial, demographic, etc.

A modern army is dependent on good transportation since men, matériel, and food must be carried to the theater of operations. There is a close correlation between the size of an army and the effectiveness of its transport. An old-style army was limited to 40,000 men because it was dependent on poor roads and horse-drawn vehicles. By the time of the Franco-Prussian War Europe was fairly well supplied with railways, and the three German armies which

invaded France had a strength of 384,000, while the French defenders numbered 250,000. The development of the motor vehicle added to the railways
made it possible to supply the millions of men in the armies of World War I.
By World War II the use of mechanized transport had been immensely extended, and the transport plane was also extensively used. In transportation,
as in the manufacture of matériel, the basis of military power is industrialization.

Conscription was first introduced by the French revolutionary government in 1793 and was imitated by Prussia in 1807. National mass armies made
their appearance on the battlefield. Subsequently France substituted a system
by which men of means could hire substitutes to take their places in the army.
Except for Prussia, most states continued to rely upon professional armies
recruited by voluntary enlistment. The defeat of the French professional army
by the German conscript army in 1870 led to the abandonment of the older
system. With the exception of Great Britain almost every European state
adopted universal military service based on conscription. Nationalism made
the change much easier, for people generally agreed that patriotism required
every citizen to prepare himself to defend his country. Great Britain adopted
wartime conscription in the latter part of World War I, and since World
War II both she and the United States have instituted compulsory military
service in peace as well as war.

Modern war has changed drastically the position of civilians. The able-
bodied male population is conscripted, with the exception of those who are
so essential that they are more valuable in some form of war work. An increasing number of women are enlisted in the armed services. The rest of the
effective male population and in some countries a high proportion of the
women are mobilized for some form of war work. Here again the strength
of nationalism has led to the acceptance of this duty. One result has been
greatly to weaken the distinction between combatants and noncombatants.
A munitions worker is as essential in the winning of the war as a soldier,
and to destroy a war plant may be more damaging than to wipe out a bat-
talion. This transformation in the role of civilians has coincided with the
development of the airplane and the guided missile. Prior to the twentieth
century the national army literally stood between the civil population and
the enemy, and it had to be destroyed before the latter could be directly
attacked. Now for the first time weapons are available which can bypass the
armed forces and strike directly at noncombatants. Out of this came the
air attacks on enemy cities which were so striking a feature of World War II.

Today it is almost impossible for a conquered country to regain its independence once its armed forces have been destroyed. It is true that under-
grounds arose in most of the countries conquered by Hitler and that in the
aggregate they did a good deal of damage through sabotage, espionage, and

ambushing small detachments. Tito and his partisans virtually liberated Yugoslavia through their own efforts, though it should be remembered that the British provided much of their equipment. This was a special case since the mountainous character of the topography made it peculiarly suited to guerilla warfare. France is much more typical in that most of it is comparatively open country. The French underground was of considerable help in the Anglo-American invasion of 1944, but it could never by itself have liberated France. Guerillas have neither the equipment nor the training to face a regular army in a pitched battle. Two centuries ago and less rebels and regulars alike were armed with flint-lock muskets. The regular had the advantages of discipline and perhaps cannon; but, on the other hand, the soldier was out in the open, a good target, while the rebel fought from behind barricades or stone walls. Today the decisive weapons are airplanes, tanks, and heavy artillery, and it is very unlikely that the modern rebel will possess them or be skilled in their use. The conqueror will, and he will have the further advantage of rapid communications. If an uprising occurs, he will learn of it in a matter of hours, and very soon he can send by air a force that will squelch the revolt. The conqueror will be all the more likely to receive early warning because, if one may judge from Nazi and Soviet practice, he will cover the conquered country with a network of secret police. A revolt to have any hope of success needs thousands of participants, and when so many know a secret, someone is sure to betray it from hope of reward, fear, or under torture. In other words, a people once conquered will stay conquered, unless it is liberated as the result of attack by a foreign power. If once the whole world were conquered, it is hard to see where the outside assistance would come from.

War is also distinguished by its steadily mounting destructiveness. France took part in most of the great wars of the modern epoch; but in the period from 1630 to 1789 the maximum of the population killed or wounded was .58 percent and the minimum .001 percent. Even in the Revolutionary and Napoleonic wars which caused an unprecedented drain on French manpower, the maximum loss was 1.54 percent. The French loss in World War I was 5.63 per cent. In World War I it is estimated that the military casualties among all the nations involved were 8,540,000 killed, and that in addition about 10 million civilians died of disease, privation, or gunfire. In World War II about 15 million were killed in battle; including civilians, the total deaths may have been 40 million. The number of civilians killed by the Germans through measures of deliberate extermination is estimated at close to 12 million. The bombing of cities by both sides was responsible for hundreds of thousands of deaths. Russian casualties have been estimated at perhaps 12 to 15 million, over half of which were civilians.

On the financial side war has become almost unbelievably expensive.

The total direct cost of World War I was estimated to be $126 billion to the Allied and Associated Powers and $60 billion to Germany and her allies. Property damage was believed to be some $37 billion. The military cost of World War II was estimated at over $1100 billion and property damage at $230 billion. Both world wars proved the impossibility of demanding from the conquered reparations which would begin to pay for the cost to the victors. The direct military costs are far more than can be paid for by taxation, and so war leaves behind it a heavy burden of national debt. To this must be added the expense of restoring property that has been damaged or destroyed, and of replacing such items as factory machinery which have deteriorated from excessive war use. Irreplaceable natural resources are depleted, like the high-grade iron ore of Minnesota. The disabled must be supported, and there is the further loss of their productive capacity as well as of those who have been killed. Industry is diverted to producing munitions which are fired at the enemy, so that victory is bought at the cost of a decrease of the national wealth. A long-term consequence of war is dislocation of world trade. Factories are unable to supply their former markets, and these either create new industries to manufacture the missing imports or else turn to another source of supply. In either event, the original supplier is unlikely to regain the whole of his former market when the war is over.

DISARMAMENT

Antiwar societies have existed for over a century, but they had little effect as long as the nations thought of hostilities in terms of old-fashioned war and regarded it as undesirable but legitimate. World War I awakened them to the realization that its character had completely altered, and from that time widespread hostility toward it developed. Conferences were held at The Hague in 1899 and 1907 to discuss the limitation of armaments, but little came of them save a Convention on the Laws of War on Land. The treatment of sick and wounded and of prisoners of war was prescribed in the Geneva Conventions of 1864, 1906, and 1929, and regulations were drawn up for the International Red Cross. After World War I the use of poison gas was prohibited by treaty, and after World War II the Genocide Convention forbade racial extermination.

Article VIII of the League of Nations Covenant stipulated that "the maintenance of peace requires the reduction of national armaments to the lowest point consistent with national safety. . . . The Council . . . shall formulate plans for such reduction." A succession of League committees was appointed which produced a plethora of plans and prepared the way for the Disarmament Conference which met at Geneva in 1932. It wrestled earnestly and voluminously with every phase of the problem, and it was doomed to fail before it ever met. The conference adjourned in 1934 without lessening the strength of the world's armies by as much as a single soldier. Each power put forward demands that coincided with its own national policy. Germany demanded equal rights, that is the abolition of the disarmament clauses of the Treaty of Versailles. She insisted that other nations reduce their armaments to her level, or permit her to rearm up to theirs. France agreed to limit her armaments if Germany were kept disarmed, and provided a heavily armed international police force was created, which would come to the aid of a victim of aggression. The United States and Britain opposed the creation of an international police force and favored the German demand for equality in land armaments. They were unsympathetic to the French thesis that security must precede disarmament and insisted that the latter must come first. France pointed out that they did not offer to reduce their overwhelmingly larger navies to the level of those of the other powers. Italy urged the abolition of all weapons such as battleships, tanks and bombing planes which she lacked the money and factories to manufacture in large quantities. If the wealthier states had adopted this self-denying ordinance, Italy would truly have become a great power. Litvinov for Russia proposed the total abolition of all weapons. The Communists knew that their proposal would be rejected, and they advanced it as a propaganda move in their war against capitalism. The aim was to show the peoples of the world that "disarmament and the abolition of war are possible only with the fall of capitalism," and so rally their support to the "proletarian dictatorship."

The principal reason for the failure was that the conference put the cart before the horse. The fashionable argument of the day was that armaments were the principal cause of war and that their drastic reduction would be a guarantee of peace. It is true that an arms race may heighten suspicion and tension which already exist and so become a contributory cause of war. But the fundamental question is: What caused the arms race? No state enlarges its armed forces from collector's mania, as an individual might buy stamps or paintings, for the hobby is too expensive. The answer to the question is that armaments are instruments of policy: they are a manifestation of the pursuit of power which is a fundamental factor in international relations. A state arms for one of two reasons: it may have a policy of aggression like Nazi Germany or Soviet Russia or it may fear that it is the destined object of attack like France between the two world wars or the Western world today. In the first case, strong armaments are essential for attack, and in the second, for defense. In other words, armaments are a symptom and not a cause of an underlying conflict of national policies. Until the root of the trouble, the conflict of policies can be removed, each state or group of states will continue to arm in order to achieve its aims.

The basic factor in interwar Europe was that France and her allies were determined to maintain the peace settlement of 1919 which gave them a position of strength. They feared and distrusted Germany, and to prevent a change in the status quo they remained heavily armed. They would modify their policy only if they were assured of armed help in case of attack, and this they failed to secure. Germany could not upset the peace settlement until she had rearmed. She, therefore, demanded equality which really meant superiority. For once the armed forces were equal, Germany with her far more extensive industrialization would be stronger than the French group of states. On both sides armaments were instruments of policy, and it was a waste of time to attempt disarmament as long as Europe was divided between the satiated and unsatiated states. A lesser reason for the failure of the Disarmament Conference was that the times were not propitious. Japan was conquering Manchuria, Hitler came to power while the conference was meeting, and Germany was openly threatening to break the Versailles Treaty unless the leading powers agreed to arms equality. France's fears for her own security were increased, and she refused to disarm unless her safety were assured. Neither the United States nor Britain were prepared to guarantee the defense of the European states. The conference also failed to solve the serious technical difficulties connected with disarmament. It wasted months trying to divide weapons into offensive and defensive, a futile occupation since any weapon can be offensive or defensive according to the way it is used.

The interwar history of naval disarmament confirms the belief that it is impracticable when national policies are in conflict. At the Washington Conference of 1922 naval equality was established between the United States and Britain, and Japan accepted a strength 60 percent of that of the others, and France and Italy were given fleets of equal size. The United States and Britain were allowed 500,000 tons for the replacement tonnage of their battleships and battle cruisers, Japan 300,000 tons, and France and Italy 167,000 tons apiece. This established a ratio of 5: 5: 3: 1.67: 1.67. Ratios were also established for aircraft carriers, but it proved impossible to reach agreement on smaller warships. In 1927 a futile attempt was made to extend this ratio to other types of ships, but a second effort succeeded at the London Conference in 1930. A ratio of 10: 10: 7 was established for American, British, and Japanese cruisers and destroyers, and Japan obtained equality in submarines with the other two powers. France declined to accept equality with Italy, and these two states refused to sign the treaty. In December, 1934, Japan gave notice that she would terminate the Washington Naval Treaty on December 31, 1936, and the London Treaty expired on the same date. The three powers began new shipbuilding programs, but the United States and Britain reaffirmed their pledge of naval equality with one another.

The United States and Britain were able to agree on parity primarily because both governments felt that war between them was inconceivable and that their navies would never come into conflict with one another. Both took very good care to maintain naval superiority over all other fleets. Japan accepted a 5:5:3 ratio for two reasons. The strength allotted to her fleet made it impossible for either the American or the British navy to attack it in the western Pacific. Moreover, the Japanese government of the 'twenties had abandoned the policy of imposing its control on China by force, and there was no risk of war with the United States. In the 'thirties the militarists regained control of the government and began a policy of armed aggression in China. This once more entailed the risk of war with the United States, and they denounced the naval limitation treaty and enlarged their fleet. Franco-Italian naval equality meant French inferiority in the Mediterranean because only part of the navy could be stationed there, the rest being required for the defense of other French possessions. Since Italy was entirely a Mediterranean power, the whole of her navy would be in that sea. Mussolini coveted French North Africa, and if war came, his naval superiority in the Mediterranean would put France at a dangerous disadvantage. The attitude of each state to disarmament was determined by whether it had a conflict of policy with other naval powers.

Two other futile attempts to prevent war should be mentioned. The Kellogg-Briand Peace Pact or Pact of Paris of 1928 aroused extravagant hopes that a great advance had been made toward the abolition of war. Sixty-one states renounced war as an instrument of policy and agreed that the settlement of all disputes which might arise between them would never be sought except by peaceful means. Henceforth all wars were renounced except defensive wars, wars in support of the League or any existing treaties of alliance, wars to uphold the Monroe Doctrine, and wars in areas vital to British interests (the British Monroe Doctrine). Apart from this formidable list of exceptions, no wars were supposed to occur; but if they did, the signatories were under no obligation even to consult one another, much less to take action. Officially, too, every nation goes to war in self-defense, and the pact has been described as a solemn resolution against sin, with sin to be defined by the sinners. The pact was no more than a moral gesture which indicated a new ethical attitude to war, but did nothing to restrain any state which had the power and inclination to wage it. In 1932 Secretary of State Stimson tried to counter the Japanese conquest of Manchuria by declaring that the United States would not recognize the legality of any situation which impaired its treaty rights in China or which ran counter to the Kellogg-Briand Pact. This doctrine of nonrecognition of the fruits of aggression was not supported by actions and had no deterrent effect. The Japanese continued to carry out their plans for setting up a puppet government and exploiting the country's resources for their benefit.

ALLIANCES

A traditional method of strengthening the power of a state is the formation of alliances. This is possible when the prospective allies have some interest in common, whether for defense or attack. The treaty stipulates that
under certain circumstances, which it outlines, the allies shall declare war.
An alliance is commonly followed by consultations between the general staffs
to concert plans for joint action in the event that the treaty obligation should
arise. A variant of the military alliance promises merely diplomatic support.
Fundamental differences of ideology have been bridged when the incentive
was strong enough. Soviet Russia condemned the League of Nations, joined
it in 1934 to seek aid from the Western powers against Hitler, and became a
benevolent neutral on the German side from 1939 until she was forced into
the war in 1941. Churchill, no friend of communism, welcomed Russia's enforced arrival in the Western camp. Unofficially he was quite candid about
his motive. "I have only one purpose, the destruction of Hitler, and my life
is much simplified thereby. If Hitler invaded Hell, I would make at least a
favourable reference to the Devil in the House of Commons." The duration
of an alliance depends upon how long each of the partners continues to
benefit from it. No government enters into such an engagement from pure
altruism, but because it forwards the interests of the state. If it ceases to do
so the alliance will not survive long. One of the oldest existing alliances is
that between Great Britain and Portugal, which has lasted for nearly 300
years. Portugal's friendship gives assurance that it will not be used as a base
for attacking British shipping passing near it. Portugal, a small and weak
country, is promised help if it is attacked.

An alliance is not pure gain: it may also become a liability. Each state
must promise to support whatever interests of its partner are covered by the
treaty, for without mutual benefit there can be no alliance. A state may thus
be drawn into a war which it would rather avoid. Hitler would have preferred not to go to war with the United States in 1941, but he did so because
the alternative was to break his alliance with Japan which he considered
essential to his victory. The plethora of alliances since 1945 shows that this
instrument of power is far from outmoded. Great powers no longer fight
singlehanded: they go to battle with as many allies as they can bring in.

THE BALANCE OF POWER POLICY

Castlereagh, the British foreign minister at the Congress of Vienna, defined the balance of power as "the maintenance of such a just equilibrium
between the members of the family of nations as should prevent any one

of them becoming sufficiently strong to impose its will upon the rest." A fuller but essentially similar definition was given by Sir Eyre Crowe, the British permanent under secretary for foreign affairs, in 1906:

History shows that the danger threatening the independence of this or that nation has generally arisen at least in part, out of the momentary predominance of a neighbouring state at once militarily powerful, economically efficient, and ambitious to extend its frontiers or spread its influence. . . . The only check on the abuse of political predominance derived from such a position has always consisted in the opposition of an equally formidable rival, or of a combination of several countries forming leagues of defence. The equilibrium established by such a grouping of forces is technically known as the balance of power, and it has become almost an historical truism to identify England's secular policy with the maintenance of this balance by throwing her weight now in this scale and now in that, but ever on the side opposed to the political dictatorship of the strongest single state or group at a given time.

The essential idea is the equilibrium represented by a pair of scales. State *A*, strong and aspiring to what Crowe called "political dictatorship," outweighs or in other words has more power than states *B*, *C*, or *D*. But if *B*, *C*, and *D* form alliances their combined weight in one pan of the scales will equal that of *A*, and so restore the balance. Actually, the situation is likely to be more complex, for *A* is probably allied with *E* and doing its best to negotiate an alliance with *F*. So *B*, *C*, and *D* will have to form alliances with a few more letters of the alphabet. Moreover, each time one of the rival leagues forms a new alliance and so increases the weight in its pan of the scales, the other tries to make still another alliance as a counterweight. The object, however, is a balance or equality of opposing forces, at least in theory.

In practice the word is often used in the sense of preponderance. States try to increase the strength of their own league so that the balance is not even, but tilted in their favor. The reason is that it is impossible to estimate exactly the power of any single state, let alone a number of them. There is an element of uncertainty, and if the miscalculation is serious, it might lead to defeat if war broke out. Therefore, the state must try to make itself so strong that even if it has made erroneous calculations it can still maintain a balance with its opponents. In other words, it must strive to create not a balance of equality but a superiority of power in its own favor. Since both of the opposing states or groups of states have this aim, there is a competition in armaments and alliances.

It is sometimes said that the object of the balance of power policy is to preserve the peace, and this is the desire of the weaker states. No nation courts a desperate and uncertain war against a powerful adversary. But peace never has been the prime purpose of the policy: its principal aim has been to preserve the independence of the threatened states. Peace if possible, but independence at all costs has been the goal. During the last four centuries of European history the policy has preserved the independence of the weaker states and overthrown the aggressors, but more often than not this has been done at the cost of war. The policy has often been condemned for this reason, and the same condemnation has been extended to armaments and alliances, e.g., the North Atlantic Treaty Organization. All three involve a danger of war, and on occasion may lead to it. The alternative is to remain poorly armed, without allies, and with no attempt to balance the power of the aggressor state. This was the policy followed by the European neutrals in World War II, and the result was that Hitler conquered them one at a time. Unfortunately the pattern is not set by the nations that want peace, but by those that intend to use their strength for aggressive purposes. There is a choice of evils, but in a world based on power politics the greater danger lies in disunity and weakness.

A common argument against the balance of power is that it is unstable and constantly changing. This is true and also unavoidable. It has already been pointed out that the power of a state depends upon a complex of factors and that they are forever altering. Russia's power aroused fear among her allies after the defeat of Napoleon. Her collapse in 1917 seemed to show that she was "a colossus stuffed with clouds." Twenty-five years later she played a major role in the defeat of Germany, and a few years afterwards her power aroused serious apprehensions throughout the Western world. The balance is always changing, and adjustments must constantly be made to restore it. Perhaps the best argument in favor of the balance of power policy is that it is inevitable in a world of sovereign states. There is no world government supported by an international army to which they can appeal for protection when a Hitler or Napoleon follows a policy of aggression. Power has to be matched against power, and the policy of the balance is an essential stabilizing factor.

Some of the smaller states owe their independence to the policy. Controlled by a strong power, Belgium and Holland are a base for an attack on Britain, France, or Germany. No one of the three can permit any other to subjugate them, and the maintenance of their independence is in the common interest. Switzerland is a road of invasion into France, Germany, and Italy. None of them can afford to allow it to be conquered, and the solution has been to guarantee its independence and neutrality in the "general interest" of Europe. Turkey, Iran, and Afghanistan owe their survival to the refusal of various Western states to permit them to come under Russian control. Occasionally the balance has been maintained by partitioning a state. In the eighteenth century Prussia, Russia, and Austria preserved their local power ratio by dividing Poland between them. Germany and Russia repeated this in 1939. The reason was that one state could not afford to allow another to increase its power without obtaining a proportionate compensation.

THE HISTORY OF THE BALANCE OF POWER

The maintenance of the balance is an application of the fundamental law of self-preservation, and it appears whenever there are independent states. The policy was practiced by the city states of classical Greece, and it was known in China, India, and the ancient empires of the Middle East. It disappeared during the centuries when Rome ruled all the world that mattered. After the fall of the Roman Empire little was heard of the policy for a thousand years, but it re-emerged among the city states of Italy in the late fifteenth century. Machiavelli explained its technique in his essay *The Prince*. The sixteenth century saw the rise of the sovereign state, and from then onwards a paramount purpose of European governments was to maintain the balance.

The great contest of the first part of the sixteenth century was between Charles V, ruler of the Holy Roman Empire of Germany and Spain, and Francis I of France. Francis shocked the moral sense of Christendom by forming an alliance with Muslim Turkey in order to prevent his Christian rival from expanding his territory. Henry VIII of England joined first one side and then the other in order to prevent either from becoming too strong. His redoubtable daughter Elizabeth I used the policy with marked success to wear down Philip II of Spain, the world power of the day. During the Thirty Years War (1618–1648) Cardinal Richelieu used the technique to weaken the Austrian Empire and tilt the balance in favor of France. Before the end of the century France under Louis XIV had become the dominant power and sought the hegemony of Europe. William III, King of England and Holland, formed one league after another to humble Louis' pretensions, and the result was the defeat of France.

During the eighteenth century the maintenance of the balance was the guiding principle of the rulers of Europe. This was the key to the bewildering medley of alliances and counteralliances, the frequent shift of a state from one league to its opponent, and the devious maneuverings. At the end of the century the growth of France's power upset the balance and came near to making Europe a French empire. Great Britain took the lead in building up coalitions which finally defeated Napoleon and broke the threat of his domination. The Congress of Vienna tried to establish a new balance of power, and its arrangements lasted without any drastic changes for nearly two generations. The only serious war of the period, the Crimean War of 1854–1856, was fought by Britain, France, and Piedmont to prevent Russia from upsetting the balance in the Balkans by defeating Turkey. In 1877

Russia again attacked and defeated Turkey, and dictated the Treaty of San Stephano which very greatly increased her power in the Balkans. The Congress of Berlin in 1878 compelled Russia drastically to limit her gains, and thus prevented her from upsetting the balance. The Monroe Doctrine was a move to maintain the balance, at least from the viewpoint of Britain, which first suggested it. The purpose was to confine the power of Russia, Austria, and France to Europe and prevent its extension to the revolted Spanish colonies of Central and South America.

The normal state of Europe in the eighteenth and nineteenth centuries was that of a multiple balance. In the central and eastern parts of the continent were Russia, Prussia, and Austria, and in western Europe, Britain, France and Spain. In the later part of the nineteenth century Italy replaced Spain. Through the permutations and combinations of their friendships and hostilities they held one another in check, and prevented any one from obtaining a dangerous ascendancy. At the end of the nineteenth century the multiple balance began to break down and be replaced by a simple balance. The start of the trouble was when Germany was allowed to defeat Austria in 1866 and France in 1870. This gave her twenty years of predominance on the continent, and her position was strengthened by her alliances with Austria and Italy. Gradually a counterbalance came into being with the formation of the Franco-Russian alliance (1894), the Anglo-French Entente (1904), the Anglo-Russian Entente (1907), and the gradual shift of Italy from the German toward the Western League. All the great powers were now aligned on one side or the other, and no scope was left for the shifts in alignment which had sometimes had a restraining influence in the earlier period. The simple is more dangerous than the multiple balance: it makes for heightened tension, an armaments race, and crises. Balance of power considerations were very influential in the decisions of the governments to declare war in 1914. The same thought was in the mind of the American government when it entered the war in 1917, for the danger that Germany might control Europe and destroy British sea power presented a threat to the United States.

The war showed that Germany had become so strong that the other great powers of Europe were no longer able to defeat her unassisted. The help of the United States was necessary. This was the first indication that the balance was ceasing to be a purely European affair, and was beginning to become global in its scope. During the interwar period the attempt was made to replace the balance of power policy by the League of Nations system of collective security. The attempt failed, and as the threat of Axis domination grew the old policy re-emerged, for no third way was known of maintaining the independence of the weaker states. Once more Britain and France drew together, and in 1939 an abortive attempt was made to bring in Russia and recreate the Triple Entente of World War I. Once again the United States gravitated toward the Western allies because an Axis victory was not in American interests.

BALANCE OF POWER AND COLLECTIVE SECURITY

The balance of power policy and the international organization, whether the former League of Nations or the present United Nations, have one purpose in common. Both are intended to preserve the independence of the weaker states. The difference is primarily one of technique. With the traditional method the maintenance of the balance is left to the states which feel themselves threatened, while those less immediately concerned attempt to remain neutral. Each group of opposing states tries to strengthen its position by persuading the neutrals to join it. Under a genuine system of collective security there are no neutrals among the members of the international organization. The prevention of aggression is everybody's business, and all are expected to join in the economic or military measures taken to halt the aggressor.

Hopes were high at the end of both world wars that collective security would supersede alliances, heavy armaments, the balance of power policy, and power politics. If ever an aggressor raised his head, he would be crushed under an avalanche of states which would go to war to uphold the international organization. Collective security to be effective requires that its supporters must have an overwhelming preponderance of force upon their side, and must be ready to use it to prevent aggression. They must be prepared to do this even if their own immediate interests are not in jeopardy. For collective security to succeed it must have the firm support of all, or at least most of, the great powers. Its effectiveness lessens in proportion to the number that are neutral, and still more so if they are actively hostile. The League of Nations never had the strength behind it which President Wilson postulated. His own country refused to join, and in the 'thirties Japan, Germany, and Italy left it. When the crucial test came over Ethiopia in 1935, the effective strength of the League was reduced to France and Britain. They did not have the overwhelming superiority which the theory of collective security assumed. Both in the Ethiopian affair and in the earlier challenge when Japan conquered Manchuria, neither the League powers nor the United States were willing to engage in a war to prevent an aggression which did not seriously threaten their own national interests. To uphold collective security required a spirit of self-sacrifice which did not animate either their governments or their peoples. The postwar record is somewhat better; but national interests are still dominant, and it would be optimistic to assume that the members of the U.N. are willing to fight any place and any time in support of collective security. Broadly speaking the world is divided into the Communist states, the neutrals, and the Western bloc led by the United States. In practice, the nations which feel themselves threatened by Russia seek for security through the creation of a global balance of power rather than through collective security, while the neutrals hope to remain aloof from the struggle.

SELECTED READING

CARR, EDWARD H., *The Twenty Years' Crisis, 1919–1939*. London: Macmillan and Company, Ltd., 1940.

CLARKSON, JESSE D., and COCHRANE, THOMAS C. (eds.), *War as a Social Institution: the Historian's Perspective*. New York: Columbia University Press, 1941.

EARLE, EDWARD M. (ed.), *Makers of Modern Strategy. Military Thought from Machiavelli to Hitler*. Princeton: Princeton University Press, 1943.

FALLS, CYRIL, *A Hundred Years of War*. London: Duckworth, 1953.

LIPPMANN, WALTER, *U.S. Foreign Policy, Shield of the Republic*. Boston: Little, Brown and Company, 1943.

MORGENTHAU, HANS J., *Politics among Nations: The Struggle for Power and Peace*, 2d ed. New York: Alfred A. Knopf, 1954.

OGBURN, WILLIAM F. (ed.), *Technology and International Relations*. Chicago: University of Chicago Press, 1949.

REYNOLDS, P. A., *War in the Twentieth Century*. Cardiff: University of Wales Press, 1951.

SCHWARZENBERGER, GEORG, *Power Politics, A Study of International Society*, Rev. ed. New York: Frederick A. Praeger, 1951.

STRAUSZ-HUPÉ, ROBERT, *The Balance of Tomorrow*. New York: G. P. Putnam's Sons, 1945.

VAGTS, ALFRED, *A History of Militarism. Romance and Realities of a Profession*. New York: W. W. Norton and Company, 1937.

WHEELER-BENNETT, JOHN W., *The Pipe Dream of Peace: the Story of the Collapse of Disarmament*. New York: William Morrow and Company, 1935.

WIGHT, MARTIN, *Power Politics*. London and New York: Royal Institute of International Affairs, 1949.

WRIGHT, QUINCY, *A Study of War*. 2 vols. Chicago: University of Chicago Press, 1942.

CHAPTER 6

TECHNIQUES OF POLITICAL PROPAGANDA

The shaping of foreign policy was very largely left to governments and small interested groups until World War I. The man in the street had taken little interest in foreign affairs, but the war taught him that it could vitally affect him personally. Since then he has insisted on having a voice in its determination, but his lack of knowledge of the issues involved often handicaps both him and his government in making wise decisions. A concomitant development has been the enhanced importance of the ordinary citizen in the work of government. A minority of the states of the world are democracies and a wide franchise gives large numbers a voice in policy formation. Even in the police states the rulers claim to be the leaders of their peoples, and feel it necessary to hold stage-managed elections where they are endorsed by a 99-percent majority. A third development has been the immense expansion of education and the revolution in communications. From the point of view of the propagandist widespread literacy has been a boon, for it has enabled him to reach a far larger audience. At the same time the nineteenth century saw the rise of cheap newspapers with large circulations, and the establishment of a world-wide mail service with inexpensive postal rates. The same century brought the invention of the telegraph and ocean cable, which meant that news could be disseminated far more quickly. The twentieth century added wireless, aircraft, radio, motion pictures, and television. All the necessary elements were present for forging the new weapon of propaganda.

PROPAGANDA

Propaganda can be defined as systematic attempts through mass communications to influence the thinking, and thereby the behavior, of people in the interest of some particular group. The activity must be conducted to benefit some group, since otherwise it is difficult to distinguish it from edu-

cation which also affects opinions. It should be noted that education may
be perverted into propaganda, e.g., under Hitler the first aim of the German
schools was to manufacture good little Nazis. The activity must be systematic because if it is not, it will have little effect and will thus defeat the
purpose of the propagandist. It seems superfluous to write that propaganda
must concern itself with controversial topics, for if there were universal agreement, there would be no point in preaching to the converted. The definition
includes the activities of private interests, for public opinion is greatly affected by pressure groups. Propaganda is also carried on by governments,
both within their own states and in foreign countries. It is not a necessary
part of the definition that the propaganda be deceitful or unscientific, though
it frequently is. But to say that everything that is honestly and logically stated
with the intention of influencing opinion in the interest of some group is not
propaganda would narrow the definition too much. It would mean that
advocating the overthrow of a foreign government by violence was not propaganda if the arguments were frank and reasonable.

Propaganda is used to influence domestic as well as foreign opinion.
It is one of the most powerful agencies in creating the feeling of nationalism.
Governments as well as private interests try to influence public opinion and
win its support for their policies. Democratic governments must do this
within the limits set by the freedoms of speech, press, and public meeting.
What totalitarianism achieves by force and misrepresentation, democracy
must try to accomplish through the free interplay of public opinion, guided
by a responsible government. It is only in time of war that a democracy
abridges the democratic freedoms, e.g., by press censorship. The dictatorships do not ignore public opinion, but they try to shape and mold it instead
of following it. For this reason the Communists like the Nazis and the
Fascists established a complete monopoly of all means of communication
in their respective states. The public are allowed to learn only what the
government wants them to know. The press and all other publications are
controlled: Goebbels, Hitler's minister of propaganda, described the German
newspapers as a trained symphony orchestra which kept perfect time to his
baton. Under the Soviet regime history has been rewritten more than once
to conform with the changing policy of the government. Eminent historians
have been disgraced because they failed to keep up with the party line
and produced works which some time before would have been highly approved, but were anathema under the new dispensation. There is a highly
organized and continuous campaign to indoctrinate the mass of the population until it accepts the ideology of the dictatorship and makes it its own.

The purpose of propaganda in international affairs is to influence public
opinion abroad in such a way that a foreign government will be compelled
to carry out a policy advantageous to the propagandist's government. This

is done by appealing to the mass of the population over the head of its government. One method tries to develop cultural relations through, for example, the publication by a government of magazines, pamphlets, and news reports which present its actions and way of life in the most favorable light. Moving picture films are prepared for the same purpose. Libraries are established in foreign cities, or cultural missions are sent abroad. Sometimes societies are established to popularize the national culture such as the Alliance Française. It established centers of French learning in many countries and heightened the prestige of France abroad. Scholarships are created for the benefit of foreign students, or exchanges are made with teachers and professors in another country. It has been said that among the measures used to strengthen peace none has proved more successful than the cultural relations program, in spite of the undeniable fact that it has been used on occasion to further political and military purposes as well as the interests of peace. Another method is to arrange conducted tours for visitors who can rarely speak the language and can be suitably impressed by showing them only the things which it is expedient that they should see. The Dean of Canterbury was powerfully affected by this technique during his visit to the Soviet Union. Most of the above methods are fairly obvious, and the persons affected by them must be aware of their origin.

Words, pictures, cartoons, songs, and many similar devices are the typical means of making propaganda. The propaganda may advocate a policy, vilify some individual or party, or extol some person or group connected with the propagandist. News is his most important tool. If it is favorable, it can be emphasized, and if it is unfavorable, it may be withheld or modified. Sometimes the propagandist uses false evidence to substantiate his charges. Hitler quoted from the forgery known as the *Protocols of the Wise Men of Zion* to strengthen his accusation that the Jews were conspiring to rule the world. It is a mistake, however, to believe that all propaganda consists of lies. A good propagandist will tell the truth if possible, since if he is convicted of untruthfulness his influence is weakened. A frequent method is to give a judicious selection from the facts, suppressing those which speak against his case. Above all, the propagandist supplies his own version of the meaning of the news. He resembles a lawyer pleading in court, working for his client's interests rather than presenting the whole truth. As a rule, the propagandist does not want his audience to reason; his aim is to convince them by sweeping them off their feet. He, therefore, appeals to basic emotions, such as fear, patriotism, desire for power or rewards, etc.: Hitler was a master of this device. The electoral success of the Nationalist party in South Africa arises from the success with which it plays upon the widespread fear of the European minority that any relaxation of white supremacy will ultimately result in control by the Negro majority.

Short and catchy slogans are often used, e.g. "No taxation without representation," "Make the world safe for democracy," "Remember Pearl Harbor," "Liberty, Equality and Fraternity," or the phrase coined by the French defenders of Verdun against the Germans in 1916, "They shall not pass." National anthems like the *Marseillaise* are often effective propaganda. Songs can serve the same purpose, such as Lissauer's *Hymn of Hate* against England in World War I. Cartoons can have influence, such as those of David Low in the London press of the nineteen thirties heaping ridicule on all proposals for urgently needed rearmament. Another device is the symbol, such as the Nazi swastika. A person can be built up till he becomes the personification of an idea—Hitler in Germany and Stalin in Russia. National heroes can be associated with an idea. Washington and Lincoln are symbols of American democracy. The use of symbols and slogans is particularly effective in stimulating the emotion of patriotism. The discrediting of opponents by insults or insinuations is a common practice: the United States in Soviet propaganda is referred to as the "capitalist imperialist warmongers of Wall Street," and another favorite term is "cannibal hyenas." The propagandist is under a certain disadvantage if he is a foreigner. If he tells of the superiority of conditions in his own nation, his information is likely to be received with skepticism. If he is attacking another country or its government, the large majority of its citizens will resent this because of their feelings of nationalism. It is a distinct gain if the hostile propaganda can be carried on by natives of the country that is being attacked, and a fifth column is a valuable asset in such an endeavor.

HISTORY OF PROPAGANDA

Prior to 1914 propaganda was usually intended to influence domestic opinion. The press of each nation was patriotic, and was one of the great formative influences in the development of nationalism. Very occasionally propaganda was used against a foreign state. During the French Revolution the Assembly in 1792 announced that it would "come to the help of all nations which might wish to recover their liberty." French soldiers went into battle with the slogan of "War to the castles, peace to the cottages." When Napoleon conquered a country, he made extensive use of propaganda to win friends and influence people. But instances of trying to sway other peoples were rare, for until the twentieth century it would have been regarded as an act of unthinkable vulgarity to appeal to the people in order to influence the policy of their government. The correct way to do that was through the traditional machinery of diplomacy.

World War I was the first occasion when propaganda assumed major importance both at home and abroad. The demands made upon the ordinary citizen were so unprecedented for military service and war work that special efforts were necessary to win his support for the government's policy and strengthen his fortitude and his willingness to make sacrifices. To sustain morale there were appeals to patriotism, hatred of the enemy was cultivated, and each nation proved that its cause was just and idealistic, while that of its opponents was the reverse. For the first time organized efforts were made by both sides to influence public opinion in neutral countries, particularly the United States. A form of psychological warfare was used to break down the enemy's will to resist. One method was to drop pamphlets and leaflets behind the enemy lines pointing out that further resistance was hopeless. As long as Germany seemed likely to win, this propaganda had little influence; but it played a considerable part in the final collapse when the country had been worn down economically by the Allied blockade and its armies had been defeated. After the war the United States, Britain, and France abolished the propaganda agencies which they had created.

INTERWAR PROPAGANDA

The Germans organized a very widespread propaganda campaign, the purpose of which was to manufacture sympathy and secure the abolition of the terms of the Versailles Treaty which imposed reparations, territorial losses, and disarmament. The attempt was remarkably successful, and a large part of the world was persuaded that the treaty should be abrogated. This attitude was a great help to Hitler when he began to break one clause of the peace settlement after another. One reason why British public opinion supported his reoccupation of the Rhineland in 1936 and his annexation of the Sudeten Germans in Czechoslovakia was because it believed that he was wiping out two of the crimes of the wicked Treaty of Versailles. German propaganda scored a striking domestic success when the army persuaded the people that it had never been defeated—actually it lost a quarter of its strength in the last hundred days—but that it had been stabbed in the back. Hitler made skillful use of propaganda to win the support of the masses for himself and his program. He established a propaganda ministry under Goebbels, who set himself to create "one single public opinion." German psychologists had made a very careful study of propaganda, and Goebbels profited from their discoveries. He also owed something to the methods used by the Western powers during World War I and to those developed in Russia. Education became a masterpiece of indoctrination, and a high degree of fanaticism was developed in the Nazi party. Mussolini likewise made an effective use of propaganda to consolidate his power at home, as well as employing it abroad.

Years before the Russian Revolution Lenin recognized the crucial importance of propaganda. The Communists showed themselves to be masters in developing its methods and appealing to different classes of the population. It was used not only to consolidate their control over Russia, but also in their campaign to promote revolution in capitalist states. At this time radio came into its own, and Lenin and Trotsky were the originators of the idea of broadcasting directly to foreign peoples. Foreign language broadcasts began from their powerful Moscow stations, despite the protests of the governments affected. After World War I international peacetime propaganda became a regular occurrence, and for some years it was practically monopolized by the dictatorships. The colonial powers began broadcasting to their empires, France in 1931 and Britain in 1932. In 1938 the British Broadcasting Company began broadcasting in German and Italian, and by 1939 it had programs in sixteen languages.

WORLD WAR II

The dictatorships had well-trained propaganda machines when hostilities began. The German government kept its people fighting long after all hopes of victory had gone. Its propaganda war on France was an effective auxiliary to the military attack. Class was set against class, and cleverly organized campaigns were carried on to weaken the morale of soldiers and civilians and arouse distrust of their British ally. Blackmail was used against persons of influence to force them to act as German agents. Intensive attempts were made to foster isolationism in the United States and keep it out of the war. Japan also used propaganda extensively. The democratic powers had no organization comparable with that of the Axis states, but in the end they proved to be the more effective. Britain established a ministry of information in 1939 and conducted successful propaganda at home and abroad. The British Broadcasting Company had a very large audience in the occupied countries of Europe, despite the severe penalties imposed by the Germans for listening. The United States established the Office of War Information in 1942. It operated several foreign-language radio stations in Europe, besides printing many pamphlets and attaching psychological warfare teams to the armed forces. Psychological warfare comprises the use of propaganda against the enemy, together with such military measures as may supplement the propaganda. The United States and Britain set up a joint psychological warfare division in the European theater of war.

POSTWAR PROPAGANDA

After the war the United States and Britain greatly curtailed their propaganda activities. Russia came out of the war with a very large and efficient propaganda machine, and her recent allies soon felt the weight of her attack. As the cold war became more intense, the United States and Britain realized the need of a counterattack. From then onward an intensive propaganda campaign has been an important phase of the strained relations between East and West. In 1948 the Smith-Mundt Act was passed "to promote the better understanding of the United States among the peoples of the world and to strengthen cooperative international relations." This gave the propaganda activities of the State Department permanent legislative status. The work was divided between the Office of International Information (named in 1951 International Information Administration), which took over the mass media functions—radio, press and publications, and motion pictures—and the Office of Educational Exchange, which became responsible for the exchange of teachers and students and the support of libraries and institutes. In 1953 the International Information Administration was separated from the State Department, and under the modified title of the United States Information Agency (USIA) was made an independent agency reporting to the president through the National Security Council. The information activities carried on abroad are known as the United States Information Service (USIS). The staff in 1954 was 9539 and the appropriation $77 million. The Voice of America is the broadcasting service of the USIA. This had a staff of 1503 and broadcast over seventy-eight short wave transmitters in the United States and abroad in thirty-four languages. Motion picture films were shown in eighty-seven countries in 1952. The International Press Service produced pamphlets, leaflets, magazines, cartoons, photographs and materials for newspapers. They were distributed abroad to newspapers and magazines, radio stations, schools, and leaders of opinion, and also through the information centers. Each of the centers had its modest library of books, magazines and newspapers. Under the Educational Exchange Service 5072 foreigners were brought to the United States in 1952, and 1687 Americans were sent abroad.

The Department of Defense has its own radio programs for American service men abroad and also provides them with publications and motion pictures. All this is passed on to the inhabitants of the countries where the troops are stationed. The most important of the private American propaganda organizations is the National Committee for a Free Europe, which was founded in 1949. It operates Radio Free Europe from twenty-two transmitters in western Europe and has a staff of about one hundred, mostly Europeans. In addition, it publishes a number of publications. The purpose is to carry on propaganda against the Communist dictatorships of the satellite states, and encourage the conquered peoples in their hope that ultimately they will regain their freedom.

British international propaganda is primarily the responsibility of the foreign office, though other ministries are concerned to a lesser degree. It controls the British Information Service which operates in thirty-six countries. This supplies publications, films, and press materials, and maintains libraries and information centers. Four periodicals are published behind the iron curtain. The foreign office also controls radio broadcasting stations in the Middle East and Germany. The bulk of the broadcasting is conducted by the British Broadcasting Corporation (BBC), a public corporation which operates under government supervision. Its overseas broadcasts are in forty-four different languages, and cover most parts of the world. The aims are to make available an impartial news service, to give the British point of view, and to describe the British way of life. The programs are printed in several BBC magazines. The British Council is a semiofficial, semi-independent corporation, established in 1934 to teach English and interpret the British way of life abroad. An American authority said of its work in cultural relations that "it is largely in consequence of the activities of the British Council that no literate European will ever again refer to the English as a nation of shopkeepers." In 1952 the Council carried on educational and cultural work in fifty-eight countries, and operated 102 libraries. Most of its financial support comes from the foreign office. The total appropriation for overseas propaganda was $27.4 million in 1953.

Russia has by far the most extensive propaganda organization that the world has ever seen. The Communists have been expanding and improving it since 1917, and have attained a high degree of skill. They have the further advantage in their operations on the home front that they have a monopoly and are not hampered by a strong tradition of free speech. From the beginning the Communists have been fully aware of the importance of ideas in their campaign for world revolution. Success depends upon enlisting the support of the masses; but one would gravely underestimate the acumen of the party if one assumed that its appeal was directed to them alone. The propagandists are all things to all men. "Communism is the most aggressive and, up to this moment, the most successful organized missionary movement of all time. We need to understand that it is aided but not caused by adverse economic conditions. It appeals to the high-born as well as the downtrodden, to the doctor of letters as well as the illiterate—and always in the form of cleverly contrived promises to set right whatever is wrong." The chief appeals are made to "hatred, jealousy, fear, a sense of injustice, racial animosity and a desire for power."

Expenditure is far greater than in any other country. The State Department estimated that in 1950 it was $928 million in Russia alone and $481 million in the satellite states, giving a total expenditure of $1,409 million. Only the most loyal party members are allowed to practise propaganda, and the number engaged in it at home and abroad is estimated to be 1.4 million, all highly trained. The broad outlines of policy are decided by the Presidium of the central committee of the Russian Communist party. Its agency for propaganda is Agitprop, the Department of Propaganda and Agitation. The foreign office in Moscow and its diplomatic representatives abroad also engage in propaganda.

Radio propaganda is prepared by the psychological warfare branch of the foreign office, which is believed to have a staff of 250. In each case a native of the country concerned assists a Russian in preparing the script. It was believed that in 1950 Russia was broadcasting in thirty-two foreign languages, and she led the world in the number of hours on the air. The number of transmitters is unknown, but there are estimated to be 1250 jammers for making unintelligible foreign broadcasts beamed to Russia. A very large volume of publications of every kind is printed in many languages and distributed by a branch of the Soviet ministry of foreign trade. The distributing agency in a foreign country is sometimes the local Communist party. In addition to books, pamphlets, and leaflets, there are magazines and newspapers. The Communist press abroad is supplied with news by Sovinformburo, and motion pictures are distributed by Sovexportfilm. Tass, an agency of the Soviet government, has a virtual monopoly of the gathering and dissemination of Russian news abroad. Voks arranges conducted tours for groups of visitors to Russia, and also sends abroad delegations of artists, athletes, and intellectuals. Another useful propaganda agency is the study groups and the Soviet Friendship Societies which exist in many countries. Camouflaged propaganda organizations include the World Peace Committee which launched the Stockholm Peace Petition, the International Union of Students, the World Federation of Trade Unions, and the Cominform. The satellite states also carry on foreign propaganda.

POLITICAL WARFARE

Political warfare is a vague term which has no exact technical meaning. It is roughly equivalent to intervention when that word is used in its loose popular sense. Political warfare covers a variety of means short of actual war which a state uses to weaken or exert pressure upon another state. The methods employed include the following: diplomacy, economic pressure, armed demonstrations, propaganda, fifth-column activities, sabotage and encouragement of revolt. The purpose of an action determines whether it is or is not political warfare. Thus propaganda which tries merely to create good will toward the propagandist's government is not political warfare, but it becomes so if the object is to coerce a foreign government into changing its policy. An embargo is not political warfare when the aim is to prevent the export of some scarce commodity, but embargoes on the shipment of American military raw materials to Japan in 1940–1941 were political warfare, since the purpose was to compel her to modify her policy of aggression. Political warfare does not end with the outbreak of military conflict but is likely to be continued in many forms in order to weaken the enemy. Thus in 1917 the Germans helped a Communist exile named Lenin to travel from Switzerland to Russia in order to start a revolution and overthrow the government which was trying to continue the war.

Diplomacy which seeks its ends by argument and persuasion is not considered political warfare, but it becomes so when it employs more or less veiled threats of the consequences which will follow a refusal to grant the demands. Particularly in the nineteenth century diplomatic arguments were sometimes supported by a show of force to emphasize that the government was in earnest. When Commodore Perry returned to Japan in 1854 to negotiate a commercial treaty, his success was due in part to his escort of a powerful squadron of seven warships. At times armies have been stationed close to the frontier of a state which is being pressed to make concessions. In 1946 Russian troops were moved close to the Russo-Turkish border in the hope that this threat would frighten Turkey into admitting Soviet garrisons. Pressure is also applied by *retorsion*, which is a legal but deliberately unfriendly act with a retaliatory or coercive purpose. A common form is a retaliatory increase in tariff rates against countries which discriminate against the products of a particular state. Another method employed quite frequently has been *reprisal*, which has become a broad principle of justification for otherwise questionable state conduct. The term covered various kinds of coercive action whereby a state attempted to secure satisfaction from another for some wrong which the latter had committed against it. Examples were the seizure of the property of nationals of the offending state, or an embargo by which its ships were forbidden to enter or leave the ports of the nation applying the pressure. There was also the pacific blockade of the ports of a weak state by a stronger naval power in order to interrupt its seaborne trade without actually declaring war. In 1902 Germany and Britain blockaded Venezuela to compel her to pay her debts. Another form of reprisal was bombardment, as when an Italian cruiser bombarded the Greek island of Corfu in 1923 to compel the government to agree to Mussolini's demands. To-day reprisal which involves the use of force is probably illegal under the U.N. Charter, so far as its signatories are concerned. The law on the subject is vague, but the probability is that reprisal would be considered legal except when it was forbidden by commitments under the U.N. Charter, arbitration treaties, etc. Political warfare includes the use of military forces to intervene in the affairs of foreign states. Such American interventions in the Caribbean region were fairly frequent in the past, but the practice was abandoned with the introduction of the Good Neighbor policy in 1933.

The technique of the fifth column is based upon the fact that no government ever has the unanimous support of the whole population. There are sure to be individuals or groups who oppose the official policy, who want power, or who, if there is a racial minority, want independence. Their support may be enlisted by offering to satisfy their desires, and their number may be increased by propaganda. Organized and helped with money or arms, a fifth column may become a powerful auxiliary of a foreign state. One of the most successful examples dates from about 1375 B.C., and can be followed in detail from the despatches found in the ruins of the foreign office of Pharaoh Akhnaton, who ruled over Palestine, Lebanon and Syria as well as Egypt. His empire was invaded by the king of the Hittites (modern Turkey), allied with Egyptian vassal princes and assisted by nobles of high rank at the pharaoh's court who appear to have been bribed. The fifth column was so effective that the pharaoh was persuaded the rebel princes were resisting the invaders, and that the princes who actually were faithful to him and were fighting to preserve his empire were traitors. The end of it all was that the loyal princes were killed in battle, the Egyptian soldiers were defeated, and the whole of Akhnaton's foreign dominions were lost. Fifth-column tactics were often used in the milleniums that followed, but never with greater success than when they destroyed the Egyptian Empire in the Middle East.

The assassination in 1914 of the Archduke Franz Ferdinand, the heir to the throne of the Austrian Empire, was an act of political warfare, for the murderer was helped by Serbian officials. One reason why Germany believed Britain would remain neutral in World War I was that she expected an Irish revolt for which she had supplied the arms. The Protestants of northern Ireland had raised an army and were preparing to rebel rather than be included in the plan for Irish self-government which the government of Great Britain was determined to carry out. When the war broke out, the Protestants postponed their rebellion in order to join the British army. During the war Germany maintained a wide network of spies and saboteurs in the United States whose chief task was to prevent munitions from reaching the European allies. The Germans were probably to blame for hundreds of mysterious fires and explosions throughout the country. One principal result was that the sabotage was a major reason why American public opinion became hostile to Germany.

NAZI FIFTH COLUMNS

Between the wars political warfare was used extensively by Nazi Germany. Hitler's methods of undermining Austrian independence from within were a classic example. The fifth column was the Austrian Nazi party, which was armed, financed, and controlled from Berlin. Camouflaged Nazis were infiltrated into key positions in the government, and the German ambassador in Vienna had early and accurate information of the plans of the Austrian dictator. A revolt took place in 1934, in the course of which the Nazis assassinated the Austrian dictator Dollfuss. This attempt was premature, but when Hitler struck again in 1938, the Austrian Nazis were an important factor in his success. The Sudeten Germans of Czechoslovakia were organized into a similar fifth column and gave Hitler his pretext for the Munich Agreement. In 1939 the Germans in Poland hampered the Polish army in its defense against the German invaders. It was estimated that Hitler spent $300 million a year to organize Germans abroad and spread propaganda. Other examples of political warfare were the German and Italian help to Franco in the Spanish Civil War and the Nazi penetration of Latin America through the medium of the Germans living there. Germany organized and financed the Spanish Fascist party, the Falange, to carry on pro-Axis propaganda and espionage in Spanish America and the Philippines. Once the war began Germany tried to prevent the United States from joining or assisting the Allies. She used disruptive propaganda, the purpose of which was to divide Americans by fomenting racial, class, and religious hatreds. Fifth-column groups were created such as the German-American Bund and Father Coughlin's Christian Front. German agents tried to infiltrate into the America First Committee, a powerful isolationist organization which opposed American entry into the war. The German conquest of Norway and France was facilitated to some extent by fifth columns. After the invasion of France began German agents worked behind the French lines issuing false orders and spreading panic among civilians so that entire populations fled, clogging the roads, with the result that French reinforcements could not reach the front.

SOVIET POLITICAL WARFARE

Throughout its existence Soviet Russia has concentrated upon the development of political warfare. After World War I it fomented unrest in the Western democracies, brought about a temporary Communist dictatorship in Hungary, and organized several unsuccessful revolts in Germany. Communists were active in the Asian dependencies of Holland, France, and Britain, and for a time in the 'twenties they had hopes of capturing control of the Kuomintang party in China. The Communists have always looked upon political warfare in the tropics as one of their best weapons. Since World War II it has been effective in China and Vietnam and is a serious danger in some other Asian countries.

The cold war that has been going on since 1945 provides a great many examples of political warfare. This and not conquest by the Red army created the European satellite states. The method was described as the technique of the inside job, and is dealt with in the chapter on Russian foreign policy. The same tactics have been tried unsuccessfully in the states of the free world. The fifth column for engineering a revolution in an anticommunist country has been the local Communist party, a branch of which has been established in almost every state. All of them receive orders and assistance from Moscow. The general policies to be followed are laid down by the Presidium, and instructions are sent to the headquarters of the national parties. They decide how best to carry out their directives in the light of local conditions, and transmit their orders to the cells or units. The link between Moscow and national headquarters may be by Moscow radio broadcasts, a direct courier, instructions from the Soviet embassy in the capital of the state, or some international congress, e.g., a peace or a cultural congress, at which representatives of the various Communist parties are present amongst the rank and file of the delegates. At no point is the original Moscow decision amended. There is considerable discussion about it, but this is limited to detailed application of a policy which has already been settled. Strong and effective leadership is considered vital to success, and promising candidates carefully selected from the different Communist parties are trained in a special school in Moscow. They are thoroughly instructed in Communist ideology, the conduct of propaganda, class war, strikes, sabotage, armed revolt, and civil war. Then they are sent to the part of the world where their natural talents and acquired knowledge will do the most good. The Communist party in each state is divided into small units or cells, most of the rank and file members of which are ignorant of the higher control and of the membership of other cells. Thus the destruction of one cell does not imperil the party as a whole.

Not every Communist carries a membership card, for there are also the crypto-Communists. These are people who are in every respect Communists and obey all instructions of the party, but who are forbidden to join it because they can give it more efficient service by appearing not to be members. A government official for example, a confidential secretary, or a journalist may be more useful if there is no documentary evidence which can connect him with the party. Outside the party also are the "fellow travelers," people who agree with its aims but have not formally joined it. "Through the cryptos and the fellow travelers, the Communist party is able increasingly to spread its influence to people and organizations remote from itself. . . . New organizations, new contacts, and a whole solar system of fellow-traveler organizations bring more and more into that circle of which the party is the centre." Infiltration has been widely practiced, and reliable party members have been appointed to important positions in the police, army, and other government services.

In the economic field the tactics have been to secure the election of Communists to the controlling positions in the trade unions. The large majority of the members are not Communists, but loyalty to their union can be counted upon to make them obey the orders of their executive. By exploiting grievances strikes are called which are very damaging to the national economy. In Great Britain, for example, the voting strength of the Communist party is about 35,000 out of 50 million, and the number who hold positions of authority in the trade unions is small. The latter have concentrated their efforts upon the unions which are vitally important in an industrialized nation that depends for its livelihood upon foreign trade, e.g., the longshoremen (a strike here can paralyze import and export trade), unions connected with the distribution of gas and oil (strikes here can paralyze road transport), electrical workers (not only lighting but unloading ships, atomic plants, and the operation of many factories depend upon electricity), and engineers (this in Britain includes the men who control the supply of power to the bulk of the factories and also extends into the shipbuilding, automobile, and aircraft industries). There have been very damaging strikes in many of these unions. In 1954 the Communists engineered a strike of the longshoremen on a trivial pretext and tied up the ports for six weeks. It was estimated that the loss in imports and exports was about $600 million. Sometimes the strikes have had political motives, e.g., to impede the production of munitions in the present armaments race. The infiltration of the unions is more serious in France and Italy than in Britain. In the American trade unions the story is one of continually dwindling Communist influence.

Another phase is found in apparently innocent organizations with laudable aims, most of the members of which are unaware that they are really under Communist control. Examples with typically innocuous names are the World Federation of Democratic Youth and the International Women's Day Committee. These societies are an essential part of the Communist propaganda machine. Of set purpose representatives of all schools of thought are admitted to their governing bodies. "What really matters is that the aims and program of these organizations should be dictated to them (without their realizing it) by the Communist party." The propaganda is very skillfully conducted, and

constitutes a ceaseless barrage against the minds of the free peoples. It is conducted through press, radio, pulpit, pamphlet, platform and, most insidious of all, carefully planned whispering campaigns. Its danger is more acute because it is not open advocacy of the Communist creed. On the contrary, one hears very little about Marxism from the skilled Red agitator. He concentrates on day-to-day affairs affecting the mass of people and preys upon their natural desires and fears. That is why words such as "peace" and "democracy" figure so prominently in the Communist vocabulary. The party's main propaganda theme is based upon the simple but outrageous premise that the Soviet Union, together with the other "People's Democracies," is fighting a battle for peace against the warlike capitalist states. Thus support for Russia is depicted as a step towards world peace. Attacks on Britain, the members of the Commonwealth, and the U.S.A. are regarded in the same light.

The Communist peace campaign is very closely linked with the industrial agitation to sabotage the defense industries of the Western powers.

The World Peace Movement arose out of a series of peace congresses held in many cities of Europe and North America in 1948 and 1949. A permanent World Peace Committee was established in 1949, composed of Communists and fellow travelers. National committees were set up in different countries to enlist popular support. Many well meaning people, lovers of peace and not Communists, supported the campaign, often without realizing its Soviet origin. One purpose of the World Peace Movement was to mobilize public opinion so that it would put pressure on Western governments to support Soviet peace proposals in the U.N. These were diametrically opposed to those of the United States and the other Western states. In March, 1950, a meeting was held at Stockholm to launch the Stockholm Resolution condemning atomic war. Its sponsors claimed that the petition was signed by 275 million persons, of whom 30 million came from Western Europe and 1.35 million from the United States. The resolution is worth studying as an example of the plausibility of Communist propaganda. It would be a mistake to underestimate its appeal to uninformed people. "We demand unconditional prohibition of the atomic weapon as a weapon of aggression and mass annihilation of the people, and that strict international control for the implementation of this decision be established. We shall consider as a war criminal that government which first employs the atomic weapon against any country."

It was strange that a peace appeal did not condemn aggression or war as such. This might have been awkward since the invasion of South Korea took place while signatures to the resolution were still being collected. In the next place the emphasis was on the atom bomb, the weapon that Russia was most anxious to abolish. No mention was made of other weapons in which Russia had a great superiority. The "strict international control" demanded could only mean the Russian proposals which most of the members of the United Nations had rejected as inadequate. According to the resolution the problem of peace was very simple: abolish the weapon in which Russia was at a great disadvantage. By implication the resolution condemned the United States as the government that might use the bomb and diverted attention from Communist aggression.

SELECTED READING

BARGHOORN, FREDERICK C., *The Soviet Image of the United States: A Study in Distortion*. New York: Harcourt, Brace and Company, 1950.

BARRETT, EDWARD W., *Truth is Our Weapon*. New York: Funk & Wagnalls, 1953.

CARROLL, WALLACE, *Persuade or Perish*. Boston: Houghton Mifflin Company, 1948.

CHASE, ALLAN, *Falange: The Axis Secret Army in the Americas*. New York: G. P. Putnam's Sons, 1943.

FRASER, LINDLEY, *Germany between Two Wars: A Study of Propaganda and War Guilt*. New York: Oxford Press, 1945.

INKELES, ALEX, *Public Opinion in Soviet Russia: A Study in Mass Persuasion*. Cambridge: Harvard University Press, 1950.

KRIS, ERNST, and SPEIER, HANS, *German Radio Propaganda*. New York: Oxford Press, 1944.

LERNER, DANIEL, *Sykewar: Psychological Warfare Against Germany, D-Day to V-E Day*. New York: George W. Stewart, 1949.

—— (ed.), *Propaganda in War & Crisis: Materials for American Policy*. New York: George W. Stewart, 1951.

MARKEL, LESTER, and others, *Public Opinion and Foreign Policy*. New York: Harper and Brothers, 1949.

MIKSCHE, F. O., *Secret Forces: the Technique of Underground Movements*. London: Faber and Faber, Ltd., 1949.

POSSONY, STEFAN T., *A Century of Conflict. Communist Techniques of World Revolution*. Chicago: Henry Regnery Company, 1953.

ROWAN, RICHARD W., *The Story of Secret Service*. London: Miles, 1938.

CHAPTER 7

ECONOMIC NATIONALISM

Political nationalism has its counterpart in the economic field: the nationalist thinks of international economic and political relations alike in terms of national interests. The state to which he gives his loyalty must be prosperous, strong, and influential in world affairs. The duty of the government is so to direct economic activity that it helps to produce this result. The welfare of the people must be sought; but where necessary, this must be subordinated to the interests of the nation. Economic nationalism has dominated the world since 1918, and writers sometimes look back wistfully to the good old times of free trade before World War I. These halcyon days, however, were only an interlude between economic nationalism and its spiritual ancestor mercantilism. So similar are the two in aims and methods that the former is sometimes called neomercantilism.

MERCANTILISM

Mercantilism shaped governmental policy during the seventeenth and eighteenth centuries. Economic activity was encouraged, but always under the overriding authority and regulation of the government. The state must be strong, and since wealth is a basic factor in strength, production and trade must be fostered. The state must aim at self-sufficiency, and nothing must be imported that could be produced at home. Colonies were acquired as a market for the manufactures of the metropolitan power and to supply food and raw materials which otherwise must be bought from foreign countries. Great importance was attached to foreign trade, and exports of manufactures were encouraged by subsidies and other devices, while imports were limited by import duties and sometimes prohibitions. So far as possible the object was to sell without buying in order to secure every year a favorable balance of trade, that is, an excess of exports over imports. Foreign buyers must pay their debts in gold or silver coin, and the inflow of bullion increased the national wealth. The attempt was made to prevent gold leaving the country. A large merchant marine was built, vested interests of all sorts were heavily protected, and consumers were neglected. The mercantilists were familiar with discriminatory tariffs, bilateralism, and tariff wars. The restrictive trade methods of modern economic nationalism have many analogies with those of mercantilism.

FREE TRADE

Adam Smith launched his attack upon mercantilism in his *Wealth of Nations* in 1776. He was followed by a group of early nineteenth century British writers, the classical economists, who worked out the philosophy of laissez faire. They advocated that all governmental control over production and trade should be abolished. There should be completely free competition of private enterprise, and government intervention in the economic sphere should be confined to punishing through the courts those who actually broke the law. The guide to conduct should be enlightened self-interest. The classical economists assumed that every man was aware of his own long-run best interests better than the government or any one else. So if every man were left completely free to pursue those interests, he would do so, to his own maximum profit and also to that of the nation.

Import duties and export subsidies should be abolished, and free trade established. The mercantilists' preoccupation with a favorable balance of trade, the import of bullion, and the power of the state were all ignored. Imports paid for exports, and in the long run a nation could sell only as much as it bought. For if merchants of country A were prevented by import duties from selling their goods in country B, then they could not acquire the currency of country B with which to pay for the commodities it wished to export. If an industry were too weak to compete with foreign imports, it was inefficient or artificial and deserved to fail. The free traders had a robust faith that with international free trade every industry and nation would get the trade to which its competitive efficiency entitled it. Such a regime would also promote international specialization. If traders were left free to pursue their own profit by buying in the cheapest and selling in the dearest market, then in the long run each country would concentrate on producing and exporting those commodities in which its costs of production were lowest and its profits highest, and each country would import those articles in which its production costs were greatest. The classical economists had little interest in using the tariff as a bargaining weapon. The enormous expansion of trade which they correctly prophesied would give opportunities to all.

The economists were supported by the rising class of British manufacturers, who saw the immense profits that were possible if they could free themselves from the outworn trammels of mercantilism. The machine and the factory were replacing hand industry, and the use of steam power was just being mastered. Costs were reduced, and output multiplied at an amazing rate. Great Britain in 1815 was in an excellent position to take advantage of the new inventions. Her position had many parallels with that of the United States at the end of World War II. Britain had been safe from invasion and had been the arsenal and paymaster of the enemies of Napoleon. She had developed production, technical skill, and financial strength. She had become practically the sole creditor country in the world—the only nation whose currency was virtually on a gold standard—and London was the leading money market. The nations of continental Europe had been impoverished and devastated by nearly a quarter century of wars, and their industrial development was far behind that of Britain.

Mercantilism was abolished as a national policy, and Great Britain and the empire adopted free trade between 1846 and 1860. Britain became the most important market in the world, and her foreign trade far surpassed that of other nations. Despite the great increase in population, standards of living rose markedly, though not evenly, and the price of food declined sharply. Wherever industrialism spread, the workmen gained more in material welfare and ultimately in political power than in any previous century. For a time the advocates of laissez faire believed that it would abolish war. They expected that with the spread of free trade national boundaries would cease to have any great economic importance and that a network of commerce would knit together the whole world in a mutually beneficial exchange of goods which it would profit no nation to disturb.

For a brief period it seemed that these hopes would be realized. In 1860 the Emperor Napoleon III agreed to an Anglo-French treaty which substantially lowered import duties on British manufactures. Britain and France negotiated similar treaties with many other European countries. The benefit of the lower tariffs was spread widely by the large number of treaties which contained an unconditional most-favored nation clause. Each contracting party assured all others with which it had such a treaty that it would apply to them tariff duties at the lowest level granted to any third state, and without requiring from them any reciprocal concessions in their tariffs. Until 1923 the United States adhered to the conditional form of this clause. When it negotiated a treaty which reduced import duties, the new lower rates would be extended to states with which America had a most-favored nation clause, only if they reciprocated by granting to American trade tariff concessions equivalent to those granted by the other party to the new treaty. After 1923 the United States adopted the unconditional form of the most-favored nation clause.

THE RETURN TO NEOMERCANTILISM

The expectation that other nations would adopt the British system of free trade lasted only a few years. In the eighteen-seventies there was a return to protective tariffs, particularly in Germany. The United States had first established a tariff to foster the development of industry in 1816, and after the Civil War it rapidly developed a high tariff. Other countries in the Americas and the British self-governing dominions began to raise their tariffs also. The usual motive was the protection of infant industries, and the development of nationalism made the acceptance of this easier. In Germany, especially, the dominant motive of economic nationalism was to increase the power of the state rather than to promote individual welfare. From this time onward tariffs slowly rose; but since they were moderate in height and were not changed too frequently, a large volume of international trade was carried on in spite of them. Only Britain maintained free trade, though Denmark, Belgium, Holland, and Switzerland had low tariff policies approximating to it. As manufacturing developed in western Europe and the United States, Britain gradually lost her head start, and in the last quarter of the nineteenth century she was ceasing to be the workshop of the world. American production overtook British in 1890, and German in 1900. Britain's exports continued to grow however, though not as fast as those of the United States and Germany. Britain was also emerging as the organizing and regulating center of world trade, finance, and investment. By 1913 Great Britain had 13.94 percent of the world export trade; Germany, 13.11 percent; the United States, 12.47 percent (by this date exports of manufactures exceeded raw materials and food); and France, 7.24 percent.

THE PATTERN OF WORLD TRADE

The whole world was gradually drawn into the trading orbit of western Europe. Its industries required raw materials in unprecedented quantities, far beyond the capacity of its limited area to produce them. As population grew, it became increasingly difficult for European countries—and particularly for Great Britain—to produce enough food to feed their peoples. This growing dependence on imported food and raw materials coincided with the settlement of the United States, South America, and the British dominions. Their economic development was made possible by the building of transcontinental railways in the later nineteenth century and the construction of faster and larger ships. In the late 'seventies meat and other perishable foods began to be brought to Europe in refrigerated ships. Speed of travel was immensely increased and the cost of freight fell sharply. A fairly complete network of telephone systems and ocean cables enabled merchants to obtain information in at most a few hours, instead of waiting for months. At the end of this pre-World War I period came the invention of wireless telegraphy, the automobile, and the airplane. The development of modern communications shrank the world enormously.

Imports to the manufacturing centers came mainly to consist of large and increasing quantities of bulky commodities such as iron ore, coal, and other minerals, rubber, cotton, and other vegetable raw materials, and food. The exports from Europe were primarily a great variety of manufactured goods, which paid for the imports. The world became economically interdependent, and every community found its prices affected to the extent that its economy was geared to world markets. "A fall in London wheat prices caused by a bumper crop in Argentina would depress prices and check exports from the United States. This would tend to pile up surpluses in the United States and to reduce the income of American farmers. These developments in turn would affect the real estate and labor markets." Under the nineteenth-century system it was impossible to stabilize domestic prices without restrictions on world trade. There were no laws intended to achieve stability of prices and no governmental machinery set up to regulate the markets. Trade was free and therefore unstable. It relied upon competitive forces to maintain equilibrium within and between markets.

The crowning economic achievement of the nineteenth century was the pattern of world trade as it existed in 1913. It was severely damaged by World War I, limped along with unsuccessful attempts to restore it in the nineteen-twenties, was broken by the great depression, and finally destroyed by the economic nationalism of the nineteen-thirties. The pattern of trade was global and was grouped into six broad divisions. The tropical countries exported more to the United States than they imported from it: the United States sent more to the British dominions and nontropical Latin America than it received from them: they in turn exported more to continental Europe: continental Europe exported more to Britain: and the circle was closed by Britain exporting more to the tropics than it imported from them. The monetary mechanism by which trade was financed prior to 1914 was the international gold standard.

INVESTMENT

Industrialization created profits on a scale such as the world had never seen before. Part of it was invested in the country of origin, but to an increasing extent it found an outlet abroad in regions which lacked the capital to develop their own resources. European, and especially British, investment was mainly responsible for developing the agricultural, mineral, and even the manufacturing resources of countries overseas. To an important extent the development of the United States was financed by British loans. When

SUEZ
CANAL

PANAMA

THE DOLLAR AREA

Modified from Jean Gottman, Geography of Europe, rev. ed., New York, Henry Holt & Co., 1954, p. 117

Ocean Trade Routes of Western Europe

the loans floated in Europe were wisely used, they increased the prosperity of the borrower besides affording a handsome return to the lender. During the first half of the nineteenth century the bulk of the loans came from Great Britain. About the middle of the century the French had sufficiently recovered from the effects of the revolution and the Napoleonic wars to play a growing role in international investment. In the latter part of the century Germany began to make investments abroad. Holland and Switzerland did the same on a smaller scale. The United States was on balance a debtor country until World War I. Its foreign investments were about $2 billion, but European investments in the United States were between $4 billion and $5 billion. Europe remained the world's banker until its capital was largely dissipated in World War I.

British foreign investments were estimated to amount to $18.25 billion in 1913. The average rate of interest was higher than on British domestic investments. Of this over 46 percent was invested in the British Empire, (34 percent in the dominions and 12 percent in India and the tropical dependencies), 20 percent in the United States, and 20 percent in Latin America. The British put little money into Europe and were much more interested in developing the new countries. They also provided the bulk of the short-term credit needed to finance the growing volume of international trade. To the London money market, wrote Feis, "you might come with a collection of treaties bearing the smeared symbols of an African chief, a survey map of properties located in India suitable for tea growing, a concession for a power plant in some South American town, the prospectus of a new bond issue of the Erie Railroad, and find some door open to you, some dim office where your treaties, maps, concessions and prospectuses would be taken as familiar chances." By 1913 the dividends from foreign investments were estimated to be $1.45 billion or 9 percent of the national income. They paid for a substantial part of the continually growing surplus of imports over exports. French foreign investments abroad in 1914 were about $8.7 billion. Of this 61 percent was invested in Europe (including 25 percent in Russia), 13 percent in Latin America, and only 9 percent in the French colonies. Unlike the British the French had a marked preference for investment in Europe and were interested only to a minor extent in investment in their colonies. German foreign investments were around $5.7 billion, of which 55 percent was in Europe, 16 percent in Latin America, and about the same percentage in the United States and Canada.

There was virtually no government control or supervision of the London money market. Before a large foreign loan was floated, there was informal consultation with the government, and on very rare occasions it exerted its influence to block the flotation. In France foreign loans required official approval, and this power was used to promote lending to friendly states and prevent it when the government disapproved for political reasons. In Germany there was close co-ordination between official policy and private trade and banking. German economic penetration abroad was closely linked with diplomacy. There were occasions when German banks were induced by the government to take up foreign investments that strengthened the policy of expansion. On occasion all governments exerted diplomatic pressure to enable their nationals to secure concessions for development, and pressure extending occasionally to the use of force was employed against weak debtor states to compel them to meet their obligations.

THE GOLD STANDARD

Every transaction in international trade requires the transfer of money from the currency of the debtor to that of the creditor. The process by which this is accomplished is termed foreign exchange, and a large number of complicated banking arrangements developed to facilitate it. In certain circumstances described below a debt was settled by the shipment of gold, but usually this clumsy expedient was avoided. This was possible because every nation imports as well as exports. There are always American importers who have debts to pay to British companies in pounds sterling, and there are also American exporters who are owed debts by British companies which they wish to convert from pounds into dollars. The function of the banks is to bring these two sets of traders together so that the American importers can pay the American exporters and the British importers can pay the British exporters. Of course, an individual importer does not pay an individual exporter: the banks balance the two sets of obligations against one another, and if imports equal exports, the whole operation can be concluded without any international transfer of currency.

London in the last quarter of the nineteenth century became the financial center not only of the British Empire but of the whole trading world. The great bulk of international trade was carried on and paid for in sterling. The monetary system on which it operated was the gold standard. It was an essential part of the system of nineteenth-century commerce in which it developed, and when this collapsed it became unworkable. Britain had been on the gold standard since 1816, and most of the other important countries adopted it between 1873 and 1897. The period during which it was fully operative was less than twenty years, from 1897 to 1914. The currency of each country had a fixed and legally defined gold content, and the value of one currency in terms of another was determined by the gold content of the standard coins. This ratio, which was known as the mint par of exchange, worked out at

One pound sterling = $4.86 = Marks 20.40 = Francs 25.25 and so on.

Actual rates of exchange fluctuated narrowly about these ratios. The limits of fluctuation were set by the cost of shipping gold from one financial center to another. For example, the cost of transport between London and New York was about three cents on the pound sterling each way. The dollar-pound exchange rate would vary between $4.89 and $4.83. These upper and lower limits of the fluctuation were known as the gold points. Suppose that the value of American exports to Britain exceeded that of British exports to the United States. The British demand for American dollars to settle the debt would then be greater than the American demand for pounds sterling, and the exchange rate of the pound would fall in terms of dollars. If the exchange rate fell below $4.83, it would pay the British debtor to ship gold to New York rather than to sell his pounds and buy dollars. Similarly if an American debtor had to pay more than $4.89, he would buy gold in New York and ship it to London to settle his debt.

The exchange rates of the various currencies were fixed within the narrow limits of the gold points as long as the nations adhered to the gold standard, and as long as their citizens were free to buy gold and export or import it as they chose. There were none of the wild fluctuations in exchange rates that followed World War I. This was a great advantage from the point of view of international trade and investment. It removed the risk that the profit on a transaction would be wiped out by a sudden change in the exchange rate, or that a foreign investment would lose much of its value in the same way. The gold standard was the nearest approach to a uniform currency the world has ever had. This stability of exchanges was one of the principal reasons for the great expansion of international trade and investment after 1870.

THE END OF LAISSEZ FAIRE

World War I undermined the nineteenth-century system of international trade. The economic position of the European belligerents was weakened, while the United States and Japan largely increased their industrial output. Markets which had been cut off from their prewar sources of supply sometimes established their own industries. In other cases they transferred their purchases to the United States and Japan, which retained permanently part of the markets they had conquered during the war. Germany lost the bulk of her foreign investments, and the British had sold over 20 percent of their most valuable holdings abroad to buy war supplies. Taxes and death duties were very heavy, and many British industries lacked the financial resources to modernize and found it difficult or impossible to obtain loans. The staple exports all suffered severely, and the merchant marine was hard hit by the competition of subsidized foreign shipping. France had the heavy burden of reconstructing the areas devastated by four years of trench fighting, and the Communist repudiation of the tsarist loans was a serious loss.

At the time men failed to realize how profoundly the war had changed economic conditions, and strenuous efforts were made to restore laissez faire, the gold standard, and the mixed regime of free trade and moderate tariffs. Superficially, it seemed by 1925 that the attempt was well on the way toward success. The productive capacity of Europe was substantially restored, and there seemed to be a ready sale for its manufactures as well as for the expanded exports of the United States, Japan, and the rest of the world. Large loans were made to Europe and especially Germany, since it was felt that its reconstruction was essential to restore world trade. The bulk of the money came from the United States, though Great Britain contributed more than was wise in view of her lessened financial resources. By 1930 the United States had about $15 billion invested abroad, nearly a third of it in Europe. The bulk of international trade was still conducted in sterling, and London made vigorous but futile efforts to regain its position as the world's financial center. It still retained its unequaled knowledge and skill, but far less money was available than before the war to finance trade and make loans. The United States was now the chief source of foreign loans, and financial leadership was divided between New York and London to the detriment of both. Great Britain remained free trade until 1931, and restored the gold standard with the pound at its prewar parity in 1925. Other countries returned to the gold standard, and agreements were made with the United States for the settlement of the war debts. The repayment of reparations seemed to have been arranged by the Dawes and Young Plans. Conferences were held to promote international economic cooperation and the lowering of trade barriers, but they came to nothing.

Genuinely to restore the prewar economy would have required far-reaching changes which were not carried out, primarily because of the growing strength of economic nationalism. The need to make the changes was disguised by the apparent growth of prosperity in the 'twenties. The real cause of the seeming recovery was the volume of foreign loans already referred to. They made it possible for the borrowing countries to obtain the foreign currencies, primarily dollars, with which to pay reparations and war debts and to import heavily, while postponing strenuous efforts to expand exports. Loans also enabled the creditor countries to export heavily while postponing the necessity of receiving payment in the form of imports. American loans however tapered off from the middle of 1928 and ended in 1930, and this was the immediate cause of the crisis and financial panic which spread over Europe in 1930 and 1931. Along with the great depression, which began with the New York stock market crash in October 1929, it marked the end of the period of apparent postwar recovery.

Reparations and war debts collapsed, there were widespread defaults in the payments due on foreign investments, agricultural production was maintained but prices collapsed, and world industrial production fell on the average by 31 percent. There was a spectacular fall in the volume of world trade and its value decreased by 65 percent, national incomes fell in most countries by 40 to 50 percent, and unemployment reached an unprecedented height. The financial panic in Europe forced Great Britain off the gold standard, and in the same year she gave up the attempt to be a free-trade oasis in a high-tariff world, and set up her own protective system. By 1936 the abandonment of the gold standard was general. In 1933 an economic conference was held to pull the world out of the depression by cooperative action. It failed because the leading powers disagreed on what measures should be adopted, especially in the monetary field. The attempt to restore the system of laissez faire was abandoned, and the nations took refuge in economic nationalism. This was a remarkable illustration of the old belief that the best cure for a dog's bite was a hair of the dog that bit him, for economic nationalism had been largely responsible for the failure to restore laissez faire. The cause of the trouble was now invoked to produce a cure.

ECONOMIC NATIONALISM

World War I had accelerated the development of the prewar economic nationalism, and it continued to grow during the 'twenties. During the war many countries established industries to supply commodities which they had formerly received from abroad. The same process continued during the 'twenties, especially in the new states created by the peace settlement. Many of the new enterprises demanded and received protection by using the infant industry argument, or at times on the ground that they were vital to the national welfare. There is truth in both arguments; but both can easily be abused. So often promising infants become adult iron-lung addicts, never strong enough to live outside a protective tariff; and almost anything can be plausibly represented to be in the national interest. The feeling of insecurity in Europe greatly strengthened the trend toward economic nationalism. The fear of a future German attack was strong in the French bloc. This gave force to the argument that key industries must be fostered and the nation become as self-sufficient as possible for the sake of national defense. Many of the war and interwar industries were uneconomic and would have succumbed if exposed to the degree of foreign competition that had existed in 1913.

Agriculture as well as manufacturing felt the influence of economic nationalism. During the war the acreage in Europe under wheat fell sharply; while there was a marked increase in that of the United States, Canada, and Argentina to supply the European need for food. European wheat could not compete in price with that from overseas, and on purely economic grounds there was a strong case for imitating Britain. In the later nineteenth century she had allowed her agriculture to become a depressed industry because it could not compete with imported grain. In Europe, however, the farmers were a strong vested interest, and also there was the fear that in the event of war German submarines might cut off the supply of food from overseas. The nations of the continent restored their domestic agriculture to its prewar dimensions and protected it against overseas competition. After Great Britain abandoned free trade she too began to revive her agriculture by protective measures. The ultimate result was a great surplus of unsalable wheat, low prices and agricultural depression in the United States and elsewhere overseas.

The American protective tariff had been appropriate to a developing and primarily agricultural debtor country. It was necessary to limit imports while expanding exports in order to meet the payments on the foreign loans and develop industry. World War I, however, had transformed the situation, and the United States had become a creditor on a large scale, as well as greatly expanding its production and exports. After the war further heavy loans were made, and the sale of American products abroad was pressed vigorously. It was necessary to enable foreign countries to earn enough dollars to meet their debt payments and pay for their purchases. This could only be done by increasing imports into the United States. Instead the Fordney-McCumber Tariff Act of 1922 raised the import duties on the very articles that might have done most to right the balance of payments. A temporary solution to the problem was found by lending European countries the credit to buy from the United States the goods they wanted and which Americans wished to export. Later the loans were discontinued, and in 1930 the Hawley-Smoot Tariff Act substantially increased import duties on 890 classes of items. This forced the United States to share with Spain the distinction of having the highest general tariff level in the world. It is estimated that in the end forty-five nations raised their tariffs against American goods, partly in retaliation and in part because they had no choice. Since the United States was determined to maintain both a creditor position and a highly favorable trade balance, other states had no alternative but to close their own markets as far as possible to American goods.

Each nation tried to sell its exports at all costs. Domestic industries which felt the foreign competition demanded protection on the ground that otherwise they would be forced out of business and so add to the growing unemployment. Their government hastily imposed higher tariffs or other obstacles to trade, in the hope that it could protect its own nationals from unemployment by passing this on to those of the exporting country, for if the latter's industries were prevented from selling, they would be compelled to contract their operations. It was a policy of beggar my neighbor, and in the long run it could not even claim to be effective. The effect on the country whose exports were prevented from selling was that it was unable to earn foreign exchange. It therefore put up its own trade barriers in self-defense in order to curtail its purchases from the nation which was shutting out its goods, thereby creating unemployment in the latter's export industries. With nation after nation raising trade barriers to protect domestic industries and at the same time trying to sell abroad, the result was that every country damaged every other country's trade and injured its own in the process. The comparatively open world market of the laissez-faire period was gone. No one nation could cope with this problem: the only way to handle it was by joint international action, and that failed in 1933.

The protracted large-scale unemployment created by the great depression confronted governments with a most serious problem which would fairly certainly lead to severe labor conflicts and might have revolutionary implications. In Germany its existence was an important factor in bringing the Nazis to power. The maintenance of full employment became and still remains a cardinal aim of policy. During the pre-1914 period the business cycle with its alternation of prosperity and depression was accepted as an inevitable law of economics, and booms and slumps spread from one country to another. After the great depression many countries tried to maintain full employment and prevent a fall in wages by insulating the national economy from the ups and downs of international trade and the vagaries of the business cycle. It was believed that this could be achieved by government control of imports and exports, foreign exchange, and investment. To do this required national planning and a degree of interference with private enterprise which varied from country to country. The effect of this preoccupation with full employment was to reinforce economic nationalism. The integrated world economy was divided into a number of imperfectly insulated national economies loosely linked together.

AUTARKY AND POWER

Another motive of economic nationalism which became prominent in the 'thirties was exemplified by Nazi Germany or Soviet Russia. This was to control national economic life in order to increase the political and military power of the state, and so make it a more effective engine of aggression. When these were the purposes of government, the well-being of the people could not be the primary object or, in Goering's phrase, "Guns before butter." There was a concentration upon imports of military raw materials in preference to those needed for peaceful trade.

The most striking characteristic of German policy was autarky. As far as possible the country was to be made self-sufficient, and economically independent of the rest of the world. This was a return to the old mercantilist contention that imports are bad. This point of view exists in other countries, as shown by the "Buy American" and "Buy British" policies. The contemporary Soviet bloc aims at autarky. One way of pursuing self-sufficiency is to develop domestic resources to the utmost, regardless of cost. A recent example is the tariff against Australian wool to assist American sheep farmers who are nevertheless unable to supply the national demand. Another method is the development of substitutes to replace imports, e.g., the refining of oil from coal and the production of synthetic rubber in Nazi Germany. Sometimes the substitute is as good as the original, but often it is more expensive and not so satisfactory.

A program of self-sufficiency in a country like Germany which has only limited resources is bound to lower the general standard of living. The discrimination against foreign imports is proof of this, for no merchant will buy from abroad goods which are more expensive or less satisfactory than the same article produced at home. Even the United States could not attain full self-sufficiency though it could come much closer to it than Germany; but the price would be a lowered standard of living. Twentieth-century scientific technology has made it necessary to use a wide range of raw materials in order to make the most efficient product. Often very small amounts only are needed, e.g., tungsten alloy in the manufacture of steel; but they are essential and economic substitutes have not been found for all of them. Raw materials are so widely dispersed that no one nation possesses all of them. The net effect of technological advances in the field of raw materials has been to make nations decidedly less self-contained. Modern industrial civilization rests upon a raw-material base that is unavoidably international.

The case for self-sufficiency is not tenable when it is examined purely from the economic point of view. As a preparation for conquest, however, there is a great deal of method in its madness. With Hitler autarky was the prelude to empire. He knew that as soon as he went to war with Great Britain a naval blockade would cut off all supplies from overseas. Partially to counteract it, he developed substitutes and stock piles. For the same reason he brought central Europe and the Balkans under German control, since they could supply some of the necessities he lacked at home. In time of peace it is not necessary to annex territory in order to buy raw materials and food: they can be obtained by the ordinary processes of international trade. But if a state intends to go to war, it is most desirable to control the countries where they exist so that the supply cannot be cut off. This was the real purpose behind Hitler's demand for *Lebensraum* or living space.

THE METHODS OF ECONOMIC NATIONALISM

Tariffs have been the traditional way of regulating imports, and when they are prohibitively high, they have the effect of an embargo, unless the commodity is so essential that it must be bought regardless of cost. During the nineteen thirties a variety of new devices were elaborated by governments. A prohibition or embargo was sometimes employed which forbade any import of a particular article. Much more frequent was the use of quotas. The government would decide what total quantity might enter the country in a given year, and would then divide this among the various countries of supply with which it wished to trade. Once an exporting nation had used up its quota, that particular market was closed to it till it received a new quota. Unlike a tariff it was not possible to pay the import duty and continue to sell as much as the market would buy. Another device which was widely employed was bilateral as opposed to multilateral trade. Bilateralism is the name of a system in which the balance of trade is achieved between pairs of countries—A and B, A and C, A and D, etc. Multilateral trade exists when trade between country A and the rest of the world is balanced, but not necessarily the trade between country A and each of the countries B, C, and D, etc.

Exchange control was widely used in the 'thirties. The original purpose was to prevent the great and sometimes extreme fluctuations in the foreign exchange rate of a nation's currency, and to give it a stable value in the international market. Exchange control operated by the government monopolizing all foreign exchange possessed by the residents of the country. Exporters who earned foreign currencies by their transactions or investors who owned foreign securities were required to surrender them to their government and be paid in local currency at rates set by it. All who wished to send money out of the country must obtain an official license to buy the necessary foreign currency. Neither investment abroad nor importing were possible without the government's permission. By giving and withholding licenses the government could secure a balance of payments equilibrium and maintain the foreign exchange rate of the national currency. Exchange control went on to its logical end of the control of foreign trade and investment. It was impossible to buy foreign goods or securities unless they could be paid for, and it was the government which decided whether this would be permitted. The inevitable sequel was state planning and control. It was necessary for the government to draw up elaborate plans for regulating, e.g., what commodities might be imported, in what quantities, and from what foreign sources, how much money might be invested abroad, etc. Ingenious schemes were devised to evade the control. To close the loopholes, the government was compelled to impose more and more stringent and detailed regulations and assume an increasingly pervasive control over the national economy.

Another development was the formation of agreements between firms in the same branch of manufacturing limiting the scope of competition. It is perfectly possible to believe in private enterprise and at the same time be skeptical whether free competition will bring the maximum profit. Often the agreements crossed political frontiers by the formation of international cartels.

Among the stipulations were limitation of output, price maintenance, the pooling of patents and processes, and the allocation of markets in which the other members of the cartel would not compete. The German cartels, greatly encouraged and later controlled by the state, were used to promote the aims of foreign policy. Cartels were also formed by the producers of raw materials, sometimes with government support, e.g., tin, rubber, copper, nitrates, etc.

The United States began to modify its high tariff policy by the Reciprocal Trade Agreements Act of 1934. The administration was empowered to negotiate treaties by which American import duties might be reduced by as much as 50 percent in return for equivalent tariff reductions on American products. The lower duties were extended unconditionally to all states with which the contracting parties had most-favored nation treaties. This was an attempt to re-establish multilateral as against bilateral trade. The United States tended to confine tariff reductions to commodities which were supplied chiefly by the country with which the treaty was negotiated. This limited the benefit to the other states to which the concessions were extended. Moreover many American import duties were so high that even a 50-percent reduction often left a formidable protective tariff. The Act continues to be one of the most important instruments of American economic policy.

Great Britain's abandonment of free trade and the gold standard in 1931 was soon followed by the formation of the sterling bloc. Britain's departure from gold had been imitated by the rest of the empire except Canada, and by a number of states such as Denmark whose currencies were really based on sterling. This grouping of countries within a common currency area was extremely loose and informal. There was no organized attempt to follow a common monetary policy, and the neutral nations left the bloc on the outbreak of the war in 1939. In 1933 and 1934 Britain made bilateral treaties with nine countries, many of which were members of the bloc. In 1932 at the Ottawa Conference reciprocal preferential treaties were negotiated between the members of the Commonwealth and Empire. As a substitute for the vanished world market Great Britain was using its new tariff and its domestic market as bargaining weapons to assure an outlet for its exports both within and without the empire.

IMPERIAL PREFERENCE

The rule in all empires was always that the metropolitan power dictated the tariffs of its dependencies. The sole exception was that the British self-governing dominions and India had tariff autonomy. Britain controlled the tariffs only of the non-self-governing tropical dependencies. So far as Britain, India, and the dominions were concerned the preferences and quotas granted to one another in 1932 were the result of hard bargaining on all sides. The preferences given by the tropical dependencies to the rest of the empire were arranged by Great Britain. About half of the colonies gave little or no preference, since they were precluded from doing so by open door treaties. The imperial preference rate of duty was less than the lowest rate extended to foreign states, and was never granted to countries outside the empire. The Ottawa Conference by no means established empire free trade or a customs union. The policy of the dominions was to fix the imperial preference rate high enough to afford substantial protection to domestic industries, and to admit freely only those empire commodities which were not produced locally. In return the dominions were given a preferred position in the United Kingdom market for food and raw materials. The tropical dependencies which produced sugar, fruit, tobacco, and wines (e.g., West Indies and some African colonies) received important benefit from the United Kingdom preferences. United Kingdom manufactures gained to some extent from the preferences which were given them in the tropical market.

The trade of parts of the empire with one another increased from 25.7 percent of their total trade in 1929 to 33.2 percent in 1938. The exports of Great Britain to the empire grew from 44.5 percent of the total in 1929 to 49.8 percent in 1938, and in the same period the imports rose from 29.4 to 40.4 percent. Some but by no means all of the increase in interempire trade was due to imperial preference: other causes were also very important. All the currencies of the empire, with the exception of Canada's, were tied to sterling. When they went off gold, the pound depreciated in terms of the American dollar and other gold standard currencies. This made it more expensive for members of the sterling bloc to buy from foreign states and cheaper to buy from one another, and this had an important effect on redirecting trade. Moreover, there were no exchange controls within the empire to hamper trade. The continued rise of trade barriers during the 'thirties excluded some empire goods from their former foreign markets and diverted them to interempire trade. Great Britain was the United States' best customer, and American sales to the empire and particularly Canada were also heavy. The American favorable balance of trade in merchandise with the empire was about $351 million yearly. The effect of imperial preference was that dominion wheat, bacon, fruit, and lumber largely replaced American in the United Kingdom. In 1936–1938, 42 percent of American exports still went to empire markets, and 36 percent of American imports came from there. To some extent the Anglo-American and American-Canadian treaties of 1938 restored American exports to their former position, in return for some reduction in the extremely high United States duties against British goods.

The abandonment of laissez faire affected British investment as well as trade. From the time of the great depression onward the government controlled the flotation of loans in London. Preference was given to borrowers in Britain and the empire, and few foreign loans were permitted. The total amount of Britain's overseas investments in 1939 was $17,943,000,000 and the annual income $850,000,000. About five eights of the total, $9,628,000,000 was invested in the empire, mostly in India ($2,129,000,000) and the dominions. Investment in Europe was $1,147,000,000, much of it frozen by exchange controls. There was no hope of restoring either commerce or investment on a pre-1914 basis. The gold standard and free trade were discredited. Entrenched behind trade barriers, the nations were trying to find some halfway house between laissez faire and the closed economy of Russia where the government monopolized economic life.

SELECTED READING

BASCH, ANTONIN, *The New Economic Warfare*. New York: Columbia University Press, 1941.

CONDLIFFE, J. B., *The Commerce of Nations*. New York: W. W. Norton and Company, 1950.

EINZIG, PAUL, *Economic Warfare*. London: Macmillan & Company, Ltd., 1940.

———, *World Finance, 1914–1935*. New York: The Macmillan Company, 1935.

ELLSWORTH, P. T., *The International Economy: Its Structure and Operation*. New York: The Macmillan Company, 1950.

GORDON, DAVID L., and DANGERFIELD, ROYDEN, *The Hidden Weapon: Story of Economic Warfare*. New York: Harper and Brothers, 1947.

HEXNER, ERWIN, *International Cartels*. Chapel Hill: The University of North Carolina Press, 1945.

HODGSON, J. G. (ed.), *Economic Nationalism*. New York: Richard R. Smith, 1931.

MEYER, F. V., *Britain's Colonies in World Trade*. New York: Oxford Press, 1948.

STALEY, EUGENE, *World Economy in Transition*. New York: Council on Foreign Relations, 1939.

CHAPTER 8

IMPERIALISM

Imperialism is the policy by which one state establishes its political and economic control over people of a different nation or race, usually by force. In its traditional sense the word "empire" implies subjection, however mild and benevolent the control may be. In every empire of history there has been a ruling race or metropolitan power which exercised authority over subject peoples. Frequently the term imperialism is confined to the tropical dependencies of the Western powers; but this is to narrow its meaning unduly. For this would mean that Hitler was not imperialistic when he overran Europe and set up an empire which he believed would last a thousand years. The essence of imperialism is the subjection of people of another race or nationality. The color of their skins and the relative hotness or coolness of their climate are immaterial.

Sometimes too it is said that there can be no imperialism without salt water. To conquer a country on another continent is imperialistic because it is separated from the metropolitan power by an ocean. But to conquer an adjoining territory which has a common land frontier is not imperialism, but merely natural expansion over adjacent continental territory. According to this theory, Russia was not imperialistic when it brought Siberia under its control, and neither was Nazi Germany. The Americans however were imperialists when they crossed the Caribbean Sea to Puerto Rico or the French when they established themselves in North Africa.

IMPERIALISM THROUGH HISTORY

Imperialism is at least as old as Sargon of Akkad, who ruled in Mesopotamia about 2600 B.C. and extended his realm by conquest from the Mediterranean to the Persian Gulf. For thousands of years imperialism has been one of the principal driving forces in the field of international affairs. From one point of view the history of European relations with Asia is the ebb and flow of imperialisms. In the fifth century B.C. the king of Persia, ruling over the Near and Middle East, tried to subjugate Greece. The counterattack of Alexander the Great reversed the situation, and for a thousand years North Africa and much of the Middle East became part of Europe. The Arabs of the seventh century restored it to Asia, conquered Spain, and were only turned back by their great defeat in 732 A.D. in southern France. To some extent the Crusades were a European attempt to regain part of the lost territory. At times the Mongol conquerors were a grave threat to medieval Europe. The Turks carried the war into Europe, until they were beaten back under the walls of Vienna in 1683. In the sixteenth century the pendulum began to swing against Asia with the conquests of Portugal and Spain, and later of Holland, England, France, and tsarist Russia. It is a mistake to say that Asia lived at peace within itself until the European came with his acts of aggression against it. Empires were founded and destroyed in the Middle East, India, China, and Java, but imperialism itself merely transferred its habitation from one state to another. There is no reason to suppose that this great historic trend has come to an end. This would indeed be a curious belief for a generation that has known Hitler and Stalin. The older imperial powers are in retreat; but their place has been taken by Soviet Russia, whose ambitions are more inordinate than those of any earlier conqueror.

PSYCHOLOGICAL CAUSES OF IMPERIALISM

Marxism declares that imperialism is purely the result of economic forces; but analysis shows that its causes are much more complex. They include imponderable psychological motives, such as the desire for power. This is one of the strongest impulses in human nature, and on occasion it is a driving force in the history of nations. Hitler had this lust for power, and other great conquerors like Napoleon have been driven by the same overmastering impulse. Sometimes whole nations have been swayed by this motive. No one can study the history of Germany for the past two generations without realizing that government and people alike felt themselves to be a chosen and a frustrated people. The Germans had convinced themselves that they were a superior, indeed a master race, and that they ought to have played a major role in history. Yet until Bismarck made them the dominant power in Europe in 1870 Germany meant nothing, while France and Britain had played a great part in world affairs for centuries. Precisely what Germany wanted was undefined, though various influential groups had different plans for annexations. Over and beyond the wish for material gain there was the desire for dominance and the imponderable satisfaction which this would bring to all patriots. Professor William L. Langer defined this motive as clearly as it can be expressed when he wrote of "the disposition of a state to forceful expansion without any special object and without a definable limit. Conquests are desired not so

much because of their advantages, which are often questionable, but merely
for the sake of conquest, success and activity." The governments of Imperial
and of Nazi Germany stimulated and led this driving national force. This
same psychological compulsion seems to have been a leading and perhaps the
principal cause of the policy which brought Japan into World War II. As in
the case of Germany, victory promised great material gains. Yet one has the
feeling that these were only rationalizations for the psychological urge to extend the power of Japan to the utmost limits. In two generations the Japanese
had turned their country from a weak feudal kingdom into a great power
and had defeated China and Russia. These striking achievements gave them
an exuberant self-confidence, an energy that had to find an outlet, and an im-
pelling desire to advance to still greater triumphs abroad.

Prestige has sometimes been a motive for imperialism. The king of France
began the conquest of Algeria in 1830 because his throne was shaky and he
believed that the glory of a successful little war would strengthen it. Mussolini
was influenced by similar considerations in Ethiopia. There was also the belief
that colonies were the hallmark of respectability, like her marriage lines to a
woman, and that a state was not fully a great power until it had secured this
visible mark of its status. This was the reason that Italy conquered Libya and
prided herself on a possession that was 90 percent pure Sahara Desert.

STRATEGIC CAUSE OF IMPERIALISM

The strategic motive runs through the whole history of imperialism.
Ancient Egypt always tried to control the upper valley of the Nile, or to give
it its modern name the Sudan, for military and economic reasons. Contemporary Egypt has the same desire as Colonel Nasser's policy has shown—a remarkable instance of continuity in national design after 4000 years. In 146 B.C.
Rome literally wiped out Carthage because its existence was believed to be a
menace to the republic. The development of the British Empire affords many
examples of territory annexed primarily to strengthen naval defense. The
prosperity of Great Britain depended upon its foreign trade, and a large navy
was necessary to protect it. To be effective a navy must have bases and fueling
stations, and over the centuries the British acquired an unrivaled collection
in most parts of the world. The Suez Canal sea route to the Pacific is guarded
by a succession of naval and air bases. Gibraltar (taken from Spain in 1704)
dominates the adjacent waters of the Atlantic and the Mediterranean. Malta
(annexed at its own request) does the same in the central Mediterranean, and
the Suez Canal was protected by the occupation of Egypt in 1882. Aden, a
naval and fueling station, occupied in 1839, blocks the narrow exit from the
Red Sea. Protectorates over the small states of southern Arabia prevent any
rival power from establishing bases there that could threaten the Indian

Ocean sector of the sea route. The defensive alliance of 1930 with Iraq and the British air bases there, had the same purpose. Ceylon was taken from Holland in 1795, partly because the harbor of Trincomalee would provide a much needed anchorage for the fleet. Lastly, the naval and air base at Singapore dominated the exit from the Indian Ocean into the Pacific.

The British occupation of Egypt was a good example of strategic imperialism at work. Napoleon had shown that Egypt could be used as a base for attacking India, and its importance was immensely increased by the opening of the Suez Canal in 1869, which largely superseded the long sea route around Africa. Whoever controlled Egypt dominated the canal, and unfortunately the government was on the verge of bankruptcy. Its khedive, Ismail, had borrowed over $500 million, largely from French and British creditors. They were pressing their governments to intervene and salvage their speculation. Britain was genuinely unwilling to do so, since it considered that British subjects who invested in a foreign country should do so at their own risk and not expect their government to act as a debt collector. France, however, intended to intervene, and Britain could not afford to allow her to do so single-handed, and thus obtain control of Egypt and the canal. The two governments established a joint financial control to safeguard the bondholders, and also to make certain that neither one obtained a monopoly of control. A revolt of the Egyptian army and a massacre of Christians in Alexandria in 1882 decided Britain to intervene to restore order. At the last moment France refused to cooperate, and Britain found herself in sole control of the country. The crowning touch of irony was that the prime minister who sent a British army to Egypt was Gladstone, a vehement anti-imperialist who held that it was more blessed to lose dependencies than to obtain them.

The United States was having difficulty in 1903 in persuading Colombia to consent to the building of the Panama Canal. So when an opportune revolt broke out in the Colombian province of Panama, President Theodore Roosevelt promptly took advantage of it. He prevented the Colombian government from sending troops, and recognized the revolutionary leaders as the *de facto* government of Panama, three days after the revolt began. The new republic leased in perpetuity a strip ten miles wide across the isthmus on which to build the canal. The United States was given the right to station troops in the canal zone and administer it "as if we were sovereign." The annexation of Puerto Rico gave the United States naval and air bases which guard the eastern approach to the canal. The American strategic trusteeship over the former Japanese mandate islands (the Marshalls, Marianas, and Carolines) is not far removed from annexation, since the U.N. Council can exercise as much or as little control as the United States chooses to permit. The islands have a negligible economic value, but have great strategic importance as part of the first line of defense confronting Asia.

Soviet imperialism is sometimes dictated by strategic considerations. One of its aims is to control the Gulf of Finland and the Baltic Sea. Consequently, Finland on the northern shore of the gulf has been made unable to resist an invasion and is therefore amenable to pressure. Estonia, Latvia, Lithuania, and part of East Prussia have been annexed. This completes control of the gulf and extends Russian naval and air power into the middle Baltic. The transfer of Germany east of the Oder to Poland makes it far harder for Germany to attack to the East than it was in 1941. If the attempt to gain control of Greece and Turkey had succeeded Russia would not only have had commercial ports on the Mediterranean, but would have been in a position to threaten the sea route through the Suez Canal. Control of Iran would give naval bases on the Persian Gulf from which the Indian Ocean sector of the same sea route could be attacked.

RELIGION

Crusading zeal has not been a monopoly of Christians: the Arab conquests of 1300 years ago which stretched from Persia to the Pyrenees were caused in part by a fanatical determination forcibly to spread their recently acquired religion. The same intolerant zeal was a driving force with the Spanish and Portuguese imperialists of the sixteenth century. For hundreds of years they had been fighting the Moorish conquerors of Spain on the twin grounds that they were foreigners and Muslims. The completion of the task left them bursting with crusading ardor and with nothing to exercise it upon. The obvious course—made possible by the discoveries of Vasco da Gama and Columbus—was to follow the heathen overseas and convert him to the true faith. Religious persuasion was made much easier if conquest had first made resistance impossible. So a strong missionary zeal was one basic cause of the formation of the Spanish and Portuguese empires.

Protestant missionary societies were formed about the beginning of the nineteenth century and began to work in all parts of the non-Christian world. At first the missionaries strongly opposed imperialism. Gradually they discovered that by themselves they were powerless to root out various abuses and barbaric practices. Muslim Arab slave traders with small armies semi-depopulated parts of east Africa in their raids. Unscrupulous white traders sold the liquid dynamite known as trade gin. The African Negroes themselves refused to give up intertribal warfare where captives were enslaved or eaten, and juju worship, which sometimes entailed black magic and human sacrifice. The missionaries came to realize that only a Western government with troops, police, and law courts could put an end to these conditions. So in the second half of the nineteenth century missionaries, powerfully supported by their national churches, brought pressure on their governments to annex the areas in which they worked.

Today the same desire to make converts is shown by the Communists. As in all revolutionary movements some of them are time servers, or opportunists who hope to rise to power by joining what they believe is the winning side. Amongst them, however, are genuine fanatics who have a crusading fervor for imposing their beliefs upon others, and are ready to use any means that will accomplish their end. An intolerant, religious zeal—if one can apply that term to a faith that denies the existence of God—is one of the causes of the creation of the Soviet bloc and of the attacks on the West.

ECONOMICS AND IMPERIALISM

The imperialism of the ancient world was simple and direct in its attitude toward the conquered. Many of them were taken as slaves along with their valuable and portable property, and an annual tribute to the ruling power was often imposed. The ruling philosophy was that to the victor belong the spoils. The attitude was much the same during the earlier period of Western imperialism. Mercantilism was the prevalent economic philosophy from the sixteenth to the early nineteenth century. As applied to colonies, it taught that they existed for the benefit of the metropolitan power. Monopoly was the keynote of the system. Colonial products, e.g., sugar and tobacco, must be sold only to the metropolitan power. A colony was required to buy all its manufactures from there, and was forbidden to establish factories of its own which would compete. Trade between the metropolitan power and its colonies was restricted to ships owned and manned by one or the other.

The effects of the industrial revolution were largely responsible for the imperialism of the later nineteenth century. The increased volume of output produced by machine industry led to a growing need for foreign trade, to dispose of the surplus which could not be sold in the domestic market. At the same time manufacturing was developing in continental Europe and the United States, and tariffs were rising to protect the new industries. The Western market threatened to contract, just at the time when a greater volume of goods was seeking an outlet and competition was growing. Exaggerated hopes were entertained of the possibilities of trade with tropical Africa and Asia. To make sure that these markets continued to be available they were converted into colonies. Annexations were often followed by the squeezing out of foreign business interests. This forced governments which like the liberal governments of Great Britain in the 1880's did not want to annex territory, to join in the scramble. As traders found themselves gradually being forced out of one part of Africa after another by colonial annexations, they successfully brought pressure upon their governments to give them protection by annexing other areas in which they were established.

Machine industry required much larger amounts of raw materials than could be produced in Europe. Toward the end of the nineteenth century, moreover, the demand for several tropical raw materials became far greater than previously, e.g., rubber, palm oil, and coconut oil. Most of the races of the tropics were content with their own low standard of living, and were only willing to produce goods for export when the spirit moved them. Their production of raw materials fell far short of Western requirements in quantity and standardized quality. Over a period of years it might have been possible to obtain the desired production by teaching the tropical races to want a higher standard of living and work harder in order to obtain it. This has been accomplished with, e.g., cocoa in West Africa. The delay would have been long however, and the development of some types of Western production such as automobiles would have been hamstrung. Industry was not prepared to wait, and Western producers went into the tropics to set up plantations and mines. The possibilities of the tropics as a market and source of raw materials were exaggerated. It was not realized how small was the purchasing capacity of the average native. Experience showed too that only a few raw materials were obtainable in important quantities. In 1938 out of the total imports into Great Britain 8.5 percent came from her colonial dependencies (this excludes the self-governing dominions), and 12 percent of her total exports went to them. In the same year 9 percent of Holland's imports came from Indonesia and 10.5 percent of her exports were sold to it. The figures for France were 27 percent and 28 percent, for the United States 18 percent and 9 percent, and for Germany (in 1913) .5 percent and .6 percent.

Industrialization produced profits far in excess of those obtainable in earlier ages, and eventually the point was reached where so much money was seeking investment at home that the rate of interest was lower than abroad. About the end of the nineteenth century for instance railway construction in western Europe brought a return of 2 percent or 3 percent, while in colonies or undeveloped foreign countries the rate might be anywhere from 10 percent to 20 percent. The risks were greater, and investors insisted on a much higher return. In an independent country there was the danger of default or repudiation, which would not be allowed to take place in a colony ruled by the creditor state. When this happened in a foreign state, the bondholders put pressure on their government to intervene. Investment as a cause of imperialism was less important than the search for new markets. In the early twentieth century only 9 percent of France's foreign investments, and 3 percent of Germany's were in their colonies. In 1913 only 12 percent of British investments abroad were in India and the tropical colonies, compared with 20 percent in the United States and 20 percent in Latin America. There are few reliable studies of the net return from colonial investments, but such information as is available indicates that they have been far less profitable than is generally supposed. The gold mines of the Rand in South Africa have usually been re-

garded as a very lucrative enterprise, but over the period 1886–1932 they
yielded an average annual dividend of approximately 4.1 percent upon the
large capital invested. Writing in 1938 of the whole of Africa (apart from the
area north of the Sahara Desert) Lord Hailey stated that "when the investments which were wholly or partially lost were taken into account the average
of earnings has almost certainly been lower than would again induce the investors to embark their capital."

THE HAVE *VS.* HAVE-NOT ARGUMENT

Nazi Germany and Fascist Italy argued that their economic troubles were
due to their lack of colonies and that a redistribution of tropical territory
would remove their discontent. More specifically Germany demanded the
return of the colonies which she had lost in World War I, particularly those
in Africa. The Germans justified their claim on the ground that they must
control adequate supplies of raw materials in territories included in the German monetary system, that they needed markets to which they had assured
access, and that they must have territory to which their surplus population
could emigrate. The former colonies could supply "a large part of the food
supplies and raw materials which we now lack." This argument grossly exaggerated the possibilities of the German ex-colonies. In 1929, their most prosperous year, their total imports were only $58,000,000, while Germany's exports
were $3,212,000,000. They could have supplied her with vanadium, a steel
alloy, more than enough sisal, nearly enough phosphates, and with a small
part of her requirements of cocoa, bananas, and vegetable oils. They could do
nothing to meet her needs in Goebbels' six "basic materials of industry," coal,
iron, oil, cotton, rubber, and copper. As for emigration, the tropics are unsuitable for European settlement on a large scale because of the climate and
because manual laborers can only obtain employment if they will take the low
native rate of wages. This means that they must accept the native standard of
living and sink to the status of poor whites. The tropics provide only a limited
number of managerial positions, such as mine and plantation managers and
business executives. In 1914 there were only 19,696 Germans (including 3,115
soldiers) in the whole of their empire. Out of the average annual German
emigration of 25,600 for the decade 1904–1913 about thirty went to the colonies
and the rest to the United States or South America, where their prospects were
much better.

Germany would have gained one important advantage from the return of
her colonies, but this was strategic and not economic. Her former possessions
were so distributed in Africa that together with the Italian dependencies, aircraft based on them could attack almost the entire continent. Submarines and
long-range aircraft operating from them could have attacked Allied shipping

both in the South Atlantic and the Indian Ocean. The Mediterranean was virtually closed to through traffic from 1940 to 1943, and ships bound for Egypt and countries east of it took the comparatively safe sea route around Africa. If they had had to run the gauntlet of enemy attack in both oceans, the strain imposed on merchant shipping and warships would have been almost intolerable.

The restoration to Germany of her former colonies would have had little effect upon her economic position. Neither would the transfer to her of the colonial dependencies of all the colonial powers. Among them they produced only about 3 percent of the world's raw materials, and provided the greater part of its supply only in rubber, tin, cobalt, and some of the vegetable oils. Colonial producers would sell their produce to any customer, irrespective of nationality, who would pay them the world price. During part of the 'thirties, for example, British rubber growers in Malaya preferred to sell to Japanese rather than British buyers because they offered slightly more than the world price of the moment. Looked at as a market, all the tropical colonies together were less than 10 percent of the world market, owing to the low purchasing power of their peoples. The bulk of the world's foodstuffs and raw materials came from the independent self-governing states, including the British dominions. The same countries were the principal markets of international trade. No one had the power to transfer them to Germany: the only way in which she could improve her commercial relations with them was by negotiating trade treaties to which they freely assented.

A metropolitan power does however have certain advantages in its colonies over a foreign state. Community of language, laws, weights, and measures inescapably work in its favor. Machinery and other capital goods are usually bought from the metropolitan power because the engineers who place the orders are accustomed to their own country's products. Colonial governments normally order supplies from national firms. In a very few instances discriminatory export duties have been imposed to canalize the export of colonial raw materials to the metropolitan power. Freedom of access to raw materials implies the right to develop as well as to buy them on equal terms. In the British and Dutch colonies foreign capital is given the same rights as national, with the exception that in Burma oil leases were granted only to British subjects. In the French colonies restrictions hamper the investment of foreign capital. Interwar schemes for limiting the output of raw materials, e.g., tin, rubber, and copper, sometimes penalized consumers for the benefit of producers, though all suffered equally, nationals of the metropolitan powers paying the same price as foreigners.

Preferential tariffs by which goods of the metropolitan power are admitted to the colonies at a lower rate of duty than foreign products have been widely employed in the American, British, French, Portuguese, and Japanese empires. The principal exception has been that the Open Door or equal treatment for all nations was guaranteed by treaties in certain areas such as mandates, Morocco, and the Conventional Basin of the Congo, which comprised the Belgian, French, British and Portuguese dependencies in tropical Africa. In the 'thirties the United States supplied American dependencies with about 80 percent of their imports and bought over 90 percent of their exports. The figures for the Japanese Empire were slightly lower. Great Britain supplied 24.5 percent of the imports into her dependencies and bought about 36 percent of their exports. The figures for the French Empire were 53 percent for imports and 66 percent for exports; and for Indonesia, 19 percent and 14 percent. Imperial preferences effectively increased the metropolitan powers' share of their colonies' import trade and lessened the sales of foreign countries.

The principal reason why Germany, say, found difficulty in buying raw materials or foodstuffs was the problem of paying for them. If a German importer wished to purchase, for example, Malayan rubber, he could not pay for it with marks. He must sell marks to buy the Malayan currency of Straits dollars needed to purchase the rubber. A British importer could do this easily since the Straits dollar was linked with the pound sterling and no difficulties in obtaining foreign exchange existed. Ability to buy a foreign currency became a problem in the interwar period when currencies fluctuated in value, trade barriers multiplied, and international trade was reduced substantially. It often became difficult for a state to obtain enough dollars, pounds, or whatever foreign currency it needed to pay for its imports because the entry of its goods into foreign markets was restricted. Limitation of sales lessened the ability to obtain the foreign exchange needed to buy raw materials. To some extent the colonies contributed to this situation by their imperial preferences. Their import duties were low, however, compared with those of the industrialized nations. The principal cause of the trouble was the independent industrialized nations which fenced off their domestic markets with trade barriers, and which were also the suppliers of the bulk of the world's food and raw materials. Germany and Italy greatly aggravated their difficulties by their exceptionally heavy demands for military raw materials required for their armament programs. The problem of freedom of access to raw materials was really a question of finding the foreign exchange to pay for them. It could not be solved by abolishing imperial preferences or transferring colonies because they accounted for only a small part of the world's trade and raw materials. The only solution was if the industrialized sovereign states drastically reduced their trade barriers, and thereby facilitated access to the raw materials of the world.

COLONIAL POLICIES

The purpose of the United States and Great Britain has been the same, to train the colonial peoples to govern themselves democratically. The method has been to make successive transfers of political power from colonial administrations to elected leaders, so that the people could learn self-government by practicing it. The goal in the Philippines was the creation of an independent republic, while in Puerto Rico it is a form of dominion status less complete than in the British Commonwealth. The United States continues to control the tariff, foreign policy, and defenses of Puerto Rico. Great Britain hopes that when a part of the empire attains complete self-government, it will voluntarily decide to remain as a partner in the Commonwealth as Ceylon did. If, however, it chooses to secede and become an independent state, Britain accepts the decision as an inalienable right of self-government, as in the cases of the republics of Burma and Eire.

The rate of constitutional progress of the colonies depends on such factors as the maturity of their civilization, the size of their population, and their economic development. There is, therefore, a wide variation in the rapidity of their political progress. Ceylon and the former mandate of Iraq belonged to what might be called the advanced backward peoples and attained complete self-government, the first in 1948 and the second in 1932. At the other end of the scale British North Borneo is largely inhabited by the grandsons of Moro pirates on the sea coast and by Dayak headhunters in the interior. The latter still have a tendency to indulge in their favorite outdoor sport despite the discouraging attitude of the local authorities. It was feared that if the Dayaks were informed that henceforth they were to settle affairs of state by counting heads, they might translate this as official permission for the more lasting solution of taking them. The first steps in political education are being taken, but a sizable period of apprenticeship will be necessary before the Dayaks will fully comprehend the democratic process. In between the two extremes are dependencies such as the Gold Coast in West Africa, which are not far removed from complete self-government, and are beginning to think about dominion status.

French colonial policy was very different from American or British, especially before World War II. The goal was not independence or dominion status, but an increasingly close association of the colonies and the metropolitan power. Unlike the American and British practice colonial electorates were carefully limited and the legislatures with restricted powers were largely advisory. They were not intended to give a training in increasing self-government. The real authority lay with the French officials, and they in turn were controlled from Paris more strictly and in greater detail than in an American or British colony. Centralization and political, economic and cultural subordination to France were the essence of the system. The relation between the French and the colonial peoples was intended to be mutually beneficial. It was to be a partnership but with the French emphatically the senior partner and supplying their "superior knowledge, directive talent, moral sense, financial resources and technique of improvement." The policy in each colony was to form a native elite of French citizens, a prerequisite being the abandonment of native modes of life. Great reliance was placed upon education in forming the elite, and its goal was the creation of men who had broken with their history and environment and had completely accepted French culture and standard of values. These Asian or African French citizens had the same rights as European French citizens. They were sharply distinguished from the French subjects, the mass of the population who had retained their traditional beliefs and way of life. The small French-educated elite were associated with the French officials as auxiliaries in the administration and in bringing to the natives who lived in traditional fashion as much of French civilization as was suited to them. The system satisfied the aspirations of the few, but it gave no real management of their own affairs to the native majority; and the native who acquired French citizenship had to abandon his racial individuality. Some members of the elite became completely French in loyalty, but with others their education stimulated the development of nationalism. Before World War II a small minority of French-educated nationalists existed in many dependencies, e.g., North Africa and Indochina, and were demanding self-government.

World War II led to a marked development of nationalism in the empire, and a much stronger demand for self-government. France granted a decided increase in colonial autonomy with wider suffrage and enhanced powers in the legislatures. The empire, renamed the French Union, was divided into three categories: (1) the Associated States of Tunisia, Morocco, Cambodia and Vietnam; (2) areas such as Algeria and Martinique which formed part of metropolitan France, elected members to the legislature in Paris and were subject to the same laws and administration as the rest of France; (3) the former colonies which were now renamed overseas territories. In addition to their own local legislatures, they were represented in the French parliament in Paris. Theoretically the Associated States were self-governing and equal partners with France in the Union; but in practice they were subject to a considerable measure of French control. None of the Associated States are content with their new status. France and the Union were represented in a new organ of government, the Council and Assembly of the Union in Paris. It debated all colonial questions and made recommendations. It was not a genuine imperial legislature however, for its powers were advisory. The final authority lay with the French national legislature, which could accept or reject all recommendations. A good deal of the prewar policy of French control over the empire survives, and the new arrangements fall far short of satisfying the demands of colonial nationalists. France does not propose to make the Union a loose league of equal partners like the British Commonwealth. On the contrary, it is to be a collection of semiautonomous units united under the headship of France.

SOVIET IMPERIALISM

The Russian Empire is markedly different from that of the other colonial powers in that the Great Russians, the dominant group, are 58 percent of the total population. The Uzbeks and Kazaks of central Asia, the largest non-Slav people of the Soviet Union, are less than 5 percent. By contrast the population of Great Britain is barely one eighth of that of India and Pakistan. The Great Russians have a numerical superiority which far surpasses that of the ruling race of any other empire and ensures Soviet domination. Moreover, climatic conditions have made it possible for them to settle in their colonies in very large numbers. In Uzbekistan they are now perhaps 20 percent of the population, and in some colonies they outnumber the original inhabitants. The result is that it would be infinitely more difficult for the Soviet subject peoples to achieve independence than, for example, Indians, Indonesians, or Africans, who amounted to over 99 percent of the colonial population. Since tsarist days Russian imperial control has been built on the solid basis of colonization by Russian workers and peasants, and the policy of settlement has been intensified since 1917. This intermixture of peoples has so complicated the situation that it is impossible to conceive of the subject races (known as nationalities in Russia) ever attaining complete self-government.

Ever since 1917 the majority of the Communist party have come from the Great Russians, and they supply most of the principal leaders. Many of the party members in the colonies are Russian settlers and do not belong to the subject races. According to Soviet legal theory the sixteen republics of the Soviet Union are fullfledged sovereign states; but in practice they are strictly controlled from Moscow. The Kremlin frankly admits that its purpose is to impose the ideals of the Russian urban workmen, as interpreted by itself, on the peasants of all the peoples of Russia. There is to be equality of subjection. Despite the democratic freedoms enshrined in the constitution, it is inconceivable that the citizens of any Soviet republic would be permitted to restore their farms to the peasants, exercise the legal right of secession, or elect a noncommunist government. The Communist administrations of the republics themselves are not allowed to deviate from the orders sent them from Moscow.

At the time of the Revolution of 1917 some of the subject races tried to regain their independence from Russian control. These nationalist revolts were crushed by the Red army, and Communist governments placed in power. In one colony after another during the interwar period they too showed that like Tito they were nationalists as well as Communists. An impressive list of premiers, cabinet ministers, and leading party officials were shot—Tartars, central Asians, Georgians, Azerbaijanis, Ukrainians, and Byelorussians—or sometimes merely dismissed by the Kremlin for the crime of national deviationism. This is a piquant contrast to the warm support which Russia has given in the United Nations to nationalist movements in French North Africa. During the Germans' invasion of Russia in 1941 some of the subject peoples welcomed them and even fought in their armies. After the war the Kremlin destroyed by deportation the Tartars of the Crimea, the Kalmucks, and the Chechens of the Caucasus mountains.

The claim has often been made that Soviet imperialism has won the loyalty of its subject peoples by fostering their cultural nationalism. This is an exaggeration, but it is equally wide of the mark to say, as a prominent Ukrainian nationalist did, that all cultural autonomy meant was that his people were allowed to keep their own traditional folk dances, and that in public comfort stations the words "Men" and "Women" were written in Ukrainian instead of in Russian. It is true, however, that the history and folklore of the subject peoples are being rewritten to glorify the culture of Russia and create loyalty to her. They are being purged of nationalistic bourgeois errors, such as treating tsarist Russia as the enemy, regretting her conquest, and glorifying leaders who fought against it. Native customs and institutions are destroyed if they do not fit in with the standardized pattern of Communist life. Stalin laid down the principle that nations have the right to preserve their national institutions, but that the Communist party has the higher right to abolish any which it considers pernicious. As for social services, the Soviet government has introduced important improvements. It has greatly reduced illiteracy, established universities and trade schools, improved medical and health services, and increased the cultivated area by irrigation works. As in other empires material benefits have not reconciled the subject races to the loss of independence. Some of the colonies, however, are among the richest parts of Russia in oil, minerals, and arable land. There has been impressive development of mines, factories, and agriculture under the Five Year Plans, and it is clear that the Soviet Government has no intention of relaxing its control.

The economic history of the Soviet satellite states in Europe shows the same policy of ruthless exploitation for the benefit of Russia. Before World War II they were producers of food and raw materials. Czechoslovakia was the only country with extensive manufacturing. The Kremlin's policy since the war has been to develop mines and factories, with special emphasis on heavy industry. There has been a marked increase in the production of steel, coal, oil, and electricity. The development is not designed primarily to help the satellite states, but for the benefit of Russia. Poland for example has important coal mines; but Poles complain that they are short of coal for heating their houses because the bulk of it is sent to the factories of northwestern Russia. Rumania used to be one of the granaries of Europe, but there have been years when Rumanians went hungry because most of their wheat was taken by Russia to relieve food shortages there. One purpose of the industrial development is to increase the Soviet war potential: this explains the particular attention given to the steel industry. Another aim is to increase the self-sufficiency of the Soviet empire and make it as far as possible independent of the rest of the world. In 1953 it was estimated that for every 100 tons of coal mined in the U.S.S.R. the satellites added 58 tons, for every 100 tons of steel they added 32.5 tons, and for every 100 tons of crude oil, 28.2 tons. A third purpose is to produce a surplus of goods which can be sold in "outside markets" for political purposes. While exports of grain to Western Europe fell to half their prewar level, large quantities were offered to Egypt, Brazil and Pakistan, where grain can be good propaganda for communism.

Before the war Eastern Europe sold little to Russia because it had so little to offer in return. The same situation still exists, but in 1952 the foreign trade of the satellites with Russia varied between 58 percent of the total for Poland and 92 percent for Bulgaria. Little was given in return, and the redirection of foreign trade away from the natural markets in the West was effected by the Communist dictatorships of the satellite states. Some of the local leaders themselves tried to oppose the orders from Moscow as injurious to the interests of their native countries. They showed that like Tito they were guilty of the crime of non-Russian nationalism. Consequently, they were removed from office or hanged. The canalization of trade and the emphasis on industry have been intensely unpopular among the peoples of the satellite states. They have caused great hardships, and there have been acute shortages of food and consumer goods. Results have been accomplished by ruthless exploitation of the workmen and peasants. Large numbers have been condemned to forced labor in the mines and factories, and in building canals and railways. To find a parallel in the imperialism of Western Europe to the remorseless exploitation of the twentieth-century Russian Empire it would be necessary to go back to the history of the Spanish Empire in the sixteenth century. The parallel would not be exact however, for the government of Spain tried to protect the Indians from the inhuman treatment to which they were subjected.

REGIONAL COMMISSIONS

Dependencies in the same part of the world frequently have similar problems, and their solution can be hastened if the colonial powers collaborate instead of each following an independent policy. The West Indian islands, for instance, all suffer from a low standard of living, inadequate revenue for social services, overpopulation, and too great a dependence on a limited number of products grown for export. In 1942 an Anglo-American Commission was created to encourage and strengthen cooperation in such fields as labor, agriculture, housing, health, education, and economics. In 1945 France and Holland joined the organization, which was renamed the Caribbean Commission. Regular meetings are held which are attended by representatives of the colonial powers and of the local inhabitants, for the discussion of common problems. A Research Council provides the commission with technical advice on health and economic and social development. A similar commission was established for the Pacific dependencies south of the equator and east of Indonesia. The members are the United States, Great Britain, France, Holland, Australia, and New Zealand, and the organization and functions are similar to those of the Caribbean Commission.

The commissions do not have executive authority: their function is to coordinate policies by mutual consultation and the giving of advice from technicians and representatives of the colonial peoples. The commissions are not accountable to the Trusteeship Council, but the members' realization that failure to carry out reforms lays them open to the criticism of foreign colleagues is a valuable stimulant.

SELECTED READING

AMERY, LEOPOLD, *The German Colonial Claim*. New York: Longmans, Green and Company, 1940.

ANGELL, NORMAN, *Raw Materials, Population Pressure and War*. Boston: World Peace Foundation, 1936.

CAROE, SIR OLAF, *Soviet Empire: The Turks of Central Asia and Stalinism*. London: The Macmillan Company, 1953.

Colonial Administration by European Powers. New York: Royal Institute of International Affairs, 1947.

HAILEY, LORD, *African Survey*. New York: Oxford Press, 1938.

———, *The Future of Colonial Peoples*. Princeton: Princeton University Press, 1944.

HALL, H. DUNCAN, *Mandates, Dependencies and Trusteeships*. Washington: Carnegie Endowment for International Peace, 1948.

KOLARZ, WALTER, *The Peoples of the Soviet Far East*. London: Philip, 1954.

———, *Russia and Her Colonies*. London: Philip, 1952.

LANGER, WILLIAM L., *The Diplomacy of Imperialism 1890–1902*, 2 vols. New York: Alfred A. Knopf, 1935.

MAC INNES, C. M. (ed.), *Principles and Methods of Colonial Administration*. New York: Academic Press, 1950.

MUMFORD, WILLIAM B., *Africans Learn to be French*. London: Evans, 1937.

POOLE, BERNARD L., *Caribbean Commission: Background of Co-operation in the West Indies*. Columbia: University of South Carolina Press, 1951.

PRATT, JULIUS W., *America's Colonial Experiment*. New York: Prentice-Hall, 1950.

PRIESTLEY, HERBERT I., *France Overseas: A Study of Modern Imperialism.* New York: Appleton Century Company, 1938.

Royal Institute of International Affairs, *The Colonial Problem.* New York: Oxford University Press, 1937.

STAHL, KATHLEEN, *British and Soviet Colonial Systems.* London: Faber and Faber, Ltd., 1951.

CHAPTER 9

GEOGRAPHY AND FOREIGN POLICY

CLIMATE AND TOPOGRAPHY

Climate, rainfall, and topography can decide to some extent the kind of life that a people lead. It would seem natural that Russia, a predominantly land power with few ice-free harbors, should build up a large army and have little interest in merchant shipping and a navy. The Eskimos evolved a civilization which was well designed for existence inside the Arctic Circle, but this so absorbed their energy and ingenuity that they never progressed any further. The Negroes of equatorial Africa never evolved a high civilization, partly because the hot, humid climate sapped the energy, and also in a way life was too easy. A low standard of living could be attained by moderate exertion and forethought, and they were content not to progress beyond this.

The most propitious conditions are found in a temperate climate, where the average temperature is somewhere between 60° and 73°. It is also desirable that there should be changes not only between the seasons, but also from day to day. These increase physical and mental vigor and resistance to disease, and they also require forethought and energy to provide food, clothing, and shelter. The climatic changes are enough to make impossible the lethargy of the tropics, and yet not so great as to monopolize human effort. Among the countries which satisfy these requirements are most of the United States, southern Canada, much of northern Europe, and Japan. These same regions have an adequate but not an excessive rainfall, and this is almost as important as temperature. In desert regions like the Sahara the lack of rain so limits the available food supply that only a scanty population can exist. The excessive rainfall of the tropics combines with the high temperature to produce the enervating atmosphere of a never-ending Turkish bath, and it also provides ideal conditions for the widespread diffusion of diseases such as malaria which themselves sap human energy.

Natural frontiers, such as rivers, mountains, and deserts, have lost much of their strategic value with the development of modern means of communication and of warfare. The German defense of the Rhine held up the Allied advance only temporarily in 1944–1945. In 1943 General Leclerc's mechanized column crossed the Sahara from south to north, capturing the Italian desert forts as it advanced. It is still true however that natural obstacles have some military importance, e.g., the mountainous terrain of Italy helped the Germans to hold out longer in 1943–1945. A river may affect international relations if more than one state is interested in it. One reason for the hostility between Israel, Jordan, and Syria is that all three need the water of the Jordan River for irrigation.

AREA AND POSITION

The two most important geographic influences on international relations are area and position. The more extensive the territory of a state the more likely it is to contain a greater quantity and variety of natural resources so that a large state tends to be more powerful than a small one. There is the all-important qualification, however, that great space is only an asset if it is linked together by an adequate network of roads and railways, and the resources are of value only if they are developed. Provided that there are potential resources which can be developed, it is not the natural environment which counts so much as the use which its inhabitants make of it. A case in point is the varying fortunes of Russia in the two world wars. In 1914 Russia was an old-fashioned, agricultural great power, with millions of troops but with factories that were utterly inadequate to provide matériel. Germany was an industrialized great power with armies excellently equipped, and it was amazing that the badly armed Russians soldiers fought hard for three years despite immense losses before they collapsed. The Soviet defeat of the German armies in World War II was due in considerable measure to the development of heavy industry under Stalin's Five Year Plans so that the Russian armies were vastly better equipped than they had been twenty-five years earlier. Similarly, one reason for the weakness of China *vis à vis* Japan was that in the former industrialization was in its infancy, while the latter with far fewer natural resources had made itself into a strong industrialized state. Contemporary warfare has immensely increased the importance of area. A modern battle requires a surprising amount of territory, and the development of air power puts a small country at a heavy disadvantage, since military targets are unavoidably crowded together.

The position of a country is of the first importance because this determines its relations with other states. A good illustration is the great gain which the British have reaped since the sixteenth century from their location at the northwest corner of Europe. The importance of position can alter with changing conditions. Geographic discoveries can bring this about, as witness the effect of the Spanish and Portuguese explorations of the fifteenth century upon England. The development of the airplane and of guided missiles is another illustration. The protective effect of the English Channel has been immensely lessened, and the traditional American policy of isolationism has become obsolete. An equally startling case is the new importance that air routes over the Arctic Circle have given to northern Canada. Position also explains why some islands have an importance out of all proportion to their size and economic resources. No one took any interest in Greenland except the aborigines until it was realized that it was on the shortest air route from Germany to the United States. The Azores, Bermuda, Midway, or Okinawa are bases from which aircraft can dominate great areas of the ocean.

GEOPOLITICS

Geopolitics attained great notoriety during World War II, and its presiding genius, General and Doctor Professor Karl Haushofer, acclaimed himself as the founder of a new science which provided an infallible guide for German imperialism. Actually, Haushofer was not an originator but a popularizer of other men's ideas. The geopoliticians had devised a new combination of geography and political science, with some concepts borrowed from biology, the purpose of which was to exalt the power of the state. The American geographer Whittlesey described the writings of the geopoliticians as an "intermixture of sound geographic and political thinking with contradictory statements, doctrinaire notions and palpably false assumptions. . . . Even the phrasing commonly used by geopoliticians is usually vague, often confusing and sometimes misleading." Haushofer and his disciples gave to Hitler's program of conquest a pseudo-scientific justification.

Haushofer was greatly influenced by Sir Halford MacKinder's Heartland Theory. This was first enunciated in 1904, elaborated in *Democratic Ideals and Reality* which was published in 1919, and appeared in its final form during World War II. MacKinder pointed out that Europe, Asia, and Africa form a single continent, which he called the World Island. The sea powers, e.g., France or Britain with their bases in western Europe, dominated the world for several centuries, but this could be replaced by the global control of the land powers Russia or Germany. MacKinder believed that the key to world domination lay in the control of the Heartland. This was the area which was immune from attack by the sea powers. In his original definition it included most of Siberia and extended as far west as the basin of the Volga River. On the north the Heartland was protected by the frozen Arctic Ocean and on the south by deserts and the complex of lofty mountain ranges that make up Persia, Afghanistan, and Tibet. A second definition was strategic, and in addition to the original Heartland took in Europe as far west as the Elbe River, Sweden, the Baltic Sea, most of the Balkans, the Black Sea, and all of Turkey except the plain along the Mediterranean. MacKinder argued that

> Who rules East Europe commands the Heartland:
> Who rules the Heartland commands the World-Island:
> Who rules the World Island commands the World.

His practical conclusion, written to advise the victorious Allies in 1919, was that they must not allow Germany to retain control of her conquests of 1914–1917 in eastern Europe. Haushofer deduced that Germany must form an alliance with Russia to dominate the World Island and later the world. Believing that Japan was the coming power in Asia, he urged an alliance between her, Germany, and Russia.

It is still pertinent to examine the validity of the theory. Russia today controls most of the Heartland as strategically defined, from the Elbe River eastward. During the past thirty years the original Heartland (roughly Asiatic Russia) has been revolutionized by the development of mines, factories, railways, and airlines, and the Soviet government hopes that eventually it will provide half of the total industrial output. MacKinder, however, thought too much in terms of land and sea power and underestimated air power. He failed to foresee the conquest of polar air by long-range aircraft and the discovery of the atom bomb and of guided missiles. He did not allow for the fact that the United States is only separated from the Heartland by the Arctic Circle, and that the shortest air routes from the United States to Siberia are over the polar ice cap. Russia can no longer safely ignore her northern seaboard, leaving it to the protection of nature as MacKinder originally assumed. In addition, there are vitally important targets which could be reached from American air bases in Western Europe, Turkey, and the Far East. They include the Baku oil fields, which provide half of Russia's oil, the Rumanian oil field, and the heavy industry of the Ukraine and upper Silesia. Moreover the loyalty of the European satellite states might not prove too reliable. The conclusion seems to be that MacKinder exaggerated the danger. Russia's control of most of the Heartland as strategically defined is a threat to Western Europe and the rest of the world. But MacKinder's belief that the ruler of the Heartland commands the World Island and the world cannot be sustained.

RAW MATERIALS

Great national wealth, power in the world of states, and a high standard of living all depend upon industrialization. The military significance is summed up in the rule of thumb that matériel is to manpower as 5 to 1. A state must either have ample supplies of raw materials within its territory, or else have assured access to them. The world's raw materials are very unevenly distributed, the most favored areas being the United States, western Europe, and Russia. The bulk of Asia, Africa, South America, and Australia are much less generously endowed. The richest areas include all the world's leading powers with the exception of Japan, and she overcame her deficiencies by trading with the United States and the British Empire and appropriating Korea and part of China's resources.

The two basic minerals are coal and iron. The former is essential for the production of iron and steel, though oil and electric power have replaced it in some forms of manufacturing. The United States is the largest single producer of coal, followed by Russia, Britain, West Germany, Poland and France together with the Saar. The United States is by far the world's principal producer of iron ore, and the large deposits now being developed in Quebec and Labrador are available for her use. By 1960 it is estimated that she may import about 35 million tons a year. The high-grade ores in Minnesota are approaching exhaustion, but there are extensive reserves of lower grade ores. The invention of beneficiating them to form a concentrate has given the Minnesota iron mines a new lease of life. In order of importance the chief iron-ore producing countries are the United States, which accounts for nearly 40 percent of the total, Russia, France, Sweden, the United Kingdom, and Germany. France is the principal producer in western Europe. The ore deposits in the United Kingdom supply about 40 percent of domestic needs and are of low grade. They are supplemented by heavy imports of high-grade ores from Sweden, Spain, and French North Africa. Sweden has extensive reserves of high-grade ore.

The United States and Russia are the only two nations which can maintain heavy industry on a very extensive scale from their own domestic deposits of coal and iron. At the present time the United States produces over half the world's steel, 101,250,000 tons in 1953. According to unofficial estimates Russian production was 38,000,000 tons in 1953. The next largest producer is Great Britain with 18,520,000, followed by Western Germany, France, and Belgium-Luxembourg. India's steel production is small, but there are quite large deposits of coal and iron ore close to one another. India is the one Asian country which seems destined to develop an important steel industry based on domestic resources. China has extensive coal deposits, but her iron ore is rather poor in quality and limited in quantity. The present prospect is that she cannot have a large iron and steel industry for a long period based on her own ores.

A group of alloys are essential for making steel with various special qualities such as hardness, tensile strength, toughness, and resistance to rust. Russia is the world's largest producer of manganese, while the United States with limited deposits is a heavy importer. Most of the other sources of supply are in the British Empire. Chrome comes mainly from Russia, the British Empire, Turkey, and the Philippines. The copper mines of the Belgian Congo furnish most of the world's cobalt. Excluding Russia, the United States produces nine tenths of the world's molybdenum. Russia is moderately well supplied with nickel, but about 94 percent of the world's supply is found in Canada. China and Burma were formerly the principal exporters of tungsten, and Russia has extensive deposits. The chief producers in the Western world are the United States, Portugal, and Bolivia. Vanadium is primarily supplied by the United States and Peru.

Aluminum is next to steel the most commonly used of all metals. Compared with the prewar period, there has been a phenomenal increase in its production, primarily because of its importance for aircraft and military equipment. The United States and Canada account for about two thirds of the world's production and the Soviet bloc for one eighth. Bauxite, the ore from which aluminum is manufactured, comes chiefly from British and Dutch Guiana in South America, the United States, Indonesia, and France. The United States is still the world's largest single producer of copper, followed by Chile, Northern Rhodesia, and the Congo. Nearly half the zinc is furnished by the United States and Canada. The United States produces over a quarter of the world's lead, followed by Mexico and Australia. Mercury is vital in wartime since it is one of the constituents of a chemical compound used to detonate explosives. Italy and Spain each provide about two fifths of the world's supply, and Russia is believed to have large quantities. Three fifths of the world's tin comes from Southeast Asia, with Malaya and Indonesia as the principal suppliers. About an eighth comes from the Congo and Nigeria, and nearly a fifth from Bolivia. Pitchblende is the main source of uranium and plutonium from which atomic energy is derived, and it is believed to exist in many parts of the world. The main deposits (excluding considerable quantities in Russia) are in the Belgian Congo, Canada, and South Africa. Czechoslovakia and Poland have important deposits, and known supplies in the United States are limited.

Southeast Asia produces over 90 percent of the natural rubber, Malaya and Indonesia each providing over 37 percent. The United States takes more than 40 percent of the world's exports and is the largest single market. Despite the development of synthetic rubber, 89 percent of which is manufactured in the United States, the sale of natural rubber is larger than before the war owing to the increased use of rubber. Russia has a large synthetic rubber industry, as had Germany prior to 1945. The four principal producers of cotton are the United States with 40.8 percent, Russia with 17.5 percent, the British Empire with 17 percent, and China with 13.1 percent. The chief exporters are the United States, Egypt and Pakistan, while the leading importers are Great Britain, France, West Germany, and Japan. Japan produces 66 percent of the world's raw silk, and the United States is the largest importer. The sterling area (chiefly Australia and New Zealand) provides 50 percent of the world's wool, Argentina and Uruguay 19 percent and the United States 7 percent.

OIL

There are two major oil-producing areas in the world. The first includes the fields in the United States, Canada, Mexico, Colombia, and Venezuela. The proved reserves of the United States are estimated to be about 20 percent and of the whole of North and South America 30.3 percent of the world total. The ownership is predominantly American, with British and Dutch companies controlling most of the remainder. In 1954 the United States produced about 46.3 percent and the Western Hemisphere 66 percent of the world's oil. The second major area comprises the Near and Middle East. The principal fields are in Iran, Arabia, Iraq, and the Russian field near Baku. Omitting the Russian field, the proved reserves are believed to be 60 percent of the world total, but production in 1953 was only 20.3 percent of the world total although rapidly increasing. Ownership of the Middle Eastern field was 42-percent American, 52-percent Anglo-Dutch, and to a limited extent French. There are small fields in southern Asia, producing about 2.7 percent of the world's supply, the ownership of which is divided between American and Anglo-Dutch companies. Europe has 7.6 percent of the world's oil, and Africa .1 percent. Important reserves, mainly undeveloped, are believed to exist within the Arctic Circle in Alaska, Canada, and Siberia. During World War II the Germans developed the refining of synthetic oil from coal on a large scale.

Russia is estimated to have perhaps 6.5 percent of the world's proved oil reserves, and her production in 1954 was estimated to be about 8.3 percent of the world total. In addition, she controls the small and declining field in Rumania and the still smaller fields in Hungary, Poland, and other satellite states. The United States, Great Britain, and Holland together account for 80 percent of the world output. The ownership is very concentrated: five American and two British and Dutch companies own 70 percent of the world's oil fields. The Middle East sends the bulk of its oil to Europe, which has little of its own, and also helps to supply Africa, India, and Australia. American consumption has grown so greatly that imports now exceed exports, and the United States draws increasingly upon Latin America. American proved reserves are substantially greater than was believed ten years ago, but it is considered that domestic supplies will become steadily more unable to meet the further expansion of consumption which is anticipated. For this reason the United States is interested in the Middle East, which has the largest comparatively untouched oil reserves in the world.

No single country of western Europe can begin to compete with the United States and Russia in variety and quantity of raw materials. The only major mineral asset of Great Britain is coal, of Germany, coal and potash, of France, iron and bauxite, and of Italy, mercury and pyrites (for sulfur). It is only when taken as a whole that western Europe becomes an important storehouse of mineral wealth. Even then it is almost totally lacking in various essentials such as oil, copper, and alloys for steel. The British Empire is self-sufficient in almost everything except oil, of which it has little except in Canada and the promising field in Borneo. To speak of the empire is rather misleading, however, since each dominion has full power over its own resources. Producers sell impartially to whoever can pay the world price, and Great Britain has no control over their actions. The empire is not an integrated economic unit under a single authority like the United States or Russia, and this greatly lessens its economic power.

The importance of the tropical regions as a source of raw materials has been greatly exaggerated. The tropics produce the greater part of the world's tin, cobalt, and rubber and an important fraction of its manganese, chrome, bauxite, phosphate (for fertilizer), and copper. They provide palm oil, coconut oil, and most of the peanut oil; but for all these, other vegetable oils can be substituted. There are also vegetable fibers such as hemp, jute, and sisal. Completing the list with foodstuffs, the tropical regions grow most of the rice, cocoa, and tea, and part of the sugar, bananas, coffee, and tobacco. The preponderant part of the world's raw materials and foodstuffs do not come from the tropics but from the independent sovereign states of the middle latitudes.

Not even the United States and Russia are self-sufficient. At the present time the United States uses from 33 to 50 percent of the world's supply of each raw material. It imports all its tin, chromium, and nickel, and varying percentages of its uranium, manganese, mercury, cobalt, antimony, bauxite, tungsten, lead, copper, zinc, oil, wool, and rubber. This list is far from exhaustive, and it is estimated that by 1975 the United States will use 60 percent more raw materials than in 1950. As domestic supplies become depleted, more and more will have to be imported. Very much less is known about Russia's resources, but here too there seems to be a considerable list of deficiencies. This paragraph is the best commentary on the policy of autarky or economic self-sufficiency. If the two most richly endowed states are not independent of the rest of the world, it is no use for smaller countries to try to attain this goal.

SELECTED READING

BOWMAN, ISAIAH, *The New World: Problems in Political Geography,* 4th ed. Yonkers: World Book Company, 1928.

DE MILLE, JOHN B., *Strategic Minerals.* New York: McGraw-Hill Book Company, 1947.

HARTSHORNE, RICHARD, *The Nature of Geography.* Ann Arbor: Edwards Brothers, 1946.

LEITH, C. K., FURNISS, J. W., and LEWIS, C., *World Minerals and World Peace.* Washington, D.C.: Brookings Institution, 1943.

MAC KINDER, SIR HALFORD J., *Democratic Ideals and Reality.* New York: Henry Holt and Company, 1942.

SPYKMAN, NICHOLAS JOHN, *America's Strategy in World Politics: The United States and the Balance of Power.* New York: Harcourt, Brace and Company, 1942.

WEIGERT, HANS W., and STEFANSSON, V. (eds.), *Compass of the World.* New York: The Macmillan Company, 1947.

———, ———, and HARRISON, R. E. (eds.), *New Compass of the World.* New York: The Macmillan Company, 1949.

WHITTLESEY, DERWENT, *The Earth and the State, A Study of Political Geography.* New York: Henry Holt and Company, 1939.

World Production of Raw Materials. New York: Royal Institute of International Affairs, 1953.

CHAPTER 10

POPULATION AND FOOD

THE GROWTH OF POPULATION

In 1800 the population of the world was probably not much more than 900 million. The birth rate was high, but the death rate was almost equally so, and the rate of increase was very slow. The high death rate was caused by the natural checks on population—famine, disease, and war. Conditions in Europe were similar to those which now prevail in China and other parts of Asia. Famines occurred periodically and were usually followed by pestilence which slew many of the survivors, who were weakened by underfeeding. Little could be done to relieve them, for the lack of good roads made it impossible to move food from the regions which had a surplus into those where there was a deficit. In the rudimentary state of medical knowledge doctors proceeded largely by guess and by God, and public health simply did not exist. A pessimist might have quoted Hobbes' remark that life was poor, nasty, brutish, and short. Wars were frequent, and since armies usually lived off the country, many of the civilians died of hunger or disease.

In 1953 the world's population was estimated to be perhaps 2,547,000,000, and to increase at the rate of about 1 percent a year. A later U.N. estimate in 1954 placed the annual increase at 30 million or slightly more than 1 percent. The population of Europe had trebled since 1800, that of North and South America had grown ninefold (partly by immigration), Asia's had more than doubled, and Africa's had increased by 75 percent. The cause was a fall in the death rate, while the birth rate remained high for about a century. This change was due to a series of revolutionary events which began in Europe and from there spread to the other continents in varying degrees. Medicine made immense advances, and public health was literally invented and evolved into what it is today. For the first time man knew the cause of disease, and also how to prevent it. Agricultural productivity was very greatly increased by improvements in farming; and good roads, railways, and steamships made it possible to move food into areas where crops had failed.

Famine was abolished in the developed areas, though it continues in countries like China where conditions roughly resemble those of eighteenth-century Europe. The industrial revolution raised very greatly the standard of living. This in itself lessened the death rate, since the predisposing condition for a fatal disease is often lack of physical vitality due to chronic underfeeding. Another effect of industrialization was that wealth and technical knowledge grew as they never had before. This provided, for example, the engineering skill to carry out great public health projects and the money to pay for them. The natural checks on population virtually ceased to operate in the developed parts of the world and to a lesser extent in the rest of it. In Europe, the United States, and the British dominions the birth rate continued high during most of the nineteenth century but began to fall toward its close so that their populations are now growing very slowly. In the rest of the world population continues to mount since the birth rate remains high while the death rate is falling. This threatens to create some of the most intractable problems that mankind has had to tackle.

The reasons for the fall of the birth rate are bound up with the rising standard of living and the great movement of population from the country to the town which was brought about by the industrial revolution. Other careers were opened to women besides marriage: a large number of children were no longer needed to carry on farm work: and the higher standard of living awakened the wish for a still better standard. One way to attain this was to cut down the expense of rearing a large family, and the discovery of modern methods of birth control coincided with this widespread and growing desire. Small families first appeared among the urban well-to-do and spread from them to the town workmen, and later to the farm population. The result by the 1930's was that over a large part of the Western world the net reproduction rate was less than one. This rate is the ratio of the child to the parent generation (ages about fifteen to forty-five). A rate of one means that the parents are reproducing themselves and the population will remain stationary. Less than one means that the next parent generation will be smaller and there will be a proportionate reduction in its production of children, or, in other words, a falling population. Moreover the point is eventually reached where the decreasing number of births can no longer be offset by further decline in the death rate, since this has already gone about as far as possible. Gradually, therefore, the total population would decline.

WORLD POPULATION SHIFTS

The net reproduction rate before World War II was less than one in most of northwestern Europe (including Great Britain, France, and Germany), the United States, Australia, and New Zealand. France had moved further along the road than the rest and had reached the point where deaths exceeded births. In southern and eastern Europe the birth rate was beginning to fall in certain segments of the population, but there was room for a considerable reduction of the death rate. The population of these countries would, therefore, grow for several decades before they went the same way as the other European countries. The most important country in this second group was Russia, and here a marked increase of population was expected before it tapered off. Assuming that the prewar net reproduction rate remained unchanged, it was estimated that by 1970 the population of the United States would have grown to 155 million, Italy's to 53 million, and Germany's with just under 70 million would have begun to decline. Great Britain's population would have fallen to perhaps 42 million and France's to 37 million. Russia's population would have risen from 170.5 million in 1939 to 251 million and that of Poland and the other Slav countries of the Soviet bloc to 85 million. To the extent that population is a factor in state power, the center of gravity in Europe would shift to the East. Russia would overshadow western Europe, though increases in North America and southern Europe would counterbalance declines there.

The most startling changes however would lie in the population ratio of Europe and North America as compared with Asia. The Asian population estimated to be 1,097,000,000 in 1939, would grow by hundreds of millions. Sometime between 1975 and 1985 Japan might have between 85 million and 95 million people, instead of the 73 million who overcrowded the islands in 1940. China's population, guestimated to be between 375 million and 425 million in 1939, might be anywhere between 585 million and 700 million in 1980. The population of India might rise from 389 million in 1941 to 680 million in 1981. In other words, the three most overcrowded countries of Asia, India, China, and Japan, which had perhaps 860 million people in 1940, might have as many as 1,475,000,000 in 1980. The explosive possibilities of this situation hardly need emphasis, especially when it is remembered that similar developments though on a smaller scale would be taking place elsewhere, e.g., the Near and Middle East and Java. India, China, and Russia would be the three most populous countries with 60 percent of the world's peoples, and of all the Western nations only the United States would exceed Japan. The Western nations would have a far smaller fraction of the total world population than in 1940. Moreover, they would contain a high percentage of older persons, while Russia, Japan, India, and China, which today have only a small proportion of old people, would show larger contingents in the military age groups of twenty to thirty-four.

There seems no reason to question these prewar calculations that the population of Russia and Asia will grow prodigiously, but it would appear that the estimate must be modified somewhat as regards the United States and the other Western powers. In most of these countries the decline of the birth rates halted during the 'thirties. Thereafter increases occurred, especially during the years following the great depression and after World War II. After 1947, or thereabouts, birth rates declined in some countries, but in nearly all of them the rates are still higher than in the 1930's. The exact significance of the change is much in dispute. Some consider that it is due to marriages temporarily postponed by the depression or World War II. Postponed war marriages however hardly seem an adequate explanation so long after 1945, and also there is a tendency to have more and earlier children than had been the custom formerly. In southern and southeastern Europe on the other hand the birth rates during the last two decades have generally continued their previous downward trend without the upsurge noted in other parts of the Western world. Whatever happens in the future, the 1970 population estimates for the Western nations previously quoted must be revised upward.

OVERPOPULATION AND *LEBENSRAUM*

Hitler and Mussolini argued that Germany and Italy were have-not nations compared with the "bloated pluto democracies," by which they meant the United States, France, and Great Britain. They claimed that they were overpopulated and did not have the resources adequately to support their peoples, and they waged a share the wealth campaign in the international field, demanding that Germans and Italians must have *Lebensraum,* that is, their fair proportion of the territory and resources of the globe. As a matter of fact, the pressure of population in Germany was less serious than in some other European countries. Germany had 372 inhabitants per square mile, while Belgium had 708. Belgium's trade with her colony of the Congo was not very large, and her one mineral asset was coal. Nevertheless, she maintained a satisfactory standard of living by intensive agriculture and through building up an important export trade in manufactures.

Prewar Holland represents another good example of a country which maintained one of the highest standards of living in Europe, although it had 642 people per square mile and very limited *Lebensraum*. Here again the principal secret of success was the energy and inventiveness with which the Dutch made the most of their few natural advantages. These consisted of a limited amount of coal and geographic position. Holland like Germany had good harbors and was on the great sea route from northern Europe to the Americas and the Far East. Originally much of the country was at the bottom of the North Sea, and it was converted into fertile farmland by centuries of unremitting toil which is still going on. Holland's prosperity was based upon five elements. Trade with her East Indian empire and the income from investments there provided about 15 percent of the annual national income. In addition, there was the European trade, and especially that up the Rhine with Germany; a sizable merchant marine; specialized production, like the electrical industry; and exports of specialized agricultural produce, such as bulbs and tomatoes.

Few things worried Hitler more than the falling birth rate. Far from taking comfort from this future solution of his problem, he launched a vigorous campaign to raise it by such measures as subsidies to large families. He increased the net reproduction rate from .70 in 1933 to .98 in 1940. Hitler gave his game away when he complained that Germany with 69 million was overpopulated and in the next breath declared that his great German empire could only be sustained if there were 250 million Germans. In other words, Hitler wanted a large population as a garrison to hold down the countries he intended to conquer, and the pathetic appeals about underprivileged Germany were intended to manufacture sympathy abroad. Mussolini, who had more reason than Hitler to worry about Italy's overcrowded condition, was equally energetic in raising the birth rate and set his goal at 60 million Italians.

OVERCROWDED ASIA

The population of Asia increased from perhaps 600 million in 1800 to an estimated 1,364,000,000 in 1953. The growth has been most marked in countries like India which were under European control, or which like Japan have partially Westernized themselves. There the birth rate has remained high, but the death rate has fallen because the natural checks on population have largely ceased to operate. The population of Java grew from perhaps 4.5 million in 1816 to over 50 million in 1941. In Japan the population rose from perhaps 30 million in 1867 to 73 million in 1940. In 1872 the population of India was probably around 256 million; by 1941 it was 389 million and increasing by 5 million a year. If censuses had been taken at an earlier date, it would probably be found that the population doubled under British rule. The explanation was threefold: India was given the longest period in her history of freedom from invasion and civil war; famines and resultant epidemics which formerly killed people by the millions were largely eliminated; and British medical and health services considerably reduced the mortality rate. From the point of view of the future, the most serious aspect of the situation is that the countries that have been under European rule are predominantly agricultural. Of them all, India is the most industrialized, and even here 80 percent of the people are subsistence farmers.

The explanation is that during the nineteenth and the early twentieth centuries the colonial powers all believed in the system of free private enterprise. Governments did not have the power or the desire to direct how capitalists were to invest their money. Apart from France, which discouraged manufacturing in her colonies in the interests of home industries, the investor was free to use his capital where and how he chose. Attracted by the cheap labor or the proximity of raw materials, a few started manufacturing in the colonies, like the Scotsmen who moved their jute factories from Scotland to Calcutta. The majority, however, were interested in Asia and Africa as sources of raw materials and established mines and plantations. Asians and Africans lacked the business and technical knowledge and usually the money to start factories themselves. The Asian and African colonies, therefore, continued to be preponderantly agricultural, producers of food and raw materials. All this while the death rate was falling and the population growing. The result today is that many of the colonies and former colonies have a very large population.

There are many reasons for the very low standard of living in Asia and parts of Africa, but the most important is that there are far too many trying to obtain a living from the land. There are tens of millions of surplus farm laborers whose competition for work drags down the level of wages to a pittance. Antiquated methods of arable and stock farming mean that the cultivator does not get the return he should from his work. Today about 30 percent of Indians are chronically underfed because the country does not produce enough food to give them an adequate diet. A large part of the peasants are heavily in debt to native moneylenders. Over wide areas the farmers are sharecroppers who pay an excessive rent. The prevalence of diseases such as malaria and hookworm means that the victims are always physically and mentally below par, and incapable of working as hard as a healthy man.

All the underdeveloped countries of Asia have elaborate plans for a comprehensive attack on the problem of poverty. They intend to expand agriculture, but everywhere the emphasis is placed on manufacturing and mining as the key to progress. This raises the problem of the effect of industrialization upon countries which are already densely populated. Will it reproduce the experience of nineteenth-century Europe, when the population trebled? The development of modern Japan—the one Asian country which has industrialized—parallels in general outlines the evolution of nineteenth-century Europe. The same sharp increase in population occurred, and at long last, in the period between the two wars, there were signs that the birth rate was beginning to fall. The death rate, however, kept falling even faster, and the result was that the population continued to grow, a process which is still going on. Therefore, it seems probable that the same development will take place elsewhere. Industrialization will create a far larger taxable capacity, and hence an enhanced revenue for the medical and health services. This means a further fall in the death rate. After some decades no doubt the birth rate will begin to fall, and finally the population will cease to increase. But by that time it is possible that the population of India will have reached the fantastic figure given earlier in this chapter. The same will probably occur in the other underdeveloped areas.

This raises the question of whether the expansion of agriculture and industry can keep well ahead of the growth of population, as it must if the present low standard of living is to be raised. There are so many unknown quantities here that the only safe answer is to say that it may, and again it may not. India is fairly typical of the underdeveloped countries, with the qualification that the prospects for industrialization are better than elsewhere. So a study of the Indian situation illustrates the complexity of the problem, and how impossible it is to be dogmatic about what is going to happen. The tilled area could be extended by perhaps 60 per cent or 70 per cent by using the "cultivable waste." The reason it is unused at present is that most of it is poor land, requiring heavy expenditure on irrigation works, soil improvement, etc., before it is worth cultivating. Another line of attack is to persuade the peasants to use better farming methods. At present the crop yield is only about a third of what it is in Japan, which is itself below the level of Western Europe. Scores of millions of conservative peasants must be persuaded to change their methods of farming. Because of their low income, the improvement, e.g., fertilizer to improve soil fertility, must be so inexpensive that they can afford to use it.

Religion as well as long-established custom is sometimes an obstacle to change. To cite an instance, there are perhaps as many as 275 to 300 million cattle and sheep, but most of them are of poor quality. There are far too many animals for the available pasture, and literally millions should be slaughtered and selective breeding promoted, but this does not occur. The cause of this is that three quarters of the Indians are Hindus, and the killing of cattle is forbidden by their religion and now by law. Incidentally, this is one reason for the underfeeding, since no orthodox Hindu can eat beef. All of the foregoing means that food production in India can be increased, but that it will not be quick or inexpensive to do so. Improvement of agriculture is also a prerequisite for a successful expansion of industry, since the market for manufactures will have to be found primarily in India itself. At present the average income is estimated to be only $60 a year, and this will have to be raised to increase purchasing capacity.

To improve the rural standard of living manufacturing will have to draw off the surplus millions of farm laborers. It must also expand fast enough to provide work for millions more who are going to be born in the coming decades. Whether it will be able to do this is not certain. Professor Warren Thompson believes that the food supply may be increased by 75 to 80 percent in the course of several decades. The population, however, is now growing at the rate of 15 percent every ten years and will continue to do so for several decades before the birth rate begins to fall. Assuming that this rate of increase continues, India will have a population of 680 million by 1981, or 75 percent above that of 1941. If the death rate should fall more rapidly than is assumed in the preceding calculations, the population by 1981 might be as much as 800 million. Professor Thompson fears that "When one asks whether the lot of the masses of the people in India will be any better in 1981, even with the rapid progress assumed above, if there are somewhere between 680 million and 800 million persons, the answer must almost certainly be that it will be little or no better, possibly even worse. The great increase in production will be consumed in keeping increased numbers of people alive at about the level of living now prevailing." At the most hopeful the per capita income will probably increase a little, but the demand for better conditions will increase more rapidly. The key to the problem is the birth rate; any substantial and rapid reduction would falsify the gloomy prediction just quoted. Unfortunately, large families are sanctioned by immemorial custom and religion, and several hundred millions must be persuaded to break with the past. The experience of Japan and of Western Europe shows that custom and religion do change, but that they do not alter quickly. Whether India can accelerate the tempo of change is the biggest unknown factor in the whole problem.

The same problem of population growth exists in many other countries, notably in Japan, China, Java, Vietnam, Egypt and much of the Middle East. Africa is trending in the same direction. Everywhere there is a similar demand for a higher standard of living, and the same race between rising population and improved agriculture and promotion of manufacturing. Sir John Russell, a British agricultural expert, summed up the problem in these words. "The root trouble is that Western medical science has outstripped world agricultural practice, and its results have been carried to non-Western peoples, lowering infant mortality and general death rates so that children grow up with no certainty that food will be available. Western methods can, I believe, provide for Western rates of increase but not for Eastern rates."

WORLD POPULATION AND FOOD

The Food and Agriculture Organization (FAO) recently made a survey of the pre-1939 food supply of seventy countries which had 90 percent of the world's population. This showed that roughly one third of the world's population was well fed. Included were the United States, Canada, northern Europe including Russia, Australia and New Zealand, and Argentina, Paraguay, and Uruguay. About a sixth was fairly well fed, including most of southern Europe and part of the other continents. Over half the world's population ate only about two thirds as much food as the well-fed group.

Moreover the diet was largely starch (e.g., cereals) which gave energy, but it was deficient in protective foods, such as meat, fish, and milk. Such an unbalanced and insufficient diet could not maintain normal health and energy. It promoted a high death rate and impaired working capacity. In this category were most of Asia, Mexico, and Central America, and probably part of South America and Africa. In the whole underfed area the average pre-1939 income was less than $100, and poverty was the principal cause of malnutrition. To put it another way, the well fed third of the global population ate two thirds of the food, and the underfed one half ate less than a quarter.

On the whole, the problem is worse today than it was before the war. The principal food-exporting countries are the United States, Canada, Australia, and New Zealand. The last two give first call upon their exports to Great Britain, which is by far the largest food-importing country. In North America alone has there been a very marked expansion in food production, and its exports have greatly increased. South America's food production has grown. But its population has increased by 24 percent, and it is eating more of its own food than before the war. Turning to the food deficit areas, Europe's agriculture on the whole has made an impressive recovery from the heavy losses caused by the war. This was particularly marked in Western Europe, owing to American help, although increased agricultural production has not quite kept pace with the growth in population. Africa has rather more than maintained its low standard of living. The great problem is Asia, for here less food is available than before the war while the population has grown. So an inadequate diet has become more inadequate than ever.

Production has not kept pace with increasing population, and World War II and its aftermath have lessened supplies. Before the war the three principal rice-exporting countries were Burma, Thailand, and French Indochina. They supplied the chief deficit areas, India, Ceylon, China, and Malaya. Today Japan has been added to the list. At the same time rice exports have fallen from 5.7 million tons to 2.9 million in 1952, because of the wars in Indochina and Burma. Thailand alone increased production moderately, and with more buyers competing for less rice the individual ration has been reduced and the price has risen fivefold. India has also obtained cereals from the United States and Australia. The much advertised Chinese shipments of rice to India in 1952 seem to have been made for propaganda reasons, and not because the country had a real surplus.

The FAO has worked out estimates of the quantity of food which will be needed by 1960, assuming that the world population increases by 25 percent and everyone has enough to eat. The percentages of increase vary from 21 percent for cereals and 46 percent for meat or fish, to 100 percent for milk and 163 percent for fruit and vegetables. The question is whether the world can meet these demands, and the still heavier ones that will arise after 1960. The general rate of population growth may be 1 percent in a year (in a few countries it is known to be higher, e.g., Java), and the world's present population may double before it attains stability. Food production must increase even faster, if the goals set by the FAO are to be attained.

The question has been asked whether Malthus may have been right after all. Writing in 1803, he argued that population increased far faster than food supply and that it would go on growing until it was reduced by the natural checks of famine, disease, and war. Any increase in food production would soon be absorbed by the growth of population so that no marked rise in the general standard of living was possible. Malthus' fears for Europe were falsified by the opening up of the virgin farm lands of North and South America, Australia, and New Zealand, by the heavy emigration to them, and by the sale overseas of Europe's machine-made products which gave it the money to buy the food it needed. Food production more than kept pace with the growth of population, and the standard of living rose substantially. There are no more empty continents where Asians can settle and grow food. Limited areas are available in Southeast Asia, but part of them will be needed for the expansion of the local populations. The Negroes of Africa are increasing quite fast, and there will not be much room there. The great basin of the Amazon River is almost uninhabited and might take large numbers of Asian immigrants, who could be kept healthy by modern tropical medicine; but the political difficulties would be great. The immigration policies of the United States, Canada, New Zealand, and Australia rule out settlement there. The conclusion seems inevitable that Asians must remain within their present borders, grow as much food as they can, and call on the rest of the world for the remainder.

At the present time about 9 billion acres or 27 percent of the earth's surface is in agricultural use—2.5 to 3 billion acres in arable farming and the rest in pasture. During the past fifty years agricultural research has enlarged the yields of many crops by from 10 percent to 25 percent and has also increased the weight and number of cattle, pigs, etc. Millions of farmers have availed themselves of these discoveries, but there are a very large number who have not. It has been estimated that if all the world's farmers and particularly those of Asia and Africa took full advantage of the knowledge already possessed, in most cases existing yields could be increased by considerably more than 20 percent. To carry out this program will not be quick, easy, or cheap. The cost is far beyond the resources of Asian and African governments and can only be met if assistance on a large scale is made available by the West. As regards the extension of the cultivated area, only about one fourteenth of the world's land surface has the necessary combination of suitable temperature, rainfall, soil, and topography for farming. It is estimated that about 300 million acres could be made available, for instance, in northern Canada, Scandinavia, and Siberia, and perhaps an additional 1 billion acres in the tropics. At a very rough estimate the total would be 1.3 billion acres more or less. Owing to our ignorance of the problems of tropical agriculture, a great deal of preliminary investigation will be needed. How necessary this is was shown by the great peanut fiasco a few years ago. A corporation set up by the British Labour government lost some $136 million and proved that while peanuts flourish in many parts of tropical Africa, it is not as easy to grow them as one might think. Very heavy expenditure will also be needed on railways, seaports, and public health.

Assuming that the whole of this program were carried out—the highest productivity on existing farms and the extension of the cultivated area—it is believed that the world could supply most of the food which the FAO estimated would be needed in 1960. Additional food could be obtained by expanding the fishing industry, especially in the Southern Hemisphere. This still leaves the question of what to do about the increase of population after 1960. Here experts differ, some arguing that Malthus was correct and others contending that if all the world's resources were fully used it could feed as many as 6 billion people. In 1954 a U.N. study estimated that in the next thirty years the world's population may increase from the present 2.5 billion to about 4 billion or more. In theory it should be possible to provide enough food. However, because of "ignorance, greed, strife, superstition, and blind tradition" the production increases that are likely actually to be achieved will probably be much smaller than those which are technically possible. As a result, there is a real danger that the standard of living of the world's peoples will fall as their numbers increase.

One final phase of the problem deserves consideration. In the previous paragraphs food needs and supplies have been considered globally. Actually there will be deficit and surplus areas. Asia promises to be the worst of the former, while the latter will be North and South America, Australia, New Zealand, and perhaps Russia. Russia presumably will not act from purely humanitarian or economic reasons, but will give or refuse food as the aims of her foreign policy dictate. What should be the attitude of the Western surplus countries? When there is an emergency as in the recent famines in India and Pakistan, they will doubtless continue to give food or lend it on easy terms. Insofar as the deficit countries can pay for food imports by the sale of their exports, they will be able to buy it. But it may be a long time before they are in a position to do this. Have the surplus countries a responsibility to provide them with food irrespective of payment? It is not impossible that this may become an important issue in international relations.

SELECTED READING

CARR SAUNDERS, A. M., *World Population: Past Growth and Present Trends*. New York: Oxford Press, 1936.

CLARK, FREDERICK, and PIRIE, N. W. (eds.), *Four Thousand Million Mouths: Scientific Humanism and the Shadow of World Hunger*. London: Oxford Press, 1951.

DAVIS, KINGSLEY, *Population of India and Pakistan*. Princeton: Princeton University Press, 1951.

HATT, PAUL K. (ed.), *World Population and Future Resources*. New York: American Book Company, 1952.

MC CONKEY, DAREL (ed.), *Food and People: A UNESCO Project*. Six pamphlets. New York: United Nations, N.D.

NOTESTEIN, FRANK H., *et al., The Future Population of Europe and the Soviet Union*. Geneva: League of Nations, 1944.

STAMP, LAURENCE D., *Our Underdeveloped World*. London: Faber and Faber, Ltd., 1953.

THOMPSON, WARREN, *Plenty of People*. New York: Ronald Press, 1949.

———, *Population and Peace in the Pacific*. Chicago: The Chicago University Press, 1946.

———, *Population Problems*. New York: McGraw-Hill Book Company, 1942.

VOGT, WILLIAM, *Road to Survival*. New York: Wm. Sloane Associates, Inc., 1948.

PART 3

BASIC FACTORS
IN DIPLOMACY, LAW,
AND ORGANIZATION

CHAPTER 11

DIPLOMACY: ITS NATURE AND OBJECTS

Governments of national states employ many methods to attain foreign policy objectives. Their choice of method reflects the elements of strength or influence at their disposal, their estimate of corresponding elements arrayed against them, the importance they attach to the objective, and their judgment of the consequences of using one method or another in terms of immediate results and long-term international relations. Upon these considerations a government may choose to employ persuasion and negotiation, propaganda, economic pressure, mediation and conciliation, invocation of international judicial procedures, collective action through international security agencies, threat or demonstration of force, forceful measures short of war, war, or self-imposed isolation. The method generally chosen to facilitate the conduct of recurrent international transactions, to adjust differences which are susceptible of compromise, or to explore possibilities of action in more difficult situations, is *diplomacy*.

NATURE OF DIPLOMACY

Varied use of the term "diplomacy" has produced some confusion. Harold Nicolson noted at least five common senses of the word, denoting respectively foreign policy, international negotiation, administrative machinery or processes to facilitate negotiation, a functional branch of the foreign service, and the personal qualities contributing to persuasive negotiation. In professional usage diplomacy is to be distinguished from foreign policy or international law and confined to the art or practice of international negotiation and the administrative management of such negotiations. "Negotiation" is here very broadly conceived; it refers not alone to the discussion and final formulation of the terms of an agreement, but also (a) to defining areas of agreement by continuous reporting of the position of the state to which a diplomat is accredited, and effective representation to it of the position of the state which sent him; (b) to building relationships of mutual confidence and understanding which will inspire agreement. Sir Charles Webster has suggested that successful diplomacy depends mainly upon three factors: producing a climate of opinion favorable to the achievement of desired ends, devising the best forms of agreement to give practical effect to these ends, and creating or recognizing the appropriate moment for a maximum effort toward agreement. Not always simple in individual transactions, the manipulation of such factors in the relations of states will often present extraordinary tests of foresight, patience, and astuteness.

It is sometimes useful to think of diplomacy, when applied to conflicting national interests, as a form of negotiation to which war stands as the extreme alternative. Quincy Wright may overstate the case in saying that "where the possibility of war does not exist . . . the term diplomacy is hardly applicable," but his remark can be understood in the sense that diplomacy seeks to achieve by explanation and persuasion a position at least as advantageous as a state's power in terms of economic and military strength, cultural leadership and influence, might entitle it to expect if these forces were thrown into direct conflict with the power of other states. Brilliant diplomacy, of course, may achieve even greater successes as one state may present its case more persuasively, may mobilize its strength more impressively or with more apparent determination to use it, or may by alliances compound with other states a force greater than it could individually command. But the strength of diplomacy as a method seems to lie in the prudential consideration that if conflicts of national interests can be accurately assessed in terms of the physical ability and determination of governments, or combinations of governments, to attain their ends by force, then it may be more sensible to agree peaceably to a result which could otherwise be painfully imposed. How far a government can actually act with such calculating prudence may, however, depend upon factors not wholly predictable or measurable, such as public opinion or the personal vagaries of political leaders.

Still, one ought not to exclude the possibility that diplomacy can be used not to avoid but deliberately to provoke a war. When Bismarck in 1870 released to the press a brusque and provocative version of the Kaiser's Ems telegram reporting his rejection of the French ambassador's demands for a guaranty that Prince Leopold would never renew his candidacy for the Spanish throne, he did so with full knowledge that this would aggravate an already bellicose French government, and as he put it to "wave the red rag before the Gallic bull." More recently it has been asserted by some writers that Franklin D. Roosevelt's diplomatic relations with Japan in the months before Pearl Harbor were deliberately calculated to convince Japan that no settlement satisfactory to it could be achieved without war. We need not

accept this view in order to agree that if the President had wished to provoke war with Japan as a "back door to war" with Germany he could no
doubt have used a frustrating diplomacy to this end.

It also seems proper to include within the term diplomacy large areas of
negotiation about matters which present little or no conflict of national interests but which may to mutual advantage be better organized or regulated.
Diplomatic negotiation to increase international trade through reciprocal tariff
concessions, to regulate international transport or communications facilities,
to provide economic, military, or technical assistance, to arrange defensive
alliances, or to develop international administrative organizations, may seem
to the participating states less a matter of reconciling conflicting interests than
of giving effect to a joint purpose. In this case there may exist no probability
of resort to force as the alternative to agreement; the alternative is simply
a less effective or profitable international relationship.

In modern political society diplomacy is distinctively an instrument of
the governments of national states. What are the implications of this?

First, that diplomats negotiate as agents of legally co-ordinate political
units, seeking to adjust the external relations of these units upon the basis
of bilateral or multilateral agreements. As representatives of governments they
bargain with the representatives of other governments, following instructions
given by their respective governments. They seldom possess discretionary
powers, unless within limits which define a range of solutions acceptable to
their governments. They do not, or at least should not, make policy; rather,
they supply facts needed by policy makers and seek to give effect to policy. To
be effective any agreements reached must engage the responsibility not only
of the diplomatic agents but of the governments they represent, and through
these governments of the states.

Second, that the manner in which diplomacy is conducted by a particular
government may reflect to some extent the peculiarities of that state's political
and economic system. Thus, the diplomacy of a democracy may be less
free to outrun public or legislative opinion than that of a dictatorship and
may be more closely tied to constitutional limitations. The diplomacy of a
state which is economically and territorially satisfied may be less aggressive
and more inclined to meet problems as they arise than that of a state with
unsatisfied aspirations.

Third, that the extent of reliance upon diplomacy tends to be in inverse
ratio to the growth of effective international constitutional or institutional
apparatus. Among independent states international agreement or action depends upon diplomacy. When these states enter into a confederation of weak
central powers of the type exemplified by the Articles of Confederation and
Perpetual Union (1778) among the American colonies or the German Confederation of 1815 the national assembly, although procedurally regulated,

continues to be essentially diplomatic in the sense that representatives of the member states negotiate and the results are not effective without the assent of the states—a kind of institutionalized diplomacy by conference results. More closely integrated federal unions, such as the United States under the Constitution of 1787, or the North German Confederation of 1867 and the German Empire of 1871, exhibit vestigial remains of diplomacy in the form of state representation in upper legislative chambers, but the method of diplomacy has given way to legislation by bodies representing also the whole body politic. Such legislation immediately controls the citizens or authorizes direct action by the federal executive. In like manner national states have entered into international administrative unions for a variety of purposes, and later into more nearly universal international organizations with multiple functions such as the League of Nations or the United Nations. These organizations are at the level of confederation rather than federation, operating through the medium of diplomacy by conference. Action taken is generally no more than a recommendation to member states which can be implemented only by their assent or ratification. In international organization we have yet to pass from diplomacy to legislation. Certain powers of direct action were vested in the U.N. Security Council, but the possibility of exercising them remains subject to diplomatic agreement. A persistent source of weakness in the United Nations has been the failure of state representatives to appreciate their responsibility to negotiate as diplomats. Many are drawn by the illusion of legislative structure to adopt tactics of sharp debate, vituperation, and speeches to their own constituencies.

EVOLUTION OF DIPLOMACY

Greece and Rome

Diplomatic practice among national states today contains elements inherited from Greek and Roman tradition, but the ancient world made no use of permanent diplomatic missions. Rather they sent emissaries upon an *ad hoc* basis to transact particular business. Even in the early Homeric poems we have a pleasant account by Antenor to Helen and King Priam of the mission of Menelaus and Odysseus to the Trojan assembly (*Iliad*, iii, 216–224; trans. from Nicolson, *The Evolution of Diplomatic Method*): ". . . the resourceful Odysseus kept his eyes on the ground when he rose to speak, and held his staff rigidly in his hand, moving it neither to right nor to left, as if he were slow-witted. You would have taken him to be either sulky or stupid. But once you heard that great voice booming from his chest, and when the words fell one after another like snow-flakes on a winter's day, you realized that Odysseus, as an Ambassador, was beyond compare." In republican Rome, and to some extent in the empire, envoys were received by and permitted to address the Senate, and were even provided lodging at the expense of the state in a building called the Graecostasis. Such a form of diplomacy scarcely accords with modern procedures, although under the Articles of Confederation the American Congress as a whole received the French minister, Gerard, who had leave to be present during foreign policy debates and to consult from time to time with the Congress sitting in committee of the whole.

The ancients accepted the rule of safe conduct and protection for diplomats, at least within the receiving state, probably conceiving it in terms of religious sanction. The Athenians and Spartans did put to death ambassadors sent by Darius to demand submission. But the Spartans concluded that they had become objects of divine wrath in consequence of this offense, and sent to Xerxes two distinguished citizens to expiate by their death the killing of the Persians. It is evidence of the universality of the principle that Xerxes declined this offer, considering it beneath him to follow the Spartans in violating the "usages of all mankind."

The modern consular officer, concerned with the protection of nationals or their interests in other countries and with advancement of commercial relations, has a prototype in the Greek *proxenos* (or, when formally commissioned, *etheloproxenos*), a citizen of one city who undertook to represent there the interests of citizens of another city. Such an arrangement was especially required in the law of Greek cities because a resident alien who had come from another city ordinarily had no legal personality unless he were enrolled as attached to a citizen patron.

Although the Romans conducted foreign relations with characteristic regard for system and ceremonial forms, they made no major contributions to diplomatic practice. Probably this was due to the unequal relationship commonly existing between Rome and the states with which she dealt, which led the Romans to impose their own notions of law and protocol as superior to barbarian practice. Yet they made use of formal embassies; had precise categories of instruments for concluding international agreements and for international arrangements of friendship, patronage, and alliance; held nice conceptions of *bona fides* in the observance of commitments; and seldom moved in matters of war or treaty without observing a set of antiquated ritual ceremonies which were the special function of the College of Fetials. Their formalized conceptions of procedure perhaps encouraged occasional resort to fictions which satisfied the forms of justice and propriety with little regard for the substance. It would have offended Roman sensibilities to make war until the *pater patratus* had gone with his fetial entourage to hurl a ceremonial spear of hardened cornel wood into the enemy territory, but these sensibilities were not disturbed by the later designation of a plot of ground before the Temple of Bellona in Rome, which by a fiction served as enemy territory for this purpose.

Medieval Period

To the Romans may be attributed the origins of diplomatic archives, which later became the core of foreign office structures. It was their practice to issue state letters of recommendation, passports, safe conducts, etc., to those authorized to travel upon imperial roads, especially to the provinces. These were called diplomas (from the Greek *diploma*, a letter folded double) because they were originally stamped upon folding metal plates. The term came to be applied generally to official documents granting some favor or privilege or embodying state commitments, and these documents were filed in archives for reference. Hence, it was natural that the term *diplomatics* came later to be applied to the science of identifying and interpreting old documents. In the medieval period such collections of documents bearing upon foreign relations were systematically organized under officers of royal households and in the papal chancery. Clerks were employed who became skillful in their use. In the Carolingian Empire an elaborate chancery was developed under an important official called the "chancellor."

In thirteenth-century England essential foreign relations documents were dispersed in several depositories in the *Chancery, Exchequer,* or *Wardrobe.* To overcome difficulties in the use of documents so dispersed the Council appointed a series of officers called *custos processuum,* or keeper of processes. The *custos* was invariably an expert in diplomatic documents who was trained also in civil law. In fact, he did assemble and study large numbers of documents in preparing for diplomatic missions, then mainly concerned with claims of the Norman kings to French feudal tenures under the Treaty of Paris of 1259. Thus the *custos* as a specialized career servant became an early type of permanent undersecretary and his office a forerunner of the British foreign office.

The *custos processuum* was an officer of the king's household, as were chancellors and keepers of rolls generally throughout the feudal period. Foreign relations were then conducted directly by kings, or kings in council, through such officials. Professional clerks and keepers of records sometimes went upon diplomatic missions, particularly when the issues were technical; at other times clerics, nobles, or knights were used. These missions continued to be special, and no resident embassies were established. Although there are some instances of resident missions at an earlier date, particularly those sent by the pope, it seems to have been the initiative of the Italian city states in the fifteenth century which cleared the way for acceptance of career diplomacy through resident missions. Because of suspicion that these would facilitate spying, the change was accepted grudgingly. As late as 1625 Grotius still asserted the right to refuse reception to resident embassies, although they were then common, as being an unnecessary innovation unknown to ancient custom. Sir Edward Coke says that Henry VII of England refused to receive ledger ambassadors.

As early as the thirteenth century Venice began a series of laws regulating the conduct of its envoys, e.g., the prohibition of 1236 against acceptance from another state of favors or profits, and the regulations of 1268 forbidding wives to accompany ambassadors for fear of gossip, requiring a cook to be taken along as precaution against poisoning, and directing that a written report of each mission be filed within a fortnight after the envoy's return. In the thirteenth and fourteenth centuries Florence began to use distinguished citizens such as Dante, Petrarch, and Boccaccio as envoys, then moved to the more professional type represented by Machiavelli and Guicciardini.

With the spread of resident missions after the fifteenth century career diplomats became a necessity. Francis I of France (1515–1547) was probably the first ruler to organize systematically a diplomatic corps. Although present notions of recruitment and training of career diplomats originated only in the nineteenth century, the whole period of post-Renaissance history witnessed a steady growth of career diplomacy as a profession attractive to men of ability and position.

Italian Renaissance Diplomacy

The conditions of diplomacy among the Italian states of the Renaissance unfortunately produced a tradition of duplicity, cunning, and unscrupulous maneuvering for advantage which has clung to diplomacy. The weakness of these states led to unstable balance of power politics characterized by endless connivance and faithless compacts to gain an illusory security. It is in this context that the writings of the great Florentine, Niccolo Machiavelli, are to be understood. He lacked neither patriotism, humanity, nor idealism. Yet his advice was that in dealing with princes who abuse candor, good faith, or honor, the way to security and stable government lies in unsentimental appraisal of the opponent's qualities and employment without compunction of any means which will checkmate him:

. . . a prudent Prince neither can nor ought to keep his word when it is hurtful to him and the causes which led him to pledge it are removed. If all men were good, this would not be good advice, but since they are dishonest and do not keep faith with you, you, in return, need not keep faith with them; and no prince was ever at a loss for plausible reasons to cloak a breach of faith. . . .

.   .   .

. . . And you are to understand that a Prince, and most of all a new Prince, cannot observe all those rules of conduct in respect whereof men are accounted good, being often forced, in order to preserve his Princedom, to act in opposition to good faith, charity, humanity, and religion. He must therefore keep his mind ready to shift as the winds and tides of Fortune turn, and, as I have already said, he ought not to quit good courses if he can help it, but should know how to follow evil courses if he must. (*The Prince,* ch. xviii).

Such baldly amoral manipulation of power in the national interest is rather appalling. Yet it is due to Machiavelli to admit that he reflected the spirit of diplomacy in his day and that other practitioners before and since have advocated similar principles, among whom may be mentioned Louis XI of France, Thomas Cromwell, and Cardinal Wolsey. Cromwell solicited the services of an agent, Michael Throgmorton, in these words: "You have bleared my eye once; your credit shall nevermore serve you so far, to deceive me the second time. I take you as you are." And Louis XI directed his envoys: "If they lie to you, you lie still more to them." If we have become morally more sensitive in diplomacy perhaps the explanation lies less in the improvement of diplomatic character than in the advance of states in the modern period from the dog-eat-dog compulsions of dynastic ambitions into some sense of European community. The international politics of the present day suggest that there is still need, not for deception and bad faith, but certainly for cool appraisal and unsentimental marshaling of forces.

Even the worst features of Machiavellian tradition have had some later currency, but we need not take as representative of that day the well-known quip of Sir Henry Wotton, jotted in a friend's album about 1604: *"Legatus est vir bonus peregré missus ad mentiendum Reipublicae causâ,"* which, so Isaak Walton tells us (*The Life of Sir Henry Wotton*), "Wotton could have been content should have been thus Englished: 'An Embassador is an honest man, sent to *lie* abroad for the good of his Country.'" The term "lie" was then as commonly used to signify "reside" as "prevaricate," although the intended pun is less apparent in the Latin form. What is really significant in the incident is the reaction of James I, who "apprehended it to be such an oversight, such a weakness, or worse, in Sir Henry Wotton, as caused the King to express much wrath against him." Two formal apologia by Sir Henry were required to restore him to grace.

French Diplomacy

Modern career diplomacy owes more to French than to Italian example. As the slippery Italian diplomacy reflected an unstable political system dominated by autocrats or oligarchs, so French diplomacy since the period of Richelieu reflected the increasing sense of constitutional restraints within the state and orderly standards in external relations. These latter were supported by a new system of international law shaped by a series of great jurists—Gentilis, Grotius, Zouche, Bynkershoek, Vattel. Responsibility and profes-

sional standards entered diplomacy. Cardinal Richelieu followed Machiavelli in conceiving national interest in terms which excluded moral or sentimental considerations, and his diplomacy was sufficiently devious, but he
did insist upon responsibility both in the careful observance by diplomats of
their instructions and in the scrupulous observance by the state of its international undertakings. He saw also the need to align public opinion in support of foreign policy. That his diplomatic practice was deliberately calculated is evident from his words:

> I will boldly say that the service which a regular and unbroken system of
> diplomacy, conducted both in public and in secret in all countries, even where
> no immediate fruit can be gathered, is one of the first necessities for the health
> and welfare of the state. I can say with truth that in my time I have seen the
> face of affairs in France and in Christendom completely changed because under
> the authority of his Majesty I have been enabled to practice this principle which
> till my time had been absolutely neglected by the ministers of this kingdom.

By 1685 the French maintained ten permanent embassies, several special
missions, and five ministers resident. Their diplomatic agents were classified
as ambassadors extraordinary, ambassadors ordinary, envoys, and residents.
Although members of noble families had to be sent to certain capitals for
reasons of prestige, an increasing use of officials was made elsewhere. Written
instructions were carefully drafted, and during the eighteenth century received ever-increasing attention to detail and literary quality. Under Colbert
economic and commercial relations became a significant focus, particularly
in the expansion of the Levant trade, and a corps of consuls was developed
for service there.

In the well-known work of François de Callières, *De la manière de
négocier avec les Souverains* (1716), we have an epitome of the standards
of the French career diplomatist of that day, and with few exceptions they
are the standards of career diplomacy today. Amateur diplomats he considers
dangerous; diplomacy is an expert craft to be practiced by men of the highest
qualities—an observant and cultivated mind, powers of concentration in the
midst of distraction, sound judgment, directness, ability to penetrate the
thoughts and motives of others, presence of mind and adroitness in speech,
an equable humor, a tranquil and patient nature, open and ingratiating manners, self-control and restraint in discussion, avoidance of mystery, courtesy
and nobility of spirit, innate dignity and selflessness, liberality in entertain-
ment, social finesse, personal courage, coolness and firmness in negotiation,
all figure in his list. So do a mastery of European history and polity, and an
easy fluency in French, German, Italian, and Spanish, as well as Latin, then
the *lingua franca* of diplomacy. A distinctive professional training he thought
essential; neither clergy, nor military men, nor lawyers, possessed the special

attitudes and experience required. De Callières was sufficiently the representative of his age to urge well-calculated but tactful gifts, even bribes, and to value the use of spies, but he denounces deceit and bad faith: ". . . a lie always leaves a drop of poison behind, and even the most dazzling diplomatic success gained by dishonesty stands on an insecure foundation, for it awakes in the defeated party a sense of aggravation, a desire for vengeance, and a hatred which must always be a menace to his foe." It is the interest of the diplomat ". . . to establish a reputation for plain and fair dealing so that men may know they can rely upon him; for one negotiation successfully carried through by the honesty and high intelligence of a diplomatist will give him a great advantage in other enterprises on which he embarks in the future; . . . he will be received with esteem and pleasure, and men will say of him and of his master that their cause is too good to be served by evil means . . ." (trans. by A. F. Whyte).

This conception of diplomacy conducted continuously by career men of exceptional competence, endowed within the limits of their instructions with wide discretion and full powers, and enjoying each other's confidence as members of a professional corps, spread throughout Europe and dominated foreign relations until the twentieth century. At its best, in the eighteenth and nineteenth centuries, it settled into a highly professionalized method which attracted practitioners of great competency in all the major states.

It is probable that much of its success stemmed from the fact that the *corps diplomatique,* essentially aristocratic in composition, became an international society with a strong corporate spirit. Career diplomats of long service came to know personally most of the diplomats of other states and in some cases several generations of diplomats of one family. In any given capital they were thrown together socially as much as professionally. Feelings of friendship and camaraderie were inevitable. Furthermore, their society was one very sensitive to niceties in conduct. Patience, serenity, unfailing courtesy were enjoined by all the ablest exponents of the art. In conducting public business a leisurely and formalized system of written communication prevailed. The style used was dignified, deferential, allusive, calculated to convey an intention without offensive expressions. Its nuances were perfectly understood by the initiated. In the nineteenth and twentieth centuries increasing use was made of oral conversations, but careful diplomats commonly prepared a minute of the substance of the talk afterward, and even submitted it on occasion to the other party for correction. These careful, courteous, and urbane relations were well calculated to avoid or to smooth over distressing international incidents, and the diplomatic profession was as a whole dedicated to peace and good relations insofar as permitted by state policy.

One can hardly imagine a diplomat of the old school, such as Malmesbury, Talleyrand, or Metternich permitting such an unfortunate ejaculation as Bethmann-Hollweg's "just for a scrap of paper" (to the British ambassador, August 4, 1914) to escape him, however great his cause for agitation. Much less would he have stooped to the deliberate scurrility and invective with which Vishinsky larded many of his remarks to organs of the United Nations. In Mowat's opinion it was even considered a reflection upon diplomatic competence in the nineteenth century to fail to negotiate a peaceful settlement of a dispute.

MODERN TYPES OF DIPLOMACY

The old diplomacy was in the nineteenth century, and has been increasingly in the twentieth, subjected to influences which have tended to modify it. The most obvious of these have been rapid transport and telecommunications. Until the nineteenth century communications were so slow and uncertain that foreign offices had perforce to rely upon diplomatic *expertise* in the field. It is said that Stratford Canning (later Lord Stratford de Redcliffe), the British minister to Turkey, received from the foreign office between 1810 and 1812 only sixteen despatches, none of which had any direct bearing upon the difficult negotiations in which he was engaged. And Edward Livingston, Secretary of Foreign Affairs under the Articles of Confederation, received no word during a period of eleven months from any of the twelve American agents in Europe. When General Washington requested information, Livingston was obliged to reply that he had none other than that to be found in the public press.

Testimony by Lord Stratford de Redcliffe, Sir A. Buchanan, Lord John Russell, and others to the Parliamentary Select Committee on the Diplomatic Service in 1861, discounted the danger that the telegraph might weaken the sense of responsibility of ministers and pointed to the brevity and frequent inaccuracy of telegraphic messages. But such considerations can hardly be urged today, when detailed instructions can be given by teletype and telephone. Although the advent of telecommunications has not rendered skill or address in negotiation useless, it has certainly enabled foreign office officials to direct even the smallest details of policy in negotiation. The instance of Secretary of State Dean Acheson in his office in Washington listening to a broadcast of the proceedings of the U.N. Security Council and holding open a telephone line so that he could speak directly to the United States delegate on the floor of the Council, presents an extreme example of the possibilities of control. The importance of the individual diplomat's capacities is no longer decisive in respect to decisions to be taken during the course of negotiations, although it may still be very great in the cogency and persuasiveness of presentation.

Personal Diplomacy

A related phenomenon, made possible by the rapidity of modern air transport and telephonic communication, is the increasing frequency of personal diplomacy by political heads of government and of conferences among foreign ministers and other government officials. President Franklin D. Roosevelt appeared to have great confidence in this sort of direct approach, feeling that misunderstandings could be cleared away quickly and agreement reached by direct conversations. If the results sometimes justified this confidence they also illustrated the dangers inherent in the practice. The Leaders' Agreement of Yalta (1945) was expeditiously concluded by Roosevelt, Churchill, and Stalin, with little intervention by diplomats or foreign office experts. But it was so poorly drafted that several clauses present major conflicts in interpretation and it is not even possible to determine from the text whether the agreement is a personal undertaking by three men to attempt to do certain things or an immediate governmental commitment. The terms of the agreement were not known even to the secretary of state, and remained secret for a year. When released, they led to much legislative and public controversy. Apart from the questions of policy involved, which must long be a matter for controversy, it may be fair to remark that the most perfect rapport between political heads of government is not the same as effective communication between governments. The latter involves the cumbersome process of ascertaining that communications are responsibly made and that agreements are not only skillfully drafted to express the sense of the negotiators, but that they express a consensus of governments as well. Deliberation and consultation in determining positions and the use of expert agents in presenting them go far to avoid pitfalls and to secure firm acceptance of the result. Perhaps convivial bonhomie among chiefs of state may hasten agreement, but only at the risk of indiscretion; the prudent policy officer will remain at his desk and in consultation with his political colleagues.

Nor is it easy to justify the frequent journeys from capital to capital of the foreign ministers of great powers since World War I. They sometimes arouse an infinity of distracting press and radio speculation, political tub thumping, and propaganda, apparently only to achieve perfunctory conversations which could hardly reveal any facts not obtainable through resident diplomatic officers. This is not to deny that such direct negotiations may sometimes be necessary in a period of crisis.

Diplomacy by Conference

A second influence which has affected diplomacy is the increasing use of international conferences. In recent years the term "diplomacy by conference" has become common. This cannot be because of any novelty in the method, for significant conferences have been held from time to time ever since the

Congress of Westphalia (1641–1648). Conference techniques had slowly to be worked out, but most of the difficulties which confronted early conferences arose over problems of protocol now long since resolved. It required nearly five years to reach agreement upon safe conducts and meeting places before the Congress of Westphalia could even convene. Because of rival claims to diplomatic precedency, two cities had to be used: the French treated at Münster, the Swedes at Osnabrück, then the two treaties were joined. There was wrangling even over the order of the procession and arrangement of chairs in the church for public prayers which preceded the opening. Then seven months were required to satisfy all parties about the full powers of the delegates. The first propositions advanced were frivolous; only after a year were genuine French demands stated, and subsequent negotiations required two years more. Much of the negotiation proceeded through written communications which mediators carried from one side to the other. Yet the conference did much, if only by demonstrating the absurdities of overemphasis upon precedency, to show the way for more expeditious procedures in later conferences. The great peace conferences of Utrecht (1713–1714), Vienna (1814–1815), Paris (1919), at approximate intervals of one century, each marked stages of increased facility in dealing with ever more complex issues, and set patterns of procedure and protocol. Precedency among diplomats has been settled by the ranks established in 1815 and 1818, and by common-sense rules of alphabetical order and seniority based on length of service at a post. The conference technique has become increasingly flexible.

Yet it would be placing the cart before the horse to assume that the greatly increased use of conferences in the twentieth century resulted from improvement in conference method. Procedural efficiency became necessary because of the increasing use of the method, which itself stems from a number of roots: the multilateral character of many recent problems, e.g., economic and technical assistance or defense arrangements; the progressive integration of the community of states into permanent international organizations which must use the conference technique; the increase of international business at the technical and administrative level, which can be negotiated better by the expert from an executive agency than by the career diplomat; the demand for open diplomacy; the encouragement to frequent conferences from rapid transportation and the possibility of direct control by foreign offices.

It is indicative of the greatly accelerated use of the conference technique that since World War II the United States has regularly participated in hundreds of conferences each year (fiscal year ending in 1946, 171; 1947, 284; 1948, 327; 1949, 269; 1950, 302; 1951, 326; 1952, 318; 1953, 285; 1954, 271). A breakdown of the data for 1954 shows 76 sessions of U.N. organs or agencies (General Assembly and its agencies, 14; Security Council and its agencies, 5; Economic and Social Council and its commissions or committees, 36; Trusteeship Council and its committees, 7; International Court of Justice, 1; other agencies and conferences, 13). The specialized agencies affiliated with the Economic and Social Council held 83 conferences (FAO, 22; International Bank, 1; ICAO, 21; ILO, 11; ITU, 3; UNESCO, 8; UPU, 1; WHO, 6; WMO, 10). Inter-American organizations held 17. Other international organizations accounted for 37, distributed among agencies for international commodities control (cotton, rubber, sugar, tin, wheat), regional organizations (ANZUS Council, Caribbean Commission, North Atlantic Council, South Pacific Commission), unions of scientific associations, and bodies to regulate fisheries, international river traffic, migrations, and reparations. The remaining 58 were mostly *ad hoc* conferences, and extremely varied, including such topics as tariffs and export controls, customs cooperation, distribution of strategic metals, control of commodities (rice, coffee, sulphur), exploration of the sea, pollution of the sea by oil, limnology, commissions of conciliation and inquiry, statistics, inland transport, tonnage measurement, zoology, veterinary science, tropical medicine and malaria, quaternary research, microbiology, agriculture, home economics, African defense facilities, international legal problems of Asian countries, low-cost housing, fairs and expositions, centenary celebrations, film festivals, aviation, and a number of political problems (Bermuda Conference, Four Power Conference at Berlin, Geneva Conference).

Such an enumeration sufficiently indicates the variety of procedural patterns lumped together in the term *diplomacy by conference.* A meeting of chiefs of state with a few advisers as at Potsdam, Yalta, or Teheran is an international conference; so is a session of the U.N. General Assembly, or Security Council, or Human Rights Commission; so also a meeting of foreign ministers in the Geneva Conference on Indochina and Korea, or in more routine planning sessions of the North Atlantic Council, or of postal administrators in the Congress of the Universal Postal Union, or of jurists in the Inter-American Juridical Committee, or of materials experts in the International Tin Study Group. It follows that the advantages and disadvantages of the method will not be applicable equally to all. Private diplomatic conversations can often explore the possibilities of agreement upon sharp political issues with less laceration of feelings or solidifying of opposition in case of failure than a highly publicized conference. On the other hand, the conference method seems appropriate and necessary in the many areas of multilateral concern where there is enough consensus to support administrative agreement and action. This has been true of multilateral tariff bargaining, of commodity agreements, of regulation of transport and communications, of economic and military aid to Europe. It may also be true at the political level within a group of like-minded states, as shown by successful conferences on European and Asian defense, and in regional organization.

Certainly the widespread use of conferences has to be accepted as a fact of international life to which a deliberate adjustment of diplomatic machinery must be made. But conferences function properly only in alliance with traditional diplomacy. Few succeed unless there has been careful planning and exchange of views through ordinary channels, so that possible lines of agreement are predictable. Conference methods are particularly efficient when coupled with standing secretariats which can lay the groundwork by preliminary studies and exchanges of views. Such arrangements are of course characteristic of international organizations. It would seem also that a new type of negotiator or negotiating team must be developed in which persuasive exposition combines with expert command of subject matter which is often technical. In the give and take of the conference it is not always possible to take time for mature reflection and consultation; therefore, position papers have to be carefully prepared in advance with an eye to all possible alternatives, and the negotiator must develop some of the skills associated with legislative committee work and debate. Finally, it seems imperative that a rational approach to publicity be made which will secure the public interest in the proceedings without subjecting negotiators to pressures which would limit flexibility of action. For this reason public opinion needs to adjust itself to the necessity for occasional closed conferences.

Popular Diplomacy

A final influence which affects modern diplomacy has been the drift toward what has been called popular or democratic diplomacy. This is frequently associated with the first of President Wilson's Fourteen Points (1918): "Open covenants of peace, openly arrived at, after which there shall be no private international understandings of any kind, but diplomacy shall proceed always frankly and in the public view." Wilson found it impossible to follow the principle of open negotiation at the Paris Peace Conference. No doubt he always realized the limitations of such a method, for he advised the Senate, "When I pronounced for open diplomacy, I meant, not that there should be no private discussions of delicate matters, but that no secret agreements should be entered into, and that international relations, when fixed, should be open, above-board, and explicit." He was protesting against the evils of secret commitments, which were still to plague the Paris Conference, and pointing toward an international community founded upon popular approval and assent.

To speak of popular or democratic diplomacy is in fact to confuse terms, for insofar as diplomacy is concerned with negotiation it is physically impossible to conduct it by popular action. What is really meant is the demand for popular control of foreign policy, but even this has serious implications for the conduct of diplomacy. It has given rise to popular suspicion of the professional diplomat and of the traditional amenities of career diplomacy, which in the United States has led to arbitrary interferences with and investigations of the career service by elected officers. It has encouraged political leaders to undertake negotiations formerly assigned to diplomats and to conduct them in the full spotlight of publicity. It has led foreign ministers increasingly to heed the vagaries of public opinion and either to adjust policy to it or to undertake time-consuming propaganda efforts to change it. It accounts in part for the recent predilection of foreign ministers for open conference diplomacy in which they sometimes can deliver policy statements or abusive criticisms of the policy of other states, designed to please their own publics rather than to facilitate international agreement.

These disturbing tendencies result in part from a natural inclination of uninformed citizens to blame the old diplomacy for the failure to avert the two world wars. They fail to realize that there was at that time an abandonment of that diplomacy, with its principles of rational accommodation and compromise to maintain a political equilibrium. The political leaders of Germany, France, and Russia before World War I were already caught up in popular national aspirations which limited their freedom of action. England might perhaps have been able to steady the equilibrium by calculated balance of power diplomacy, but Grey temporized until it was too late. The passions let loose by the war determined the vindictive character of the peace, which in a time of immense dislocation provided an argument for Hitlerism. Again, there may have been opportunities for postwar adjustments in the interest of stability or for firm restraint of the territorial aspirations of dictators before the resurgence of German power, but the missing of these opportunities reflected closely the bondage of statesmanship to a vacillating and uncertain public opinion.

No one would question that representative government implies the right of the people through their elected representatives to determine foreign policy. It follows that policy issues should be publicly discussed and that information necessary for such discussion should be available to the public. But it does not follow that a responsible government should abdicate its responsibility to make decisions, or hang upon every turn of public attitude, or make the conduct of its international negotiations a subject of public knowledge, irresponsible discussion, and emotional reactions. That we have drifted so far in these directions may be partly the result of cold war, in which the weapon of propaganda dominates and no sincere desire for accommodation exists. Nevertheless, the consequences of releasing and stimulating popular fears and passions have been very destructive of rational diplomacy and make even the smallest adjustments increasingly difficult.

DIPLOMACY AND THE BALANCE OF POWER

It is sometimes suggested that the old diplomacy was by its characteristics peculiarly adapted to be the instrument of balance of power policies, and that the collective security principle is sharply at variance with balance of power principles and associated with open diplomacy. Among the "Four Principles" which Woodrow Wilson formulated in his speech of February 11, 1918, as a philosophy underlying the more detailed prescriptions in the Fourteen Points, was the following:

2. Peoples and provinces are not to be bartered about from sovereignty to sovereignty as if they were mere chattels in a game, even the great game, now forever discredited, of the Balance of Power.

Instead, territorial settlements were to be made upon the basis of national self-determination. And in the "Five Particulars," of September 27, 1918, Wilson emphasized that there should be ". . . no leagues or alliances or special covenants and understandings within the general and common family of the League of Nations," nor any ". . . special selfish economic combinations within the League . . . [or] employment of any form of economic boycott or exclusion," except as a collective security sanction—that is, that balance of power maneuvering should not be removed from general diplomacy only to be brought within the diplomatic forum of the League of Nations. In conformity with these views many sincere advocates of collective security have tended to think of it as a revolt against "power politics" and to equate balance of power diplomacy with selfish and predatory foreign policies. The student should avoid such facile generalizations until he has considered some of the implications of the history of balance of power outlined in the chapter on force.

At once a semantic difficulty appears. There are nearly as many meanings of the phrase "balance of power" as there are writers upon the subject. In a useful review of the literature Ernst B. Haas has distinguished eight primary uses of the phrase, and has further described four different types of intention which may motivate those who use it. There are even those who, like Cobden, deny that the term has any meaning at all:

The balance of power is a chimera: It is not a fallacy, a mistake, an imposture—it is an undescribed, indescribable, incomprehensible nothing; mere words, conveying to the mind not ideas but sounds, like those equally barren syllables which our ancestors put together for the purpose of puzzling themselves about words . . .

Sometimes the phrase is used in a descriptive rather than a policy sense, either as a synonym for power politics generally, or as a term for distribution of power. In the latter sense it may bear a pleasant connotation when applied to a distribution supposed to be in the interest of stability, an unpleasant one when applied to shifting, unstable distributions. There are also those who conceive of balance of power as a universal law of history or politics. Here the implication is that a kind of natural law of political behavior first constrains states lacking in material resources, or galled by treaty restrictions, or responding to internal drives toward imperialism, to adopt aggressive tactics against their neighbors. The latter are then driven to use balance of power diplomacy to check the revisionist or expansionist states and fall naturally into the usual patterns—treaty guaranties of boundaries, defensive alliances, interventions, compensations to offset gains by rival states (e.g., acceptance by Austria of part of Poland, not because she favored partition, but because a unilateral land grab by Prussia would disturb the balance; also the division of Africa by the powers in the nineteenth century). There may certainly be something in this, but it seems a little pretentious to talk in terms of universal laws when we are only upon the threshold of scientific study of political behavior. The extremely varied evidence of history scarcely enables us to spell out the detailed workings of the principle with any confidence.

In terms of policy it is sufficient for the present discussion to distinguish two purposes: (1) balance of power in the sense of an equilibrium within a community of states deliberately sought by combinations designed to check undue aggrandizement of any one state or coalition of states; (2) balance of power in the sense of hegemony sought by a deliberate effort to tip the balance in one's own favor.

The second sense is no doubt an etymological perversion of "balance," which should mean "equilibrium," and it may be a political perversion of the policy. This could certainly be said of the cynical attitude of Frederick the Great when after seizing Silesia from Austria with the help of France he treacherously concluded a separate peace at Breslau (1742), leaving the French committed in untenable positions in Bohemia and Austria, from which they extricated themselves with the greatest difficulty. "Prudence seemed to require he should hold a middle line of conduct, by which he might establish an equilibrium between the houses of Hapsburg and Bourbon." Aggressors can be expected to explain themselves as defenders of equilibrium, just as war is generally waged in the name of peace.

But a more serious difficulty lies in the capacity of states to delude themselves into supposing their policies are merely defensive when in fact they upset equilibrium. As Nicholas J. Spykman said:

> There are not many instances in history which show great and powerful states creating alliances and organizations to limit their own strength. . . . The truth of the matter is that states are interested only in a balance which is in their favor. Not an equilibrium, but a generous margin. . . . Whatever the theory and the rationalization the practical objective is the constant improvement of the state's own relative power position. The balance desired is the one which

neutralizes other states, leaving the home state free to be the deciding force and the deciding voice. (*America's Strategy in World Politics*)

It would be more generous to conclude that these unhappy results sometimes occur not because statesmen are universally cynical and do one thing while they say another but because they cannot accurately assess power or measure political equilibrium and are therefore prone to err on the side of that supposed margin of safety which really continues imbalance.

Despite these difficulties, which ought not to be minimized, history is full of testimonies to altruistic intent in balance of power policies. The classic statements of the principle in terms of preserving equilibrium express it not as a policy of individual jockeying for position but as a principle of public order in the general interest. "The interest of France and of the whole of Europe is involved," said Richelieu in 1624; "the union of the separated states of the house of Austria outbalances the power of France, which secures the liberty of Christianity." In the reign of that great disturber of European equilibrium, Louis XIV of France, Fénelon wrote:

To hinder one's neighbor from becoming too strong is not to do harm, it is to guarantee one's self and one's neighbors from subjection; in a word, it is to work for liberty, tranquillity, and public safety; . . . excessive aggrandizement of one may mean the ruin and subjection of all the other neighbors . . . This attention to the maintenance of a kind of equality and equilibrium between neighboring states is what assures peace for all.

Even more significant are the peace settlements of Westphalia (1648), Utrecht (1713), and Vienna (1815), which sought to restore and guarantee equilibrium after long periods of disturbance to the balance of power. Their provisions clearly conceive of European equilibrium as a principle of public law collectively affirmed.

The territorial arrangements of the Peace of Westphalia were a conscious adjustment of the balance of power designed to permit continuation of the contending states in a variable form. Use of the combined force of all the signatories was guaranteed against any state which violated these arrangements and persisted in aggression for a space of three years although exhorted by its victim "not to come to any Hostility, . . . [but to submit] the Cause to a friendly Composition, or the ordinary Proceedings of Justice." (Treaty of Münster, Arts. 123, 124.)

The framers of the Treaty of Utrecht expressly stated that the division of Spanish lands between Hapsburg and Bourbon was made "to preserve equilibrium in Europe." Even before Utrecht there had been a convention between England and the States-General (1711), whereby the parties, in contemplation of peace, engaged to enforce the settlement. In the event that an infraction could not be prevented or a dispute over construction of terms amicably resolved within two months, they agreed that "the common forces of the Confederates who shall subscribe this convention, shall be united together, and such a number sent to act either by sea or land against the disturber, whosoever he be, as the greatness of the danger shall require, till satisfaction be made to the party injured, and until there be an entire prospect or provision for renewing and securing the publick peace and tranquility."

These treaties of guaranty appear to rest upon a philosophy of live and let live and to pose equilibrium as the principle of action. A further step toward joint action was taken at the Congress of Vienna, where Europe was resettled after the Napoleonic wars by the creation of the European Concert. Great Britain, Austria, Prussia, and Russia allied themselves in 1815 (Quadruple Alliance) to see that stipulations of the treaty should be fully observed, but further "agreed to renew their Meetings at fixed periods, either under the immediate auspices of the Sovereigns themselves, or by their respective Ministers, for the purpose of consulting upon their common interests, and for the consideration of the measures which at each of those periods shall be considered the most salutary for the repose and prosperity of Nations, and for the maintenance of the Peace of Europe." This arrangement, to which France became a party at Aix-la-Chapelle in 1818 (Quintuple Alliance), created no permanent machinery, but the obligation to consult did supply a framework for concerted action. It was indeed the initiation of conference diplomacy, which is thus seen to have been associated at the outset with the principle of equilibrium.

In the minds of the public the Concert was also associated with the Holy Alliance, which, however, was a separate treaty whereby sovereigns accepted the Tsar Alexander's pietistic proposal to regulate both foreign and domestic polity according to the tenets of Christianity. A more realistic association might connect the Quintuple Alliance with conservative and legitimist policies, for Metternich and the Tsar sought to use the system of consultation to authorize interventions against disturbances of the status quo. This interpretation of the Alliance was, however, resisted by Great Britain. She succeeded in blocking in 1815 the Tsar's proposal to guarantee the throne of Louis XVIII, and in 1818 his demand for a treaty guaranteeing all thrones and frontiers of Europe. When the eastern powers at Troppau and Laibach (1820, 1821) asserted the right of the Alliance to repress revolutions, Castlereagh protested.

In practice, however, the continental powers did win their point in several incidents, including the suppression by Austria, as agent of the Alliance, of revolutions in Naples and Piedmont (1820), and the authorization to France to intervene in the Spanish revolution (1822). Great Britain opposed these interventions and then blocked support for Spain in the revolutions of her American colonies. She also stimulated announcement by the United States of that part of the Monroe Doctrine which declares against extension to

America of interventions by the European Concert. "It is impossible," said Monroe, "that the allied Powers should extend their political system to any portion of either [American] continent without endangering our peace and happiness; . . . It is equally impossible therefore that we should behold such interposition with indifference." Canning, as the instigator of the British-American position could say with justice, "I called the new world into existence to redress the balance of the old." Great Britain withdrew from the Quintuple Alliance and thereafter pursued for years an individual policy.

During the century about twenty important conferences were held, in many of which England participated. Probably the Concert had its greatest success in dealing with Near Eastern disturbances. It localized the Serbian-Bulgarian war of 1885, the Cretan War of 1897, the Balkan wars of 1912–1913. It intervened also to quiet disorder in parts of the decadent Ottoman Empire, e.g., Egypt, yet failed to prevent the Crimean War in 1854 or the Russo-Turkish War of 1877, although Turkey had itself been "admitted to participate in the advantages of the public law and system (*concert*) of Europe" by the Treaty of Paris (1856). The powers did intervene on Turkey's behalf at the Congress of Berlin in 1878 to rewrite the Russian-dictated Treaty of San Stefano.

Nor was the success of the Concert in Europe remarkable. It was effective in protecting Portugal from Spain in 1826, in guaranteeing Belgian neutrality in 1830, and in securing the neutralization of Luxembourg in 1867. But it did nothing to prevent France's annexation of Nice and Savoy in 1860 as the price of its consent to unification of the north-central Italian states with Sardinia, nor could it prevent Bismarck's successful wars against Denmark in 1864 (annexation of Schleswig-Holstein), against Austria in 1866 (creation of the North German Confederation, excluding Austria), and against France in 1870 (cession of Alsace-Lorraine; creation of the German Empire).

The changes which occurred during the century in the power structure were extraordinary. The German Empire under Prussian hegemony, and the Kingdom of Italy, had emerged in response to a unifying surge of nationalism. That same nationalism tended to weaken polyglot empires like Austria, Turkey, and Russia. In America the United States and in Asia Japan became new powers in a system which had burst the confines of Europe. Finally, the last great wave of European imperialism brought the powers into conflict in Africa and Asia. The arena was expanding and a new world balance of power was clearly in the making. To cope with these problems was beyond the competence of the European Concert although it attempted in some measure until World War I to find solutions for a continuing series of disturbances. Meanwhile Europe moved into a fresh alignment of strength in the Triple Alliance of Germany, Austria, and Italy (1882), and the Triple Entente of France, Russia, and Great Britain (1907). The desire for a balance continued, but the alliance system lacked flexibility to adjust to the great pressures upon European equilibrium. By drifting into rival armed camps the powers committed themselves to involvement in the mistakes of others and thus to a great war which none really wanted. In the alliance system they lost the principle of equilibrium upon which the Concert was based.

We have not emerged from this difficulty. To be sure we can think no longer in terms of European equilibrium or the Concert of Europe; we have moved on to a world stage. Indeed, Western Europe almost ceased after World War II even to be a factor in the world balance of power, so complete was European collapse. One could almost say with Pope:

> Now Europe's balanced; neither side prevails,
> For nothing's left in either of the scales.

But the principle of equilibrium had passed into institutional forms first in the League of Nations, then in the United Nations. Each was developed as a form of conference diplomacy designed to maintain world equilibrium in an improved sense—i.e., not simply the status quo but a status adjusted through peaceful change. On the other hand, the power struggle continues, and with it the alliance systems. To date the modest successes of the League and the United Nations in adjusting disputes have scarcely touched the issues between the great powers upon which the uneasy balance depends.

What can be said of the relation of diplomacy to these historical events? As between those who speak disparagingly of the balance of power—"forever discredited"—and those who see in it either a law of politics or a guide to sound policy, there seems to be mainly a difference of formulation. Where President Wilson denounces the "bartering of peoples" in the name of balance of power, another might conceive this was taking the name in vain. If equilibrium within a system of states be the goal, this carries no implication of violence to self-determination. Nor does the association of the "old diplomacy" with balance of power policy suggest that it was simply a tool for the aggrandizement of greedy dynasties. It was that diplomacy which first formulated balance of power principles in terms of European equilibrium and stability, which sought security for this equilibrium in treaty guaranties, which placed conference diplomacy and consultative action at the service of the same principle. If some of its products were less commendable, we need not be surprised, for diplomacy is at best an instrument and cannot be more enlightened than those who employ it. But thinking of the expressed objects of the Treaty of Münster—not to permit any signatory ". . . to pursue his rights by force and arms; but if any difference has happen'd or happens for the future, every one shall try the means of ordinary justice, and the contravenor shall be regarded as an infringer of the peace. . . ." (Art. 124)—we may wonder whether the objects of enlightened diplomacy in 1648 were really inferior to our own.

SELECTED READING

BERNARD, MOUNTAGUE, *Four Lectures on Subjects Connected with Diplomacy.* London: Macmillan and Company, Ltd., 1868.

CALLIÈRES, FRANÇOIS DE, *De la manière de négocier avec les souverains* (1716), trans. by A. F. Whyte as *The Practice of Diplomacy.* London: Constable and Company, Ltd., 1919.

CAMBON, JULES M., *The Diplomatist.* London: P. Allan, 1931. (Trans. of *Le Diplomate.* Paris: Hachette, 1926).

CUTTINO, G. P., *English Diplomatic Administration.* New York: Oxford University Press, 1940.

HAAS, ERNST B., "The Balance of Power: Prescription, Concept, or Propaganda?" in *World Affairs,* V: 442–477 (July 1953).

HEATLEY, D. P., *Diplomacy and the Study of International Relations.* Oxford: Clarendon Press, 1919.

JUSSERAND, J. J., *The School for Ambassadors and Other Essays.* New York: G. P. Putnam's Sons, 1925. Title essay, pp. 3–61.

MACHIAVELLI, NICCOLO, *The Prince* (trans. by Vivian Hill Thomson), 3d ed., Oxford: Clarendon Press, 1913.

MATTINGLY, GARRETT, *Renaissance Diplomacy.* Boston: Houghton Mifflin Company, 1955.

MOWAT, R. B., *Diplomacy and Peace.* New York: Robert M. McBride and Company, 1936.

———, *The European States System.* London: Oxford University Press, 1923.

NICOLSON, HAROLD, *Diplomacy,* 2d ed. London: Oxford University Press, 1950 (Home University Library).

———, *The Evolution of Diplomatic Method* (Chichele Lectures, University of Oxford, November 1953). London: Constable and Company, Ltd., 1954.

PONSONBY, ARTHUR, *Democracy and Diplomacy.* London: Methuen and Company, Ltd., 1915.

REINSCH, PAUL S., *Secret Diplomacy: How Far Can It Be Eliminated?* New York: Harcourt, Brace and Company, 1922.

VANSITTART, LORD, "The Decline of Diplomacy" in *Foreign Affairs,* 28 (2): 177–188 (January 1950).

WEBSTER, SIR CHARLES, *The Art and Practice of Diplomacy.* London: London School of Economics and Political Science, 1952. Reprinted in *American Foreign Service Journal,* 29 (11): 16 (November 1952).

CHAPTER 12

FORMATION AND CONTROL OF FOREIGN POLICY

An important and often perplexing factor which affects a state's conduct of its external relations is the character of its governmental institutions for this purpose, and the position of those institutions in its general social apparatus for determining and effecting public policy. Even if one can assume that the "national interest" of a state is upon some point perfectly clear, it may happen that its government is so organized that it cannot promptly set into motion foreign policies reasonably designed to secure that interest. Whether it can or not may depend upon the interplay of many agencies—public opinion, political parties, interest groups, bureaucratic influence, distribution of powers among governmental agencies, systems of legislative representation, executive-legislative relations, administrative facilities, and others. A skillful estimate of the probable international behavior of other governments always involves a detailed knowledge of the institutional framework and political forces within that state so that a study of comparative government becomes essential to the practical conduct of international relations. Diplomatic reporting is regularly concerned with analysis of foreign political systems. It is because of its inability to take such factors into account that the general public often feels frustrated by what seems to it the persistent obtuseness of other countries.

The problems to be considered must here be dealt with very briefly. They fall under three general captions: (1) the formation and control of foreign policy; (2) domestic administration of foreign affairs; (3) external administration and foreign service. The first will be considered in this chapter, the second and third in the succeeding chapter.

THE UNITED STATES

Only a partial understanding of the formation and control of American foreign policy can be gained from examination of formal governmental institutions. To a quite remarkable degree the system is diffused and incoherent, depending heavily upon informal processes and extragovernmental elements for integration. The formal institutions and processes of representative government are in themselves significant, but their functioning is intelligible only within this larger framework.

An examination of the Constitution of the United States suggests at once that the conduct of foreign affairs is an exclusive preserve of the national government, for not only are all enumerated powers in the field of foreign relations allocated to agencies of the national government, but also Article I, Section 10, specifically forbids states to enter into treaties, alliances, or confederations, or without consent of Congress to make agreements or compacts with foreign powers, to grant letters of marque and reprisal or keep troops or warships in time of peace, to issue money or currency, or to levy duties on imports or exports. Thus control of the important areas of war, foreign trade, and international agreements is effectively foreclosed to the states.

The enumerated powers nowhere vest the control of foreign affairs as such in any single agency. The "executive power" is indeed vested in the President, and it might have been argued in 1787 that foreign relations were traditionally regarded as within the executive power. However, the Congress is given a significant share in their control. The President is made commander in chief of the armed forces and hence may direct their operations, but these forces are only such as the Congress is willing to provide and maintain. War may be declared only by the Congress, a power of diminishing value in an age in which wars are often fought without declaration. President Truman felt that the obligations of the United States under the U.N. Charter were a sufficient authority for a major armed intervention in Korea without a declaration of war, and a survey by two Senate committees in 1951 disclosed "at least 125 incidents in which the President, without congressional authorization, and in the absence of a declaration of war, has ordered the Armed Forces to take action or maintain positions abroad." Perhaps the injunction may be understood thus: wars may often be fought without declaration, but if there be a declaration, Congress must make it. Nevertheless, congressional jealousy of its prerogative led to the careful phrasing of the North Atlantic Treaty, in which the only obligation undertaken by each signatory in the event of armed attack upon another signatory is to take "such action as it deems necessary, including the use of armed force"; and similarly of the Southeast Asia Collective Defense Treaty and other Asian defense pacts, in which the undertaking is "to meet the common danger in accordance with its constitutional processes." This avoidance of any advance commitment to use armed forces in defense of allies was hardly required by the Constitution, but was necessary to satisfy senatorial opinion.

The President is authorized to nominate, and with the advice and consent of the Senate to appoint, officers, including "ambassadors, other public ministers and consuls"; also to receive the ambassadors or public ministers accredited to the United States by other governments. From these powers and the inferred power of presidential removal of most officers, coupled of course with the general executive power, stem the President's control of the administration of foreign affairs. Since the President chooses, directs, and may remove from office the policy officers, higher administrators, and overseas agents, he is placed in effective control of the executive machinery for communicating or negotiating with other governments. Mr. Justice Sutherland, speaking for the Supreme Court, referred to the power in this way (United States *v*. Curtiss-Wright Export Corporation, 299 U.S. 304 [1936]):

   . . . In this vast external realm, with its important, complicated, delicate and manifold problems, the President alone has the power to speak or listen as a representative of the nation. He *makes* treaties with the advice and consent of the Senate; but he alone negotiates. Into the field of negotiation the Senate cannot intrude; and Congress itself is powerless to invade it. . . . We are here dealing . . . with . . . the very delicate, plenary and exclusive power of the President as the sole organ of the federal government in the field of international relations—a power which does not require as a basis for its exercise an act of Congress, but which, of course, like every other governmental power, must be exercised in subordination to the applicable provisions of the Constitution. It is quite apparent that if, in the maintenance of our international relations, embarrassment—perhaps serious embarrassment—is to be avoided and success for our aims achieved, congressional legislation which is to be made effective through negotiation and inquiry within the international field must often accord to the President a degree of discretion and freedom from statutory restriction which would not be admissible were domestic affairs alone involved. Moreover, he, not Congress, has the better opportunity of knowing the conditions which prevail in foreign countries, and especially is this true in time of war. He has his confidential sources of information. He has his agents in the form of diplomatic, consular, and other officials. Secrecy in respect of information gathered by them may be highly necessary, and the premature disclosure of it productive of harmful results. . . .

   If the President and his agents serve as eyes, ears, and mouthpiece of the government in its international transactions, it, of course, follows that the President may greatly influence the course of these transactions, for he acts as an independently elected officer vested with executive authority. The extent to which he is in practice free to decide, of course, is subject to normal political forces and the interplay of legislative and presidential powers in what is called a system of checks and balances. The checks are more apparent than the balances. The President might decide that the national interest required military intervention in a trouble spot. He possesses the legal competency to determine the facts through his agents, to decide what to do, to assure other governments that the United States will intervene, even to set armed forces in motion. Yet his freedom of action is limited, for he must rely upon congressional appropriations to support such a military enterprise and must therefore assure himself of congressional agreement with the policy. He must also correctly estimate public support or risk the political fortunes of himself and his party. Although President Eisenhower considered the advisability of armed intervention in Indochina, he carefully disclaimed any intent to use his executive discretion in this matter. In fact he had been forced into this position by the vigor of his party's attack upon President Truman's Korean intervention. Similarly, it would be wholly within the legal competency of the President to recognize a new government by sending and receiving diplomatic agents or by a diplomatic note. But no one supposes that such a controversial issue as recognition of Communist China will be decided without full consultation of congressional leaders, or that the Executive could, in a practical political sense, now recognize that government in the face of known congressional opposition.

The treaty power poses one of the most difficult problems of executive-legislative relationship. We learn from the Constitution that treaties made under authority of the United States are part of the supreme law of the land, and that they are made by the President, although he cannot ratify them until he has obtained the advice and consent of the Senate, two thirds of the Senators present concurring (Const., Art. VI, Section 2; Art. II, Sec. 2, Clause 2). Perhaps the "advice" of the Senate was intended to suggest a consultative function of that body during the process of negotiation, but the unhappy experiences of George Washington in trying to consult orally with a body which insisted upon using a legislative process to determine its answers put an early stop to this conception. Mr. Washington was reported to have said, on leaving the Senate chamber, that he would "be damned" if he ever came there again. Apart from informal consultation with Senate leaders, and occasional use of legislators as negotiators, the Senate has now to await submission of the draft treaty, and confines its advices to suggesting amendments of the text or reservations in the nature of qualifying interpretations, upon which it conditions its consent to ratification.

Even so, its influence in treaty making is often decisive. It may reject the executive's work altogether or insist upon significant (occasionally quite unacceptable) changes. It may unconscionably delay its assent. Thus, the Isle of Pines treaty languished upward of twenty years in the Senate, and was itself once called up by Senator Borah in the Foreign Relations Committee as a means of delaying consideration of adherence to the Statute and Protocol of the Permanent Court of International Justice. The defeat of the Versailles Treaty is a well-known example of a Senate check to executive policy. Indeed, some executive officers have come to regard the Senate's attitude toward treaties as characteristically obstructive. "A treaty entering into the Senate is like a bull going into the arena," said Secretary of State John Hay. "No one can say just how or when the final blow will fall. But one thing is certain— it never will leave the arena alive." The truth is that the Senate acquired this reputation by killing a few treaties of great political significance, but in fact has approved without change over 70 percent of all treaties submitted, required amendments (frequently to the benefit of the treaty) in only 16 percent of the cases, and by rejection or delay has blocked only 10 percent. A good deal has been accomplished in recent years to avoid sharp conflict between the President and the Senate by inviting greater senatorial participation at the negotiating stage.

The President has also the option of resorting to executive agreements rather than treaties. The former are referred to only obliquely in the Constitution. If they were once thought appropriate only for temporary or minor administrative agreements, it cannot be said that recent practice shows any clear differentiation of treaties and executive agreements upon the basis of subject matter. Use of them has increased surprisingly, both absolutely and relatively to the use of treaties (1789–1839, 60 treaties, 27 executive agreements; 1839–1889, 215 treaties, 238 executive agreements; 1889–1939, 524 treaties, 917 executive agreements; 1940–1950, about 80 treaties, 1107 executive agreements). Such important matters as the German and Japanese surrenders (1945); the Atlantic Charter (1941); the Moscow (1943), Teheran (1943) and Yalta (1945) Agreements; the Rush-Bagot Agreement (1817); the Boxer Rebellion Protocol (1900); the Open Door in China (1899–1900); the Gentlemen's Agreement concerning Japanese immigration (1907); the Lansing-Ishii Agreement (1917); the recognition of the Soviet government (1933); the annexation of Texas and Hawaii; numerous reciprocal trade agreements and wartime Lend-Lease agreements; economic aid, military assistance, and technical assistance agreements; international aviation, transport, and communications agreements; have all been arranged by executive agreement rather than treaty.

Some have concluded this is a deliberate by-pass of the use of treaties to avoid the necessity of obtaining Senate consent to ratification. But the facts hardly support this assumption. Although the President can conclude executive agreements without consulting Congress, he seldom does so except in the case of wartime military arrangements. Many agreements are made under prior legislative authorization, e.g., the reciprocal trade agreements, agreements for health and sanitation aid to American states under the program of the Institute of Inter-American Cooperation, technical assistance agreements, economic aid programs, international postal agreements. Others provide implementing regulations to carry out a policy agreed upon by treaty, e.g., the air transport agreements supplementary to the International Civil Aviation Agreement signed at Chicago in 1944, and the military assistance agreements with NATO countries. Even when Congress gives no advance authorization, it often shows approval of executive agreements by subsequent resolution or by voting appropriations to carry out the agreements. It has recently been estimated that about 95 percent of all executive agreements obtain congressional authorization or assent in some manner. If the accelerated use of executive agreements is not a means of by-passing the Senate, what then is the explanation? It lies in the vast increase in international relationships at a level requiring detailed administrative regulation. These are much more appropriately and flexibly managed by executive agreement than by treaty.

Recently, Senator John W. Bricker and others have made persistent efforts to obtain an amendment of the Constitution which would prohibit treaties inconsistent with or not pursuant to the Constitution, and would stipulate that no treaty or executive agreement could take effect as internal law in the United States unless given effect by legislation valid in the absence of the treaty. To the first of these propositions there is no objection in principle, but most constitutional lawyers agree that it is superfluous as a mere restatement in rather unsatisfactory form of existing law. Although the supremacy clause of the Constitution includes within the supreme law of the land statutes made in pursuance of the Constitution, but treaties when made under the authority of the United States, the distinction was made only to avoid the implication that treaties made before the Constitution (e.g., the peace treaty with England) would be excluded. The Supreme Court has repeatedly declared that treaties inconsistent with the Constitution will be held void. The second proposal involves a change of much significance and no merit. Our government could hardly make treaties affecting individuals unless it could carry them out in internal law. If this can be done only by a statute valid in the absence of the treaty, it would mean that the treaty could not be given effect by Congress unless it dealt with subjects within the enumerated legislative powers delegated to Congress. A treaty affecting the reserved powers of the states, for example, a treaty giving aliens the right to acquire property or engage in business within a state, or one allowing extradition of offenders then within state jurisdiction, or an atomic control agreement involving inspection and control of local production, could be given effect as internal law only by the individual legislative action of the forty-eight states—a most improbable event. The present system, in which treaties may deal with reserved power subjects when they affect foreign relations but presumably not when they are of exclusively local interest, seems preferable. Apparently the substantial support which Senator Bricker's proposals have gained in Congress reflects some failure to appreciate the practical effect of the plan and an exaggerated fear that treaties will be used to allow international agencies to encroach upon domestic jurisdiction.

The constitutional arrangements thus far discussed may suggest that the division of foreign relations powers between executive and legislative branches, and the constitutional checks each may apply to the other, provide little basis for an integrated foreign policy program. There is a measure of truth in this, for the integrating elements must be sought outside the constitutional framework and processes. They are not built into the formal institutions of government, nor do they operate automatically. Some conscious effort must be made by executive officers and congressmen to meet each other halfway if there is to be harmonious development of foreign policy. Conversely, if there is basic disagreement between executive and legislative branches about policy, the means are at hand for them to exhaust each other in fruitless bickering and obstruction. In recent years there have been some remarkable examples of deliberate collaboration and carefully cultivated consultation, as in the legislative action on UNRRA, the U.N. Charter, and the European Recovery Program. On the other hand the relations between executive officers and Congress with respect to Asian policy have been marked by suspicion, backbiting, and heckling investigations. Congress even tried by voting unwanted appropriations to impose its view of economic and military aid policy upon the President.

As a chief executive of large powers, elected by the people, and usually acknowledged as leader of one of the two major political parties, the President has thrust upon him the responsibility for administration leadership. Therefore, he must frame a legislative program and seek congressional support for it. If his party enjoys a secure legislative majority, his task will be greatly facilitated by use of the machinery of party control which functions in both houses of Congress, although more effectively in the House of Representatives than in the Senate. When party strength is narrowly divided in one or both houses, as has happened in recent years, the administration must seek support for its program in both parties. In the field of foreign policy this is generally less difficult than in domestic, for some feeling of bipartisanship prevails; in a period of continuous crisis Congress may unite in "stopping partisan politics at the water's edge." It would be a little naive, however, to attribute bipartisanship wholly to patriotic sentiment. It is, after all, the interest of the administration to secure as many votes from the opposition as possible by wooing its more sympathetic leaders, and calling the resulting coalition bipartisanship. Not many instances can be cited in which the bipartisan base was obtained by deliberately compromising the administration program. Even more significant, however, is the fact that American political parties are not traditionally aligned so as to divide upon foreign policy issues, nor have such issues until the last quarter century often dominated national elections. Both parties are loose conglomerations of every sort of economic and social interest, formed upon a basis of varied local groups which move within the national party with a minimum of central discipline or conformity. Members of the Congress come up through local politics and generally find it more profitable to take their stand upon issues of particular interest to their own communities or states. Such issues may certainly involve foreign affairs but as often do not. It is only in the case of the President and Vice President that elections may with some consistency take account of national foreign policy issues, and even there these have sometimes been avoided by agreement of the candidates in the name of bipartisanship. Consequently, it is not surprising that party divisions in Congress afford no clear indication of division upon foreign policy legislation and that other combinations can be made under so pleasant a caption as bipartisanship without disturbing party sensibilities.

The practical process of legislation depends heavily upon committee action. For foreign affairs questions the Senate Committee on Foreign Relations and the House Committee on Foreign Affairs are the primary bodies, but account must also be taken of others. Because much of postwar American foreign policy has involved loans or grants to carry out programs of economic, military, and technical assistance, or appropriations for military, intelligence, and information programs, it has been possible for the appropriations committees in each house to intrude themselves into foreign policy by reexamining the policy of programs already adopted for which they are asked to recommend appropriations. Occasionally other committees may assert a claim to consider foreign affairs measures, and jurisdictional conflicts are not uncommon. Even worse, the left hand may not know what the right hand is doing. For example, foreign trade policy since it involves tariffs falls to the House Ways and Means Committee and the Senate Finance Committee. Agricultural products fall within foreign trade, but domestic agricultural programs, which may stimulate surpluses which require exportation and dumping, are determined by the two agriculture committees. Economic aid bills, which ought surely to be related to import policy, pass to the Foreign Affairs and Foreign Relations Committees. Petroleum policy in the House is of interest to the Interstate and Foreign Commerce Committee as well as to the Foreign Affairs Committee.

In dealing with congressional committees the executive branch has marked advantages of position in that most important foreign policy bills will have been initiated and drafted in executive agencies, and that most of the expert testimony about such measures must be obtained from executive officers. The committees do have small permanent staffs to assist in research and drafting, and may obtain some help from the Legislative Reference Service of the Library of Congress, but these staffs must spread themselves very thin to cover all the legislative problems presented. It is, therefore, a necessity for the committees to apply to executive agencies for information and to rely heavily upon the views expressed by them. At this point there is a substantial opportunity for bureaucratic influence to assert itself, especially at the technical level. Nor are individual members of the Congress usually well situated to deal with executive officers on even terms. Apart from the insufficiency of staff resources at their command, they are caught in a system which subjects them to the heaviest pressures upon time and energy. Constituents press them into special service as intermediaries in governmental contacts to an extent which led Robert Ramspeck, former congressman and Civil Service commissioner, to suggest that there should be two sets of congressmen, one for legislative business, the other to run errands for constituents. Few have time for detailed study of measures, and so they must rely upon those among them who have established leadership in particular areas, or follow some outside lead—whether from party, administration, or special-interest groups. It is perhaps in part from some sense of frustration and suspicion in dealing in this unequal fashion with the executive branch that the Congress has sought compensation in frequent investigation of executive officers and agencies. In ordinary circumstances a well-co-ordinated and persistently advocated administration program occupies a strong position. By the same token a failure or division in executive leadership may open the way for confusion and permit legislative cliques to exert disproportionate influence.

Governmental and party machinery of course operates in a larger context of public opinion and of special-interest groups. To define the role of American public opinion in foreign policy is difficult, but certain characteristics of it may be noted. It is only rarely possible for it to assume any initiative in pressing a policy upon the government, although this happened in the case of the Kellogg-Briand Pact (1928) for the outlawry of aggressive war. Certainly no complicated legislative measure can be initiated by public opinion. Rather it operates by reacting favorably or negatively to proposals made by the government or by action groups. These reactions tend to define the area within which the government may pursue a policy or program. At times public opinion imposes sharp restraints upon administration policy, as when it failed to respond to the interventionist desires of President F. D. Roosevelt from 1939 to 1941. Although he was able with difficulty to support the Allies by such measures as the destroyer-naval base agreement, the defense of Iceland, the Lend-Lease Act, and convoy of shipments, public opinion remained predominantly non-interventionist until Pearl Harbor. On the other hand, public opinion seemed fully prepared for the Marshall Plan and perhaps even ahead of congressional opinion. Of course, much will depend upon leadership and executive skill in carrying opinion along a desired course. This was done with consummate skill by President Wilson, who campaigned in 1916 upon the slogan "He kept us out of war!" yet was able to lead the country into war in 1917 with the enthusiastic support of the people. His messages in this period seemed seldom to anticipate the public's reactions to the war, yet they took full advantage of them.

Some attention has been given in Chapter 4 to peculiarities of opinion, tradition, and ideology which distinguish peoples. Naturally, these are implicit in any estimate of the probable course of public opinion, but need not be reviewed here. A brief comment may be ventured upon the mechanics of reaching public consensus on foreign policy. These vary from country to country in accordance with variations of social structure. In no country can it be said that the percentage of total population which participates in foreign policy discussions is very large. Ignorance and apathy exclude the majority. Immense outlays for public education in the United States have so far produced in a population of 160 millions only 10 million high school graduates, and little more than a million college graduates. On the basis of public opinion polls it has been estimated that on the average about 30 percent of the electorate are wholly unaware of important issues of foreign affairs, another 45 percent are aware of them in the sense of being conscious that issues exist but are uninformed about them and therefore incapable of any reasoned judgment upon the facts, while only 25 percent possess sufficient knowledge and interest to make some positive contribution to public discussion or to react rationally. This is not a very encouraging datum of democracy. We must assume then that about a quarter of the electorate is involved in what is called public opinion on foreign affairs, except that a larger group may be led by emotional appeals or propagandistic use of symbols to react irrationally upon some issue and must therefore be considered as not a merely neutral but a potentially dangerous element.

How does that 25 percent of the electorate which is informed about foreign affairs reach judgments about the issues? It appears that this segment of the population is better educated, better read, better provided with newspapers, books, television sets, and other sources of information than the rest, and especially addicted to membership in voluntary associations which have special interests in foreign policy. American society contains such a number and variety of voluntary associations representing groups or interests—occupational, patriotic, religious, veterans, nationality, economic, political, social, beneficial, and other groups—and so many of these concern themselves at times with political issues, that we are prone to take this activity for granted. Yet it is, at least in the degree found here, a quite unique social phenomenon, only approached in England and quite foreign to French and other continental societies. It is these associations which assume the initiative, much more than political parties, in developing and debating the issues of foreign policy and in seeking to impress their views upon the government. The debate proceeds through all the channels of mass communications but presumably falls upon stony ground except in the case of the 25 percent, where it may take root and bring forth fruit in the form of a foreign policy consensus. Needless to say, this is a procedure which can be democratic only to the extent that all points of view are reasonably well presented, and of this there can be no assurance. Interest groups are not all uniformly alert and active in participating in the debate, and the enterprise or resources of some may catch the others napping. Government officials may also seek to persuade the public, and here again the President enjoys a marked advantage over members of Congress, for his smallest thoughts are impressed upon millions of his countrymen by every resource of modern communications. If he does not succeed in leading public opinion, it is from no want of facilities.

When one considers the American system—almost a lack of system—of policy formation, he must inevitably be impressed by its variety and unpredictability. This is due largely to the fact that systems of representation and collaboration are only partly institutionalized. The representativeness of Congress is in fact very imperfect due to overrepresentation in the House of rural areas as against urban, underrepresentation in the House of southern Negroes, equal representation in the Senate of states irrespective of their population, and disproportionate influence of special-interest groups able to lobby effectively. In any case the neat picture of the sovereign people acting through its representatives, duly chosen through the agency of responsible and disciplined parties which have taken their stand upon issues and selected candidates with reference to them, is a euphemistic misrepresentation of the American political process. It is far more haphazard and informal than this would suggest, far more a matter of individual leadership, bureaucratic influence, and extremely varied nongovernmental pressures.

GOVERNMENTS OF WESTERN EUROPE

The usual type of government in western and northern Europe is parliamentary democracy, which has also spread to the states of the British Commonwealth, Japan, the Republic of Indonesia, and elsewhere. Its characteristic feature is a strong legislative chamber elected to represent population units, from which the leaders of the dominant political party or coalition of parties form a cabinet to control executive-administrative functions. The cabinet also provides legislative leadership but must continue to enjoy the confidence of the legislative body to remain in office. Generally there is a second legislative chamber which in unitary states is often a vestigial remain of aristocratic class representation but in federal states may be used to give representation accompanied with substantial powers to the member states or provincial governments. A formal head of state, either monarch or president, is also provided, to assure legal continuity between governments and to discharge certain formal duties and symbolic functions. This general pattern is subject to numerous institutional variations in different countries, and their political institutions must, as in the case of the United States, be considered in terms of broader social patterns. For foreign policy purposes it will be sufficient to comment upon the British, French, and West German governments, which exhibit sharp contrasts.

Great Britain

In Great Britain, as in the United States, there are only two major political parties, Conservatives and Labour, the Liberals and other minor parties having polled only 4 percent of the vote in the general election of May 26, 1955. The Liberal party after World War I was still a tolerably strong third party which might hope to hold the balance of power, and did so in the two Labour ministries of Ramsay MacDonald, but in recent years it has apparently receded beyond hope of revival. In its biparty system the British situation differs from that of continental governments, which are based upon multiparty systems. Compared with American parties, the British parties are more centralized and disciplined. Although they rest upon local constituency associations, or in the case of the Labour party upon a mixture of trade union, socialist, and constituency associations, they are actually dominated by permanent central offices. In the Labour party the annual party conference is also a significant policy-determining body, and the Executive Committee chosen by the conference directs the work of the Central Office. Local party organization is not as professionalized as in the United States, probably because of British antipathy to bossism and corrupt machine politics and because rewards for such activity in the form of political patronage are negligible. Nor is local autonomy in the choice of candidates so marked. The lack of a local residence requirement for candidacy and the practice of assigning able candidates to districts in which they do not live, naturally enable the central offices to make recommendations to local units. Locally nominated candidates also require the endorsement of the Central Office. After election the party group in the House of Commons is tightly held together for legislative purposes. Persistent deviation from party policy may result in suspension or even expulsion from the party and in having to face a party-approved candidate at the next election who at the least would so split the party's vote as to elect the opposition candidate.

In the general British social structure the parties appear to be a relatively more significant agency for public policy formation than their American counterparts. There are numerous voluntary associations in Great Britain, but they are less active in producing foreign policy consensus. Perhaps this is due to the fact that the parties are themselves more genuinely voluntary associations and not, as in the United States, cliques of career politicians. There are also many political clubs which ally themselves with one party or another. In the case of Labour party politics the socialist societies and the trade unions are very important. The latter meet in annual congresses which concern themselves closely with political policy issues. Communications media also lend themselves less readily to a potpourri of group opinions. Local papers have lost ground to the great metropolitan dailies, and each party has important organs (Conservatives, Beaverbrook's *Daily Express* and Rothmere's *Daily Mail;* Labour, the *Daily Herald;* Liberal party, *The Manchester Guardian;* independent but always close to government sources, *The London Times*) which carry its official positions into every hamlet.

How do these characteristic features of party organization affect foreign policy? It must be admitted at once that certain basic British foreign policies, such as maintenance of a sound foreign trade position, close relations with the Commonwealth nations, naval strength, opposition to dominance of the continent and especially the Low Countries by any aggressive power, are common to both parties. But the Labour party contains substantial pacifist elements, and as a whole has been more strongly committed than the Conservative party to disarmament and pacific settlement of international disputes, including support of the League of Nations and the United Nations. Although it now supports rearmament and defense alliances, it finds these policies distasteful expedients thrust upon it by the conditions of the cold war. To the Conservatives such policies are not necessary evils but the normal requirements of a policy of strong empire defense and balance of power diplomacy. The Labour party has traditionally been less imperialist than the Conservatives, and although neither party could today be called imperialist, some difference of emphasis remains. Thus Labour granted full independence to India against sharp Conservative opposition. Labour has also appeared less resigned to a close association with United States policy and more sympathetic to a soft policy toward communistic states. It is probable that its positions in this respect are influenced by its left wing, composed of Bevanites and Fabian socialists, who hardly comprise a fifth of the party strength (the rest lying in the more conservative trade unions) but who are nevertheless highly vocal and influential. Party discipline has certainly been employed where feasible, as in the expulsion of Platts-Mills in 1948 and Zilliacus in 1949, but it has not been possible to deal so decisively with Richard Crossman or Aneurin Bevan, who have a more substantial following. Bevan has been twice suspended from party membership, but his continuing separatism is a source of embarrassment to the Labour party. It is reluctantly facing the fact that it must either find a policy compromise broad enough to embrace him or must disown him.

The decisive influence of the parties in foreign policy probably lies in their relationship to the government, i.e., the cabinet. For the party division in the House of Commons determines the formation of the ministry, which will be formed by the leaders of the majority party except in the rare case of a coalition government. In the nature of things they cannot become party leaders or continue as such unless in sympathy with the policy positions of the party. This is apparent from the dropping of Ramsay MacDonald from Labour party leadership after he formed a coalition ministry, and from

Aneurin Bevan's withdrawal from the cabinet in 1951 because of dissent on the rearmament issue. The dropping of Sir Samuel Hoare from the cabinet in 1935, on the other hand, was a result of popular antagonism to the Hoare-Laval Pact (pp. 370, 530) rather than of party discipline, and did not result in a change of the cabinet's basic position with respect to League of Nations intervention. It is not often that the parliamentary party group will have occasion to chasten members of the ministry but this is because they are the embodiment of its essential positions. It follows that the broad lines of the party's foreign policy positions will demarcate the area within which the ministry's discretion—admittedly a very broad one—can operate.

When we turn to executive-legislative relationships, we find a situation very different from that which prevails in the United States. The exercise of all powers of sovereignty is vested in the Parliament, which in effect means in the House of Commons, for the Lords have only a suspensory veto of action by the Commons. The queen as formal head of state may, of course, be said in a formalistic legal sense to be sovereign, and still sends and receives ambassadors and approves treaties, but the substance of power has long since passed to the Parliament, and the queen acts only in accordance with the views of her ministers. Some personal influence she may still exert in counsel, and this may be substantial in the case of an experienced and sagacious monarch. This was certainly true in the field of foreign affairs of Edward VII and George V. The monarch does have the advantage of a continuous view of politics from a nonpartisan position, and especially in foreign affairs has valuable sources of information from diplomatists and royal family connections—although less so than in the period before World War I. Queen Victoria, whose prince consort was a statesman of first rank in foreign policy, still insisted upon her constitutional prerogative to have all out-going foreign office dispatches submitted to her for alteration or assent, after first passing to the prime minister for his comments. Palmerston, when he was foreign secretary, was flagrantly derelict in complying, probably because his views were out of harmony with those of the queen and prince consort, and he was temperamentally impatient of constraint. However, he was first reproved, and afterward, because he continued to ignore the queen, was removed from office with the full approval of the cabinet. Yet the royal prerogative which was thus defended against impudence was not long proof against the mounting pressure of business. Even in Victoria's lifetime it became necessary at times to send dispatches before she had approved them, although in deference to her feelings she always received a copy marked "Draft." Later sovereigns have not tried to reassert a regular right of review. Today the queen has no claim to be continuously consulted upon foreign policy; such views as she may offer will be heard with deference and respect, but the ministers will decide.

Since the House of Commons possesses an undivided legal authority and could even change political institutions by a legislative act, there is nothing comparable to the American conception of separation of powers or checks and balances. On the contrary, the integration of the several branches of government under control of the Commons is built into the constitutional system. This does not mean that there is no separation of functions. In fact this is in some respects more complete than in the United States. For foreign affairs it involves cabinet, Commons, and civil service. Some attention will be given to the last named in connection with foreign affairs administration, but the bureaucracy also has an influence upon foreign policy. This is most notable in the foreign office, where the career officers' experience and judgment can be brought to bear effectively through the Permanent Under Secretary for Foreign Affairs, a long-time career officer, upon his political chief, the Secretary for Foreign Affairs. The latter has the responsibility for political direction and the former the duty to carry out the directives received, but it would be unwise to discount the persuasiveness of a seasoned expert in foreign affairs in advising a political officer who is pretty sure to be able and well grounded but who has not the leisure or independent sources of information to study all questions *de novo*. The permanent under secretary and his staff must expect to satisfy the major foreign policy premises of the cabinet and party in power as expressed by the foreign secretary, but this will leave open important areas for professional influence. In this respect the English career service is probably better situated than its American counterpart, for in executive agencies of the United States the break between political and career officers occurs at a lower level, so that a considerable body of political appointees who frequently lack specialized training or experience is superimposed upon and mingled with the career officers. It is true that permanent under secretaries of departments in the British government are as a class recruited in terms of exceptional managerial capacity and broad intellectual competency, so that they often are more noted for powers of administration than for command of particular professional fields. In the foreign office, however, the permanent under secretary has characteristically united administrative competency with diplomatic experience and exceptional grasp of foreign policy. His qualifications may on occasion be so formidable that a sharp difference of opinion between him and the foreign secretary renders their relationship unworkable. Anthony Eden requested that Sir Robert Vansittart be relieved of his duties as permanent under secretary and assigned to the special position of "Chief Diplomatic Adviser to His Majesty's Government," probably mainly because of his identification with the Hoare-Laval agreement.

By all odds, the most important element of government, for foreign policy as for domestic, is the cabinet. It consists of those ministers who head the more important executive agencies, plus a few ministers without portfolio

—usually sixteen to twenty persons designated by the prime minister from the larger number of ministers and junior ministers he has placed in control of departments. The prime minister is designated by the crown but must be the acknowledged leader of the majority party in Parliament. The ministers and cabinet members are also chosen as party leaders in the Parliament who have risen upon their own merits. In effect, they are an executive committee of the majority party which undertakes the executive-administrative functions of government as well as the legislative leadership. The cabinet members, themselves members of Parliament, determine administration policy, present a legislative program, defend it upon the floor of the Houses and in committees, whip up party support for its enactment, and direct its administrative management. They may exercise direct executive power without legislation; as a body they become members of the Privy Council and can act through orders-in-council, sometimes an important device in foreign affairs.

In this group the prime minister is the most powerful and the foreign secretary is always important, but it is more useful to think of the cabinet as a whole, for the principle of cabinet solidarity and responsibility requires that they speak with one voice and hold themselves responsible to the Commons as a group for the administration program. If a cabinet member dissents seriously from the views of his colleagues, he must be dropped; if he remains, they must be prepared to support his policies in Parliament. As a whole the cabinet must resign if it loses the confidence of the Commons; or, in the alternative it may go to the country, i.e., request the crown to order a general election which will determine whether its or the Commons' position enjoys popular support. In ordinary circumstances it will be the foreign secretary who in consultation with the prime minister determines the foreign policy of the government, but his colleagues in the cabinet must be informed and may be expected to take a close interest in matters of importance. Diplomatic information is regularly circulated among them. A close relationship of confidence must, of course, exist between the prime minister and the foreign secretary. Eden's disagreement with Prime Minister Chamberlain's appeasement policy with respect to Hitler led to Eden's resignation from the cabinet.

What of the House of Commons? It is certainly not a rubber stamp for the cabinet—the opposition party sees to that—yet it may almost be said that the cabinet governs England during the sufferance of the Commons. Without entering into the details of the legislative process, it may be said that it affords few opportunities for the special-interest lobbying, arbitrary committee action, or minority obstructionism which are so common in the Congress of the United States. Yet it requires the cabinet continuously to explain and defend its legislative program and also its conduct of administration. Major debates upon foreign policy occur at intervals during the sessions of Parliament, usually in response to demands that important new developments or undertakings be explained. They provide opportunities for the foreign secretary and his colleagues to present the government's policy and defend it against opposition criticisms. Divisions are not taken unless a proposal or motion of censure is before the House, but the government can in any case obtain some sense of the degree of support its views command. Foreign policy debates in the House of Lords are of little consequence in determining consensus but sometimes evoke distinguished contributions to analysis of a position. In the House of Commons there is also the well-known institution of the question hour, in which ministers are required to respond to an infinite variety of queries of the most pointed type. Sometimes the foreign secretary and his parliamentary assistants, the two ministers of state for the foreign office and the two parliamentary under secretaries for foreign affairs, are freer from this barrage than their colleagues, for they may decline to answer questions when disclosures are considered contrary to the public interest. However, a persistent evasion of questions would provoke the sharpest criticism. The cabinet is free to approve a treaty and it can be ratified by the crown upon advice of the appropriate minister without reference to Parliament. Nevertheless important treaties are usually laid before the Commons, particularly when legislative action is required to implement them. Although the Labour party at one time advocated debate of all important treaties before signing, this has not been the practice even during Labour ministries. Parliamentary debate of ratification is not likely often to result in a negative recommendation, since in view of the government's having signed the treaty this would have to be treated as an expression of lack of confidence. Similarly, parliamentary approval is not required for exercise by the cabinet of the crown's war power, but would certainly be obtained in any serious conflict. The executive-legislative relationship is indeed a remarkable product of experience which permits a strong centralized executive power within a framework of responsibility and representative institutions. But the principles of solidarity and responsibility which make the relationship workable depend upon much deeper qualities of political responsibility and forbearance which are a part of the tradition of the British people and its officials.

France

When we turn to France, we encounter a political system which seems designed to frustrate efficient executive action. The reason is understandable, for the constitution of the Fourth Republic was made in the shadow of the Vichy experience and was designed to avoid the danger of executive domination. Therefore, it placed the powers of government squarely in the hands of the popular branch of the legislature, the National Assembly, gave no real power to the formal chief of state, the president, and subjected the premier (properly styled the president of the Council of Ministers) to the Assembly's whims in a manner which discourages executive leadership. However, the new frame of government is in a process cf experimental change which may produce some improvement.

The character of the central government can be understood only in terms of the political party structure. In contrast with the situation in the United States and Great Britain there are many parties and by no means all of them are even committed to the present form of government. The two largest parties, the Communists and the Gaullists (RPF, or *Rassemblement du Peuple Français,* Rally of the French People) hold between them 35 percent of the seats in the National Assembly but fortunately can agree upon only one point, the necessity to change the present constitution.

Although an amendment of the system of proportional representation in 1951 has built up the parliamentary strength of the moderate parties, it by no means assures stable government, for none of these parties has enough strength to dominate the group; and the coalitions which must be formed to set up a ministry divide upon many points of party policy and are therefore vulnerable to both internal and external attack. These moderate parties include the Socialists; the MRP (*Mouvement Républicain Populaire,* Popular Republican Movement), a new Catholic social party which emerged from the war and which is based upon Catholic trade unionist and middle-class elements, with some conservatives; the RGR, or Rally of Left Republicans, of which the Radical Socialist party is the principal component (a name, by the way, which is now a misnomer, for the party was "radical" in the sense of late nineteenth-century politics and now occupies a middle position in the political spectrum); and finally a number of small conservative parties and individual deputies who are loosely grouped as Independents and Moderates. It must be added that these parties are poorly disciplined. Issues are all too frequently presented to the voter in terms of a logical or philosophical position but dimly related to practical politics, and the personal element is strong. Deputies within a party group in the Assembly may differ widely, and they feel little constraint about defection from the party. Nominations are upon a local basis, campaigns are carried on without much benefit of central party organization and upon a highly personalized basis. Newspapers are numerous and associate themselves frequently with individual candidates. It would appear also that the individualism of French voters and the general indifference in rural France to national politics favors personalized politics and weak party discipline.

What are the consequences of this party system in the National Assembly? In a word, to disintegrate it into petty units which cannot hope to coalesce into effective working groups unless the governmental system overcomes their naturally divisive tendencies. In fact it does not. The constitution provides for a president, a ministry, and a second chamber, the Council of the Republic, but places none of these in a position to strengthen the government.

The president is not popularly elected but chosen by a joint session of the Assembly and Council for a term of seven years. The powers assigned to him seem at first impression moderately significant, but upon examination most of them are found to lack substance. He designates the premier, cabinet ministers, councilors of state, ambassadors, and other officers, receives foreign ambassadors, presides at meetings of the Council of Ministers, promulgates statutes and may request reconsideration of them, is commander in chief of the armed forces, instructs diplomatic representatives, makes treaties, and even may dissolve the National Assembly. But he is only a titular chief executive. All his acts, save the naming of a premier, must be done upon authority of the ministers. Although he "commands" the armed forces, the direction of them is assigned to the premier. Although treaties are made in his name, all important ones require parliamentary ratification. All his appointments and instructions are really the acts of his ministers; and his suspensory veto of legislation is almost ludicrous, for it must be upon advice of the ministry, which would presumably have resigned if it had unsuccessfully opposed the legislation in the Assembly. In the choice of the premier he has indeed some latitude by reason of the party structure, for the ministry must be a coalition of parties in which several persons have approximately equal claims to consideration. It is also true that his long term of office, which can be once renewed, coupled with the fact that most legislative and diplomatic papers come under his scrutiny, places him in an excellent position to exert influence as an adviser, and the traditions of the office are favorable to this.

As for the second chamber, it was omitted altogether from the first draft of the constitution but this was a major reason for its rejection by the people. However, the present Council of the Republic has no independent powers. It may exercise only a suspensory veto of Assembly legislation. If, however, it amends an Assembly bill by absolute majority, the Assembly can override the amendment only by a like majority. The Council has debated most foreign policy issues and probably exerts somewhat increasing influence by reason of the fact that its relatively conservative composition matches the drift of French politics, which is sometimes more coherently expressed in the Council than in the Assembly.

What of the premier and his ministry? Having been chosen by the president, the premier must attempt to form a ministry by drawing together leaders of several party groups. Since he cannot appeal to them all in terms of policy, he must dangle the bait of offices before them, and parties have actually come to feel that certain ministries in the work of which they are most interested are a kind of private party preserve to be regularly allocated to them. The specific importance of this in foreign affairs is that the foreign ministry has been regularly allocated to the MRP and therefore held alternately by its leaders, Georges Bidault and Robert Schuman. This was not unnatural, for the party arose in anti-Vichy resistance and was therefore clean in foreign policy terms. The necessity for exclusion of the Communists, and the suspect character of some leaders of older center parties helped. A good deal of American comment has pointed to the long tenure of two men in the foreign ministry as showing basic stability in the French government, but it is rather a result of the bargaining position of the MRP. This has detracted from the power of premiers to control foreign affairs fully. The French ministry has been likened to a game of musical chairs; the frequent fall of ministries is the signal for a scramble for place, but when the players sit down again the ministry looks much the same.

The most important aspect of the matter lies in the relationship of the ministry to the Assembly. Here the procedure seems to be confusion worse confounded. Far from minimizing the influence of minority party obstructionism, it subjects the ministry to it at every turn. The system of proportional representation is carried into the committees where endless bargaining results. At frequent intervals, and at the instance of a minor party or even an unaffiliated deputy, the ministry can be made to defend its program in reply to interpellations (formal questions in writing). In a context of numerous parties, with little party discipline in the center group, this means the ministry is involved in a perpetual Donnybrook Fair and subjected almost upon a day-to-day basis to danger of disintegration and loss of confidence. Nor can it in that event save itself by dissolution of the Assembly and appeal to the electorate, for the right of dissolution is restricted to an event unlikely to occur, i.e., defeat of two ministries in succession by absolute majorities of the Assembly.

The applicability of these difficulties to the conduct of foreign affairs is immediate, for foreign policy has provided dominant issues since the war over which many ministries have been broken. Neither of the extremist parties collaborates in foreign policy. The Communists opposed the European Recovery Plan, the North Atlantic Treaty, French aid in Korea, the European Defense Community; they advocated rapprochement with the Soviets and reduction of Germany to impotence. The Gaullists have demanded a strong, independent France in control of its own defense, a Western European federation under French hegemony, large French rearmament. How they would achieve these goals is not clear. With both these parties sniping at the center parties, and the latter far from unified upon the details of foreign policy, it has been difficult to move. The foreign ministry, in the hands of MRP, has seized the initiative brilliantly with its proposals for the

European Iron and Steel Community and the Defense Community, but a succession of French premiers has struggled against the Assembly's demands to hedge these arrangements with restricting amendments. Even Pierre Mendès-France, who sought with apparent popular support to gather the reins into his hands, unify the ministry, and cut through the foreign policy and financial impasse, was broken by the party differences over colonial policy.

To understand the position of French foreign policy at any moment it is necessary to take account of the shifting party alignments. For a short time after World War II an effort was made to form cabinets by a coalition including Communists, Socialists, and MRP. Since there was fundamental and growing disagreement among these parties, ministries could function at all only by dividing the ministerial posts into nearly autonomous party groupings. It was in this way that the MRP monopoly of foreign affairs began. In such a situation the cabinet hardly functioned as a unified ministry but was rather a device for bargaining and compromise among the parties. Strong leadership by the premier was hardly possible.

In 1947 the Communists were expelled from the ministry because they failed to support a motion of confidence on the government's wage and price control policies. Thereafter ministries were formed by coalitions of centrist parties, excluding Communists on the left and Gaullists on the right. This made possible a degree of coherence and executive leadership by the premier, for these parties have a good deal in common; but it also dangerously narrowed the voting strength of the ministry in the Chamber of Deputies and exposed it to the difficulties of maintaining a united front by holding together the least disciplined parties. In particular, the Radical Socialist Party re-emerged as a necessary but undependable element of coalitions, and small right parties had to be included, e.g., Independents and Peasants. The only disciplined party remaining in the ministries was the MRP. In terms of foreign policy this meant that its control of the foreign ministry became increasingly difficult. After 1950 the policy of Western European integration so consistently pursued by Schuman as foreign minister had to be compromised to take account of the demands of rightist elements in the coalition. In personal terms the succession of Georges Bidault to the office of foreign minister represented the shift toward compromise and devious maneuvering in this sphere. MRP found itself increasingly to the left in government coalitions.

The ministry of Mendès-France endeavored to shift again toward the left to recapture support from the Socialists, who had passed into opposition, but failed to secure support for its policies. That of Faure was a swing again to the right with inclusion of Gaullist ministers. It managed to maintain itself through the crisis of North African revolt and the restoration of the deposed sultan of Morocco, Sidi Mohammed ben Youssef, but only by the most tortuous parliamentary maneuvers, for in a series of confidence votes the government support was in each case differently compounded. Faure's decision to hold elections six months before the end of the Assembly's normal term was sustained only by support from the Communists. This decision was apparently taken to forestall efforts of Mendès-France to realign a left-center coalition and secure changes of the electoral laws which might favor increasing its strength. On the colonial question Faure with difficulty found a formula satisfactory to foreign Minister Pinay, who represented moderate rightist elements, and was unable to satisfy his Gaullist supporters, who left the ministry. In the end the Communists also withdrew their support, and the ministry was defeated by absolute majority, as that of Mendès-France had been. This enabled Faure to dissolve the Assembly and thus force early elections. Unfortunately they only weakened the position of the moderate center parties. Thus it is apparent that the pursuit of a consistent French foreign policy has been increasingly difficult and is now directly involved in the problem of cabinet coalitions. It is unlikely greater stability can be achieved unless a general improvement of conditions lessens the Communist and Gaullist strength and thus relieves the center parties from such sharp bargaining pressures.

Germany

The government of the Federal Republic of Germany has been in operation only a short time and under circumstances quite unique, especially in foreign relations. Therefore, it is doubtful whether any conclusions concerning its governmental characteristics in the formation and control of foreign policy will be a reliable guide for the future. Certain points will be mentioned because they need to be kept in mind in following the progress of events.

The first is that the party structure seems to reflect postwar compulsions more than it is likely to do in the long run. Neither the Communists nor the neo-Nazi parties have shown strength. Reaction to the measures taken in East Germany may largely explain defections from the Communist party, and latent Nazi strength has naturally bided its time. Both these parties, as well as minor factions generally, also receive less than proportional representation under the electoral law. It seems possible, however, that the achievement of independence, the progress of rearmament, and the increasing emphasis in East-West politics upon the issues of neutralism and unification may open possibilities for the resurgence of such parties. It also seems apparent that many Germans have not actively identified themselves with parties in the postwar period, and that these have been largely dominated by aging prewar leaders. This popular indifference is understandable in view of widespread disillusionment. Many Germans associate parliamentary democracy with the difficulties and frustrations under the Weimar constitution, and perhaps with some of the postwar floundering of occupation governments in the western zones. To this must be added the general apathy toward politics which followed in the wake of the Nazi frenzy and ultimate exhaustion and defeat. Whether the parties have been adequate vehicles of general opinion is therefore not clear.

The nearly equal strength in the *Bundestag* (lower house) of Adenauer's CDU/CSU (Christian Democratic and Christian Socialist Unions) and the Social Democrats (SPD), or Socialists, until the 1953 election, threw the balance of power to the Free Democrats (FDP), who entered the government coalition with the CDU/CSU. In 1953 the latter gained 45 percent of the votes and further improved its position by adding the German party and the All-German Bloc (a new refugee-expellee party) to the coalition. Thus the government commanded the two-thirds majority necessary to amend the Basic Law to permit rearmament and thus to make ratification of the European Defense Community and the Contractual Agreements possible. Nevertheless, the party lines in the Bundestag had remained tightly drawn, for German parties exhibit tight discipline and small disposition to compromise, the Socialists opposing these measures bitterly. Throughout the period there has been an unfortunate absence of any spirit of collaboration or interchange between government and opposition parties, which if pursued in a period of more balanced distribution of strength among a number of parties might produce a stalemate.

The governmental institutions have been devised to follow the tradition of the Weimar constitution while avoiding the weaknesses in it. With what success remains to be seen. Under occupation pressure a federal system was installed, the German states (*Länder*) designating representatives who comprise the Federal Council (*Bundesrat*) of the national parliament. However, the federal principle has not produced a division of powers with respect to foreign affairs; these are assigned exclusively to the national government. The Länder can enter into treaties with foreign states in certain areas of concurrent jurisdiction if not contrary to or occupied by national legislation or treaties, and in legislation as to taxation and finance the assent of the Bundesrat is required. Changes in the Basic Law require two-thirds majorities in each House. In the situation created by the need to amend the Basic Law as a prerequisite to ratification of the treaties of Bonn and Paris the votes of one of the Länder in the Federal Council nearly blocked action. Yet this is not to be understood in terms of opposition between Länder and Reich. The party organizations function in the legislative assemblies of the Länder as in the national parliament, and the Socialists simply found this the most promising method of trying to block rearmament. Apart from such occasional opportunities the powers of the Bundesrat are negligible, and the centralizing tendencies of German government have been continued through the strong powers assigned the national government, and through the chancellor's control of patronage and the well-integrated, powerful bureaucracy.

The chancellor is clearly the central figure of the government, and the office has thus far been conducted by Dr. Adenauer with Bismarckian firmness, although very different temper. It seems probable that the large powers of the chancellor, beneficently employed by Adenauer, would become a problem if they ever again fall into the hands of a nationalistic demagogue like Hitler. Neither the president nor the Bundestag has adequate controls over the chancellor. The president may propose a chancellor to the Bundestag, but the Bundestag elects him. Having done so, it cannot easily be rid of him, for a vote of censure must be accompanied by the election by absolute majority of his successor. Should this be impossible, the chancellor could continue in office without parliamentary support until he chose to ask the president to dissolve the Bundestag or could request the president to declare a state of legislative emergency for a period up to six months, thus suspending Bundestag action. The president as chief of state has only formal functions, his actions giving effect to ministerial decisions.

Much will depend upon the disposition of the Bundestag. It has effectively debated foreign policy questions such as the Schuman Plan, the European Defense Community, and rearmament. Its Foreign Affairs Committee has played a significant role in discussing postwar treaties and foreign policy decisions, and its views have on occasion affected executive action. Thus the chancellor was led to postpone for six months the signing of the agreement reached at the New York Conference of Foreign Ministers in 1950 for restoration of German autonomy in foreign affairs because the committee objected to the undefined obligation expressed in his acknowledgment of the prewar debts of the German Reich. Nevertheless, the foreign policy of postwar years has been dominated by Chancellor Adenauer, who has at all times held the initiative firmly in his hands. At times he has been less than frank in his disclosures to the Bundestag and in effect has played a devious and skillful diplomatic role between it and the foreign governments with which he dealt. On the highly controversial question of German rearmament and contribution to the European Defense Community he submitted a secret memorandum to the Occupying Powers on August 29, 1950, prior to the New York Conference of Foreign Ministers, in which after requesting an increase in the strength of their forces in Germany he offered "in the event of the formation of an international West European Army, a contribution in the shape of German contingents." The important Petersburg Agreement of November 22, 1949, was not submitted by him for ratification, a position, however, in which the chancellor was later supported by the Federal Constitutional Court. The stronger position of the government coalition after 1953 of course simplified the chancellor's problem, and he obtained approval of the EDC treaties from both houses of the parliament although this was not constitutionally required. After the creation of a ministry of foreign affairs in 1951, Chancellor Adenauer also held that post, until the appointment of Dr. Heinrich von Brentano as foreign minister in 1955, and has continued to dominate personally the field of foreign policy and administration. With some few exceptions the Bundestag has not strongly asserted the responsibility of the chancellor to it.

Nor is the chancellor merely *primus inter pares* with respect to the cabinet. The fourteen ministers are appointed by the president upon nomination by the chancellor. As a cabinet, they do not follow the British principle of solidarity and responsibility to the legislature; rather, as in the cabinet of the United States, they are responsible to the chancellor, and he alone to the Bundestag. It cannot directly censure or dislodge individual ministers. Since the chancellor cannot be overthrown unless the Bundestag can agree upon a successor by absolute majority, it is in practice impossible for the legislative body to make a serious issue of the conduct of a particular minister. There has also been a continuation of the strong bureaucratic element of the government at all levels. At the present time, therefore, it is hard to avoid some misgiving about the future of democratic control in Germany. If it is to become firmly established, it will require more responsible popular participation, clearer development of the principle of cabinet solidarity and ministerial responsibility to the parliament, and less emphasis on centrally controlled bureaucracy. These goals may not be out of reach. However, the tendency toward strong, centralized, executive control, fully understandable in the situation confronting the Adenauer government, may continue. If so, the results will depend upon the quality of the chancellor.

THE SOVIET GOVERNMENT

Although the ideological preconceptions of communism, as modified by Leninist-Stalinist interpretation and reconciled with certain traditional aims of Russian policy, may provide a set of fairly constant objectives, they leave sufficient latitude of tactics to open a wide range of foreign policy choices. These characteristically fluctuate according to circumstances from the undermining tactic of infiltration and organization of proletarian elements in "capitalist" states, to outright collaboration or alliance with democratic capitalist states in struggles against fascistic or feudalistic capitalist states. More recently the first method seems to have been broadened in Asia to draw in both proletarian and bourgeois support against "Western imperialism," postponing the Marxist social revolution until the Asian state can be drawn firmly within the Soviet orbit. Thus, Soviet foreign policy has occasion to use an even greater range of methods than traditional Western diplomacy,

for it employs diplomatic relations or external force at times but also intervenes systematically in the domestic affairs of other states in trying to weaken
their political and economic systems.

The formation and control of Soviet foreign policy cannot be understood
simply in terms of the formal structure of the governments of the U.S.S.R.
or its satellite states. The institutional systems of these states do not develop
policy through such channels but through party organization. The party in-
fuses formal governmental structures at every level and utilizes them as instruments of action or propaganda or to stimulate consensus. It also crosses
political frontiers to provide international unification of communist action.
Governmental structures appear on the surface to provide a complete system
of representative democracy in the hierarchy of elected soviets or councils
(from base to top, village and city ward soviets, rural district and city soviets,
regional soviets, Union Republic Supreme Soviets, U.S.S.R. Supreme Soviet),
and Communists certainly refer to their systems as "people's democracies."
But if these terms are understood in a traditional sense, the elected soviets
are in both manner of election and in functioning a mere travesty of representative government.

There is only one party, the Communist party, and it comprises the hard
corps of trained, indoctrinated, highly disciplined revolutionaries. From time
to time its ranks have been ruthlessly purged of those considered to deviate
from ideological purity, and others have been recruited. It is an elite corps
with restricted membership, deliberately kept small and mobile. Even after
substantial wartime recruitment the party in the U.S.S.R. does not exceed 6
to 7 million members. Its structure of committees corresponds at each level
to the hierarchy of "legislative" soviets and to a similar hierarchy of government "executive" committees, thus permitting systematic control of the latter
structures by the party workers. The communist doctrine of dictatorship of
the proletariat in fact resolves itself into dictatorship by the party, since only
under party direction can the proletariat act. "In *this sense,*" Stalin declared
in 1940 (*Problems of Leninism*), "it could be said that the dictatorship of
the proletariat is *in essence* the 'dictatorship' of its vanguard, the 'dictatorship'
of its party, as the main guiding force of the proletariat." The party deliberately shapes and leads public opinion. This does not imply that there is no
independent opinion in communist countries, but adverse opinion has no
facilities for consensus or action. There are indeed frequent party admonitions
to assess public attitudes carefully, and sententious advice to the party members as teachers of public opinion not to forget that they can also learn from
it, but these cannot disguise the fact that instruction and influence follow a
one-way street from party to public. Those of the public who do not submit
with enthusiasm, or at the least with passivity, find there are stern sanctions
against nonconformity. The party itself maintains a close unity, promoted

by rewarding doctrinal conformity and effective party service and by systematic elimination of deviates and failures.

Direction proceeds from the Central Committee, or from the smaller Presidium of the Central Committee, of the party to lower level committees. In theory, policy is determined under the principle of democratic centralism, which calls for unified, centralized execution of a policy after it has been democratically determined. But it is quite clear that the emphasis is now upon centralism, not democracy, and that policy comes from party leaders. The leaders themselves are recruited for higher party organs not by election but by co-optation upon the basis of proven merit. Therefore, the dictatorship, with control of all policy, in the end centers in the small group of men in the Presidium of the Central Committee (which has officially succeeded the former Politburo), and is implemented under direction of the Central Committee Secretariat. Party congresses hear extensive political reports from the Central Executive Committee, which always include an appraisal of the international situation and a recapitulation of foreign policy objectives. The details of instructions to Soviet diplomats by the Central Committee (or its working collegia, the Political and Organizational Bureaus and the Secretariat) have been open to delegates to the congresses but have never been discussed during sessions. Actually there has been less discussion on foreign policy questions than on any other major topics. Speeches are confined to remarks praising the Central Committee's conduct of policy, and resolutions on such subjects are nearly always unanimously approved. Stalin dominated the controlling group in the Presidium of the Central Committee as a dictator, and there was continuous jockeying for position as successor to his power. However, there is at least a possibility that direction can be shared collegially. Malenkov attempted to control the situation after Stalin's death and failed. Although Khrushchev seems now to be the dominant personality, there is some evidence that Bulganin also plays a positive role in shaping policy in the field of foreign relations. It may be that no one has yet succeeded in fully occupying Stalin's place.

The mechanics of party control of government are simple and thorough. Only party-approved candidates may stand for election, and usually there is only one candidate. Elections are not intended as an apparatus for free choice, since the result is a foregone conclusion, but rather as a means of explaining party, and hence government, policy to the electorate and of drumming up support. Those elected may not be wholly party members, but at least will have demonstrated their worthiness. "Legislative" procedures in the elected soviets consist mainly in listening to explanations of policy by party leaders and then ratifying their suggestions. This is true even of the Supreme Soviet of the U.S.S.R., which finds it necessary to meet for only a week twice yearly to transact all its legislative business. It devotes most of this time to hearing reports by party leaders, expressing its satisfaction with them, ratifying various ministerial measures and electing (again, really ratifying party choice of) its Presidium and the U.S.S.R. Council of Ministers. In foreign relations it has been inactive, serving principally as a tribune for foreign policy reports or declarations by party leaders. These are not actively debated. The usual practice has been to dispense with debate and vote unanimous approval upon motion by a prominent deputy who refers to the exhaustive clarity of the report and the consistency of the foreign policy of the government.

Under the Constitution of 1936 the Presidium of the Supreme Soviet possesses significant powers in the field of foreign relations. When the Supreme Soviet is not in session, the Presidium may proclaim a state of war in the event of attack upon the U.S.S.R. or if necessary to fulfill obligations under defensive alliances, and may order mobilization. It ratifies and denounces international treaties, appoints and recalls Soviet envoys to foreign states, and receives the credentials of foreign diplomats accredited to the U.S.S.R. It also appoints ministers. These powers have been used fully. Although it functions in theory subject to the legislative direction of the Supreme Soviet, the latter has in fact enacted few statutes, and almost none relating to foreign affairs. On the contrary, the Presidium has been very active in issuing decrees, and the Council of Ministers in issuing ordinances and instructions, so that these last must (apart from technical quibbles over what constitutes legislation) be considered the real legislative organs. They produce, as Towster put it, the bulk of the "obligatory, state-enforced, activity-guiding norms in the Soviet system." The policies developed by these executive organs are ratified complaisantly by the Supreme Soviet, which is thus mainly an organ for policy announcement and dissemination. Nor is the Presidium to be understood as a mere interim committee of the Supreme Soviet. It includes as vice chairmen the chairmen of the presidia of the supreme soviets of all the constituent republics of the U.S.S.R., as well as some members elected from the federal Supreme Soviet. It is regarded as a collegial executive. In fact, many members cannot attend regularly, and many functions, including those in connection with foreign relations, are carried out by the chairman (referred to outside the U.S.S.R. as the Soviet president) and secretary in the name of the Presidium. It is symptomatic of party controls in this organ that the chairman is the only member who sits also in the Presidium of the Central Committee of the Communist party. There is of course no problem of separation of powers as between "legislative" and "executive" branches. In the case of neither is the term descriptive, and both are merely vehicles of party policy.

The Council of Ministers (called until 1946 Sovnarkom, Council of People's Commissars) is the highest executive-administrative organ. Since it operates continuously and produces numerous ordinances and directives, it is in practice the most important organ for legislative as well as for executive and administrative functions. It co-ordinates the work of the ministries within policy lines specified by it. In the field of foreign relations it is authorized by the constitution to exercise general supervision. In fact, it guides the ministries of foreign affairs, foreign trade, armed forces, armaments, munitions, aviation industry, shipbuilding industry, and others essential to the implementation of foreign policy. It enacts the specific measures required, extends recognition to foreign states or governments, severs relations, appoints and instructs negotiators of treaties or executive agreements not requiring ratification, confirms executive agreements and gives preliminary approval to treaties, orders acts of reprisal, appoints trade representatives. So important a body must of course respond sensitively to all changes of party line and transmit these to the administrative staff. This is assured because there are usually five or six members of the Presidium of the Central Committee of the Communist party who act as a directorate for the Council of Ministers and themselves assume important ministerial posts, always including the ministry of foreign affairs.

There seems to be no difficulty in the conduct of foreign relations by reason of the federal structure of the U.S.S.R. The federal government has competency with respect to nationality and the rights of aliens. Under the constitution of 1936 it controlled defense and foreign relations generally, and still controls Soviet Union treaties, foreign trade, state security, the decision to make war, and the direction of military forces. It may also establish "the general procedure governing the relations of Union Republics with foreign states." The constitutional reform of 1944 granted the constituent republics the right of direct representation in foreign affairs and the right to maintain separate military establishments. Probably the motivation for this change was the desire to make a case for membership of these republics in the United Nations. The Western powers did as a concession to the U.S.S.R. grant membership to the Ukrainian S.S.R. and Byelorussian S.S.R. These changes seem to be something of a showpiece to impress the innocent. They have not altered the fact of central control of foreign policy. Nor is there any evidence of separate military formations within the constituent republics. No doubt the changes have some political significance, for commissariats of war and foreign affairs were abolished in Union republics in 1923 and their re-establishment was firmly resisted until 1944. But the significance lies probably in the assurance that the party structure is so firmly in control of policy that the government feels no apprehension that such concessions will lead to inconsistent policies or deviation of member states from the party line.

A more difficult problem seems to arise in the relations between the U.S.S.R. and Communist states which are not members of the Union. It seems clear that party centralization has been effective in the satellite states of Eastern Europe to secure uniform foreign policy. The cases of Yugoslavia and Communist China certainly suggest the possibility of separate Communist states which pursue autonomous policies, but it is too much to suppose that the separation is likely to be a fundamental one. Tito broke with Stalin in part because he advocated that more aggressive tactics than those favored in Moscow be pursued in advancing European communism in the postwar period, and because of his desire to run his own show. In this he succeeded because his native party organization had attained sufficient strength during the war to resist infiltration and domination by Russian Communists, a fact not true of other Eastern European states. Yet there is no question that the Yugoslav policy is a communist policy, and the willingness of Tito to receive Western aid and to enter into defensive arrangements which strengthen his independence of action does not mean a compromise upon communism or a desire for permanent coexistence with free enterprise states. Mao Tse-tung was long regarded as a deviationist in his emphasis upon building a peasant communist movement. This background and the independent strength of China led to some question whether Russian leadership would be welcomed there. But Chinese Communists have apparently decided to imitate the Soviet pattern and have conducted a great propaganda campaign to improve Chinese attitudes toward Russia. Mao Tse-tung has shown signs of less patience in the struggle with the West than Stalin and his successors have displayed, but this hardly means opposition to the U.S.S.R. as such. If there is some chance of separate, autonomous communist states, there is probably very little possibility that communist states will actively oppose each other.

The peculiarities of Communist social, party, and governmental structure seem to present, at least for the present, an almost complete negation of those theoretical objectives of the classless society and the withering away of the state which are held to justify the system. The people's democracies turn out in fact to be tightly controlled dictatorships with all the possibilities for flexible policy maneuvering and rigid internal controls associated with dictatorship generally. This has been quite apparent in the opportunistic twists of Soviet foreign policy. What is not always so clear in view of the conspiratorial character of the system is the set of compulsions which at any time may lead the party oligarchs to embark upon a new turn of policy.

SELECTED READING

ALMOND, GABRIEL A., *The American People and Foreign Policy*. New York: Harcourt, Brace and Company, 1950.

BAILEY, THOMAS A., *The Man in the Street*. New York: The Macmillan Company, 1948.

BORKENAU, FRANZ, *European Communism*. New York: Harper and Brothers, 1953.

CHEEVER, DANIEL S. and HAVILAND, H. FIELD, JR., *American Foreign Policy and the Separation of Powers*. Cambridge: Harvard University Press, 1952.

CORWIN, E. S., *The President's Control of Foreign Relations*. Princeton: Princeton University Press, 1917.

DAHL, ROBERT A., *Congress and Foreign Policy*. New York: Harcourt Brace and Company, 1950.

DANGERFIELD, ROYDEN J., *In Defense of the Senate: A Study in Treaty Making*. Norman: University of Oklahoma Press, 1933.

ELLIOTT, WILLIAM YANDELL, *et. al., United States Foreign Policy: Its Organization and Control* (Report of a Study Group for the Woodrow Wilson Foundation). New York: Columbia University Press, 1952.

FAINSOD, MERLE, *How Russia is Ruled*. Cambridge: Harvard University Press, 1954.

FRIEDRICH, CARL J., *Foreign Policy in the Making*. New York: W. W. Norton and Company, 1938.

FURNISS, EDGAR S., JR., *The Office of the Premier in French Foreign Policy-Making: An Application of Decision-Making Analysis*. Princeton: Princeton University, Organizational Behavior Section, 1954 (Foreign Policy Analysis Series No. 5).

———, *Weaknesses in French Foreign Policy-Making*. Princeton: Princeton University, Center of International Studies, 1954 (Memorandum No. 5).

GOGUEL, FRANÇOIS, *France Under the Fourth Republic*. Ithaca: Cornell University Press, 1952.

HOWARD, JOHN ELDRED, *Parliament and Foreign Policy in France: A Study of the Origins, Nature and Methods of the Parliamentary Control of Foreign Policy in France During the Third Republic with Special Reference to the Period from 1919 to 1939*. London: Cresset Press, 1948.

JENNINGS, SIR IVOR, *Cabinet Government*, 2d ed. Cambridge: Cambridge University Press, 1951.

LANGFORD, R. VICTOR, *British Foreign Policy; Its Formulation in Recent Years*. Washington: American Council on Public Affairs, 1942.

LEITES, NATHAN, *The Operational Code of the Politburo*. New York: McGraw-Hill Book Company, 1951.

LONDON, KURT, *How Foreign Policy is Made*, 2d ed. New York: D. Van Nostrand Company, 1950.

SEABURY, PAUL, *The Wilhelmstrasse; A Study of German Diplomats under the Nazi Regime*. Berkeley: University of California Press, 1954.

SNYDER, RICHARD C., and FURNISS, EDGAR S., JR., *American Foreign Policy; Formulation, Principles, and Programs*. New York: Rinehart and Company, 1954.

STRANG (LORD), *et al., The Foreign Office*. London: George Allen and Unwin, Ltd., 1955; New York: Oxford University Press, 1955. (The New Whitehall Series.)

TOWSTER, JULIAN, *Political Power in the U.S.S.R., 1917–1947; The Theory and Structure of Government in the Soviet State*. New York: Oxford University Press, 1948.

CHAPTER 13

FOREIGN AFFAIRS ADMINISTRATION

The administration of foreign affairs is not in practice neatly separated from the determination and control of foreign policy, although it perhaps ought to be. In a representative government elected officers ought certainly to determine policy, and modern opinion leans to administration by career civil servants chosen upon the basis of merit. But between the elected officers and the career civil service some governments have one or more layers of higher level executive officers who are neither fish nor fowl. They are political appointees and therefore part of the representative system, yet their indirect choice removes them from a sense of direct responsibility to the electorate. If they are more numerous and their assignments more varied than can readily be comprehended within the "span of control" of a single chief executive, they may become too independent to be genuinely representative. On the other hand they are not career officers who wish to devote their lives to the mastery of a special field and may therefore be presumed incompetent to give expert advice or direction in the technical areas of foreign affairs administration.

This situation may be illustrated by comparison of British and American practice in the foreign office and the Department of State, respectively. In the former the entire officer personnel is composed of career men, up to and including the permanent under secretary of state for foreign affairs. The political appointees are the Secretary of State for Foreign Affairs, two ministers of state whose duties are likely to be concerned with United Nations and international conference problems, and two parliamentary under secretaries who assist in presenting the government's foreign policy program to the Parliament. None of these political officers is involved in the foreign office in an administrative sense; administrative direction of the career service rests with the permanent under secretary. He also serves as a funnel through which ministerial directives to the foreign office and foreign office advice to the ministry must pass. Only the foreign secretary can override the advice of permanent officials of the foreign office: junior ministers, such as parliamentary under-secretaries, are specifically forbidden to do so without consulting the minister.

By contrast the Department of State's political officers include the Secretary of State, sometimes but not regularly the Under Secretary of State, the two deputy under secretaries, one for substantive matters, one for administration, and the whole body of officers having assistant secretaryships or posts of comparable rank, such as the Legal Adviser and the Special Assistant for Intelligence. There is a tradition, usually observed, which reserves the post of Under Secretary for a career man, and this is often true of the post of Counselor of the Department of State and invariably of the director of the Policy Planning Board. Except for this modest intrusion of career men at the higher levels the whole administrative management of the department down to bureau and office chief levels is in the hands of political appointees, and it must be added they are as often as not persons without special training or experience in foreign affairs administration. It appears to be assumed, as George Kennan has recently remarked, "that 'management' is something wholly divorced from function," and that one who has demonstrated his administrative capacity in the Home Loan Bank Administration should encounter no difficulties as Assistant Secretary of State for Near Eastern, South Asian, and African Affairs. The need for both foreign affairs competence and management ability at the higher levels is clear, but it would seem that the proper way to obtain this is to select from the experienced career officers those who demonstrate management competency, and bring them forward, after additional in-service training in administration if needed, to the higher posts. The American practice penalizes the career officer by closing the higher ranks to him, and confuses the relationship of administration to policy, which properly should be to give expert advice to the policy officer and to administer effectively the policy directives which come from him.

DOMESTIC AGENCIES OF FOREIGN AFFAIRS ADMINISTRATION

The central agency for the administration of foreign affairs is everywhere the foreign office, and usually so called (sometimes foreign ministry), although the corresponding agency in the United States is called the Department of State because it originally had many, and still retains a few, domestic functions. Foreign offices are often popularly designated by place names, as Whitehall for the British foreign office, the Quai D'Orsay for the French ministry of foreign affairs, and (regrettably) Foggy Bottom for the Department of State.

Perhaps the simplest key to the structural problems of foreign offices is a consideration of the functions for which organization must be provided. Until the present century these were conceived mainly in terms of political relations with other countries; that is, the foreign office was simply the home base of the diplomatist, which translated policy into notes, despatches, memoranda, and instructions, drafted agreements, carried on necessary legal and historical research, sifted information coming in from the field, and in general did the preparatory work for negotiations with other governments. This preoccupation with diplomacy, scarcely qualified except for some attention to problems of foreign trade, permitted a very simple, compact administrative structure, so that foreign offices were for centuries among the smallest of important government agencies. Castlereagh's staff at the foreign office in 1821 included only 27 persons, and the Department of State staff was then about one third that number. By 1909, after a major reorganization, it had grown to no more than 35 officers, 135 clerks, and 40 minor employees. On the eve of World War I the personnel was less than 500, before World War II less than 1000. But the great pressure of wartime and reconstruction activities brought personnel to a postwar peak of about 9000, from which it had dropped to 5500 in 1954, prior to the integration of State Department and Foreign Service personnel recommended by the Wriston Committee.

United States

In the United States the structure of the department during the nineteenth century consisted of the Secretary of State, a Chief Clerk, and a small group of clerks who seem to have been first permanently assigned to specific duties in 1818 in the secretaryship of John Quincy Adams, then grouped into seven bureaus by the reorganization plan of Louis McLane in 1833, elaborated to thirteen units by Hamilton Fish in 1870. The first assistant secretary was authorized in 1853, a second in 1866, a third in 1875. There was no under secretary until 1919. This was all the organization required even during the difficult years of the Civil War, when Secretary Seward merely added extra clerks and a temporary bureau for political prisoners and rebel correspondence. In the reorganization planned by Assistant Secretary Huntington Wilson, begun by Secretary Elihu Root in 1908 and completed by Secretary Philander C. Knox in 1909, the State Department first moved toward a more complex organizational pattern. The core of it was a group of four politico-geographical divisions, which assumed the diplomatic business for Western Europe, the Near East, the Far East, and Latin America, respectively. With some adjustments these divisions have continued and have subdivided themselves as business increased into subregional units, in turn subdivided into country desks. Thereafter there was continuing elaboration of structure but little fundamental change until the 'thirties, when the expansion into new functional areas began

with the addition of an economic adviser and staff, and the creation of a
Division of Cultural Relations.

World War II involved the department heavily in wartime economic
activities, most of which had to be assigned to separate agencies such as the
Board of Economic Warfare, the War Production Board, the Office of Lend-
Lease Administration, and the Office of Foreign Relief and Rehabilitation
Operations. Some effort was made to co-ordinate these activities under the
policy guidance of the State Department, but jurisdictional conflicts led the
President to draw most of them together into a large independent agency,
the Foreign Economic Administration. This was only a stop-gap solution,
for continuing economic functions had to be reassigned after the war. Many
were returned to the Department of State, others assigned to new agencies.
Most notable in this group are the economic aid and technical assistance functions. The former were first placed in the Economic Cooperation Agency,
which gave way after the development of the military assistance program to
the Mutual Security Agency, created in 1951 to handle both economic and
military aid. Technical assistance was first divided among the Technical
Assistance Administration of the State Department, the Institute for Inter-
American Cooperation, and the Mutual Security Agency. In 1953 a new independent agency, the Foreign Operations Administration, succeeded the
Mutual Security Agency and assumed the economic aid, military aid, and
technical assistance functions of that agency and of the department. It has
proved to be short-lived, however, for it was terminated in 1955 and its functions and personnel returned to the State Department, where an International
Cooperation Administration has been set up.

Mention has been made of the beginnings of a State Department program
of cultural relations before World War II. Since the war it has developed into
a substantial program of educational exchange of students, instructors, and
cultural materials. The department also acquired in 1945 the functions and
personnel of the Office of War Information and set about developing an
international information program. The merger of these two programs produced the department's Office of International Information and Cultural
Affairs (or later Educational Exchange). After the Smith-Mundt Act of 1948
very substantial appropriations were given to the information program but
there was never a wholly clear conception of its function, which moved
gradually from President Roosevelt's notion of giving "the world a full and
fair picture of American life and of the aims and policies of the United States
Government," to something approaching psychological cold warfare. The
shift seems to have stemmed from the effectiveness, or assumed effectiveness,
of American propaganda in influencing the Italian election of 1948. Congress
was never satisfied with the State Department's conduct of the information
program, even after it was turned over to a semiautonomous International

Information Administration, and in 1953 created a separate International Information Agency. This agency was to receive policy guidance from the Secretary of State, but its administrative channel to the President lay through the National Security Council. Whether these arrangements can long endure seems doubtful. The function may well return to the State Department in time.

Still another novel postwar function has been intelligence research. In a sense the State Department has always performed this function, for diplomatic and consular agents regularly report their observations in the field and these reports have been studied by department officers, particularly in the geographical divisions. Modern intelligence research, however, is a much more systematic effort to draw together information not only from field agents but from all printed sources in answering specific problems. In 1945 the President transferred the staff of a wartime intelligence research agency, the Office of Strategic Services, to the Department of State, and thus gave it a nucleus from which its Office of Intelligence Research (OIR) was developed. For some time the personnel of this office seemed to work at cross purposes with that of the geographical offices, but this difficulty has gradually subsided since better contact was established by placing intelligence liaison officers in the geographical units. This State Department activity must not be confused with the new independent agency, the Central Intelligence Agency (CIA), created to provide intelligence research for all departments of the government and to utilize information obtained from them.

One other new function must be mentioned. During the war the department set up a special division on postwar planning which conducted the studies needed for postwar international organization. This staff did the preliminary work for the conferences at Dumbarton Oaks and San Francisco, which produced the U.N. Charter, and for the Bretton Woods Conference on international financial agencies. After the division had completed this preliminary work of planning and the United Nations and new specialized agencies had taken form, it was natural that the division should be transformed into a unit to conduct United States relations with international organizations. It was apparent that the old geographical agencies did not provide a suitable framework for dealing with global problems. The solution was to add to the four geographical divisions (by then called offices, and later bureaus) a fifth unit for international organization problems. It is now called the Bureau of International Organization Affairs and concerns itself with developing United States policy, expressed in position papers, to be followed by United States delegates to organs of the United Nations, the specialized agencies, and international conferences.

These new functional areas in the administration of foreign affairs—economic affairs, international information and educational exchange, intelligence research, and international organization problems—when added to a vast increase of the traditional work of the department and such temporary functions as occupation government and rehabilitation activities, serve to explain why the Department of State has been in an almost continuous process of reorganization since the war. The Hull-Stettinius reorganizations of 1944 and 1945 were designed chiefly to rearrange departmental units into functionally coherent groups, to provide clear lines of authority and responsibility, and to strengthen the direction of the department. The number of assistant secretaries was increased, an executive secretariat and a long-range policy planning board were added, and some effort was made to relieve top officers from administrative pressure by interposing a new layer of offices between the assistant secretaries and the divisions. Perhaps the most significant point in relation to the new functions was the recognition of them in new office structures parallel rather than subordinate to the older geographical offices.

This conception was attacked by the Hoover Commission in 1949. It argued that the department was essentially a foreign policy agency which should transfer operational functions other than diplomacy to other agencies and devote itself to formulating foreign policy in consultation with these operating agencies. In the newer functional areas it would require only small staffs of experts for advisory and consultative work. These would be subordinated to the geographical and international organization offices, which would again become the core of the department and its only operating units. Some effort was made to carry out these recommendations. The geographical and international organization offices were given a preferred status as bureaus. The other offices were somewhat reduced, and liaison officers from them assigned to the bureaus. But it has not been possible to give full effect to the plan because no such complete devolution of operating functions as that contemplated has been feasible. Nor is it clear that this is the soundest approach. A State Department confined to diplomatic operations but charged with foreign policy direction of a number of independent agencies performing other foreign operations must find the means of making its directives effective. Relations between independent agencies are not such as to make this easy.

In the United States the problem of co-ordinating executive agencies within a unified foreign policy has proved perplexing. This does not result from any absence of legal authority in the executive branch, for the President clearly has complete power to control the agencies. The difficulty is rather a practical one resulting from the immense pressures upon the President's time and energies, the number of independent agencies involved, and the nearly equal strength and influence of the larger ones. The Hoover Commission concluded in 1949 that there were about forty-five executive agencies participating in the conduct of United States foreign relations. Although this is symptomatic of the excessive proliferation in the executive branch, we need not take it too seriously in terms of policy co-ordination. Most of these agencies were involved in specialized administrative functions for which policy had been firmly established. In postwar years that problem has involved primarily the relations of the State Department with (a) security and defense agencies and (b) economic agencies.

In the first category the core agency is the Department of Defense. It contains a number of planning units which impinge upon foreign policy, notably the Armed Forces Policy Council, the Joint Chiefs of Staff, the Office of the Assistant Secretary of Defense for International Security Affairs, and the Munitions Board. Subordinate to the Department of Defense are the three Departments of the Army, Navy, and the Air Force, each of which contains units concerned with military aspects of foreign policy. The related functions of defense mobilization, which affect many agencies, have since 1953 been drawn together into the Office of Defense Mobilization in the Executive Office of the President. Control of atomic production, including weapons, rests with an independent agency, the Atomic Energy Commission. Military intelligence in the sense of strategic or tactical intelligence rests with the military services, but broader security intelligence is the function of the Central Intelligence Agency, already mentioned. Propaganda, the instrument of psychological warfare, is the function of the International Information Agency, the separation of which from the State Department has been mentioned. Finally, it must be noted that military assistance to allies, a most important aspect of American security policy, has involved the Defense Department for procurement and specifications, the Foreign Operations Agency for planning, contracts, and overseas operations, and the State Department for diplomatic negotiations and general policy.

How have these numerous agencies been drawn together with the Department of State under a common foreign policy canopy? No one would suggest that teamwork has been uniformly impressive, but in security policy substantial unity has been achieved through the National Security Council. This body, created by statute in 1947, is in form an interdepartmental committee, now composed of the President, Vice President, Secretary of State, Secretary of Defense, and Director of the Office of Defense Mobilization. It has a broad mandate to advise the President "with respect to the integration of domestic, foreign, and military policies relating to the national security," so as to promote interagency cooperation in this area. Actually, there are at present few broad questions of foreign policy which do not relate to security so that the Security Council must be considered one of the most important focal points for integrating foreign policy. Unlike most interdepartmental committees it has its own secretariat and also draws in representatives at the technical level from participating agencies. The secretariat does the spade work of preparing position papers and projects for consideration by the Council.

Thus, although it is an interagency committee the Council is almost an independent agency in itself. This conclusion is fortified by the fact that the Central Intelligence Agency operates under the direction of the Council; the International Information Agency has an administrative connection with it; and since 1953 a new interdepartmental committee, the Operations Coordinating Board (also equipped with a secretariat), has been added to its instruments. This last board attempts through consultation to integrate at operating levels security programs involving several agencies. This whole development of the Security Council and its affiliates is disconcerting to those who still think in the tradition of the State Department as *the* foreign policy agency, but given the terms of interdepartmental relationships in the security area it is probably inevitable.

In the field of economic affairs the distribution of operations is even wider, although the need of integration may be less urgent. In the promotion of foreign trade two units are significant, the Office of International Trade in the Department of Commerce, and the Office of International Trade and Resources in the Department of State. But this would involve tariff questions and therefore draw in the United States Tariff Commission, the Bureau of Customs in the Treasury Department, and an interdepartmental Committee on Trade Agreements. If control agencies concerned with quality of goods, plants, or animals imported into the country were included, we should have to add the Bureau of Narcotics in the Treasury Department, the Antitrust Division in the Department of Justice, the Bureau of Animal Industry and Bureau of Entomology and Plant Quarantine in the Agriculture Department, the Food and Drug Administration and the Public Health Service in the Federal Security Agency, and the Federal Trade Commission. When we enter the area of transport, we find the United States Maritime Commission, the Civil Aeronautics Board, the Civil Aeronautics Administration of the Department of Commerce, and the Office of Transport and Communications of the Department of State. If the question be one of foreign loans, exchange, or financial policy, we find the Office of International Finance in the Treasury Department, the Office of International Finance and Development in the State Department, and the Export-Import Bank of Washington. International labor problems concern the Office of International Labor Affairs in the Department of Labor and the Office of International Economic and Social Affairs in the State Department. There is an Office of Foreign Agricultural Relations in the Department of Agriculture. Agencies for economic aid and technical assistance have been mentioned elsewhere. These are by no means all, but they suffice to show the complexity of structure for economic operations. Many of these agencies participate also in policy.

There is no single device for assuring foreign policy integration in this area. The notion of the Hoover Commission that the State Department should be the policy agency and guide operations performed by other agencies has to some extent been followed and explains the rather complete paraphernalia of economic offices in the department. But there are agencies which are not readily amenable to such policy direction. Here a common device is the interdepartmental committee. Such committees may be formed at various levels and for a variety of purposes. They have sometimes been very effective co-ordinating devices. This has been true of the Committee on Trade Agreements, which approves the list of commodities used in tariff bargaining, the National Advisory Council on International Monetary and Financial Problems, primarily concerned with foreign loan policies, the Air Co-ordinating Committee, which co-ordinates civil aeronautics policy, and the less formal committees which developed the details of the Marshall Plan for European economic aid. Still another co-ordinating technique was tried by the Truman administration. Mr. Averell Harriman was given a post as special assistant in the White House with the task of presiding over interagency co-ordination. There were some advantages to this, since as the immediate representative of the President he possessed an authority which interdepartmental committees may lack. Unfortunately his role was somewhat confused by the fact that he served simultaneously as the Mutual Security administrator. President Eisenhower has used several special assistants in the foreign relations field, e.g., C. D. Jackson and Nelson Rockefeller for foreign policy, Dillon Anderson for national security problems, and Harold Stassen for disarmament. In his reorganization plans Mr. Eisenhower has tried to define carefully by executive directive what the working relationships between agencies shall be. This was done when FOA was set up, and when the International Information Agency was removed from the State Department. The President's role in direction and co-ordination is limited by the immense pressures upon his time and energy. These might be reduced by adoption of former President Herbert Hoover's proposal of a second vice president to direct 35 or 40 of the administrative agencies less important in terms of policy.

There appears to be one other method of dealing with the problem which merits more consideration than it has thus far received. This would be the reorganization of the State Department as a small superdepartment upon the model of the Department of Defense, grouping within it a number of separate agencies to deal respectively with diplomacy or political relations, foreign economic relations, and international information. Such a structure might assure the Department of State of its central position in foreign affairs and considerably simplify the machinery of co-ordination.

Great Britain

The British foreign office occupies a position in the government corresponding closely to that of the Department of State in the United States. Its functional area has been defined by the gradual elaboration of offices which have separated out one or another of the functions originally vested in the office of the secretary of state, which has existed from the reign of Henry III. In 1782 a division was made between a secretary of state for home affairs (English and Welsh) and a secretary of state for foreign affairs, whose province was external relations generally. In 1794 military affairs (other than naval, already vested in the Board of Admiralty) passed to the secretary of state for war. Administration of colonies, which had passed first to the Home Office, was transferred to the War Office, where it remained until the creation in 1854 of the office of the secretary of state for colonies. A separate India office under a secretary of state for India also existed until 1947, when India and Pakistan became independent members of the British Commonwealth of Nations. Other colonies had passed earlier to the status of dominions and then became autonomous members of the Commonwealth. Hence it became necessary to create the office of secretary of state for dominion affairs in 1925, later renamed secretary of state for Commonwealth relations. The foreign office is therefore not primarily responsible for colonial, Commonwealth, or defense policy, although it necessarily consults regularly with the offices concerned with these functions. Nor does it have administrative responsibilities in the field of foreign trade, which is the function of the Board of Overseas Trade, although it has been necessary to maintain a few economic departments in the foreign office. In one respect the foreign office pattern differs sharply from that of the Department of State; the former has assumed full responsibility for the overseas information and cultural relations programs and has four departments to conduct them.

Within the foreign office the basic units are departments, of which there are thirty-eight, exclusive of the corps of inspectors and the legal advisers. Most of these are grouped under eight assistant under secretaries of state and two officers of comparable rank—the director of communications and the director of research and librarian. However, there are three deputy under secretaries of state, who also supervise departments directly. One of these directs seven administrative departments. A second is concerned primarily with international organization relations. The third supervises the Western department (diplomatic relations with Benelux countries, France, Germany, Switzerland, and Eire), and the nonsecurity aspects of the European regional and North Atlantic Treaty organizations. Assistant under secretaries, with one exception, report directly to the permanent under secretary rather than to deputy under secretaries. The latter are distinguished chiefly by the fact that, in addition to duties of departmental supervision, they represent the foreign office on senior interdepartmental committees and undertake special assignments. One is the United Kingdom representative on the Permanent Commission of the Brussels Treaty Organization. For some years after 1947 there were also a permanent under secretary and deputy under secretary for German affairs, but the elimination of occupation government functions has made it possible to dispense with these. Political departments follow a geographical arrangement which to some extent still perpetuates traditional terminology. The Northern department (Scandinavian and Baltic countries, U.S.S.R. and its east European satellites) and the Southern department (Austria, Balkan countries, Turkey, Spain and Portugal, Vatican) take their titles from an early division of European diplomatic business although the original lines are no longer followed. The Western department has been mentioned, and there is also an Eastern department (Iran, Persian Gulf states, Saudi Arabia, Yemen). This last is grouped with an African department and a Levant department (Iraq, Israel, Jordan, Lebanon, Syria; also a secretariat for the interdepartmental committee on Middle Eastern affairs, which deals with technical assistance and defense questions in the Middle East). Other geographical departments are the American, the Far Eastern, and the South-East Asian. Staff services, apart from housekeeping functions, include departments for communications, archives, claims, consular affairs, passports, passport control, protocol, treaties and nationality questions, and security. A special feature is the strong position of the Library, traditionally the center of research and drafting functions of the foreign office.

The achievement of interagency co-ordination in the British government requires somewhat less artificial devices than in the United States because the cabinet system is itself a co-ordinating mechanism which needs only to be elaborated. The principle of cabinet solidarity imposes a necessity of reaching agreement by persuasion or compromise, with resignation of dissident ministers as the alternative. In so important an area as foreign affairs, resignations might invite a party split and endanger continuation of the cabinet. Great effort will therefore be made by the prime minister and foreign secretary to obtain a united front in foreign policy. There are, nevertheless, very serious problems in securing a unified administration, for foreign policy is inextricably bound up with foreign trade, defense measures, and many domestic issues outside the jurisdiction of the foreign office, as well as with problems of Commonwealth relations.

Agencies of co-ordination include the cabinet secretariat and the cabinet committees. The former, begun during World War I, was a borrowing of the methods developed by the Committee of Imperial Defense. It provides a permanent secretariat, with technical economic and statistical services at its disposal, which assumes responsibility for preparation of agenda, circulation of minutes, memoranda, and reports, and assistance to cabinet committees. The committees are designated by the prime minister according to need, although a few have come to be standing committees. They bring together the group of ministers concerned with particular areas of policy, and are regularly used both to study problems and submit recommendations to the cabinet, and for co-ordination of policy and administration among ministries. For example the standing defense committee, headed by the prime minister, includes the minister of defense, the lord president of the council, the foreign secretary, the chancellor of the exchequer, the minister of labour, the minister of supply, the first lord of the admiralty, and the secretaries of state for war, air, Commonwealth relations, and colonies. It is advised by the joint chiefs of staff of the armed services. Thus, in a different context, something very like the apparatus of the National Security Council of the United States exists in the British government.

In recent years the practice of assigning to several ministers additional tasks of co-ordination in principal policy areas has been tried. In the case of defense a new ministry of defense was created to which the admiralty, war office, and air ministry were subordinated. Although they retained most of their operating responsibilities and the ministry of defense concerned itself briefly with co-ordination, priorities, and certain joint operations, the subordinate agencies lost their seats in the cabinet. The idea of the superdepartment has not been applied elsewhere. Three co-ordinating ministers were designated by Attlee, including the foreign secretary, who was charged with general oversight of Commonwealth and Empire problems. This practice has continued, although it raises certain questions of responsibility since all the ministries thus supervised by a co-ordinating minister are still represented in the cabinet.

At the ministerial and official level there is also a good deal of less formal co-ordination. The foreign secretary is able to use his junior ministers to some extent for this purpose, and there are very many interdepartmental committees at the technical level. The treasury also endeavors to eliminate overlapping functions or agencies through its control of budget estimates and thus to rationalize the administrative structure.

Continental Governments

The foreign offices of the French Republic, the German Federal Republic, and the U.S.S.R., follow generally the pattern of the British foreign office, but the relationships in which these offices stand to the political branches of government vary a good deal. It is also in this relationship that one finds the answer to problems of co-ordination rather than in the administrative structure itself.

French Republic. In France the minister of foreign affairs, like the British foreign secretary, is a political rather than a professional officer. Nevertheless, the peculiarities of the cabinet and party system have led to long tenures in this office, even by ministers whose foreign policy views were not agreeable to the premier and other colleagues in the ministry. To an unusual degree

French foreign ministers have therefore been able to develop technical proficiency and knowledge of the details of foreign affairs administration and to perform technical duties as well as policy direction. They have also at their disposal a distinctive agency called the minister's cabinet, a kind of personal staff. This can hardly be compared with anything in American government, unless it might be the staff of a United States Senator or Congressman. It somewhat resembles the parliamentary under secretaries and ministers of state of British practice, but is a more highly organized body with wider functions. Functioning under a director and a *chef de cabinet* it includes a number of persons of extensive experience in the ministry of foreign affairs and diplomacy, as well as special communications facilities and couriers. This staff assists the minister in his relations with the parliament, the press and public, and the career officers of the ministry, performing many routine duties in facilitating correspondence, conferences, interviews, review of career officers' proposals, travel, and the like. The cabinet is clearly a factor in smooth co-ordination of administration.

The foreign ministry is composed almost wholly of career officers, although designation of the higher permanent officials is by the minister in consultation with the cabinet. Foreign office and foreign service personnel are interchangeable, and it is possible to make political appointments to important posts, but this has in practice been done only when compelling reasons exist. Career officers are therefore characteristically found in charge of all the offices and divisions of the ministry of foreign affairs. At their head is the secretary general, the French equivalent of the British permanent under secretary, whose office was created in 1920. He is certain to be a career expert of broad diplomatic and administrative experience, who possesses exceptional qualifications to advise the foreign minister. His office includes secretariats which deal with special problems, conferences, United Nations and UNESCO relations, and the work of the ministry.

The organization of the ministry itself includes eight offices with numerous divisions. Of these offices five are concerned primarily with staff functions, i.e., administrative affairs; personnel, accounting, and supplies; protocol; cryptography and codes; and archives. The others are political affairs; economic, financial, and technical affairs; and cultural relations. The first is organized upon the usual geographical lines, with divisions grouped into four principal directorates for America, Europe, Asia and Oceania, and Africa-Levant. To the last are assigned additional functions as to the protectorates of Tunisia and Morocco. The economic divisions include a directorate handling economic and financial negotiations and relations with international economic organizations; a directorate of technical accords to protect economic interests abroad and deal with problems of international transport; and a directorate for economic cooperation projects. The cultural relations office is well developed and the oldest large-scale effort in that field by a principal state. France has long expended substantial sums to improve attitudes toward it in the Near East and Far East.

Co-ordination of administration in France seems rather more probable than co-ordination of cabinet policy. Within the ministry of foreign affairs it would appear that adequate facilities for it exist in the cabinet of the minister and the office of the secretary general. In interdepartmental relations, given a firm policy line upon which the cabinet and deputies agree, it is possible through the cabinet secretariat, the direct contacts of ministers and their cabinets, and various committees to correlate action. The real danger of dis-unity lies primarily at the political level, in the party bargaining which has enabled one party to control the ministry of foreign affairs and to operate it as an autonomous preserve for a number of years while other parties kept a like control of other important ministries. This situation made any co-ordi-nation of action among ministries difficult and subject to political bargaining.

Federal Republic of Germany. The resumption of foreign affairs admin-istration by the Federal Republic of Germany occurred so recently that its arrangements for this purpose cannot be considered to have reached a defini-tive form. The Occupation Statute proclaimed by the Allied military governors in 1949 reserved important rights as to disarmament, demilitarization, foreign affairs, foreign trade and exchange control, and other matters. However, the establishment of German consulates was allowed by the Petersburg Agreement of November, 1949. In September, 1950, the New York conference of the foreign ministers of the United Kingdom, United States, and France au-thorized the Federal Republic to establish a foreign ministry, terminated the state of war, and guaranteed West German territory against armed aggression. In April, 1950, an "office for foreign affairs" had been established in the office of the chancellor, thus providing a nucleus for the ministry of foreign affairs created March 16, 1951. Chancellor Adenauer himself assumed the post of minister of foreign affairs. Consulates general were opened in London, New York, and Paris in 1950. Two years later the consuls general became chargés d'affaires. In the summer of 1953 they were given the personal rank of am-bassador. Diplomatic missions have since been established throughout the noncommunist world. The Federal Republic has also entered about thirty international organizations. The Occupation Statute ended May 5, 1955.

The new ministry of foreign affairs has been organized upon conventional lines. Under the foreign minister is a secretary of state for foreign affairs, who with the help of a legal adviser, press officer, and a group of *Referenten,* directs the office. It contains staff divisions for protocol, personnel and administration (organization and maintenance, representation services, payments and ac-counts, cryptography and codes, translation, library), and legal work. Line functions are assigned to a political division, a division of commercial policy, and a cultural relations division. A training academy is conducted at Speyer.

Foreign policy has been controlled by Chancellor Adenauer, who uses the ministry less for policy consultation than as an administrative group to carry out his instructions. Although the chancellor appears to rely upon Dr. Hallstein, who is the secretary of state for foreign affairs, he has not delegated discretion in matters of policy. He has also conducted many negotiations personally and possesses remarkable qualifications even for technical direction. Under these circumstances the ministry has not yet developed strongly as an autonomous agency capable of exerting much professional career influence upon political officers. Co-ordination and direction of foreign policy administration has been primarily the function of the office of the chancellor. Although this reflects the dominant position of Dr. Adenauer, it also results from the strength of the office of chancellor and the dependence of the ministries upon it. It is unlikely that relinquishment of the post of foreign minister by Adenauer to Brentano will much affect the situation.

U.S.S.R. The Soviet ministry of foreign affairs (*Minindel,* formerly *Narkomindel,* People's Commissariat for Foreign Affairs) is the administrative unit which carries out the directives of the Council of Ministers in matters of foreign policy. Its personnel is interchangeable with diplomatic agents, and officials of the ministry have from time to time represented the U.S.S.R. in negotiations. The foreign minister, who directs the ministry, is usually a party member of high though not necessarily the highest standing. Molotov, as an old Bolshevik and party leader, undoubtedly has participated in major policy councils although he probably never dominated them. Vishinsky was not among the inner circle, although he was respected for his remarkable legal and forensic talents. Litvinov was almost outside the policy line and never enjoyed full confidence. No doubt the choice of the foreign minister has reflected the Russian view of the seriousness of the problems to be undertaken and the spirit the government wishes to cultivate at the moment in foreign relations.

Soviet ministers are unlike the ministers of parliamentary democracies in many respects. Although formally elected by the Supreme Soviet, they are in no sense an executive committee of legislative leaders. The Council of Ministers does not form a cabinet responsible to the legislative body. Rather the Supreme Soviet ratifies a choice of ministers made by the party headquarters. These continue to be at all times sensitive to the party line and devoted to administrative implementation of it. They present policy to the legislative soviets rather than take their cue from them. Some of them will be members of the party center able to issue policy directives to their ministries. Others will be technical and administrative experts whose influence does not go beyond advice to the party managers. In either case, they usually are or become specialists capable of technical as well as administrative direction of their ministries.

The collegial principle has prevailed in the organization of ministries as in other Soviet executive structures. This began in the early period of the commissariats, when a collegium for each commissariat was appointed by the Council of People's Commissars. Decisions were to be taken after discussion by the collegium and minister. This principle underwent modification. Direct management passed to the minister subject to the right of the collegium to appeal from his decisions to the council. Then in 1934 Stalin abolished the collegia, only to restore them a few years later in reorganized form. They are appointed by the Council of Ministers and include the minister, his deputies, and important ministry officials—perhaps five to nine in all. But the collegium acts only in the name of the minister and with his assent. If there are differences of opinion, members of the collegium may appeal to the Council of Ministers and the Central Committee of the party. The principal function of the collegium is not policy direction but administrative management in executing policy, which in theory leaves some scope for policy direction by the minister. It is apparent, however, that the collegium is a means of surveillance and review, so that deviation from the party line could not go long unquestioned. Other controls exist through the secret police and the limitations imposed by planning and budget controls and the checks of a "ministry of state control."

The internal organization of *Minindel* is apparently much like that of Western European foreign offices, with a regional breakdown of political divisions and a number of staff services. An unusual emphasis seems to be placed upon intelligence activities and upon the in-service training of personnel.

Interdepartmental co-ordination is certainly not a problem in the U.S.S.R. since the party is the co-ordinating mechanism which assures conformity throughout the government. The Council of Ministers responds directly to the party center and is the principal policy and management body. Here any problems of co-ordinated action by several ministries can be readily adjusted. This is important for the Soviet scheme of foreign policy since the ministry of foreign affairs must maintain close relations with the ministry of defense and the ministry of defense industry, with *Agitprop* (the Administration of Agitation and Propaganda), with the ministries of internal and foreign trade, culture, transport, communications, and others. Proliferation of new ministries during the war necessitated the creation of a small state committee of defense, which acted as a co-ordinating war cabinet from June 30, 1941, to September 4, 1945. This included Stalin, Molotov, Voroshilov (replaced by Bulganin), Beria, Malenkov, to which later were added Mikoyan, Voznesensky, and

Kaganovich. After the war some reduction in the number of ministries was made by Stalin, and after his death a further consolidation with reduction to twenty-five, so that co-ordination through the Council of Ministers is now a problem of manageable proportions.

Fainsod reports (*How Russia is Ruled,* p. 282) the comments of an informant acquainted with the Politburo's methods of control of the commissariat of foreign affairs under Litvinov in the late thirties. The Politburo maintained a subcommittee on foreign affairs of which Molotov was chairman, Mikoyan specialist in foreign trade questions, and Zhdanov in Comintern (later Cominform) affairs. Detailed directives were issued by the Politburo to the commissariat, which could move autonomously within the areas covered by them. But if issues arose which could not be resolved by reference to directives they had to be referred to Molotov as chairman of the subcommittee. When he thought them of sufficient importance they were referred to plenary meetings of the Politburo for discussion, and the commissar then reported and offered recommendations. Otherwise the subcommittee decided. The Politburo also obtained memoranda from the foreign section of the Central Committee secretariat, which had sources of intelligence not always available to the commissariat. This picture of continuous, detailed direction of the commissariat's work by the inner circle of party leaders is undoubtedly approximately correct for the present conduct of the ministry.

Since 1944 the ministry of foreign affairs has been a Union-republic ministry, i.e., it comprises a central ministry in contact with individual foreign affairs ministries in each of the sixteen republics. The usual administrative pattern of these ministries contemplates the use of the republic ministries as offices for regional operations. It must be remembered, however, that the extension to the constituent states of rights of overseas representation did not in fact produce any foreign affairs activity by them other than membership of the Byelorussian and Ukrainian S.S.R.'s in the United Nations. It may be assumed that the central ministry holds a tight rein in foreign affairs administration and that the local ministries are used only for routine consultation, informational facilities, and internal execution of treaty obligations. Representatives of *Minindel* are attached to republic ministries to assure proper co-ordination.

The actual conduct of Soviet foreign relations in the field also exhibits evidence of close party control. Soviet negotiators persistently follow with tactical skill and concentration a policy line determined by the party center, and can seldom respond to overtures of other governments. Annoying evasions or delays pending receipt of new instructions are therefore a usual feature of their negotiations. Shifts in party strategy may also produce surprising changes of front which Soviet negotiators must present with composure however inconsistent they may be with positions previously asserted.

FOREIGN SERVICE ADMINISTRATION

Classification of Agents

In regulations adopted at the Congress of Vienna in 1815, to which additions were made at the Congress of Aix-la-Chapelle in 1818, diplomatic agents were divided into the following classes:

1. Ambassadors; legates (papal ambassadors extraordinary upon special missions, always cardinals); nuncios (papal ambassadors resident, never cardinals).
2. Envoys and ministers plenipotentiary.
3. Ministers resident, accredited to the sovereign.
4. Chargés d'affaires, accredited to the minister for foreign affairs.

This classification was followed by the United States for designation of its envoys in a statute of March 1, 1893. The titles now employed are ambassador extraordinary and plenipotentiary, envoy extraordinary and minister plenipotentiary, minister resident, chargé d'affaires.

Agents of the first class in the Vienna rules are said to possess representative character, i.e., to represent directly the formal chief of state of the sending state, not always identical with the political head of government. Thus a British ambassador technically represents the queen, although in practice directed by her government. And President F. D. Roosevelt's reference to "my ambassador," although it provoked some witticisms, was legally quite accurate. Agents of the first three classes are accredited to the formal chief of state of the receiving state, and therefore must be received by him before they have leave to enter upon their duties. These initial receptions by the sovereign or president are still sometimes occasions for stately ceremonial reminiscent of a day when monarchs really controlled foreign relations. But the form alone remains. For every practical purpose the diplomat's business now lies directly with the foreign office.

It should be noted that consuls are not classified as diplomatic agents. They are, in fact, certified to the foreign office of the receiving state, which issues a document called *exequatur,* which is their authorization to exercise consular functions. However, they do not upon appointment report to the government of the receiving state but proceed directly to the consular district within that state or its dependencies to which they have been assigned. There they establish relationships with local officials and businessmen.

The foreign service of a state may also include a variety of other agents. Military, naval, and air attachés are commonly detailed from the armed services to advise diplomatic officers. They also report military information directly to their own services. Information officers conduct, sometimes in conjunction with diplomatic establishments but often separately, programs of international information, educational exchange, and propaganda. Technical problems which confront diplomatic establishments require a variety of special attachés, e.g., economic analysts, agricultural experts, minerals and petroleum specialists, press officers. A variety of administrative officers (budgeting, accounting, purchasing, custodial, etc.) may be needed to discharge the housekeeping functions of the larger embassies, legations, and consulates.

A distinction must be made between the international terminology of the Congress of Vienna and the classifications which a particular state may choose to use within its own personnel systems to designate officers for foreign service. Thus the Foreign Service of the United States as defined in the Foreign Service Act of 1946 includes a number of distinct groups: chiefs of mission (partly political appointees, partly career officers); Foreign Service officers, in six numbered classes and the unnumbered class of career ministers; Foreign Service staff officers and employees, in twenty-two numbered classes of which Classes 1–9 are considered officers; Foreign Service reserve officers; alien clerks and employees of the overseas establishments; consular agents. These classifications relate even more to the terms of recruitment and tenure than to functions. A Foreign Service officer may be assigned to diplomatic duties as first, second, or third secretary of embassy, counselor of embassy, or if of career minister rank, as an ambassador or minister. He may also be assigned to consular duties as vice consul, consul, or consul general. Or he may be, and frequently is, assigned to mixed diplomatic and consular duties. Foreign Service staff officers usually have administrative assignments but may on occasion be commissioned as consuls. Reserve officers are appointed for temporary service for periods up to five years (changed in 1955 from four years) upon the basis of specialist competencies, and may not be reappointed for a year after completing a tour of duty.

As these categories are authorized by statutes, a limited use of all may continue, but the integration program recommended by the Wriston Committee in 1954 contemplates the future staffing of most officer posts both in Foreign Service establishments and in the Department of State with Foreign Service officers. This move toward a unified foreign affairs service follows a trend in which the United States has lagged behind other major powers. In England the personnel of the foreign office and the diplomatic service were amalgamated, on the basis of recommendations of the Royal Commission on the Civil Service (1911–1914), immediately after World War I, and the "Eden Reforms" of 1943 provided for integration of the diplomatic, consular, and commercial diplomatic services. Continental powers preceded the English-speaking countries in such integrations of foreign service personnel. According to a study made by the Bureau of the Budget and the Department of State in 1947 twenty-nine of thirty-four countries which were examined had interchangeable departmental and field personnel. In all but six, these services

were at least formally a part of the general civil service, although some differentiation probably resulted in practice from the frequency of separate recruitment. Of the six which deliberately provided a separate foreign affairs service,
Great Britain was the most important.

The United States further complicates its personnel arrangements by
maintaining a number of overseas staffs which are separate from the Foreign
Service. This practice had been nearly eliminated, except for a few small
groups, such as Treasury Department agents, when the overseas commercial
and agricultural services were brought into the Foreign Service in 1939. Unfortunately, the demands of postwar programs of military occupation, economic aid, military assistance, technical assistance, international information,
and intelligence acquisition could not be met by the limited personnel of
the Foreign Service, and many separate staffs were created. There are now
in excess of twenty distinct personnel systems for different types of overseas
service. A separate agricultural service was recently recreated. The effect of
these tendencies has been not only to confuse foreigners who have to deal with
American overseas agencies, but to create difficult problems of co-ordination
of action and administrative control among such agencies. To some extent
the situation may be expected to improve with the elimination of temporary
agencies, but a more fundamental reorganization seems to be indicated in
view of the complexity of the overseas operations which the United States
must expect to continue. There are limits, however, to the scope of such reorganization. It cannot be expected that the overseas civilian employees of
the military services can be integrated into a general service, nor is it clear
that field staffs engaged in economic aid and technical assistance projects could
properly be drawn into Foreign Service officer status even if it should come
to include specialists. Their present status as separately recruited groups assigned to Foreign Service staff and reserve officer ranks may, in view of the
temporary and *ad hoc* character of their projects, be preferable.

It should be added that some use has been made by the United States,
especially in wartime, of special executive agents outside the framework
of the Foreign Service. These are usually confidential presidential representatives, of whom Colonel House in the Wilson administration and Harry
Hopkins in Franklin D. Roosevelt's administration are the best known. There
are advantages in the practice but also some dangers unless the President is
careful to keep the Department of State advised; otherwise the official diplomatic mission and the confidential agent may not speak with one voice. Thus
it was disconcerting to Charles Francis Adams, when he was minister to
England during the Civil War, to find that his government had sent two
bankers to try to outbid the Confederate States of America in purchasing
ironclad ships against the construction and sale of which Adams was officially
protesting. When in 1940 President Roosevelt decided without consulting

Secretary of State Cordell Hull to send Under Secretary of State Sumner Welles on a mission to Europe, a misunderstanding resulted which contributed to the final estrangement of Hull and Welles. On the other hand, there is a definite place for professionally qualified special agents used in proper relationship to the regular diplomatic establishment, for they can act as trouble shooters and can deal with the broader problems which are beyond the scope of a mission to a particular country. Prentice Gilbert, Norman Davis, Hugh Gibson, and more recently Philip Jessup, have done excellent service in this capacity. The tendency in recent years has been to designate such agents as ambassadors at large.

The danger to be avoided in the use of special executive agents may be illustrated by the extreme example of *Le Secret* of Louis XV of France. That monarch seemed often to be at cross purposes not only with his ministers but even with himself, undoing with the left hand what he was contriving with the right. He created a kind of secret foreign office under his immediate supervision, which, as David Jayne Hill remarked, amounted to "an organized conspiracy against the King's own official diplomacy." The Prince de Conti and the Count de Broglie were successively the secret ministers (*les vizirs de poche*) in charge of this organization, which also had as its secretary the first clerk of the foreign office and as field representatives certain members of the regular diplomatic service acting independently of it upon orders of the king and some special correspondents outside the service. It was not uncommon to have the regularly accredited French envoy to another government maintaining one position under instructions from the foreign office, while a representative of *Le Secret* (perhaps one of the envoy's own secretaries) undid his work by presenting inconsistent views of the king privately transmitted. It requires an almost psychopathic personality to achieve such an absurdity, but as international politics have not been wholly free even in recent years from such personalities, it seems desirable to have administrative structures and practices which minimize irresponsibility.

There is a customary relationship between titles and posts. Regular diplomatic establishments, or missions, may be either embassies or legations. The chief of mission assigned to an embassy is an ambassador; if assigned to a legation, a minister. Until 1893 the United States did not send or receive ambassadors. Thereafter it accredited ambassadors to a small group of countries with which it had important relationships, sending ministers to others. The number of embassies was increased slowly until recent years, when it was thought desirable to gratify the *amour propre* of governments by accrediting ambassadors to nearly all of them. In 1955 the United States accredited ministers as chiefs of mission only to Hungary, Iceland, Laos, Luxembourg, Rumania, and Yemen, and the last named was not a separate post but only an additional duty of the ambassador to Saudi Arabia. At three of its largest embassies (London, Paris, Rome) it had a minister in addition to the ambassador, and also a minister-consul general in Hongkong. Ten counselors of embassy at important posts had the personal rank of minister but were not so accredited to the receiving state. Several special assignments were made, the United States high commissioners to Germany and Austria, the chief of the United States Mission to the North Atlantic Treaty Organization and European Regional Organizations, and the diplomatic agent to Tangier. The first three were ambassadors, the last a minister. A consul general has charge of a consulate general, which will be found only in the more important commercial cities. A consulate is under the direction of a consul, or at some minor posts of a vice consul. In some commercial towns where it is not thought practicable to have a consular establishment, a consular agent may be designated.

Whether an agent is to be regarded as a diplomat depends, not upon his status in the personnel system of his own state, but upon assignment to perform diplomatic functions. Usually this will mean that the diplomatic officer is designated as an ambassador, minister, chargé d'affaires, counselor of embassy, secretary of embassy, embassy or legation attaché, although in some cases other titles may be used. In the first flush of proletarian triumph the U.S.S.R. for a time refused to use the traditional titles of decadent diplomacies. It styled all of its diplomatic agents *Polpreds* (political representatives). By a decree of the Presidium of the Supreme Soviet dated May 9, 1941, the Soviet government reverted to the traditional ranks of ambassador, minister, and chargé d'affaires. The Soviet *Torgpreds* (trade representatives) occupied an intermediate status specially defined by treaty. As representatives of a state trading monopoly empowered to negotiate commercial treaties or agreements, they sometimes obtained diplomatic immunities. It is not, therefore, the title which is conclusive, but the character of the duties assigned. We are, however, saved from much uncertainty by the practice most states follow of publishing a *Diplomatic List,* in which are shown the names of diplomatic agents of other states who have been officially received as such. The *Diplomatic List* serves as *prima facie* evidence of a right to claim diplomatic privileges and immunities. Generally speaking, diplomatic status will be accorded to those who have a diplomatic assignment even though they have also some nondiplomatic duties.

Functions of Agents

What, then, are diplomatic duties? It is usual to range them under four headings: representation, negotiation, reporting, protection.

By *representation* is meant not only the conveying of diplomatic messages to a government, but also the function of acting as spokesman, interpreter, and symbol of one's country at occasions official and private, ceremonial and informal, and cultivating friendship and understanding through such contacts. This is essentially a public relations function and makes very heavy demands upon diplomatic officers, who are frequently caught up in a round of social functions, official calls, speeches, dedications, commemorations, to the great prejudice of rest, digestion, and systematic office routine. Yet the time and effort must be accounted well spent if it produces a better understanding of official positions and public attitudes among the opinion leaders of the two countries. To the extent that a country's program of "international information" consists only in an honest and temperate effort to give, in the words of President Franklin D. Roosevelt, a "full and fair picture" of its way of life and its government's aims and policies, this would seem consistent with diplomatic representation and properly within the functions of a diplomatic establishment. But a program of false or slanted propaganda, or one involving interventions of questionable legality into another government's domestic politics, cannot be conducted by diplomats without destroying the confidence they should cultivate. If such programs are considered essential devices of cold war, they should at least be organized under nondiplomatic auspices. The practice of states varies. Although the International Information Agency of the United States became in 1953 an independent operating agency subject to the policy guidance of the Department of State, its staff members both in Washington and the field hold appointments as Foreign Service officers (a few), Foreign Service staff officers, and Foreign Service reserve officers. With the exception of the Foreign Service officers, however, they do not have additional diplomatic or consular duties and carry on their functions separately. Many of these functions, e.g., library and reference services, are hardly propagandistic.

Negotiation signifies the process of reaching through exchange of views, conversations, or formal conference, agreements which can be expressed in precise terms, generally written, as international agreements which the governments legally obligate themselves to observe. The most formal of international political agreements are frequently called treaties, the texts of which are carefully worked out by negotiation. Others may be termed conventions (usually administrative or technical matters), protocols, acts, general acts, final acts (of conferences), statutes, declarations, arrangements, accords, concordats, *modi vivendi* (usually informal or temporary). The titles chosen are somewhat arbitrary and are not significant of differences in international legal character, although they may affect constitutional requirements of particular states as to ratification or domestic legal status. A binding international agreement may be, and often is, effected by a simple exchange of notes between governments. And the Permanent Court of International Justice in the *Eastern Greenland Case* (P.C.I.J., Series A/B, No. 53 [1933]) gave effect to an agreement between Denmark and Norway on the ground that the foreign minister of Norway had made an oral commitment in response to an oral inquiry by the Danish minister to Norway, which was established from minutes each had made of the conversations. As has been indicated, the function of negotiation has in considerable degree passed from the hands of resident diplomats to special diplomatic agents or negotiators sent from foreign offices, particularly in multilateral agreements and questions of technical or administrative character. Still, negotiation must be considered a primary function of professional diplomacy, and effective negotiation is indeed an end product of all diplomatic effort.

Although much comment can be found, even by professional diplomats, upon the techniques of negotiating or the principles of diplomacy in general, it hardly appears that these constitute a special professional art peculiar to diplomacy. They apply as well to any transactions in which one seeks to persuade others to accept his views, and are probably better learned by practice than by precept. "Take snuff often and slowly," advised the experienced diplomatist Kolle, "sit with your back to the light, and speak the truth; the rest you will learn by observing your older colleagues." Pleasant, courteous relationships, clear marshaling of facts and arguments, persuasive conversation, may well be recommended to the apt but are as likely to elude the inept. One can hardly do better than quote the sensible comments of Professor Mountague Bernard, made nearly a century ago (*Four Lectures on Subjects Connected with Diplomacy,* pp. 149–150):

> Cardinal Janson, who distinguished himself as *chargé d'affaires* at Rome, was asked by Louis the Fourteenth where he had learnt to negotiate so well. "I learnt it, Sire," answered he, "when I was Bishop of Digne, and had to trot about with a lantern to canvass for the election of a maire of Aix." To know exactly what you want; to see quickly and clearly what is practicable; to take everything by its right handle; never to be in a hurry; not to contradict; not to irritate; not to threaten; not to seek mere triumphs in argument, or assert principles which lead to nothing; above all, to remember that the person you are dealing with probably knows his own interest as well as you know your own, that the real end of negotiating is to find a point at which the interests of both parties can be made to coincide, and that by the dexterity which over-reaches or over-persuades nothing is gained in the long run;—all this is good advice, but it is almost as good at a parish vestry as at a conference for the pacification of Europe. The difference is rather in the weight and magnitude of the interests concerned than in their special character.

Reporting is the preparation by diplomats for the use of their governments of detailed information and data about the country to which they are accredited, with interpretative analysis designed to clarify policies, attitudes, and probable reactions of government leaders, organized groups, and general public. Since this information is intended to guide the diplomat's government in determining its policy, it is imperative that it be comprehensive and accurate.

In part it will consist in regular periodical reports of a routine character, in part of special reports upon particular problems or in response to inquiries. Capacity for effective reporting is hardly an ability which can be taken for granted in diplomatic agents, and much casual, inadequate, and purely impressionistic comment has been sent in. Governments now try to secure better reporting by systematic training of career diplomats and by detailed guidance in the preparation of reports. Thus, the United States Department of State now issues for the use of its Foreign Service officers a detailed manual on political reporting and another on economic reporting. The collaboration of specialist attachés in the more technical reports has also produced a more sophisticated analysis. Governments do not, of course, rely exclusively upon diplomatic agents for information but often develop specialized intelligence services, e.g., the Central Intelligence Agency of the United States. Until recent years intelligence agencies were concerned mainly with security information. Although this continues to be their focus, the scope of their inquiries has become broader since World War II.

Protection of nationals and their interests may be thought of as primarily a function of consuls at the administrative level and of diplomats at the policy level, but diplomats find it impossible to avoid intervening in the practical difficulties of their nationals to secure their personal and property rights or to give procedural assistance in redressing violation of them. This involves a great variety of time-consuming inquiries and representations. At the policy level it is of course the diplomat's function to protest any conditions, legislation, or regulations which unjustly discriminate against his nationals and to try to obtain changes.

The duties of diplomats necessarily overlap those of consuls, who are concerned principally with commercial relations and protection of the interests of nationals. However, the consuls work at the local level, whereas diplomats are intermediaries of national governments, seeking to effect better relations, economic or political, in terms of national governmental policy. *Consular functions* are varied and often technical, including the following: (a) authentication of foreign documents required for legal transactions, service of legal documents, taking and authentication of protests, depositions, or declarations; (b) issuance (now only in special cases) and visa of passports or travel permits, checking of invoices and certificates of origin of goods destined to the consul's home state as an aid to its customs officials; (c) registering of vital statistics concerning the consul's nationals residing abroad in the consular district, for use in case of need to evacuate them or to enforce draft laws, etc.; (d) as far as permitted by local law to adjust differences between the consul's nationals (formerly even sitting as a court having extraterritorial jurisdiction over them in certain Asian and Middle Eastern states) and to assist them when arrested or detained by the receiving state or involved in legal proceedings there; (e) to take steps to protect and secure administration of estates in the consular district left by deceased nationals; (f) to protect the interests of absent, incompetent, ill, or minor nationals in the consular district; (g) to visit and inspect vessels of the sending state when in ports of the consular district, taking custody of ship's papers, adjusting problems of seamen's wages or tenure, complaints against the master, or disputes effecting the internal order or discipline of the ship; (h) to provide for salvage of vessels of the sending state or their cargoes when in distress in waters off the consular district, and to safeguard the interest of nationals in claims arising from wreck or salvage; (i) to inspect any vessels bound for ports of the sending state in order to enforce its sanitary laws or other regulations with respect to emigrants, goods and produce, or animals to be carried there; (j) to protect nationals, their property or interests, from injury within the consular district, or to help them obtain redress for injuries; (k) to study conditions within the consular district and to report to the sending state, or respond to inquiries by businessmen, upon trade conditions, business opportunities, and the like.

Privileges and Immunities of Agents

It has long been recognized that the efficient conduct of foreign relations by governments requires that their diplomatic, and to a lesser degree their consular, agents should be accorded special privileges and immunities in the countries to which they are accredited. Most of these rights are defined by international law. Probably they originated in the representative character of ambassadors and ministers, which led rulers to consider molestations of their agents as personal affronts to themselves and to demand for them rights equivalent to those which they would themselves enjoy if they visited another country. It has often been said that diplomats have extraterritorial rights in the states to which they are accredited and that an embassy or legation is a kind of enclave within a foreign jurisdiction. This is a fiction. The special position of the diplomat results not from the extension of the territorial jurisdiction of the sending state into the receiving state, but rather from a grant by the receiving state of a personal exemption from its normal territorial jurisdiction to the extent that usage has established this as necessary to facilitate international relations. Upon this basis it is easier to understand that the immunity from entry and search regularly accorded to diplomatic premises is not absolute, but related to the agent's duties and dependent upon his good faith and respect for the rights of the receiving state in discharging them.

Thus a Canadian court refused to exclude from evidence papers which had been removed from the office of the military attaché of the Soviet embassy by an embassy employee when the government offered this evidence in a criminal action against a member of the Canadian Parliament for conspiracy in supplying classified information concerning atomic weapons to the embassy

(Rose *v.* The King. [1947] 3 Dominion Law Reports 618). Although the court remarked that a Soviet diplomatic agent would enjoy personal immunity from criminal prosecution even though he organized espionage or sabotage against the receiving state, it declared that

. . . the offended Government has the right immediately to take every repressive measure, any initiative which may annihilate or destroy the acts of disloyalty endangering the public as a result of the abuse of office of such Embassy. And these measures of repression or protection could go as far as expelling the ambassador, or putting his mansion, his documents and archives under a sort of seal . . .

An investigation of Soviet espionage by a Canadian commission revealed at least five separate channels of communication centered in the U.S.S.R.'s mission at Ottawa: diplomatic reporting to the commissariat for foreign affairs, commercial reporting to the commissariat for foreign trade, military intelligence reported to the director of military intelligence in Moscow by military attachés, reporting by the NKVD to its Moscow headquarters, and party communication through the political section of the embassy to the Central Committee in Moscow or to Canadian Communist leaders. The atomic secrets espionage which was uncovered was conducted by military intelligence personnel. It was no less an abuse of the privileges of the embassy, since conducted under its auspices and with the use of its facilities. Such activities inevitably arouse distrust and hostility prejudicial to the legitimate conduct of diplomacy.

It might indeed be difficult to place any sharp limitation upon a government's right to expel a foreign diplomat. Since it need not receive him in the first instance, it can properly desire to be rid of him if he becomes *persona non grata* for any reason. Usually the sending state will respect the wishes of the receiving state and withdraw such an agent, knowing that he could not continue to serve effectively. But requests for withdrawal are sometimes declined when they are thought abitrary, and expulsion follows. One or two examples may clarify this. In 1888 the British minister to the United States, Lord Sackville-West, was tricked into answering a private letter, purporting to come from a former British subject, inquiring which candidate in the presidential election might be more favorable to friendly relations with Great Britain. The correspondence was published, and the United States requested Sackville-West's recall. When the British government refused to recall him without further inquiry, he was instantly dismissed. It has been said that this decisive action was taken to placate the Irish vote, but it seems to have been warranted in view of the envoy's interference in domestic politics. In 1952 George F. Kennan, the United States ambassador to the U.S.S.R., made a speech in Berlin in which he likened diplomatic service in Moscow to the internment of diplomats in Germany after Pearl Harbor. The Soviet government termed this a slanderous attack and demanded Kennan's recall. The United States complied even though the government took occasion to express its agreement with Kennan's statement. These incidents suggest that even though the motivations for demanding recall may be thought political, there is little to be gained by refusing.

Although a government may rid itself of an unwelcome diplomat, it has a legal obligation during his period of accreditation to protect his person from injury, obstruction, detention, or indignity, and to guarantee his immunity from criminal or civil suit or compulsion to appear as a witness. Neither his felonies nor his misdemeanors can be prosecuted, nor can his unpaid grocer or landlord invoke the aid of the courts, nor his discontented wife obtain a divorce in the courts of the receiving state. This immunity from local jurisdiction is designed to assure the unimpeded conduct of public business and therefore continues from the diplomat's entry into the receiving state through his entire tour of duty and such additional period as may reasonably be required for him to remove himself and his household from the country. Immunity is also granted to diplomats accredited to other states (except perhaps unrecognized states) who may be passing through a country *en route* to or from their posts. By agreement a similar immunity is usually allowed to officials of and representatives to the United Nations and other international organizations, and also to judges of the International Court of Justice. In national capitals the special status of diplomats is well understood and regularly respected by police and magistrates; elsewhere there are occasional incidents attributable to lack of experience with such matters, as in the arrest and temporary detention of the Iranian minister by the police of Trenton, New Jersey, in 1937 for speeding, or the insistence of a magistrate of Westchester County, New York, upon fining a chauffeur driving Trygvie Lie, Secretary-General of the United Nations, for a similar offense in 1946, despite certification of immunity by the Department of State. Diplomatic immunity from jurisdiction may be and not infrequently is waived, but this must be done by the chief of mission or by the foreign office of the accrediting state. A limited immunity, not very precisely defined, extends to the servants of the diplomat—cook, chauffeur, valet, clerks, etc.—upon the assumption that interference with them would in some measure impede the work of the diplomat.

In the case of consuls there is no immunity from criminal prosecution, nor from civil suit unless it can be shown that the injury complained of occurred in the course of public business—what may be called a line of duty offense. When the Princess Zizianoff sued Mr. Bigelow, the director of the passport service at the United States consulate general in Paris for defamation in 1928, he contested the court's jurisdiction upon the ground that the alleged defamation consisted in informing the press, in response to an inquiry why he had refused visa of her passport, that she was a Soviet secret agent who had carried on espionage work among American patriotic organizations. He considered that since his duties required him to refuse the visa he could hardly avoid public explanation and was therefore entitled to state the facts. However, the court concluded that his duties did not extend to public statements of the reasons for his decisions, and assumed jurisdiction.

Consuls are usually not required to attend as witnesses in civil cases. In criminal cases they may be summoned, and this is sometimes done in the United States because of the constitutional right of the accused to confrontation of witnesses. Where possible, depositions are used to avoid injury to consular dignity or interference with public functions, and a refusal to respond as to matters affecting public interest would usually be respected. In the well-known Dillon case (1854) a subpoena *duces tecum* (i.e., requiring the bringing of documents or papers) was directed by a court to the French consul at San Francisco. He pulled down his consular flag and complained to the French ambassador. After a long diplomatic controversy the United States finally agreed to redress the indignity done the consul by a formal exchange of salutes when a French ship or squadron should appear in the harbor of San Francisco.

Both diplomats and consuls enjoy in the receiving state exemption from national or local taxes upon their persons, their salaries or incomes from sources outside the state, and their interest in movable property or buildings used for residence or public business, except as these last may be assessments for services or local improvements. They may also import any articles for personal or official use which are not prohibited by law without payment of customs duties.

It should not be inferred that the privileged positions of diplomatic and consular agents lead to unrestrained conduct by them. There have been abuses of hospitality, but foreign service officers generally are meticulous in complying with local laws and regulations and appreciate the public purpose which justifies their privileges and immunities. Chiefs of mission usually will not tolerate improper conduct by members of their staffs, and the *doyen* of the diplomatic corps at a particular capital might occasionally exert himself to restrain exceptionally provocative conduct. Abuses will usually be terminated by disciplining offenders as soon as attention is drawn to their misconduct by the receiving state, and such action sometimes terminates foreign service careers.

Foreign Service Recruitment and Training

Governments find the problem of selecting, training, and retaining suitable personnel for effective foreign service a perplexing one. Indeed, the spread of egalitarian tendencies in government has probably increased the difficulty, for reliance can no longer be placed upon selection from an internationally homogeneous aristocratic class as assurance of an acceptable measure of taste and gentility. In general it has been more difficult to test candidates for foreign service for qualities of character and personality than for specific intellectual achievements. Some differences exist in the approach of governments to this problem.

Great Britain recruits its foreign service from university graduates who have obtained first- or second-class honors in their final examination. Until the rise of the Labour party to power in the present century, candidates came almost wholly from a background of preparation at a public school (a British term for a private school—Eton, Harrow, etc.), followed by university training at Oxford or Cambridge. As they came for the most part from the same social stratum and had passed through the same rigorous classical training, it was possible for a foreign office board composed of persons perfectly familiar with this pattern to select by interview the candidates having the required personal traits. These were subjected to the comprehensive and stiff Foreign Office-Diplomatic Service examination, a series of essays and translations designed to test for high academic attainments and literary skill. The following random selection of questions from the 1933 examination may suggest its spirit:

Write a congratulatory ode to the Gas Light and Coke Company on the completion of a new 250 foot gas-holder.

Illustrate Pope's skill in satire, aphorism, description, and compliment.

What traces are there in Latin literature of a belief in the immortality of the soul, and what forms did it take?

"Benthamism has really a closer affinity with Economics than with Ethics." Do you consider this estimate of Benthamism sound?

It was assumed, with some reason, that successful candidates would be able to fend for themselves in the foreign service with a minimum of in-service training. Given the conditions of candidacy, results were excellent, but they did unduly limit the sources of available personnel by emphasizing a particular pattern of formal training. In recent years the British government has moved to a new type of examination designed to broaden the base. Candidates are now less narrowly confined to the Oxford-Cambridge graduates and emphasis is increasingly upon innate intelligence, capacity, and personal adaptability rather than command of subject matter. A preliminary written examination involving essays, intelligence tests, and mathematical problems eliminates 40 percent of the candidates. The remainder take a civil service selection board residential type examination, in which they are under the scrutiny of a board of assessors for two days. This was formerly done at a country house, but now in London. The testing involves examination of data concerning the candidate, interviews, questionnaires, projection tests, exercises in speaking, debate, and group discussion of problems. A rating is assigned each candidate after review of his qualities by the board. A final selection board, which includes civil service commissioners, foreign office representatives, and two or three people from industry, trade unions, or universities, conducts the final interview and makes the choice. It is perhaps too early to say whether this method will prove wholly satisfactory, but given a group of candidates of somewhat diversified background it has marked advantages in testing personal qualities over the old half-hour interview.

Selection methods in the United States have followed British notions pretty closely. Since the reorganization of the foreign service by the Rogers Act (1924), it has been customary to give a rather comprehensive three-day written examination which specifically tested training in economics, history and government, and one or two foreign languages, but placed greater emphasis upon a general examination of ability to read difficult passages with accuracy and comprehension in a limited time, skill in expression and composition, understanding of graphic and statistical representation, ability to work with logical and mathematical relationships, and the extent of the candidate's fund of cultural data. Those who were successful in the written examination were orally interviewed by a board in Washington in order to form some estimate of personal qualities. A quite able group of Foreign Service officers was recruited in this way, but the effectiveness of the system was somewhat limited by continuance of separate recruitment upon different bases of the administrative officers of the Foreign Service staff corps, the specialist attachés of the Foreign Service reserve corps, and several groups of overseas employees outside the Foreign Service who worked in such fields as agriculture, finance, international information, and economic assistance.

As a result of the Wriston Committee's recommendations the Department of State instituted a simplified one-day written examination for Foreign Service officers in 1955, which will place greater emphasis upon testing of intelligence and aptitude and may permit candidates of varied specialist training to pass. This change is in conformity with recommendations for an integrated service in which there will be opportunity for appointment and advancement of the specialist in agriculture, or minerals, or propaganda, or economic analysis, or engineering, as a Foreign Service officer, as well as for the candidate trained more generally for international relations and diplomacy. Whether this mode of examination will prove successful remains to be seen. The method of recruitment will probably mean that more in-service training will need to be given by the Department of State's Foreign Service Institute, or perhaps that government supervision of part of the candidate's university training will be attempted. The problem of overseas personnel systems outside the Foreign

Service also continues, although the indications are that attention will soon be given to it.

In contrast with the British and American tendency to recruit students of general or varied university training, the French government has moved toward specific career training. From 1871 to 1945 recruitment for foreign service was almost entirely from candidates trained at a private institution, the *École Libre des Sciences Politiques.* In 1945 a basic change in the recruitment of civil service officers was instituted. Institutes of political studies were established at the Universities of Paris and Strasbourg for preliminary training in politics and public administration. For students unable to pay tuition, state subsidies are provided. Those wishing to enter the foreign service or higher civil service posts generally must proceed to the National School of Administration for three years of additional training. Admission to this school is by competitive examination, for which graduates of the institutes or civil servants who have had five years of appropriate experience are eligible. The examinations, which are both written and oral, test specifically knowledge of politics, economics, and diplomatic history. Admission to the National School of Administration is probationary and constitutes a form of government employment, for all students receive stipends. They are required, subject to financial penalties, to continue in service twelve years. Nevertheless, they have no assurance they will be permitted to complete training or to enter the foreign service. Although account is taken of their preferences, the government reserves the right to shift them from foreign affairs training to some other branch of the civil service. Those who complete the foreign service training take final examinations and may choose in the order of their standing from the posts then available. Thus the government controls the whole course of training and can focus it much more directly upon subjects relevant to the functions to be performed in its service.

A proposal for a comparable Foreign Service academy, following the pattern of our military academies, has recently attracted some support in the United States Congress, but the Department of State has opposed it. The Wriston Committee properly observed that such a project would be far more expensive than subsidized training in existing educational institutions. The Federal Republic of Germany has established an academy at Speyer where foreign service recruits are given eighteen months of training for the intermediate grades. This was necessary because the Federal Republic has had to overcome rapidly a shortage of qualified personnel, especially in the higher grades, imposed by the Nazi disruption of the career services. The government was sharply criticized for using older diplomats from the Hitler regime and academic personnel from a few universities. A campaign by the Frankfurter *Rundschau* led to a parliamentary investigation of this, after which some of the personnel was dismissed and recruitment reorganized.

Problems of Foreign Service Tenure and Status

Selection of able personnel, although of first importance, will not in itself assure the efficient functioning of a foreign service. It is necessary also to provide conditions of salary, advancement, housing, education of children, travel allowances, home vacations, medical services, retirement benefits, which will attract competent persons to remain in foreign service in preference to competitive opportunities. Certain aspects of foreign service are everywhere interesting and challenging, but these duties are not all performed amid the social gaieties of Paris and Rome. There are also consular invoices to be examined and trade reports to be compiled in grubby tropical ports, unending lines of travelers and emigrants whose papers must be processed, Communist states in which diplomatic service is a form of internment, posts which are unhealthy, remote, dangerous, understaffed. Officers who remain for years in foreign countries often find themselves out of touch with their own native culture, unable to find suitable schools for their children, and confined to a somewhat artificial society. After the first flush of novelty fades, and the "precious minuet of diplomacy" turns out to be the routine tedium of compiling reports and performing services for insistent fellow nationals, there are many whose eyes turn toward the more lucrative professional opportunities at home. If experienced men are not to be lost, it is necessary to give them varied assignments, opportunity for occasional home service, promotion on a fair basis with opportunity to reach the highest diplomatic and foreign office posts, and adequate compensation. The details of these problems could be examined at some length, but this is rather the province of more specialized books on foreign service administration. Progress has certainly been made in these directions in recent years in the foreign services of principal countries. In the United States such improvements have included the system of impartial promotion boards, elimination of officers placed in the lowest category by three successive boards or failing of promotion for a period of ten years, provision of housing or allowance for quarters, allowances to equalize cost of living differentials, increased representation allowances for official entertaining, salary increases, and appointment of career men as chiefs of mission in many countries (62 percent of the posts in March, 1955).

A perplexing problem in the United States service stems from temporizing with the basic issue of the relationship of the Foreign Service to the personnel systems of the State Department, of other foreign affairs operating agencies, and of the general civil service. The basic conception of the Rogers Act of 1924 was an elite corps of career officers of broad training and varied experience, capable of adapting themselves to any requirements of diplomatic and consular service and of rising to posts involving managerial responsibility and policy discretion. This formula seemed reasonably adequate even with the

assimilation in 1939 of several specialist groups. There was no interchangeability with Department of State personnel, but Foreign Service officers were
used in some of the key positions in the geographical offices. World War II and
the cold war which followed posed a series of problems which placed too
great a strain upon both the numbers and the versatility of Foreign Service
officers. These problems were postponed rather than solved during the war
by recruitment of a Foreign Service Auxiliary composed primarily of specialists, and of course by developing some new operations in special wartime
agencies. After the war it was necessary to provide for staffing the international
information program, and later the programs of economic aid, military assistance, and technical assistance. Since these functions had become the main
stream of American foreign operations, there was something to be said for
placing the policy direction of them in the State Department and the operations in the Foreign Service. Neither was possible without a complete revamp-
ing of personnel to allow for such specialized work. Unfortunately, the
Foreign Service Act of 1946 provided little framework for such specialization,
for it only authorized a staff corps and a reserve corps which were less attractive
in their terms of tenure than the Foreign Service officer corps, and from which
lateral entry into the latter with advanced standing was difficult. Nor was
any greater provision made for use of departmental or general civil service
personnel in the Foreign Service.

Under these circumstances recruitment for important areas of foreign
affairs had to be to secondary corps which provided little career incentive.
In the field some of these functions were conducted under direction of agencies
separate from the State Department, although supervision by chiefs of mission
was also provided, at least formally. Much confusion from divided lines of
responsibility followed. Economic recovery programs were conducted by
country missions directed at different stages by the European Cooperation
Administration, the Mutual Security Administration, or the Foreign Operations Administration. Their personnel included staff and reserve officers and
their work was supposed to be correlated with that of the diplomatic mission.
A similar arrangement existed for military assistance groups, except that the
Defense Department was necessarily involved in most questions of procurement of military items. Defense Department overseas staffs dealt with NATO
problems. Some effort to draw all these threads together in European countries
was made in 1952 by creating the office of the Special Representative in Europe,
jointly appointed by the secretary of state, the secretary of defense, the director
for mutual security, and the secretary of the treasury. Information programs,
utilizing staff and reserve officers in the field, were subject to diplomatic
supervision. Their home agency was for a time in the State Department but
later became separate, although still subject to policy direction. Technical
assistance teams have been drawn from many agencies and either paid at

rates provided for Foreign Service reserve or staff officers according to a conversion table for civil service positions, or actually transferred to reserve or staff corps, or employed by organizations under contract with the government. These complicated structural arrangements, which by no means exhaust the list of overseas operations, point to an inability upon the part of the State Department to assume all the lines of foreign policy and administration. Even less was the Foreign Service equipped to conduct a unified overseas administration comprising such diverse elements.

As we move toward more settled arrangements, it will become increasingly desirable to simplify and integrate agencies. Termination of the Foreign Operations Administration has returned its functions of economic, military, and technical assistance to the State Department. It is not improbable that international information will follow. In the department and in the field it will become increasingly important to develop flexible personnel systems which will find place for the generalist and the specialist alike and provide career incentives for both. It will have to be recognized that economic and informational functions must take their place with diplomacy. Free interchangeability between the department and the field seems already projected under the Wriston Committee recommendations. Substantial lateral entry from the reserve and staff corps into the Foreign Service officer corps has also taken place. It is too early to foresee the final form of an integrated foreign affairs corps, but it is beginning to take shape.

One other question deserves attention in connection with departmental and Foreign Service personnel. The necessity in recent years to screen personnel carefully for security purposes has been generally recognized. Unfortunately, the procedures became a political football, and annoyance in Congress over the frustrations of the international situation vented itself in toleration of Communist witch hunting by some of the least responsible legislators. The Internationl Information Administration was subjected to bizarre "investigations" which drove able and experienced officers to distraction or resignation. Security checks of State Department and Foreign Service officers were individually conducted, but have produced several very disquieting cases.

In the case of John Stewart Service there was a clearance by the Loyalty Security Board of the Department of State, but a Civil Service Loyalty Review Board felt that the release by Service of confidential reports he had prepared while on duty in China to Philip Jaffe, editor of *Amerasia,* created a reasonable doubt of his loyalty. His services were therefore terminated. The reports in question apparently contained nothing harmful to national security, and the background information in them had already been given, with official authorization, to American correspondents in China and to various persons and groups in this country. The Loyalty Security Board had held release of them to Jaffe a "serious indiscretion," but not an indication of disloyalty. A question was raised whether the nature of Service's reporting or his personal contacts suggested Communist leanings, but he was cleared of this charge.

John Carter Vincent had served in China from 1924 to 1936 and thereafter until 1947 in key positions in China and Washington, becoming a principal adviser upon Far Eastern policy. The State Department's Loyalty Security Board examined evidence of Communist affiliations or connections, and of his reporting which was critical of Chiang Kai-shek's government and praised the Chinese Communists. It found no sufficient reason to question his loyalty and affirmed this position upon two rehearings. However, a Loyalty Review Board held that the whole course of Vincent's conduct as a policy officer raised a reasonable doubt of loyalty and recommended termination of services. Secretary of State Acheson felt that some of the Review Board's expressions raised serious questions and set up a special panel to reconsider the evidence and advise him. When Secretary Dulles succeeded Acheson, he discontinued this inquiry, and after personal review of the case accepted Vincent's resignation. Oddly, he found that Vincent was not shown to be a security risk nor was reasonable doubt of loyalty established, but he concluded Vincent's reporting and evaluation of facts, and his policy advice, showed "a failure to meet the standard which is demanded of a Foreign Service officer of his experience and responsibility at this critical time." Yet Vincent's work had led to his promotion to the rank of career minister and his assignment to very responsible posts in the Department.

John Paton Davies, Jr., was subjected to nine hearings and cleared by the first eight. However, he was re-examined under the changed criteria of Executive Order 10450 of May 27, 1953, and upon the ninth review a Security Hearing Board concluded that his continued employment was not "clearly consistent with the interests of the national security" because of demonstrated lack of judgment, discretion, and reliability. Secretary Dulles followed the recommendation of the board, indicating that no question was raised of Davies' right to report as his conscience suggested, but that his observations, evaluations, and policy recommendations, his critical attitude toward existing policy and lack of forbearance in expressing dissent "outside privileged boundaries," fell below the standard required of Foreign Service officers. The demeanor of Davies as a witness was said not to inspire confidence in his reliability, and his responses to questions to be "less than forthright."

It is clearly impossible for anyone who has not examined the evidence in these and other cases to reach conclusions about the propriety of the results. On the other hand, it is disturbing to find men relieved from service after being several times cleared of any imputation of disloyalty upon grounds that suggest indiscretion or incompetency, when these men have been highly regarded in the service and have received steady advancement. Such a result cannot but leave a doubt whether the unpalatable character of their opinions as reflected in their reporting or policy recommendations has influenced the result. This doubt has been expressed by distinguished career officers, who have emphasized the danger which would result from a feeling by officers in the field that they could not afford to report as their critical faculties suggested when their conclusions might be politically distasteful.

It must be added that the criteria of Executive Order 10450, according to which officers must show that their continued employment is "clearly consistent with the national security," are in large part inconclusive or irrelevant. These go far beyond evidence of disloyalty. Any showing of past mental or nervous disorder, criminal conduct, immorality, bad associations, excessive use of intoxicants, drug addiction, sex perversion, may raise the presumption which the officer must rebut to show that his conduct is clearly consistent with security. Yet there is no known body of data which suggests that the incidence of treason or disloyal conduct has been higher among sex deviates, drug addicts, or even those species of criminals motivated by passion or commercial advantage. The danger of such an approach lies in subjecting faithful officers to defense against malicious innuendo and envious backbiting, and to opening suspicions which no possible burden of inquiry can quiet, however unfounded they may be.

Care for the rights of officers is one thing, lack of needed vigilance quite another. The British government apparently had substantial evidence connecting Donald D. Maclean and Guy F. deM. Burgess with the continuous loss of secret information to the Russians. The personal habits of these officers were also so irregular as to raise serious doubts of their reliability. Yet investigation was unduly delayed. The men were not even under surveillance, and they escaped from the country. The government's handling of the matter as shown in a white paper reviewing the case was considered by many members of Parliament to be inexcusably careless. There seems no reason why competent criminal investigation and apprehension of officers guilty of subversive acts cannot be conducted without passing to the extreme of unprofessional investigations which prejudice the careers of loyal officers.

SELECTED READING

ASHTON-GWATKIN, FRANK T., *The British Foreign Service*. Syracuse: Syracuse University Press, 1950.

The Brookings Institution, *The Administration of Foreign Affairs and Overseas Operations*. A report prepared for the Bureau of the Budget. Washington: Government Printing Office, 1951.

CECIL, ALGERNON, "The Foreign Office," Ch. VIII (pp. 539–630) in Vol. iii of Sir A. W. Ward and G. P. Gooch (eds.), *The Cambridge History of British Foreign Policy 1783–1919*. New York: The Macmillan Company, 1923.

CHILDS, J. RIVES, *American Foreign Service*. New York: Henry Holt and Company, 1948. Appendix B covers British and French foreign offices and foreign services.

CRAIG, GORDON A., and GILBERT, FELIX (eds.), *The Diplomats, 1919–1939*. Princeton: Princeton University Press, 1953.

"The Department of State, 1930–1955: Expanding Functions and Responsibilities," in *Department of State Bulletin*, Vol. xxxii, No. 821 (March 21, 1955), 470–486, No. 822 (March 28, 1955), 528–544.

GOSSES, FRANS, *The Management of British Foreign Policy before the First World War*. Leiden: A. W. Sijthoff, 1948.

Harvard Research in International Law, Draft Codes on "Diplomatic Privileges and Immunities" and "Legal Position and Functions of Consuls." *American Journal of International Law*, Supplement to Vol. 26 (1932).

HERTSLET, SIR EDWARD, *Recollections of the Old Foreign Office*. London: John Murray, 1901.

KENNAN, GEORGE F., "The Future of Our Professional Diplomacy," in *Foreign Affairs*, 33 (4): 566–586 (July 1955).

MACMAHON, ARTHUR W., *Administration in Foreign Affairs*. University: University of Alabama Press, 1953.

MC CAMY, JAMES L., *The Administration of American Foreign Affairs*. New York: Alfred A. Knopf, 1950.

PLISCHKE, ELMER, *Conduct of American Diplomacy*. New York: D. Van Nostrand Company, 1950.

SATOW, SIR ERNEST, *A Guide to Diplomatic Practice*, 3d ed., by H. Ritchie. London: Longmans, Green and Company, 1932.

STRANG (LORD), *et. al., The Foreign Office*. London: George Allen and Unwin, Ltd., 1955; New York: Oxford University Press, 1955. (The New Whitehall Series.)

STUART, GRAHAM H., *American Diplomatic and Consular Practice*, 2d ed. New York: Appleton-Century-Crofts, 1952.

———, *The Department of State: A History of Its Organization, Procedure, and Personnel*. New York: The Macmillan Company, 1949.

TILLEY, SIR JOHN, and GASELEE, STEPHEN, *The Foreign Office*. London: G. P. Putnam's Sons, Ltd., 1933.

Toward a Stronger Foreign Service: Report of the Secretary of State's Public Committee on Personnel, June 1954. Wriston Committee report. Washington: Government Printing Office, 1954.

CHAPTER 14

LAW
IN THE INTERNATIONAL
COMMUNITY

SUBJECTS OF INTERNATIONAL LAW

International law is that body of rules which regulates relations among states and other entities which possess international legal personality, that is, international organizations and perhaps to a very limited degree private persons. It is the law of the international community, but since this community has no political organs authorized to enact legislation, international law is based upon custom and upon treaties—the latter constituting a kind of direct legislation by the members of the community. It is systematized and developed by judicial interpretation and application, by juristic writing, and by private and official codification.

The term international law usually means "public" international law, i.e., rules governing public relationships. The term private international law is sometimes applied to rules governing relationships between individuals of different states, for example, with respect to international contracts, sales, agencies, business associations, etc. The term is misleading, however, and in common law countries "conflicts of law" is preferred, for this law is actually national law. Thus, if a New York merchant enters into a contract of sale with a London buyer and there is later a dispute over it, an action might be brought either in New York or London. In either case the preliminary question will be whether American or English law applies to the contract. This choice of law question will be settled in New York under the New York rules of conflict of laws, in England under the English rules. The court to which application is made will either proceed with the case and apply its own law or will declare the contract is a foreign one and refuse to assume jurisdiction.

The only international aspect in this example is the transaction itself. States have indeed moved toward greater uniformity in their rules of conflict of laws, but uniform national laws are not the same as international law. Efforts have been made to reach uniformity in such fields as negotiable instruments, sales, contracts of carriage, warehouse receipts, and other areas of commercial law. Maritime law, or admiralty, is another related body of national law in which some international uniformity has been achieved.

The traditional conception of international law as applicable to states is not severely strained by extending this law to international organizations, since the extent of their international personality is usually defined by the member states in the constituent instrument (treaty) creating the organization. Not to regulate such institutions according to international law would be inconvenient, for their functions are such as to bring them into regular relationships with the governments of states. Since World War II their activities have so increased as to lead to the differentiation of a body of "international constitutional law," concerned with legal problems in the interpretation and application of the treaties which serve as the constitutions of these organizations. The Charter of the United Nations is especially important in this respect, for it is the basis of much of the international law affecting collective settlement of disputes. Consideration will be given to this subject in Chapter 16.

The problem of the individual in international law is more difficult. The traditional view was that states were subjects of international law, but that individuals were merely objects. They might be affected indirectly in that the state's rights or duties under international law would require regulation of its nationals, but they did not as individuals possess rights and duties under international law. This concept is undergoing some revision because it hardly meets all the facts. One or two illustrations will demonstrate this. In the law of international claims the object is to provide redress for an injury to an individual, suffered in a foreign state, for which no local remedy can be obtained there. Let us assume that Smith, a national of the United States, enters into a contract with a Mexican company to sell it certain machinery at a list price of $5000. Smith delivers the machinery in Mexico, but the company fails to pay for it. Smith then brings a suit in a Mexican court alleging breach of contract, but the court shows obvious bias by arbitrarily excluding Smith's evidence and finds for the company. Appellate tribunals affirm the judgment. It is now open to Smith, since he has exhausted remedies available in Mexico and has been denied justice there, to ask the government of the United States to present an international claim against the government of Mexico, which will be heard by the United States–Mexican Claims Commission, established for that purpose. So what began as a private claim against a private company has become a claim of one state against another, and this upon the theory that denial of justice to any national is an injury to the United States. If so, one might expect compensation to be measured in terms of the injury to the United States, but not so—what the United States actually collects from Mexico, which had nothing to do with the original injury but is at fault in denying justice, will be measured by Smith's injury, i.e., $5000. To add to the confusion the United States is under no legal duty to pay over the award to Smith, although it will do so. Clearly the theory that states alone are subjects of international law capable of bringing international actions is here applied in a fictitious manner. The sovereign state cannot act as the agent of its own national, yet the whole substance of the claim it brings is a private one. It may well be urged that claims tribunals should be provided in which individuals could directly prosecute such actions against foreign states. To date this has not been done.

Another area in which the individual seems directly involved with international law is that of crimes. There are certainly very few crimes in international law, the best known being piracy, war crimes, and the new crime of genocide, not yet universally accepted. Nor is there an international criminal court, although a proposal for one is under consideration. The situation has been that international law recognizes and defines these crimes but leaves prosecution and punishment to states, authorizing a universal jurisdiction, so that a state may deal with an offender irrespective of his nationality. In the case of piracy most states even used their own definitions. The trials of major war criminals at Nuremberg and Tokyo were conducted by what were called International Military Tribunals. However, the defeated states were not parties to the treaties which created these tribunals and did not have judges in them. In part the offenses charged were war crimes long accepted and codified by the Hague and Geneva Conventions, but other counts charged crimes against humanity and instigation of aggressive war, neither of which was an internationally defined crime at the time the acts were committed. Although open to the criticism of *ex post facto* action as to these counts, the proceedings have probably given further impetus to international criminal law, particularly as the results were codified by the International Law Commission of the United Nations. This was done at the request of the General Assembly.

These examples hardly suggest that the place of the individual as a subject of international law is a large one, but they show he has not been wholly excluded. Universal jurisdiction, as applied to pirates and war criminals, is unlikely to be freely extended. If an international criminal court should be created, it is probable it will have jurisdiction only over persons turned over to it by their own states.

THE BASIS OF OBLIGATION IN INTERNATIONAL LAW

In Chapter 2 some attention was given to the position of the state in the international community and to the implications of the theory of sovereignty for legal limitations upon states. The doctrine of absolute, irresponsible sovereignty developed by Hobbes and Austin, in which law is regarded as the mandate of the sovereign, and the sovereign as the person or group able to compel obedience, would mean that a sovereign state is not itself subject to law, hence that there can be no international law imposed upon it without its consent. Yet we have only to observe the conduct of states to become convinced that they do habitually observe certain international rules with substantial uniformity and regularity, that they are careful to justify their conduct in terms of law, and that breaches of the rules of international law not infrequently do lead to redress through diplomatic or judicial channels.

The contrary impression is sometimes popularly held, but usually by persons who are generalizing from instances of breach of particular treaties by aggressors or from violations of rules governing the conduct of hostilities or the status of neutrality. It would certainly be foolish to gloss over such matters or to dismiss them lightly, but their significance requires some evaluation. In part they must be ascribed to changing modes of warfare, which by tacit consent have been thought to make certain rules governing the conduct of warfare obsolete. For example, the Hague Convention rule requiring advance notice of bombardment so as to permit removal of civilians cannot be followed in aerial bombardment without inviting destruction of planes by antiaircraft batteries. The rule requiring visit and search of ships on the high seas to determine whether they are carrying contraband has given way to forcing them into control ports for examination because radio and aircraft make it dangerous for a ship to lie to for an hour or more as a target while conducting a search. Nor do submarines fit easily into traditional rules requiring removal of passengers and crew before sinking merchantmen. They are thin-skinned craft which an armed merchantman could readily sink, and they lack space for passengers; hence the temptation is great to sink ships upon radar contact without surfacing. Again, old rules distinguishing absolute and conditional contraband in terms of military or civilian consignees are outmoded, for in total war a state commandeers any goods it wants. There is even a rule forbidding weapons "calculated to cause unnecessary suffering," but does any one suggest it will prevent use of atom bombs?

These instances show the difficulty which technical advances in warfare have caused. States will not risk defeat in order to observe obsolete standards. In general, war is an appeal to force and, therefore, an institution outside law, to which states resort when legal settlement has broken down. Consequently, it is a little incongruous to expect it to be conducted as decorously as a cricket match. To attain universal settlement according to law it is necessary to be rid of war. Aggressive war has indeed been declared illegal, but a good deal of practical definition and political implementation are required to accomplish its actual outlawry as an institution. It must, therefore, be admitted that war still stands as an alternative to international law, which limits its range of effectiveness.

In the relations of states in time of peace the situation is more promising. Some rules, such as those concerning diplomatic agents, have been followed for centuries. Substantial bodies of law exist with respect to recognition of states or governments and its consequences, nationality, state succession to rights and obligations, the jurisdiction and jurisdictional immunities of states, the conclusion, application, and termination of treaties, international claims, and other subjects. Gaps certainly exist in the body of rules and uncertainties abound, yet courts and governments find it possible to deal with such subjects rather effectively in terms of generally received rules. Some further indication of the law in these fields will be given presently.

How is it possible to have such a development in the absence of any enforcement agency superior to states? In what sense are states bound by international law and what are the sanctions against noncompliance? The answers to these questions may be easier if one asks what are the sanctions of law generally. Certainly a body of rules or precepts must have some effectiveness in application to be properly called law. But effectiveness may result not simply from the anticipation of executive and judicial enforcement by police or sheriff or courts but from more complex motivation—habit, moral compunction, social standards and the consciousness of community censure, self-interest in maintaining such standards in order to secure protection of one's own rights. Who can say that he desists from murder, rape, arson, and larceny only because he fears to be hanged or imprisoned? Most people so thoroughly embody in their own moral codes the social standards of their community that they never even contemplate such offenses and would not commit them although well assured they could escape detection. Were this not so the problem of enforcement would be impossible. Historically, it is clear that the common law felonies were all developed and received judicial application upon the basis of community standards before there was any strong central executive or government. These were not law because enforced by the state, but rather were enforced by the state because law.

If we disabuse ourselves of the artificial conceptions flowing from the Hobbesian doctrine of sovereignty and consider states simply as institutions created by men for purposes which although broad are yet limited, then there is no reason to suppose that the reasons for state subjection to law are different from those which obligate individual men or other human institutions. States are composed simply of men, as are corporations, churches, and trade unions.

If these are obligated to observe legal limitations, so may the state be. The source of the obligation is not in the legal system itself but in the moral or social compulsions which lie behind it. In this sense we have not come much farther than medieval man, who explained his sense of obligation in terms of natural law and claimed for himself certain "natural rights." Today we may, according to taste, explain the matter in terms of ethical or philosophical presuppositions, Kantian or Hegelian or Social-Utilitarian, or prefer to seek in economic, psychological, and sociological analysis the compulsions which move men living in a society. In one way or another we arrive at a system of values which lies behind the legal system and provides the reason for its obligatory force.

The practical difficulties in subjecting states to international law are principally two. First, the state is an institution which possesses great power and if disposed to act lawlessly may racket about very destructively in the international community for years before the forces of law and order can bring it to book. In this it differs not in kind but only in degree from organized crime within a state, which at times has become sufficiently powerful (e.g., gangsterism of the prohibition era) to set local law at defiance. Nazi lawlessness in international relations was prolonged and flagrant, but did not in the end escape redress. Second, we have today such differences in the value systems of major states in the international community that they do not all subscribe wholeheartedly to the traditional assumptions about legal relationships among states. It is not that they challenge the existence of a binding international law, but that they disagree about its principles. Soviet jurists have expressed several inconsistent notions. Korovin argued that during the period before the final victory of communism over free enterprise international law would reflect the compromise between the competing systems. Pashukanis saw it as an instrument of the state to be used in the struggle. In recent years the view generally held has been that of Vishinsky, who considered that international law must take account not only of struggle between rival systems but also of cooperation between the U.S.S.R. and certain capitalist states. The practical meaning of this seems to be a system which blows hot and cold in terms of the emphasis the U.S.S.R. chooses to place upon the revolutionary struggle. It is certainly not a sound basis for international law, which must apply irrespective of state policy, and its weakness is betrayed by heavy Soviet emphasis upon state sovereignty and the consensual basis of international law. Observance of treaties, equality of states, nonintervention, national self-determination, definition of aggression, punishment of warmongering, have all been stressed, but in view of the persistent misconduct of the U.S.S.R. they must be taken as mainly a propaganda line. We are thus in some danger of losing, as between East and West, that minimum consensus among states which justifies speaking of international community at all, and if so, might be forced back into a predicament like that before the nineteenth century, when international law was confined to European states and others moved outside its orbit in ill-defined relationship. For the present, however, the schism is not this complete, and we seem again to be in a period of Soviet emphasis upon cooperation.

The emphasis upon sovereignty and equality of states in the nineteenth century did not prevent agreement upon principles of international law but did lead to efforts to explain it in terms of state consent to be bound explicitly by treaty or impliedly with respect to customary law. In this theory international law would not be effective within the state, i.e., in applications to individuals, unless given effect by statutory incorporation into national law. There seems to be a fundamental fallacy in such consent theories. Either states are bound by international law or they are not bound. If they consent to be bound and have sovereign power to withdraw their consent at any time, then they are not really bound. Nor is implied consent a satisfactory ground for subjecting a state to a rule which has never been drawn to its attention. If states do concede the obligatory force of international law, it must be that it is a genuine limitation upon their freedom of action and that state sovereignty is susceptible of such limitation. Upon no other principle can we have international law.

There is indeed a difference of professional opinion among international lawyers whether there continues to be an international community in the sense of common interests and values sufficient to support a system of international law. H. A. Smith (*The Crisis in the Law of Nations* [1947]) and Thomas Baty (*International Law in Twilight* [1954]) have concluded there is not. Others are only slightly more encouraging. Julius Stone (*Legal Controls of International Conflict* [1954], p. 37) remarks:

. . . However it be as to more limited orders, that of international law as a world system is still, on critical questions, "law in the books" rather than "law in action." . . . Such major principles as appear to find a universal acceptance, do so partially, with misunderstanding, misinterpretation and prejudices, and plain distortion to sectional interests; and in a manner not yet susceptible of integration into a coherent system of value judgments shared by mankind.

Percy Corbett (*Law and Society in the Relations of States* [1951]) also finds a large gap between the dogmas of international legal orthodoxy and the actual conduct of governments when considerable interests are at stake. He feels that international law lacks compulsory organs of interpretation and enforcement, a lack springing from absence of international community ("present in the international sphere only in a highly rarified form"); hence, that much of international law might better be termed merely international usage. He believes the future of international law to be one with the future of international organization, and both dependent upon the growth of international community.

Even if a more optimistic view be indulged as to the strength of international law or the existence of a universal value system capable of supporting it, one must agree with these writers that the "law in books" needs to be rigorously tested against the facts of international practice. Nothing is gained by an unrealistic assumption of legal rules which fail under pressure to satisfy rudimentary tests of effectiveness. There is genuine need for the sociology of international law urged as early as 1910 by Max Huber, but only in recent years has any serious effort been made to consider legal rules in the context of the social and psychological determinants of action at the international level. Corbett and Stone, in the works just mentioned, move in this direction, as have Quincy Wright (*A Study of War* [1942]), Charles DeVisscher (*Théories et Réalités en Droit International Public* [1953]), and Dietrich Schindler (*Contribution à l'Etude des Facteurs Sociologiques et Psychologiques du Droit International* [1933]). The techniques of behavioral research might throw needed light upon the existence or nonexistence of individual attitudes and value patterns in national societies sufficient to support international law as a limitation of sovereignty.

DEVELOPMENT OF INTERNATIONAL LAW

A few points concerning the history of international law will cast light upon the character of the system. As a legal system it has been associated with the national, territorial state of the modern period for about 400 years, but its roots go deeper. There was a species of international, really intermunicipal, law among the city states of ancient Greece. It included rules on diplomatic immunity, treaties, international conferences and confederations, arbitration, and warfare. Ancient oriental peoples also developed rules of international conduct. Rome expanded into a great empire and therefore steadily contracted its international relations by bringing foreign peoples within the empire. It tended to develop its own rules of diplomacy and war without much reference to international standards; rather it set the standard. Some reference to these rules, which were a part of the Roman fetial law, was made in Chapter 11.

More significant for the future was the body of rules which the Romans called *ius gentium,* i.e., the law of peoples or nations. "Law of nations" is a term now used interchangeably with "international law," but we must not confuse the Roman usage with the modern application of the term. It seems better on that account to use the Latin term *ius gentium.* This was originally a special body of Roman law administered by a judge called the *praetor peregrinus,* who had jurisdiction of legal actions between two aliens (*peregrini* means strangers, or aliens) or between a Roman citizen and an alien. The older Roman civil law (*ius civile*) was an exclusive law belonging only to citizens, and citizenship was not freely extended to conquered peoples. The early *ius civile* was also burdened with highly formalistic pleading and procedure which could not fairly be applied to strangers unfamiliar with it. Therefore the *praetor peregrinus* applied to aliens a body of rules drawn from Roman law but divested of formalistic elements. To some extent he may have been influenced by information about the alien's own law in considering how to adapt Roman law to his needs. Thus the *ius gentium* was not international law but rather a liberalized version of Roman law. Nevertheless, its simplified form and general application led people eventually to think of it as a universal system which would be considered just in any country. It was in fact a very superior system of law which influenced the later development of the *ius civile*. No doubt the tendency to think of it as a universal system was also strengthened by conceptions of natural law (*ius naturale*). These were not of much consequence in Roman juristic thought but appear in perfunctory references in legal materials of the late republic and empire, having apparently been introduced by philosophic writers like Cicero. It was inevitable that the *ius gentium* and *ius naturale* came to be associated, upon the assumption that a universal system of law must reflect principles of justice recognized by all reasonable men. This association was to endure for centuries. *Ius gentium* was of course a system of private law, but the term was also occasionally used in a general sense by jurists in reference to diplomatic immunity, the laws of war, and international boundaries, matters certainly not within the jurisdiction of the *praetor peregrinus*.

Rome as a great empire transmitted to later Europe a tradition of universality. The principal vehicles which sustained the tradition were (a) the Holy Roman Empire, which however broke up into feudal regimes and became little more than a symbol of unity, certainly of little effect in France or England; (b) the Roman law, which was codified by jurists of the Emperor Justinian in the sixth century, A.D. (the *Corpus Iuris Civilis Iustinianiae*), and in this form was revived in the twelfth century and became the basis of legal study in the Italian universities and later throughout Europe, thus providing juristic conceptions widely received as a framework in which common law could be systematized; (c) the Roman Catholic Church, which as a really effective universal institution, drew together most of the threads of universalism. Its canon law, based upon Roman law, provided a code for the whole ecclesiastical community and was influential in an even wider area. The church became identified with natural law as a kind of official interpreter, the more so as it claimed to be the keeper of the consciences of kings. On this ground popes and bishops asserted the right to arbitrate the disputes of lay rulers. As natural law contains the notion of private rights exempt from public interference, and this is also found in Roman law, the church tended to become the champion of these rights. When the decline of feudalism and the rise of the modern state created again a public or political capacity distinct from the private capacity of subjects, private rights were posed as a limitation upon the state. This explains why it was that the Spanish jurist-theologians of the sixteenth century were so concerned with the rights of the American Indians in the face of the Spanish conquest, an interest which produced Vitoria's lectures on the subject, since regarded as an early classic of international law. The Roman Catholic Church also made some contributions to international law upon humanitarian grounds, as in the prohibition of the use of crossbow and ballista (weapons "calculated to cause unnecessary suffering"?) and the suspension of private wars by the "truces of God" from sunset Wednesday to sunrise Monday.

The impetus to development of the modern system of international law came from a combination of circumstances. The universal systems of the middle ages became ineffective with the rise of strong national states. Although these states received the Roman law, it had become mingled with common law elements so that the resulting systems were national in character. The influence of the Roman Catholic Church was eliminated in some countries after the rise of Protestantism. The empire lost all pretense of universal character and became a union of Catholic states (Spain, Austria, Germany). At the same time the need for international controls became even greater. One reason was that the religious wars introduced a new element of intense feeling and consequent lack of restraint not present in feudal wars. Perhaps even more important was the entry of states into commercial promotions, overseas ventures, and competition for colonial areas. There had been international mercantile contacts before, but medieval traders were a kind of international fraternity who under license of kings developed their own rules. These are to be found in the maritime codes of trading cities, e.g., the Rhodian Sea Law, the *Rolls of Oléron,* the *Consolato del mare* of Barcelona, and in the law of the piepowder (i.e., *pied poudreux,* dusty foot) courts set up at medieval fairs. The great state-chartered trading companies like the British and Dutch East India Companies, the subsidized voyages of discovery, and the public grants of land for colonization to companies of merchant adventurers, introduced an element of state interest and control requiring firmer international regulation. This indeed remained for a long time inadequate. It was this context which provided the motivation for the great jurists who shaped the new system of international law. It was no accident that they appeared in the north European Protestant countries which were most keenly alive to these problems—in England, Gentilis, Zouche, Selden; in the Netherlands, Grotius and Bynkershoek; in Germany, Pufendorf, Wolff, Vattel, Moser.

This is not the place to examine the particular contributions made by these writers of the seventeenth and eighteenth centuries. Their significance for international law as a system was that they provided for it a theoretical foundation attuned to modern conceptions, and proceeded to systematize the materials, many of them old but others collected from modern judicial decisions, treaties, and diplomatic practice. They were not all important for the same reasons. Grotius, often called the father of international law, is important not so much for the analysis of particular problems, as for his statement of the jurisprudence of international law, i.e., the underlying juristic conceptions and the principles which should animate legal relations among states. His system lumps together public and private international relations, applying to both the same natural law principles. He distinguishes natural law and *ius gentium* but does not maintain the distinction carefully. Further, he divorces natural law from any necessary connection with divine revelation and thus makes it a secular rule of reasonableness. It is his intention to apply this rule to all relationships outside national law. As a universal rule, he felt it could be established from classical history and Christian literature and was at no pains to develop the modern practice of states. Gentilis, Zouche, Bynkershoek, and Moser, on the contrary, were less theoretical and more concerned with examining the international practice of states, aiming to discover what rules they accepted rather than to justify these rules in moral terms. Thus they founded the positivist school of international law, which became dominant in the nineteenth and twentieth centuries. Pufendorf, Wolff, and Vattel continued the natural law emphasis, with variations, although Vattel was also distinguished by a practical command of diplomacy. These and other important writers have established a tradition in international law which attaches more than ordinary weight to juristic writing. In a field of law in which the paucity of judicial decisions, and the inconclusiveness of diplomatic exchanges, have left many uncertainties, this has not been an unmixed blessing. The authority of jurists has asserted a number of propositions which have been assumed to be law but which have not in the end proved tenable when tested in practice.

As in any other developing field of law, the juristic materials have increased with accelerating rapidity. These include (a) decisions of national courts in cases involving international law; (b) decisions of international tribunals, beginning with the arbitrations under the Jay Treaty of 1795 and progressing through a number of important bilateral arbitrations to the multilateral Permanent Court of Arbitration set up at The Hague in 1899, then to standing international courts, first the Permanent Court of International Justice (1920–1946) and now the International Court of Justice (1946 to date); (c) treaties, of which many thousands are in force, including a substantial number of multilateral treaties designed to state or restate rules of international law; other thousands have provided legal issues of earlier days; (d) diplomatic papers which reveal the positions taken by governments or their legal advisers upon questions of international law; (e) materials of international organizations bearing upon legal questions. These materials, with the comments of publicists upon them, provide a tremendous quarry as yet only partly worked, for many governments have not yet published some substantial portions of the relevant material. The United Nations at the suggestion of its International Law Commission, is endeavoring to increase the availability of such materials.

During the last century there has also been a good deal of codification, that is, the systematic restatement of existing law. This began with draft codes prepared by individual scholars or by private professional organizations, for example, Francis Lieber's *Code for the Government of Armies* (1863), Bluntschli's general reduction of international law (with some of his personal opinions) to the form of a code (1868), and the numerous resolutions and drafts of the *Institut de Droit International* and the International Law Association since 1873. Official codification began in the field of the law of war. International conferences developed the Geneva Convention of 1864 on care of sick and wounded in warfare and the two sets of Hague Conventions of 1899 and 1907 dealing with conduct of land and naval warfare and neutral rights and obligations. These last have shown a marked tendency to obsolescence, already noted. After the creation of the League of Nations more ambitious efforts were made. After elaborate preparations, which in the United States led to an unofficial but very valuable compilation of materials and draft codes by the Harvard Research in International Law, conferences were held to work on topics in the law of nationality and territorial waters. The results were disappointing and revealed sharp differences of opinion even in areas which had been thought well settled.

The United Nations has created an International Law Commission composed of technically competent persons, which regularly works on projects of international law codification in fields of its own choice (to date, the high seas and territorial waters, treaties, and arbitral procedure) and also some projects referred to it by the Assembly (the law of the Nuremberg trials of major war criminals and a Declaration of the Rights and Duties of States). It has also the function of "progressive development of international law," that is, the proposal in the form of draft treaties which might be ratified by member states of rules supplementary to existing international law. The commission has made a useful analysis on the new law of the continental shelf, and has proposed (with substantial dissenting voices) a plan for creating an international criminal court. In general it seems doubtful that many fields of international law are ripe for codification; there are as yet too many gaps and differences of opinion among states. Some useful contributions may be made toward progressive development, but there is also danger that efforts to anticipate the proper direction of international law development may prove unrealistic. International law has not yet reached that stage of development characteristic of the civil law of Europe and the common law of English-speaking countries in which legislative elements rather than judicial have become preponderant and codification therefore natural, but it may be that the pressures upon it will force acceleration of the normal development.

THE SCOPE OF INTERNATIONAL LAW

This is not the place to attempt a detailed statement of the rules of international law. What follows is intended only to indicate the principal topics covered and to convey some sense of the possibilities and limitations of the system as a regulatory device for the international community.

Recognition of States and Governments

Since the primary components of the international community are states, and these function politically through governments, it is important for international law to define the terms upon which states and governments may participate in the rights and duties which the system stipulates. This has been treated somewhat as if admission to the international legal community were an election into membership of a gentlemen's club, to be determined by vote of the members themselves, and at least partly in terms of their personal preferences. This is not true in theory, for it would be generally admitted that a state has rights and duties under international law simply by reason of statehood. However, statehood is determined only by recognition extended by existing states to new states which have emerged by revolution or by combination of two or more states. There is no central agency to make such decisions, nor any definitive set of criteria other than the usual attributes of statehood mentioned in Chapter 2. There is also difference of opinion whether the act of recognition is actually constitutive of legal rights or merely declarative of a status which exists *de facto*.

It should be noted that this is a question distinct from recognition of a new government which supplants a former government without any change in the state. Thus there are two Chinese governments, the Communist People's Republic and the Nationalist government. They have not agreed upon a division of the territory and people of China into two states, but each claims to be the government of the whole of China. Consequently, other governments have only to decide which of the two governments they will recognize; they do not have to decide whether China is a state. In contrast to this we have many recent cases in which new states have emerged: the Republic of Indonesia proclaimed itself in 1945 in revolt against the Netherlands; India was separated into India and Pakistan in 1947, and the two states were granted independence by act of the British Parliament; Israel proclaimed its independence in 1948 while the United Nations was trying to decide what disposition to make of the area, formerly under British mandate. These and other postwar instances of the creation of new states led the governments of existing states, in considering whether or not to recognize the new ones, to determine whether the conditions of statehood were met.

Decisions taken in such cases have not afforded precise standards. The reason is that the normal consequence of recognition is the establishment of diplomatic relations between the two countries, and governments frequently allow their political attitudes to affect a decision which has such consequences. In some cases they are led by sympathy or policy into premature recognition before it is clear that criteria of statehood have been satisfied. In 1932 Japan set up a puppet government in Manchuria, which had long been Chinese territory, and recognized the new "state" of Manchukuo. However, most other states continued to regard the area as part of China; only El Salvador formally recognized Manchukuo, although the U.S.S.R. probably did so in-directly by concluding a treaty with the Manchukuoan government. It might be questioned whether Israel so clearly satisfied the requirements of statehood when it proclaimed its independence as of 6:01 p.m. on May 14, 1948, as to justify recognition by the United States at 6:11 p.m. the same day. At that time sovereignty over the area was still being actively contested with the Arabs. A well-known older example occurred in the revolt of Panama against Colombia, November 3 and 4, 1903. The United States on November 2 and 5 ordered war-ships to maintain transit across the isthmus and to prevent the landing of armed forces or the advance of Colombian troops from Colon to Panama. On November 6 the United States recognized Panama. Of course, this whole proce-dure constituted an intervention by the United States in violation of the rights of Colombia.

There are also situations in which the new state pretty clearly does have the qualities of statehood but is not recognized by certain other states for rea-sons of policy. Thus, the Arab states do not recognize Israel although its con-trol of its territory and population has long been established. Nor does the United States recognize the absorption of the Baltic republics of Estonia, Lat-via, and Lithuania by the U.S.S.R., although the fact of the extinction of those states is hardly open to question. It would seem that the decision should turn upon the question whether the absorption of the territory and population into another state or the separation of it from an existing state and incorporation into a new one is a *fait accompli* or is still being actively contested. The fact that a mother country continues to grumble about the loss of a colony it is powerless to recover, or that a few exiles from a state which has been absorbed still style themselves a government, will hardly suffice.

The international law principle in these matters assumes that once a state has been recognized, that recognition is irrevocable. If, thereafter, there should be a revolutionary change of government, or a civil war not yet con-cluded between two governments, while the state itself continues with the same territory and population, a failure to recognize the new government is taken as continuing recognition of the old one. Great Britain recognized the Communist Peoples Republic as the government of China in 1950 and withdrew recognition from the Nationalist government of Chiang Kai-shek, which had been forced to withdraw to Formosa. But the United States took no action and therefore continues to recognize the Nationalist government as the government of China. The British attitude has been that the Communist Peoples Republic controls effectively the whole mainland area of China and therefore is entitled to recognition. The United States admits this effective control but stands upon the failure of the Communist Peoples government to act in a responsible fashion in international relations, as shown by seizure of United States consular properties, detention of consuls and of military and civilian personnel, and assistance to aggressors in Korea. This is certainly not a pointless position, but it shows an extension of one criterion of statehood—the capacity to enter into foreign relations, to include the disposition to do so in a responsible manner, accepting international legal obligations.

Thus, there appears to be a difference of opinion as to the proper grounds for preferring one government to another. The policy of the United States has not been consistent. For many years it was based almost wholly upon effective control by the government. Then President Wilson in dealing with the Huerta government of Mexico, took the view that since capacity of the government to represent the state and to carry out its international responsibilities was essential, it would be improper to recognize a government which had seized power by force until it became clear that the people acquiesced in its control. The Stimson doctrine of nonrecognition, applied by the League of Nations to Manchukuo, followed this view. The government of the United States also refused to recognize the government of the U.S.S.R. until 1933, although there had long ceased to be any rival government. The United States continued to recognize the Kerensky government, which maintained no more than a theoretical existence. Reasons assigned for delay were that the Soviet government had sought by propaganda to undermine other governments, and had repudiated state debts contracted by the tsarist government. Yet recognition was given in 1933, although only an empty gesture toward satisfying these objections had been made.

It must be said that international law, while presumably accepting the premise that a government should be representative of the state and prepared to discharge the state's legal responsibilities has not prescribed *de facto* control on the one hand or proof of popular acquiescence on the other as the test to be applied. An area of political judgment is thus left to governments which is outside international law. This is unfortunate, for the decisions taken upon political grounds in recognizing new governments have significant legal consequences.

Governments not infrequently attempt to reserve judgment with respect to a new regime by extending to it *de facto* rather than *de jure* recognition, thus implying some doubt that its factual control will be permanent or will be exercised with regard for international obligations. But the practice seems unsound. Recognition *de facto* is no less complete or qualified recognition than *de jure* recognition; it merely adds a needless comment about the government's character. As soon as the extent of control has become sufficient to justify the conclusion that the government represents the whole state, it would seem sufficient to justify recognition *de jure*. One might conceivably argue that Great Britain prematurely recognized the Communist Peoples' Republic as the government of China because that government does not yet control Formosa, but he could hardly on that account argue that recognition should have been *de facto* rather than *de jure*.

The practical significance of recognition of a state or government, apart from the exchange of diplomatic agents, is to grant it immunity from legal process in the recognizing state and to lead the latter to concede the validity of acts of that government *within its own territory*. In some cases validity may even be conceded retroactively to the beginning of the regime even though recognition is delayed, but this seems unwise since it may have the effect of divesting private rights. A well-known example was *Luther* v. *Sagor* ([1921] 1 K.B. 456, and 3 K.B. 532), in which timber in Russia belonging to an English company had been taken by the Soviet government under an expropriation law, and by it sold to the defendant, who brought it into England. At the time of the transaction the U.S.S.R had not been recognized by the British government; therefore the court declined to recognize the effectiveness of its acts and ordered the timber restored to the original owner. By the time an appeal was heard, however, *de facto* recognition had been given to the Soviet government, from which the Court of Appeal concluded that it must retroactively recognize the validity of the confiscation and transfer of title by the Soviet government, since this occurred in Russia. This case serves to explain why recent expropriations such as the Mexican seizure of oil lands of American companies in 1936, or the Iranian nationalization of the properties of the Anglo-Iranian Oil Company in 1951, gave rise to no challenge of the legal effectiveness of these acts of recognized governments, but only to claims of compensation based upon the standard of justice due to alien owners.

Since there is continuity of the state, even when changes of government occur, and international obligations are considered to be undertaken by the state rather than by the government, it follows that any government which secures control succeeds to certain rights and obligations of the state. Whether other states will grant the rights may depend upon recognition; the United States before 1933 allowed representatives of the defunct Kerensky government to gather up Russian assets in the United States (albeit under agreement to pay them into the Treasury of the United States against Russian debts). Funds of the state-controlled Bank of China on deposit in San Francisco were awarded with some hesitation to the Nationalist Government (Bank of China v. Wells Fargo Bank and Union Trust Co. [1952] 104 F. Supp. 59; [1953] 29 F. (2d) 469). We have seen that willingness by a government to assume state obligations may be the condition of recognition. In general it succeeds to contract obligations, including debts, rather than to tort obligation, unless liability for the tort has been adjudicated and thus transformed into a debt. Public debts are frequently a subject for special treaty arrangement after division of a state or federation of several states. Conquering states often decline to assume debts of conquered states, especially if incurred in fighting the war.

Territory

States acquire the right to exercise jurisdiction over particular territory in a number of ways to which international law gives some definition. Unclaimed territory, called *territorium nullius,* may be acquired by effective occupation, i.e., the exercise of governmental functions to an extent proportioned to the needs of the society in the area claimed. This is a relatively recent rule; until about 1800 claims were often founded upon discovery followed by symbolic acts of annexation such as planting flags, erecting monuments, or ceremonial taking of possession in the name of the sovereign. These are now considered insufficient in themselves. An unoccupied wasteland or island, or an uninhabitable Arctic or Antarctic area, of course, requires fewer governmental acts to establish effective occupation. The Permanent Court of International Justice, in dealing with rival claims of Norway and Denmark to portions of eastern Greenland in 1933 (P.C.I.J., Series A/B, No. 53), was satisfied that colonization of coastal areas by Denmark plus statutes, administrative regulations, and treaty agreements purporting to apply also to inaccessible areas, sufficiently established Danish sovereignty over the whole. These principles have little practical significance today except in Arctic and Antarctic areas, and there many of the interested powers claim upon grounds which have little or no standing in law, such as propinquity, discovery and mapping without settlement, or the sector theory under which adjacent states claim all territory enclosed by the extension of their most easterly and westerly meridians to the pole. All these claims have been rejected by the United States and remain unsettled. There is some possibility that a division may be effected through negotiation.

Territory may also be acquired by one state from another state. This might be done by annexation with the assent of the state annexed. Or it may be done by cession, either after purchase or land exchange or conquest. Conquest is ordinarily followed by a formal act of cession, and there is some disposition among international lawyers to assert that conquest alone, in view of formal agreements purporting to outlaw aggressive war, would not be sufficient in the absence of a cession. However, it is doubtful that we have yet reached this point. Continued occupancy of the area by the conquering state, especially if eventually recognized by other states, would seem sufficient. Military occupation before an armistice does not transfer sovereignty, but the exercise of the sovereignty is temporarily undertaken by the occupying power. A good deal of local autonomy is usually allowed if consistent with military necessities, and there are rules of international law designed to prevent undue interference with private rights. Occupation after surrender, pending a final peace settlement, seems to follow different principles at the discretion of the occupant. Certainly the occupation of Japan by the United States and of Germany by the United States, Great Britain, France, and the U.S.S.R. after World War II, led to major constitutional changes, adjustment of property rights, and reeducation programs. The status seems, therefore, to follow the rights of conquest.

Land boundaries between states are defined by treaty so that the contribution of international law is confined mainly to problems of treaty interpretation. Most of the special rules of boundary law relate to fluvial and marine frontiers. Where rivers are specified as boundaries, the law now presumes that the *thalweg*, i.e., a line down the middle of the principal navigable channel, is intended. The outward boundary of the territorial seas off a country's coast was long supposed to be three marine miles from the low-water mark, following the sinuosities of the coast. However, a number of states have in recent years asserted limits of ten or twelve miles, so that the three-mile rule is now generally accepted only in the sense of a minimum limit. To this rule exception is also made in the case of bays, which have often been held to be territorial waters when they penetrate deeply into the land territory and the opening between their headlands is narrow, say ten miles or less. Upon ground of historical practice some bays of much greater size have been considered territorial, e.g., Chesapeake Bay, Hudson Bay, especially when they constitute important interior waterways or are essential to defense. Islands at some distance from the coast have their own territorial waters, but integrated island chains or groups may sometimes be treated as units, with marine boundaries drawn from the outermost points. The International Court of Justice recently sanctioned Norway's use in place of the low-water mark of straight base lines drawn from points some of which were on the mainland but others on headlands of islands in the "rock barrier" (*skjaergaard*) which runs along the coast, often at some distance from the mainland (*Anglo-Norwegian Fisheries Case*, I.C.J. Reports, 1951, p. 116). This may probably be regarded as a special instance supported by historical claims and peculiar geographical configuration. Airspace superjacent to land or water territory is also considered to be territory of the state, so that alien aircraft may be excluded from it or permitted to enter only upon conditions specified by law or treaty. Foreign military aircraft, except of allies, are of course generally excluded, and many international incidents have occurred in recent years because of their straying or alleged straying into prohibited areas.

State jurisdiction may within reasonable limits be extended beyond territorial waters to the high seas when this is necessary to support national law enforcement. The conceptions of territory and jurisdiction seem at times to be confused in claims with respect to the "continental shelf." The term itself is not precise, but rests upon the fact that the subsoil of the ocean often shelves slowly downward under shallow water for a considerable distance before dropping off abruptly into the ocean deeps. The drop-off frequently occurs at a depth of about 100 fathoms (600 feet). In 1945 President Truman issued a proclamation in which the natural resources in the continental shelf contiguous to the coasts of the United States were said to "appertain" to the United States, "subject to its jurisdiction and control." Conservation and prudent utilization of these resources were assigned as reasons for this step. If this be a claim to territory, it is only with respect to subsoil, and intent to interfere with fishing and navigation in superjacent waters was disclaimed. However, the use of off-shore oil-well derricks is clearly contemplated, and the United States is now engaged in erecting permanent radar stations upon huge cement-filled tripods driven into the ocean bed in waters about fifty feet deep and 100 miles or more from the Atlantic coast. *Quaere,* will these be artificial islands entitled to their belts of territorial waters? Other states have made even more ambitious claims, which include the resources of the waters as well as of the subsoil and extend to considerable distances from the shore without regard to depth. Thus Peru, Ecuador, and Chile, with a view to monopolizing whaling and fisheries, claim the continental shelf and resources of superjacent waters of whatever depth to a distance of 200 miles from shore. Actually there is little shelving there; the drop off comes only a few miles from the coast. These claims have been contested, and no final rule has yet evolved.

Nationality

Many questions of jurisdiction and rights turn upon the relationship of individuals to the state. Either they are nationals, in which case they may in United States practice be citizens or noncitizen nationals; or they are aliens, resident or nonresident, friendly or enemy; or they are stateless persons, possessing no nationality. There are also cases of dual and multiple nationality. Nationality may be generally defined as a relationship between state and individual in which the individual owes allegiance to the state and the state protects the individual. Citizenship is sometimes used in the same sense but may, as in the United States, entitle one to certain political rights in addition to protection. A nonnational is an alien; he may be a national of another state or a stateless person.

It seems desirable that each individual should be a national of a state in order to be assured of protection, but that he should not be a national of more than one state in order to avoid conflicts of jurisdiction over him. Obviously this can be the case only if all states accord nationality upon some exclusive but uniform basis. At the present time, however, international law has imposed no such single standard, but leaves to each state the definition of its nationality requirements. Possibly there are some unstated limits to this freedom; protests would no doubt be made if the United States claimed as its nationals all persons in the world who have red hair, or all whose I.Q.'s exceed 140. The present practice of states is to confer nationality at birth upon one or both of two grounds, either birth within the territorial limits of the state (nationality *jure soli*), or birth anywhere as the child of parents one or both of whom are nationals (nationality *jure sanguinis*). Either principle is subject to many minor variations. Unfortunately, the two bases are not mutually exclusive and therefore open the possibility of dual nationality. For example, Italian law claims as nationals all children of Italian parentage wherever born. Upon this basis Italian nationality can be transmitted through several generations of non-resident Italians, and most of the large Italian colony in New York are Italian nationals, although also United States nationals by reason of birth here. The consequence is that if they happen to visit Italy they can be subjected to requirements affecting nationals, such as military service, and the United States, although it protests, cannot extricate them.

Nationality may also be acquired by naturalization, which must depend upon satisfaction of the requirements of the naturalizing state. But naturalization may be impeded or may result in dual nationality unless the state of origin permits expatriation and emigration for permanent residence. Communist states do not do so, nor did Nazi Germany and Fascist Italy. There is no rule of international law asserting a right of expatriation.

Statelessness generally results from statutory provisions which deprive a person of nationality, frequently as a penalty, without his having acquired another nationality. The United States, for example, deprives persons of nationality who take an oath of allegiance to or are naturalized in a foreign state; but also those who serve in the armed forces or a public office or participate in a political election, in another state; or who formally renounce their United States nationality; or are convicted of desertion in time of war from the armed forces, or of treason, or of draft evasion by leaving the country (Immigration and Nationality Act of 1952, Sec. 349). Some states divest the nationality of persons who marry aliens. More serious are the many cases since World War I in which politically disaffected persons in communist and fascist states have been deprived of nationality. Many others become stateless through territorial changes. This meant they could not obtain passports and often found it difficult to enter other countries and to become naturalized there. The international "Nansen passport" was devised by the League of Nations to assist such stateless persons. Some efforts have been made by treaties to avoid these unfortunate situations, but the achievements to date have been rather slight.

Jurisdiction

The principles governing the jurisdiction of states flow from the conception of them as sovereign entities, independent and equal before the law, and from their control of their territory and their nationals. Because of practical difficulties involved and the probable impairment of good relations a state does not usually take jurisdiction over a foreign government or its instrumentalities, property, or possessions, or over a personal sovereign or diplomatic agents, but allows them sovereign immunity from suit in its courts. For example, the sultan of Johore traveled incognito in England in 1885, styling himself Albert Baker. In this guise he gained the affections of an English lady who later sued him for breach of promise of marriage. He pleaded sovereign immunity. After consulting the Colonial Office the court allowed the plea, and that despite the fact Johore was a protected state which had surrendered control of its external relations to Great Britain; even internal sovereignty was thought sufficient basis for immunity. (*Mighell* v. *Sultan* of Johore [1894] 1 Q.B. 149).

All questions of immunity are not so simple. Public armed ships of another state are invariably granted immunity. The principle was extended for a long time to all ships publicly owned or possessed, and this is still done in some states. But states have increasingly undertaken the direct operation of merchant vessels, competing with private owners in the carrying trade. To grant them immunity from suit in a function traditionally regarded as private, and thus to improve their already unequal competitive position, has been distasteful to free enterprise states. As a result, many now deny immunity. John Marshall was under the impression that the immunity extended to diplomatic agents (see Chapter 13) and to public armed ships should apply also to military forces passing through or stationed in another state (*Schooner Exchange* v. *McFadden* [1812] 7 Cranch 116). His authority has been invoked to challenge the propriety of the NATO Status of Forces Agreement (1951; ratified by United States 1953), which allows the immunity only when offenses are committed in line of duty or at a military post or station; otherwise local criminal jurisdiction prevails. Actually, Marshall's conclusion reflected treaty arrangements rather than general international law, and more recent agreements have tended away from complete immunity.

State jurisdiction is basically territorial. This means that states have jurisdiction over persons and things within their territory, whether land, marine, or aerial, as the limits of that territory have already been defined. Resident nationals, aliens, and stateless persons are all included, unless in a category entitled to special immunity. In territorial waters account must be taken of ships of other states. The immunities of public ships have been mentioned. Merchantmen are subject to the territorial jurisdiction, but international law has developed the rule of not assuming criminal jurisdiction unless the offense in question is of such gravity as to disturb the peace of the port. Since ships enjoy the right of innocent passage through the territorial waters of other states, it is not customary to subject them to civil suits unless with respect to obligations incurred for the purpose of that passage.

Jurisdiction is also extended outside territorial waters to the extent that this may prove necessary for effective enforcement of internal law. This principle was first clearly announced in a dictum of John Marshall in Church *v.* Hubbart (2 Cranch 187 [1804]), and has become the basis for statutory authorizations of jurisdiction at considerable distances from shore over smugglers, rum runners, and ships hovering off the coast with intent to violate the local law. For such purposes a twelve-mile belt, or a one-hour sailing distance from shore at the speed of the ship or contact boat, have been used. The United States Anti-Smuggling Act of 1935 authorized seizures within fifty marine miles outward from the outer limit of customs waters, which extended twelve marine miles from the coast. Some of these claims have been contested, and exact limits of such jurisdiction seem not yet to have been stated by international law.

States also have jurisdiction over nationals and ships having national character when upon the high seas, and may extend criminal jurisdiction over them into other states if territorial jurisdiction is not assumed and if assistance can be obtained to get custody of them by extradition or otherwise. Jurisdictional conflicts may result in criminal cases when one state wishes to assume jurisdiction because the offense was committed in its territory, the other because it was committed by its national. The result may often depend upon which state has physical custody of the offender. This situation is further complicated by statutes of a few states authorizing jurisdiction over nonnationals who commit offenses outside their territory, if the offenses injure the state or its nationals. These "state interest" and "passive personality" theories cannot be admitted as primary grounds of jurisdiction, but the Permanent Court of International Justice found that injury to nationals was a basis of jurisdiction not forbidden by any rule of international law (*The Steamship Lotus,* P.C.I.J., Series A, No. 10 [1927]), and injury to states has been used as a basis in anticounterfeiting treaties.

In a very few cases, already mentioned, a universal jurisdiction may be exercised by any state which captures the offender, irrespective of nationality or situs of crime. Piracy and war crimes are the notable instances. In the case of the major war criminals tried at Nuremberg and Tokyo there was a choice of jurisdictional principles. As the military occupants of those countries the victor states were actually the governments of Germany and Japan at the time and could have proceeded on the basis of nationality of the offenders. However, they particularly wished to assert that what they were doing was consistent with international law and a contribution to it; hence, the specially created "international military tribunals." In this they opened themselves to criticism, for if the trials were conceived as an application of international law by an international jurisdiction, then it must be said that two of the counts (aggressive war, crimes against humanity), did not reflect crimes then defined by international law. This objection would not apply to a third count on traditional war crimes.

Intercourse

Some account has already been given of rules of international law affecting diplomatic intercourse of states, which are mainly concerned with defining a set of privileges and immunities which will assure free dispatch of the diplomat's work (see Chapter 13).

Formal relationships among states depend upon treaties and other types of international agreement, and international law contains a number of rules designed to test the validity of treaties in terms of competency of governments to act and the voluntary character of their acts. A treaty made under coercion may be considered void, if by that is meant coercion applied to negotiators or to individuals involved in the ratifying process. A British mission to Bhutan in 1864 was grossly insulted and roughly handled by the Bhutanese, who knew little of the outside world. Ashley Eden, the envoy, felt compelled to sign an offensive treaty they drafted in order to get the members of his mission out safely, but beneath his signature wrote the words "under compulsion." The next year the British sent a military expedition into Bhutan which corrected Bhutanese impressions of the British Empire. In concluding and obtaining ratification of a treaty with Haiti in 1915, United States Admiral Caperton used military pressure at stages of the negotiation, influenced individual members of the Haitian National Assembly, impounded bank notes needed by the Haitian government, promising they would be immediately available upon ratification, and threatened military control of Haiti if ratification failed. Probably neither procedure satisfied international law standards. However, we must not assume that treaties are invalid merely because one state is in an unequal bargaining position, as in the case of a defeated state making a peace treaty. Here the compulsion rests in the circumstances and not in pressures upon individuals. Such treaties are not likely to become invalid until aggression can be effectively curtailed.

International law also prescribes rules concerning "full powers" of negotiators; the effect of signing, ratification, and exchange of ratifications, i.e., when the agreement becomes binding; reservations; accessions by other states; termination either by fulfillment of stipulated terms, by agreement, by intervention of forces rendering performance impossible, by abrogation, or by change of essential conditions; and the effect of war upon treaties. Some general principles affecting interpretation of treaties have been advanced, but technical rules upon this subject have not been established. For present purposes it seems unnecessary to enter into the details of any of these topics.

Communications and commercial intercourse among states rest upon the assumption of a right to trade and intercourse, which was asserted at least as early as Vitoria. How far this is a legal right and not just a general practice is doubtful; certainly there have been hermit states, e.g., Nepal and Japan, which for centuries excluded foreigners and refused to trade. In any case, international law contains no customary rules upon the subject, leaving its regulation to a vast network of treaties which prescribe the conditions of communications and commercial intercourse. In recent years we have moved increasingly toward more nearly uniform practice expressed in multilateral conventions, often accompanied by international supervisory or regulatory organizations. These include the International Civil Aviation Organization, Universal Postal Union, International Telecommunications Union, Inter-Governmental Maritime Consultative Organization, and upon a regional basis, especially in Europe, international river and railroad commissions. A projected International Trade Organization has not yet been established, but multilateral tariff bargaining has been accomplished under the General Agreement on Tariffs and Trade. It appears then that an impressive body of conventional international law is emerging in these fields. Its character can be considered more conveniently in Chapter 15.

International Disputes

The earliest advances made toward the pacific settlement of international disputes were in the field of diplomacy. Collective interest in the maintenance of order led other states to tender their *good offices* in providing an avenue of communication whereby the disputants could negotiate a settlement, then to proffer suggestions as a form of *mediation* which might lead to agreement upon a basis of settlement. There is no law involved in these political procedures unless it be the conventional rule of The Hague Conference of 1907 that a tender of good offices or mediation cannot be considered an unfriendly act.

The next development was the creation of *commissions of inquiry* designed to investigate and fix the facts of the dispute, upon the assumption that clarification of them will lead to agreement between the disputants. This procedure merges into *conciliation,* in which a commission, either specially created or permanent, after determination of the facts recommends a basis of settlement, which, however, is in no sense binding upon the disputants. An undertaking to refer disputes to international commissions of inquiry was inserted into the Hague Convention on Pacific Settlement of International Disputes (1907), and such commissions were formed in three cases. The most notable instance was the *Dogger Bank Case* (1905), involving firing upon English fishing boats during the Russo-Japanese War by the Russian Baltic fleet under the misapprehension that they were Japanese torpedo boats. A number of treaties were negotiated by William Jennings Bryan when he was secretary of state which authorized permanent conciliation commissions and included the unusual feature of a "cooling time" provision, i.e., the parties agreed to submit disputes to the commission and not to resort to war before its report was made. These commissions have not been used but may have suggested certain pacific settlement provisions of the League of Nations Covenant and the United Nations Charter (see Chapter 16). Permanent commissions of inquiry and conciliation were established by the Convention on Inter-American Conciliation of 1929.

The method of *arbitration* goes a step beyond conciliation in that the parties agree in advance that they will accept the award of the arbitral tribunal. This award is supposed to be made by an application of the rules of international law to the facts presented in evidence. International claims tribunals make a special application of arbitration. Arrangements for arbitral tribunals are made by treaty, with details of the terms of submission often reserved for a supplementary agreement called a *compromis*. A sole arbitrator is occasionally used, as in the arbitration by President Coolidge of the Tacna-Arica dispute between Chile and Peru (1925), but tribunals are commonly formed by each party's appointing either one or two arbitrators and letting these choose a third or fifth to serve as umpire. These sit as a court, hear evidence and arguments upon the law presented by agents of the disputant states, and enter an award usually supported by a detailed opinion stating their conclusions upon the facts and the law. They differ from regular courts only in the manner of appointment, informal rules as to evidence and procedure, and the *ad hoc* character of their proceedings.

Arbitration has been widely employed in the nineteenth and twentieth centuries, especially since the Alabama Claims arbitration of 1871. The Permanent Court of Arbitration created by The Hague Conference of 1899 was not an actual tribunal but a panel of judges from which tribunals could be formed to deal with particular cases. Nearly a score of arbitrations, some of substantial importance, were completed under these arrangements. A large network of bilateral arbitration treaties also exists, but with the exception of international claims commissions arbitral tribunals have not been used very frequently in recent years. Nor is the method one which can be employed in situations in which the parties are adamant or undisposed to compromise, for arbitration treaties often contain so many loopholes and qualifications as to be no more than agreements to try to agree upon a submission. Use of arbitration in sharp political issues is of uncertain merit. Mussolini submitted the boundary dispute at Wal Wal to arbitration but used this as a method of postponing discussion of the larger issue created by his mobilizing Italian forces upon the frontier of Ethiopia. Hitler refused to arbitrate his demands upon Poland in 1939 despite the provision for this in the Locarno Treaty.

The final stage of pacific settlement techniques is *international adjudication,* that is, the submission of disputes to regularly organized international courts having a defined jurisdiction. The first of these (apart from a short-lived Central American Court of Justice) was the Permanent Court of International Justice (1920–1946), of which the existing International Court of Justice is a continuation. The name has been changed; the administrative association of the Permanent Court of International Justice with the League of Nations for budget and election of judges has given way to a like association of the International Court of Justice with the United Nations; and some minor changes in the statute made. The court is composed of fifteen judges, of as many nationalities, elected for nine-year terms by the U.N. General Assembly and Security Council, voting separately. Only states may be parties in cases before it, although information relevant to cases may be requested of, and must be received when submitted by, international organizations. They must also be notified of proceedings involving construction of their constituent instruments. Advisory opinions are given by the court upon request of the General Assembly or other U.N. organs and specialized agencies designated by the Assembly. Virtually all have been designated. Such opinions have in recent usage been requested mainly to obtain a construction of powers and functions of U.N. organs and agencies. Questions arising from disputes between states then before the Security Council or Assembly have also been submitted, but these sometimes pose the question whether the court is not in effect passing upon a dispute when the parties are not before it.

The jurisdiction of the International Court of Justice extends to all cases the parties refer to it and to matters specially provided for in treaties. Many treaties do contain provisions for submission to the court of questions arising under their terms. As to states, jurisdiction is dependent upon voluntary submission of a dispute, but they may under the "Optional Clause" of Article 36 file statements accepting, with or without qualification, the jurisdiction of the court without special agreement in cases with other states which have done the same. Most states parties to the statute of the court have accepted the Optional Clause, but often with reservations. The United States has reserved questions essentially within its domestic jurisdiction "as determined by the United States," which largely negates its acceptance.

In deciding cases the court applies (a) international conventional law, (b) international custom as evidence of a general practice accepted as law, (c) the general principles of law recognized by civilized nations, (d) as subsidiary authority, judicial opinions and teachings of publicists. If the parties agree it may (e) decide *ex aequo et bono,* which probably means it may extend legal principles into new areas on the basis of equity and justice. Although the court's judgments have no force as precedent, they have great persuasive value, and the advantage of a continuing jurisprudence. Their cumulative effect should be of considerable value in developing and systematizing international law. Whether it can make any contribution to the settling of political disputes must, of course, depend upon the willingness of states to submit such disputes to the court. To date, they have been reluctant to do so. Two of the more significant cases of this sort before the International Court of Justice were the *Corfu Channel Case* (I.C.J. Reports [1949], 4–169) involving responsibility of Albania for the mining of the Corfu strait and consequent damage to British ships, and the *Anglo-Iranian Oil Co. Case* (I.C.J. Reports [1952], 93–171) which arose from nationalization of the company's property by the government of Iran. In the first case, after unsuccessfully trying to evade the court's jurisdiction, Albania refused to pay the judgment entered against it. In the second the court found that it had no jurisdiction for want of Iranian consent.

LAW IN INTERNATIONAL RELATIONS

What can be said in conclusion? Certainly international law is not at present able to assure order and harmony in the world. Neither, however, can diplomacy, international organization, or even plain force. But it hardly appears that the marked indifference toward international law now so characteristic is justified. It is a system of law which is neither complete, nor mature, nor always certain. But in this it merely reflects the condition of the international community. International law is no more than the normative element in all international relations—that part of them which has hardened into rules of conduct generally accepted and enforced. To expect that law can substantially raise the moral tone of international relations is therefore to propose they raise themselves by their own bootstraps. On the other hand, international relations cannot continue without producing law; it is a thread which runs through every aspect of them—commerce, diplomacy, international organization, even war—and must be understood accordingly.

If it is not the sole instrument of international order, it is, nevertheless, a significant and necessary instrument, as are diplomacy, international organization, and force. And if the explanation of the foundations of law given in this chapter be correct, it has always one distinct advantage over these other instruments in that they represent policy, whereas law represents, to borrow a phrase from a recent address of Dr. Eelco N. van Kleffens, "the average of what is right, nationally or internationally." As a general standard of justice which can be opposed to special claims of national interest it provides a needed point of reference in assessing the propriety of state conduct. Law, along with the human conscience, is with us to stay, whatever its nature and in spite of its blind spots.

SELECTED READING

BRIERLY, J. L., *The Law of Nations: an Introduction to the International Law of Peace,* 5th ed. Oxford: Clarendon Press, 1955.

———, *The Outlook for International Law.* Oxford: Clarendon Press, 1944.

BRIGGS, HERBERT W., *The Law of Nations: Cases, Documents, and Notes,* 2d ed. New York: Appleton-Century-Crofts, 1952. Especially the editorial notes throughout text.

CORBETT, PERCY E., *Law and Society in the Relations of States.* New York: Harcourt, Brace and Company, 1951.

DICKINSON, EDWIN D., *Law and Peace.* Philadelphia: University of Pennsylvania Press, 1951.

GIHL, TORSTEN, *International Legislation: An Essay on Changes in International Law and in International Legal Situations* (trans. by S. J. Charleston). London: Oxford University Press, 1937.

HUDSON, MANLEY O., *International Tribunals, Past and Future.* Washington: Carnegie Endowment for International Peace and Brookings Institution, 1944.

JESSUP, PHILIP C., *A Modern Law of Nations—An Introduction.* New York: The Macmillan Company, 1948.

KEETON, GEORGE W., and SCHWARZENBERGER, GEORG, *Making International Law Work,* 2d ed. London: Stevens and Sons Ltd., 1946.

KELSEN, HANS, *Principles of International Law.* New York: Rinehart and Company, 1952.

LAUTERPACHT, H., *The Function of Law in the International Community.* Oxford: Clarendon Press, 1933.

NIEMEYER, GERHART, *Law without Force: the Function of Politics in International Law.* Princeton: Princeton University Press, 1941.

NUSSBAUM, ARTHUR, *A Concise History of the Law of Nations,* rev. ed. New York: The Macmillan Company, 1954.

STONE, JULIUS, *Legal Controls of International Conflict.* New York: Rinehart and Company, 1954. Esp. Introduction and Book I.

VAN KLEFFENS, EELCO N., "The Place of Law in International Relations," in *United Nations Review,* 1 (7): 20–23 (January 1955).

CHAPTER 15

THE GROWTH
OF INTERNATIONAL
ORGANIZATION

When they think of international organization, most people today think of the United Nations, which has in fact drawn together the converging lines of many historical threads of organization, some of which are very old. Collectively these threads comprise a network of some complexity, a great part of which is concerned with administrative functions seldom publicized. Although attention is now focused upon political and security questions considered by the General Assembly and the Security Council of the United Nations, these are relatively new areas of activity. The historical growth of international organization stems from efforts to make the procedures of international law and diplomacy more effective.

Some attention was given in the preceding chapter to the progression through the stages of good offices, mediation, commissions of inquiry, conciliation, and arbitration to judicial settlement. This was not indeed a historical sequence of development, for arbitration was used rather frequently by the ancient Greeks, and occasionally in medieval Europe. However, its use had lapsed and was not revived until the arbitrations under the Jay Treaty of 1795, nor much in vogue until after the Alabama Claims settlement in 1872, so that the order is roughly chronological for the development of machinery of pacific settlement among modern states.

In the discussion of balance of power diplomacy in Chapter 11, it was shown that the effort to maintain European equilibrium produced three innovations: treaties of guaranty, conference diplomacy, and the Concert of Europe. These marked a growing sense of the need for collective action against aggressors. Treaties of guaranty need not, of course, be collective undertakings, but they seem to have moved in that direction, as shown by the British-

Dutch agreement (1711) to guarantee the Treaty of Utrecht, the guaranty by the European powers of the Saxon cessions and the neutrality and integrity of Switzerland in 1815, the British-Austrian-French guaranty in 1856 of the independence and integrity of the Ottoman Empire, the multilateral treaties guaranteeing the neutrality of Belgium in 1839 and of Luxembourg in 1867, the four-power guaranty of the independence and constitutional order of Greece in 1863, and others. These treaty undertakings involved no machinery other than consultation in the event of circumstances evoking the guaranty, and some of them did not even specify consultation. Lord Derby argued in 1867 that the collective guaranty in the Luxembourg convention did not obligate the British government to intervene in support of the neutrality of Luxembourg unless the other parties to the convention also acted, but this interpretation would seem to render the guaranty illusory. It has not been the usual view. In a sense it may be said that the collective security undertakings of the League of Nations Covenant and the United Nations Charter are a generalized form of the principle of guaranty, with detailed arrangements for consultation and pooling of forces.

Conference diplomacy was a natural technique in situations of general concern, such as the great European peace settlements of 1648, 1713, 1815, and 1919. These would not as *ad hoc* congresses have had much significance for international organization but for the fact that they created a pattern for collective action with respect to questions of European equilibrium, and therefore suggested the advantage of regularizing consultation and joint action in that area. However, no machinery was created until 1815, after the French Revolution and the Napoleonic wars had aroused the apprehensions of all the major dynasties of Europe and driven them into a defensive coalition. The question at the Congress of Vienna was how to continue the coalition for the collective guaranty of the settlement, and the answer was the Concert of Europe. The continental powers would have preferred a specific collective guaranty against internal revolution as well as external aggression, and made great efforts to persuade Great Britain to participate. The tsar suggested an international navy attached to an international agency for suppression of the slave trade (presumably as a sop to British interest in suppressing this traffic) and Prussian generals proposed a European army under Wellington's command, to be based on Brussels. But Castlereagh was disturbed by the conservative dynastic interests which the continental governments wished to secure through the Concert and counseled against specific commitments. In his opinion a collective guaranty against domestic revolution must postulate internal peace and justice within the countries guaranteed; "nothing would be more immoral or prejudicial to the character of government generally than the idea that their force was collectively to be prostituted to the support of established power without any consideration of the extent to which it was abused." Nor would he pledge intervention even to guarantee the new frontiers. In a parliamentary government, he argued, the question of intervention must be considered when the occasion arose, and a prior commitment would antagonize the House of Commons. In view of the British attitude, the Concert had to be reduced to an undertaking to consult. Yet Castlereagh became convinced of the value of the conferences in which he participated, reporting to the cabinet that little embarrassment and much solid good came out of them: "It really appears to me to be a new discovery in the European government, at once extinguishing the cobwebs with which diplomacy obscures the horizon, bringing the whole system into its true light, and giving to the counsels of the great Powers the efficiency and almost the simplicity of a single State." However, regular meetings were abandoned after 1822. The partial success of the Concert in dealing with a series of European problems has already been noted. It was hardly an early form of the League of Nations, but it was a necessary experience preliminary to such an arrangement.

The use of conferences also suggested the possibility of employing them as legislative bodies to develop by treaty more effective rules in certain areas of international law. Some of the acts already mentioned, whereby guaranties of independence, integrity, or neutrality were given in order to settle the position of Switzerland (1815), Belgium (1831), Luxembourg (1867), Turkey and the Balkans (Congress of Berlin, 1878), Morocco (Conference of Algeciras, 1906), were in effect legislative as creating by a collective mandate a new international legal status intended to be permanent. Several law-making treaties regulating privateering, blockade, and contraband (Declaration of Paris of 1856), the care of the sick and wounded in war (Geneva Conventions of 1864 and 1868), and the conduct of land and naval warfare (Hague Conventions of 1899 and 1907) were the work of major conferences. The principle of freedom of navigation upon the Rhine was urged by the Congress of Paris in 1814, and an Annex to the Act of the Congress of Vienna in 1815 applied the principle to European international rivers generally. In the Treaty of Paris of 1856 reference was made to the Vienna rules as part of the public law of Europe, and the same instrument created an international control of the Danube and admitted Turkey to the advantages of the public law and Concert of Europe. It is evident that the powers had come to conceive of a European legal community (capable of extension more widely), of which the Concert was a political and legislative organ, however rudimentary.

INTERNATIONAL ADMINISTRATIVE UNIONS TO 1914

Not all of the conferences of the nineteenth century were concerned with territorial settlements or political questions. The rapid expansion of foreign commerce and travel posed urgent problems of regulation. In this area the interest of all countries in effective administration was clear, and it quickly became apparent that this could not be done upon a national basis. What was done is of particular interest in the development of international organization because it proved to be possible to create permanent secretariats or administrative bureaus to deal with some of these problems. The public administrative unions which emerged usually combined such apparatus with annual or occasional conferences of representatives of the member states to revise the basic regulations but used the permanent secretariat to do the preparatory work for the conferences and to exercise the administrative and regulatory functions for which the union was formed.

In the period before World War I organizations of this sort developed in at least five functional areas: (1) communications and transport; (2) industry and commerce; (3) public health and sanitation; (4) morals and crime; (5) financial, police, or political controls. They varied widely in their purposes and in the extent of the powers vested in them. Some were merely supervisory and intermediate, designed to co-ordinate government administrations; others had autonomous powers of some scope and conducted separate international administrations. Leonard Woolf, who examined them in some detail in 1916 enumerated the following and distinguished four categories (*International Government*, 159–161):

I. Permanent deliberative or legislative organs working in conjunction with administrative organs: 1. The Telegraphic Union; 2. The Radio-telegraphic Union; 3. The Universal Postal Union; 4. The Metric Union; 5. The International Institute of Agriculture; 6. La Commission Penitentiaire Internationale; 7. The Sanitary Councils and International Office of Public Hygiene; 8. The International Geodetic Association; 9. The International Seismological Union; 10. The Pan-American Union; 11. The Central American Union.

II. Periodic conferences in conjunction with permanent international bureaus or offices: 1. Railway Freight Transportation; 2. Industrial Property; 3. Literary and Artistic Property; 4. Pan-American Sanitary Union; 5. Slave Trade and Liquor Traffic in Africa.

III. Conferences and conventions with the object of unifying national laws or administrations (partial list): 1. Conferences Internationales pour l'Unité Technique des Chemins de Fer; 2. Automobile Conference; 3. Latin Monetary Union; 4. Scandinavian Monetary Union; 5. Central American Monetary Union; 6. Conference on Nomenclature of Causes of Death; 7. Legal Protection of Workers; 8. Submarine Cables; 9. Commercial Statistics; 10. White Slave Traffic.

IV. Special international organs of a permanent character: 1. Permanent Sugar Commission; 2. Opium Commission; 3. Plague Surveillance in China; 4. International Committee of the Map of the World; 5. Hague Tribunal and Bureau; 6. Central American Court of Justice; 7. International Bureau for the Publication of Customs Tariffs.

This list included only regimes which he thought to be commonly regarded as public international unions. However, those in the third category
depended upon periodic conferences and had no permanent organs. On the
other hand there should certainly be included in the fourth category a number of control commissions possessing financial, police, or more general administrative powers, in Turkey, Albania, Greece, Egypt, the Congo Free
States, Spitzbergen, and the Suez Canal area; and about a score of regulatory
commissions for international rivers running between or through two or more
states (or in the case of China national rivers of interest to other states)—in
Europe the Rhine, Danube, Scheldt, Meuse, Elbe, Oder, Pruth, Dniester,
Niemen, Vistula, Guadiana, Tagus, Douro; in Africa the Congo; in China the
Hwang-ho and Pei-ho; in America the St. Lawrence, Rio Grande, Amazon,
and Rio de la Plata. Thus the total array of prewar international administrative unions with permanent organs was probably in excess of fifty, without
counting the ten conventions which merely imposed uniform state action. It
is impossible here to give a comprehensive account of them, but some of
the more significant will be described briefly.

River Commissions

The most notable of the river commissions were those created to enforce
uniform tolls and rules of navigation for the Rhine and the Danube. The
Octroi Convention of 1804 between the arch chancellor of the Holy Roman
Empire and France established on the Rhine the first international organ for
river control. Toll stations and navigation police operated under a director
general and a group of inspectors and receivers. Judicial appeals could be made
from local rulings on breaches of regulations to a commission composed of
the French prefect at Mayence, a representative appointed by the arch chancellor, and a jurist chosen by these two. At the Congress of Vienna the river
was declared open to all riparian states and a Rhine Commission composed
of one representative of each riparian state created. This was a weak body
which met only once a year, leaving regulation of navigation and toll collections to a group of inspectors. Voting was generally equal but on some
questions weighted according to the length of the state's river bank. A right of
appeal to the commission continued. By later treaties the regulatory powers
of the commission were increased, and special courts established to interpret
regulations. The Central Commission for the Navigation of the Rhine still
exists.

The European Commission of the Danube was established in 1856 by the
Treaty of Paris. In this case the commission was not confined to representatives
of riparian states but included seven, later eight, states which had an interest
in the river traffic of the lower or maritime Danube. It could rely upon some

degree of financial independence from fees for services and also levied dues and floated loans which enabled it to make improvements in the river by dredging and dock facilities. Its regulatory powers included licensing of boats and pilots, navigation rules and collection of fines for violations, toll charges, supervision of channel markings, lighthouses, and docks. Thus it had legislative and judicial competence. It employed a permanent staff of clerical, technical, and financial personnel, and a river police, and had its own flag. Unlike other river commissions it was not just a supervisory and co-ordinating body for national administrations but a genuine international administration. This important commission continued to function autonomously for many years and proved to be highly effective. After World War I it was decided to internationalize the whole of the Danube from Ulm to its mouth. The European Commission continued its jurisdiction of the maritime Danube, and a new International Danube Commission of ten states was created for the "fluvial Danube." It was, however, a much weaker agency, confined to preparatory and supervisory functions. After World War II the lower part of the river fell wholly under Communist control. A conference at Belgrade in 1948 attempted to reach agreement upon a new river regime but divided as between the United States, Great Britain, and France, on the one hand, and the seven riparian states led by Russia. A convention providing for free navigation subject to regulation by a unified commission for the whole river was adopted by the votes of the communist states. The commission would be a weak one operating "in accordance with the sovereign rights of the Danubian States," and of course under domination of the U.S.S.R. The Western states contend that the older conventions cannot be legally modified in this way and of course have refused to recognize the jurisdiction of the new agencies over the upper Danube.

Railway Transport

The large amount of railway traffic across national boundaries in Europe naturally suggested the desirability of international arrangements permitting through traffic with minimal regulations. International conferences upon this subject were held in 1878, 1881, 1886, and 1890. The last produced a convention which created an international administration of railway transport of merchandise. It operated through an Administrative Bureau without benefit of any regular congress or conference. Amendment of the convention required the special convening of a conference on demand of one fourth of the states. However, the principal European states did by the convention agree that their railway administrations would accept goods other than those in certain prohibited classes for through transport under a *lettre de voiture,* specifying rules as to packing, transport, charges, distribution of receipts, and accounting among railway administrations. Claims for loss or damage could be brought in courts of the state of the railway administration affected; disputes between administrations were subject to arbitration by the bureau. A by-product of through traffic was a movement to standardize gauge of track and construction of cars. Conventions of 1886 and 1907 on these subjects were ratified by most European states. Consideration was given to extending the system of through traffic to passengers and baggage but this had not been accomplished before World War I.

Universal Postal Union

"To the ordinary man in the twentieth century," as Alfred Zimmern remarked, "it seems little less than a Law of Nature that a letter stamped and addressed to a foreign country should reach its destination." Yet it was only in 1875 that international arrangements for handling mails at low, uniform rates were established. Before that arrangements were chaotic. Some bilateral arrangements existed between particular countries, private postal systems such as that operated by the princes of Thurm and Taxis were used, and postal rates were extremely confusing, involving the computation of charges to be made by each postal administration along the route. Rates varied widely according to the choice made from alternative routes, but were in general very high. There was further confusion when the several postal administrations involved attempted to divide receipts upon the basis of proportionate costs of carriage. The General Postal Union created in 1875, renamed Universal Postal Union in 1878, was the result of an agreement between twenty-two states. It includes postal administrations not only of independent states but also of their dependencies, and has grown to be really universal with eighty-eight members. Its effect is to create a single postal administration for foreign mails which functions through pooling the services of national administrations, all of which have agreed to the free movement of mails upon specified conditions of carriage and postal charges. The union functions through a congress which meets at intervals of about five years and which sets maximum postal rates and conditions of collaboration among postal systems. As each state retains its own postal receipts there is no elaborate accounting procedure required. Arrangements for arbitration are included in case two or more states disagree as to the construction of the convention. A striking feature is the fact that modifications of the basic regulations are made by a majority vote of the congress, which consists not of diplomats but of technical people from postal administrations, and although conventions must be ratified, the union puts these changes into immediate effect. This derogation from sovereignty is tolerated because the regulations are not involved in power politics and because the services rendered by the union are so essential that withdrawal from the union over a disagreement about terms of carriage would be unthinkable. The Congress of the United States has by statute authorized the Postmaster General to conclude postal treaties and conventions, which are ratified by the President without submission to the Senate—the only instance of such congressional complaisance. Administrative functions of the Postal Union are vested in a smaller international bureau, or secretariat, located in Bern, Switzerland, and staffed by Swiss. They publish a journal in several languages, act as a clearing house and adjust accounts among the member postal administrations, collect and distribute information, give opinions upon questions of interpretation, and prepare proposals for consideration by the Congress.

International Telegraphy

The formation of an International Telegraphic Union in 1865 preceded the Postal Union and the general lines of organization were similar. Provision was made for a conference and a bureau. The former differed from the congress of the Universal Postal Union in that it did not have power to amend the basic convention but only the *Reglèment* or regulations issued under it. However, this sufficiently empowered it to deal with technical requirements in transmitting messages, hours during which telegraph offices should be open, tariffs of charges, and clearance of accounts among administrations. These arrangements proved satisfactory as far as they went, but it soon became apparent that further regulation was needed to protect international interests in submarine cables and in wireless telegraphy. Both were politically sensitive instruments, since they were involved in power relationships.

Great Britain entered the cable field early (first cable 1851, first transatlantic cable 1858) and attained a virtual monopoly, aided by her control of gutta percha, one of the materials needed in manufacturing cables. After 1894 a determined effort was made by Germany to break the British monopoly. Permission to connect early German cables in the Atlantic area with the British world-wide network was refused. In the Pacific Germany purchased the Mariana and Caroline Islands, where the Island of Yap became a cable center with lines to the Celebes, Guam, and Shanghai, constructed by a joint German-Dutch corporation. No disposition was shown by Great Britain to enter into an international pooling or linking up of cable facilities, but some progress was made in obtaining international rules to prevent damage to or breaking of cables by fishing boats and ships.

Wireless telegraphy was first developed in 1897 by a British company holding the Marconi patent. This firm sought for a few years to monopolize the field by a contract with Lloyds and the Italian government under which telegraphic service between ships and shore was established but messages would not be sent to or received from any ship not using the Marconi system. Although the British attended a conference on wireless telegraphy in 1903, they were not yet prepared to make any concession. But in 1906 they abandoned this position and in the interest of safety of shipping agreed to a convention creating a Radiotelegraphic Union similar to the Telegraphic Union and utilizing the same bureau. Provision was made that all shore and ship stations must respond irrespective of the system used, and that coast stations must be connected by special lines with the main telegraphic system. Other controls affected technical arrangements and charges.

Commodity Agreements—International Sugar Commission

An unusual experiment with commodity control through international regulation of tariffs was made with the establishment of the Permanent Sugar Commission in 1902. A number of European states had artificially stimulated sugar production by bounties to producers which enabled them to dump their product upon the world market at prices below that of West Indian sugar. The British government wished to avoid permanent injury to the West Indian sugar industry, and in time the bounties became so onerous that European governments were willing to assent to an arrangement for their elimination. The first agreements failed for want of any device to secure enforcement. In the Convention of 1902 this was provided: the signatories agreed to abolish bounties, to impose no import duties upon nonbounty sugars beyond a specified maximum, and to impose a countervailing tariff upon imported bounty sugars. A bureau was set up to gather statistics and information on sugar legislation, but the real powers were placed in a commission of one delegate from each signatory. This body, among other things, determined whether signatories accorded any direct or indirect bounty, what bounties existed in nonsignatory states, and what countervailing tariffs should be applied to sugar from the latter. It acted by a majority vote. Thus one of the most characteristic exercises of national sovereignty—the fixing of a tariff—was surrendered to an international body. The commission succeeded in eliminating the bounty system, but its very success led England to withdraw in 1913 because as a sugar-importing state she had no interest in keeping prices up once the bounty system was destroyed.

Public Health and Sanitation

A field which proved exceedingly difficult to bring within international administrative regulation, despite a universal and compelling interest, was the prevention of epidemics of bubonic plague and cholera. Europe even in the nineteenth century was periodically swept by devastating epidemics introduced from the Orient by commercial shipping or sometimes spread by the great religious pilgrimages to shrines in the Near East. The methods of infection were well known—cholera by contamination of water by diseased persons, plague by rat fleas which have bitten diseased persons—but there were persistent differences of national policy in trying to meet the danger. Many European governments sought to do this by quarantining vessels which entered their ports for such a period as was conceived to assure their freedom from contamination. The method proved lamentably ineffective and had the further inconvenience that cargoes were often ruined needlessly by delay or decontamination measures. Great Britain felt it could not afford to deal with shipping in such a way and refused to use quarantine, relying instead upon expeditious inspections and immediate isolation of infected persons in port hospital facilities and decontamination of infected goods. Other persons and goods were not detained. While this was a more sensible approach to the problem, it did not save England any more than quarantine did the continental states from epidemics. The reason was that in the absence of regular notification of infection at points from which ships came it was impossible to focus inspection sharply enough. The corrective for this was clearly an international program of public health information, but this was long delayed because the continental states did not accept the British premises and the British feared to become involved with the continental view favoring quarantine. When all finally became convinced of the ineffectiveness of quarantine, action became possible.

The Convention of 1893 was in part a negative document—that is, it stipulated maximum periods of quarantine and listed articles which could be subjected to detention or disinfection. In effect this met the British position by limiting the use of quarantine methods. On the positive side it established an obligation to notify health administrations of other states when infection was discovered. International Sanitary Councils were set up by a Convention of 1892 to provide exceptional controls at points important in the movement of pilgrims—Constantinople, Alexandria, Tangiers, and Teheran. Those at Alexandria and Tangiers were reasonably effective; the others appear to have failed because of diplomatic backbiting between the Germans and the British. The provisions of both conventions were incorporated into the Convention of 1903, which defined in greater detail the measures of inspection and regulation to be applied at the Suez Canal, Persian Gulf, and pilgrim control points. The convention authorized an International Office of Public Health, which was established in Paris in 1907. It collected public health data and documents for the information of signatories and published a monthly bulletin of statistics, laws, and regulations. It was also authorized to correspond with the sanitary councils and to propose amendments of the convention.

Pan-American Union

In the Western Hemisphere a unique experiment in general regional organization slowly evolved. Simón Bolívar, the leader of the Latin American revolution against Spain and liberator of Venezuela, Colombia, Ecuador, Peru, and Bolivia, urged a general security organization of American states and succeeded in convening the first Pan-American congress in 1826. But the revolution had been won and the impulse to collective action was no longer sufficiently strong to support Bolívar's ambitious project for a general arbitration pact. The United States and Chilean delegates did not even arrive in time for the meetings, and a British delegate was authorized only to act as an observer. The conference adopted a pretentious final act, but it secured only one ratification. No bureau or secretariat had been created, and there were only occasional evidences in later years of desire to pursue the matter farther. In 1881 Secretary of State James G. Blaine, whose interest was mainly in closer commercial collaboration, suggested a general congress, but he left office and the project was abandoned until 1889. The United States Congress then renewed the invitation, and the First International American Congress assembled in Washington. It adopted a number of recommendations upon scientific and commercial collaboration, extradition, and arbitration, and for the first time set up a permanent agency—the Commercial Bureau of the American Republics—to collect and distribute information on trade, tariffs, and commercial legislation. The bureau proved so active and useful that its work was enlarged in 1896, and a permanent international executive committee was formed to supervise it and collaborate with the Secretary of State in choosing its personnel. The Second International Conference of American States (1901) considered a very broad program of projects in the fields of arbitration, commerce, and transportation, trade marks and copyrights, health and sanitation, professional exchanges, and others, and again enlarged the permanent establishment by creating a Governing Board representing all signatory states, enlarging the International Bureau, and authorizing its director to attend meetings of the board and its committees. Provision was also made for international conferences at regular intervals of five years. At the third conference the duties of the bureau were further expanded, it became a depository of records of conferences and the Governing Board, and an administrative unit to carry out their decisions. The director was required to attend sessions of the board and to prepare agenda. In 1910 the title of the bureau was changed to the Pan-American Union.

World War I induced in subsequent conferences a renewed interest in arbitration and collective security arrangements, developed in a series of impressive conferences at Havana (1928), Montevideo (1933), and Lima (1938). Interest has continued, however, in problems of health, communications, law, and more recently cultural exchange and technical assistance. In terms of treaties concluded and resolutions or declarations adopted the union has been immensely active, although it must be added that ratification and active implementation of these instruments has often lagged. Still the extent of hemispheric solidarity achieved through the years was amply demonstrated for security purposes during World War II and after, when joint action was taken as to the neutrality zone; in breaking diplomatic relations with the

Axis; in an integrated system for pacific settlement of disputes framed in the Act of Chapultepec (1945), which also provided for joint consultation in case of aggression against any American state; and finally in the implementation of the latter principle by the Treaty of Reciprocal Assistance signed at Rio de Janeiro in 1947. A final change of organizational pattern came in 1948 with the creation of the Organization of American States, which functions through the quinquennial Inter-American Conference, consultative meetings of foreign ministers, the Council of the Organization, composed of ambassadors of member states to the United States, three bodies subsidiary to the council—the Inter-American Council of Jurists, the Inter-American Cultural Council, and the Inter-American Social Council. The Pan-American Union continues as the permanent central organ and secretariat of the Organization of American States.

THE LEAGUE OF NATIONS

One purpose of reviewing the development of international organization in the century before 1914 is to place the League of Nations, which was created by the Conference of Paris after World War I, in a proper perspective. No one who is familiar with this earlier growth will be likely to make the common mistake of supposing that the League of Nations was an idealistic or theoretical conception without historical roots. It is probably true that some of the statesmen at Paris were not as familiar with the historical antecedents as they should have been in order to give full effect to the voice of experience, but it is also true that one will look in vain for novel elements in the Covenant of the League of Nations which were not present or suggested in earlier organizations. The idea of collective guaranties was not new; nor were large conferences of member states for political, economic, or social planning; nor limited concerts of strong states for collective security action; nor technical bureaus or secretariats in the fields of communications, transport, cultural relations, economic and social welfare, health, statistics, etc., nor even the notion of permanent international courts. The only novelty of the League lay in its comprehensive character as a framework for encompassing many of these functions. Early organization had followed the piecemeal approach of what has been called the functional principle of organization, i.e., providing specific machinery as the demands of a particular problem suggest the need. For the first time the League of Nations put together some of these pieces as an integrated structure and thus drew them to the attention of the world. It provided a more general membership base and therefore a more general application, and somewhat enlarged the range of subjects and techniques. These were at most quantitative changes. The only qualitative change was the obligation imposed upon member states by Article 16 to break off all commercial, financial, and personal relations with a Covenant breaker, and this proved unenforceable.

It is unnecessary here to trace the steps in the actual formulation of the Covenant of the League of Nations or of the constituent instruments of its related organizations, the Permanent Court of International Justice and the International Labor Organization. Although the personal prestige of President Wilson was an important factor in emphasizing the Covenant, it does not appear that there was in fact any resistance to the plan in Europe at all comparable to that encountered in the United States. Several governments contributed plans which influenced the final drafting. The Hurst-Miller Draft, which was the basis of discussion at Paris, derived from a foreign office memorandum, modified in the light of a French plan and of a paper by General Smuts of the Union of South Africa, whose conception of the structure of the League Council and views upon mandates proved persuasive. Another main line of planning began with the report of the Phillimore Committee to the foreign office, which was utilized by Colonel House in preparing a plan for President Wilson. House added points on an international court, disarmament, and the principle that a threat to the peace is a matter of concern to all states (a point also suggested by Elihu Root). His paper was largely redrafted by President Wilson in several revisions. Plans were also submitted by Italy and Japan but these received little attention. The Covenant was made an integral part of the treaties of peace (Part I in each case), as was the Statute of the International Labor Organization (Part XIII). It was the presence of the Covenant in the Treaty of Versailles which led, under the conservative leadership of Henry Cabot Lodge, to rejection of the treaty by the United States Senate.

Structure of the League of Nations

Membership in the League of Nations was intended to be nearly universal. In an annex to the Covenant thirty-two original members, signatories of the treaty, were named. All but two, the United States and the Hedjaz (later united with the Nejd in the Kingdom of Saudi Arabia) accepted membership. So did thirteen other states listed there as invited to accede to the Covenant. Any other "fully self-governing" state which would give "effective guarantees of its sincere intention to observe its international obligations" and accept League prescriptions as to its armaments, could be admitted upon application by a two-thirds vote of the Assembly. The right of withdrawal, subject to two years' notice and fulfillment of all obligations was recognized. Expulsion of a member by the Council was also authorized in the event of violation of the Covenant. During the life of the League twenty states were admitted upon application. Certain applicants were rejected either as not self-governing

(Armenia, Azerbaijan, Georgia, Ukraine) or "on account of their small size" (Liechtenstein, Monaco, San Marino). Twenty states withdrew from membership, the most notable instances being Japan in March 1933, as a result of League action in Manchukuo; Germany in October 1933, ostensibly because of dissatisfaction with the handling of disarmament but evidently as part of Hitler's general program to flout legal restraints; and Italy in December 1937, because of League sanctions in the Ethiopian incident. In one case a member was expelled: on December 14, 1939, the Council declared the U.S.S.R. no longer a member because of its aggression against Finland. At the final session of the Assembly in April, 1946, there were thirty-four states represented.

The absence of certain states from the League presented special problems. Germany was not admitted until 1926, the U.S.S.R. until 1934, and the United States never joined. Failure to recognize the liberal Weimar government of Germany perhaps delayed the realistic approach to its problems which was needed. The absence of the U.S.S.R. before 1934 fed a Communist propaganda line that the League was a reactionary instrument. Of course, its presence later led to leftist demands for sharp action against fascism, which probably alarmed conservative opinion and distorted a problem which should have been considered in terms of breach of the Covenant or of international obligations generally. This tendency to divide the League in terms of ideologies, although not so shattering a conflict as the later East-West schism in the United Nations, weakened its effectiveness in security cases. Had the United States joined it might have added an element of disinterestedness and impartiality in the consideration of these problems. What it would have meant in bolstering sanctions is not clear, for the isolationist temper of the United States during much of this period might have prevented participation in them in any case.

The principal organs of League action were an Assembly, a Council, and a permanent Secretariat. They represent, respectively, the principles of the general conference, the concert of great powers, and the bureau, as developed in earlier organization. The Assembly consisted of not more than three representatives from each member state, casting one vote. The Covenant specified that the Council should include representatives of the Principal Allied and Associated Powers (United States, Great Britain, France, Italy, and Japan), plus four members chosen and replaced from time to time by the Assembly. The British wished to exclude small states completely, but President Wilson's early approval of the Smuts proposals on this point (later, he moved toward the British view), and the willingness of France and Italy to satisfy the small states, made a compromise necessary. The conception of a concert of great states was further compromised by amendment. In 1922 the Assembly added two additional nonpermanent seats, moved by the fact that the retention in the Council of Belgium, Spain, Brazil, and China seemed for different reasons desirable and that other states were pressing for membership. When Germany joined the League, she was given a permanent seat, but the dictatorial governments of Spain and Brazil refused to consent to this unless given permanent seats also. Their request was not met, and in consequence they withdrew from the League, but the effort to find a compromise produced a plan in which the elected members were increased to nine, chosen for three-year terms, with the qualification that not more than three of these might be reelected. These "semipermanent" seats were intended for Poland, Spain, and Brazil. When the U.S.S.R. entered as a permanent member, the Council had six permanent, three semipermanent, and six nonpermanent seats. The withdrawal of Germany, Italy, and Japan and the expulsion of the U.S.S.R. left only two permanent members. Probably it would be a mistake to conclude that the formal possibility of outvoting of permanent by elective members was in practice significant, for great powers can generally align the votes of lesser powers, but it was highly significant that the Council had only for a few years a sufficient membership of great powers to form a true concert.

In powers the Assembly and Council were co-ordinate, being authorized in identical terms to deal "with any matter within the sphere of action of the League or affecting the peace of the world." As the Assembly met only annually, the Council was in effect an interim body with full powers. The basic voting requirement in both bodies was the requirement of unanimity for decisions, but action by a majority was permitted in matters of procedure, "including the appointment of committees to investigate particular matters." The unanimity rule was conservative, for there had been many instances of majority action in earlier organizations. However, the rule adopted was conceived in terms of security action, in which the unanimity rule of the diplomatic assembly was naturally followed, and the framers doubtless had an eye to calming apprehensions among those (e.g., the Senate of the United States) who feared loss of sovereignty. Although a complicating factor in a procedural sense a unanimity requirement should not be regarded as an insuperable obstacle to agreement, for it is often possible to exert pressures to secure the abstention from voting of states which are opposed to but not materially affected by a proposal. Nevertheless, it would appear that the application of so strict a rule to all types of business was a retrogression. In practice, however, it was offset in several ways. In the first session of the Assembly a rule was established that a majority vote would suffice for the adoption of resolutions expressing a wish (*voeu*), as distinct from decisions. This meant that League practice approximated the later rule of the U.N. Assembly, which requires at most a two-thirds majority but which has no action powers and can therefore only express wishes or recommendations. The second League Assembly also concluded that amendments to the

Covenant could be initiated by a majority vote, a rule more flexible than that of the United Nations. Finally, one must bear in mind the development of the six standing committees of the League Assembly (constitutional and legal matters; technical organizations; armaments; administrative and financial matters; social and humanitarian matters; mandates, minorities, and political matters). These committees found it highly inconvenient, especially in the financial committee's handling of the budget, to use a unanimity rule, and all fell into the practice of recommending resolutions sent to the plenary sessions of the Assembly by majority vote. There opposing states usually abstained in deference to the committee recommendation, so that much routine business was expedited in this way.

In dealing with security problems the vote of parties to the dispute was not counted, and there was and is much to be said for unanimity among the others, or at least among the great states, which must bear the brunt of sanctions. The decision to participate in an application of sanctions, other than mere breaking off of commercial intercourse, to a Covenant breaker was left to the individual decision of the member states, to which the Council could only recommend contributions. Article 16 of the Covenant did brand aggression in violation of the Covenant as an act of war against all members, but as it takes two parties to convert an act of war into a state of war this hardly implied compulsory participation in sanctions. Under the circumstances unanimity of action could hardly be expected without unanimity of voting.

The Covenant said little about the Secretariat beyond providing for a secretary-general and such secretaries and staff as might be required. The first secretary-general, Sir Eric Drummond, was named in the Annex to the Covenant; successors were to be appointed by the Council with the approval of a majority of the Assembly. There seems to have been little consideration of the proper scope or form of such an organization, and the modest bureaus of earlier organizations afforded little guidance. Probably the leaders at the Paris Conference were impressed by the success of interallied councils for food, munitions, and shipping control, and by the efficiency of the war cabinet secretariat in London, directed by Sir Maurice Hankey, who had contributed much to the organization of the Paris Conference. They offered the post of secretary-general to him, and he drew up a paper outlining his conception of the proposed Secretariat. However, he declined the post. Drummond was important in developing the conception of a truly international Secretariat, for which no real precedent existed, and demonstrating that such a heterogeneous body, comprising nationals of over thirty states, could be devoted, well integrated, and highly efficient. He was aided at the outset by an extraordinary group of principal officers, who had distinguished themselves in national civil services. In the later years of the League the quality of the personnel declined somewhat under pressure of member states to secure proportionate representation in the Secretariat.

Drummond was also responsible for the basic plan of organization. Under two deputy secretaries-general and two under secretaries he grouped a number of sections headed by directors, which were designed to deal with the special tasks imposed upon the League by the Covenant, including Article 24, which suggested that existing international bureaus be placed under the League's direction if the parties consented; and if not, that the Secretariat should collect and secure relevant information and render any assistance to them which might be desirable. There was a Mandates Section, an Economic and Financial Section, a Section for Transit and Communications, a Section for Social Problems, such as the drug and white slave traffics, a Political Section to aid the Council in security problems, boundary questions, etc., a Legal Section to advise upon legal points and to register and publish treaties, an International Bureaus Section to deal with other international agencies, an International Commissions Section to assist special League regimes such as those in the Saar and Danzig, a Minorities Section to assist the Minorities Commission in supervising guaranties in minorities treaties, a Disarmament Commission, a Health Section, an Information Section, and a treasurer, librarian, and registrar of archives. Beginning with 121 officers the Secretariat grew to more than 700 at its peak and established patterns of international administrative activity which have been continued in the U.N. Secretariat.

The Permanent Court of International Justice (see Chapter 14) and the International Labor Organization may be considered as parts of the League system but both functioned as wholly autonomous agencies. The International Labor Office has its own annual General Conference representing the governments, employers, and labor of all member states, a Governing Body (executive council) which meets quarterly, and the International Labor Office, a permanent secretariat. It seeks to improve conditions of labor by securing adoption of international conventions setting minimum standards and by exchange of information. The Court, created mainly to hear actions between states, made a direct contribution to the work of the League by its advisory opinions upon legal questions referred to it by the Assembly or Council.

Work of the League of Nations

To describe in any detail the work of the League of Nations during the quarter century of its existence would require a volume in itself. Here it is possible only to make some illustrative comments concerning matters other than security problems, reserving the latter for the next chapter, so that comparison can be made with United Nations procedures.

Although the Covenant contained no provisions for an economic or financial program, and President Wilson warned against such activities, the League was obliged to enter this field because of the problems posed by economic dislocations of the war and the peace settlement. An Economic and Financial Organization was formed, which included several advisory committees: economic, financial, fiscal, statistical, co-ordinating, and loan contracts. These units arranged many international conferences upon problems of tariffs, customs procedures, protection of industrial property, monetary problems, counterfeiting, and the like. Several world economic conferences of general scope were also convened but achieved little. More striking was the financial reconstruction of Austria, Hungary, Greece, and Bulgaria. These countries had exhausted their credit and were near collapse. The Financial Committee was able upon the basis of the internal reforms it suggested to arrange for new loans under League supervision and to stabilize currencies. An International Relief Union was formed under League auspices which provided disaster relief in a number of countries stricken by earthquakes, flood, or famine. A Communications and Transit Organization was established which drew together activities to improve maritime, river, air, railway, and motor transport. It convened a number of special conferences and formed a permanent secretariat. Notable achievements were the comprehensive Convention on the International Regime of Railways (1923) and the Statute on the Regime of Navigable Waterways of International Concern (1921). Recommendations for an international bank produced no action except that the need for a clearing arrangement for payment of reparations by Germany under the Young Plan led to the creation of the Bank for International Settlements.

In the social field the League also sought to correlate many activities under an Advisory Committee on Social Questions. An improved convention for suppression of traffic in women and children was concluded in 1921, which was widely ratified. Extensive collection of data concerning violations and measures for suppression was also made, and suggestions made to governments found to be derelict. A Child Welfare Information Center was created in the Secretariat which collected and published information and studies concerning illegitimacy, juvenile delinquency, and adoptions. To judge the effectiveness of such work is difficult; it has to be measured by eventual improvement of national standards. The League's Health Organization continued the earlier work on prevention of epidemics. A great deal was done to improve epidemiological intelligence by securing standardization of reports from national health administrations and relaying information by radio as well as in periodical publications from Geneva to port and national health authorities. A Singapore Bureau was set up which was successful in establishing contact with 180 Asian ports. Another major contribution of the Health Organization was its work on biological standardization, i.e., the setting of standard units of potency of drugs and antitoxins so that uniform terminology can be employed in exchange of medical data, prescriptions, etc. Extensive studies of nutrition were undertaken in collaboration with the International Labor Organization and the International Institute of Agriculture. A Mixed Committee was created, which produced a notable report on the whole field of nutrition. From this has come activity by national nutrition committees set up by twenty-one governments. This activity has led directly into the work of the Food and Agriculture Organization and the World Health Organization of the United Nations. Much work was done also in assisting certain national health administrations to improve training facilities and methods. Finally, it should be noted that the League achieved a genuine success in an old and frustrating field of regulation—control of narcotic drugs—opium, morphine, and heroin. An international drug convention had been concluded at The Hague in 1912 but was not brought into force until after the war. It stated principles of control without providing machinery. The League established an Opium Advisory Committee, which developed a plan of import and export certificates to control shipments of narcotics. This and provision for a Permanent Central Opium Board were incorporated into the Geneva International Opium Convention of 1925. The Board was a kind of watchdog of narcotics production and trade, which could report any evidence of illicit traffic or abnormal production to the Council for action by embargo or otherwise. A convention of 1931 finally secured agreement upon limitation of manufacture, and a 1936 convention upon international co-ordination of facilities for apprehension and punishment of offenders. These conventions were almost universally ratified, and excellent governmental cooperation has been achieved in giving effect to them.

In the political field, apart from security questions, the principal efforts made were in disarmament, protection of minorities, and administration of mandates and supervised areas, i.e., Danzig and the Saar. Attention has been given in Chapter 5 to the failure of the elaborate League effort to find a formula for disarmament. This failure was not without incidental benefits, for it showed clearly that governments will not agree to disarm unless they feel that security against aggression has been otherwise assured. Disarmament is therefore not a technical but a political problem. Madariaga properly remarked of it: "There are no technical questions. There are only political questions in uniform." The only successful disarmament agreement, the Washington Naval Conference Treaty of 1922, was made possible by the achievement of political agreement in the Four-Power Pacific Pact and the

Nine-Power Pact. Japan accepted naval inferiority because of the United States agreement not to fortify Guam or strengthen the Philippines—thus neither could carry a naval attack to the other.

This point was not lost upon the technical commissions which the League set up to prepare disarmament proposals. It explains why they were diverted in 1923 into the preparation of a Draft Treaty of Mutual Assistance to come into force upon acceptance of a disarmament treaty. This project was adopted by the Assembly but rejected by the British government, which hesitated to give military commitments. The next year arbitration, common action against aggression, and disarmament were all joined in the Geneva Protocol. This too was adopted by the Assembly but defeated by the British government. As a partial substitute the Locarno Treaties of nonaggression and guaranty were concluded, and upon this basis Germany was brought into the League. The Preparatory Disarmament Commission then worked from 1926 to 1930 to prepare a draft disarmament convention for consideration by the General Disarmament Conference, finally convened in 1932. This conference failed, but its failure was again not on technical grounds. There seemed indeed some prospect of agreement after the United States consented to consultation in the event of an aggression and to waive rights of neutral intercourse with an aggressor. At that point the decision was made to deny equality in armament to Germany for a probationary period of four years, and she left the conference and the League. At no time thereafter was the situation in Europe one to encourage disarmament. As the security problem could not be solved, the disarmament problem could not be solved.

The League's function with respect to minorities arose because of the creation of a system of treaties after World War I in which more than a dozen defeated or succession states in Europe accepted certain standards of equal treatment of minorities as to personal and political liberty, protection of law, language and religion, schools, employment, and the like. These obligations were placed under the guaranty of the League Council. The mode of operation was in general to permit minority groups which believed their rights had been violated to present petitions to the League. These were first reviewed by the minorities section in the Secretariat, and unless pronounced "nonreceivable" were considered by Committees of Three, which determined whether they should be brought before the Council. Legal issues arising from construction of the treaties could be referred to the Permanent Court of International Justice. The Council if convinced of abuse requested the state to comment upon the situation, and was of course free thereafter to take any steps it thought necessary. Presumably these procedures were of some utility, but the consensus of observers was that they proved far from sufficient. There were many reasons. The Committees of Three sometimes felt justified in dropping cases because governments assured them situations would be adjusted. The Council tolerated very long delays in awaiting answers from governments. When it did issue cautionary words or corrective mandates, it sometimes failed to inquire later what action had been taken. But the basic difficulties were intrinsic in the situation. The treaties did not automatically produce a change in internal regulations, and some of the governments were not of a complexion likely to take these obligations seriously. If the League was to meet them upon their own ground in a matter of domestic law enforcement affecting individuals, it required a far greater force of inspectors and police than it could muster. It is doubtful that a function of this sort can properly be undertaken by a governing body which lacks direct jurisdiction over persons.

The mandates system attracted wide attention as a unique political experiment in the colonial field. An early effort in 1884 to establish an international regime in the Congo by a treaty commitment without supervisory machinery had failed miserably. This error was not repeated. Fifteen colonial areas ceded by Germany and Turkey to the Allied and Associated Powers after World War I were placed under administration of various states (mandatories) subject to the terms of agreements between them and the League of Nations, which assumed supervision of the administrations in order to assure that the interests of the natives were secured according to the tenor of the agreements. These areas were classified as A, B, and C mandates, the A category comprising areas taken from Turkey (Palestine, Transjordan, Iraq, Syria, and Lebanon) which were so advanced that immediate local autonomy and rapid achievement of statehood were contemplated; the B category areas in Africa (Tanganyika, Togoland, Cameroons, Ruanda-Urundi) which required administration by the mandatory, under conditions assuring native rights, with some prospect of eventual advancement at least to political autonomy; the C category areas taken from Germany in the Pacific (New Guinea, Western Samoa, Nauru, Mariana and Caroline Islands) and German Southwest Africa, which for various reasons —small size or population, remoteness, or contiguity with the mandatory— were to be administered as integral parts of the mandatory's territory. League supervision was vested in a Permanent Mandates Commission.

This regime may be accounted partially successful. Iraq became an independent state. So did Syria, Lebanon, Palestine (Israel), and Transjordan; but there were forces independent of the mandates system which contributed in those cases. The open-door principle was successfully maintained, and the interests of the natives probably taken more into account. On the other hand, the procedures exhibited several serious defects. Only a formalized right of petition by peoples of the mandate to the commission was provided—in writing and channeled through the mandatory. Reports by mandatories were required, but their content could not be verified by direct inspection. Hence, the Japanese fortification of the Pacific islands in violation of terms of its mandate could not be officially noticed, for Japan blandly denied it in its reports. Nor did the commission have any rights of intervention; it could only offer criticisms and suggestions and hope that force of opinion would induce the mandatory to comply.

It is generally said that the League of Nations failed, but this judgment is based upon the failure of its security procedures to avert World War II. With that we shall deal in the following chapter. With respect to the varied functions just discussed one can hardly pass a judgment of failure. Nor can they be dismissed as minor functions; they lie at the core of the permanent objects of government. Certainly the success was not unqualified, but when the resources and instruments available to the League are considered its achievements will surely bear comparison with those of national governments.

THE UNITED NATIONS

One purpose of this review has been to overcome an impression common in the United States that international organization began with the United Nations. In fact, there are few things in its organization or conception which present any novelties, and virtually all of the problems which confront it can be understood better if one knows how they evolved in the experience of the earlier organizations. There was indeed something to be said for continuing the League after World War II with amendments of the Covenant to take account of its deficiencies, but the bad odor into which it had fallen as a result of failure to solve the security problem suggested some advantage in a fresh departure, if not in structure at least in name. This was rendered the more compelling by the direction of United States leadership.

Sufficient agreement was reached among the Allies in the Quebec, Moscow, and Teheran conferences during the war as to creation of a new security organization to enable the State Department to proceed with detailed planning. A special division for that purpose was created under the direction of Leo Pasvolsky, and elaborate committee structures drew in much expert opinion both official and private. Although Prime Minister Churchill and President Roosevelt were inclined to emphasize regional organization, opinion finally shifted to support a renewal of the universal-type organization in the pattern of the League. Drafts were prepared and exchanged among the powers, and in August, 1944, a conference was held at Dumbarton Oaks, near Washington, which reached agreement upon most issues. The outstanding differences of opinion over the disposition of the mandates, the voting rule in the Security Council, and Russia's demand that all Soviet republics be given membership, were resolved at the Yalta Conference, so that it was possible in 1945 to proceed with a full-scale conference representing fifty governments to draft the United Nations Charter at San Francisco.

Structure of the United Nations

The Charter, approved on June 26, 1945, created a structure in many respects parallel to that of the League of Nations. The principal organs reappear but in somewhat altered relationship. The General Assembly composed of five representatives of each member, casting one vote, corresponds to the League Assembly. The Security Council, composed of five permanent members (United States, U.S.S.R., Great Britain, France, China) and six members elected for two-year terms by the Assembly, corresponds to the League Council. However, it is clear that the Security Council was not conceived as a general executive organ as in the League but was instead assigned "primary responsibility for the maintenance of international peace and security." (Art. 24.) For this purpose it was to have direct powers of action through a Military Staff Committee and an international police, but the latter has never been formed. Perhaps the large states had in mind to concentrate control of security questions in the Council to the exclusion of the Assembly, but the clauses specifying Assembly powers were amended at San Francisco to make it clear that all questions within the scope of the Charter or relating to functions of any organ may be discussed by it (Art. 10). Recommendations upon security matters may also be made provided the Security Council is not then considering them (Arts. 11, 12). The Assembly has also special mandates to initiate studies and recommendations to promote international cooperation in all fields (Art. 13) and to recommend measures of peaceful change (Art. 14). We shall return in the next chapter to the relations between the two organs in security questions. Consideration must also be given there to the voting rule in the Security Council, which greatly affects its procedure. In the Assembly voting is by two-thirds majority upon specified "important questions," otherwise by simple majority. Since the U.N. Assembly has no action powers, this is not an advance from League procedure, for the League Assembly adopted recommendations by simple majority.

The Trusteeship Council and the Economic and Social Council (ECOSOC) are both organs which act under the authority and supervision of the Assembly. It elects the eighteen members of the latter for three-year terms, choosing six each year. Representatives of separate international administrative unions affiliated with ECOSOC as specialized agencies, are often invited to participate in its discussions and its commissions. There is also a novel arrangement whereby nongovernmental organizations are authorized to send representatives as consultants. These consultative organizations are classified as A and B, the first consisting of a few which have a broad interest in most activities of the council and an important place in the economic and social life of the area represented (e.g., International Chamber of Commerce, International Cooperative Alliance, World Federation of Trade Unions), the second including a large number of organizations of special competency (e.g., Inter-American Statistical Institute, International Federation for Housing and Town Planning; International Federation of Teachers Associations, International Union for Child Welfare). Their representatives may attend public meetings of ECOSOC or its commissions, submit documents or statements, or present views orally. Category A representatives may also propose items for the council agenda. Thus ECOSOC is a directive and co-ordinating body for a large number of agencies. In the League structure there was no counterpart of the Economic and Social Council, but the idea was developed there. A committee headed by Stanley Bruce had studied the proliferation of League agencies in these fields in 1939 and had recommended creation of a Central Committee for Economic and Social Questions, with control of its own budget and personnel to supervise the economic and social commissions. This was virtually a blueprint for ECOSOC. Further consideration will presently be given to its structure of commissions and specialized agencies.

The Trusteeship Council, of course, inherits the functions of the Permanent Mandates Commission of the League. It is composed of the member states administering trust territories, those permanent members of the Security Council who do not administer trust territories, and additional members elected by the Assembly for three-year terms in sufficient number to balance the council between those who do and those who do not administer trust territories. It enjoys a more autonomous position than the Mandates Commission, has greater supervisory authority, and has extended its interests to non-selfgoverning territories other than trust areas.

As to the two remaining organs, the International Court of Justice is an almost exact counterpart of the Permanent Court of International Justice, and the U.N. Secretariat follows closely the structure of the League Secretariat. It appears, however, to have achieved a somewhat better integration. It now includes the Executive Office of the Secretary-General, under direction of an executive assistant; eight departments, each supervised by an assistant secretary-general; and the Technical Assistance Administration, under a director-general. All these units are under the direction of the secretary-general, who is appointed by the Assembly upon recommendation by the Security Council for a term of five years. As the Charter gives the secretary-general the right to bring to the Council's attention matters affecting security (Art. 99) and directs him to make an annual report to the Assembly on the work of the organization (Art. 98), he is in a position to express his opinions and offer proposals. The men who have occupied the post have not hesitated to do so, thus making the office a good deal more than a position of administrative management.

A few other changes deserve consideration. Pressure from small states led to inclusion in the Charter of a preliminary enumeration of purposes and principles of the United Nations. These reaffirm the standards of justice and international law, the principle of equal rights and self-determination of peoples, and cooperation in meeting cultural, economic, social, and humanitarian problems. They urge respect for human rights and fundamental freedoms "without distinction as to race, sex, language, or religion." The interests of the member states are affirmed by recognizing their "sovereign equality," pledging them to refrain from threat or use of force "against the territorial integrity or political independence of any State," and to settle disputes by pacific means. There is also a prohibition (Art. 2, Sec. 7) against intervention by the United Nations "in matters which are essentially within the domestic jurisdiction of any state," unless by way of sanctions against an aggressor. These principles may be useful to define the spirit and purpose of the organization; they are somewhat hortatory and imprecise if intended as legal definitions of powers and limitations. In the following chapter some attention will be given to the meaning of the domestic jurisdiction limitation, particularly as it affects U.N. interventions in disputes.

Another new departure is the specific recognition and approval of regional organizations not inconsistent with the purposes and principles of the Charter. This resulted from a compromise between the views of those who favored the universal type of international organization (e.g., Cordell Hull, and the State Department planners generally) and those who considered regional organizations with co-ordination through a concert of powers a more realistic approach (e.g., Winston Churchill, Franklin Roosevelt, Sumner Welles). The terms of the Charter (Arts. 52, 53, 54) specify that enforcement action shall not be taken in security cases by regional agencies without prior authorization by the Security Council, whereas they are free to use pacific settlement techniques upon their own initiative, later reporting the steps taken. Article 51, drafted by the committee on regional arrangements to satisfy the desire of the American republics for a freer hand for regional action along the lines suggested by the Act of Chapultepec (1945), actually prescribed a "right of individual or collective self-defense" against armed attack until such time as the Security Council "has taken the measures necessary to maintain international peace and security." This was not in terms limited to regional action and was later separated from the chapter on regional arrangements and placed at the end of the preceding chapter dealing with threats to the peace, breaches of the peace, and acts of aggression. Its significance with respect to security action will have to be explored in the following chapter.

The basis of membership has been somewhat modified from that used by the League, and the change has not been a happy one. Apart from the original members, who participated in the San Francisco Conference, membership is open "to all other peace-loving states which accept the obligations contained in the present Charter and, in the judgment of the Organization, are able and willing to carry out these obligations." Admission is by the General Assembly upon recommendation of the Security Council (Art. 4). This last provision, coupled with the fact that the criteria stated are merely matters of opinion, has caused great difficulty. The voting rule in the Security Council enables any permanent member to defeat a motion to recommend admission, since this is considered a substantive question, with the result that the U.S.S.R. vetoed admission of friends of the western bloc and the United States, Great Britain, France, and Nationalist China vetoed admission of friends of the Communist bloc. Advisory opinions by the International Court of Justice made it clear that only the criteria stated in the Charter should be used in voting, and that a recommendation by the Council to the Assembly meant a positive recommendation. As no member need disclose what motivates his vote, this did not prove helpful. Nor did the Council heed any of the numerous pleas by the Assembly to eliminate politics from its consideration. Nearly a score of applicants were rejected. Occasional proposals for a bargain between East and West to admit some candidates supported by each attracted support but were several times rejected partly because the International Court had excluded trading as a proper criterion in voting. Finally, during the tenth Assembly a proposal was made to admit eighteen states, of which five were communist, thirteen non-communist but with a few exceptions inclined toward neutralism in the East-West struggle. Although widely supported this proposal was defeated in the Security Council because Nationalist China vetoed admission of Outer Mongolia and in reprisal the U.S.S.R. then vetoed all the non-communist applicants. A compromise was reached later by dropping Outer Mongolia and Japan and admitting the remaining sixteen. Presumably the U.S.S.R. will attempt to obtain concessions with respect to Communist China before agreeing to the admission of Japan. There will also be a difficult problem with respect to admission of Germany unless the powers can agree upon its reunification. Some progress has been made toward universality of membership but only by subordinating the criteria of the Charter to political bargaining.

The problem of membership should not be confused with the question of seating of delegates presented by the existence of the Communist Peoples' Republic and the Nationalist government of China, each claiming to represent the state of China. If two delegations appear to claim China's seat, this does not involve any question of Chinese membership in the United Nations, which has existed from the outset. It is just a question of determining which is the properly accredited delegation. This is done by each organ on the basis of the report of its own credentials committee. However, in order to avoid the embarrassment which would occur if one organ should seat the Nationalist Chinese, and another the Communist Chinese, the General Assembly suggested in 1950 that it (or when not in session its Interim Committee) should consider such questions first and that other organs should take its conclusions into account. To date, the representatives of Nationalist China continue to be seated despite frequent explosions from and protest withdrawals of Russian delegates.

Although the Assembly does not have to contend with the veto, it does have instances of bloc voting. This has probably been given more emphasis than it deserves, for the only really consistent instance of it occurs in voting by Communist states. There are blocs of Arab, Asian, and Latin American states which hold together upon appointments and elections, but not very tightly on political questions unless they are such as peculiarly affect the group. The Arab bloc can be expected to show some unity upon Palestine questions; a split between colonial and noncolonial countries occasionally appears, e.g., on questions of French policy in North Africa and Indochina; and the Communist-Western split, with Asian-Arab neutralists in a noncommittal role, is familiar. But these alignments vary from one question to another.

Economic and Social Agencies

Three organs are involved in United Nations work in the economic and social field: the General Assembly, the Economic and Social Council, and the Secretariat. The work of ECOSOC has been regularly reported to the Assembly, which examines and debates it at length and frequently returns suggestions or directions. ECOSOC has at its disposal three regional economic commissions, for Europe, Asia and the Far East, and Latin America, respectively; also nine functional commissions dealing with the following subjects: (1) Fiscal Matters; (2) Human Rights; (3) Narcotic Drugs; (4) Population; (5) Social Questions; (6) Statistical Matters; (7) the Status of Women; (8) Transport and Communications. There are also four standing committees: the Technical Assistance Committee (a committee of the whole), the Committee on Negotiations with Specialized Agencies, the Council Committee on Non-Governmental Organizations, and the Interim Committee on Program of Meetings. *Ad hoc* committees are set up when the Council thinks it necessary.

ECOSOC is charged by the Charter to enter into agreements with existing specialized international administrative agencies in the economic, social, cultural, educational, health, and related fields, and to make recommendations for co-ordination of their policies and activities. It may also propose new agencies to the member states. Reports are obtained by ECOSOC from the specialized agencies, there is an exchange of representation (without vote) for consultation, and proposals for agenda are made by each to the other.

ECOSOC may also perform services within the scope of its functions at the request of either the specialized agencies or the member states, and it regularly attempts to integrate the services of the agencies into its projects. The specialized agencies now involved are the International Labor Organization (ILO), the Food and Agricultural Organization of the United Nations (FAO), the United Nations Educational, Scientific, and Cultural Organization (UNESCO), the International Civil Aviation Organization (ICAO), the International Bank for Reconstruction and Development (BANK), the International Monetary Fund (FUND), the Universal Postal Union (UPU), the World Health Organization (WHO), the International Telecommunication Union (ITU), the World Meteorological Organization (WMO), and the Inter-Governmental Maritime Consultative Organization (IMCO). The International Refugee Organization (IRO) was discontinued in 1952. The projected International Trade Organization (ITO) has not yet been set up, although many states have participated in multilateral tariff bargaining under the General Agreement on Tariffs and Trade (GATT).

Several of these organizations or their predecessors have been discussed already. No effort will be made to consider the others in detail. However, it should be noted that several are new agencies which are attempting to provide services in fields not previously occupied by international agencies, such as FAO, UNESCO, ICAO, BANK and FUND. FAO is closing with one of the great long-range problems of international relations—how to supply food for a rapidly growing world population which already outruns the supply. It has collaborated with many other agencies, notably WHO and UNESCO, in essential studies in the fields of pest control, soil and fisheries conservation, fertilizers, distribution of farm machinery, nutritional aspects of child feeding, and education of primitive agricultural peoples in improved methods. It has created new agencies to assist it, such as the International Rice Commission, several forestry commissions and fisheries councils. UNESCO has undertaken a very ambitious program in elimination of illiteracy, exchange of cultural materials, a program of translations, services to professional associations and founding of several new international associations, international seminars on the correction of history texts, and many other fields. ICAO is a more technical group concerned with working out the detailed application of the Chicago Civil Aviation Convention (1945) with respect to carriage of goods and persons in international commerce, standardization of flight regulations, let-down procedures, and the like. The FUND is an exchange mechanism, the BANK a lending agency for state development projects which has usually viewed financing conservatively, reserving its loans for projects likely to yield quick returns in increased production.

Even conceding the immensity and importance of the economic and

social field it hardly appears that such a proliferation of machinery can be efficiently administered. There should be no assumption that ECOSOC administers or should administer all of it. Its task is rather that of a consultative, planning, and co-ordinating agency. But its agenda are extremely heavy and its sessions protracted. There continues to be some overlapping and some mismating of functions. A. Loveday, M. Laugier, and others have argued for a functional reorganization. Mr. Loveday suggests that the Human Rights Commission, which is not economic and social but political, be transferred to the Assembly, where it would contribute in common with the Interim Committee and the International Law Commission to the purposes of Article 13 of the Charter. The Economic and Social Commissions would be confined to the co-ordination of the work of the specialized agencies. The other commissions might be placed under a new policy-determining body with separate headquarters in Geneva.

As an example of an ECOSOC commission the work of the Human Rights Commission may be considered. That body first devoted itself to the formulation of the Universal Declaration of Human Rights (1948), an attempt to state a set of standards which all states should try to observe. The declaration was approved by the Assembly "as a common standard of achievement for all peoples and all nations," but has no other legal standing than this might give it as a recommendation. However, it has been inserted into some national constitutions and has influenced statutes and court decisions. It is a noble document but appears to be cast in a distinctively Western European, and especially Anglo-American, institutional mold. Thus, it specifies the right of full and free consent of intending spouses, the right to own property and to be secure from arbitrary deprivation, the right to take part in government directly or through freely chosen representatives. These are surely foreign to a number of societies whose representatives voted for them without demur.

After completion of the declaration the commission spent about five years in shaping two draft treaties, a Covenant on Civil and Political Rights and a Covenant on Economic and Social Rights. It is proposed to open these for ratification by member states if approved by the Assembly. The first is formulated in terms of real obligation to enforce, although enforcement is left to state jurisdiction, subject to a Human Rights Commission for receipt of complaints by other states. This commission would investigate the problem, try to conciliate the parties, and report to the United Nations. It would have no enforcement powers. The second draft treaty does not even contain a legal obligation to observe the standards expressed; it speaks rather of an ultimate goal states would pledge themselves to try to attain. Progress reports would be made to ECOSOC. Comments of governments were asked before discussion of the draft covenants by the tenth Assembly. It postponed

action due to opposition to provisions to secure self-determination of peoples. The government of the United States, probably to appease Bricker amendment supporters, has announced in advance it will not ratify. Rather it favors a long-term program of education based upon the Universal Declaration. In the formulation of both the declaration and the covenants the commission frequently submitted partial drafts to ECOSOC, and ECOSOC submitted them to the Assembly, so that directions were given by these bodies to the commission as to the lines to be followed—e.g., the separation of a single original covenant into the two covenants in order to take account of the different degrees of consensus and possibilities of implementation with respect to civil and political rights, on the one hand, and economic and social rights, on the other.

It should not be assumed that the structure of ECOSOC agencies is such that all human rights questions are assigned to the Human Rights Commission. On the contrary, the Genocide Convention was developed by an *Ad Hoc* Committee on Genocide appointed by ECOSOC, the draft statute for an International Criminal Court was the work of the International Law Commission, functioning under the Assembly, the Convention on the International Transmission of News and the Right of Correction was drafted by a subcommission of the Human Rights Commission but the companion Convention on Freedom of Information had to be reworked by a special Assembly committee. The Convention on the Status of Women came from the commission of the same name. Another Subcommission on the Prevention of Discrimination and the Protection of Minorities under the Human Rights Commission worked on minorities problems for a time, but its conclusions were later merged with the covenants on human rights.

In the economic field the most significant step has been the development of a program of technical assistance whereby teams of expert advisers are made available to economically underdeveloped countries to assist them in setting into motion projects for which they can supply manpower, materials, and most of the budget, but not technical direction. This emerged from the effort to give some coherence and integration to work being done by a number of agencies, and received emphasis after President Truman created the Point-Four Program (1949). Technical assistance is peculiarly a matter involved in the co-ordination of work of many agencies. In the field a project, say to improve agricultural production, may encounter a health problem which requires assistance from WHO, such as the elimination of malaria or yaws among natives, or may necessitate training of illiterate natives through techniques developed by UNESCO, or require drainage of land or provision of fertilizers for which a loan by the BANK is desired. Thus administration of such programs is a problem of co-ordination, the problem of ECOSOC

in miniature. To deal with it three new agencies have been set up, which conveniently for memory are called TAA, TAB, and TAC—i.e., the Technical Assistance Administration, a unit of the Secretariat which makes the detailed plans and arrangements for particular projects; the Technical Assistance Board, composed of heads of appropriate U.N. and specialized agencies, which co-ordinates the contributions to be made by different agencies; and the Technical Assistance Committee of delegates of all members of ECOSOC, which serves as a reviewing and evaluating agency.

Projects are initiated by proposals or requests from governments desiring assistance. In some cases preliminary survey teams have been sent to work out a plan of economic development which will take account of the resources and needs of a country. In other cases all that is required is a body of advisers to a functioning local project. But the typical case of technical assistance is the request for an operating mission of experts to go to the country and work with local personnel in setting the project into motion. Projects vary widely. They have included such things as swamp reclamation, housing developments, forestry planning, statistical services, census techniques, reform of public finance and customs administrations, surveys of agriculture, industry, geology, mining, and transportation, reorganization of civil service, crop rotation, fertilization, improvement of strains, agricultural mechanization, fisheries controls, and many others.

In work of this type the United Nations has certain advantages not shared by programs at the national or regional level, like the Point-Four Program of the United States or the South and South-East Asian Colombo Plan. Many countries which need assistance are peculiarly sensitive to what they consider the imperialistic designs of private capitalists or of other governments. Consequently, it has been difficult to restore the flow of private capital into underdeveloped areas since the war because of unwillingness to give it reasonable protection or inducements. Governments of former colonial states have also looked with suspicion upon aid from an international agency. In addition, the U.N. can draw technicians from a wide range of member states, including small states which might otherwise be overlooked, and can frequently find personnel in Asian countries which has a better conception of local conditions and problems and how to adapt new methods to them than the Western technicians.

To date, the great problems have been the scarcity of able and adaptable technical experts with knowledge of native languages and, even more, the insufficiency of the funds allocated to technical assistance programs. Since advance commitments by governments cannot be obtained, it is not possible to plan very far ahead on the basis of probable resources. The attitude of the Congress of the United States, the largest contributor, accentuates the diffi-

culty. In 1954 it appropriated enough only to carry through the calendar year, leaving uncertainty whether a supplementary appropriation would be made for the remainder of the fiscal year.

Dependent Peoples

The U.N. trusteeship system, under the supervision of the Trusteeship Council, has followed the general lines of the mandates system, with some improvements suggested by that experience. It can be applied to former mandated territories, to territories detached from enemy states as a result of World War II, and to other territories voluntarily placed under the system by states which control them. However, no areas in the last category have been placed under the system, and in consequence of this the council has sought to exercise some supervision over non-self-governing territories not within the system. All of the former mandates which had not become independent states were brought within the trusteeship system with the exception of former German Southwest Africa, a C-mandate of the Union of South Africa.

The Southwest Africa mandate had presented a difficult problem because of its immediate proximity to the Union and because of the disposition of 10,000 German colonists there to advocate a termination of the mandate and restoration to Germany. This was encouraged by the German Government. South African and British settlers (about 20,000) therefore increasingly urged direct integration of the area into the Union. At the end of World War II Prime Minister Smuts proposed annexation of the mandate and declined to place it under trusteeship, although repeatedly urged to do so by the United Nations. This attitude of the Union was not one peculiar to any particular government, but the accession of the nationalist government of Malan produced a more forthright insistence upon it. In 1947 the Union had agreed to maintain the mandate and to make its mandatory reports to the Trusteeship Council. However, its attitude stiffened in the face of persistent criticism, and in 1949 it attached the area to the Union with representation in the dominion Parliament and declined to continue reporting. Upon the basis of unofficial representations on behalf of some native tribes by the Reverend Michael Scott and others, the Council and Assembly apparently concluded that some discriminatory practices and prevention of free petitions or appeals to the United Nations had occurred. A request was made to the International Court of Justice for an opinion as to the legal status of the area. In 1950 the Court replied that the Union was under no obligation to place the mandate under trusteeship, but if it elected not to do so, it would continue subject to the obligations of the mandate agreement, with the United Nations substituted for the League for supervisory purposes. Nevertheless, the Union has declined to resume reporting, although the Assembly set up a committee

to deal with it, or to permit Africans to make statements to U.N. agencies. It has offered to negotiate with the remaining Allied and Associated Powers of World War I (France, United Kingdom, United States) a modification of the mandate agreement. During the tenth Assembly it withdrew its delegation in protest against renewed U.N. inquiries.

The Charter authorized (Art. 82) creation of strategic areas under trusteeship agreements, in which case the supervision of the administration falls to the Security Council rather than to the Trusteeship Council, and no field inspections occur. Only one strategic trust has been authorized, that of the United States in the former Japanese mandated islands of the Pacific (Marshalls, Marianas, and Carolines).

The principles governing trusteeship are similar to those of mandates in most respects. Article 76 specifies as objectives the furtherance of peace and security; promotion of "political, economic, social, and educational advancement of the inhabitants of the trust territories, and their progressive development towards self-government or independence"; respect for human rights and fundamental freedoms of the inhabitants without distinction as to race, sex, language, or religion; and an open door for members of the United Nations and their nationals, with equal treatment and legal protection for the latter. There is no longer a prohibition against fortification or raising of native troops, as there was in the mandates system. Experience had shown that the defenseless state of New Guinea in World War II merely facilitated Japanese conquest. Article 84 provides that the trust territory "shall play its part in the maintenance of international peace and security." The trusteeship agreements between the administering state and the Assembly (or Security Council, for strategic trusts) invariably contain a careful recitation of the rights of the inhabitants and the purposes of the trust, which serve as a standard for exercise of the Council's supervisory functions.

Supervision is exercised through an apparatus of petitions, questionnaires and reports, and inspections. In 1947 the Trusteeship Council prepared an elaborate questionnaire containing 247 questions in twelve sections, with a statistical annex in thirteen parts, to serve as a basis for annual reports by administering states. This has at least the virtue of discouraging the glossing over of unpleasant details. Upon the basis of the reports written questions, frequently very sharp ones, are put to representatives of the administering powers, answered in writing, after which there is oral questioning and debate. The council's information is increased by petitions received from the trust area. These may come from tribal groups or individuals and no longer have to be channeled through the administering power. A great flood of petitions is received, creating a difficult problem of examination and evaluation. Periodic visits of inspection are made by representatives of the council to the trust areas. Some of these tend to be rather formalized, like an an-

nounced military inspection for which every one polishes his brass and puts his best face forward. However, some have resulted in critical examinations. Upon the basis of the questionnaires, reports, and inspections the Council makes its reports to the Assembly and frequently directs suggestions for improvements in administration to the trust powers.

The Charter includes in Chapter XI (Arts. 73–74) a declaration regarding non-self-governing territories. The members recognized that the interests of the inhabitants of dependent areas is paramount over their own interests as colonial powers and accepted "as a sacred trust" the obligation to promote the well-being of dependent peoples and to assist them in progressive development of self-government "according to the particular circumstances of each territory and its peoples and their varying stages of development." The colonial powers also agreed to submit to the secretary-general "for information purposes" reports on the economic, social, and educational (but not the political) conditions in the dependencies. There was no indication of an intention to authorize any sort of intervention or supervision by the Trusteeship Council.

However a strong bloc of anticolonial states has pressed for extension of U.N. supervision over such dependencies. This has included the Arab and Asian states, abetted by the Communist bloc, and usually supported by Latin American states. The United States has been torn between its anti-imperialist attitudes and the necessity not to weaken or alienate the colonial states of Western Europe. The colonial powers of course resisted any extension of supervision as a violation of the Charter and of domestic jurisdiction. In this they were clearly right. Nevertheless, the Assembly in 1947 developed a detailed questionnaire to be used by the colonial governments in reporting, and in 1946 set up an *ad hoc* committee of sixteen, which has been renewed from time to time, to examine the reports and any other data about non-self-governing territories and make procedural and substantive recommendations to the Assembly. A Division of Information from Non-Self-Governing Territories has been developed in the Secretariat. With these aids the Assembly's Fourth Committee has regularly examined problems relating to the dependencies, and the Assembly has sent inquiries and recommendations to the colonial powers in much the same spirit as if it were dealing with trust area administrations.

The colonial powers have been indignant at this treatment, and have felt with some reason that it is not only illegal but is being pushed by states which tolerate internally economic and social conditions worse than those in the colonial administrations they criticize. Their view is shared by Francis B. Sayre, formerly United States representative in the Trusteeship Council:

Often the administering powers are urged by the majority to carry out policies which the majority would refuse to carry out in relation to their own peo-

ples; . . . political independence is not synonymous with human freedom. . . .
Men can be as effectively manacled by economic and social forms of servitude as
by political oppression. . . . The premature grant of political independence before a people have had adequate economic and social preparation, can do them
untold harm. Indigenous leaders . . . can exploit their own compatriots as ruthlessly as aliens, or even more so. Nor is the cause of international peace served by
giving full independence to a people who are not able to defend themselves.

THE PRESENT STAGE OF INTERNATIONAL ORGANIZATION

Consideration will be given to the security functions of the League of
Nations and the United Nations in the next chapter, and this material must
enter into any evaluation of them. In the light of the preceding account it
seems clear, however, that a steady process of consolidation of agencies and
elaboration of functions in the international field has been in progress for
more than a century. The League and the United Nations mark striking
reorganizations in this historical development rather than changes in pattern.
Although the structures are increasingly elaborate, they have not departed
from the basic pattern of confederation as instruments of sovereign states.
If there is any accession of power to the United Nations, it lies more in the
facts of organic growth and increasing reliance of governments upon United
Nations services than in any deviation from the characteristic legal pattern.

In one respect there is even a divergent tendency, for the period since
World War I witnessed the growth of regional organization among American states to a position of substantial effectiveness both in social and economic areas and in maintenance of peace. Since World War II there has
been a marked increase in regional organization elsewhere. The Arab League
has not been particularly well integrated except as a vehicle of opposition
to Israel, although it has been used for social and cultural collaboration to
some extent. But in Europe the movement toward functional organization
has been significant. It has included the Schuman Plan creating a European
Coal and Steel Community (discussed elsewhere); a number of customs
unions; a European Payments Union for monetary clearance; the Green
Pool, a projected agricultural organization; the European Defense Community, related to the North Atlantic Treaty Organization; the Organization
for European Economic Cooperation, set up in connection with the Marshall
Plan; as well as older organizations in the field of river navigation and rail
transport.

There is also a Council of Europe which may provide a political framework for gradually drawing together the functional organizations. It includes
fifteen West European governments and has two principal organs, the
Council of Ministers and the Consultative Assembly. The ministers as
government representatives were given the power of deciding the agenda

of the Assembly, which consists of 132 delegates unequally apportioned to states and appointed so as to represent various points of view. The Assembly has increased in importance and challenged the control of its agenda, obtaining some concessions. When the British elected to enter the Defense Community upon the basis of a relationship through Western European Union with the Council of Europe, its position was further strengthened. There is a movement of uncertain dimensions for European federation, which has been pushed by some states. Meanwhile, the Council is likely to become a co-ordinating and planning body of increasing importance.

But if federation at the regional level may soon be possible in some places, it is certainly premature to suppose that it is at hand at the world level. Whatever the advantages and disadvantages of greatly increased powers in a world government might be there is little indication of a significant trend in that direction.

SELECTED READING

BURTON, MARGARET E., *The Assembly of the League of Nations*. Chicago: The University of Chicago Press, 1941.

CHAMBERLAIN, JOSEPH P., *The Regime of the International Rivers: Danube and Rhine*. New York: Columbia University Press, 1923.

CHEEVER, DANIEL S., and HAVILAND, H. FIELD, JR., *Organizing for Peace, International Organization in World Affairs*. London: Stevens and Sons Ltd., 1954.

Concise Handbook of the Council of Europe. New York: Manhattan Publishing Company, 1954.

DAVIS, HARRIET EAGER (ed.), *Pioneers in World Order, An American Appraisal of the League of Nations*. New York: Columbia University Press, 1944.

DUNN, FREDERICK S., *Peaceful Change*. New York: Council on Foreign Relations, 1937.

EVATT, HERBERT VERE, *The United Nations at Work*. Cambridge: Harvard University Press, 1948.

Everyman's United Nations: A Ready Reference to the Structure, Functions and Work of the United Nations and Its Related Agencies, 4th ed. New York: United Nations Department of Public Information, 1953.

FELLER, A. H., *United Nations and World Community*. Boston: Little, Brown and Company, 1952.

GOODRICH, LELAND M., and HAMBRO, EDVARD, *Charter of the United Nations, Commentary and Documents*, 2d ed. Boston: World Peace Foundation, 1949.

HALL, H. DUNCAN, *Mandates, Dependencies and Trusteeships*. Washington: Carnegie Endowment for International Peace, 1948.

HILL, MARTIN, *The Economic and Financial Organization of the League of Nations. A Survey of Twenty-Five Years' Experience*. Washington: Carnegie Endowment for International Peace, 1946.

LEONARD, L. LARRY, *International Organization*. New York: McGraw-Hill Book Company, 1951.

LEVI, WERNER, *Fundamentals of World Organization*. Minneapolis: University of Minnesota Press, 1950.

LIE, TRYGVE, *In the Cause of Peace; Seven Years with the United Nations*. New York: The Macmillan Company, 1954.

LOVEDAY, A., "Suggestions for the Reform of the United Nations Economic and Social Machinery," in *International Organization*, VII (3): 325–341 (August 1953).

MANGONE, GERARD J., *A Short History of International Organization*. New York: McGraw-Hill Book Company, 1954.

POTTER, PITMAN B., *Introduction to the Study of International Organization*, 5th ed. New York: Appleton-Century-Crofts, 1948.

RANSHOFEN-WERTHEIMER, EGON F., *The International Secretariat. A Great Experiment in International Administration*. Washington: Carnegie Endowment for International Peace, 1945.

REINSCH, PAUL S., *Public International Unions*. Boston: Ginn and Company, 1911.

ROSS, ALF., *Constitution of the United Nations*. New York: Rinehart and Company, 1951.

SAYRE, FRANCIS BOWES, *Experiments in International Administration*. New York: Harper and Brothers, 1919.

SCHWEBEL, STEPHEN M., *The Secretary General of the United Nations*. Cambridge: Harvard University Press, 1952.

VANDENBOSCH, AMRY, and HOGAN, W. N., *The United Nations: Background, Organizations, Functions, Activities*. New York: McGraw-Hill Book Company, 1952.

WALTERS, F. P., *A History of the League of Nations*, 2 vols. London: Oxford University Press, 1952.

WOOLF, L. S., *International Government, Two Reports . . . Prepared for the Fabian Research Department*. London: George Allen and Unwin Ltd., 1916.

World Organization, A Balance Sheet of the First Great Experiment. A Symposium on World Organization. Washington: American Council on Public Affairs, 1942.

ZIMMERN, ALFRED, *The League of Nations and the Rule of Law, 1918–1935*. London: Macmillan and Company, Ltd., 1936.

CHAPTER 16

COLLECTIVE SECURITY

Although the function of international organization is not solely to keep peace, there is a sense in which that function must be considered primary. As in any other community, order in the international community is a prerequisite to growth of stable institutions. The immensely destructive character of modern weapons, the powerful forces now challenging the established order, and the consequent impossibility of localizing wars, make it imperative to strengthen security mechanisms wherever possible. This is not a problem which can be solved in a simple manner by any panacea. The notions of doctrinaire persons who see a complete solution in pacifism or passive resistance or world federalism ignore an essential element of institutional growth, the human factor. Political institutions become effective only when widely and firmly accepted by people as the way in which things must be done. It is, therefore, a matter of little moment to propound a paper scheme, however logical, which runs wholly counter to experience and habitual action. We can go forward, but only from the point where we now are. For this reason it is important not to slough off imperfect but accepted methods impatiently, but rather to improve them in the light of experience. We may perhaps be overtaken by calamity before the forces of order are strong enough to save us, but predictions of doom have been so common in the history of the world that we are entitled to assume there is still a chance we may win through.

Nor is it sensible to dismiss collective security as a complete failure requiring a fresh departure. In fact, it has not been a complete failure, and in those cases in which it did fail, we have to ask whether this resulted from deficiencies in the machinery or from failure to use it, i.e., failure of participating states to meet their obligations. Of course, it is fair to press the question whether the obligations imposed upon member states are so unrealistic or radical that it would be visionary to expect punctual discharge of them. If so, the system itself is at fault and requires amendment. But we ought to be cautious about concluding that a system which sometimes works and sometimes does not is necessarily ill conceived. It seems to be characteristic of all political systems, national and local as well as international, that they pursue an erratic course—sometimes succeeding, sometimes failing, and still out-living failure. This is not, of course, an argument for complacency, which in the light of two world wars would be a strange attitude. It is rather a suggestion that careful study of existing and earlier security systems may suggest some opportunities for social engineering short of revolution.

PACIFIC SETTLEMENT OF DISPUTES

Some account was given in Chapter 14 of procedures for pacific settle-ment of international disputes by good offices, mediation, commissions of inquiry and conciliation, arbitration, and judicial settlement. If these tech-niques could be regularly applied, settlement upon the basis of agreement or of law would often result. Therefore, both the League of Nations and the United Nations have sought to make the acceptance of pacific modes of settlement in place of force an obligation of membership. In practice, their organs have frequently intervened in disputes only in the sense of suggesting or directly applying such methods, although it must be added that their success in persuading disputant states to accept pacific settlement has some-times been connected with their apparent disposition to take more extreme steps if necessary.

Disputes before the League of Nations

Article XI of the Covenant declared that any war or threat of war would be "a matter of concern to the whole League," and authorized member states to draw threats to the peace to the attention of the Council or Assembly. Members pledged themselves (Art. XII) to submit disputes likely to lead to a rupture either to arbitration or judicial settlement or inquiry by the Coun-cil and not to resort to war until three months after the award by the ar-bitrators, or the judicial decision, or the Council's report. They also agreed (Art. XIII) to submit to arbitration or judicial settlement any dispute suitable for settlement by those methods, which had not yielded to diplomatic settle-ment, particularly disputes of the sort enumerated in the statute of the Per-manent Court of International Justice as falling within its jurisdiction. Further, they agreed to carry out in good faith any award or decision ren-dered, and not to resort to war against a member which complied therewith. If disputes likely to lead to a rupture were not submitted to arbitration or judicial settlement, the parties agreed (Art. XV) to submit them to media-tion by the Council. In the event of a report unanimous except for the dis-putants' votes, all members of the League agreed not to go to war with a disputant which complied with the recommendations.

Of sixty disputes considered by the League, thirty-five were settled in accordance with procedures in the Covenant, and all of these by pacific settlement rather than application of sanctions. The three efforts to settle disputes by application of sanctions, to be discussed later, were unsuccessful. A few examples will show how the League machinery was used.

In a case involving the rival claims of Sweden and Finland to the Aaland Islands, which while under Russian control had been lumped with Finland for administrative purposes and then granted independence as a unit, the Council used a Committee of Jurists to examine the legal status and a Committee of Inquiry as to other matters. It assumed jurisdiction on the jurists' advice the matter was not a Finnish domestic question, yet affirmed the sovereignty of Finland, subject to neutralization of the islands and protection of the basic rights of the Swedish population. Their desire for annexation by Sweden was ignored upon various practical grounds. The Council also regarded the Spanish Civil War as a domestic matter and took no steps against outside assistance to Franco, partly because the states concerned tried to deal with the question by a nonintervention pact.

In several cases advisory opinions were requested from the Permanent Court of International Justice. In the British complaint (1922) about the application to its subjects of French nationality decrees in Tunis and Morocco, the Court's opinion that such decrees were not solely a matter of domestic concern led to further negotiation and a settlement between the parties. In two boundary cases, those of the Jaworzina district between Poland and Czechoslovakia (1923–1924) and the Mosul area between Iraq and Turkey (1924–1926), the Court's opinions merely upheld the right of the Council to decide. It did so, but its award was accepted only in the first case; Turkey reopened negotiation as to Mosul and settled the boundary directly. The Court's advisory opinion in 1931 that an Austro-German customs union would violate treaty obligations was given after the parties had announced abandonment of the plan, but consideration of the case probably influenced this result.

Two cases of border disputes in the Balkans were successfully controlled by the Council. While the Allied Conference of Ambassadors was considering the boundaries of Albania, the Yugoslavs entered the area (1921). The Council left settlement of the boundary to the ambassadors but appointed an investigating commission. The commission followed the case and after the fixing of the boundary was able to report evacuation by the Yugoslavs. Perhaps the most striking League success occurred in the dispute between Bulgaria and Greece over the Demir Kapu area (1925–1926). In the face of a mobilization of forces on the border, Aristide Briand, as the president of the Council, took the initiative by asking that both states withdraw their forces and submit the matter to the Council. The Council supported his action and demanded assurance within twenty-four hours of withdrawal of troops behind frontiers. A military commission was appointed to supervise this. Then a Commission of Inquiry was sent to the area to determine responsibility and assess damages. Greece was ordered to pay $210,000 to indemnify Bulgaria.

On the other hand, there were several cases in which League action was inconclusive or unsuccessful. In the dispute between Poland and Lithuania over Vilna (1920–1922), Poland seized the city in defiance of a military commission sent to draw a demarcation line, a Council recommendation of a plebiscite, and an effort by the president of the Council to mediate. Poland had taken the town from Russia, which recaptured it and then ceded it to Lithuania. A Polish general then occupied it, ostensibly without government authority, and continued to hold it. The Council was not prepared to take strong action against Poland, which was collaborating in the war against the Bolsheviki, and took no steps to change the situation.

The assassination of Italian members of a boundary commission sent by the Allied Conference of Ambassadors to delimit the frontier between Albania and Greece, produced an abrupt ultimatum to Greece by Italy demanding heavy indemnity (1923). When Greece replied proposing submission of the dispute to the League, Italy bombarded and occupied Corfu as a reprisal. The Council considered the murder of the Italians and concluded that Greece should pay the indemnity. Mussolini was not censured for his act, although a committee of jurists was asked to study the legal status of such measures by a member of the League. They concluded that some "coercive measures" could be taken which did not constitute war within the meaning of the Covenant. Neither Great Britain nor France was prepared to move against Italy at that time for reasons extraneous to the dispute.

In 1935 Germany reintroduced compulsory military service and began to build an air force. This led to a condemnation by the Council and appointment of a committee to consider strengthening collective security, but no direct action against Germany seemed feasible. In the war between China and Japan (1937–1945) the Council concluded that the Japanese were violating treaty obligations but left it to member states whether to apply sanctions individually. By then the European situation had become too threatening to divert forces, and nothing effective was done. In the case of Russia's aggression upon Finland (1939) and seizure of territory in Karelia, the League did find that Russia had violated the Covenant. The Council, therefore, expelled her from the League. It was in no position to undertake other measures against her.

These incidents leave a mixed impression. In general, it appears that inclination to take action was in inverse ratio to involvement in more pressing political problems. It also lagged against great powers. The attitude of particular states was also conditioned by the directness of their interest in the area affected. When the Council was moved to intervene, the apparatus of investigation and mediation was freely used, and was quite successful in certain disputes between small states. The standards of the Council were the standards of a diplomatic conference, but something was certainly gained because it was immediately available, capable of rapid action, and subject to ample publicity. A good deal of use was made of the Permanent Court in clarifying legal issues. Arbitration continued to be used with some frequency during the interwar period. A recent comprehensive collection of arbitral reports in that period discloses sixty cases, not including actions before claims tribunals. However, there were not many which stemmed directly from suggestions by the Council, nor is it clear how far obligations under the Covenant affected resort to arbitration.

Modifications of League Machinery

Some effort was made to define more specifically the obligations of member states not to resort to war and to strengthen pacific settlement techniques. French insistence upon mutual security guaranties as a prerequisite to disarmament led to the preparation of the Draft Treaty of Mutual Assistance (1923) which proposed to give the Council authority to determine the aggressor in a dispute and to determine the forces each state should contribute for Council action. This draft was approved by the Assembly and referred to member states for their observations, but was rejected by the British government. An effort had been made by the Scandinavian countries to amend the draft to limit the application of mutual security guaranties to countries which accepted arrangements for compulsory arbitration. This was only one of several efforts they had made to remove conciliation and arbitration procedures from the Council, which they regarded as too political a body to handle them, and to vest them in commissions, subject to an absolute duty to arbitrate.

In the Fifth Assembly (1924) these proposals were taken up and incorporated into the scheme of the Geneva Protocol (Draft Protocol for the Pacific Settlement of Disputes), which attempted to unite in a comprehensive plan disarmament, security, and arbitration. If a party to a dispute requested it, the matter was to be referred to a committee of arbitrators chosen by the parties. If the parties could not agree upon the arbitrators or terms of submission, the Council was authorized to appoint them. The arbitrators were not required to be jurists, for the plan was conceived in terms not of legal but of political issues; hence the term "arbitrators" is a little misleading —mediators or conciliators would be more apt. If neither party asked for "arbitration," the Council would act and a unanimous decision by it would be binding. However, if its recommendations were not unanimous, the dispute would be submitted to arbitrators selected by the Council. The award of this panel would be binding, and failure to observe it would lead to the application of sanctions. Other provisions of the protocol defined aggression as failure to observe obligations under the Covenant or the Protocol, and authorized the Council to determine sanctions and call upon members to apply them. Every member was obligated to comply. This plan would have plugged a number of gaps in the Covenant, but again the British government rejected it. Thereafter, local security arrangements were made in the Locarno Treaties and the general arbitration plan was dropped. It reappeared later in some of the provisions of the United Nations Charter.

In 1928 a further step was taken in the General Act for the Pacific Settlement of International Disputes. Under the act governments agree to submit any disputes not settled by diplomacy to a Conciliation Commission, authorized to examine the facts and propose a settlement but not to compel acceptance of it. All legal disputes were to be submitted to arbitration or to the Permanent Court of International Justice.

Outside the League the network of Locarno Treaties (1925) involving Germany, Great Britain, France, Italy, and Belgium, involved nonaggression commitments by Germany and guaranties of the German-Belgian and German-French frontiers by Great Britain and Italy. In the event of differences, the parties agreed to pacific settlement through resort to conciliation, the League Council, or the Permanent Court.

Mention should be made also of the Pact of Paris of 1928 (Kellogg-Briand Pact), whereby states pledged themselves to renounce war as an instrument of national policy and never to seek solution of disputes or conflicts except by pacific means. This is a statement of principle, but it provides no criteria for testing compliance. After World War II it was used by the Nuremberg Tribunal to establish the fact that acts initiating an aggressive war constitute a crime, but this could hardly have been the original intention of the framers. Some effort was made by interpretation to read into it certain sanctions and thus to "give it teeth," but these suggestions produced no practical consequences.

Provisions of the United Nations Charter

One of the most notable features of the U.N. Charter is the strengthening of the procedures for pacific settlement. In Chapter VI an effort was made to draw all pacific settlement techniques together into an integrated pattern. Virtually all of them are recited in Article 33, whereby parties to a dispute likely to endanger international peace and security, undertake to "seek a solution by negotiation, enquiry, mediation, conciliation, arbitration, judicial settlement, resort to regional agencies or arrangements, or other peaceful means of their own choice." The Security Council may also call upon the parties to use such means, and may investigate any dispute or situation likely to lead to a dispute to determine whether it may endanger the maintenance of international peace and security (Art. 34). Such disputes or situations may be drawn to its attention by a member, or by a nonmember if willing to accept the obligations of pacific settlement with respect to them (Art. 35). The Council is authorized at any stage in such disputes or situations to act as a mediator in proposing procedures of adjustment, taking into account what the parties have done and the desirability of referring legal issues to the International Court of Justice (Art. 36). If pacific settlement measures fail, the parties undertake to refer the dispute to the Council which may, if it considers the situation dangerous, act either under Article 36 or by directly recommending terms of settlement (Art. 37).

Before examining the applications of these provisions it is necessary to refer to three points affecting procedure: the relationship of the General Assembly to security questions, the so-called "veto" in the Security Council, and the effect of the reservation of questions of domestic jurisdiction to the member states.

Security powers of General Assembly. Although the Security Council is given "primary responsibility" for maintenance of peace and security (Art. 24), "primary" seems to be used in a chronological rather than a qualitative sense. The General Assembly can discuss any questions within the scope of the Charter or of the functions of other organs, including the Security Council's (Art. 10); it has no power of direct action but may make recommendations with respect to such questions either to the Council or to member states, except that it cannot do so with respect to a problem then under consideration by the Council unless the Council requests this (Art. 12). If a majority of the members of the Council wish the issue to be transferred to the Assembly, they can make this possible by simply dropping it from the Council agenda, for this is considered a procedural question. The effect of these provisions is that the Assembly is potentially a very active security organ, although hampered by the fact that it can only recommend and never order action.

The Veto. Under Article 27 the Security Council must proceed under a unique voting rule, which was advanced by the United States at the Yalta Conference to satisfy the U.S.S.R. Decisions on procedural matters are made by an affirmative vote of any seven of the eleven members. Decisions on other matters require "an affirmative vote of seven members including the concurring votes of the permanent members." Hence, a negative vote by any one of the permanent members blocks action; it is this which has been referred to as the veto. The article does not make clear whether it means the concurring votes of the permanent members *present and voting,* but it was probably formulated in the light of the League practice, in which abstention from voting when present was held not to break unanimity. The application of the veto has been quite frequent not only with respect to applications for

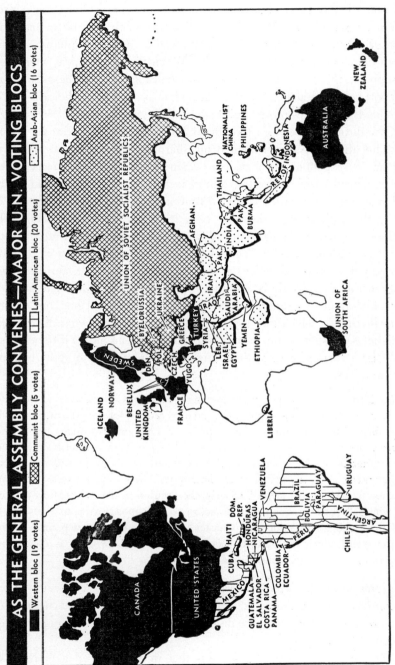

AS THE GENERAL ASSEMBLY CONVENES—MAJOR U.N. VOTING BLOCS

Western bloc (19 votes) Communist bloc (5 votes) Latin-American bloc (20 votes) Arab-Asian bloc (16 votes)

From The New York Times, Oct. 19, 1952

353

admission, already noted, but also in security questions. Given the schism between Communist and Western states, it is extremely difficult to act upon any security question without affecting the real or supposed interests of one or both blocs and thus inviting the veto. When the Charter was framed, it was supposed that there would be sufficient harmony among the great states to support collective action, but this has seldom proved to be the case.

What is meant by "procedural matters" and "other matters"? In a rough sense, the distinction between procedural and substantive questions is meaningful, but the line between them is not sharp. Is it a procedural matter to order an investigation into a dispute, when this may develop facts which make a particular course of action almost inescapable? At San Francisco the small states tried to obtain a clearer definition because they were hopeful of limiting the application of the veto. They formulated a list of twenty-three questions directed to the delegates of the sponsoring governments (United States, Great Britain, U.S.S.R., and China), each involving a type of decision which might be proposed under the terms of the Dumbarton Oaks draft, and asked whether each would be considered procedural or substantive. In reply the sponsoring powers ignored all the specific points except one, but offered a general criterion which they suggested would make clear what the answers should be. A question would have to be regarded as substantive if the decision could start a chain of events which might result in a need to apply enforcement measures.

To illustrate: in ordering an investigation, the Council has to consider whether the investigation—which may involve calling for reports, hearing witnesses, dispatching a commission of inquiry, or other means—might not further aggravate the situation. After investigation, the Council must determine whether the continuation of the situation or dispute would be likely to endanger international peace and security. If it so determines, the Council would be under obligation to take further steps. Similarly, the decision to make recommendations, even when all parties request it to do so, or to call upon parties to a dispute to fulfill their obligations under the Charter, might be the first step on a course of action from which the Security Council could withdraw only at the risk of failing to discharge its responsibilities.

With some justice Dr. Herbert Evatt, the delegate of Australia, summarized this construction as meaning ". . . that, without veto, the Council can only discuss whether a dispute can be discussed, and can only investigate whether it should be investigated."

The one specific answer given was that in the event of a preliminary question whether another question was to be considered procedural or substantive, this preliminary question would be substantive. From this arises the "double veto," for the preliminary question, "Resolved that the motion before the Council shall be considered a procedural question," if vetoed, would force a substantive vote on the principal question. In one case, however, involving the charge that the transfer of the United States Seventh Fleet to the Straits of Formosa constituted an aggression upon China, a resolution to invite a representative of the People's Republic of China to attend obtained eight affirmative votes but Nationalist China and the United States voted against it. Sir Gladwyn Jebb, as president of the Council, declared the resolution adopted, thus treating this vote as procedural. A protest by China was not sustained. The San Francisco interpretations are not a part of the Charter, and can hardly be regarded as official construction of it. Although they have in practice usually been followed, it is open to the Council to reach its own interpretations. The point is one upon which there continues to be a major difference of opinion both as to the meaning of the present rule and as to what the rule should be. Although the government of the United States does not wish to eliminate the veto altogether, it has said it would be willing to redefine procedural questions to include the pacific settlement decisions under Chapter VI, limiting the veto to decisions under Chapter VII.

Domestic Jurisdiction Limitation. Among the general principles at the beginning of the Charter is Article 2, Section 7:

Nothing contained in the present Charter shall authorize the United Nations to intervene in matters which are essentially within the domestic jurisdiction of any state or shall require the members to submit such matters to settlement under the present Charter; but this principle shall not prejudice the application of enforcement measures under Chapter VII.

This clause was suggested by a limitation in the League of Nations Covenant applied only to Council action with reference to disputes. In the Charter the limitation is a general one applicable to all organs and functions, from which only enforcement measures under Chapter VII, i.e., sanctions, are excluded. Thus, it applies to pacific settlement procedures by either the Security Council or General Assembly.

It cannot be said that the meaning of the limitation is at all clear. In the Covenant the clause reads "a matter which by international law is solely within the domestic jurisdiction," but the Charter refers to no international law standard and substitutes "essentially" for "solely." It may be conceded that there is little international law upon the point, but it may nevertheless be wiser to refer such questions to courts rather than political bodies so that judicial decisions can gradually build up dependable criteria. "Essentially" domestic might be taken to refer to matters "preponderantly" domestic, where there are mixed domestic and international interests, or to matters essential to state sovereignty, two quite different conceptions. The meaning of the term "intervene" is also obscure. As a term of international law it signifies interfering in the affairs of another state by force or threat of force. But this is clearly not the sense intended, for the present form of the clause resulted from an Australian amendment, and Dr. Evatt explained that he intended thereby to make it clear that the limitation applied to recommendations under Article 39 and excluded only "enforcement measures." But if the limitation applies to interferences in domestic affairs which do not involve force, where is the line to be drawn? Goodrich and Hambro (*Charter of the United Nations* [2d ed.], 120) suggest that "while discussion does not amount to intervention, the creation of a commission of inquiry, the making of a recommendation of a procedural or substantive nature, or the taking of a binding decision constitutes intervention under the terms of this paragraph." This may be a very reasonable view, but it is not a necessary conclusion from the words of the Charter.

Cases Involving the Domestic Jurisdiction Limitation

Several instances of United Nations practice suggest that no uniform standard with respect to domestic jurisdiction has emerged and that criteria of political convenience prevail.

In 1946 complaint was made to the Security Council that the Franco regime in Spain was a cause of international friction and a threat to peace. It did not appear whether this meant an outright threat to peace in the sense of Article 39 or a "situation which might lead to international friction or give rise to a dispute" in the sense of Article 34. Certainly the character of the Franco government was wholly a domestic matter unless it could be shown that it necessarily disturbed international peace. The Council disagreed. Upon referral to the Assembly a resolution was adopted recommending that the Franco regime be barred from U.N. agencies and affiliated international organizations, and that member states withdraw diplomatic agents from it. These recommendations were carried out but proved ineffective. They were revoked in 1950.

The Nizam of Hyderabad complained to the Council in 1948 that India threatened intimidation, invasion, and economic blockade. India replied that Hyderabad was not an independent state; India was only suppressing domestic disorder. Later India notified the Council that the Nizam had capitulated to Indian forces and wished to withdraw his complaint. This message was confirmed by the Nizam, who withdrew his representative. Although the Council retained the item on its agenda, it took no action.

After the expropriation by the government of Iran of properties of the Anglo-Iranian Oil Company in 1951 an application was made to the International Court of Justice by Great Britain for a declaration that the government of Iran was obligated to submit the dispute with the company to arbitration as provided in the concession agreement or alternatively that a denial of justice to the company had occurred for which compensation should be paid. The court ordered certain interim measures designed to protect company interests and operations until a decision should be reached. When these orders were ignored by Iran, the British government applied to the Security Council. Objection was made by the U.S.S.R. and Yugoslavia to inclusion of the item on the agenda because expropriation must be considered a domestic question. Great Britain argued that Iran's conduct was a threat to the peace. The item was deferred pending a ruling by the International Court of Justice upon its competency to assume jurisdiction. However, the court decided it could not proceed for want of a voluntary submission to jurisdiction by Iran, and therefore did not pass upon the question whether the Iranian expropriation was wholly a matter of domestic jurisdiction.

A bloc of Asian-Arab states in 1951 and 1952 requested the Security Council to examine the situation in the French colonies of Tunisia and Morocco as endangering international peace and security. The burden of the complaint was that the prime minister of Tunisia charged violation by France of its obligations under the Treaty of 1881 to take steps toward Tunisian autonomy. Complaints of violations of human rights and state independence in Morocco were made. France opposed inclusion of the Moroccan question in the Assembly agenda in 1951 and succeeded in persuading the Assembly to postpone the matter without deciding its competency. In 1952 the Tunisian case was taken to the Council, where France argued that even a substantive discussion would violate Article 2 (7). A resolution to include the matter in the agenda failed. Then both cases were placed before the Assembly, where France opposed consideration in the First Committee and refusd to participate in discussions in the plenary sessions. As it was not politically feasible to take any direct action, the Assembly merely adopted euphemistic resolutions expressing confidence and hope that France would endeavor to further the effective development of free institutions in Tunisia and Morocco. No formal decision upon competency was reached. At the tenth Assembly in 1955 France again opposed consideration of its handling of the Algerian situation. By a narrow vote, 28 to 27, the Assembly rejected the recommendation of its General Committee and decided to debate the question, although the vote made it clear it would not be able to take any action more decisive than its earlier resolutions. Protesting against the Assembly's decision, Antoine Pinay declared his government would not accept any U.N. intervention and considered void any recommendation it might make with respect to Algeria. The French delegation then withdrew from the Assembly. Its action proved effective; in order to coax the French to return the Assembly dropped the Algerian question from its agenda.

Some of the sharpest discussions of the domestic jurisdiction reservation have occurred on complaints about South African discriminatory legislation. India complained to the Assembly in 1946 of violations of human rights of

South African subjects of Indian origin. It was said that discriminatory legislation directed against the Indians violated the Cape Town Agreement of 1932 between India and South Africa, and threatened to impair friendly relations between the two states. South Africa denied there were any international agreements applicable and argued the Assembly was incompetent to consider the charge under Article 2 (7). It urged without success submission of the question of competency to the International Court of Justice. The Assembly did not specifically decide upon its competency but appeared to feel the treatment of nationals by a state might fall within Assembly jurisdiction if it led to the impairment of international relations or breach of international commitments. In 1952 the Assembly authorized a commission to study the racial situation within the Union of South Africa, i.e., the *apartheid* policy applied to natives. This had been vigorously opposed by the Union as a violation of Article 2 (7). The Assembly's theory appeared to be that the Union's legislation violated human rights obligations under the Charter and created a socially explosive situation threatening peace. The Union considered the resolution void and refused to cooperate. The apartheid policy was again taken up by the tenth Assembly, but after the withdrawal of the South African delegation in protest, the Assembly dropped the question from its agenda.

Equally intransigent were Bulgaria, Hungary, and Rumania when charged in 1949 with violating the human rights provisions of the peace treaties by trials of church leaders and statutes authorizing state control of courts, expression of opinion, and exercise of religion. The Assembly noted the obligations expressed in the treaties and urged compliance. In 1950 it expressed concern over the refusal of the three governments to cooperate in examination of the charges by appointing representatives to commissions authorized by the treaties. It requested an advisory opinion of the International Court of Justice upon the question whether there was a legal obligation to appoint the commissioners and whether, if one member were not appointed, the others could act. When the court advised that there was a positive obligation to appoint commissioners but that action could not be taken by a rump commission, the Assembly formally condemned the three countries for willful refusal to discharge their obligations.

A method of avoiding the domestic jurisdiction limitation was suggested by the disposition of the African colonies relinquished by Italy. Under Article 23 of the Italian Peace Treaty disposition of the colonies was to be made within one year by France, Great Britain, the United States, and the U.S.S.R., but if they could not agree the matter was to be referred to the Assembly and its decision accepted as conclusive. The question was referred to the Assembly, which in 1949 provided for the independence of Libya by January 1, 1952, the continuance of Somaliland for ten years (until 1960) as a trust territory under Italian administration, and the federation of Eritrea with

Ethiopia as an autonomous unit with a constitution drafted under U.N. supervision. These arrangements thus avoid domestic jurisdiction limitations by obtaining advance commitments of states to accept U.N. recommendations in a domestic matter.

These cases do not seem to present any standard of domestic jurisdiction. Assembly and Council have apparently felt they could construe Article 2 (7) without recourse to the International Court of Justice, but they have done so only by implication. One must consider the action taken rather than any formal decision upon competency. The looseness of language in Article 2 (7) seems to allow very flexible United Nations action, and raises no specific barriers to such action. The possibility of strong action in pacific settlement is thus enhanced, but at the risk of arbitrary action. There seems to be merit in the suggestion of Abba Eban, delegate of Israel, that the article be amended to make clear that discussion is not prohibited but that intervention by institutional action within a member state is.

Other Pacific Settlement Cases in the United Nations

In addition to the cases which have been mentioned to illustrate the domestic jurisdiction reservation, the United Nations has had to deal with a number of important security problems, most of which were unsettled business remaining from war situations.

In Iran the Soviet forces which had been stationed in Azerbaijan to protect a supply line to their eastern front lingered until 1946, although at the Teheran Conference in 1943 it had been agreed to withdraw them when the war ended. In January, 1946, Iran complained to the Council, which discussed the matter without getting beyond procedural questions. The Russian delegate insisted no dispute existed because agreement had been reached with Iran upon a withdrawal date in March. He withdrew from the Council when his proposal to postpone consideration was rejected. Nevertheless, the Council adopted a resolution directing the parties to report on May 6 whether withdrawal had been completed. The troops were actually withdrawn in May. What the original intentions of the Russians may have been is not clear, but the publicity in the Council seems at least to have hastened withdrawal.

Several applications were made to the Council in connection with disturbances in Greece. The first was a Russian complaint in 1946, no doubt in retaliation because of the Iranian complaint, that continuance of British troops in Greece was a source of tension endangering the maintenance of peace. The matter was discussed inconclusively and set aside. Then in August, 1946, the Ukrainian S.S.R. charged that Greek forces, encouraged by the presence of the British, were fomenting disorder on the Albanian frontier. A resolution to set up a committee of investigation was vetoed by the U.S.S.R., and all other resolutions failed. The Council then moved to other business.

Finally, in December, 1946, the Greek government complained that Albania, Bulgaria, and Yugoslavia were waging guerrilla warfare on the frontiers and stirring up Greek Communists. All parties were invited to present their views, including Albania and Bulgaria, which were not members of the United Nations. After hearing them the Council decided to send a commission of inquiry to Greece. After its preliminary investigation an observation group was left in Greece to report any changes in the situation. The politics of the case were further complicated by the Truman Doctrine (1947), which led to United States military and economic aid to Greece and Turkey. It proved impossible to obtain agreement upon any action in the Council due to Russian vetoes; consequently, the case was dropped from the agenda. This enabled the Assembly to take it up and to establish the United Nations Special Commission on the Balkans (UNSCOB), designed to assist the disputant states in reaching agreement and solving minority questions in the frontier area. It was not received except in Greece but continued to observe and report the situation. A Conciliation Committee appointed in 1948 accomplished little. Eventually the problem was eased through the Yugoslav break with the U.S.S.R. and subsequent resumption of normal diplomatic relations with Greece and through the strengthening of the internal position of the Greek government. It can hardly be said that the United Nations solved the Greek problem but it did throw a great deal of light on what was happening there and thus aided the Greek government to deal with it upon more nearly equal terms.

The Syria-Lebanon case of 1946 again arose from a complaint that troops had not been removed, that their continued presence was inconsistent with the sovereignty of the two states, and that removal had been made subject to conditions inconsistent with the Charter. Great Britain and France denied that there was a dispute or that they were parties to a dispute, thus injecting a procedural problem, for under Article 27 parties to a dispute may not vote whereas no such rule exists in the investigation of a situation. However, the two powers did not press the point, but replied to the charges and abstained from voting. A resolution proposed by the United States to express confidence in their avowed intention to withdraw was vetoed by the U.S.S.R. However, Great Britain and France indicated they would act in the spirit of the majority view and later notified the Council of withdrawal of their forces.

One of the most important cases arose from the Indonesian independence movement. During the war the Japanese had occupied the Dutch East Indies. The interval after Japanese surrender before British forces could take control was sufficient to permit Indonesian nationalists to proclaim the independence of the Republic of Indonesia. Negotiations between the nationalists and the government of the Netherlands disclosed no common ground; each wanted full control. The matter came to the Council in January 1946 upon complaint by the Ukrainian S.S.R. that British forces in Indonesia were using Japanese troops against the independence movement. After brief discussion it was dropped. However, the Dutch were unable to restore order, despite an agreement at Linggadjati in 1947 whereby the *de facto* authority of the republic over Java, Madura, and Sumatra was conceded and an Indonesian federal state in a Netherlands-Indonesian union was projected. This agreement was differently construed by the Dutch and Indonesians and widespread fighting continued. In July India and Australia drew the Council's attention to the matter—India as a situation endangering peace, Australia as a breach of the peace calling for enforcement measures under Article 39. The Council called for a cease fire; this was ordered, but was imperfectly observed. The Council also requested the consuls of its members stationed in Batavia to make joint reports on the situation and authorized a Committee of Good Offices to attempt to find a basis of settlement. Through this mediation a truce agreement was reached in January 1948 (Renville Agreement), which stipulated eighteen principles as a basis of settlement. The implementation of the agreement proved difficult and negotiations broke down. In December the Netherlands denounced the truce agreement and resumed military operations. The Council again called for a cease-fire, for immediate and unconditional release of Indonesian leaders held by the Dutch, and renewal of negotiations. A new mediating committee, the United Nations Commission for Indonesia was created. The Dutch accepted the cease fire, released the republican leaders, and proposed a round-table conference at The Hague to settle the status of Indonesia. With the aid of the commission the parties succeeded in conferences at Batavia in working out measures for cessation of guerrilla fighting, release of political prisoners, and arrangements for the round-table conference. This conference reached agreement upon transfer of sovereignty to the Republic of the United States of Indonesia and the incorporation of the republic into a Netherlands-Indonesian Union, i.e., a personal union under the Netherlands crown. The agreement was approved by a majority of the Council, although its resolution was vetoed by the U.S.S.R., and it has been put into effect. The intervention of the Council in this case seems to have been of real value in inducing continuation of negotiations, and the framework of the United Nations action also helped to direct pressures upon the Dutch, such as the conference of Asian, Australasian, and Middle Eastern States at New Delhi and the cutting off of United States economic aid to the Netherlands allocated for use in Indonesia. A good deal of initiative and flexibility in creating agencies was shown by the Council.

A much less successful effort was made to settle the dispute between India and Pakistan over Kashmir. This was one of the protected princely states which upon the separation of India and Pakistan had an option

whether they would join one or the other. Because of the Muslim character
of the population and the Indian preferences of the Hindu prince the choice
was difficult. Kashmir was placed provisionally under India subject to later
plebiscite, but border raiding preceded and followed this decision. India reported to the Council invasions by Muslim tribesmen in 1948 and accused
Pakistan of inciting them. Pakistan denied this and charged that India had
obtained control illegally and stirred up Hindu attacks upon the Muslims.
The Council appointed a Mediation Commission to investigate the situation
and supervise withdrawal of troops and nonresident tribesmen. A plebiscite
administrator (Admiral Chester Nimitz) was unable to carry out his task
because India and Pakistan never agreed upon troop withdrawal or the conditions of the plebiscite. The Mediation Commission reported failure. It was
later replaced by a sole mediator. Sir Owen Dixon and Dr. Frank P. Graham
in turn sought unsuccessfully to obtain agreement to demilitarization and
arbitration. Although the parties came somewhat closer together upon points
of procedure, they were unable to agree upon the number and character of
forces to be left on either side of the cease-fire line at the end of demilitarization. There appeared to be no real desire by India to facilitate a plebiscite,
from which it had little to hope. The sum of the Council's achievement has
been to quiet active fighting and obtain a partial troop removal.

The problems of Palestine have been the special concern of the Assembly,
although five organs of the U.N. were involved in various ways. The situation was created by the heavy migration of Jewish refugees into Palestine, a
British mandate, and consequent economic and political dominance of Jew
over Arab. The effort of the British to reconcile Arab and Jewish views about
the political organization of the state failed. They, therefore, requested the
Assembly to make recommendations for the future government of Palestine.
A United Nations Special Committee on Palestine (UNSCOP) was appointed to conduct an investigation and report. UNSCOP suggested partition
into Arab and Jewish states, although a minority favored a federal state.
Upon this basis the Assembly drew up a plan for partition and requested
the Security Council to deal with any threat to the peace in putting it into
force, the Economic and Social Council to work out plans for economic
collaboration between the two states, and the Trusteeship Council to undertake the administration of Jerusalem. A U.N. commission was appointed to
take over the administration when Great Britain relinquished the mandate
in 1948. Heavy fighting between Arabs and Jews followed. The Council
requested a cease fire but also expressed doubt that it possessed authority to
impose the Assembly plan. At this stage the United States suggested that a
trusteeship in Palestine might be a preferable arrangement. However, the
Assembly adhered to its plan and appointed a mediator (Count Folke Berna-

dotte), who succeeded in obtaining a temporary cease fire. He could not bring the parties together upon substantive matters. Meanwhile, the State of Israel proclaimed its independence on May 6, 1948, and was promptly recognized by the United States. Fighting continued, and the Security Council, finding a threat to the peace under Article 39, ordered governments to stop military intervention. Count Bernadotte was assassinated and succeeded by Ralph Bunche, and later by a Conciliation Commission. Bunche succeeded in negotiating armistice agreements. However, difficult problems have continued. An elaborate Assembly plan for international administration of Jerusalem failed completely. Arab refugees from the new state of Israel have required relief and rehabilitation for which sufficient funds are not available. And border incidents between Arabs and Israelis have been common. Recent purchase of arms from Czechoslovakia by Egypt may portend greater trouble. Although the United Nations made a great effort in the case, it is difficult to assess the effectiveness of its achievement. The partition of the area was accomplished by Israel's attainment of independence and not along the lines contemplated by the Assembly. But the work of the mediators proved effective in stopping hostilities.

Conclusions on Pacific Settlement

It appears that the Charter has proved a flexible instrument for pacific settlement techniques. The Assembly as well as the Security Council has found it possible to move freely as far as powers and machinery are concerned, and both have created subordinate agencies as circumstances suggested. Thus the Assembly developed the observation commission in Greece, the mediator in Palestine, and a variety of commissions. It showed facility in directing several organs to contribute to its planning in Palestine, although the plans were not accepted. The Council has proved able to move rapidly upon occasion; has employed investigation, observation, truce, and consular commissions, has mediated directly and through good offices commissions; and has been able to focus a good deal of pressure upon disputant states. The greatest handicap has been the voting procedure of the Council, which has certainly blocked action in many cases and in instances where rather petty motivation rather than vital national interest dictated the negative vote. Basic to this problem has been the fact that so many trouble spots remained after the war and so little harmony existed between the East and the West in settling them. Had a major postwar settlement been possible, the situation would have been less difficult, but it was kept deliberately fluid in a continuing struggle for position. The process of settlement has in consequence been markedly political, with little tendency toward utilization of the more dispassionate methods of arbitration and judicial settlement. States have not really sought the arbitrament of law, but rather to bargain for an improved political position. Under these circumstances the results have been perhaps as satisfactory as could be expected.

There has been little disposition to effect systematic improvement of the machinery of mediation and conciliation despite the flexible experimentation evident in its use. The Interim Committee of the Assembly did undertake studies of pacific settlement processes and made a number of recommendations. At its suggestion the General Act for the Pacific Settlement of International Disputes, adopted by the League of Nations Assembly in 1928, has been made operative as to organs of the United Nations. A panel for inquiry and conciliation, composed of persons nominated by member states has been set up, from which commissions of inquiry and conciliation can be formed. To date, however, this seems to have remained a paper structure. The Assembly was led also to suggest that the Security Council consider the appointment of a special conciliator or mediator in disputes, and suspend consideration until he reported the success of his efforts to bring the parties together. It is perhaps an evidence of the temper of the times that so little attention is voluntarily paid to the availability of conciliation apparatus of this sort.

There remain some questions concerning the relative position of the Council and the Assembly, the relationship of regional to United Nations security processes, and of peaceful change to pacific settlement, which can better be discussed after some account of the use of sanctions has been given.

SANCTIONS

Both the Covenant of the League of Nations and the Charter of the United Nations provide for the application of diplomatic, economic, or military sanctions to states which use force against other states in violation of international obligations. Although little use has yet been made of these provisions, they are available as an ultimate resort in the event of outright aggression or inability to settle disputes peacefully because of the recalcitrance of one of the parties.

League of Nations

Article X of the Covenant pledged member states to preserve the territorial integrity and political independence of members against external aggression. At the Paris Conference the British had argued against this as implying a commitment to go to war, but President Wilson insisted they must show they "meant business." A compromise was reached by adding a clause proposed by the French which negatived the assumption that any automatic obligation was created by providing that the Council should "advise upon the means by which this obligation shall be fulfilled." Probably the

French understood the word *aviser* in the sense of "look to" rather than "advise," but this was not the intent of the English-speaking delegates. Later sentiment so far veered away from absolute commitments that the Assembly unanimously adopted in 1923 an interpretative resolution according to which the Council should, in discharging its function, "take account, more particularly of the geographical situation and of the special conditions of each State," and each member state could itself decide "in what degree the Member is bound to assure the execution of this obligation [to preserve the territorial integrity and independence of other members] by employment of its military forces."

The plan of the Covenant, as has been seen, pledged the member states not to resort to war without attempting to find a solution for their disputes either by arbitration, or by judicial settlement, or by mediation of the Council, and waiting at least three months after the arbitral award, or judicial decision, or recommendations (if unanimous) of the Council (Art. 12). This left certain "gaps" for wars not covered by this prohibition, as when the Council was not unanimous or the other party failed to accept such pacific settlement, but these gaps did not affect any cases which in fact arose. The Covenant then assumed that a member which deliberately resorted to war in disregard of these covenants committed a particularly heinous offense, and should "*ipso facto* be deemed to have committed an act of war against all other members of the League." They, in turn, undertook "immediately to subject it to the severance of all trade or financial relations, the prohibition of all intercourse between their nationals and the nationals of the covenant-breaking State, and the prevention of all financial, commercial or personal intercourse between the nationals of the covenant-breaking State and the nationals of any other State, whether a Member of the League or not" (Art. 16). It then became the duty of the Council to recommend to member states what effective military, naval, or air force they should contribute for sanctions against the Covenant-breaker. Mutual assistance among members to prevent any special hardship to one from these measures was also provided.

Thus there was an immediate and direct obligation upon members of non-intercourse with the Covenant-breaker, but the choice whether to participate in a program of military sanctions was to be made voluntarily by each member upon the basis of the Council's recommendation. Even these commitments appeared too strong to the British when it became apparent that the United States would not enter the League, and in consequence of misgivings expressed by Lord Balfour at the eighth meeting of the Council an International Blockade Committee was set up to consider the means of carrying out Article 16. Its report formed the basis of proposals for amendment of the Covenant which were not in fact adopted, but which received the approval of the Second Assembly and thereafter were generally taken as an authoritative construction of Article 16. These explicitly stated that neither Council nor Assembly could call upon members to apply sanctions, that each member must itself decide whether the Covenant had been violated and if so, what form of sanctions it would support. Sanctions should also be progressive in severity, from diplomatic to economic to military.

Three cases arose which deserve some comment: the dispute between Paraguay and Bolivia over possession of the Chaco Boreal area (1928–1935), the Sino-Japanese conflict in Manchuria (1931–1933), and the Italo-Ethiopian war (1935–1936).

The Gran Chaco case was negligible as an example of sanctions; only an arms embargo was used, and it did not affect the result. The case may be dismissed with two comments. The first concerns the definition of the aggressor. The war in the Gran Chaco had been in progress for several years before the first appeal was made to the League of Nations by Paraguay. It did so because after early successes and a period of truce it was then suffering reverses. As a group of American governments had tendered good offices, the Council merely appointed a committee to follow their efforts. The tide of war again turned, and Paraguay recovered lost ground, captured a dozen forts, and took the Bolivian headquarters. Two Bolivian governments fell in quick succession, and Bolivia was forced to resume negotiations with the help of the American mediators. Because progress was desultory, the Council authorized an investigating commission to go to the Chaco. Before it arrived (nine months later!) Paraguay had again declared war. The League commission managed to secure a brief armistice and drafted a proposed treaty which both parties thought objectionable on many points. Nevertheless, it was reported to the Council as a basis of settlement and adopted. By this time Bolivia had nothing left to lose and feared a proposed arms embargo because she imported all her munitions. Therefore, she invoked Article 15 and accepted a report of the League Committee calling for evacuation of a zone at the front followed by a peace conference, or if that failed, by reference to the Permanent Court. Paraguay, which was in possession of the Chaco, rejected the report, and on that account was held to be the aggressor and subjected to the arms embargo. Under all the circumstances this decision must be considered arbitrary, although in accordance with the Covenant provisions.

The second comment is that the position of the Council was complicated by the efforts of American states. The Pan-American Conference on Conciliation and Arbitration had appointed a committee of five to extend good offices, which were accepted. A nine-member Commission of Investigation and Conciliation was then set up, which was able to effect the first truce. After resumption of hostilities this committee, rechristened the Committee of Neutrals, again sought a basis of settlement. The American states also applied in unison the Stimson Doctrine of nonrecognition of the fruits of aggression. After the Council decision Paraguay withdrew from the League and Argentina and Chile induced the belligerents to agree upon an armistice and negotiate a peace. As Article 21 of the Covenant took special notice of the validity of regional understandings like the Monroe Doctrine, it was natural that the League should hesitate to take any initiative while the American governments were actively seeking a settlement. No specific rules governing the relationship of regional and League security processes had been stated.

The Manchurian dispute began with the occupation of Mukden and other points by Japanese forces. The official Japanese rationalization was that this was a defensive war to protect Japanese nationals in Manchuria whom the Chinese government failed to protect. China drew the matter to the attention of the Council as early as September 21, 1931, and several times thereafter. The Council requested withdrawal of troops and assumption by China of responsibility for the safety of Japanese subjects. On the basis of the disputants' obligations under the Kellogg Pact, Secretary of State Stimson declared the United States "would endeavor to reinforce what the League does," and would participate in the Council's discussions of the case. However, the theater of war expanded steadily. On December 10 the Council authorized a Commission of Inquiry (the Lytton Commission) to investigate the dispute on the spot. By January the fighting had reached major proportions and Stimson announced his Doctrine of Nonrecognition. Soon after the Japanese attacked Shanghai, which led to an emergency session of the Council and a demand for a cease fire and troop withdrawal. The League also adopted the Stimson Doctrine. In fact the Japanese found Shanghai too costly an effort and withdrew in May but made no concession in Manchuria. Japan set up and recognized the puppet state of Manchukuo in September 1932.

While all this was going on, what of the Lytton Commission? It had not reached the Orient until the end of February, and then consumed seven months in its investigation, reporting on October 2, 1932. Its admirable, if rather tardy, report contained a dispassionate review of the whole situation, designed not to wound the sensibilities of either belligerent. It recommended dissolution of the puppet state and creation of an autonomous Manchuria under Chinese sovereignty, with new treaties to guarantee the rights of both states. Whether this would at any stage have been acceptable to the Japanese is doubtful, but it certainly was not at that late date. The Assembly considered the report in December, and through a Committee of Nineteen tried vainly to persuade Japan to submit the dispute to a conciliation commission. Finally, the Assembly was obliged to consider the report on its merits and to accept it, thus condemning Japan and committing the League to the myth of Chinese sovereignty in Manchuria.

An Advisory Committee was created to concert action against Japan, and with it the United States collaborated. But neither the United States nor Great Britain would participate in an active intervention; hence sanctions were confined to the diplomatic variety. They included nonrecognition of Manchukuo and its legal ostracism from such international conventions as the Universal Postal Union. Japan gave notice of withdrawal from the League. It need hardly be said the sanctions proved ineffective.

The Italo-Ethiopian war provided the greatest challenge to the League collective security system. The ultimate failure, or rather withdrawal, of the economic sanctions used against Italy was a decisive blow to the League which shattered confidence in its value as a security agency. Therefore, it is important to understand what happened.

Ethiopia appealed to the Council on January 3, 1935, because of a border incident at Wal Wal, but no action was taken beyond reminding the disputants of their general arbitration treaty concluded in 1928. Outside the League there was a good deal of diplomatic activity. The announcement of German rearmament had been followed by the Stresa Conference of 1935, where Italy, France, and Great Britain sought a common front against Hitler. Laval of France held conversations with Mussolini and reached an understanding, presumably on the basis of a free hand for Italy in Ethiopia. The British were disturbed by the German situation, by the possibility that communications through the Mediterranean could be cut by Italian aircraft and submarines if Italy should be driven to make common cause with Hitler, perhaps by the pacifist strength shown in an English peace ballot. It was, therefore, inevitable that some appeasement of Italy's territorial thirst should be considered. However, Great Britain and France persuaded Mussolini to accept arbitration of the Wal-Wal dispute. He finally did so but delayed action by objections to the composition of the commission and its terms of reference. Meanwhile he moved the Italian army to Africa, thus creating a question much broader than the Wal-Wal incident. Nevertheless, the Council postponed the issue pending conclusion of the arbitration. In July the Council adjourned to permit Great Britain and France to seek a basis of settlement. Conversations were held on the basis of a treaty of 1906 allocating spheres of influence in Ethiopia. However, no basis of settlement was found, and the movement of Italian troops continued. In September the Wal Wal commission reported neither state was responsible for that incident. The Council finally was induced by Ethiopia to discuss the case in September. A Committee of Five suggested a plan under which Ethiopia would accept foreign advisers (including Italian) in her public services. Italy was not satisfied. The Council then reverted to Article 15 and appointed a Committee of Thirteen to draft a report. It refuted Italian claims of Ethiopian barbarism and asserted Italy's obligation to refrain from force. But the rainy season had ended in Ethiopia, and the Italian invasion had begun. Ethiopia invoked Article 16,

The resolution arouses mixed feelings. In part it seems to be a paper structure, for few members have set aside any forces to implement Assembly recommendations, and none would be under compulsion to do so. Only such minor powers as Turkey, Greece, and Denmark expressed willingness to allocate special units for U.N. service. The United States and a number of other states suggested that their military components in regional defense arrangements might be made available in appropriate cases and subject to later decision. Nor is it easy to put national contingents from different countries together quickly. The possibility certainly exists that a group, like the NATO powers, which has a joint force in being might offer its services, provided the circumstances suited its interest, but this might inject an element of regional or bloc bias that was not intended. The work of the Collective Measures Committee in attempting to project the principles upon which political, economic, or military measures might be concerted is interesting but necessarily rather general, and smacks of academic exercise. On the other hand, the Peace Observation Commission, with a Panel of Field Observers placed at its disposal, can be used by either the Assembly, the Interim Committee of the Assembly, or the Security Council, and it should prove a useful resource. The plan does afford, at the least, a possible framework of action in the not too improbable event that the Security Council should be hamstrung by the veto at a critical juncture. The arrangement suggests a remarkable reversion to the voluntary sanctions programs of the League of Nations.

Collective Defense and Regional Security

Article 51 of the Charter contains a provision preserving to member states the right of individual or collective self-defense if an armed attack occurs against a U.N. member, unless the Security Council has taken measures to maintain peace and security. The provision is no doubt intended to cover the interval before collective security measures can be set in motion. But the existence of the veto and the lack of international police make it perfectly possible that the interval may be stretched to indefinite duration through inability of the Council to act. In that case it would seem that Article 51 may afford authority for concerted preparations for collective self-defense of a substantial type.

This at least is the construction which has been put upon the article in such notable defensive alliances as the North Atlantic Treaty (1949), the South East Asian Collective Defense Treaty (1954), and the Inter-American Treaty of Reciprocal Assistance (1947). Each of these treaties, stipulating reciprocal assistance in the event of armed attack upon signatories, states that it was concluded in the spirit of Article 51 to carry out the inherent right of collective self-defense and will be administered in a manner consistent with that article, i.e., that a report of any defense action taken will be made to the Security Council. Thus a formidable group of alliances of special blocs has been tied in with the Charter, at least in a formalistic sense. This seems a surprising companionship for a universal system of collective security.

Articles 52–54 of the Charter refer with approval to regional organizations and encourage the development of pacific settlement of local disputes through such organizations. Use by the Security Council of regional arrangements or agencies for enforcement action under its authority is also contemplated. In this case, however, the prior authorization of the Council is required. If it is not quite clear how a "regional" organization should be defined, it is nevertheless clear that the Organization of American States, the European Defense Community, and the Arab League are regarded as regional organizations. A possibility of some integration of their security machinery and procedures with the United Nations system therefore exists. Little has been made of this as yet, but the Security Council has deferred to the Organization of American States (OAS) in recent Central American disputes.

A complaint by Costa Rica in 1948 that its territory had been invaded by Nicaraguan forces was not placed on the agenda of the Security Council, apparently because the chairman of the council of OAS stated that it was already taking action with respect to the matter. Other incidents have been referred by Caribbean states to OAS, which has duly informed the Security Council of its actions. During the successful revolution of Colonel Castillo Armas against the government of Guatemala in 1954 that government complained to the U.N. Council that Honduras and Nicaragua were aiding the rebels and therefore engaged in "an act of criminal aggression." Guatemala was not formally a member of OAS; it had ratified its charter with a reservation which prevented deposit of ratification. However, this reservation did not refer to its obligation to resort to Inter-American procedures of pacific settlement. In fact, Guatemala did not deny this obligation but argued that it did not in this case preclude an immediate application to the Security Council because the issue was not a dispute within the meaning of the OAS charter but an externally supported aggression or invasion. In the Security Council the Guatemalan position was supported by the U.S.S.R., which vetoed a resolution otherwise generally supported to refer the case to the OAS. Thereafter a resolution was adopted calling for termination of acts likely to cause bloodshed and requesting all members of the United Nations to refrain from giving aid to such action. Soon after Guatemala charged Honduras and Nicaragua with such acts in giving aid to the rebels and asked the Security Council to enforce its resolution. The Council met, but for want of seven affirmative votes failed to adopt its agenda. Meanwhile the OAS Peace Committee had received a Guatemalan complaint against Honduras and Nicaragua, then a request to postpone investigation because of the reference of the matter to the Security Council. Later the Guatemalan government agreed to the investigation, but the government fell and the new government of Armas withdrew the permission because of the mediation of the United States and El Salvador. The council of OAS also scheduled a meeting to consider possible measures to meet aggression or a situation endangering peace, but canceled the meeting because of the success of the revolt. Although somewhat inconclusive these incidents suggest a general disposition in the United Nations to defer to the procedures of the regional organization, and an intent in the OAS to carry out its functions. In the event that security systems as detailed as that of the OAS should become general throughout the world, it would seem desirable that some more systematic division of labor should be considered. The regional security organization can count upon one advantage in assurance of interest on the part of participating states by reason of proximity.

Collective Security and Peaceful Change

Finally, it must be observed that a system of collective security cannot be effective in a situation in which an unjust or unacceptable political and economic status is perpetuated. Peace in such a situation may be maintained by force for a time, but the process will become increasingly difficult unless some provision for peaceful changes in the status quo operates. It was one of the great weaknesses of the League of Nations that no provision was made for peaceful change other than the statement in Article 19 of the Covenant that the Assembly might from time to time "advise the reconsideration by Members of the League of treaties which have become inapplicable and the consideration of international conditions whose continuance might endanger the peace of the world."

The U.N. General Assembly is better situated under Articles 13 and 14 of the Charter. It is enjoined to initiate studies to promote international cooperation in the political, economic, social, cultural, educational, and health fields and to encourage progressive development and codification of international law. This authority has led to creation of the Interim Committee of the Assembly and the International Law Commission, as well as the commissions under the Economic and Social Council. These bodies are interested in general changes, e.g., structural organization or legislation, rather than injustices or inequalities in the position of particular states. To some extent the Assembly has shown interest in the latter problem. Thus in the case of Palestine or of the Italian colonies it did not confine itself to maintaining peace but proposed detailed plans for administration and political and economic structure. It is to be hoped that work of increasing value will be done in this field. If so, the number of collective security cases will diminish.

Conclusion

What has been said should indicate the diversity and complexity of the problem of increasing the effectiveness of collective security. As presently organized, a dispute arising from a conflict of interests between two states is referred to U.N. organs which must act by reconciling the conflicting interests of eleven or fifty states. A sense of responsibility and impartiality must gradually grow up in the system before this can be avoided and dispassionate procedures and criteria can be applied. Present deficiencies merely reflect the disorder and paucity of genuine community that exist in international affairs. But progress has been made, and it certainly appears that a genuine group concern for the security of all states in the community is growing. It must grow at the popular as well as at the governmental level to assure that responsible participation becomes habitual. Meanwhile the system is quite certain to have its ups and downs for a long time, with the risk of a catastrophic failure. It is not on that account an absurd effort. "What is there ridiculous about collective security?" asked Mr. Churchill, and answered very properly, "the only thing that is ridiculous about it is that we have not got it."

SELECTED READING

See also readings at end of preceding chapter.

ARECHAGA, EDUARDO JIMÉNEZ DE, *Voting and the Handling of Disputes in the Security Council.* United Nations Studies, No. 5. New York: Carnegie Endowment for International Peace, 1950.

BRIERLY, J. L., *The Outlook for International Law.* Oxford: Clarendon Press, 1944.

CONWELL-EVANS, T. P., *The League Council in Action: A Study of the Methods Employed by the Council of the League of Nations to Prevent War and to Settle International Disputes.* London: Oxford University Press, 1929.

DICKINSON, EDWIN D., *Law and Peace.* Philadelphia: University of Pennsylvania Press, 1951.

EVATT, HERBERT VERE, *The Task of Nations.* New York: Duell, Sloan and Pearce, 1949.

GOODRICH, LELAND M. and SIMONS, ANNE P., *The United Nations and the Maintenance of International Peace and Security.* Washington, D.C.: The Brookings Institution, 1955.

GREEN, L. C., "The Security Council in Action," in *Year Book of World Affairs,* II: 125–161 (1948).

HAVILAND, H. FIELD, JR., *The Political Role of the General Assembly.* United Nations Studies, No. 7. New York: Carnegie Endowment for International Peace, 1951.

JESSUP, PHILIP C., *International Security.* New York: Council on Foreign Relations, 1935.

KELSEN, HANS, "Organization and Procedure of the Security Council of the United Nations," in *Harvard Law Review*, LIX: 1087–1121 (1946).

———, "The Settlement of Disputes by the Security Council," in *International Law Quarterly*, II: 173–213 (1948).

LISSITZYN, OLIVER J., *The International Court of Justice, Its Role in the Maintenance of International Peace and Security*. New York: Carnegie Endowment for International Peace, 1951.

MACLAURIN, JOHN, *The United Nations and Power Politics*. London: George Allen and Unwin Ltd., 1951.

Royal Institute of International Affairs, *International Sanctions*. London: Oxford University Press, 1938.

THOMPSON, KENNETH W., "Collective Security Reexamined," in *American Political Science Review*, XLVII (3): 753–772 (September 1953).

PART 4

POLICIES OF THE
LEADING POWERS

The Great Powers
in World Affairs

The nineteenth century has often been described as the century of nationalism. There is a general notion, part belief and part hope, that today nationalism is gradually diminishing and that little by little it is being replaced by internationalism. This idea was particularly strong at the end of World War II when the United Nations was established, just as it was thirty years ago when the League of Nations was set up. National interests and ideologies wrecked the League, and the same forces have largely paralyzed the United Nations. The war strengthened nationalism as well as internationalism and created it in regions such as tropical Africa, where in 1939 it hardly existed.

World War II taught the lesson that no one nation could live to itself and defend itself successfully, and that a larger unit was necessary for national survival. In Western Europe, where modern nationalism first developed and grew to maturity, it has weakened to some extent. Evidences of this are seen in the Schuman Plan, and the proposals for an international army and a federation of Western Europe. At the same time the opposition to all these measures, on the ground that they injure national interests, is proof of the continued vitality of nationalism. In Asia, Africa, and the Western Hemisphere nationalism seems to be gaining in strength. It appears fairly certain that it will play a dominant role in the twentieth as it did in the nineteenth century. To write this is not to deny the importance of internationalism. These two great forces act and react upon one another, as can be seen by even a cursory study of the proceedings of the United Nations.

Every state has vital interests which it tries to promote, and to this end has evolved its national policies. To a very considerable extent the international events reported in the newspapers are due to the interaction and sometimes the conflict of national policies. Sovereign states differ enormously in material power, and therefore in the extent to which they can achieve their purposes by their own unaided strength. This is the element of inescapable truth in the phrase "power politics." The small group of states known as the great powers far outstrip the rest in their degree of material strength. Prior to World War II there were seven of them—the United States, Great Britain, Germany, France, Russia, Japan, and, by courtesy, Italy. Today there are two super great powers—the United States and Russia. Italy has been dropped

from the list, and the others for varying reasons are not in the same class as
the first two. China and perhaps India may enter eventually into this group.
There are also a few states, sometimes referred to as middle powers—Canada
and Italy are good examples—which exert a disproportionate degree of influence because of their geographic position, natural resources, or extent of
industrialization.

International relations are to a large extent shaped by the policies of the
leading powers, in alliance or sometimes in antagonism toward one another.
For in the last analysis only they have the strength to make their will prevail.
A small power cannot successfully oppose a determined great power unless it
has the support of another great power. This does not mean that the world
of states is merely an arena for a survival of the fittest, an all in fight with no
holds barred. It all depends on which of the great powers is immediately
concerned. None of them is without reproach, but some have a much better
record than others. Some impose restraints upon themselves, and on the
whole respect the rights of weaker states. Others, and Soviet Russia is the
best contemporary example, ride rough shod over their neighbors whenever
they can get away with it.

The policies of the great powers are a manifestation of nationalism, since
each state is primarily concerned with the advancement of its own interests.
Sometimes the policies themselves are older than modern nationalism, e.g.,
British reliance on sea power, and the effect of the latter is to increase the
strength of the support which they receive from the population at large.
Along with national policies goes a varying support of internationalism, exemplified by the attitude which each state follows in the United Nations.
Sometimes the internationalism is carried to a point where it is allowed to
interfere with national interests. At others, e.g., by discreet lobbying for
votes, the United Nations itself is made to serve as an instrument for carrying
out the national policies of some of its members.

SELECTED READING

Atlantic Alliance: N.A.T.O.'s Role in the Free World. New York: Royal Institute
    of International Affairs, 1952.
BUTLER, HAROLD, *The Lost Peace.* New York: Harcourt, Brace and Company, 1942.
FULLER, MAJOR GENERAL J. F. C., *Second World War, 1939–1945.* New York: Duell,
    Sloan and Pearce, 1949.
GATHORNE-HARDY, G. M., *Short History of International Affairs, 1920–1939,* 4th ed.
    New York: Oxford Press, 1950.
LANGER, WILLIAM L., *European Alliances and Alignments, 1871–1890.* New York:
    Alfred A. Knopf, 1931.
MANSERGH, NICHOLAS, *The Coming of the First World War, A Study in the Euro-
    pean Balance 1878–1914.* London: Longmans, Green and Company, 1949.

MIDDLETON, DREW, *Defence of Western Europe*. London: Muller, 1952.

MORGENTHAU, HANS J., *Politics Among Nations: The Struggle for Power and Peace*. New York: Alfred A. Knopf, 1948.

MOWAT, R. B., *The Concert of Europe*. London: Macmillan and Company, Ltd., 1930.

NAMIER, L. B., *Diplomatic Prelude 1938–1939*. New York: The Macmillan Company, 1948.

———, *Europe in Decay, A Study in Disintegration 1936–1940*. London: Macmillan and Company, Ltd., 1950.

———, *Facing East*. New York: Harper and Brothers, 1948.

REITZEL, WILLIAM, *The Mediterranean*. New York: Harcourt, Brace and Company, 1950.

SCHMITT, BERNADOTTE E., *The Coming of the War. 1914*. New York: Charles Scribner's Sons, 1930.

———, *Triple Alliance and Triple Entente*. New York: Henry Holt and Company, 1934.

SCHWARZENBERGER, GEORG, *Power Politics: A Study of International Society*. New York: Praeger, 1952.

TOYNBEE, ARNOLD J., *et al.*, *Survey of International Affairs*. London and New York: Oxford Press, 1920 *et seq*.

WARD, BARBARA, *Policy for the West*. New York: W. W. Norton and Company, 1951.

———, *The West At Bay*. London: Allen and Unwin, Ltd., 1948.

WHEELER-BENNETT, JOHN W., *Munich: Prologue to Tragedy*. London: Macmillan and Company, Ltd., 1948.

WIGHT, MARTIN, *Power Politics*. London: Royal Institute of International Affairs, 1946.

WILMOT, CHESTER, *The Struggle for Europe*. New York: Harper and Brothers, 1952.

There are excellent articles in *Foreign Affairs,* New York, and *International Affairs,* Royal Institute of International Affairs, London. Consult also the Foreign Policy Association's *Headline Series.* For specific areas consult the *Far Eastern Survey* and *Pacific Affairs,* New York, *The Middle East Journal,* Washington, D.C., and the *Round Table Quarterly,* London (for the British Empire).

CHAPTER 17

THE UNITED STATES

TRADITIONAL POLICIES

The policies of isolation and the Monroe Doctrine were well suited to the conditions of the nineteenth century. The obvious national interest was to settle half a continent and develop its resources. Here the United States was peculiarly favored by geography and the political conditions of the times. Its predominance in the Western Hemisphere was assured, for no other state in North or South America had comparable natural resources and the hope of evolving into a great power. The United States could determine its course of action without too much consideration for the reactions of its neighbors. The contrast with contemporary Europe was striking where there were six powers of roughly equal strength. None of them could embark on any policy without first calculating its effect upon the others. The balance of power policy was as inevitable in Europe as it would have been out of place in the Western Hemisphere.

The protection afforded by the Atlantic and Pacific Oceans placed the United States almost beyond the reach of invasion prior to the invention of long-range airplanes and guided missiles. Coupled with the absence of a rival great power in the Western Hemisphere, this gave America the immunity from attack that was enjoyed to a much lesser degree by the British Isles. The principal difference was that since the ocean was so much wider than the English Channel the sense of isolation was proportionately greater. The final factor in American nineteenth-century security was the domination of all the oceans of the world by the British navy. After the destruction of the French and Spanish fleets at the Battle of Trafalgar in 1805 its supremacy was unchallenged until the building of the German navy in the early twentieth century. Land wars could occur in Europe, but they could not spread overseas unless Great Britain allowed it. To permit them to do so was contrary to the interests of Britain as a manufacturing and trading nation. There were a good many intra-European and colonial wars in the nineteenth century, but there were no world wars. The Monroe Doctrine itself affords a good illustration of this British policy. In 1823 the Holy Alliance was considering the dispatch of a Franco-Spanish expedition to subdue the revolted Spanish colonies. Canning, the British foreign minister, suggested a joint Anglo-American veto of the policy. President Monroe preferred a single-handed declaration that the re-establishment of European control over any American colonies which had gained their independence would be contrary to the interests and peace of the United States. It was known, however, that if necessary Britain would assist in its enforcement. Altogether isolationism was the obvious and natural policy for the nineteenth century. That it persisted after the conditions which justified it had begun radically to change is another example of the time lag which often occurs before an obsolescent policy is brought up to date.

American Far Eastern policy was in marked contrast to the isolationism which was followed toward Europe. Interest in China was the result partly of trade which dated from the early nineteenth century, and also of the extensive activities of American missionaries there. The aims of American policy were to maintain equality of commercial opportunity and the territorial integrity of China. Carried to their logical conclusion they could have ended in active intervention, since they ran counter to the ambitions of some of the other powers, especially Russia and Japan. Until the present century the American government confined its support of the Open Door policy to diplomatic measures. Ultimately, however, the insistence that Japan abandon the fruits of her invasion of China was one reason for the attack on Pearl Harbor in 1941. Prior to that date the conquest of the Philippines during the Spanish American War of 1898 was the only exception to the rule that the advancement of American interests in the Far East was sought through diplomatic negotiations. Exaggerated hopes were entertained of the importance of Manila as a commercial base from which the United States could capture an ever larger share of the trade of the Orient.

THE UNITED STATES AND WORLD WAR I

The United States had held itself aloof from the years of heightening tension and crisis in Europe which preceded the outbreak of war in 1914. When the struggle began the desire to remain neutral was almost universal. At the same time various factors worked in favor of the Entente powers. Public opinion tended to sympathize with Britain and France because they were democracies, and to look on Germany with disfavor as an autocracy. The German violation of Belgian neutrality in 1914 made a deep impression, and there was a strong sentimental sympathy for France dating from the American Revolution. In the 1930's the belief became widespread that the United States had been brought into the war through the machinations of American bankers and munitions makers who had a financial interest in the victory of the Entente powers. American involvement in the war was also attributed to the skill with which the British conducted their propaganda. There was truth in both these explanations, but it was by no means the whole truth.

Far more important was the strong and growing anger at the unrestricted German submarine warfare, which cost many American lives. The British naval blockade of Germany aroused great indignation because it contravened the traditional policy of neutral rights of trade. The British, however, only interfered with property, while the Germans destroyed American lives. The actual *casus belli* in 1917 was the resumption of unrestricted submarine warfare. Combined with it was resentment at the conditions under which Germany offered to allow American ships to sail the seas unmolested. The effect was reinforced by the disclosure of Germany's attempt to persuade Mexico to attack the United States and reconquer her lost territory in Texas, New Mexico, and Arizona. A final cause of American entry into the war was that a small but influential group realized the extent to which the British navy had contributed to American security. It feared that if Germany won, her dominance of Europe would compel the United States to protect itself by arming on an unprecedented scale. "Unperceived by many Americans, the European balance of power is a political necessity which can alone sanction in the Western Hemisphere the continuance of an economic development unhandicapped by the burden of extensive armaments."

THE RETURN TO ISOLATIONISM

After 1918 there was a desire to return to prewar conditions and a failure to realize that this was impossible. Isolationist sentiment revived, and with it the old hostility to the close association with Europe which membership in the League of Nations would require. This aversion was heightened by the contrast between the idealistic aims set forth in President Wilson's wartime speeches and the actual terms of the peace settlement. Other causes of President Wilson's defeat were his failure to include any prominent Republicans in the delegation which he took to Versailles in 1919 and the personal animosity toward him of some of the Republican leaders. In spite of all this, the peace treaties and the League Covenant received a majority in the Senate, but not the two-thirds majority required for ratification. In 1921 separate peace treaties were signed with Germany, Austria, Hungary, and Turkey. The Republican administrations at first ignored the League of Nations, but after 1925 cooperated in its humanitarian activities such as the suppression of the international trade in opium. Owing to the opposition of the isolationists, the United States did not join the Permanent Court of International Justice.

By the negative policy of abstention the United States helped to make impossible the establishment of an assured peace in Europe.

THE GOOD NEIGHBOR POLICY

For many years there had been hostility in Latin America to the policy of the United States, and particularly to the armed interventions in the Caribbean republics carried out under the Roosevelt Corollary, the early twentieth-century interpretation of the Monroe Doctrine. This was resented as an implied protectorate which the United States had proclaimed by its own single-handed action. There were many allusions to "Yankee imperialism" and domination by the "Colossus of the North." President Hoover adopted a conciliatory policy toward the Latin American republics, and by publishing the Clark Memorandum disavowed the Roosevelt Corollary. President Franklin D. Roosevelt went much further and laid down the "Good Neighbor Policy." In 1933 he announced that from then onward the United States was opposed to armed intervention, and by the end of 1934 there were no more American troops in any Latin American state. A resolution was adopted at the Montevideo Conference of American republics and approved by the United States in 1934 that "no state has a right to intervene in the internal or external affairs of another." A treaty with Cuba in 1934 terminated the American legal right of intervention under the Platt Amendment of 1901.

In 1938 the President took a further important step in continentalizing or internationalizing the Monroe Doctrine. Hitherto it had owed its validity to the sole action of the United States. By the declaration adopted at the Lima Conference of 1938 the American republics reaffirmed their intention to consult with one another concerning any threats to the peace or territorial integrity of the states of the Western Hemisphere. This meant in effect that if any European power attempted conquest in North or South America, it would meet with joint opposition. Hemispheric defense was no longer the sole task of the United States: it became a joint responsibility of twenty-one equal American partners. When World War II began in 1939, the foreign ministers of the American republics met at Panama and declared their neutrality. The effects of the Good Neighbor policy showed themselves after Pearl Harbor. The United States called a meeting of the foreign ministers at Rio de Janeiro in January 1942. They stated that an act of aggression against one of them was equivalent to an attack upon all, and recommended that American states break off diplomatic relations with the Axis powers. By January, 1943, all except Argentina had either done this or else declared war on the Axis countries.

INTER-AMERICAN ORGANIZATION

The states of the Western Hemisphere are far too jealous of their sovereignty to consider any form of federal union, though gradually they are increasing their degree of cooperation. Linguistically and culturally the Latin Americans are far closer to Spain and France than they are to the United States. Then, too, the export trade of most of the Spanish American republics is principally with Europe. Apart from coffee and some raw materials their products are competitive and not complementary with those of the United States. This restricts exports, and so in turn limits their capacity to import American manufactures. Canada, too, as a member of the British Commonwealth has traditionally held aloof from the Pan-American system. The first conference of American states was held at Washington in 1889, but little was accomplished because of the Latin American distrust of the United States. The conference, however, created the Organization of American States with a headquarters at Washington known as the Pan-American Union. Later conferences were held at irregular intervals. One of the most important accomplishments was an agreement that all disputes not settled diplomatically would be brought before permanent commissions of investigation and conciliation, and juridical conflicts would be submitted to arbitration.

The machinery of the Organization of American States was revised at the ninth conference at Bogotá in 1948. The charter states that the Organization is a regional agency within the United Nations, and that its functions are to strengthen the peace and security of the continent, provide means of pacific settlement of disputes and of common action against aggression, and promote cooperative solutions of American problems. Every five years the member states are to hold a conference to decide general policy and consider matters affecting friendly relations between them. The organ of consultation is the meeting of the foreign ministers of the American republics. It may come together at any time to discuss any question of importance. The Council, composed of one representative from each of the twenty-one member states, is the executive committee of the Organization. It has many duties, among them the drafting of recommendations for submission to the various conferences, and acting as an interim organ of consultation before the foreign ministers take over in case of a threat to the peace. The Council supervises the Pan-American Union in Washington, which is the general secretariat of the whole Organization.

Wartime cooperation culminated in the adoption of the Act of Chapultepec in 1945. It declared that every attack on the territory, sovereignty or political independence of an American state would be considered an act of aggression against all. If this occurred, there would be mutual consultation, and each of the signatories promised to help in meeting the attack. The act did not provide a specific guarantee of military assistance in case of its violation; and the only clear obligations were consultation and unspecified aid. Two years later the solidarity of the hemisphere was carried further by the Inter-American Treaty of Reciprocal Assistance, which was signed at Rio de Janeiro in 1947. The signatories agreed to submit every controversy that might arise among them to peaceful settlement within the inter-American system before referring it to the U.N. They repeated the promise of assistance in case of attack given in the Act of Chapultepec, and defined the area to which this obligation applied as including the whole of North and South America and Greenland. The foreign ministers would determine what help should be given. If the decision were supported by representatives of two thirds of the signatories, it was binding upon all, with the important exception that no state could be required to use armed force without its consent.

PEACE BY NEUTRALITY

The growing tension in Europe in the 1930's aroused fears that the United States would become involved in a European war as it had been in 1812 and 1917. It was assumed that America was drawn in by the activities of munitions makers and bankers. Public acceptance of this explanation was strengthened by the investigation of the munitions industry in 1934–1936 by a Senate committee headed by Senator Nye of North Dakota. It revealed that among other practices armaments firms had sold arms to both sides in a war, stimulated armaments races, organized lobbies to frustrate disarmament conferences, and made agreements with foreign competitors for the division of markets. The remedy seemed to be to abandon trade with the belligerents and give up the traditional demands for neutral rights of trade and freedom of the seas. The practical difficulty was that a modern war requires not only munitions but also such a variety of raw materials and foodstuffs as to cover almost every article of commerce. Completely to insulate the United States would have meant the abandonment of virtually the whole of its foreign trade. This would have had a disastrous effect upon important groups such as cotton growers and wheat farmers. It was agreed that the embargo should be confined to armaments and not include raw materials.

Italy's attack on Ethiopia led to the passage of the first Neutrality Act in August 1935. It was renewed in February 1936 with the addition that loans to belligerents were forbidden. The law did not apply to civil wars, and when Franco revolted, it was legal to supply arms to the Spanish government. When Congress convened in January, 1937, it promptly complied with the President's wishes by authorizing him to lay an embargo on loans and the shipment of munitions to either side. In May, 1937, a permanent act replaced the former temporary legislation. It applied to civil as well as foreign wars, forbade loans, and required that the shipment of munitions but not raw materials be forbidden. No Americans were allowed to travel on belligerent ships, and the arming of American merchant vessels was prohibited. The President was given discretionary authority to place trade in commodities other than munitions on a cash and carry basis. They could be exported to belligerents provided that the purchaser obtained full legal title before they left the United States, and if they were not carried in American ships. Congress had drawn up the law with Europe in mind, but three months later Japan began an undeclared war against China. To apply the cash and carry clauses would help the Japanese who had a merchant marine and harm the Chinese who had not. The President used his discretionary authority and did not proclaim that a state of war existed. When war was declared in September, 1939, the President issued a proclamation of neutrality which imposed an embargo on the sale of munitions to all the belligerents alike.

Americans in general desired two incompatibles—Allied victory and American neutrality. On September 21 President Roosevelt summoned a special session of Congress for revision of the neutrality legislation. The isolationists opposed all change, but eventually the Neutrality Act of 1939 was passed which allowed the export of all commodities including munitions to any belligerent on the basis of cash and carry. The act forbade loans to belligerents, American travel on belligerent ships, and the arming of American merchantmen. It allowed the President to proclaim combat zones into which American ships, aircraft and citizens could not go. As Hitler overran one neutral country after another in the spring of 1940, the President extended the combat zones until finally American shipping was banned from the North Atlantic. As long as Britain and France had money, they could buy all they needed, but what would happen if they exhausted their dollar exchange and were in danger of defeat?

BELLIGERENT NEUTRALITY

American public opinion favored the European democracies, since there was a growing feeling that they were friends while the Axis powers threatened United States interests. The fall of France was a totally unexpected shock, and the imminent peril to Great Britain aroused strong apprehension of the danger to the United States if the British navy were captured by Germany. William Allen White's "Committee to Defend America by Aiding the Allies" rapidly increased in membership, and had much influence in arousing public opinion and exerting pressure on Congress. The isolationists organized "America First, Inc." and conducted a vigorous counteroffensive. During 1940 Congress authorized the expenditure of $12 billion for defense, and in

September peacetime conscription was introduced for the first time in American history. By the President's order half the new production of arms was allotted to Great Britain. In August fifty over-age American destroyers were transferred to Britain, and the United States received ninety-nine year leases of naval and air bases in Newfoundland, Bermuda, and various West Indian islands. Thanks to the interwar naval disarmament policy Britain very badly needed the destroyers. The transfer of the bases greatly increased American security, since in years gone by they had been the stepping stones by which the United States could be attacked from Europe.

Up to November, 1940, Britain had paid for everything received from the United States to a total amount of about $5 billion but she had only $2 billion left. The need for American supplies was rapidly expanding, but the cash and carry clauses would soon put an end to Britain's purchases. The Neutrality Act forbade her to float American loans, and even if she had been able to do this, it would have meant a repetition of the war debts problem that followed World War I. President Roosevelt's solution was the Lend-Lease Act, which became law in March, 1941. It gave the President emergency authority to make the United States the "arsenal of democracy." He could manufacture and "sell, transfer, exchange, lease, lend or otherwise dispose of" any defense articles to the government of any country the defense of which he deemed vital to the safety of the United States. The following month the United States obtained bases in Greenland, and in July American troops took over the defense of Iceland. In May the President proclaimed an "unlimited national emergency" which required that the defenses be put in a state of readiness to repel any acts of aggression against the Western Hemisphere. When Hitler invaded Russia in June, Lend Lease was extended to the U.S.S.R. Several American merchant ships were sunk, and naval escorts began protecting convoys of shipping. In November Congress authorized the arming of American merchantmen and their sailing to ports of belligerent nations. Step by step the dictates of American security were driving the country closer to war.

Hitler was anxious to avoid war with the United States as long as possible, being already fairly fully engaged with Great Britain and Russia. Japan was his ally however, and in 1941 Japanese-American relations were approaching a crisis. Japan would have been glad to avoid war with the United States if she could have got what she wanted without opposition. The United States could not accept Japan's dominant position in China without abandoning the whole of its traditional Far Eastern policy. Equally it could not afford to let Japan take Southeast Asia because the loss to Great Britain would have been so serious that it would have gravely increased the danger of a German victory in Europe. So Japan attacked at Pearl Harbor, and Hitler declared war because he believed that Japan's alliance was essential to his victory.

RUSSIA AND THE WEST

Wartime cooperation between the United States and Britain was close and on the whole cordial, while with Russia it was at arm's length. Nevertheless, it was reasonably effective, and there were high hopes that it would continue after the war. Nothing could so effectively ensure peace, for no aggressor would dare to challenge a combination of the United States, Russia, and the British Commonwealth. Along with this there was an enormous fund of good will and some uncritical admiration for Russia among the Western powers. Not till later did they come to realize that it was only Hitler's attack which had driven Russia over to their side, and that the events of the war had put her in a position where she could be a threat to the free world and to Europe in particular. The war destroyed the balance of power in Europe through the weakening of France and Britain and the complete overthrow of Germany. It left a colossal power, Russia, who had extended her control over the whole eastern half of the continent. In considerable measure this was unavoidable, but the decisions reached at the wartime conferences aggravated the situation.

Geography dictated that the Russian attack on the Axis would be made in eastern Europe, and that of the United States and Britain in the west. Nothing could have prevented the Red armies from occupying eastern Europe in 1945. This was the prerequisite for establishing the satellite states, for no Communist dictatorship gained power unless the country had first been "liberated" by Russia. The one exception was the victory of Tito's Communist-controlled Partisans in Yugoslavia. If Churchill's proposal to send an Anglo-American army from Italy into central Europe had been adopted at the Teheran Conference in 1943, Russia could not have attained her present position of dominance in that part of the continent. It was rejected, and by the time the Yalta Conference convened in February, 1945, the fate of eastern and central Europe had already been settled. At this meeting President Roosevelt, Stalin, and Churchill signed an agreement that the three governments would cooperate in assisting the peoples of eastern and central Europe "to create democratic institutions of their own choice." The weak point in this formula was that Russia and the Western powers attached diametrically opposite meanings to the word "democratic." Stalin went ahead with his plans to bring the whole area under his permanent control by assisting Communist dictatorships to seize power. American and British protests were ignored since no Western troops were on the spot to lend weight to their remonstrances.

FROM ONE WORLD TO TWO

The lessons of the war had decisively weakened American isolationism, and there was acceptance of the fact that the country must assume leadership in world affairs. The Senate ratified American membership in the United Nations by an overwhelming majority. But participation was expected to consist of nothing more than collaboration with like-minded nations. The Axis aggressors had been overthrown and power politics, imperialism, and the balance of power policy were ended. Russia was peace loving and wanted nothing save security against another German attack. Armaments were unnecessary, there was a clamor to "bring the boys home," and along with Great Britain the United States embarked upon a policy of singlehanded disarmament.

The awakening came fairly quickly, and no small part of the credit for it belongs to Moscow. Lord Vansittart described its diplomatic manners as "the style of an aggressive drunk." If the Kremlin had been less abusive in its language and more conciliatory in its actions, the United States would have been a good deal slower to appraise the situation realistically. One concession after another was made at the postwar conferences by the American and British governments, but they failed to evoke a corresponding willingness to compromise. Rather they stimulated the Kremlin to advance fresh demands. A lavish use of the veto began to reduce the U.N. to impotence. The Yalta Agreement was broken, and ten European states became a Soviet sphere of influence, while Finland retained a precarious semi-independence. The Potsdam Agreement was not carried out, and Russia began to make her zone of Germany another satellite state. By 1947 it was clear that the hope of one world was gone, and that the Russian bloc was engaged in an offensive against the West, with the Communist party in each country as its local fifth column. The overthrow of the Czech democracy in 1948 was a violent shock and a warning to the Western powers. Probably it did more than any other single event, except the Korean war, to draw the West together in self-defense. Participation in world affairs had become a necessity for sheer national security, and this meant that American economic and if necessary military power must be thrown into the scales of world affairs. This was power politics, and it required too that a global balance of power must be recreated as a counterpoise to the strength of the Soviet bloc.

THE TRUMAN DOCTRINE

The American government's reply to Russian imperialism was containment. It accepted that communism regarded capitalism as an irreconcilable enemy which it intended to overthrow after it had gone far toward destroying itself through its own greed and stupidity. Until that propitious time arrived the main purpose of Soviet policy was to defend and strengthen Russia. The Kremlin had great respect for material strength, and would not risk failure by hasty or premature action. It did not hesitate to retreat when confronted by superior force so long as its prestige, to which it was very sensitive, was not endangered. The main element in American policy must be "a long-term, patient but firm and vigilant containment of Russian expansive tendencies." Soviet encroachments on the Western world could be "contained by the adroit and vigilant application of counterforce at a series of constantly shifting geographical and political points, corresponding to the shifts and maneuvers of Soviet policy . . . a duel of infinite duration."

The first occasion for the exercise of this policy was in Greece and Turkey, which occupy a position of great strategic importance in the eastern Mediterranean. Crete and the Greek islands in the Aegean Sea threatened the Mediterranean sea route, as Germany had shown in World War II. In Soviet hands they would also be a first line of defense against a Western navy steaming toward the Dardanelles. Turkey meant not only control of the straits that led from the Black Sea to the Mediterranean, but also a base from which warships and aircraft could threaten the Mediterranean-Suez Canal sea route. Russia's legitimate interests had been safeguarded by the Montreux Convention of 1936, but this did not give the complete control sought by the Soviet government, which followed its tsarist predecessor in this desire. The convention gave merchant ships free passage through the straits in peace and war when Turkey was neutral. When it was a belligerent, freedom of passage was restricted to neutral merchantmen. Warships of Black Sea powers such as Russia could pass freely in time of peace, while non-Black Sea powers could send only 15,000 tons of warships at one time into the Black Sea. During war the warships of belligerents could not pass through the straits. What Russia wanted was that her warships should have free passage both in peace and war, and that non-Black Sea powers should never be allowed to send warships into the Black Sea. Russian troops and aircraft must also be stationed in Turkey to "protect" its "independence." Turkey refused in 1945 to become a satellite state, and Russia began a war of nerves to wear down its resistance. The Turks regarded the Russians as hereditary enemies, and were fatalistically determined to go down fighting but not to surrender. They were first-class soldiers, but from lack of revenue the army was poorly supplied with modern equipment. Great Britain had been arming them as far as her straitened financial resources allowed, partly because of the Anglo-Turkish alliance of 1939 and partly because the traditional British policy was to keep Russia out of the Mediterranean.

Greece and Britain had been friends for 120 years, and when the Greek government-in-exile returned to Athens in 1944 after the German withdrawal its microscopic army was accompanied by a small British force. Opposition came from EAM—the National Liberation Front—a coalition of leftist parties which was dominated by the Communists and had its own party army named Elas. It tried to seize power by force in December, 1944, and was defeated by the Greek and British troops. Elections were held in 1946 which were watched by American, British, and French observers, who reported that the voting was as free from intimidation as could reasonably be expected in a country whose political passions ran so high. The royalist party obtained a majority, and the king was brought back from exile after a plebiscite in which 65 percent of the electorate voted for his return. In the autumn of 1946 the Communists, who numbered perhaps 15 percent of the population, started a guerilla-type civil war which lasted until 1949. In addition to the cost of creating an army, the government had a colossal task of economic reconstruction, since the Germans had laid waste the country with particular thoroughness. Great Britain gave economic assistance as well as military equipment.

In 1947 the British informed the American government that it could not afford the cost of continued help to Greece and Turkey. This meant that in all likelihood the Communists would win control of Greece, since they were being assisted by Yugoslavia, Bulgaria, and Albania; and the threat to Turkey would be increased. The strategic importance of Greece and Turkey was so far reaching that their conversion into Communist states would mean a dangerous shift of power from the West to Russia, and this was not in American interests.

This consideration moved President Truman in March, 1947, to deliver the message to Congress in which he laid down the Truman Doctrine. He asked that $400 million be appropriated for economic and military aid to Greece and Turkey, and that military missions be sent to train their forces. He justified the demand on the ground that "one of the primary objectives of the foreign policy of the United States is the creation of conditions in which we and other nations will be able to work out a way of life free from coercion. . . . We shall not realize our objectives however unless we are willing to help free people to maintain their free institutions. . . . I believe that it must be the foreign policy of the United States to support free peoples who are resisting attempted subjugation by armed minorities or by outside pressure. . . ."

With American help the Greek army was enlarged and equipped. In 1949 the Communists ended the war, partly because of a very heavy military defeat and in part because Tito, who had now broken with Russia, stopped giving them further help. The United States has made remarkable progress in economic reconstruction in Greece and is trying permanently to raise the standard of living through industrialization and improved agriculture. The building of American airfields in 1954 extended the network of bases that covers all of Western Europe. In Turkey the armed forces have been greatly improved, and airfields, military roads, and a military and naval base at the seaport of Alexandretta have been built.

EUROPE ON THE VERGE

In 1945 it was realized that substantial gifts and loans were needed to relieve destitution and assist economic reconstruction in Western Europe; but there was a grave underestimate of the extent of the injury that the war had done. Between 1945 and the commencement of Marshall aid the United States lent or gave the countries of Western Europe help to the value of $9,526,000,000, and Great Britain contributed something less than $3 billion. During 1947 Britain came to the end of her dollar resources and was compelled to curtail drastically her help to foreign nations. The most disheartening aspect of the whole problem was that the situation was worse in 1947 than it had been in 1945. The position in France was typical, and with local variations the following account would have applied to many other countries of Western Europe. There was a scarcity of all the things that were normally considered essential. Especially in the towns the food that could be obtained on the official ration cards was often so inadequate that it was necessary to pay the extortionate prices of the black market. The scarcity was worsened by the phenomenally bad harvests of 1945 and 1946. For most people their prewar stocks of clothes, shoes, and household linen were worn out. Replacements were hard to find and very expensive. Houses damaged or destroyed numbered 1,236,000. It was often impossible not only to obtain materials to rebuild but also to get the materials to make a building weathertight. In addition, buildings could not be adequately heated because of the scarcity of coal. As well as the immediate needs, there was the long-term problem of restoring productive capacity. One reason for the lack of food was that no fertilizer had been available since 1940, and the flocks and herds had been reduced to feed the Germans. To remove the scarcity of consumer goods the factories must sometimes be rebuilt, or supplied with machinery, and they must also have coal and raw materials. It was exceedingly difficult to move freight because of the breakdown of communications. Apart from the scarcity of rolling stock, bombing attacks had destroyed bridges, canal locks, freight yards, and harbor works.

To a large extent the scarcity was due to causes beyond the control of the European governments. What they needed did not exist inside their own territories. They had to be imported from overseas, a great part of them from dollar countries, and the money to pay for them was lacking. In 1947 France, for example, needed $100 million a month of imports, but her exports were only $10 million a month because of the fall in production. The deficit was covered partly by American aid, and in part by using up two thirds of the reserves of gold and foreign exchange. For Europe the adverse balance of trade was over \$4 billion in 1946 and over \$5.5 billion in 1947. The Communists were zealous to point out every governmental sin of omission and commission, plus a good few that existed in their own imaginations. They drew the moral that democracy naturally meant inefficiency and exploitation, while these things were better managed in the workers' paradise. Men who were under-fed, ill clad, and cold were not overly critical, especially when things were going from bad to worse. The feeling was growing that a Communist dictator could not make things any worse and might do better than the democratic governments. An American observer wrote that "The whole continent re-mains debatable ground for ideas and ideologies. The old ideas of the French Revolution have not regained possession of the heart and mind of Europe, and the new principles of Lenin and Stalin have not established themselves in their stead. . . . You cannot eat either *Das Kapital* or the Declaration of the Rights of Man." There was a real danger that Western Europe might go Com-munist, not from ideological conviction but from growing "fedupness" with economic distress.

Altogether apart from humanitarian considerations, it was not in Amer-ican interests that Western Europe should be added to the Soviet bloc. The world has two developed and one potential workshop—the United States, Western Europe taken as a whole, and the Soviet bloc. A developed workshop is one where industry, agriculture, mining, sea, land, and air transportation, and banking are fully developed, and the population has a high degree of technical skill, as in the United States. A potential workshop is one where all these foundations of material power are in the early stages of development— like the United States a couple of generations ago, to use a very rough analogy. An indication of development and degree of power lies in the output of steel, since steel factories are potential war plants. In 1947 American heavy industry could produce about 90 million tons of steel a year, while that of the Soviet bloc would be about 35 million tons when the current five-year plan was completed. The European production of 1947 was far less than in 1938, when it had been 50.4 million tons of steel. Ultimately the war damage would be repaired, and then the output would be at least as large as in 1938. If European output were allied with American production, the power ratio would be 140 million tons against the Communist 35 million, and the global balance of power would be tilted very comfortably in favor of the West. (In 1953 the United States produced 101 million metric tons of steel and west-ern Europe 58 million, making a total of 159 million as compared with 47 mil-lion for the Soviet bloc.) But if Western Europe went Communist, then the ratio would be 90 million tons American *versus* 85 million tons Russian-controlled. The balance would be so nearly even that World War III would become an imminent possibility—especially when one considers that a dictatorship can devote much more of its steel to military purposes than a democracy. If a democracy drastically reduces the output of such items as automobiles and refrigerators to increase armaments, there are such vehement protests that the government is very likely to give in to the public demand. A dictator phones orders to the chief of his secret police, the population of the concentration camps is notably increased, and quiet is restored on the home front. The Marshall Plan was a generous and idealistic attempt to relieve distress, but it was also an outstanding example of enlightened self-interest.

THE MARSHALL PLAN

On June 5, 1947, General George C. Marshall, Secretary of State, outlined his government's plan in a speech at Harvard University. He said that "Our policy is directed not against any country or doctrine but against hunger, poverty, desperation and chaos"; and he offered help to the Soviet states as well as those of free Europe. Marshall emphasized the need to "provide a cure rather than a mere palliative." Short-term charity would relieve immediate want, but in the long run would leave the European recipient no better off than when it began. The purpose was to rebuild the productive capacity of Europe so that it would again be able to provide for its own needs and would not require further assistance. This meant more than merely restoring the prewar volume of output. It must be increased since the population was larger than in 1939. Europe must be able to produce enough to satisfy the needs of its postwar population, and in addition to manufacture sufficient exports to pay for its imports. Marshall asked the nations of Europe to draw up a statement of their needs so that the United States might consider how much help it should give.

The British, French, and Russian foreign ministers met in Paris on June 27, and Molotov condemned the offer as an imperialistic threat to the economic independence of Europe. Czechoslovakia which had wistfully eyed the American siren was ordered to remove itself from temptation. The Soviet bloc refused to participate, but sixteen nations of Western Europe met on July 12 to draw up a list of their needs for the next four years. They were Great Britain, France, Austria, Belgium, Denmark, Eire, the Netherlands, Greece, Iceland, Italy, Luxembourg, Norway, Portugal, Sweden, Switzerland and Turkey, and they were later joined by Trieste and Western Germany. In September the conference requested $22.4 billion of American aid. This amount was reduced by President Truman's advisers and Congress. The Marshall Plan, later renamed the European Recovery Program, or ERP, provided a net amount of $14,007,000,000 by the end of 1951, when the emphasis was changed from economic to military assistance.

The Foreign Assistance Act of 1948 created the Economic Cooperation

Administration or ECA to administer the aid. Very wide discretionary power was vested in it, though Congress exercised some control through a joint committee of senators and representatives and the debates on appropriations. The United States agreed to give or in some cases lend money to each European government, which would buy commodities through private channels of trade and sell them to its citizens, receiving local currency which was paid into a counterpart fund. Five percent of the latter was reserved for the American government, e.g., to purchase strategic raw materials. The remaining 95 percent was for the use of the European government, but could be spent only with the approval of the ECA. The counterpart funds were used to reduce domestic debts, rebuild railways, improve public health, etc. ECA delegated much of the task of allocating funds to the Organization for European Economic Cooperation (OEEC), an association of the eighteen Marshall Plan nations. It was placed on a permanent basis in 1948 by a treaty which gave it a governing body. The members agreed to reduce trade barriers, stabilize currencies, and continue the OEEC after the expiration of Marshall aid. ERP deserves a major share of the credit for halting the further expansion of Russian influence in Western Europe. The best recruiting ground for communism is hunger and want, and in these respects there was a notable improvement. Taking the 1938 output as 100, in 1954 the agricultural production of the ERP countries was 120 and their industrial production over 150. There was a considerable increase in foreign trade, though most of this was between the countries of Europe. The hope that the European economies would become self-supporting was not realized. Marshall aid very considerably lessened the adverse balance of trade of the ERP countries with the United States, but it did not wipe out the "dollar gap" as had been hoped. Restrictions on imports from the dollar area have been relaxed, but how to balance accounts between Western Europe and the United States continues to be one of the most intractable problems of world trade.

THE MUTUAL SECURITY PROGRAM

The purpose of the Marshall Plan was purely economic, but since 1950 the American and European governments have embarked on an intensified program of rearmament. The Korean war in 1950 brought home the dangerous weakness of the Western powers in armed strength. Productivity in the ERP countries was making a remarkable recovery, but it had not reached the point where it could provide for a heavy armaments program in addition to manufacturing for peacetime purposes. The volume of exports was insufficient to pay for the increased quantity of imports, swollen by military raw materials. The munitions needed could only be obtained by diverting factories from peacetime production. There was the danger that rearmament might bring back the conditions of scarcity and discontent which had existed in 1947, and which the Marshall Plan had been introduced to remove. There was no sense in bolting the front door against communism, and at the same time giving it entrance by the back. The remedy lay in a revival of military lend lease. Just as in World War II, Western Europe was America's first line of defense, and it was in her interests to have well-armed and politically reliable allies.

From 1950 onward economic aid under ERP declined, and military assistance grew. Originally it had been intended that ECA should continue until June 30, 1952; but it was terminated on December 31, 1951, and replaced by the Mutual Security Agency (MSA). This agency took over the economic programs of the ECA in addition to co-ordinating the military aid to foreign countries. By far the heaviest expenditure for military and economic aid was made in Europe. Moderate amounts were allotted to Chiang Kai-shek's regime, and French Indochina received an increasing amount of military equipment. The military assistance included armaments and raw materials, technical and training assistance, and machine tools.

A MSA report for 1951 gave a note of warning:

The defense build up undertaken by the European members of N.A.T.O. has produced signs of strain. Inflation since the outbreak of hostilities in Korea, twice as great as that suffered in this country, represents a danger signal which cannot be ignored. Western Europe is like a sick man who has only recently arisen from his bed. A threat to his very survival has forced him to assume heavy burdens after a very brief period of convalescence. The situation is so dangerous that he has no alternative than to do everything he possibly can. At the same time there will be little advantage to him if the burdens he takes on are so heavy as to cause a total relapse.

The economic and financial strain proved to be too great, and in 1952 Britain and the other European states announced that the rearmament program would have to be spread out over a longer period of time than originally contemplated. Another reason for the change of plan was the general belief, shared by the American government, that the threat of attack was not an imminent one, to meet which the strongest possible defense must be prepared quickly regardless of consequences. Rather it was a danger which would hang over the West for years to come, so that the problem of defense was a long-term and not a short-run affair. By 1954 defense expenditures for the European members of NATO were leveling off at about $11 billion a year, roughly twice the amount spent prior to the Korean war.

During the decade from the end of World War II to the middle of 1955 the net amount given by the United States in grants and loans was $49,711,-000,000. Nearly 80 percent of this was in grants for which repayment was not required. Of the total sum, $35,055,000,000 was economic and $14,576,000,000 military aid. By far the larger part of the former was given between 1945 and 1951; after that period economic help declined rapidly while military aid sharply increased. The distribution of the aid showed the much greater emphasis placed by American policy on Europe than on the rest of the world. Western Europe received approximately $25.1 billion in economic and $9.8 billion in military aid, or 70 percent of the total. Asia and Africa received roughly $7 billion in economic and $4.6 billion in aid which was primarily military though in some cases it would assist economic development, or 23 percent of the total. Latin America's share was about 2 percent. Since 1951 Europe has received only a small and declining amount of economic aid, and since 1953 the appropriations for military aid have been tapering off.

During the same period economic and military aid to Asia has been increasing. In 1954–1955 only about 25 percent of the total appropriation went to Europe and 72 percent to Asia and Africa. The same trend was evident in President Eisenhower's request to Congress for 1955–1956. He asked for $3,530,000,000, of which 60 percent was to be spent on the free Asian nations from the Middle East to Japan. The change in emphasis was not due to loss of interest in Europe. There the national economies had recovered to the extent that only limited help was needed, and also the danger from Russia had lessened. In Asia, however, the outcome of the cold war was still uncertain, and it was urgently necessary to counteract the threat of communism by improving the standard of living and strengthening the defenses.

THE NORTH ATLANTIC TREATY ORGANIZATION (NATO)

In 1948 the Senate by a vote of 64 to 4 accepted a resolution of Senator Vandenburg that the United States should progressively develop regional or other treaties for individual and collective self-defense. This was a far cry from traditional isolationism: for the first time in its history the nation was moving in time of peace toward a defensive alliance. The reasons were given by Secretary of State Acheson in 1951.

No nation including our own is strong enough to stand alone in the modern world. . . . We are dependent on other areas for many vital raw materials. The oceans which have shielded us in the past have dwindled to lakes in the sweep of modern technology. Even our unparalleled industrial establishment, mighty as it is, could not match the industrial power which would be levelled against us if a major part of the free world should be incorporated within the Soviet empire.

Diplomatic negotiations were begun, and the North Atlantic Treaty was signed and ratified in 1949. Originally it consisted of twelve nations—the United States, Canada, Great Britain, France, the Netherlands, Belgium, Luxembourg, Portugal, Iceland, Norway, Denmark, and Italy. In 1952 Greece and

Turkey were added, and the treaty's protection was extended to the Federal Republic of Germany. In 1955 Germany became the fifteenth member. Iceland and Norway were included because as World War II had shown they were of great strategic importance in the battle of the Atlantic. The same consideration applied to Portugal and its important possession the Azores in the center of the North Atlantic. In addition, there was the traditional alliance with Great Britain. Italy, Greece, and Turkey have much importance for the control of the Mediterranean.

The alliance, which was to last for twenty years, declared that an armed attack against one would be considered an attack against all. If it occurred, the allies would consult one another and each of them "will assist the Party or Parties so attacked by taking forthwith, individually and in concert with the other Parties, such action as it deems necessary, including the use of armed force, to restore and maintain the security of the North Atlantic area." Legally the treaty did not obligate the United States to go to war in case of an attack upon an ally, but merely to consult and take such action as the American government should deem necessary. This wording was adopted from fear that the Senate would refuse to ratify a treaty which expressly bound the United States to engage in hostilities, on the ground that it violated the constitutional allocation to Congress of the right to declare war. The treaty obligation might be discharged by providing, e.g., military equipment if the American government should decide that this was adequate to repel aggression. More likely than not, however, the "necessary" action would include the use of force, and the treaty imposed a moral obligation to go to war.

NATO is not a superstate for each government has retained its own sovereignty, and decisions have to be reached by mutual agreement. At the head of NATO is the North Atlantic Council. Each state is represented by cabinet ministers, together with a permanent delegate. Cabinet ministers usually attend two or three times a year, and the other meetings held continuously throughout the year in Paris are composed of the permanent representatives. The International Staff, headed by the secretary-general, prepares reports, sees that decisions of the Council are carried out and generally assists its work. The Council also controls a complicated system of committees, of which the principal is the Military Committee, composed of the chiefs of staff of the NATO countries. Its main responsibilities are to advise the Council on military matters: to develop plans for the unified defense of the North Atlantic area; and to provide general guidance to the Standing Group. The last is the permanent executive agency of the Military Committee. It meets in Washington and consists of special representatives of the American, French and British chiefs of staff. It is authorized to give guidance and instructions to the various NATO armed forces.

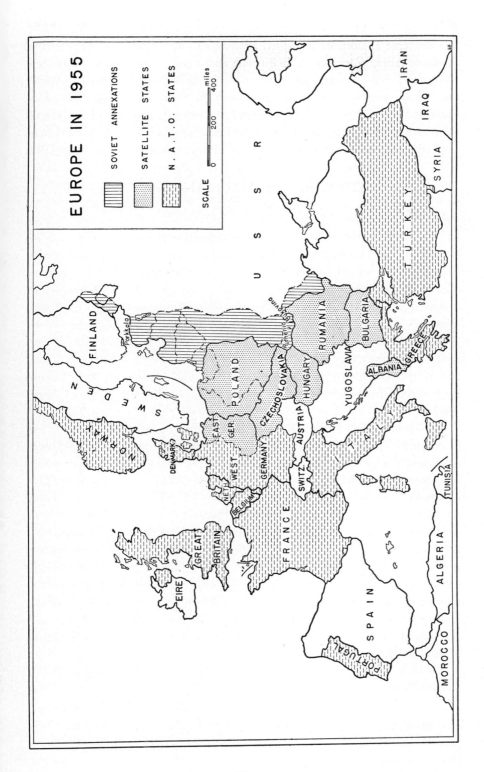

EUROPE IN 1955

SOVIET ANNEXATIONS

SATELLITE STATES

N.A.T.O. STATES

SCALE

miles
0   200   400

Supreme Headquarters, Allied Powers, Europe (SHAPE), includes the Supreme Allied Commander in Europe and a staff drawn from the armed forces of the NATO countries. It directs the integrated NATO forces in Western Europe, subject to orders received from the Standing Group. The forces controlled by SHAPE are contingents of national armies and air forces (American, British, Norwegian, etc.), which are ultimately controlled by their respective governments but have been placed under the command of SHAPE.

OTHER DEFENSIVE ARRANGEMENTS

Spain

Franco was the only fascist dictator to survive the war, and because of his ideology and his pro-Nazi attitude various penalties were imposed in the hope that they would lead to his overthrow. Spain was excluded from the United Nations and its specialized agencies, the members withdrew their ambassadors, and Marshall aid was refused. Franco flourished under this treatment, for it gained him the support of many Spaniards who opposed his regime, but became patriotically indignant at what they considered foreign interference in their domestic affairs. In 1950 the U.N. rescinded its resolutions against the presence of ambassadors in Madrid and on Spanish participation in the specialized agencies. In 1955 Spain was admitted to the United Nations.

American, British, and French military men urged the inclusion of Spain in NATO on strategic grounds. Her naval bases and airfields would have much importance in another Battle of the Atlantic: Gibraltar could only dominate the Atlantic exit from the Mediterranean if Spain were at least benevolently neutral: and the Pyrenees Mountains could be made one of the strongest defensive positions in Europe. Spanish soldiers had shown that they were excellent fighters, but their usefulness was immensely lessened by their lack of modern equipment. On the other hand, leftist political parties in the United States and Western Europe were bitterly opposed to any cooperation with fascism. The American solution was to negotiate a separate alliance in 1953 with Franco, the purpose of which was to make Spanish naval and air bases available for American forces. In return the United States has been supplying military equipment and also economic help of which Spain is very greatly in need.

Yugoslavia

Tito's exchange of a Soviet for a Western attachment is strictly a marriage of convenience. Tito prides himself on being a better Communist than Bulganin, and the similarity of his methods of government to those of Franco shows that the police state is the same whichever ideological label is attached to it. On the other hand, as long as Stalin lived, he was determined to destroy this audacious rebel if possible, and there were solid reasons why the West should intervene to prevent this. Tito's defection pushed Russia back from the Adriatic, isolated Albania and lessened its strategic value, and helped to bring about the defeat of the Communist rebellion in Greece. His successful defiance of the Kremlin might encourage Communists elsewhere, who like him were also nationalists, to go and do likewise. Finally, Tito's thirty odd divisions would at least pin down an equal number of satellite troops, and would fill the gap in the NATO defense that existed between Italy and Greece and Turkey. For all these reasons the United States, with some help from Britain, has given military equipment and economic help to Tito. The common danger drove Yugoslavia, Greece, and Turkey to sign a treaty of alliance in 1954.

The Far East

The United States has emphasized economic help and the creation of strong defenses in Europe more than in the Far East because Soviet control of the former was considered far more disastrous to the West than Communist success in the latter. China is still a potential workshop, and even when her plans for industrialization are carried out, it is doubtful whether her production will be comparable with that of Western Europe. Japan's steel production at its height in 1944 was only 14 million tons, but she is the most heavily industrialized state in Asia. Owing to this and her strategic position, a Communist victory there would make a most serious gap in the American trans-Pacific line of defense. Treaties provide for the maintenance of American troops in Japan and the re-creation of Japanese armed forces. There are alliances with the Philippines, Formosa, Australia, and New Zealand. In 1954 Washington took the lead in forming the Southeast Asia Treaty Organization (SEATO) for the defense of Southeast Asia.

The former Japanese mandate islands in the western Pacific—the Marianas, Marshalls and Carolines—have little economic value, but strategically they are part of the American defenses against an attack coming from Asia. After World War II there was strong pressure in the United States that the islands be annexed outright. This somewhat embarrassed the administration since the Atlantic Charter had committed the United States to the principle of no territorial annexations. A solution was found in placing the islands under a U.N. strategic trusteeship on terms drawn up by Washington. The United States has administrative, legislative, and judicial authority, and has power to establish naval and air bases and to recruit naval forces. While the U.N. has the right to supervise the administration of a trusteeship, Washington may forbid visits of inspection on the grounds of military security. Moreover, the islands are under the control of the Security Council where the United States has the veto power, and not of the Trusteeship Council where it has none.

The Arctic

The risk of air attack over the Arctic Circle has led to collaboration with Canada for mutual defense. The Danish colony of Greenland has an important role in these arrangements. American troops first occupied the island in 1941, and in 1951 the United States and Denmark signed a treaty for its

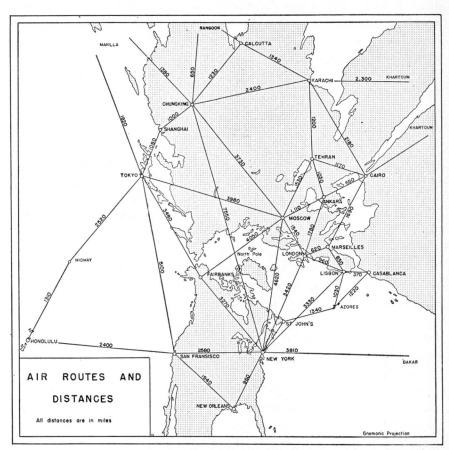

Based on the Great Circle Airways map by Richard Edes Harrison, Fortune *Magazine, May, 1943*

joint defense as long as NATO continues. The air bases in Greenland form part of the interceptive barrier against air attacks on North America. In the event of war the island would again as in World War II be of great importance as a relay station for planes on their way to Europe, as a naval base for warships guarding the North Atlantic shipping routes, and as a source of weather information.

A GLOBAL BALANCE OF POWER

The central fact of our age is the fall of Europe from the dominating position in world affairs which it occupied for several hundred years. The change began long before the present century with the growth in wealth and power of the United States. The much later development of Russia was another cause. The two world wars hastened a process which was in any event inevitable because of the extent to which they weakened the European combatants. Throughout modern history Europe consisted of a varying number of great powers of roughly equal strength, around which the second-rate powers tended to group themselves. The balance of power altered as the strength of the various states grew or declined, but it was always re-established. Since World War II power has shifted from the nations of Europe to the United States and Russia, one of which is an American and the other only a semi-European state. The strength of the two super powers is so superior to that of the rest that the former leading states of Europe have been reduced to the position of secondary powers. A balance of power no longer exists in Europe. Even if it were possible to combine the whole of free Europe into an effective alliance, it would not by itself be a match for Russia or the United States. The continent, however, is not a negligible factor: as one of the two developed workshops of the world it still plays a most important role in the world balance of power.

The overthrow of the Axis and the creation of the United Nations has not abolished the need for a balance of power as Cordell Hull expected. The idea in 1945 was that the peace-loving states, working through the U.N. and led by the United States, Britain and Russia would have such a predominance of power that they could overawe and if necessary crush an aggressor. In other words, the U.N. was to be an organization where the balance of power was tipped decisively in favor of collective security. There were two grave miscalculations in this theory. Aggression was not confined to Germany, and the peace-loving members of the U.N. did not have the necessary preponderance of power. This really means that power politics is an inescapable element in international affairs. Power politics in the legitimate sense of the term is not militarism or aggression. It is merely a prudent recognition that in a world where aggressor states materialize from time to time, even the most peace-loving nation must maintain sufficient power to defend itself. One reason why Russia became a danger to the Western world was that she was not restrained by a balance of power. The war destroyed it in Europe, and the only Western nations which were heavily armed in 1945, the United States and Britain, adopted a policy of singlehanded disarmament. Russia did not follow their example, but strengthened her armed forces and built up those of her satellites. As a result, the balance tilted strongly in her favor and encouraged her to continue a policy of imperialism.

The United States has taken the lead in devising countermeasures. These include rearmament, the North Atlantic Pact, the integration of Western Germany into this combination, and links with Spain and Yugoslavia. The Turkish-Iraqi-Pakistani alliance has been welcomed with the hope that it will be joined by other Arab states and so build a stronger barrier against Soviet imperialism in the Middle East. In the Pacific the United States is aligned with Japan, Australia, New Zealand, and several of the smaller Asian countries. The general purpose behind all the alliances is to create a worldwide league of states that will be a counterweight to the Soviet bloc. The essence of the balance of power policy is that the states which feel themselves threatened come together to contain the power of the aggressor. What has been taking place the last few years is that a balance of power on a global scale is in process of being established.

SELECTED READING

ARMSTRONG, HAMILTON FISH, *The Calculated Risk*. New York: The Macmillan Company, 1947.

BEMIS, SAMUEL F., *A Diplomatic History of the United States*, 4th ed. New York: Henry Holt and Company, 1955.

——, *The Latin American Policy of the United States*. New York. Harcourt, Brace and Company, 1943.

Britain and the United States: Problems in Co-operation. New York: Harper for the Council on Foreign Relations, 1953.

DEAN, VERA M., *Europe and the United States*. New York: Alfred A. Knopf, 1950.

DULLES, JOHN F., *War or Peace*. New York: The Macmillan Company, 1950.

KENNAN, GEORGE F., *American Diplomacy, 1900–1950*. Chicago: University of Chicago Press, 1951.

LANGER, W. L., and GLEASON, D. E., *The Challenge to Isolation 1937–1940*. New York: Harper and Brothers, 1952.

Major Problems of U.S. Foreign Policy, 1947 *et seq*. Washington, D.C.: Brookings Institution.

PERKINS, DEXTER, *The American Approach to Foreign Policy*. Cambridge: Harvard University Press, 1952.

CHAPTER 18

GREAT BRITAIN

No country shows the influence of geography upon foreign policy more than Great Britain. The three traditional policies of naval supremacy, isolation and the balance of power are largely based upon Britain's position as an island off the northwest corner of Europe. The English Channel and the North Sea give a greater degree of security from invasion than is enjoyed by any nation on the continent of Europe. They have literally wrecked many raids and invasions by their own unaided efforts. The protection of the sea has never been absolute, however, as was proved by a long succession of invaders culminating in William the Conqueror. Security required that the natural defense be supplemented, and for an island the obvious addition was a navy. For four centuries the combination of channel and fleet gave security, and this to a considerable extent was the reason why next to the Americans the British became the world's most pronounced isolationists. British isolationism was never as strong as American, however, for the reason that twenty-one miles of salt water were less of an obstacle to an invader than the 3000 miles of the Atlantic Ocean. The British were never able to disinterest themselves from European affairs as completely as Americans could before there were airplanes and guided missiles, and out of this arose the policy of the balance of power.

EUROPE'S GREATEST SEA ROUTE

The second great geographic influence, the position at the northwest corner of Europe, could not become operative until the discoveries of Columbus and Vasco da Gama. As long as commerce, power, and civilization centered around the Mediterranean, Britain lay on the road to nowhere. Beyond it was only Iceland, and even the Scandinavians had lost all desire to emigrate there. The discovery of the New World and the sea route to Asia gradually made the Atlantic and not the Mediterranean the center of the wealth and power of the Western world. This gave Britain a competitive advantage over all of Europe except France and Spain, since she lay further

409

out into the Atlantic and therefore closer to the markets and regions of settlement across the oceans. France was as well placed geographically as Britain, but she could never decide whether she preferred to be the leading colonial and naval power or the dominant military state on the continent. By aiming at both she attained neither and lost the race to Britain and Germany. Spain failed to make proper use of her position.

Of all the ocean routes of the world the one which carries the largest tonnage of merchant shipping goes down the English channel. One branch has its beginning in the upper Baltic, and gathering up en route the trade of Finland, Sweden, northwestern Russia, Poland, and Germany, it makes its way via the Kattegat and Skagerrak into the North Sea. Here it is joined by the other branch which originated in the White Sea and came down the Norwegian coast. Once clear of the English Channel the route divides, branches going to Canada and the United States, the West Indies and the Pacific, South America, Africa, the Mediterranean, and the short route via the Suez Canal to India, Australia and the Far East. At the beginning and end of the voyage all the ships are concentrated in the English Channel. Here is where Britain's position shows its effect. Rotterdam, the principal port of Holland, is 188 miles east of London. The German port of Hamburg is 448 miles to the east, while Leningrad is 1368 miles from the Atlantic. In supplying overseas markets British shipping has a natural advantage in shorter length of voyage and lower freight rates. Strategically too the British navy blocks the road of rival fleets through the narrow seas to the Atlantic.

From the sixteenth century onward the British took advantage of their geographical position and concentrated more and more on manufacturing for overseas markets, increasing merchant shipping, and colonization. Immunity from invasion helped the trend since unlike continental countries the expansion of manufacturing was not set back by the destruction caused by invading armies. The culmination came in the nineteenth century when Britain became the workshop of the world. A powerful business class developed whose interests were bound up with the expansion of overseas trade and peace. Wars in Europe were bad for business since they meant higher taxes and therefore sale prices and also dislocation of markets. Manufacturers and merchants threw their influence in favor of peace and therefore of isolation. In 1914, for example, powerful groups urged that Britain remain neutral and make money by trading with both sides. And in 1939 the businessmen, typified by Chamberlain, were in favor of peace at almost any price.

CHANNEL, FLEET, AND AIR FORCE

The first English ruler to realize the implications of Britain's island position was King Henry VIII in the early sixteenth century. The king felt that England should "seek her future upon the great waters" by trade, and emphatically should have a fleet stronger than any possible opposing navy. Henry VIII evolved the formula that the English Channel plus the fleet equaled security from invasion, and until the 1930's this was enough to ensure the safety of the island. No European general would risk sending troop transports and store ships across the channel in the face of a superior navy. Even if by a fluke the original contingents landed safely, it would not be possible to ensure supplies and reinforcements. The prerequisite for an invasion was the destruction of the English navy, and if it were larger than the opposing force, it ought to be able to win the victory.

Other circumstances strengthened reliance on the fleet as the basic safeguard. The standing army was numerically far inferior to the great forces on the continent, and since conscription was not introduced until 1939 there were not the millions of trained reserves. The reason Britain usually lost the first battles was that she began her wars with a glorified police force and trained her troops after the fighting started. If the navy were destroyed and a large continental army landed in Britain, the defending forces would be too few to protect the island. Between wars the British frequently reduced their army below the level of safety, but they never dared to carry naval disarmament so far. A world-wide commerce meant that thousands of merchantmen were always at sea and must be protected from attack. Moreover, from the early nineteenth century the effect of the growth of manufacturing and population was that the island was increasingly incapable of feeding itself. If it were compelled to live off its own resources, it could support about 18 million instead of the 48 million of 1939. By the twentieth century Britain produced only a third of its food. Two thirds of the food and the bulk of the raw materials had to be imported, while manufactures must be sold abroad to pay for imports. To surface raiders the twentieth century added submarines and long-range aircraft. The answer was to send the ships in convoys protected by destroyers, corvettes, frigates, and small aircraft carriers. Since no other nation is so dependent on imported food, Britain needs a much larger number of small warships than any other power.

The last time that Henry VIII's formula worked was World War I, when Britain raised an army of several million men after the war began behind the protection of the navy. The development of the airplane compelled a modernization of the formula, which by the 'thirties took the form that channel plus fleet plus aircraft equaled security from invasion. This was the combination that defeated Hitler's Operation Sea Lion in the summer of 1940. The plan was to land an army on the southeast coast, follow it up with reinforcements and supplies, and capture London. The British navy was overwhelmingly superior, and there was a small but powerful air force. The German air force outnumbered it by nearly four to one. The British admiralty itself admitted that the Germans might land 100,000 troops without being intercepted, but the real difficulty would be to send over reinforcements. The more the German army and navy studied the problem the less they liked it, and they informed Hitler that the invasion was not possible unless the German air force had air supremacy over the channel and the landing points. Goering was requested to destroy the Royal Air Force, and since the Battle of Britain went the other way, the invasion was indefinitely postponed.

The development of guided missiles which began in 1944 has modified the formula of 1940. Neither channel nor fleet can interfere with a guided missile which is launched from perhaps somewhere near the Elbe River and suddenly falls from the stratosphere upon a British target. To prevent launching platforms from being established within effective range of their target, Britain is committed to the defense of Western Europe as never before in her history. The major emphasis has shifted to the air force and army, but this does not mean the end of the British navy, though it will have to operate in close cooperation with air power. Merchant shipping and the British Empire have still to be protected, and armies and supplies must still be sent overseas in case of war. The building program announced in 1954 shows that the navy will be a strong force of aircraft carriers, cruisers, and a large number of small, fast ships for convoy duty, antisubmarine work, and mine sweeping.

THE POLICY OF ISOLATION

Isolation may be dated from 1557 when the French recaptured Calais and deprived England of her last possession on the continent. A century passed before she understood her good fortune, but when the truth finally dawned isolation became the preferred policy. Henry VIII's formula of channel plus fleet could only work if the English stayed on their own island. If they made annexations on the mainland, they placed themselves where their enemies could attack them. After the seventeenth century England engaged in many continental wars and could often have taken conquered territory. She always refused to do so, not from altruism but from enlightened self-interest. Land across the channel meant war to defend it sooner or later, and this was not profitable to a nation which increasingly lived by trade. Colonies or trading rights overseas were another matter, for there the navy could be depended on to prevent European interference. The nineteenth century was the golden age of British isolationism: from 1823 to 1904 the country avoided continental commitments as far as possible. Yet even during this period isolation was not complete. There were for instance the standing alliance with Portugal and the guarantee of Belgian neutrality in 1839, which was the immediate cause of the entry into World War I. On the whole, however, the description of

Lord Salisbury, the prime minister, held good, that "British policy is to float lazily downstream, occasionally putting out a diplomatic boat-hook to avoid collisions."

Britain's foreign policy between the two world wars cannot be understood unless one remembers that isolation had become almost instinctive with the people and to a considerable extent with the government. Feeling secure in their own island, they knew little and cared less about European affairs. So far as they concerned themselves with the world outside, their interest lay in the British Empire and foreign trade. Their own phrase was that they were in Europe but not of Europe. There was a good deal of truth in the apocryphal story that when all the cross-channel boat services were discontinued because of fog the London papers had the headline: "Europe cut off from England." The interwar attempt to return as far as possible to the isolation of the nineteenth century was defeated by the airplane.

Since 1945 Britain has taken part in continental affairs much more intimately and continuously than ever before. To some extent the British still feel that they are in Europe but not of Europe. Both the Labour and Conservative governments have made it clear that Britain cannot be purely a continental power, because of her membership in the British Empire and Commonwealth and her world trade. These last come first, and they will be given priority over European demands.

THE BALANCE OF POWER POLICY

Protected by the channel and the navy, Britain usually felt secure; but since she was only twenty-one miles from the continent, her safety might be endangered if a great power dominated the whole of Europe. Until recently there were six great powers in Europe, and Britain preferred that no one of them should be markedly stronger than the others. Periodically this approximate equilibrium of force was upset by the growth in strength of one of the leading powers. Eventually this created a counterweight, for a coalition was formed by the states which felt themselves endangered by the dominant state. The power of Britain was great enough to give the superiority to the side which she joined, so that she was the holder of the balance. It was contrary to her interests to allow one nation to overshadow the continent, and normally her practice was to support whichever was the weaker side. By thus making it impossible for any state or alliance of states to dominate the others, Britain preserved her own independence as well as that of the other states. As keeper of the balance, it was necessary that neither her friendships nor her hostilities should be eternal. The enemy of the moment was whichever state threatened to control Europe, but on another occasion the two might combine against some other state which had become a menace.

In the sixteenth century Henry VIII rather bungled his application of the balance of power technique, but Queen Elizabeth used it to bring about the defeat of Spain. A century later the same technique was used effectively against Louis XIV and a hundred years after that against Napoleon. In the early twentieth century Sir Edward Grey, the British foreign minister, employed the same policy against Imperial Germany. In 1939 when Neville Chamberlain tried to form an alliance with Russia he called it a Peace Front and desperately hoped it would be, but in his blundering fashion he was harking back to the policy of Queen Elizabeth. The forms of government or ideologies had no bearing on keeping the balance: it was concerned solely with whichever was the strongest and most aggressive power on the continent. Churchill pointed out that the British should not be afraid of being accused of being pro-French and anti-German. If the circumstances were reversed, they could equally be pro-German and anti-French.

Britain at the height of her power was never in a position to impose her will on the other great powers. Her strength lay in her navy, her empire, and her trade, and she never dominated Europe as Germany did from 1871 to 1890. She never willingly fought alone, for as a sea power she was compelled to seek allies who could provide the armies and the European land bases that she herself lacked. In one respect there is nothing unusual in the present situation when Britain is dependent for her safety upon a coalition of the Western nations. What is unprecedented is the immense disparity in strength between Britain and her ally the United States; that and the fact that the only other great power left in Europe is Russia.

BRITAIN AND GERMANY, 1870–1914

Germany upset the balance of power established by the Congress of Vienna in 1815, by her defeat of France in 1870 following upon that of the Austrian Empire in 1866. By replacing France as the leading military power Germany won the virtually unchallenged primacy of the continent. The bases of this position were the admitted superiority of the German army and Bismarck's pre-eminent talent for diplomacy. Britain made no move to restore the balance and on the whole accentuated Germany's predominance by usually supporting her against France and Russia. Bismarck in the 1860's had been an aggressor until he attained his goal in Europe. Beyond this he had no further ambitions and he devoted the last nineteen years of his career to keeping what he had gained. From his point of view further wars were foolish since if Germany won, there was nothing she wanted, and if she were defeated, she lost what she had already gained. Bismarck, therefore, used his skill in diplomatic combinations and the implied threat of the German army to maintain the status quo in Europe. None of this presented any danger to the security of Britain, and as a trading power she thoroughly approved of peace.

The alteration came with the accession to the throne of the young Kaiser William II and his dismissal of Bismarck in 1890. This was more than a change of personnel: it also marked the advent of a new policy which slowly aroused the uneasiness and distrust of the United Kingdom. In his flamboyant fashion the Kaiser typified the new generation which had grown up in Germany. It was no longer satisfied to dominate Europe but aspired to become a world power, in fact *the* world power with an appropriate empire and navy. The weapons of the new policy were a clumsy and provocative diplomacy backed by the threat of German armed strength. In the first decade of the twentieth century the German government engaged in what the Kaiser called saber-rattling. France, Russia, and Austria had their share of responsibility for the incidents that arose. But the factor that turned one incident after another into a crisis was vague and ominous threats that the German army might come into action unless Germany got whatever she wanted at the moment. Slowly the aggressive policy and the veiled threats changed British confidence in Germany's peaceful intentions to fear and suspicion.

The building of the German navy was the principal reason for the change in attitude. Bismarck had resisted all the pressure of the German advocates of a big navy and had deliberately kept the fleet small. He told them that on these terms alone Germany and Britain could be friends because power was divided between the two elements of land and water. Neither could effectively attack the other; therefore, neither need fear the other, and therefore they could be friends. Bismarck warned that if ever Germany, supreme on land, tried also to become supreme at sea, she was heading for a war with Great Britain. Control of land and sea was too much power concentrated in the hands of a single state, and even if all its citizens were angels, other nations would feel their safety endangered. The British would have added the further argument that while a big navy was a luxury for Germany, it was a necessity for Britain. It was true that in case of war with Britain Germany would lose her colonies and her seaborne trade; but while this loss would be damaging it would not be fatal. If the microscopic British army invaded Germany, to quote Bismarck's remark in 1864, the government would call out the police and have it arrested. But if Germany gained the mastery of the seas, she could starve Britain into surrender and invade the island with an overwhelming force. So when the Kaiser sponsored the naval construction laws of 1898 and 1900, Britain began to move along the path which led to the Triple Entente and the World War of 1914.

By the early 1900's the German navy was the second largest in the world and expanding rapidly. Britain began to lay down new ships, and before long a naval race was in full swing. Various proposals of the British government for a mutual postponement of naval construction were rejected, and the pace grew hotter. The belief spread in Britain that some day Germany would use her navy to attack. This fear was strengthened by her aggressive foreign policy, and by the jealousy and hostility toward Britain and the strength of the war feeling that were widespread in Germany. All these and especially the naval threat were the determining factors in ending the British policy of isolation.

In 1904 the British and French governments settled their colonial disputes and formed an Entente Cordiale (friendly understanding) by which they agreed to give one another diplomatic support. In 1905 Germany took advantage of the growing French control of Morocco to provoke a serious international crisis. She hoped to extract territorial compensation from France and frighten Britain into drawing back from so dangerous an entanglement. The result was to frighten them closer together, for in 1906 the French and British general staffs began military conversations, planning a joint defense in case the German threats ended in war. Subsequent crises led to the continuance of the military conversations, so that the French plan of defense was based on the assumption that the British army would hold the left of the line near the North Sea. In 1912 the British met the German naval threat by withdrawing their ships from the Mediterranean to the North Sea and relinquishing their interests there to the protection of the French fleet. France transferred her navy to the Mediterranean, leaving her channel and Bay of Biscay coasts exposed to a German naval attack unless they were protected by the British fleet. No defensive alliance was ever signed, but by 1914 Britain was under a moral obligation to enter the war on the side of France. In 1907 Britain and Russia settled their conflicts in Iran and elsewhere, and agreed to give one another diplomatic support. Russia and France had made a defensive alliance in 1894, and thus the agreement of 1907 created the Triple Entente of Britain, France, and Russia. The hard core was the Franco-Russian Alliance, and this was supplemented by the British moral obligation to France and the more tenuous commitment to Russia.

Looked at in terms of the balance of power, the record read like this. In 1870 Bismarck upset the balance with the tacit approval of Britain. In 1894 the dominance of Germany was weakened by the Franco-Russian Alliance, but this did not re-establish a balance. Apart from her own strength, Germany was supported by her alliances with Austria Hungary (1879) and Italy (1882), and the Triple was incontestably stronger than the Dual Alliance. Britain's formation of the Triple Entente in 1904–1907 was a belated attempt to restore the balance and atone for her blunder of 1870. Superficially it seemed that an equality of power had been re-established; but the events of World War I showed that this was not so. Germany completely defeated Russia in

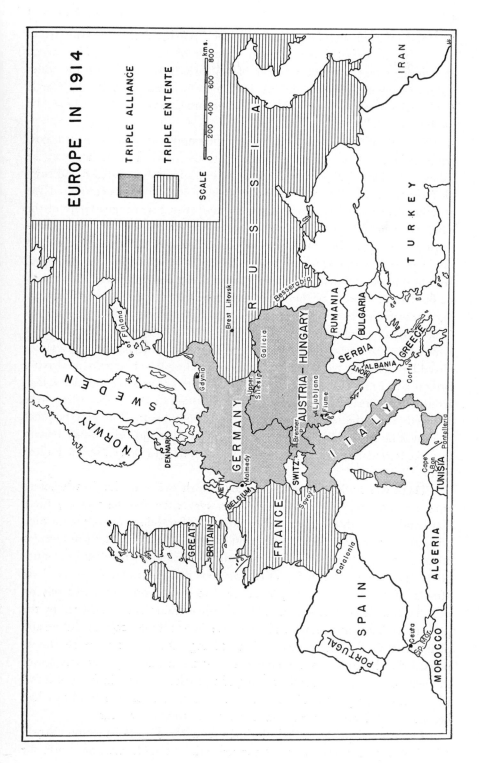

EUROPE IN 1914

TRIPLE ALLIANCE

TRIPLE ENTENTE

SCALE
0 200 400 600 800
kms.

NORWAY

SWEDEN

G. of Finland

RUSSIA

DENMARK

Gdynia

Brest Litovsk

GERMANY

Upper
Silesia

Galicia

Besserabia

RUMANIA

NETH

Malmedy

BELGIUM

GREAT
BRITAIN

FRANCE

SWITZ

Savoy

Brenner

AUSTRIA - HUNGARY

Ljubljana

Fiume

SERBIA

MONT.

ALBANIA

BULGARIA

GREECE

Corfu

TURKEY

IRAN

ITALY

Cape
Bon

Pantelleria

TUNISIA

SPAIN

Catalonia

PORTUGAL

Ceuta

Sp. Mor.

MOROCCO

ALGERIA

417

1917 and inflicted such heavy losses on the French and British armies that they only just defeated the German offensive of March 1918. The arrival of American troops in the summer of 1918 was necessary to tip the scales against Germany. This was the first indication—confirmed by World War II —that Britain was no longer able to play her traditional role as the holder of the balance.

This recital of events is likely to give the impression that the British government had a clear-cut policy which led to the move from isolation to the balance of power. This is a misleading simplification of a confused and complex situation. Sir Edward Grey, the British foreign minister, shared the growing distrust of Germany's intentions and was increasingly aware of the danger of war. At the same time he resisted the efforts of France and Russia to turn the Triple Entente into a defensive alliance. Grey feared that this might precipitate the very war he was trying to avoid. Moreover, he hoped, not too confidently, that by leaving Britain's relations with France and Russia fluid and rather vague, he would gain time that could be used for arranging a peaceful settlement between the Triple Entente and the Triple Alliance. Grey always denied that he was following a balance of power policy, though some of his cabinet colleagues so described it. The international crises provoked by Germany had great influence in molding developments by driving Britain and France closer together. The military conversations and the fleet arrangements created a moral obligation on Britain to join France if she were attacked. Since the two governments periodically assured one another that there was no legal obligation, Grey continued to say and believe that Britain was free to remain neutral. The reality was that in 1914 Britain was not a free agent.

There was no long-term and settled British policy in the decade before 1914, any more than there was in the interwar period. On the contrary, there was hand to mouth improvisation, a devising of solutions to cope with each crisis as it arose. The British are most unwilling to commit themselves in advance to a set course of action in readiness for some vague future contingency. They prefer the short to the long view and like to let the future look after itself. So the very strong tendency is to wait upon events and rely on expedients to meet emergencies. This attitude of mind is strengthened by the pressure of daily business, which leaves little time to think about the future and plan for it. Grey once remarked that "during his term of office he was so pressed that he could not remember having taken any step that was not of immediate urgency and for the solving of a problem directly in front of him." By the interwar period this pressure of overwork upon the ministers had become much more marked than in the early twentieth century.

The general public took little interest in foreign affairs before World War I, though it was alarmed at the strength of the German navy. On the whole, the British people were opposed to a continental alliance until it was clear that there was a direct and immediate threat to the security of the United Kingdom. Isolationism was particularly strong among the supporters of the Liberal government of the day, and the formation of an alliance with France or Russia would have split the party and brought about the fall of the government. Grey always felt that for reasons of domestic politics an alliance was not practicable. He did not deliberately and clearly adopt the balance of power policy. Yet as he told the House of Commons on August 3, 1914, he realized that Britain could not afford to allow Germany to conquer France and Belgium and "dominate the whole of the west of Europe opposite to us." He was moved half unconsciously toward the creation of a counterweight to Germany. This was the balance of power technique, whatever the foreign secretary may have thought he was doing.

INTERWAR PUBLIC OPINION

The public's former indifference to foreign affairs was destroyed by the discovery that an assassination in Serajevo could bring about the death in battle of 900,000 British. There was determination that this must never happen again. Diplomacy was distrusted as sinister and secret, and war was no longer the legitimate weapon of a nation's policy which most had considered it in 1914. It was now looked upon with horror and by many as a crime. An outstanding characteristic of interwar Britain, as of the democratic world in general, was its pacifism and its unwillingness to fight any war, whether on behalf of the League of Nations or anything else. This was combined with a desire to support the League, and the feeling that the collective security of fifty-six nations united at Lake Geneva could maintain peace without effective armaments. There was a strong desire to return to isolation and be free from all entanglements in Europe, now that the German navy was at the bottom of the North Sea. Apart from this, wishful thinking led to the belief that Germany was now a peace-loving democracy, and that the only disturber of the peace was "militaristic" France which wanted to dominate Europe by force of arms. War hatred of Germany was rapidly replaced by a mounting sympathy which led the British to vie with the Germans in their condemnation of the crimes of the wicked Treaty of Versailles. The Munich Agreement was the high-water mark of British pro-Germanism. The Anglo-French Entente had been a marriage of convenience and not of affection on both sides. There were only a limited number of Anglophiles and Francophiles, and temperamentally Anglo-Saxons and Latins in the mass got on best when they did not see too much of each other.

Despite the British public's determination to influence foreign affairs it knew little about them. When it made its voice heard, its combination of

excellent intentions, ignorance, and muddled thinking often had a very unhappy effect upon foreign policy. Witness the elector who wrote to a cabinet
minister at the time of the Ethiopian affair that he would always vote for
him as long as he worked for sanctions against Italy and disarmament. A
democratic government can ignore public opinion only at its peril. To lead
it in the way in which it does not want to go may mean the loss of the
next election. Too many democratic leaders, and not in Britain only, felt
that the victory of their opponents would be such a national disaster that they
must not jeopardize their chances by telling the voters what they did not want
to hear. They agreed with the Duke of Plaza Toro that

> In enterprise of martial kind
> When there is any fighting,
> I lead my regiment from behind
> I find it less exciting.

BRITAIN AND THE LEAGUE OF NATIONS

There were high hopes in 1919 that peace and justice would be assured
by the authority of the League. In 1920 the American Senate rejected the
League Covenant and the rest of the peace settlement, and returned to isolation. The British idea had been that John Bull and Uncle Sam, would-be
isolationists and reluctant interventionists, should jointly commit themselves
to European entanglements while holding hands for mutual support. The
secession of the major isolationist had disastrous effects upon the morale of
the minor.

The most likely cause of future war was an attempt by Germany to upset the peace settlement in fifteen or twenty years' time when she had recovered from her heavy defeat. This was the particular nightmare of France
and the other states which feared and distrusted Germany. They considered
that the principal value of the League was that it could be used as an instrument to guarantee their security. Its weakness was the uncertainty whether
the sanctions would be enforced against an aggressor, and the French bloc
took the lead in attempts to strengthen them. If this were done, it was
obvious that Britain as the strongest great power in the League was unanimously elected to do the bulk of the fighting; and government and people
alike regarded this with a notable lack of enthusiasm.

President Wilson and other League idealists had misinterpreted the
widespread aversion to war and the enthusiasm for the League which followed the victory of 1918. They thought it meant that internationalism was
stronger than nationalism and that if ever an aggressor state broke the Covenant, governments and peoples alike would enforce the sanctions by means

of collective security. The interwar period showed that national interests were still stronger than international ones. The majority, particularly of the older citizens, formed their ideas in the pre-1914 period when the rule was that each state concerned itself with its own interests and gave diplomatic or military aid to others only if self-interest dictated. They failed to see that they had any obligation to support collective security except in the spirit. What they overlooked was that there cannot be peace without security, and that justice is powerless unless it is supported by force.

Isolationism and pacifism were among the factors which led Great Britain to water down the obligations under the League Covenant. The abstention of the United States was another cause, since as a nonmember America had no obligation whatever to support sanctions. From 1914 to 1917 there had been a very bitter diplomatic dispute between the American demand for neutral rights of trade and the British claim to interrupt it by the naval blockade. Since Washington still maintained its position after the war, Britain feared that if the navy ever imposed a League blockade against an aggressor the old controversy would be revived. The British government announced that it would never agree to compulsory sanctions as long as the United States adhered to its claim of neutral rights of trade. Another strong influence upon Great Britain was the mounting opposition to sanctions in the British dominions. Protected by the oceans, they were isolationist and antiwar. In 1924 the Canadian delegate opposed the Geneva Protocol because "In this association of mutual insurance against fire, the risks assumed by the different states are not equal. We live in a fireproof house, far from inflammable materials." The United Kingdom was most unwilling to incur any League obligations which might compel it to go to war while the dominions remained at peace, since it was feared that this might break up the British Commonwealth.

The result of all these influences was the interpretative resolutions introduced at the League meetings of 1921 and 1923, expressing the meaning which the members attached to their obligations under the Covenant. These were declared to be optional, and in case of a breach of the Covenant, it lay entirely with the governments of the member states and not with the League Council to decide what action should be taken against the aggressor. The effect of these resolutions was strengthened by the rejection by Britain and the dominions of the Draft Treaty of Mutual Assistance of 1923 and the Geneva Protocol of 1924, both of which tried to strengthen the security provisions of the Covenant. It became clear that the British Commonwealth valued the League purely as a convenient means of consultation, and as an agency for settling disputes and controlling such international problems as the drug traffic. What the Commonwealth would do if a League member were the victim of aggression was left completely uncertain.

MODIFIED ISOLATIONISM

The Locarno Treaties of 1925 were an important modification of the British policy of isolation. The government had come to realize that the distrust and ill will between France and Germany were more likely to end in war than the millenium. Since Britain could not allow one country to control western Europe, it seemed wiser to give a guarantee of help, in the hope that this would improve relations between them. The Locarno Treaty of Mutual Guarantee stipulated that if war broke out between France, Belgium, and Germany, the League Council must unanimously (apart from the votes of the combatants) designate the aggressor. Britain and Italy were then required to give armed help to the victim of aggression. From the point of view of British policy the significance lay in the acceptance of limited intervention on the continent. Henceforth, Britain was under an obligation to take part if war broke out in western Europe. As Prime Minister Baldwin put it, her frontier was now on the Rhine. The refusal to give a similar promise of help to France's allies, Czechoslovakia and Poland, meant that British policy would still be isolationist in central and eastern Europe, and foreshadowed the attitude at the time of the Munich Agreement. Britain still thought that the peace of Europe was divisible into watertight zones, and that what happened 600 miles away in Czechoslovakia or further afield could not affect the security of the United Kingdom.

SINGLEHANDED DISARMAMENT

The reduction of the armed forces was partly a measure of economy and in part a response to the popular pressure for disarmament. There was very wide support for the view urged, especially by the Labour and Liberal parties, that armaments were the principal cause of war. Therefore, peace and security could be assured by reducing them to the lowest possible level. This ignored the reality that armaments are instruments of policy and are far more a symptom than a cause of tension. It takes two to keep the peace, and a state which follows the policy of singlehanded disarmament, as Britain did, merely plays into the hands of a heavily armed aggressor. By 1922 the British armed forces had been cut to the limit of safety in a world where there was not the slightest risk that any aggressor would challenge the victors of World War I. They were held at substantially the same level long after the assurance of peace had vanished, and it was not until 1935 that rearmament was hesitantly begun amid a loud chorus of condemnation from the Labour and Liberal parties. By this time the Royal Air Force with 688 machines in Britain was inferior to those of all the other great powers, including Germany, and was comparable with that of a second-class state. The navy was far too small for the work it had to do, and a high percentage of the ships were obsolescent. The army was smaller than in 1914, and as late as 1938 it was very short of modern equipment.

Attlee, the head of the Labour party, said that he rejected altogether the claim to parity in the air with Germany, and some Labour leaders urged that the air force be abolished as unnecessary and provocative. As late as April, 1939, the Labour and Liberal parties voted against the introduction of conscription. At the same time they insisted that the government firmly oppose the dictators, which meant war at least from 1938 onward. They tried to reconcile their inconsistency by saying that their intuition told them that Hitler, who had the equipment and knew his enemies had not, would not dare to fight. Baldwin, the Conservative prime minister, was slow and hesitant in rearming and made no attempt to waken the public from its delusions. Even in 1938 British military expenditure was only $1,520,000,000, while Germany's was at least $7.5 billion. In 1936 Baldwin frankly admitted that if he had appealed to the voters on the issue that it was necessary to rearm, "I cannot think of anything that would have made the loss of the election from my point of view more certain." So several vital years were thrown away. This contributed in no small measure to the diplomatic defeats of the later 'thirties, and to the deadly peril in which the country found itself in 1940. During the Battle of Britain in 1940 the approximate daily average of British fighter planes available for operations was 704 and of German 2682.

The one attempt at disarmament which succeeded was the establishment of Anglo-American naval equality at the Washington (1922) and London (1930) Disarmament Conferences. The technical difficulties were very serious and caused the failure of the Geneva Conference of 1927. For instance, Britain wanted a large number of small cruisers while the United States needed a small number of large cruisers. Add the point that one large cruiser was probably the equal in combat of two or three small ones, and the difficulty of establishing mathematical equality can be seen. One cause of the success was that if the United States were determined to embark on a naval race, it could afford to outbuild Great Britain. An equally important reason was that the two governments agreed that there were no serious conflicts of policy and that war between them was inconceivable. In that event the two navies would never come into conflict, and it would make no practical difference if the American navy were slightly stronger in heavy and the British in light cruisers. In this way an approximate equality in strength was established. The League of Nations sponsored a series of land and air disarmament conferences and all of them failed. The basic reason was that the French bloc would not disarm or allow Germany to rearm unless this threat to its security were compensated by a clear promise of armed help from Britain or the United States or both. These two powers urged the virtues of disarmament, were sympathetic to German claims, and critical of French "militarism," and refused to give any guarantees of armed assistance. This led a French delegate to remark that the British were twenty-one sea miles more disinterested than the French, and the Americans 3000 sea miles more so than the British.

Britain and France drifted apart during the interwar period, and despite the Locarno Treaties there was more recrimination than cooperation. The British could not understand the preoccupation of France and her allies with security. Secure for four centuries across the channel, the British could not appreciate what it meant to have a foreign country just over the river, behind which some military threat might be secretly preparing. There was nothing in the British experience to justify that perpetual nervousness and distrust of their neighbors that was common to all Europeans. Another British grievance was the French refusal to imitate the British singlehanded disarmament and in the League Disarmament Conference of 1932 to permit Germany to rearm. France and Britain also came into conflict over the maintenance of the terms of the peace treaties. Britain urged their modification in the belief that this would remove German grievances and assure peace. France and her allies usually blocked these efforts because any change, e.g., a union between Germany and Austria, would strengthen Germany and so they felt imperil their security. Since the peace treaties could not be altered without the consent of the signatories, all France had to do was to uphold the terms as drawn up in 1919 and refuse to allow changes. The growing British sympathy for Germany and the belief that the Versailles Treaty was a crime made Britain even more critical of France.

APPEASEMENT

Appeasement is a policy that ought to succeed but usually does not. Doubtless it would be excellent in a world where everyone was perfect. The theory of the appeaser is that war can be avoided and good relations restored by sedulously seeking out and removing the grievances of the appeasee. The logic is perfect, for if there are no grievances, there is nothing about which to fight. In the negotiations the appeaser displays his freedom from selfish nationalism, his ability to see the appeasee's point of view, and his anxiety to go halfway or even three quarters of the way in order to reach a compromise. The belief is that so striking a display of meekness and justice will evoke a like response from the appeasee; but in practice it seems to arouse his worst instincts. He assumes that no one makes concessions from love of justice or peace but only from fear. The inference is that the appeaser is afraid to fight and the conclusion drawn is that a reasonable settlement would be folly, since a frightened man can be coerced into making larger and larger concessions. The appeasee tends to overplay his hand as Hitler did, and make such large demands that the appeaser is not able to agree to them, and decides that war is the lesser of two evils.

Like all principles of diplomacy this is subject to exceptions, for many wars have been avoided by forbearance and patient search for a reasonable compromise. One essential is correct judgment of the aims and character of the appeasee. Chamberlain failed to see that in Hitler and Mussolini he was dealing with a pair of would-be Napoleons, and that their desire for empire could not be satisfied by the removal of the comparatively minor grievances which they put forward as camouflage to conceal their real purposes. It is also true that one cannot appease from weakness to strength. The appeaser is more likely to succeed if he is heavily armed, and if it is known that he will fight rather than make excessive and damaging concessions. But since Hitler knew that Britain was disarmed below the level of safety, and since he wrongly believed that the people were too decadent to fight, the appeasement policy never had a hope of success. Appeasement was far older than Neville Chamberlain: probably its first appearance in recorded history was with Pharaoh Akhnaton who ruled from 1375 to 1358 B.C. His attempt to counter foreign aggression by pacifism led to the loss of Egypt's empire in the Middle East and ruined the king's domestic policy of religious reform. It is also true that appeasement did not die with Chamberlain, for in the early postwar years the Western powers followed the same policy toward Russia with identical results.

Chamberlain inherited the policy from his predecessors Ramsay Mac-Donald and Baldwin, who began to practice it about 1933 when Hitler came to power. Examples were the British insistence that France agree to equality of armaments with Germany and the Anglo-German Naval Treaty of 1935, which sanctioned as large a fleet of submarines and surface craft as the German shipyards were capable of building. This treaty not only condoned another breach of the Versailles Treaty but it ignored the naval interests of France and Italy. Chamberlain's innovation, apart from giving a name to the policy, was that he pursued it more energetically and with a greater sense of urgency than his predecessors. During their tenure of office British and French armaments combined were superior to German. When Chamberlain became prime minister in 1937, the situation was changed, and no time was to be lost if peace were to be saved by agreement.

The personal character of Neville Chamberlain also played its part. If Churchill had been prime minister, war would have come earlier, or else an outraged public would have hurled him out of office. Chamberlain was autocratic, narrow, honest, obstinate and completely confident of the correctness of his own views. He had a deep and genuine hatred of war, and he believed that he had a special and personal mission to preserve the peace of Europe. He felt that the only consideration that would justify war would be the clear revelation that Hitler intended to dominate the world by force, and he persuaded himself at Munich that this was not his intention. He saw too that if Britain fought, she was in grave danger of being defeated; but to postpone war by concessions and so gain time to rearm was a secondary and not the principal motive of his actions. He knew nothing of foreign affairs, and he never realized that Hitler did not have the same standard of values as himself. He could not believe that anyone could prefer war when he could get all he said he wanted by peaceful negotiations. Wishful thinking seems to have played its part. At times when Hitler broke his word, Chamberlain had secret doubts whether he could trust him. But he wanted so desperately to bring about "that general appeasement which alone can save the world from chaos" that he seems to have reassured himself that "here was a man who could be relied upon when he had given his word."

In a way the conflict between Nazi Germany—and one might add Soviet Russia—and the West was a clash between two different civilizations with fundamentally opposed standards of conduct. Chamberlain was a typical example of the Western democratic leader whose formative years bore the indelible imprint of the later nineteenth century. This meant that in international affairs he believed in the sovereignty of individual states and in the right of each nation to follow its own interests first and foremost. War was so destructive that it should be resorted to only in the most extreme cases, and as a rule peace should be preserved by a diplomatic compromise. It was taken for granted that governments even of great powers would exercise a decent self-restraint. Above all society was governed by the rule of law, written and unwritten. On the whole treaties were kept. Illogical but humane laws of war were evolved to protect prisoners and civilians. The code was open to exceptions, yet in a vague but cogent fashion it was taken for granted that there were some things that civilized men did not do.

The Nazis and Communists did not seek merely to overthrow the peace settlement of 1919. They prided themselves that they were in revolt against the whole code of Western civilization. The attack on the churches was merely the most publicized phase of a comprehensive assault. Humanitarianism domestic or foreign was dismissed as weak sentimentality, as witness the persecution of the Jews and the kulaks. Justice was what benefited the state, and terrorism was adopted as a normal process of government. In international affairs no state had a title to independence unless it was strong enough to maintain it by force. Treaties lasted while it paid to keep them. The only deterrent to war was the uncertainty of winning, and once it had begun it was an all in fight with no holds barred. The conquered might be enslaved, transported, or exterminated at the sole convenience of the conqueror. The new regimes could not be fitted into any system based upon respect for law and upon self-restraint because they recognized no law and no limitations.

It is not surprising that the rulers of the Western nations failed to recognize at first that they were confronted with a revolutionary situation which nothing in their training had taught them to comprehend. Nazi Germany was explained as a psychological reaction against the wicked Treaty of Versailles— all perfectly understandable if one had read Freud. Similarly, as late as the 1940's, Russia was leftist and therefore presumed good, and whatever she did was the pardonable extravagance of reformers on the road to the millennium. It is comprehensible that men whose minds had been bred in the traditions of the nineteenth century should blunder badly in coping with what was, as Hitler said, a new order.

ANGLO-ITALIAN AGREEMENT

Chamberlain hoped that by removing Italy's fears and grievances he could induce Mussolini to withdraw his troops from Spain and perhaps weaken the Rome-Berlin Axis, which had not yet hardened into a military alliance. The terms of the agreement of 1938 are a good illustration of the futility of appeasement. Mussolini had lamented loudly and frequently that Italy was a prisoner in the Mediterranean, since Britain controlled both Gibraltar and Egypt, and from them could close the exits to the oceans. So Chamberlain gave assurances that Britain desired peace and friendship with Italy, and recognized that her interests in the Mediterranean were "vital." Both governments promised not to interfere with the free passage of shipping. All this could possibly mean was that Britain did not want to go to war, and would not dream of preventing the voyage of Italian ships as long as the two countries were at peace. But, of course, if Italy attacked Britain, the inevitable result would be that she would be bottled up in the Mediterranean. Now what Mussolini really wanted was to expel the British and French navies, make the Mediterranean an Italian lake, dislodge the British from Gibraltar, and annex Malta and Egypt besides a few assorted French possessions and Greece. He had an understandable delicacy about voicing these aspirations to Chamberlain, and so dissembled them by professing fears which the British prime minister accepted at their face value. As to weakening the Axis, by 1938 the only outlet left for Mussolini's ambitions was the Mediterranean, and his sole hope of achieving them was through German assistance.

THE MUNICH AGREEMENT

The Czechs and Slovaks both belonged to the Slav race and linguistically their languages were very similar. Politically they had been separated for centuries since Slovakia had been part of the kingdom of Hungary from its conquest in A.D. 1031. For several centuries the Czech kingdom of Bohemia was independent, and its kings encouraged the immigration of German settlers whose descendants were to provide the pretext for the Munich Agreement hundreds of years later. Eventually Bohemia was annexed to the kingdom of Austria, and in spite of revolts in the fifteenth and seventeenth centuries it did not regain its independence until the collapse of the Austrian Empire in 1918. The Czechs and Slovaks were then united in the independent republic of Czechoslovakia under the peace settlement of 1919. The largest minority was the 3,232,000 Austrians who twenty years later were to become known to the world as the Sudeten Germans. They were included despite their objections because the majority of them lived in the frontier districts adjoining Austria and Germany, and this was the only defensible military position in the Czech country. The new state included other minorities, and according to the census of 1930 it was composed of 7,447,000 Czechs, 3,232,000 Germans, 2,309,000 Slovaks, 692,000 Hungarians, 549,000 Ukrainians or Ruthenians, and 82,000 Poles in the coal mining district of Teschen. Czechoslovakia signed a Minorities Treaty in 1919, by which it agreed not to discriminate in any way against the minorities but to give them equal political, economic, religious and cultural rights with the Czechs. The treaty was substantially adhered to in all essentials although the Czechs were favored in minor points. The Nazi charge that hundreds of Germans had been hanged, thousands thrown into jail, and thousands had fled to Germany to save their lives was Goebbels at his worst.

The real grievance of the Germans was that they, the superior race, were ruled by the inferior Slavs. This was the inevitable result of majority rule in a democratic state where the Czechs outnumbered the Germans by more than two to one, and where most men voted according to race, Germans for German candidates and Czechs for Czechs. The principle of majority rule works successfully in a homogeneous nation like the United States where the electorate is not separated by deep and irreconcilable differences. It breaks down when the voters divide according to race or religion, as in Czechoslovakia, Ireland, and India. Eventually the very large majority of the Sudeten Germans joined the Nazi party and were organized and controlled as a fifth column from Berlin under the leadership of Henlein. After the annexation of the Czechs in 1939 the Sudeten Germans were restored to their old position as the ruling race. They were responsible for many of the wrongs inflicted on the Czechs during the German occupation, but after the war they pleaded to be allowed to remain in the country where they had lived for centuries. The Czechs replied that the Minority Treaty of 1919 by giving the Germans equal rights had laid upon them the implied duty of supporting the republic. By their actions they had shown that their loyalty was to Germany, and therefore about 3 million were deported. The few hundred thousand Sudeten Germans who had been loyal to the republic against Hitler were allowed to remain, but all the special rights which permitted them to retain their German language and culture were abolished. Henceforth, they were to be assimilated to the Czech majority.

Hitler's real reasons for demanding the liberation of the Sudeten Germans were political and strategic. Czechoslovakia was the only reliable ally left to France, and a successful attack on her would seriously weaken the position of her protector. Secondly, the occupation of Czechoslovakia would fatally compromise the independence of the neighboring states, particularly Poland and Hungary. Poland was the flat plain at the northern foot of the mountains of Slovakia, and on their southern slope they were the mountain rim while Hungary was the broad valley bottom. A German army established in the mountains would dominate Poland and Hungary. Moreover, Czechoslovakia had rich deposits of coal and iron and an important steel industry. It included the Skoda munitions works, one of the largest in the world. The armaments race was now in full swing, and if Hitler could get control of Czech production, he would have scored an important point.

Hitler believed that he could subjugate Czechoslovakia without a general war, since he was certain that Britain would not fight and that therefore France would not. In April, 1938, his agent Henlein demanded autonomy of so sweeping a nature for the Sudeten Germans that Czechoslovakia could not accept it without sacrificing her independence. France was bound by the alliance of 1925 to defend the country, but the majority of the people and the government were most unwilling to carry out their obligation. Premier Daladier was torn between his unwillingness to expose France to a repetition of her enormous losses of 1914–1918, and his feeling that she had a debt of honor to Czechoslovakia. He was not prepared to adhere to the treaty unless he received clear assurance of British support, and he put the onus of making the decision upon Chamberlain. The latter refused to make any promise, and from that time onward the French consciously or unconsciously wrote off their own obligations. Increasingly Chamberlain took the initiative which belonged by rights to Daladier, while the latter slipped into the position of a follower.

Britain had always refused to give a promise of help to Czechoslovakia, and Chamberlain was not bound by any treaty obligation. His dominant obsession was that he must save Europe from war; compared with this it seemed to him a very small thing that 3 million Sudeten Germans should be removed from Czech control. He knew that the French were unwilling to fight, and that the British public was opposed to war from a mixture of isolationism, pacifism, and sympathy for the German demands. Many felt that the inclusion of the Sudeten Germans in the Czech republic was another crime of Versailles, and that Hitler was only demanding for them that same right of self-determination which had given Czechoslovakia its freedom. If war came, all that Britain could send to France was two divisions of troops and 150 obsolescent airplanes. The Royal Air Force had only 666 fighter planes, of which 573 were out of date, against 1200 modern German bombers. British cities were very ill prepared to resist air attacks, and the French air force was weak. There was a good chance that if Britain and France fought, they might be defeated.

Russia had made a defensive alliance with Czechoslovakia in 1935 and volunteered help, but Chamberlain distrusted her so profoundly that he heavily discounted her offer. The United States was so wedded to neutrality that only moral support could be expected, and it would be a couple of years before the British dominions could train and equip troops. On the other hand, there was a good chance that Italy and Japan would join Germany, so that the balance of power was tilted heavily against Britain and France.

Military and air force opinion was sharply divided as to the validity of Chamberlain's opinions. The odds in the air were somewhat less unfavorable in 1939 than in 1938, though the German air force was still more than twice as strong as the French and British put together. In 1938, however, the Anglo-French army was much larger than the German, and the Siegfried line, the Rhineland fortifications, was not completed. By 1939 the trained reserve had been so greatly expanded that the German army outnumbered the combined French and British forces. Churchill argued that war in 1938 would have been less of a gamble than it was a year later.

Chamberlain's conclusion was that if Hitler meant what he said—that all he wanted for the Sudeten Germans was the justice denied them in 1919—he should not be opposed even though his methods were deplorably forceful. Blinded by his hatred of war, he shut his eyes to Hitler's record of broken promises, and deluded himself into believing that he was a man of "sincerity and good will." Rejecting all advice that conflicted with his own wishful thinking, Chamberlain had a childlike faith that Hitler would keep the Munich Agreement. He determined that the Czechs must be persuaded or compelled to satisfy Germany's demands. As the danger of war increased, he subjected them to growing coercion with the tacit support of France. Hitler made it clear that unless the frontier districts inhabited by the Sudeten Germans were transferred to him he would go to war, and Chamberlain with the support of Daladier forced the Czechs to agree. The final details were arranged at Munich on September 29, and subsequently Poland and Hungary obtained parts of Czechoslovakia. Chamberlain and Hitler signed a separate agreement in which they stated their determination to settle by negotiation any questions at issue between Britain and Germany, and to continue their efforts to assure the peace of Europe. This was the agreement which convinced Chamberlain that he had brought back from Munich "peace for our time." He found himself the most popular man in Britain, for peace was what the very large majority of the people wanted.

THE END OF ISOLATION AND PACIFISM

On March 15, 1939, the German army occupied Bohemia, and Hitler virtually annexed the Czechs by proclaiming a German protectorate. Slovakia became an independent puppet state under German control, and Hungary seized its Ukrainian province. The annihilation of Czechoslovakia revolutionized the attitude of the British government and people. Hitler had reiterated that he sought only for justice to Germans and that he did not want to annex foreigners. He had also promised that there would be no more forcible changes in the map of Europe. All this was stultified by his action of March 15 which showed that his real aim was to create a great German empire, and that sooner or later Britain herself would be attacked. The realization of this killed isolationism, pacifism, and sympathy for Germany. Chamberlain had general support for every step that he took to prepare for the war that was now regarded as inevitable. The only doubt in the mind of the public was whether he was too old and too slow, and ought to be replaced by Churchill.

On March 21 Hitler made demands on Poland which were a threat to its independence, and on March 30 Chamberlain announced that Poland had accepted a British offer of help against Germany. Shortly afterward similar guarantees were given to Greece and Rumania, and these were followed later in the year by the Anglo-Turkish Alliance. This was a complete reversal of the policy followed since Locarno that Britain's frontier was on the Rhine and that she would not intervene in central and eastern Europe. The weak point of the new departure was that she did not have the troops to act effectively. In April the Chamberlain government passed a law for compulsory military service, despite the bitter opposition of the Labour and Liberal parties. The British had always considered that peacetime conscription was undemocratic, and it was very significant that the measure was generally approved.

Poland alone was no match for Germany, and as soon as war began, the latter would close the Baltic so that it would be impossible to send supplies. The one country which could give help was Soviet Russia whom Chamberlain had rebuffed the previous year over Czechoslovakia. Negotiations were begun for a defensive alliance of Britain, France, Russia, and Poland, and by the end of July the prospects of concluding it seemed very favorable. They ended on August 23 when Russia announced the conclusion of a pact of neutrality and nonaggression with Germany. The promise of Russian neutrality made it certain that Germany would attack Poland, France, and Britain, since it assured Hitler and his general staff that they would not have to fight a war on two fronts.

The full story of the negotiations has not yet been made public, and it is only tentatively that one can set forth the reasons for what took place. Chamberlain believed that Russia wished to provoke a European war from which she would remain aloof so that capitalism would collapse from the strains of the contest and she could establish a communist police state on the ruins. He also doubted the military effectiveness of the Red army, while he over-estimated that of the Polish forces; and his conduct of the negotiations was dilatory and disdainful. Stalin believed that the whole world was the enemy of communism. He was always fearful that Britain, France, and Germany might reconcile their quarrel and unite in an attack on Russia. If war came, he doubted whether the British or French armies had either the will or the strength to give him effective help. It was hard to form a firm alliance for a life and death struggle when the prospective allies felt nothing but distrust and hostility toward one another. If Stalin did fight, he was determined to regain the territories which Russia had lost after World War I to Poland, Rumania, Estonia, Latvia, Lithuania, and Finland. Britain and France refused to con-sent because they felt that they would be accomplices in a Soviet imperialism that was as bad as Germany's. Poland declined to allow the Red army to cross her frontiers. Hitler was so anxious to gain Russian neutrality while he dis-posed of France and Britain that he was willing to buy it by agreeing to Stalin's territorial demand.

The loss of the Russian alliance had no effect on Chamberlain's determin-ation to go to war if Germany attacked Poland. In an effort to make this clear to Hitler an Anglo-Polish Agreement was signed on August 25, which con-firmed and strengthened the alliance of the previous April. Hitler continued to hope that in the end Chamberlain and Daladier would agree to a second Munich, but he was determined to carry out the conquest of Poland even if it meant war with the West. Up to the last, Chamberlain tried to persuade Hitler to agree to a negotiated settlement, combining this with warnings that he would honor his treaty obligations. On September 1 the German armies in-vaded Poland, and on September 3 Britain and France declared war. Hitler badly underrated Chamberlain: beneath his passionate desire for peace lay a very hard core.

A marked parallel existed between the British policy of the 'thirties and that of the early twentieth century. There was the same pacifism and desire for isolation, though the former was stronger after World War I than before it. In each case foreign policy was strongly affected by public opinion, though here again the influence was greater in the 'thirties. There was the same slow-ness and reluctance to make commitments in Europe and to adopt the balance of power policy, since the division of the continent into opposing blocs might increase the risk of war. Force of circumstances drove Britain in this direc-tion on both occasions, though Chamberlain like Grey refused to admit that this was his policy. When he was attempting to win the Russian alliance in 1939, he insisted that he was building up a peace front strong enough to deter Hitler from war. In other words, he was trying to restore the balance of power. The motive which led Chamberlain to this course was the same as Grey's—that is, the threat to the security of Britain. Each time the danger came from a great power with a dominant army and an aggressive foreign policy which aroused increasing fear and suspicion. The only difference lay in the form of the threat. The first time it was the German navy, and the second the air force. By the 'thirties Henry VIII's formula that security from invasion was assured by the English Channel and the fleet had been broadened to include the airplane.

POSTWAR BRITAIN

The decline of Great Britain from the position of power that she had prior to 1914 has been one of the most significant developments of the last forty years. One of the reasons for this has been the change in the global distribution of sea power. What enabled her to use her fleet so decisively prior to 1918 was the presence of all her naval rivals in Europe close to British bases. As long as Britain held the seas around the continent, she could blockade her opponent in his home ports, deny him access to countries overseas, and herself draw freely upon their resources. After World War I the situation completely changed with a hostile naval power, Japan, 12,000 miles away from Europe. The distance made it infinitely more difficult to cope with than it was in World War I when all that was necessary was to bottle up the German navy with the British fleet and its bases only 700 miles away. Danger could now fall directly on distant colonies, and to make matters worse the industrial strength and the armed forces of the empire were largely in Britain. Moreover, Japan was in alliance with Germany and Italy, and the combination of power and global distances was too much for Britain to handle alone after the fall of France.

The importance of size as an element of power has been immensely increased by the change in the character of war since 1939, owing to the development of mechanization and air power. The gainers are the United States and Russia, and the losers are Britain and all the other countries of Europe. One reason the Russian armies survived the German invasion of 1941 was that they were able to retreat over 850 miles and still have a vast expanse of friendly territory behind them. If the British and French had tried the same maneuver in 1940, they would have been in the Atlantic Ocean. To lessen the effect of air attack a very large area is needed for the dispersal of troops, supply bases, and war factories. Great Britain is at a heavy disadvantage with innumerable targets concentrated on an island of 93,000 square miles, rather smaller than Oregon. A large population to provide troops and workers in war industry is another essential where Britain is at a disadvantage compared with the United States and Russia.

Traditionally Britain was a naval but not a military power. In war her contribution was her fleet, limited expeditionary forces, and generous financial subsidies toward the cost of her allies' armies. The development of huge conscript armies during the nineteenth century compelled Britain for the first time in her history to raise a force of several million men in 1914. In addition, she had to maintain a supreme navy and lend heavily to her allies. In World War II a large air force had to be created in addition. All this imposed too great an economic burden on a nation of (in 1939) only 48 million. Armaments had to be paid for by the sale of exports and foreign investments. But to be strong on sea, land, and air more and more men and women had to be withdrawn from peacetime production to war factories or the armed forces. The statistics are enlightening as showing the effect of contemporary war on a nation of limited population and resources. Britain had a male population of working age (aged fourteen to sixty-four) of 15,910,000. Of these, over 15 million were mobilized, 5,896,000 in the armed forces and the remainder in industry (the majority in production connected with the war directly or indirectly). Of the 16 million women of working age, 7.1 million were in the armed forces or in industry. By 1944 of those employed in manufacturing only four were engaged in production for export, compared with fifteen before the war. The volume of exports in 1944 was only 31 percent of 1938. Partially to fill the gap and pay for imports about a quarter of the overseas investments were sold. By 1941 Britain had almost exhausted her supply of dollars and she would have been compelled drastically to curtail her war effort if it had not been for the creation of American Lend Lease.

The import of food and raw materials and the export of manufactures was the basis of Great Britain's pre-1939 economy. Since her imports considerably exceeded her exports, she paid for the deficit by invisible exports, such as the income from foreign investments. World War I gravely weakened and World War II destroyed this economy. Henceforth, exports must pay for imports, and this required an immense increase in manufacturing. Merely to accomplish this could absorb all the energies of a nation of 50,850,000. But the international situation requires the maintenance of heavy armaments by land, sea and air which absorb 12.5 percent of the national income. The total number in the armed forces in 1956 is 772,000, of whom 80 percent serve overseas in Germany and elsewhere. This is a far larger peacetime strength than was ever maintained before 1939, when the country was much more able to support the burden. If a future war were to require an effort comparable with that of the last, revival of American Lend Lease would be unavoidable. Rearmament aggravates the nation's problem of paying its way, since it diverts men from industry and agriculture to the armed forces, and requires many factories to produce munitions instead of goods for export. One illustration of how the economic situation affects the international position of Great

Britain was her inability to send arms and economic help to Greece and Turkey after 1947, although the maintenance of their independence was of the first importance. Economic weakness is a principal cause of the postwar weakening of the international position of Great Britain.

The traditional role of Britain was to tip the balance decisively, but since 1945 she is no longer able to do this. The balance of power is no longer confined to Europe and has become global—the United States and its allies *versus* the Communist bloc. Possibly Great Britain might still be able to act as the holder of the balance if she controlled the British Empire. But by the deliberate policy of 100 years she has encouraged each unit of the empire to go its own way in foreign affairs as well as domestic. The result is that the empire is rather like the description of Mussolini at a review of his troops, when he mounted his horse and galloped off in all directions. The government of Britain can never be sure whether it represents a quarter of the human race or the 50 million of the United Kingdom. In 1939 Britain was not certain until after war had been declared whether she would be supported by the self-governing dominions or whether they would declare their neutrality like Eire (the present Irish Republic). The result is that the empire is strong in war but weak in peace, owing to uncertainty as to the dominions' course of action.

The attainment of self-government by India and Pakistan has further weakened Britain. For 150 years the Indian Ocean had been a British lake, the principal reason being that the key to its control was India. Nehru cannot afford to create a navy and air force that could replace Britain's, and his policy of neutrality prevents the British from using their former bases. The defensive alliance between Britain and the dominion of Ceylon is not an adequate substitute, for a naval base and air fields on a small island are not equal to those on a subcontinent. In 1939 the army in India was composed of 45,000 British and 140,000 Indian troops. During the war this was increased to over 2 million by purely voluntary enlistment. Insofar as this force was not needed to defend India, it was sent to those countries which might be used as a base for invading India. In both the world wars these were Egypt, Iraq, and Iran, and Burma and Malaya were added in World War II. It is completely uncertain whether these forces would be available in future, and the defense of the Middle East is seriously weakened.

POSTWAR INTERESTS

The war has not radically changed the vital interests of Britain. First and foremost comes the preservation of her own independence, and this involves the defense of Western Europe to a far greater degree than ever before. The safety of Britain is no longer ensured by supporting the independence of Belgium, Holland, and France as in the pre-1914 period. The second interest is the maintenance of the British Empire. To do this and to assure the continuance of foreign trade in time of war, it is as necessary as it ever was to protect the ocean routes. This involves Britain in a multitude of commitments, all the way from her 300-year-old ally Portugal to her outpost of Hong Kong, including en route Mediterranean, Middle Eastern, and African territories, Malaya, and the southwest Pacific.

The Middle East is an important interest, though not for the reason usually given. The sea route through the Mediterranean and the Suez Canal is the shortest passage from Britain to her possessions and trading areas in Asia and the Pacific. If it is closed, the loss is very serious but not fatal. Before the war only between 9 percent and 14 percent of the imports into Britain came via the Suez Canal. To take the old route around the Cape of Good Hope adds to the cost of trade by the loss of time and higher freights. The closer the country to the canal, the greater the saving in using it. For an oil tanker from the Persian Gulf the passage via the Cape increases the length of the voyage by 80 percent, while from Hong Kong the added mileage is 37 percent, and from Sydney, Australia, 10 percent. The Axis virtually closed the canal route from 1940 to 1943 by its control of the central Mediterranean, but Britain survived both the economic and the military consequences. On the military side, General Wavell declared that Malaya was lost by six weeks, this being the extra time needed to send reinforcements from Britain via the Cape. As against this, Montgomery's army in Libya won its war although its supplies had to come 14,000 miles via the Cape of Good Hope, Indian Ocean, and Red Sea. Altogether apart from the Suez Canal, the Middle East contains the traditional roads of invasion by which armies can move from Russia to India or Africa, and from Germany to India or Africa. If the Indian Ocean coast of the Middle East were in hostile hands it would threaten the sea route from Britain to the Pacific. Then there is oil, and also the global air routes of the Western nations which have to pass over the Middle East on their way to the Pacific and to southern Africa. For all these reasons combined the preservation of the independence of the Middle East is a leading British interest.

POLICY SINCE 1945

The British socialist government (the Labour party) came to power in 1945 with a strong predisposition to seek for close and friendly relations with Russia, and a belief that this could be accomplished because "Labour can talk with Labour." There was also a tendency on ideological grounds to look upon the United States with some suspicion and disapproval, since it was the leading capitalist country. This matched the American tendency to regard socialist Britain in the same way for the reverse reasons. Primarily through the actions of the Soviet government itself the Attlee cabinet was driven to reverse its policy and draw closer and closer to the United States. The result was the curious spectacle of socialists and capitalists in close working agreement against Communists. With differences of emphasis the foreign policy of the Labour Foreign Minister Bevin was not very dissimilar from that of his Conservative successor Eden. The only dissentients were the Labour left wingers who eventually united under the leadership of Aneurin Bevan. They were critically distrustful of American policy, and favored less close and friendly relations between the two countries. They insisted that rearmament must be drastically curtailed in order still further to expand the welfare state, and they denied that this entailed the risk of a Russian attack. It is clear that Bevan has considerable support from the rank and file of his party.

Understandably Britain has not relished taking second place to the United States in sea and air power, but her attitude is utterly different to what it was toward Germany. Then Britain had the strongest suspicions of German aims, while now she is sure that the United States does not wish to dominate the world. Her aim is to foster increasingly close relations between the two countries, so that a Western bloc under American leadership is a counterpoise to the Soviet bloc. The balance of power policy is reviving on a global scale as the cold war goes on and the United Nations continues to disappoint the early hopes that clustered around it. Apart from the Bevanites both British political parties recognize that in a dangerous world there is more hope of security in creating a balance than in allowing the preponderance of actual power to remain heavily in favor of Russia. Close cooperation with the United States is a fundamental principle of British policy. In part it is based on self-interest as all policies are, but at the same time there is a genuine and long standing feeling in Britain that the United States is in a different category from other foreign countries. If the North Atlantic Treaty Organization ever develops into an Atlantic Community, Britain would feel more at home in it than in a purely European union.

Isolation is much weaker than before the war: it was killed by the educative effects of Germany's air blitz of 1940–1941 and the guided missiles of 1944–1945. The Englishman does not love all Western Europeans as brothers; but he recognizes that if they do not hang together, they are likely to hang separately. There is always the pull of the empire, however, and while the British are prepared to cooperate closely with Europe in defense and economics, they are not willing to merge themselves in a United States of Europe. Both political parties supported the defensive alliance with France in 1947, the larger alliance of 1948 that brought in Holland, Belgium and Luxembourg as well, and the North Atlantic Treaty Organization of 1949. Both agreed that British troops should be maintained in Europe as long as they were needed for its defense. There was the same bipartisan approval of aid to Turkey and Greece to resist communism and of the American-Japanese alliance of 1951. Both parties agreed upon the treaties which restored to Western Germany her position as an independent state and legalized the recreation of the German army. Eden, when he was the Conservative foreign minister, worked out arrangements for close collaboration with the Schuman Plan organization without actually joining it.

Britain is a world as well as a European power, and this explains the attitude of "Thus far and no farther." She is resolved to maintain the integrity of the British Commonwealth. This is a loose confederation of eight equal and self-governing partners, all of which have different policies. Only two of them—Britain and Canada—feel that their own self-defense requires them to station troops in Western Europe. The dominions are determined to maintain the Commonwealth, but it is inconceivable that at the present time they would federate with one another or with any Western European federation that might be set up. If Britain joined a European federation, she would have to surrender control of her foreign policy and armed forces and become a local government like, say, the state of New York. One of the purposes of the British army is to act as a strategic reserve for the whole Empire, and during the past few years troops have been sent to the Middle East, Malaya and Hong Kong as well as to Korea. The British government could not have ordered any of these movements if it had surrendered control of its forces. If any problem of Commonwealth foreign policy or defense arose, Britain would have to tell her partners that she could not cooperate with them until she had received the permission of the European international authority. This could well lead to the break up of the Commonwealth, and that is why Churchill said that "The British Commonwealth of Nations is not prepared to become a State or a group of States in any Continental federal system on either side of the Atlantic."

Support of the United Nations is a principle of British policy. There is the hope that it will avoid war by the peaceful settlement of disputes, and that if war comes, collective security may prove to be a reality. The British attitude is not entirely based on self-interest: there is a genuine element of idealism about it, a feeling that the U.N. embodies a high purpose which deserves support for its own excellence. The disappointing record of the U.N. has made Britain hope for the best while not altogether expecting it. She continues to support it, tries to strengthen it, and submits her own disputes to its settlement. But realism requires that the uncertain performance of the U.N. be supplemented by more dependable guarantees such as the North Atlantic Treaty Organization.

SELECTED READING

BRINTON, CRANE, *United States and Britain,* rev. ed. Cambridge: Harvard University Press, 1948.

British Security. New York: Royal Institute of International Affairs, 1946.

BULLARD, SIR READER, *Britain and the Middle East.* New York: Longmans, Green and Company, 1951.

CHURCHILL, SIR WINSTON S., *The Second World War,* 6 vols. Boston: Houghton Mifflin and Company, 1948–1953. Especially Vol. I, *The Gathering Storm,* 1948.

FEILING, KEITH G., *Life of Neville Chamberlain.* New York: The Macmillan Company, 1947.

KAHN, ALFRED E., *Great Britain in the World Economy.* New York: Columbia University Press, 1946.

LEEPER, SIR REGINALD, *When Greek Meets Greek.* London: Chatto and Windus, 1950.

WEBSTER, SIR CHARLES, JACOB, GENERAL SIR IAN, and ROBINSON, E. A. G., *United Kingdom Policy, Foreign, Strategic, Economic.* New York: Royal Institute of International Affairs, 1950.

WELLESLEY, SIR VICTOR, *Diplomacy in Fetters.* London: Hutchinson and Company, Ltd., 1944.

CHAPTER 19

THE BRITISH COMMONWEALTH AND EMPIRE

The British Empire in the days of George III was an empire in the traditional sense of the term; but it has long been as dead as the King himself. Throughout history empire has meant control: always there has been a king or ruling race who gave orders, and subjects who obeyed. The British Empire began to break away from this pattern nearly a century and a quarter ago, and the development has continued until the word "empire" has become almost completely misleading. This is why the rather clumsy phrase "Commonwealth and Empire" is the only accurate description. Commonwealth implies equality and empire subjection, and both terms are true of different parts of the British possessions. The division is not according to race but depends on political, economic, and social maturity. The Commonwealth includes Great Britain and the completely self-governing dominions of Canada, Australia, New Zealand, South Africa, India, Pakistan, and Ceylon. The empire is made up of tropical areas such as the African colonies, Malaya, and Hong Kong, and a few naval and air bases like Gibraltar. Most of them have a varying degree of local self-government, but the final authority lies with the government of Great Britain. These possessions are an empire in the traditional sense. British policy is to abolish the empire as quickly as is wise and substitute complete self-government in each colony. The rate of progress depends upon the degree of political advance of the population.

DEVELOPMENT OF SELF-GOVERNMENT

The principle of the policy was laid down by Lord Durham in his report on the Canadian rebellion of 1837. He advised the government of

Britain that the way to hold the empire together was to let it go. If Britain refused any demand for self-government, the eventual result would be a rebellion and the loss of the colony. But if every demand were granted, there would be no reason to revolt and the dependency would remain within the empire. The advice was acted upon from 1847 onward, and parliamentary democracy on the British model was set up. One power after another was transferred from the control of the government of Britain to that of Canada, when the demand arose that this be done. The same rights were granted to other colonies as they developed, and they were encouraged to join in larger units called dominions. Canada became a dominion in 1867, Australia in 1900, and South Africa in 1910. By 1914 a dominion had virtually complete control of its internal affairs, defense, and trade policy. The one major limitation was that Great Britain alone controlled foreign policy apart from trade relations. This restriction was swept away during World War I and the decade that followed it. Thereafter the dominions shared equally with Britain in deciding the policy of the Commonwealth.

A dominion is free to determine its own foreign relations, and none has the power to dictate to another. Each dominion is the sole judge of how far it will cooperate with the rest. So in 1939 Eire remained neutral, while the other dominions of their own accord entered the war. The only legal link holding the Commonwealth together is the common allegiance to the Crown, and in 1949 this was weakened when India became a republic with an elected president. He and not Queen Elizabeth is the head of the state; but at the same time India remains inside the Commonwealth by accepting the Crown as the symbol of the free association of its independent member nations and as such the head of the Commonwealth. The right of secession was formally admitted by Britain in 1942 and exercised by Eire and Burma when they became independent republics. The dominions have always refused to create anything in the nature of a Commonwealth legislature and executive since this would lessen their complete freedom of action. The principal constitutional machinery is the periodical meeting in London or some other capital of the Commonwealth's prime ministers, or sometimes other members of their cabinets. Britain cannot compel the assent of the dominions, and neither can a majority bind a minority. The meeting depends for its success on free discussion and persuasion. There is a single Commonwealth policy only on the rare occasions when the dominions and Britain all decide of their own free will to follow the same course of action. The Commonwealth can best be described as a loose confederation of sovereign states which cooperate when they feel like it. They hold together because at bottom they want to do so. With all the Commonwealth's weaknesses it is the world's nearest approach to an effective United Nations.

THE ASIAN DOMINIONS

Prior to World War I the development of dominion status, to use the technical term, was confined to the parts of the empire which had a population that was predominantly of European descent. India and the tropical dependencies were an empire in the traditional sense of the term, under the ultimate control of the government of Great Britain. In 1917 the British government announced a revolutionary change of policy. British control was gradually to be abolished, and power transferred to the elected representatives of the local populations. The landmarks of the new departure in India were the Montagu-Chelmsford reforms of 1919, the constitution of 1935, and the final transfer of the powers still remaining in British hands in 1947. The abolition of British control after World War II was not a sudden development but the completion of a policy which had been in operation for thirty years. The causes of division between Hindus and Muslims were so numerous and serious that the choice lay between civil war and partition. At the last moment the leaders agreed to separate peacefully, and India was divided into two dominions—the Hindu Republic of India and the Muslim Republic of Pakistan. In 1948 the former tropical colony of Ceylon completed its peaceful evolution from British control to dominion status, and graduated from the Empire to the Commonwealth.

CANADA

The development of regional foreign policies by the dominions was beginning to show itself during the interwar period, but it has become much more pronounced since 1945. This was to be expected with countries scattered so widely over the globe and affected by very different geographic, strategic, and economic influences. Canada, the premier dominion, has an area of 3,624,-853 square miles and a population of 15,236,000. About 47 percent are of British ancestry. French Canadians are 31 percent, and 20 percent are of European or American descent. Those of British ancestry feel a strong affection toward Great Britain—a feeling not shared by the French Canadians, whose attitude toward France is also critical and not too friendly. They have developed a strong French Canadian nationalism which centers primarily upon their own province of Quebec. As long as Canada is not invaded, their trend is toward isolationism. No dominion government can ignore a third of the electorate. This explains why Canada did not have conscription for overseas service in World War II and relied upon volunteers, who came mostly from the English-speaking part of the population. Canada has been powerfully affected by the proximity of the United States culturally, economically, and politically. It is the only part of the Commonwealth which does not belong to the sterling bloc. In foreign affairs Canada is insistent that Britain must not follow any policy which is disapproved by the United States. At the same time there is strong determination not to be absorbed or dominated by the more powerful neighbor, and to retain Canada's separate identity. Canada's attitude toward the Commonwealth and the world is molded by a complex of forces—strong Canadian nationalism, a warm attachment to Great Britain, the necessity of close and friendly relations with the United States, and French Canadian isolationism.

Canada's nationalism is shown in the strong opposition she has displayed for a generation to any proposal to improve the not very effective machinery for consultation between the members of the Commonwealth. At the same time reasonably close liaison has been maintained between the British and Canadian governments, and generous economic help was given to Great Britain during and after World War II. Isolationism was greatly weakened by the war and the development of long-range aircraft. Canada played an important part in the creation of NATO, and a brigade of troops was sent to Germany. Apart from Great Britain, Canada's principal interest outside North America lies in Western Europe. She is much less concerned about Asia, though Canadian troops fought in Korea. World War II brought about a virtual alliance between the United States and Canada. In 1940 an advisory Permanent Joint Board on Defence was established. This was followed by the building of airfields in Canada and the Alaska Military Highway, and the coordination of war production in the two countries. The collaboration has been continued owing to the growing tension between the Western world and Russia. The shortest air route from Russia to the United States lies across the Arctic Circle, and in the event of war Canada would be in the front line. This has led to the conduct of joint exercises for the defense of northern Canada.

AUSTRALIA AND NEW ZEALAND

Australia has a population that is 96 percent of British descent. It is spared the racial complications which compel the Canadian government to walk delicately between French- and English-speaking Canadians. There is a strong feeling of affection and loyalty toward Great Britain, and this is strengthened by the proximity to Asia. Australians feel themselves to be "of the West and not part of it; of the East but not in it." They are a small outpost of Western civilization on the edge of a vast and perhaps not overly friendly continent, and in the event of war their survival would depend on help from overseas. Australians like to point out that what to Americans and British is the Far East is to them the Near North. Japan is only 3900 miles away, while help from the United States would have to come over

6000 miles, and from Britain 11,000. British sentiment and a sense of insecurity combine to produce a stronger desire for close cooperation with Great Britain than in Canada. In 1939 troops were raised as a matter of course and sent to fight in Egypt. This does not mean that Australia is a docile satellite. There is a robust nationalism which was strengthened by World War II, and this would resist any attempt at interference. The people are Australians first and British second. If Great Britain makes a proposal the reply of Canada tends to be "Perhaps, but probably no," while Australia is likely to answer "Yes, damn you."

Until 1941 Australians took it for granted that if Japan attacked, they would fight a delaying action until Britain came to their help. The United States hardly entered their consciousness—an attitude which was reciprocated. When the war came, Britain was strained to the uttermost in Europe and Africa, and was herself defeated in Malaya and Burma. Australia was saved by American help. This experience profoundly affected the Australians' outlook. They have no intention of seceding from the British Commonwealth; on the contrary, they would like to strengthen it. But the old blind reliance on Great Britain has gone, and a realistic attitude has replaced it that the United States must be the major protector against the dangers of the future.

Australia's regional interests lie primarily in the western Pacific and to a lesser extent in the Middle East. She is not intimately concerned with Western Europe, except insofar as events there affect Great Britain. Her Pacific interests are economic, political, and strategic. The bulk of her trade is with Great Britain, but before the war there was substantial commerce with eastern and southern Asia, which Australia hopes to expand. There are only 8,829,000 Australians in a continent of 2,974,581 square miles, and close by are the overpopulated countries of Asia. Although 23 percent of the land is desert and a further 37 percent offers poor prospects of close settlement because of uncertain rainfall, it could easily maintain quite a large Asian population. All parties support the white Australia policy, the exclusion from permanent settlement of all Asians, on the ground that their admission would lower the high Australian standard of living. This has caused a good deal of resentment in Asia, and has aroused the fear that attempts might be made to colonize the sparsely populated continent by force.

Australia emerged from the war determined to assert her right to a voice in the shaping of policy. In the United Nations she was a leader of the small states in the attempt to limit the authority of the great powers, and in the Pacific she demanded that she be accepted as the spokesman for the whole Commonwealth. In 1944 Australia and New Zealand signed the Canberra Agreement, in which they laid down a co-ordinated policy for the south Pacific. The defense of this area should be undertaken by the two dominions, the United States, Britain, and the other interested powers in equal partnership. Naval and air bases should be available to all on a basis of reciprocity, and Australia refused to transfer to the United States Manus Island in the Admiralty Islands north of New Guinea, where during the war the American navy had built a first-class base at a cost of $400 million.

Australians are troubled by the threat of communism in Asia, but they are even more concerned about the possibility of a renewal of the threat from Japan. They are skeptical whether it has become either democratic or peace-loving, and they are fearful of the ultimate results of the American policy of restoring its economic and military power as a counterpoise to the Communist states in the Far East. In 1951 a defensive alliance, the Anzus Pact, was signed between the United States, Australia, and New Zealand. Each stated that armed attack in the Pacific area on any one of them would be a danger to the peace and security of all. Each pledged itself to take action in accordance with its constitutional processes in the event of hostilities. The treaty was so worded that it included an armed attack upon, e.g., Okinawa which the United States is administering or on the American forces stationed in or about Japan under the Security Treaty of 1951 with that country. In the event of war Australia and New Zealand also count on help from Great Britain to the extent that she is able to provide it. This is on the unwritten principle of the Commonwealth that if any part is attacked there is a moral obligation to assist. Australia was a signatory of the Southeast Asia Treaty Organization (SEATO), or Manila Pact, of 1954 for the defense of Southeast Asia and the western Pacific. She accepted military commitments in a plan for collective security; but as in World War II, she feels that her own safety is more bound up with the defense of Malaya than with that of the other countries on the mainland.

The rise of nationalism in Asia and the threat of communism have made Australia particularly anxious to cultivate friendly relations with the Asian states. She was very active in the United Nations in sponsoring the independence of Indonesia during the struggle with the Dutch. But since the government of the republic is weak and might fall under Communist control, Australia supports Holland in her refusal to surrender Dutch New Guinea or Irian. Advance in that quarter would give the republic a common frontier with Australian New Guinea. Australia also sent a contingent to the U.N. army in South Korea. In Malaya a small detachment of the air force is serving with the British forces against the Chinese Communist rebels, and in 1955 it was decided to send reinforcements. Next to the western Pacific, Australia is particularly interested in the security of the Middle East, where her armies fought in both world wars. The Suez Canal route is the shortest sea connection with Great Britain, and Australia is very sensitive to any threat to its safety. During the negotiations of 1951–1952 to create an army for the defense of the Middle East, Australia and New Zealand stated that if it were attacked, they would send troops. Necessarily this was coupled with the proviso that there must be peace in the Pacific.

New Zealand has a population of 2,093,000 and an area of 104,000 square miles. Despite their nationalism the people are more strongly pro-British in sentiment than in any of the other dominions and have been least changed by the effects of World War II. New Zealand stresses Commonwealth cooperation rather than independence, and prides herself on the overwhelmingly British descent of her population. Whenever Britain is in difficulties, there is a strong disposition to give whatever help is possible. In economics the policy is to buy British and to sell to Britain. The principal regional interest is the western Pacific. This means distrust of Japan, alliance with the United States as well as reliance on Britain, a New Zealand contingent of troops in South Korea, and membership in the Manila Pact.

THE UNION OF SOUTH AFRICA

South Africa (including the former mandate of South West Africa) has an area of 790,219 square miles and a population of 13,840,000. Of these about 2.5 million are of European descent, 300,000 are Indians, and the rest Negroes or half castes. Of the Europeans, about 57 percent are of Dutch and 34 percent of British descent, the former being known as the Boers. Their common fear of the large Negro majority tends to make their native policy similar. Like the American Indians, the Negroes were allotted reserves in the nineteenth century where they could live by agriculture, but the bulk of the cultivable land was assigned to Europeans. The British put an end to tribal wars and introduced medical and health measures, with the result that the Negro population increased beyond all expectations. At the same time their antiquated farming methods caused a serious decline in the fertility of the reserves. The result was that these became increasingly unable to support the growing population. More and more Negroes were compelled to seek work on the European farms and in the mines and factories of the cities. The Europeans are completely dependent upon the Negroes for manual labor, and without them the economic life of South Africa would collapse. The Indians were brought into the province of Natal between 1860 and 1911 to work on the sugar plantations. Their descendants are laborers, shopkeepers, landlords of urban properties, and business and professional men.

The Europeans are outnumbered by about five to one, and the numerical disparity is increasing. The basic principle of any government is the maintenance of white supremacy, and this is felt to be in danger. The nearest parallel to the South African situation is to be found in South Carolina and some of the other southern states. In industry the color bar confines Negroes to unskilled manual labor, while skilled employment is reserved for the European trade union members. The vote is limited to Europeans, with the exception of the 1 million half castes. The Nationalist government is determined to remove them from the common electoral roll, and give them separate representation in the Union Parliament. The Negroes are represented there by a few Europeans. The native policy of the two leading political parties, the Boer Nationalists, who gained control of the government in 1948, and the United party differs in emphasis rather than in essentials. Both support the policy of white supremacy, and any deviation from it would be political suicide. The United party has been more conciliatory and readier to make minor concessions. The Nationalists propose to maintain white supremacy by Apartheid or racial separation. The goal appears to be that Negroes and Europeans shall inhabit different parts of the country, except when the former are temporarily brought into the European areas to do the essential work assigned to them under the color bar. At other times the Negroes will live on their reserves, where they will develop their own culture and government under European control. But the reserves are far too small for this to be practicable, and the vague unrest among the Negroes is growing.

The Europeans of British descent have reason to fear that the Boer Nationalist government intends to reduce them to the position of second-class citizens. The quarrel between the Boers and British South Africans is nearly 150 years old, and culminated in the British conquest and annexation of the two Dutch republics of the Transvaal and the Orange Free State after the Boer War of 1899. In 1907 Great Britain restored to the Boers complete self-government, and in 1910 the Union of South Africa was formed by the free decision of the two European races. The basis of the agreement was that Boer and British would cooperate on the basis of complete political and cultural equality. This became the policy of the United party, which was supported by the moderate Boers and the majority of the British. The Nationalists represent the section of the Boers who are still fighting the Boer War of fifty years ago. Their creed is a fanatical mixture of narrow Boer patriotism and religious bigotry. They are convinced that God is on their side, and that His chosen people are those Boer Calvinists who refuse to compromise with the British, the Negroes, and the Indians. Their aim is to create a South African republic where the Boers would be the master race, the Negroes would be paternally but very firmly held down in Apartheid, and the British (so far as they remained in the country) would be treated as an inferior variety of white man. This politico-religious creed has obvious resemblances to that of the Nazis, with whom some of the Nationalists frankly proclaimed their sympathy during World War II.

This complex situation has explosive possibilities which have already brought repercussions far beyond the borders of the Union, and are certain to cause more trouble. India has been aroused, partly by the discriminatory treatment of Indians and also because she wishes to end the rule of Western peoples over colored races in Africa as well as in Asia. A bitter quarrel between dominions causes understandable apprehension in Great Britain. A further reason is that the Negroes of British tropical Africa are well aware of events in South Africa, and this gives rise to distrust of Britain. There is precisely nothing that she can do about it since no part of the Commonwealth can give orders to another. The U.N. Assembly attempted to compel a change in the Apartheid policy. This was regarded by South Africans as an illegal interference with their domestic affairs, and strengthened the government's position.

THE REPUBLIC OF INDIA

It is important to understand the climate of opinion in India, since this greatly affects official policy. The leaders share many of the views of their fellow countrymen. Even if they disagree, they cannot get too far out of touch with public opinion because the Asian dominions have democratic and not dictatorial governments. India particularly deserves study, both as a leader of the Asian bloc in the U.N. and because the views held are often very similar to those in other countries of South Asia. Two points which the West must always remember are the very strong and hypersensitive nationalism and the easily aroused suspicion of Western motives. Any suggestion that the West has a feeling of racial superiority causes bitter resentment, e.g., the position of Negroes in the United States or South Africa. There is intense hostility to imperialism, and the determination to do everything possible to end it in Asia and Africa. This attitude does not extend to Russian or Chinese imperialism. Nehru gave all the moral support in his power to the Indonesian Nationalists in their struggle against Holland, and regarded the French in Indochina as unregenerate imperialists with Bao Dai as their puppet. Public opinion was strongly sympathetic to the Communist-dominated Vietminh on the ground that it was fighting for freedom. The government approved of Mossadegh's nationalization of the Anglo-Iranian Oil Company's property, and it has several times in the U.N. attacked the policy of South Africa. India voted for the U.N. decision to give military support to South Korea when it was invaded in 1950, but the attitude changed when the U.N. army carried the war into North Korea. India also disapproves the retention of American troops in Japan under the terms of the peace treaty of 1951.

Asians generally are suspicious of the presence of Western troops anywhere in Asia, however strong the reasons may be, lest the real motive should be to impose Western control. It was said that American troops were sent to South Korea because the United States intended to fight Russia on Asian soil. It was added that she was extending her bases too far into Asia and was indifferent to the loss of Asian life in war. Many believed that the United States acted quickly in Korea not because of her U.N. obligation to oppose aggression but because her own strategic interests were threatened. The point to notice is that these charges have been made and believed. They illustrate how easily actions that seem innocent and praiseworthy to Americans can be given a totally different interpretation in Asia.

Very often the United States is more suspect of imperialism than Great Britain. The British are regarded as comparatively reformed characters, apart from which their losses in World War II have made them less capable of relapsing into original sin. Americans have the power and Indians fear the inclination to use it. What they are particularly afraid of is economic imperialism. In his *Glimpses of World History* Nehru pointed to Central and South America as an example of the new style of imperialism, "invisible and economic," which gains control not by the old method of armed conquest but by the more subtle technique of economic penetration. He went on to say that by trade and investment Americans had won effective control of markets and natural resources and exploited them to their own advantage, although the Latin American republics remained outwardly independent. The result is that India, like other Asian states, both seeks American financial and technical aid and yet is afraid that it may insidiously impair her independence. She is suspicious lest it be made conditional on the nation's subordinating its foreign policy to that of the United States. There is resentment that the great bulk of American aid has gone to Europe, and a demand that more attention be paid to Asian needs. There is a genuine desire to attract private investment, coupled with the fear that it will exploit India to its own selfish profit. "If the West gives aid, it will be feared for its imperialism; if it withholds aid, it will be denounced for its indifference; if it establishes garrisons, it will be attacked as expansionist; if it keeps its troops at home it ensures the success of aggression in Asia and . . . In other words . . . we are damned if we do and damned if we don't." South Asian opinion is desperately afraid of Americans bearing gifts. This mixed attitude greatly increases the difficulty of carrying out the American policy of containing communism.

In the past Indians like most other Asians have come in contact with European but not with Communist imperialism. On the whole, they do not realize that the former is in full retreat and that the threat to their independence comes from the latter. India and much of South Asia are not convinced that communism is aggressive. If it appears to be, it is because it is frightened and misunderstood. There is widespread acceptance of the Chinese leaders' assurance that they have no intention of interfering in other countries. Faith in their word is strengthened by the feeling that they are fellow Asians. It is very important that in southern Asia the Communists have soft pedaled Marxism and have posed as nationalists and economic reformers. They have collaborated with the genuinely nationalist parties, and have put in the fore-front of their program the liberation of the country from foreign rule and the improvement of economic conditions, especially among the agricultural majority. "Shoot the landlord and the moneylender and own your own farm free from debt" has been a very persuasive slogan to land-hungry and debt-ridden farmers in the Philippines, China, Indochina, Burma, and parts of India. Asians as a whole are far less well informed than Americans about real conditions inside Russia and the way in which the Communists gained control of Czechoslovakia and other satellites by the technique of the inside job. Apart from widespread illiteracy, an abundance of Communist propaganda and a lack of up-to-date books on the other side contribute to the Asians not realizing the true situation. Many Indians are attracted by the undeniably great material advances which Russia has made in industrialization under the Five Year Plans, but they do not realize the price that has been paid in human misery. Industrialization plays a great part in their own plans to improve living conditions quickly. The present standard of living in the United States is the result of a century of economic development, but India does not propose to wait a fraction of that time. Many believe that Russia has discovered the secret of a short cut to the welfare state. An added spur is that during the years that Nehru's Congress party was opposing the British it promised a vast improvement in material conditions when it came to power. Since 1947 the Congress party has been the government, and it has fallen far short of satisfy-ing the expectations it had aroused. This has led to a growing volume of dis-illusionment and dissatisfaction, which might in time bring another party to power.

The argument that Russia's success was achieved by a ruthless exercise of dictatorship is not as effective in India as in America. The traditional form of government was autocratic, and the good ruler was the benevolent despot. For about a century the ideas of democracy were taught to a minority in the English schools, and they were practised during the last generation of British rule. This is not long enough to erase the far older indigenous tradition, especially when it is believed that the reward will be a rapid rise in the standard of living. Also men who have as little as scores of millions of Indians —the average annual income is estimated to be $60—are more interested in fuller stomachs than in the democratic freedoms.

The foreign policy of the Indian government is more understandable when set against this background of public opinion. India is determined not to align herself with either side in the cold war. She hopes that by mediation she may be able to bring the Western and Soviet blocs into harmony. Typical in-stances were the attempts to arrange a settlement of the Korean and Formosan problems by negotiations. Nehru describes it as an independent rather than a neutral policy. This is combined with a feeling of greater friendliness toward the United States and Great Britain than toward Russia. The government realizes that it lacks the armed strength to defend India against a major power. It needs too a long period of peace so that it can devote its resources to the improvement of material conditions. It has no intention of forming part of any Pacific defensive alliance, and it has encouraged the other states of Southeast Asia to join India in a neutrality bloc.

The inconsistency of the government's attitude was shown when China reconquered Tibet. This large but weak mountain state on the Indian frontier is far removed from the centers of Chinese power. It has a population of about 3.5 million and an area of 764,000 square miles. When the government of China is strong, it imposes its control, and when its strength decays, the Tibetans throw off their allegiance. Tibet had been virtually independent since 1911; but in 1950 a Chinese Communist army "liberated" the country and established effective control. The security of India is affected, since if air fields were established on the Tibetan plateau long-range bombers could use them for attacks on Indian cities. Communist agents could also be infiltrated into India. Nehru accepted China's action and expressed himself as satisfied with the situation, although part of the press was not so happy. Nehru gave diplomatic recognition to the Communist government of China in 1949. He advocated that it be given China's seat in the U.N. Security Council, and that Formosa be returned to it. At the Bandung Conference of Asian and African states in 1955 he supported China's assurances that she seeks only peaceful coexistence with other countries. India supports the U.N., but primarily as a forum for discussion rather than as an organization for resistance to aggression. If the U.N. Council should eventually give a decision on the Kashmir dispute of which India disapproved, it is uncertain whether the government would accept it.

THE REPUBLIC OF PAKISTAN

Pakistan is the largest Muslim state, and has an area of 370,311 square miles with a population of 75,842,000. The description given of Indian public opinion would apply in general to the Pakistanis, but with significant qualifications. The most important is that the 900-year-old hostility between Muslims and Hindus has survived independence. Pakistan being the weaker state, there is fear of "Hindu imperialism" and a suspicion that India may some day try to annex the country by economic pressure and perhaps by force. As a result Pakistan will not follow India's lead in foreign policy, and is quite likely to do the opposite. This attitude has been stimulated by the quarrel over Kashmir.

Kashmir is a mountainous state adjoining Pakistan and India. It has an area of 80,000 square miles and a population of 4 million, of whom 80 percent are Muslims, but the maharaja or prince was a Hindu. When India was partitioned, fighting soon broke out between the maharaja's Hindu army and his Muslim subjects, and large numbers of the latter were killed. They appealed to their Pathan kinsmen, fanatical Muslim mountaineers who live near the Khyber Pass and are hereditary fighters and looters. They promptly came to the rescue and the loot. The maharaja fearing for his throne promised to join India if help were sent. Nehru disliked the prince (who has since been dethroned), but he wanted Kashmir. Indian troops were flown in just in time to prevent the Muslim rebels from capturing the richest part of the state. In 1948 the Hindu regular troops seemed likely to defeat the rebels, so Muslim soldiers from Pakistan were sent to redress the balance. The United Nations arranged a cease fire, and since then, year after year the two armies have been engaged in a sit-down war about a mile apart. Periodically tension mounts, and there is a danger that the guns will go off by themselves. This would most likely lead to all-out war between India and Pakistan, in which the strongest anticommunist forces in Asia would be fatally weakened. Meanwhile, India spends 50 percent and Pakistan 70 percent of its revenue on defense, to the great detriment of plans for raising the standard of living.

Both sides agree in principle that the Kashmiris themselves should decide by a plebiscite which state they want to join, but so far every attempt of the U.N. mediators to arrange the conditions for holding it have failed. Pakistan has shown much more willingness than India to accept the United Nations proposals, perhaps because she feels reasonably certain of winning the plebiscite when 80 percent of the voters are Muslims. Meanwhile the years drag on and a pro-Hindu Muslim government consolidates its hold on the richest part of Kashmir. National feeling is seriously inflamed in Pakistan and India, and this would make it dangerous for the two governments to agree to a compromise such as the partition of Kashmir. Apart from the Pakistanis' sympathy for their brother Muslims, they feel that their strategic position would be hopeless if their more powerful Hindu enemy occupied the Kashmiri mountains to the east of them as well as the long and indefensible southern frontier across the plain of northern India. Pakistan depends on irrigation for its crops, and the headwaters of many of the rivers are in Kashmir. The Pakistanis will not entrust the control of their water supply to India.

The Indian subcontinent is open to invasion from three directions—by sea, the road of the European invaders; across the eastern frontier from Burma as in World War II; and through the Khyber Pass or one of the other mountain passes on the North West Frontier into Pakistan. Protection by sea depends on the British navy, and its task is made very difficult by the absence of bases in India. Southeast Asia is India's first line of defense against an invasion from the east, and at present she does not have the power to protect it. If Ho Chi-minh should extend his rule over South Vietnam he would have little difficulty in bringing the rest of French Indochina, Thailand, and Burma under Communist control. This would be a decided threat to the security of India. The traditional road of invasion for 4000 years has been from Russian central Asia through Afghanistan and the passes of the Himalaya Mountains into Pakistan. An alternative but less satisfactory route goes through Iran. Even when India was united under British rule and the revenue of the whole country could be drawn on, it was far too small to provide an adequate defense. The Indian army was intended merely to take the first shock of an attack while reinforcements were brought from Great Britain. Today Pakistan, the smaller and by far the poorer state, has inherited the sole responsibility of guarding the northern frontier with an army of only six divisions. Owing to the Kashmir dispute, most of it is pinned down on the Indian-Pakistani frontier watching the Indian (Hindu) army of nine divisions. If Pakistan were overrun, India, which has no defensible frontier, would be invaded. The whole subcontinent has become a zone of weakness.

The situation will be remedied to some extent by the American agreement of 1954 to supply equipment to the Pakistan army and by the defensive alliance between Pakistan, Turkey, Iraq, Iran, and Britain. One reason for the latter is that Pakistan like Turkey does not subscribe to India's policy of neutrality. Another is that Pakistan, being a Muslim state, is greatly interested in the affairs of the Middle East. The weak point of the alliance is the limited military resources of the allies. They hope to persuade the other Arab states to join their alliance, and this would make it somewhat stronger. A Middle East-Pakistan defensive league would be warmly welcomed by the United States and Great Britain. Needless to say India strongly disapproves of American aid to Pakistan.

THE DOMINION OF CEYLON

Ceylon has an area of 25,332 square miles and a population of 8,155,000. Between 1920 and 1948 it progressed by stages from British control to complete self-government, with exactly the same rights and powers as the other dominions. The government of Ceylon negotiated a defensive alliance with Great Britain, which authorized the latter to station in Ceylon such naval, military and air forces as may be mutually agreed on. This gave the British fleet the use of the important harbor of Trincomalee, the only naval station left to it between Aden at the mouth of the Red Sea and Singapore. The government of Ceylon felt that nationalism was perfectly compatible with attachment to the Commonwealth. Moreover it distrusts India and wants the assurance of help to preserve its independence if necessary. While in general it supports Nehru's policy of neutrality, it does not share his belief that only the West is imperialistic.

SELECTED READING

BIRDWOOD, LORD, *A Continent Decides*. London: Hale, 1953.

BREBNER, J. BARTLETT, *North Atlantic Triangle*. New Haven: Yale University Press, 1945.

BROWN, WILLIAM NORMAN, *The United States and India and Pakistan*. Cambridge: Harvard University Press, 1953.

COUPLAND, SIR REGINALD, *India, A Restatement*. New York: Oxford Press, 1945.

GLAZEBROOK, G. P. DE T., *A History of Canadian External Relations*. London: Oxford Press, 1950.

GRATTAN, C. HARTLEY (ed.), *Australia*. Berkeley: University of California Press, 1947.

HODSON, HENRY V., *Twentieth Century Empire*. London: Faber and Faber, Ltd., 1948.

HOFMEYR, JAN H., *South Africa*, 2d ed. by J. P. Cope. London: Ernest Benn, Ltd., 1952.

JENNINGS, SIR WILLIAM IVOR, *The Commonwealth in Asia*. New York: Oxford Press, 1951.

LEVI, WERNER, *Free India in Asia*. Minneapolis: University of Minnesota Press, 1952.

MANSERGH, NICHOLAS, *The Commonwealth and the Nations*. London: Royal Institute of International Affairs, 1948.

——, *The Multi-Racial Commonwealth*. London: Royal Institute of International Affairs, 1955.

ROSINGER, LAWRENCE K., *India and the United States*. New York: The Macmillan Company, 1950.

SHIELS, SIR DRUMMOND (ed.), *The British Commonwealth: A Family of Peoples*. London: Odhams, 1952.

SOWARD, FRANK H. (ed.), *The Changing Commonwealth*. Toronto: Oxford Press, 1950.

WALLBANK, THOMAS WALTER, *India in the New Era*. Chicago: Scott, Foresman and Company, 1951.

CHAPTER 20

FRANCE

Suspicion and fear of Germany have been the principal key to French foreign policy since the Franco-Prussian War of 1870. The explanataion lies in the history of France, along with her geography and demography. This attitude has not been extinguished by the defeat of Germany in 1945, even though statesmen on both sides of the frontier have elaborated plans to replace the traditional enmity with friendship and cooperation.

THE INFLUENCE OF HISTORY

Wars between the two countries began nearly 450 years ago, when Germany, Austria, the Low Countries, and Spain were united under the rule of the Hapsburg Emperor Charles V. On the abdication of the emperor his dominions were divided, his son Philip II being the king of Spain and Holland and his brother becoming the emperor of Austria and Germany. The struggle went on, the object of the kings of France being to extend their territory to the Rhine River, and thus obtain a better military frontier. The power of Spain and the house of Hapsburg declined in the seventeenth century, and after that time French policy had the additional aim of the hegemony of Europe. This ambition was defeated by means of the balance of power policy, and the only substantial gain to France was the annexation of Alsace and Lorraine and some other frontier provinces in the seventeenth and eighteenth centuries. In the later nineteenth century Germany became more powerful than France, and this change in their relative positions was signalized by the complete defeat of the latter in 1870 and the annexation to Germany of Alsace Lorraine. German superiority was emphasized by World Wars I and II.

The legacy of centuries of conflict is that French and Germans regard one another as hereditary enemies. The French of the twentieth century have had no ambition to expand their territory once they recovered Alsace Lorraine in 1918. They have, however, the fatalistic feeling that what has happened again and again since the early sixteenth century is likely to continue into the future, however unwanted it may be. The attitude toward war with Germany is that it is like winter: it may come sooner or later than usual, but nothing can prevent its arrival. When it does come, the French feel that they will be defeated unless they receive help from outside. Three times in a single lifetime France was invaded by the German army. The Franco-Prussian War of 1870 was a straight fight between France and Germany, and the completeness of the German victory made the French aware that they could not hope to oppose their enemy beyond the Rhine without foreign aid. France was on the winning side in World War I, but she realized that the victory had been won by the Allied coalition and that without this it would have been 1870 over again. The catastrophic defeat of 1940 shattered French confidence and reinforced the fear of Germany.

DISPARITY IN POPULATIONS

Numerical inferiority is one reason for the French feeling of weakness. In 1801 France with 27,349,000 was the second most populous country in Europe, but by 1939 she had fallen to fifth place. After 1800 the population increased, but more slowly than in Europe generally. The French birth rate began to fall after 1880, while in Europe generally this did not occur until the twentieth century. World War I cost France 1,320,000 soldiers and 240,000 civilians killed in addition to the children who never were born. These losses were made good by the recovery of Alsace Lorraine with its population of 1,900,000. Between the two wars France's population grew by 2,700,000, but the average yearly increase was only 55,000 while it was 336,000 in Germany. The census of 1936 showed a population of 41,600,000, while Germany had about 67,000,000. World War II cost France 600,000 killed (170,000 troops and members of the underground and 430,000 civilians). These losses while heavy were not catastrophic as in the previous war. They may be compared with the German losses of about 3,500,000 troops and 700,000 civilians killed. In addition to the killed the imprisonment of hundreds of thousands of captured French troops in Germany adversely affected the birth rate, though not as much as had been expected. The census of 1946 gave France a population of 40,780,000. A sharp reversal of the previous downward trend in population began in 1945. The number of births was the highest for fifty years and the death rate fell. To some extent this could be explained by the return to France of the prisoners of war and the large number of marriages. Other factors were also present, however. The government greatly increased its expenditure on social security and family allowances, and the payments were graded so that they favored families of several children. In addition, the attitude toward bearing children seems to have changed. The number of births has now declined somewhat but continues to be markedly greater than before the war.

In 1954 the population had risen to 43,000,000. It is clear however that France will remain much inferior to Germany in manpower.

This means that the French army can only be about two thirds the size of the German and that the labor available for French war industries will be very much less than in Germany. Remembering the rough formula that matériel (equipment) is to manpower as five to one, the German army is likely to be far more extensively equipped than the French. As regards army strength the following figures speak for themselves. In 1870 when the populations were more nearly equal France had 4,400,000 men of military age (twenty to thirty-four) and Germany 4,700,000. In World War I France had 4,500,000 and Germany 7,700,000. In World War II France had only 4,300,000 and Germany 9,400,000 (including Austria).

THE FRENCH EASTERN FRONTIER

The weakness of the French eastern frontier also causes disquiet. Starting from the southeast, that is where France, Switzerland, and Germany join, the first sector is the upper Rhine. Properly fortified this is as reasonably effective a barrier to attack as can be expected in the twentieth century. The second sector of the defense begins where the frontier leaves the Rhine and cuts across country to Longuyon, approximately the point where France, Luxembourg, and Belgium meet. This was protected by the Maginot Line, and was as impregnable as military engineering and lavish expenditure could make it. Whether the Maginot Line was impregnable will never be known since the Germans never made a frontal attack on it but outflanked it. The third and weakest sector of the frontier stretched from the end of the Maginot Line to the North Sea. This was defended by the Maginot Line Extension which emphatically was not the Maginot Line. It consisted of field works on the model of World War I, strengthened at intervals by concrete pill boxes containing light guns. The section nearest to the Maginot Line was the hilly and wooded country of the Belgian Ardennes, where the Germans made their successful attack in 1940. Marshal Pétain had declared it to be impassable; therefore, it was weakly defended. North of the Ardennes lay the plain which stretched from Northeastern France to the Ural Mountains. The rivers presented no serious obstacles to troop movements, and for several centuries the armies of western Europe by common consent regarded it as ideal ground for campaigning. It is known as "The Cockpit of Europe," and it was here that the Germans invaded in 1914. Altogether this was a difficult frontier for the weaker side to defend, and its unsatisfactory character was accentuated by the location of French industry.

A large part of the coal, including the highest grade of coking coal for smelting iron, is found in the districts of the Nord and Pas de Calais near the

Belgian border. This is a leading center of the iron and steel industry, as well as of other forms of manufacturing. The Germans captured it in 1914 and held it until 1918. The same thing happened in 1940, and was one reason why General Weygand, the commander in chief, urged surrender. It would be uneconomic to move the steel industry to the iron fields in Normandy or Lorraine, and France is compelled to make the best of a heavy strategic liability.

FRANCO-GERMAN HEAVY INDUSTRY

The final reason for the fear of Germany is her marked superiority in coal and heavy industry, with all that this implies in capacity to produce war equipment. The largest coal fields of western Europe stretch from the Ruhr

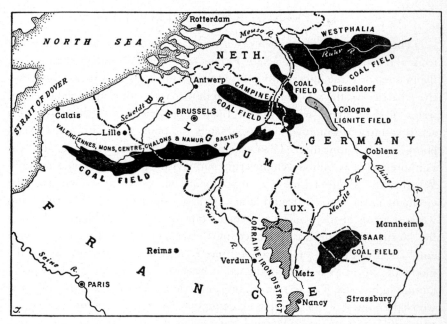

From Jean Gottmann, A Geography of Europe, *rev. ed., New York, Henry Holt & Co., 1955, p. 106*

through the Crefeld area west of the Rhine, over a corner of Holland and across Belgium into northeastern France. There is also a smaller coal field divided between the German Saar and French Lorraine. The Ruhr is by far the most important field and is also the main source of coking coal. Of the total pre-1939 output of coal western Germany provided 64 percent: Holland 6 percent: Belgium 13 percent: Nord, Pas de Calais, and Lorraine in France 16 percent. Both France and Germany have coal fields of lesser importance in other parts of the country, e.g., Silesia in southeastern Germany (transferred to Poland in 1945), but their most important source of supply is the Rhineland and eastern France. Germany is not only self-supporting but also exports large amounts of coal. France does not produce sufficient for her needs, and the greater part of it is inferior to Ruhr coal in coking quality. In 1938 Germany (including the Saar) mined 186,186,000 metric tons of coal (75 percent of it from the Ruhr) and exported about 15 million tons of coal and 2.75 million tons of coke. France in 1938 produced 46.5 million tons of coal and imported 20.5 million tons principally from Great Britain, Germany and Belgium. On the average France imported 55 percent of her coke prior to 1939.

Germany's resources in iron ore are much inferior to those of France, which has in Lorraine the largest deposits in Europe. The Lorraine iron deposits are close to the Saar coal field and extend into Luxembourg. The ore is of low grade (average iron content about 30 percent), and high-grade ore has long been imported from Sweden (iron content 55 percent to 68 percent) and other countries both by France and Germany. Before World War II the average production of the Lorraine fields was about 10 million tons (iron content) and of Luxembourg 1.5 to 2 million tons. The French iron and steel industry used only part of the Lorraine ores and the rest was exported, much of it to Germany, where it formed the bulk of the supply.

The German iron and steel industry has been much larger than the French for a variety of reasons which seem to be permanent. This means that the ability of France to produce war equipment cannot be made equal to that of Germany. Heavy industry finds its principal market not in an agricultural but in a manufacturing area, and this tends to develop near a coal field since any factories which use coal for power are built as close as possible to their source of supply. Historically the development of the market has usually preceded the establishment of heavy industry, which naturally gravitated to an area where it could obtain customers as well as the coal which it needed. Roughly speaking to smelt one ton of iron ore in Europe requires somewhat more than one-and-a-half tons of coal and about one ton, for example, of limestone, which tends to be found near coal, although there are many exceptions. Therefore, it is in general cheaper to carry iron to coal, apart from the fact that to reverse the process would usually mean to remove the steel plant from its best market. Hence, the coal fields of northeastern France and the Rhineland were naturally destined as centers of French and German heavy industry. The important concentration of steel plants near the iron mines of Lorraine is close to the coal fields of the Saar and the Ruhr. Once the plants have been built, they tend strongly to remain where they are, since they are so costly to build that the expense of removal is almost prohibitive. German heavy industry has been much more extensive than French because the Rhineland offered a larger market and had more and on the whole better coal. Further help was given to German expansion by the cheap transportation provided by the Rhine and the canal system. The German industry also arose earlier than the French, and the German annexation of the Lorraine iron field from 1871 to 1918 gave increased impetus to development. The return of Alsace Lorraine to France in 1918 did not materially alter the situation since she did not have coal enough to match her output of iron ore. Large quantities of Lorraine ore continued to be shipped to Rhineland smelters. In 1938 Germany (including the Saar) produced 22,656,000 metric tons of steel and France 6,216,000 tons.

FRANCO-GERMAN RELATIONS 1870–1914

The principal aims of Bismarck's foreign policy from 1871 to 1890 were to maintain German predominance in Europe and keep France helpless in isolation. In various ways Russia, the Austrian Empire, Italy, and Great Britain were linked with Germany. France was afraid of another German attack, and there was also the desire for revenge for the loss of Alsace Lorraine. The annexation of these provinces was perhaps Bismarck's greatest blunder. The people of Alsace were German in race and language and those of Lorraine were largely of French culture. The long period of tolerant French rule had made both of them French in patriotism. The primary reasons for the annexation were to obtain the Lorraine iron mines and to give France a weak military frontier. Bismarck had believed that the French would become reconciled to their loss, but he miscalculated badly. In all the years between the Franco-Prussian War and 1914 the one certain factor in European affairs was that France would never side with Germany so long as she kept the two provinces. The desire for revenge should not be overemphasized. It was strongest with the generation which had fought in 1870. By 1914 France would never have gone to war specifically to recover Alsace Lorraine, since she felt that the attempt would not be worth the losses it would entail. In 1894 France was able to make the Franco-Russian defensive alliance, which partially restored the balance of power. In 1904 came the Entente Cordiale with Great Britain, which developed into a British moral obligation to support France in the event of war.

FRANCE AT VERSAILLES

Two defeated nations were at the peace conference of 1919, Germany and France. France had 10 percent of her active male population killed and 11 percent wounded, the heaviest percentage of any major belligerent. The war had devastated ten of the most populous and most highly industrialized departments. France realized that only allied help had saved her from a repetition of 1870, and what she sought above all else was security against a future German attack. Clemenceau, the premier who had saved France from collapse in 1917, and the principal French delegate at Versailles, was the embodiment of the national attitude. He demanded that the German territory west of the Rhine be made into a separate and autonomous state under French control, and that French troops should hold the line of the Rhine as the best military frontier for defense against a future attack. Clemenceau agreed that the creation of another Alsace Lorraine would give Germany a bitter grievance, but he argued that her defeat and the thwarting of her ambitions had already given her ample incentive for a war of revenge. The excellence of his plan, he contended, was that the loss of most of her coal and heavy industry would make it impossible for her to avenge her grievance.

President Wilson and Prime Minister Lloyd George vetoed this proposal, but as an alternative they negotiated the Anglo-American Guarantee Treaty by which both nations undertook jointly to come immediately to the assistance of France in the event of any unprovoked aggression against her by Germany. Furthermore, the Versailles Treaty provided for the permanent demilitarization of Germany west of the Rhine and for fifty kilometers east of the river. Within this area Germany was forbidden to build fortifications or maintain troops. An inter-Allied force was to occupy the Rhineland for fifteen years. The Saar, a highly industrialized area of 700 square miles and 650,000 inhabitants, was separated from Germany and placed under a Governing Commission of five members controlled by the League of Nations. As compensation for wrecking the French coal mines in 1918, Germany ceded the Saar mines to France, and the district was to be within the French customs boundary. After fifteen years the Saarlanders were to vote on their future political status —continuance of League control, union with France, or reunion with Germany. If the last were chosen, Germany was to repurchase the mines. The Saar was only thirty miles from the iron mines of Lorraine, and in 1913 it had produced about 13 million tons of coal. By the transfer Germany would lose only about 6 per cent of her prewar output, while French production would be considerably increased.

The most important guarantee by far of French security should have been the Anglo-American promise of armed help. It was intended to be an essential part of the peace settlement. In 1920, however, the American Senate rejected it, the British government refused to give a single-handed guarantee of help to France, and the treaty thereupon lapsed. It is unprofitable to argue about the might have beens of history, but it does seem that the collapse of the Anglo-American Guarantee Treaty marks the point at which the Western world took the path that led eventually to World War II. Clemenceau's chief argument to President Wilson and Lloyd George was that if they gave this guarantee they would never have to honor it. Germany would never dare to go to war with the three Western powers. But if the guarantee were refused, Clemenceau believed that some day Germany would attack. Then, he predicted, America and Britain would be forced to fight a second time, since they could not afford to allow Germany to become dominant in Europe. Furthermore, if the treaty had been ratified, France would have felt secure and would have been more willing to agree to modifications of the peace settlement to conciliate Germany. The United States and Britain would have been able to insist on this attitude by warning that otherwise they would not continue their guarantees.

THE FRENCH BLOC

France was left all alone in Europe with Germany. Russia was an enemy, America and Britain had returned to isolation, and very quickly Germany began to evade the disarmament clauses of the Versailles Treaty. France fell back on her original policy of trying to hold Germany down in self-defense. Between 1920 and 1927 she negotiated alliances with all the states which were likewise fearful of the future. These were Belgium, Poland, Czechoslovakia, Yugoslavia, and Rumania. Until about the middle 'thirties the French bloc was an important factor in France's hegemony in Europe. On many points the members adopted a similar foreign policy, such as their refusal to disarm or allow Germany to rearm unless their security were guaranteed. Germany was encircled by France and her allies, and dared not risk a war. She had 100,000 troops but no tanks, and at most a few hundred passenger planes which could be converted into bombers. The destruction of all fortifications in the Rhineland left her completely open to a French invasion. As late as 1933 the French bloc had over 1,500,000 first-line troops, 12,660,000 trained reserves and 5000 aircraft. France's motive was not desire for power or glory as in the eighteenth century but fear. As the result of the war, she had the German tiger by the tail, and she was terrified of what would happen if she let go.

The armed predominance of the French bloc was the only real guarantee of peace. It was not preserved by the League, nor by an isolationist America or a semi-isolationist and disarmed Great Britain. The weak point was that France with her limited resources had obligated herself to maintain not only the Versailles Treaty with Germany but the whole European peace settlement of 1919. This was the price which she had had to pay for her allies, since they had agreed to help her only on condition that she supported them. Poland had about as much to fear from Russia as from Germany. Czechoslovakia, Rumania, and Yugoslavia were less concerned with Germany than with Hungary, whose ambition to restore the pre-World War I kingdom of Hungary required their dismemberment. Yugoslavia regarded Italy as her prime enemy, while Rumania was afraid that Russia might try to regain her former province of Bessarabia, which Rumania had seized in 1918. Rumania and Yugoslavia had another enemy in Bulgaria. The strength of France was not enough to support the burden which she had shouldered in her search for

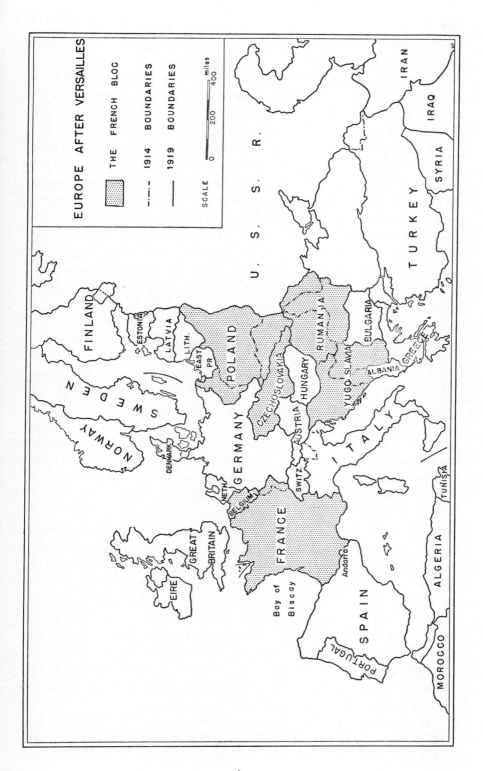

EUROPE AFTER VERSAILLES

THE FRENCH BLOC

— · — 1914 BOUNDARIES

—— 1919 BOUNDARIES

SCALE

miles

0   200   400

463

security. Her policy succeeded as long as Germany, Russia, and Italy were weak, but once they became strong it collapsed.

France's estimate of the value of the League depended upon how far it could be used to strengthen her security against Germany. From its first inception she had been skeptical since it seemed to her that the members' obligations to take action against an aggressor were too vague and uncertain. Her doubt was increased by the American refusal to join the League, and the interpretative resolutions introduced at Geneva in 1921 and 1923 which made it completely uncertain whether the League would take effective action against an aggressor or not. The attempts to strengthen the sanctions article by such proposals as the Geneva Protocol failed. The effect upon the French bloc was to force it to depend increasingly upon its own armaments and alliances and refuse Germany's demand of 1932 that she be allowed to rearm up to the French level. The inter-war attempt to strengthen peace by disarmament foundered on the insistence of the French bloc that there could be no disarmament without security.

FRANCE'S GERMAN POLICY

France's insistence on heavy German reparations was due in part to considerations of security. It was felt that as long as Germany was burdened with debt payments, she could not afford to rearm. The demand was also the result of the serious financial situation in France. The system of taxes was complicated and hopelessly out of date. Reform was urgently needed, but politicians evaded tackling so explosive an issue. The war had been financed largely by borrowing, the national debt had quadrupled, and inflation was serious. On top of this came the necessity of spending billions to restore the departments devastated by the war and of repaying the American war debt. The French government and people were united in the determination that Germany must pay the utmost possible. This policy brought France into conflict with Great Britain and the United States, both of whom favored lenient treatment of Germany. Estrangement reached its height in 1923, when France occupied the Ruhr because Germany had defaulted in deliveries of reparations. During this period France also encouraged the Separatists, who wanted to set up an independent Rhineland republic. When it became obvious by 1924 that the movement lacked popular support, the French withdrew their assistance, and the artificial agitation collapsed. In the same year the Ruhr occupation was ended, and a compromise settlement of reparations was temporarily reached in the Dawes Plan that worked successfully for several years.

In 1925 Franco-German relations were temporarily improved by the Locarno Treaties. Compulsory arbitration treaties were signed between Germany and Poland, Czechoslovakia, Belgium, and France. On this foundation was erected the Treaty of Mutual Guarantee, which applied only to Western Europe. Germany, France, and Belgium promised never to go to war with one another or to alter the frontier laid down by the Versailles Treaty (including the demilitarized zone). If war broke out, the League Council was to determine by a unanimous vote (apart from that of the belligerents) which was the aggressor. Great Britain and Italy were then bound to enter the war on the side of the victim.

The immediate beneficiary was Germany, who at that date was militarily weaker than France. She was guaranteed that there would be no more Ruhr occupations; she became a member of the League of Nations in 1926. The evacuation of the Rhineland by Allied troops began in 1925 and was completed in 1930, five years earlier than the Versailles Treaty required, and in 1927 the Allied Control Commission for German disarmament was withdrawn, despite the systematic evasions of the disarmament clauses of the Versailles Treaty. The British government hoped that France would now feel assured of security, and would adopt a more conciliatory policy toward Germany. This expectation did not materialize for several reasons. By 1925 it was believed that Germany was more likely to attack Poland than France, and Great Britain had refused to extend her promise of help to it. Yet a German attack on Poland would compel France to attack Germany because of her treaty obligations. This could create a very intricate problem in international law. If Germany set the ball rolling by attacking Poland, but France was the first to violate the Treaty of Mutual Guarantee by invading Germany—who was the victim of aggression, Germany or France? The decision was to be given by a unanimous vote of the League Council, and this would have been close to a miracle. Yet unless a unanimous vote were given, Britain and Italy were not compelled to enter the war. Hence, France had no certainty of British help. What she wanted was a straightforward promise of the pre-1914 type that if Germany attacked, Britain would aid France. Moreover, by 1925 Britain had so completely disarmed that even if she wished to she could give little help to France in ground troops or air force. Consequently France refused to regard the Locarno Treaties as a complete guarantee of security against Germany.

The Locarno agreements have been described with some exaggeration as "a most effective and formidable looking scarecrow." At the time they made a tremendous impression, and during the rest of the 'twenties the pacts did considerably improve Franco-German relations. However, the underlying feeling of insecurity remained. A significant evidence of this was the opposition of the French bloc to the British attempts to modify the terms of the peace settlement in order to remove German grievances. The British belief was that if this were done, the danger of war would be removed since Germany would no longer have any desire to reverse the Versailles Treaty. France and her allies were willing to make minor concessions, such as evacuating the Rhineland in

1930 and decreasing reparations payments (after it had become patently impossible to collect a larger amount). On all essentials, however, the French
bloc stood pat on the terms of the peace treaties, and refused to allow any
modifications unless it received stronger guarantees of security. The reason was
that any change would strengthen Germany and therefore weaken the French
bloc. This is because power is relative, and if one side becomes stronger the
other is automatically weaker.

CHANGING POWER RATIOS

The middle 'thirties were the turning point from peace to war because the
only guarantee of peace was breaking down. France was seriously weakened
by the depression. The strength of the French bloc was declining, and simultaneously Germany was rapidly rearming. The French bloc began to drift
apart until by 1938 Czechoslovakia was the only thoroughly reliable ally left.
In 1934 Poland signed a ten-year treaty of nonaggression with Germany. The
alliance with France continued, but no one was certain whether it would be
effective if put to the test. German influence grew in Yugoslavia and Rumania, and in 1936 Belgium abrogated her alliance and reverted to her former
policy of neutrality. The one Frenchman who saw the danger clearly was Foreign Minister Barthou. He believed that it was useless to make concessions to
Germany in the hope of appeasing her. France must strengthen her defenses
and be prepared to fight if necessary. In 1934 Barthou tried to tighten the alliances of the French bloc and to bring in Russia, which was beginning to fear
Nazi aggression. In 1935 alliances were signed by Russia with France and
Czechoslovakia. Barthou's wider plans for the defensive encirclement of Germany ended with his assassination by a Croat terrorist in 1934, and his policy
died with him. Laval's attempt to form an alliance with Italy was frustrated
by the Ethiopian affair. The armed strength of the French bloc gradually lessened, particularly in modern equipment. France's armament production fell
as Germany's rose, and by 1937 it was estimated that she had only 1100 airplanes ready for immediate service, most of which were obsolescent. As late
as 1938, however, she still had far more ground troops than Germany. Hitler
began to rearm rapidly in 1933, and by 1936 he had a powerful army although
his trained reserves were limited, since conscription was only reintroduced in
1935. By 1935 his Luftwaffe was as large as the Royal Air Force, and by 1940 it
was considerably stronger than the British and French air forces combined. In
1936 came the German reoccupation of the Rhineland and the beginning of its
refortification.

Inside France there were ominous developments. While young Germans
were lamenting that the Versailles abolition of conscription deprived them of
the joy of army drill, pacifism became widespread in France. The Maginot

Line, built at immense cost and believed to be impregnable, was symptomatic. It implied that if war came France would abandon her allies in central and eastern Europe and stand on the defensive, since the fortifications could be of no use to an army advancing into Germany. Yet if Germany attacked Poland or Czechoslovakia, the only way in which France could help would be by an invasion. French antiwar feeling increased with the growing strength of Nazi Germany, and with it an aversion to the treaties which bound France to her allies. Poland's realization of this had much to do with her acceptance of Hitler's offer of a nonaggression treaty in 1934. When the Munich Agreement was signed, Leon Blum, the leader of the Socialist party, wrote that he was ashamed and also relieved. Peace through the appeasement of Germany dominated the foreign policy of France after 1935. Some favored peace at almost any price as long as someone else, for example, Czechoslovakia, paid the price, but they were willing to fight in 1939 when they realized that France herself must pay. Others like Premier Paul Laval were prepared to sacrifice even France if their personal interests were favored. Even in 1939 there was a strong group of appeasers in the cabinet and the nation who deplored the declaration of war. Only a minority agreed with the murdered Barthou that France must stand her ground and fight.

The class divisions within French society reacted upon foreign policy. The French conservatives unlike those of Great Britain had never accepted change as inevitable nor did they take a prominent part in bringing it about. The more extreme royalists condemned the whole idea of parliamentary democracy and saw in fascism a means of overthrowing it. Hostility to the republic was enhanced by the unedifying behavior of some politicians of the interwar period. The propertied classes generally were most unwilling to pay taxes and strongly opposed the development of the social services because of the heavy expenditure they entailed. By "propertied classes" is meant not merely the "two hundred families" of the very wealthy who were popularly supposed to control France, but all those who had anything to lose. France was the paradise of the "small man" with a little business which the owner had built up from nothing into a modest competence by a lifetime of saving and self-denial. In the early 'thirties the social services of France were much below the level in other countries, and reforms were years overdue. Gradually during the twentieth century a strong industrial proletariat had grown up in the manufacturing and mining areas. They wanted expensive social services, and since the older political parties did not provide them, they turned to the Socialists and Communists.

The great depression sharpened the rising antagonism between Left and Right. The membership of the Communist party grew from 25,000 in 1932 to 329,000 in 1936. The propertied classes and especially the *rentiers* (those living on fixed incomes) were hard hit and fearful for the safety of their possessions.

Their worst apprehensions seemed to be realized when the election of 1936 resulted in a victory for the Popular Front, a coalition of Communists, Socialists, and Radical Socialists (moderately well-to-do members of the middle class who were radical in theory but rather conservative in practice). The Popular Front government hastily enacted many overdue reforms. These were accompanied by a wave of lightning strikes, where the sympathies of the government were patently with the strikers. The propertied classes thought they saw the first step toward a Red revolution and the establishment of a Communist state on the Russian model. Fear created hatred, and the bitterness of the class struggle divided France so deeply that national unity was undermined. Many Frenchmen became blinded to the German danger and were more interested in fighting one another than in opposing Hitler. Even the outbreak of the war in 1939 was unable to restore unity as the German threat had done in 1914. The belief was widely held that World War II would be followed by the collapse of capitalism everywhere and the global victory of communism. Therefore, war with Germany must be avoided by appeasement. Extreme conservatives looked favorably on Hitler because they thought they saw in him a protector of private property against the Communist threat. On ideological grounds strong opposition to the 1935 Russian alliance existed. The government realized that it spoke for a divided nation and hesitated to oppose Germany firmly. At each successive crisis provoked by Hitler its attitude was always the same—protests, appeals to the League Council, neatly drafted exposures of German illegality or face-saving formulas, but of action none.

THE RHINELAND OCCUPATION

The Ethiopian fiasco gave Hitler the demilitarized zone of the Rhineland. Laval's halfhearted participation in the League's sanctions against Italy destroyed his hope of a Franco-Italian alliance against Germany. At the same time the refusal of France to cooperate vigorously against Italian aggression widened the existing breach between her and Great Britain. This was the moment that Hitler chose to move 30,000 German troops into the demilitarized Rhineland in March 1936. The Versailles and Locarno treaties amply justified France in invading Germany and forcing the troops to withdraw, and Locarno also obligated Great Britain to support France. It is now known that the Germans would have retreated, since their armed forces were too weak to risk war with France. Hitler gambled for high stakes and won. The majority of the French cabinet, the army leaders, and the public were unwilling to fight unless the British entered the war with them. The British public sympathized with Hitler's action, holding that it was another crime of the wicked Treaty of Versailles to demilitarize the Rhineland and forbid German troops to garrison it. The fashionable explanation was that the iniquities of the peace settlement together with France's "militaristic" determination to dominate Europe had led the Germans to brood over their "coolie status." This acting on the "strain of instability in their characters" had put them into "an extremely neurotic frame of mind" where they blindly followed Hitler, "this gentle, imaginative and unreliable man." If he acquired what he wanted in the Rhineland, he offered to duplicate the Kellogg Pact (which Germany had already signed) and not fight any one for twenty-five years. So one must be constructive and seize "The Chance to Build," to quote the headline in the pontifical *Times* and the Liberal *News Chronicle*. Britain was determined not to fight, and finally persuaded France to take no action beyond filing a complaint with the League Council. The British government followed the lead of public opinion, and the French cabinet was content to find in British pacifism an excuse for its own.

The League passed a resolution that Hitler had broken another treaty, and soon afterward he began to build the West Wall or Siegfried Line along the French and Belgian frontiers. This was the beginning of the end for France's allies Poland and Czechoslovakia. The heavy casualties that would be incurred in breaking through the belt of fortifications made France much less willing to help them if they were attacked. This was one factor in deciding the government to sign the Munich Agreement, and it was a partial explanation of the sit-down war of September, 1939, to May, 1940. The last chance of stopping Hitler without a major war had been thrown away, and France and the French bloc were seriously weakened.

FRANCE AND THE MEDITERRANEAN

The three North African dependencies of Morocco, Algeria, and Tunisia are the most valuable part of France's whole empire. They have a combined population of 21,200,000, of whom 1,650,000 are Europeans and the rest Berbers and Arabs. There is a good deal of French capital invested, and the French settlers control the colonial economy. North Africa is also a valuable recruiting ground for the French colonial army. In case of war, the troops mobilize in the seaports and are moved to southern France. It is essential that France be strong enough in the western Mediterranean to prevent any interference with the sea passage. A large part of the French navy is normally stationed there with bases in southern France, Corsica, and North Africa.

Mussolini particularly coveted Tunisia (which had a sizable Italian minority) and Corsica, and he wished to extend Italian naval power from the central to the western Mediterranean. France had no intention of surrendering her position, and this at times led to strained relations. The London Naval Disarmament Conference of 1930 was a failure as far as France and Italy were concerned. Mussolini insisted on naval equality between the two, while France was equally determined to maintain superiority in fleet strength. Since Italy was purely a Mediterranean power, the whole of her navy would be concentrated there. France had also to defend her English Channel coast and colonies all over the world. Only part of her fleet could be kept in the Mediterranean so that naval equality meant naval inequality in that vital area. In the event of war with Germany Mussolini might bottle up France's colonial army in North Africa. Since France was wealthier than Italy, she was able to outbuild Mussolini's fleet and maintain her naval superiority. In the end Mussolini's Mediterranean ambitions brought him into the war on the side of Germany.

THE FALL OF FRANCE

First and foremost the catastrophe was a military defeat. The troops were beaten because, given their leadership and tactics, they never had the ghost of a chance of winning. The army was well led and equipped to win World War I, but it was totally unprepared for the *blitzkrieg* tactics of 1940. The responsibility for this rests with Pétain, Weygand, and Gamelin, who one after another commanded the army during the twelve years that preceded the outbreak of the war. All were members of the defensive school of military thought. Basing their doctrine on Pétain's successful defense of Verdun in 1916, they taught that an entrenched army, well provided with artillery and machine guns, could withstand almost any frontal assault even if supported with tanks and bombers. There would be an unbreakable stationary front maintained by defensive fire power. Behind it all the nation's industries would be mobilized to provide a never-ending supply of munitions. The essence of French strategy was defense, and the Maginot Line was its most complete embodiment. Consequently, when the war broke out, the French prepared to settle down to a defensive war of attrition in which Germany was gradually to be exhausted by futile attacks and the slow economic strangulation of the naval blockade.

The defensive school dismissed the possibility of a war of movement and greatly underestimated the potentialities of the airplane and the tank. It believed that their effectiveness would be minimized by antitank and antiaircraft artillery. Tanks should not be employed for offense, but should be used in close support of infantry. Therefore, most of the tanks were not formed into tank divisions, but split up into small detachments scattered along the whole front. This was the absolute negation of the German theory of the *blitzkrieg*—an offense spearheaded by tanks, dive bombers, and mechanized troops, and followed up by masses of infantry. French military orthodoxy found its principal critic in an obscure young colonel named Charles de Gaulle. In his two books he argued that defense meant defeat. In high French military circles he was regarded as a heretic and a dangerous crackpot.

At the time of the Battle of France, in May–June, 1940, the Germans had about 155 divisions. Owing to Stalin's benevolent neutrality, 126 divisions, in-

cluding all of the 10 tank divisions, were in the West. The French had 94 and
the British 9 divisions—a total of 103. If the Belgian and Dutch troops are
included, there was a grand total of 135 Allied against 126 German divisions.
Apparently each side had about 4000 tanks, though some estimates give the
Germans 3000 and the French 2300. The German superiority here was far
less in numbers than in tactics. The Luftwaffe had at the least a three to one
superiority over the combined British and French air forces, and qualitatively
the French aircraft were inferior to the German. Neither the French nor
the British had dive bombers. In other types of weapons there seems to have
been approximate equality between the contending armies. The French leaders were elderly veterans of World War I who believed that history would
repeat itself. When instead they were confronted with a tank war of movement, they no longer had the mental elasticity to adapt themselves quickly
to *blitzkrieg* situations which their training told them could not possibly
occur, but which did occur. They had been sure that tanks could not break
through the front and that if they did they would be destroyed. German
tanks, however, were constantly advancing from behind the French armies
where it was believed danger could not possibly exist. The French troops
had been taught to fight on the defensive, and they lacked the training and
often the equipment to meet the totally unforeseen tactics of 1940. Many of
them fought bravely, and a few like General de Gaulle won local victories.
But as far as the Battle of France was concerned, the issue had been decided
before the war began.

Behind the military defeat lay profound and widespread social and economic reasons for the fall of France. Among these was the deep-seated class
division, which has already been described. The Communists followed the
party line and worked against the national war effort. During the nine
months of the sit-down war they had some success in undermining the morale
of the troops, with the result that certain units collapsed when the Germans
attacked in May, 1940. Only in June, 1941, when Hitler invaded Russia did
the Communists reverse themselves and take a prominent part in the underground resistance to Germany. Part of the propertied classes also bore
their share of responsibility. They wished above all to safeguard their possessions and play safe, and they regarded the war as the forerunner of a
communist revolution. When the French army was defeated, they had no
stomach for a last-ditch defense. The sensible thing was to save one's property by coming to terms with Hitler. This school of thought was strongly
represented in the Vichy government. The antidemocrats drew the lesson
that the republic had so weakened itself that it could be overthrown and replaced by an authoritarian regime. Frenchmen of this way of thought looked
upon Marshal Pétain as the man to reform public life. Since his retirement
from the army, he had accepted the role of an Old Testament prophet, and

periodically scourged the republican politicians of their sins. He was known to be upright and honest, and as the victor of Verdun he had immense prestige. What they did not know was that at eighty-five he was beginning to go senile and that he was only the figurehead of the Vichy government.

The Communists and the propertied classes were poles apart in their aims, but for totally different reasons they both bear a share of the guilt for their country's defeat. This raises the question, Why could Frenchmen of all shades of opinion unite in 1914 but not in 1939? At the earlier date the class struggle was not so bitter; thus all classes could form the Sacred Union. The principal cause of the change was the growth of communism. In 1914 it was a theory held by the extreme left of the socialist parties. In 1939 it was the established government of the U.S.S.R., with a strong and growing fifth column in France. Communism threatened the very existence of the propertied classes as the pre-1914 labor leaders had never done. There was no longer a General Will in France.

A few years before the war a foreign observer described the French as a nation of democrats with a complete contempt for democratic leadership. The antidemocrats were a minority, and the large majority with their strong individualism were hostile to dictatorship. They were clear sighted and realistic, and they had no illusions about the caliber of the men who governed the Third Republic. Most of these were professional politicians, and the public took it for granted that democratic politics and corruption were inseparable. This belief was exaggerated, but it had a solid basis of fact. Patronage and jobbery were part of the French democratic process. Periodic financial scandals which seemed to point toward the highest political circles increased public disillusionment.

French governments notoriously had a short expectation of life. Between 1875 and 1939 there were 100 different ministries, with an average duration of less than eight months. One cause was the multiple party system under which no one party ever had a clear majority of seats in the Assembly. Every government had to be a coalition, usually short-lived, since sooner or later some party deserted its allies and the ministry lost its majority. The practical impossibility of dissolving the Assembly and holding a fresh election encouraged irresponsibility, since once a deputy was elected he was assured of his seat for the next four years. Especially after World War I politics became increasingly a struggle for place rather than for principle. Irresponsible politicians intrigued for power, and grave and contentious problems were evaded if possible since any solution would offend part of the public. All subscribed to the politicians' prayer "From losing votes good Lord deliver us." The democratic process tended to resolve itself into pulling down the government, reshuffling the political cards to put one's self and friends in power, and then countermining for as long as possible the sapping and mining of the Outs who were determined to become the Ins. The public felt neither respect nor confidence in their leaders. When the army was losing the Battle of France, there was no political leader who like Churchill could appeal successfully to the people to follow him in a fight to the death.

Another reason for the defeat was a psychological weakness which is hard to assess accurately but is very important. The staggering losses of 1914–1918 had indelibly imprinted themselves on the public consciousness, and government and people alike were determined that never again must France be bled white. This was reinforced by a feeling of the uselessness of the war. The one thing that the French hoped to gain from it was security against Germany; but they felt that they had won the war and lost the peace. They remembered vividly the collapse of the Guarantee Treaty, the watering down of League sanctions, the reluctance of American and British bankers to make loans to France while they were lavish in lending to Germany, the Anglo-American lectures on French "militarism," and the sympathy for the German breaches of the Treaty of Versailles.

The end of it all was that Clemenceau's prophecy of 1919 had come true, and once again France was in deadly peril. The United States made it clear that never again would it repeat the blunder of 1917 and enter a European war. Britain had provided in full all the troops and airplanes for which the French army had asked, but the fact remained that she had only between 300,000 and 400,000 men in France compared with over two million French on the eastern frontier. It was taken for granted that losses would be on the scale of 1914–1918, and there was no confidence that even at such a price France would gain the security that she craved so desperately. So the country entered the war not with the grim determination of 1914 but without enthusiasm and in a mood of desperation.

POSTWAR POLITICS

The left-wing parties are stronger than before the war, though they are balanced by the revival of the conservatives in the 1950's. In between come the middle of the road, moderately reformist parties of the center. None of these three sections of the Assembly has a majority, and each of them is made up of several parties with conflicting programs. The multiple party system has reappeared with all its prewar characteristics, and there is the same procession of weak and short-lived coalition governments. The postwar constitution has done nothing to correct this situation, but has aggravated it. The public seems to have the same poor opinion of its elected leaders as before the war, and the politicians show the same unwillingness to reform themselves. On the economic side some important industries were nationalized soon after the war, and France is a halfway house between capitalism and socialism.

The membership of the Communist party at its maximum was 819,000 in 1946, and its voting strength rose from 14.9 percent of the electorate in 1936 to 26.5 percent in 1951. In all the postwar elections the Communist poll has fluctuated around this figure, and in 1951 there was a moderate decline. It seems clear that they cannot win a majority by democratic methods, but their influence is still strong. Five-sixths of their supporters are not members of the party. They win many votes because they appeal to the desire for peace, to patriotic opposition to German rearmament, or to the workmen's discontent with high prices and inadequate wages. After the war the Communists gained control of the CGT (the General Confederation of Labor), which had 5 million members in 1946. The Communists used this control to bring about strikes like those of 1947 and 1948, which were attempts to overthrow or discredit the government. As a result some of the unions seceded from the CGT, and its present membership is estimated at some 2 million. The men have shown themselves increasingly unwilling to take part in blatantly political strikes. The party contains a hard core of 200,000 to 300,000 militant fanatics. Some of them have been trained as saboteurs and guerillas, and the party has concealed stocks of arms. Special troops and police have been prepared to deal with this threat. The Communist leader Thorez announced that in the event of war with Russia the Communists would support the Red army. The Communist party is a danger, and it will continue to have a large following as long as the workmen have economic grievances and are embittered by the prosperity of the peasants and manufacturers. The party, however, can no longer paralyze the economic or political life of France. But by the mere fact of its existence it makes impossible a complete union of the French people in support of their government's pro-Western policy. As in the 'thirties, there is no General Will in France.

INDUSTRIALIZATION

French industrial production has been far outstripped by that of the United States, Great Britain, and Germany. In part the shortage of coal is a cause, but another reason is that for several centuries France has tended to specialize in luxury goods and leave the more workaday articles with wide mass appeal to the other nations. A large part too of the manufacturing is carried on in small factories often owned by a single family. Frequently the owners have little inclination to expand production and modernize their methods, preferring to sell a limited output at a high price in the domestic market which is secured to them by high tariffs. In pre-1939 France there were few large and efficient factories. In 1939 industrial output was at the same level as in 1912. World War II inflicted enormous damage, a conservative estimate placing the loss at $70 billion. No less than 165,700 factories were damaged or demolished. The defeat shocked France into a realization of her industrial backwardness, and the Monnet Plan was prepared to modernize and expand production. One of its aims was to lessen the military inferiority of France by enlarging heavy industry. The goals set have not been reached, but in 1954 industrial production was 151 percent of what it had been in 1938. In 1954, excluding the Saar, the production of coal was 56,-300,000 metric tons and of steel 10,626,000 tons, the latter being 174 percent of 1938. The war potential is considerably above 1939, but is less than it should be for the safety of France.

FRANCE AND SECURITY

The defeat of 1940 had a very serious effect upon national morale. It shattered confidence in the ability of France to defend herself. The nation felt that it must win security through foreign alliances and by preventing Germany from again becoming a military power. The attitude toward the United Nations was one of hopeful skepticism. France trusted that it would succeed and was prepared to do what she could to forward this, particularly as a means of preventing a German attack. But until the U.N. proved itself it was merely a noble experiment, and France remembered another noble experiment, the League of Nations, which had failed. Therefore, she would hope for the best not too confidently, and meanwhile she would place her chief reliance on alliance rather than collective security. And so in 1944 General de Gaulle as president of France negotiated a defensive alliance with Russia.

No one has ever accused the general of being a fellow traveler. It is illuminating to ponder why he preferred Russia as an ally to the United States and Great Britain, and why a large section of public opinion agreed with him. Germany was *the* enemy, and when she recovered from her defeat, no Frenchman would be surprised if she again attacked. The United States and Great Britain were addicted to isolationism and might return to it as in 1920. (Today this belief is much weaker in France and Western Europe than in 1944; but any move that looks like a return to isolationism, e.g., a proposal to withdraw American troops from Germany, awakens the old forebodings). Moreover, the interwar period had shown that the United States and Great Britain were predisposed to be more sympathetic to Germany than to France, and a revival of this attitude was dismally anticipated. Russia, on the other hand, was a companion in adversity, on the same continent with Germany and with no English Channel or Atlantic Ocean to protect her. Along with France she had had two German invasions in a generation. Therefore, France and Russia were natural allies, and so de Gaulle, the enemy of communism at home, became the ally of Communist Russia abroad.

This alliance remained the mainstay of France's foreign policy until about 1947, and then gradually she turned to the United States and Great Britain. It was realized that the French Communist party was a blatant Russian fifth column. It was doing its best on orders from Moscow to undermine the elected government of the republic which was Russia's ally. In 1947 France and Britain signed a treaty of alliance, and in March 1948 the fifty-year Treaty of Brussels was negotiated between Britain, France, Holland, Belgium, and Luxembourg. If any of the five were attacked in Europe, the others would give it all military and other assistance in their power. While Germany was specifically mentioned, the treaty applied equally to any state which attacked one of the signatories—a diplomatic euphemism for Russia. The armed forces of the five allies were placed under unified command. The next step was taken in April, 1949, when the United States, Canada, the five Brussels Treaty powers, and five other states of western Europe signed the North Atlantic Pact. The North Atlantic Treaty Organization (NATO) was established to carry out the purposes of this defensive alliance of the Western nations against Russia.

THE RHINELAND AND THE SAAR

France's views on the future of Germany frequently conflicted with those of the United States and, to a lesser extent, Great Britain. Washington in particular took the attitude that Germany had learned her lesson and would never do it again. As the tension with Russia increased, American policy tried more and more to conciliate Germany and enlist her as an ally in the Western bloc that was coming into existence. The French pointed out that the United States and Britain had been equally optimistic about German regeneration in 1919 and that France, as Germany's nearest neighbor, had been the first to suffer from their miscalculation. The immediate threat came from Russia, but quite a few French felt that in say fifteen years' time the situation might be very different.

France's aim was to weaken Germany's war potential. One proposal was that the coal mines and heavy industry of the Rhineland should be taken away from their German owners and possession vested in an international organization under the United Nations. The existing owners, such as Krupp, had financed Hitler's rise to power, cooperated wholeheartedly in his rearmament program, and played their part in the plundering of German-occupied Europe. France argued that it was dangerous to leave these men in the control of the greatest concentration of heavy industry in Western Europe. The United States opposed such interference with the rights of private property, and was supported in its stand by Great Britain. France was compelled to give way, and the Western powers left it to a future German government to decide on the disposition of the property. This had a curious sequel in 1952. In 1946 Alfred Krupp, the head of the family, was convicted by an American court of using slave labor in his factories during the war and of plundering occupied countries. He was condemned to twelve years imprisonment and the forfeiture of his property. In 1951 the American high commissioner in Germany released him and restored his property. In 1953 the Western powers negotiated an arrangement with him by which he agreed to sell about 75 percent of his holdings and never again engage in the coal and most forms of the steel industry. In return he would receive over $60 million from the sale of his properties and an annual royalty of about $2,380,000. The German government refused to guarantee enforcement of the contract on the ground that the constitution granted every citizen the right to enter any form of business. The disclosure of this situation was not welcomed by the French and British parliaments. In 1949 the Western powers accepted another French proposal that Rhineland coal mines and heavy industry should be placed under the control of an international commission, which would fix production quotas and also the types of steel goods that might be manufactured. The mineral and industrial resources of the area could then be used to promote the prosperity of Germany and Western Europe, and at the same time be prevented from equipping the armies which had destroyed that prosperity twice in a generation. An International Authority for the Ruhr was established, but was abolished when the Schuman Plan came into effect.

The United States and Great Britain agreed that the Saar should be politically independent of Germany and economically attached to France by a monetary and customs union, although the final disposition of the area would be postponed till the peace conference. Defense and foreign policy would be controlled by France. She adopted a very conciliatory policy toward the Saarlanders, while at the same time she was determined to sever all the political and economic ties which had bound them to Germany. The Saarlanders profited economically from their union with France, and local self-government was established. In the election of 1952 the two leading political parties, which supported the French program, received about 75 percent of the vote. By 1953 coal production of 16,418,000 metric tons and steel of 2,684,000 tons were above prewar levels. An agreement was negotiated with the Saar government in 1950 by which France was granted a fifty-year lease of the coal mines, under the joint management of French and Saarland directors. In 1950 the Saar at its own request, and with French support, was made an associate member of the Consultative Assembly of the Council of Europe.

France's motive in her Saar policy was to increase her security by enlarging her coal and steel production while decreasing those of Germany. There was no desire to annex 980,000 indigestible Germans who would resent direct French control and quite possibly have an abiding nostalgia for Germany.

The above arrangements gave France what she wanted. The Saar's elected leaders declared that they were satisfied with the position in which the country was neither a German nor a French state but a semi-independent entity. The West German Republic never reconciled itself to the loss of the Saar. Opposition was encouraged by the anxiety of the Western powers to enlist Germany in NATO. France refused to give way for it would alter the balance of power in the Schuman Plan for the unified control of the coal, iron, and steel industries. Membership in the governing bodies is allocated in accordance with the production of each member, and the Saar's representatives form part of the French delegation. Germany now accounts for 35 percent of the coal and steel: France and the Saar together for 34 percent: and Holland, Belgium, Luxembourg and Italy for the remaining 31 percent. If the Saar were transferred to Germany, she would have 42 percent and France 27 percent. France proposed that the Franco-Saar economic union should be maintained, but that the Saar should be Europeanized by becoming the headquarters of the institutions of the Schuman Plan. In this way it would not form part of either nation. Germany accepted the principle of Europeanization, but demanded that the Saarlanders be allowed to ask for their return to Germany within five years. France made it clear that she would not agree to Germany's admission to NATO until the question was settled, and late in 1954 the two governments came to an agreement.

The Saar would continue to be represented in the Council of Europe and the organs of the European Coal and Steel Community, and the headquarters of the latter would be established in the city of Saarbrucken. A neutral European commissioner would be appointed by the Council of Ministers of the European Union, and would be responsible to it. He might not be French, German, or Saarlander. He would represent the interests of the Saar in foreign affairs and defense, and would be empowered to see to it that the agreement was carried out. In all other respects domestic self-government would continue as before. Pro-German political parties might henceforth be established, so long as they received no financial or other aid from Germany. The present economic union with France would continue, but in the future economic relations between Germany and the Saar would be created providing they did not endanger those with France. The agreement would be submitted to the Saarlanders as a referendum. The French and German governments also came to an understanding which could have important consequences if it is carried out. They agreed in principle that there should be extensive cooperation between France and Germany in the economic field. They examined the possibilities of expanding their trade with one another, and of encouraging the collaboration of French and German capital in industrial development in Europe and the French colonies.

Three pro-German parties were formed in the Saar with support from

Germany, and they conducted an intensive campaign against the Franco-German agreement. The issue was presented to the voters as a choice between loyalty to Germany and support of internationalism. Nearly 68 percent of the electorate voted against the agreement, and the government which supported it resigned. In the ensuing election the three pro-German parties received 64 percent of the votes. Their aim is to reunite the Saar politically with Germany, and powerful elements among them make it clear that they intend to whittle away France's economic rights. The French and German governments intend to reopen negotiations for a new agreement. Both are anxious to avoid a rupture which could have serious effects upon the unity of Western Europe in the cold war, but each has to take account of national feeling in its own country. It seems probable that Adenauer will propose economic concessions to France in return for political incorporation of the Saar in West Germany; but he may run into opposition from German patriotism in Germany and the Saar. It would appear that France will agree to the political union of Germany and the Saar, but will insist that she cannot afford to give up her economic rights for the reasons explained above. If a compromise of this nature cannot be arranged the Schuman plan might collapse and, to put it mildly, there could be a serious deterioration in Franco-German relations.

THE SCHUMAN PLAN

Far-sighted Frenchmen realized that for all time they and the Germans must live side by side. If their relations were punctuated by an endless series of devastating wars both suffered, and particularly France. Was it not possible to close the book of the past and make a fresh start in a friendly and cooperative spirit rather than with fear and distrust? The growing realization that Russia was a menace to France and Germany alike was an argument that the two ancient enemies should work together against the common danger. Gradually the government of France moved in the direction of friendship. This did not and could not mean that suspicion was dead; the attitude was rather to hope and work for the best but not expect it too blindly. The government too must be very careful not to get too far in advance of public opinion, which does not see as clearly as its leaders the need for a rapprochement.

In 1950 French Foreign Minister Schuman made a remarkably bold and statesmanlike proposal. He suggested that the coal, iron and steel industries of France, Germany, Italy and Benelux (Belgium, Holland and Luxembourg) be placed under supranational control, and he hoped that Great Britain would join the scheme. The revolutionary nature of the plan becomes clearer when one studies its economic and military implications. France is a heavy importer of Ruhr coal, while Germany imports both French and Swedish iron ore. Belgium is a considerable coal producer but imports some coal from Germany and all her iron ore from France and Luxembourg. Luxembourg imports all her coal from Germany but has considerable iron ore, which she increases by imports from France. On this basis Belgium and Luxembourg have developed an important iron and steel industry. Holland has no iron and not too much coal, but produces a fair amount of steel by means of imports. The whole area is really a single interdependent region for coal, iron, and steel, which is cut across by five frontiers. Italy has little coal or iron and is a heavy importer of both. Great Britain has ample coking coal and large reserves of low-grade iron ore (iron content about 28 percent), which she supplements by imports of higher grade ore from Sweden, French North Africa, Sierra Leone, and Newfoundland. Most of the above countries normally exported about one third of their steel manufactures, selling the remainder in their domestic markets, which were heavily protected. A potential continental market of 150 million was split five ways.

All would benefit from freer trade, and the danger that Germany might rebuild her armies for an aggressive war would be lessened if her neighbors could gain some control over the volume and varieties of German steel production. Attempts to attain this by ending Germany's control of Rhineland industry had been thwarted, but the same result might be obtained by cooperation. Thirdly, the aim of federating Europe might be advanced by what is known as the functional approach. A full-blown and immediate federation on the American plan is extremely difficult to achieve in a continent of separate nations where divisions are buttressed by centuries of patriotism, rivalries, and entrenched national interests. But suppose that one could establish cooperation in restricted fields where a combined effort might solve a common problem, such as coal, iron, and steel, and later on defense, railways, agriculture, etc. Common action might be achieved piecemeal, and on this foundation a United States of Western Europe might be set up. All these considerations were in the mind of the French government when it proposed the Schuman Plan in 1950.

A European Coal and Steel Community was to be established for fifty years, open to all the countries that wished to participate in it. It would ensure that the common market was regularly supplied with raw materials and steel, by assuring to all consumers equal access to the sources of production. It would also promote the development of exports. The national production of coal and steel would no longer be subject to the legislation of the different states, but would come under the direct jurisdiction of the community. The High Authority or executive of the community was to be composed of eight members appointed by the governments of the participating states, plus a ninth elected by the other eight. It would direct the general program, issue orders binding upon both individual enterprises and governments, fine firms

violating its orders, facilitate investment programs by granting loans, intervene when large-scale market fluctuations occurred by, e.g., production quotas, limitation of imports, etc., and work out programs for modernization and
the expansion of productive capacity. It was to be assisted by a Consultative
Committee composed of representatives of producers, consumers, and workers.

The High Authority would not be able to rule by edict. The Council
of Ministers, composed of one from each participating state, would be a
liaison between the powers of the High Authority and those retained by
each government. The Council and the High Authority would collaborate
regularly. The Common Assembly would be composed of seventy-eight members appointed by the national legislatures as follows: France, Germany, and
Italy eighteen apiece; Belgium and Holland ten each; and Luxembourg four.
It would review the High Authority's work annually. The Court of Justice, composed of seven judges appointed by the member states, would hear appeals presented by the governments against the decisions of the High Authority. The intention of the plan was to forbid cartels and foster free competition. No discriminatory or unfair practices such as dumping were allowed.
Instead of five separate markets a single market of 150 million consumers was
to be established by abolishing all trade barriers, subsidies, and discriminatory
practices. This would involve the closing of some high-cost and inefficient
coal mines and steel plants, and the High Authority was empowered to help
workers in the inevitable readjustment. One aim was to raise the standard
of living of employees to the same level. Because of the difference in production costs in the participating countries a transitional period of five years was
to be allowed before the full plan came into operation. It is not yet possible
to pass judgment on the Coal and Steel Community, but the prospects appear
hopeful. Broadly speaking, competition between the steel manufacturers and
coal producers of the six countries now resembles that of rival firms within
a single common frontier: it is no longer a trade battle conducted between
the industries of rival nations.

Great Britain refused to join the plan, and this caused considerable fear
in France and other countries that the ultimate effect might be to give the
stronger German industry dominance over those of the other participants.
In July, 1952, however, the six governments ratified the Schuman Plan Treaty,
and the International Authority for the Ruhr and the restrictions imposed on
German steel output were abolished. The Churchill government proved more
cooperative than the Labour party had been. It refused to join the plan, but
appointed a permanent delegation to the High Authority. Its purpose was to
deal on a day to day basis with the many problems of common interest that
must arise between the British and continental coal, iron, and steel industries.
The delegation was also to lay the foundations for an intimate and enduring
association between the community and Great Britain. Anglo-European dis-

cussions would normally take place in the Permanent Council of Association, composed of four representatives each of the British government and the High Authority. Occasionally, too, a British minister would meet with the Council of Ministers.

EUROPEAN UNION

Hitler's conquests convinced many Frenchmen that the division of Europe into twenty-seven separate sovereign states was out of date. After the war the preponderance of the giant American and Russian powers gave fresh strength to the idea of unity. Strategically it is obvious that no single European state could possibly defend itself. The trade barriers that divide the continent limit large-scale production and often prevent a rational organization of industry. Political union might be one way of attacking the problem of making an end to the traditional hostility between France and Germany. France, therefore, welcomed the creation of the Council of Europe or European Union in 1949, and agreed in 1950 to the admission of the West German Republic and the Saar as associate members. Germany was thus reintegrated into the political community of Western Europe.

Influential groups in France and other countries were critical of the Council of Europe because of its limited powers. Some urged that the problem be tackled piecemeal by means of the functional approach already discussed. Others advocated a union of Western Europe under a federal government which would have power to pass laws and levy taxes. Great disappointment existed because of Great Britain's refusal to join the Schuman Plan and the European army, or to consider a political federation. Fear of Germany reinforced the desire of France and the smaller nations like Belgium to have full British participation. Germany is so much more populous and powerful than the other states of Western Europe that they are afraid she may dominate the proposed federal government and the other organizations. There might be the ironical result that Germany would gain peacefully that control of Europe for which she fought World War II. Britain was badly wanted as a counterweight, since by working with France she could prevent the establishment of German dominance. By 1952 many of the supporters of federation decided to go forward with their plans without Britain and run the risk that Germany would overshadow the federal government.

NEUTRALISM

The older word for neutralism is defeatism. It is not confined to France but is found also in Germany and other nations of Western Europe. There is no organized party of any importance, but a considerable number of voters are influenced by neutralist arguments. In part the cause is psychological: the attitude exists in the countries that were defeated in World War II, both among those that were occupied by German armies and also in Germany herself. Confidence that the nation can defend itself has been shattered, and the magnitude of the Russian danger creates the fear that another war would be a repetition of the last one. It is significant that neutralism is not found in nations such as Great Britain which defended themselves successfully. Psychologically it comes down to a feeling of grim self-confidence as against one that resistance is hopeless.

In France there is the belief that war means the end of European civilization and above all of that of France. Occupation is feared almost as much as invasion, and liberation as greatly as either of them. Frenchmen remember vividly the wholesale robbery, the forced labor, the Gestapo, the shooting of thousands of civilians, and the harnessing of their economy to the German war machine. They realize that a Russian army of occupation would behave at least as badly. Then there was the damage which the Americans and British inflicted in the course of the liberation, and the belief that next time it would be worse because of the use of atom bombs. The French feel that by the time Europe was liberated a second time there would be nothing worth liberating.

Another factor making for neutralism is the weakness of Western compared with Russian armaments. There is doubt whether the West can successfully defend France, Germany, and the Low Countries, or whether the Americans and British will retreat across the English Channel and the Pyrenees until they have built up their strength for a counterattack. So, German capitalists, for instance, subsidized the Communist party as a reinsurance policy, and many hesitated to oppose it lest they be marked down for vengeance later. Some of the socialists and intellectuals are traditionally pacifists and antimilitarists. Others fear that intensive rearmament will cause so much inflation and social misery that it will create more Communists than soldiers. In some circles there is distrust of American intentions and methods and a readiness to believe that the United States and Russia are equally to blame for the cold war. The result of all these causes is the conviction that war must be avoided at all costs. Neutralism is gradually declining as Western armed forces are strengthened, and the possibility of a successful defense grows brighter. Morale is improving as convalescence proceeds; but the patient still requires delicate handling. For instance neutralism is increased by an isolationist speech in the United States or any suggestion that American ground troops in Europe may be replaced by air power. On the other hand the immediate intervention of the U.N. and the United States in Korea in 1950 reassured Europeans that they could hope for prompt help if they were attacked.

THE EUROPEAN DEFENSE COMMUNITY (EDC)

The one thing France desired to prevent above everything else was the recreation of the German army; but ultimately she was compelled to accept the idea, primarily because of American pressure. The United States first proposed the rearmament of Germany in 1950 to strengthen the defenses of Western Europe against Russia. Great Britain accepted the proposal without enthusiasm, since no other expedient could be found for filling what Churchill called "that awful gap" in Western defenses. Public opinion is sharply divided on the long-run advisability of the policy, and the chief argument of its supporters is that it is the lesser of two evils. In 1952 it was believed that Russia had twenty-two divisions in Eastern Germany (ten armored, eight mechanized, and four rifle), with 5000 tanks and 5000 aircraft. In addition, there was the Communist-controlled East German army which the Russians had been building up since 1948. It was believed to number over three divisions, about 85,000, supplied with tanks and artillery, and there was also the nucleus of an air force and navy. There were probably another 153 active divisions in Russia and a total of 20,000 aircraft, about half of them jet planes. Mobilization of the trained reserves would give the army 400 divisions within thirty days after mobilization. The satellite states had eighty divisions, not yet fully equipped and trained. The combined strength of the Russian armed forces was believed to be 4,750,000, and the satellites 1,190,000. There have also been "remarkable developments in the fields of atomic, chemical and biological warfare and guided missiles."

The NATO army in Western Germany in 1952 had eighteen divisions, of which eight were armored (six American, five French, four British, two Belgian, plus Canadian, Norwegian, and Danish brigades amounting to another division) and 1800 jet aircraft. In reserve and available after varying periods of time were about six more French, Belgian, and Dutch divisions, and American and British bombers based in Britain. The NATO army was strong enough to fight a delaying action, but not to defend Europe west of the Elbe River (the boundary between the Russian and western zones of Germany). NATO military leaders insisted that security required at least fifty to sixty active divisions. (By 1955 the total force available was about 100 first line and reserve divisions. Some of the latter were not up to standard in numbers, equipment and training, and air power was inadequate. The goal of 5000 modern aircraft had not been reached.) The economic weakness of Western Europe made it impossible to raise an adequate force from the countries already contributing to the NATO army. Commitments in other parts of the world also lessened the troops available for Europe. Britain had 80,000 men locked up in the defense of the Suez Canal, and about 60,-000 more in Malaya, Hong Kong, and Korea. France had the equivalent of ten divisions in Indochina, plus three more in other parts of her empire. The hope had been that France would be the continental mainstay of the NATO army, but nearly half her troops were in Vietnam. The only country which could provide additional troops was Western Germany, and it was proposed that she raise twelve divisions. The war plants dismantled by the victorious allies would have to be rebuilt.

Making the best of a bad job and hoping also that it might lead to the reconciliation of the two nations, France proposed the creation for fifty years of the European Defense Community, or EDC, of about forty-three divisions. The plan placed the armies and air forces of France, Italy, West Germany, Belgium, Holland, and Luxembourg under international control. It was greatly desired that Britain would join the EDC, to prevent West Germany from having a preponderance of strength in the international army, but this she refused to do. Since the scheme covered the armed forces of the six nations in Europe but not in their colonies, it included the whole of the West German army, but not the French colonial troops. The governments of the six states would no longer have any control over their European forces, which would be put under the command of a single supranational authority resembling that of the Schuman Plan. This authority would also control the production and purchase of arms. Military expenses would be paid out of a common fund made up from the contributions of the member states. A Defense Board, the members of which were drawn from the six allies, would have the same authority as a minister of defense over the national forces of his own country. To some extent the board would be controlled by a Council of Ministers appointed by the six governments and a European Parliamentary Assembly elected from the six member states. A Supreme Court was to be created to settle any legal problems that might arise.

The French proposed that national general staffs be abolished and replaced by a single international staff drawn from the six allies. The divisions would be dependent on an international formation for supplies, heavy artillery, etc. This would lessen the ability of the German divisions to operate independently. France had forebodings that under the innocent guise of creating a contingent to the EDC the German army would prepare itself as it did under the Weimar Republic for the same rapid expansion that took place under Hitler. The only men who were competent to lead the new formations were the ex-officers of World War II. This meant the resuscitation of the German Officers' Corps. It was the principal support of militarism and aggression in Imperial Germany, under the Weimar Republic, and to a lessened extent under Hitler's regime owing to his dislike and distrust of it.

Looking to the future, the French saw further possibilities. Once the twelve divisions were trained they feared that there would be a demand that the size of the army must be increased. There were the arguments that Western Germany had a larger population than France, and that she was in the front line in the event of a Russian attack. France feared also that the Ruhr industrialists would demand successfully that the limitations on types of armaments that could be produced in Germany should be abolished. The French suspected that in a few years Germany would be the strongest military power in Europe west of the iron curtain. Once that happened the French doubted if it would be possible to prevent Germany from breaking away from EDC and controlling her own national army. Behind all this was the belief that the reunification of Germany was the main political aim of the people of West Germany. Once this was achieved, they would wish to recover the territory lost to Poland. France was apprehensive lest Germany try to do this by pulling the Western world into a war with Russia, or else by making a bargain with the Soviet government. Remembering the Russo-German co-operation of the 'twenties and the Hitler-Stalin Pact of 1939, France did not think that another rapprochement was out of the question.

The result was a growing unwillingness to ratify the EDC treaty unless the United States and Great Britain would agree to obligations which were more specific than they were prepared to undertake. The American and British governments in 1952 refused the demand for a guarantee against Germany's withdrawing from the EDC. They stated that they would regard such action as a threat to their own security and would consult one another as to possible action. This was not definite enough to reassure France, and she was also dissatisfied because the promise was made as a declaration of intentions, and not in the more binding form of a treaty. Britain in May, 1952, signed a treaty which promised to provide automatic military assistance to any member of EDC which was attacked. The obligation to each of the six nations would remain binding as long as it continued to be a member of EDC, and Britain belonged to NATO. This was considered unsatisfactory since the duration of the NATO alliance was twenty years and of the EDC treaty fifty years. Apprehensions were aroused by reports in 1953 that part of the American ground troops in Germany might be withdrawn and greater reliance placed on air power. They were strengthened by a speech of Secretary of State Dulles late in 1953 in which he hinted that if the EDC treaty were not ratified soon, there might be an "agonizing reappraisal" of how to carry out the NATO alliance. Renewed French efforts were made to persuade the United States and Great Britain to promise that their troops would remain in Europe for fifty years, but a binding commitment was refused. President Eisenhower and the British government declared that when the EDC treaty was ratified they would continue to maintain in Europe such units of their armed forces as might be necessary to contribute their fair share of the troops needed for the joint defense of the area. On the point of a time limit they stated that the NATO treaty "was regarded as of indefinite duration rather than for any definite number of years." The troops would not be withdrawn so long as the threat existed to the security of Western Europe and the EDC. The American and British governments made no precise commitments as to exactly how many troops would be kept in Europe and for how long. They promised to consult their allies and work closely with them, but each retained in its own hands the final right to decide the disposition of its armed forces.

The French Assembly decisively rejected the EDC treaty in August, 1954. With it fell the Bonn Conventions for the ending of the Allied occupation and the restoration of German sovereignty, for the two had been interconnected so that the one could not be brought into force without the other. Premier Mendès-France warned that the United States and Britain were determined to rearm Germany and restore her sovereignty. The French leaders who had sponsored EDC had moved too far in advance of public opinion. With the exception of the Communists and the Gaullists who opposed the EDC the parties were divided in their attitude. The principal reasons for the rejection of the measure were distrust of Germany—in which the members of the Assembly mirrored the opinion of a large part of the voters—and nationalism. There was widespread fear that if West Germany were allowed even a small army, her militarists and extreme nationalists would eventually regain power and the history of the interwar period would be repeated at the expense of France. French nationalists argued that if France surrendered direction of her army she would lose control of her foreign policy, for "the latter without military backing will be powerless." France should not do what Britain refused to accept.

German troops were needed for the defense of Europe, but if the United States and Britain ignored France and authorized Adenauer to rearm, they ran the risk of weakening NATO. Their action might well have increased the strength of neutralism in France, and Germany and Western Europe could not be defended successfully without her whole-hearted support. It was equally true that West Germany could not indefinitely be deprived of sovereignty and armed forces, especially when Russia had granted both rights to her German satellite. The real alternatives were whether Germany would rearm in friendly collaboration with the West, or in spite of it. Adenauer warned that a Western refusal would mean "a return in Germany to an exaggerated nationalism. . . . If Germany is rebuffed by the West and wooed by the East, do you not think that the new nationalism will look to the Soviet Union? This is a great danger." The chancellor demanded the restoration of complete sovereignty including the right to rearm, without the restrictions laid down in the Bonn Conventions. It was primarily the work of British Foreign Minister Eden that a way of escape was found from this potentially dangerous situation.

A conference was held in London which worked out a substitute for EDC. Germany recovered her sovereignty without restrictions and was admitted to NATO as its fifteenth member. Western troops would remain in West Germany with the consent of its government and not as an army of occupation. Germany agreed not to manufacture atomic, chemical, or biological weapons, but was given the right to use nuclear fuels for industrial purposes. The West German army, navy, and air force were to be of the same size, 500,000 men, as agreed in EDC. They would be under the control of the German government with its own general staff, for the international control proposed by EDC was dead. To quote Eden, "The alternative we had to find in our new situation after EDC was rejected had therefore to be something less rigid, demanding less of the member states, but yet offering as nearly as possible an equally adequate system of control." The solution found was the broadening of the Brussels Treaty of Alliance of 1948 between Britain, France, Holland, Belgium, and Luxembourg to include West Germany and Italy. The clause specifying mutual assistance in case of a German attack was discreetly omitted, and the revised alliance was renamed Western European Union.

Under the Western European Union the seven allies would set up a Council which would fix the maximum contributions to NATO of all its members. Their size could only be increased by unanimous consent. The Council would also decide the strength and armament of the police and internal defense forces of the six continental European members of the alliance. France thus received assurances that the German government could not of its own volition increase the size of its armed forces. France insisted most strongly on the control of German armaments, and a compromise was arranged which gave her much of what she demanded. The allies created an agency to ensure that the prohibited types of armaments were not being manufactured and to control the level of stocks and the production of other munitions of the six continental members of the alliance. Britain was the only ally excluded from this control. Germany would provide NATO with twelve divisions, France fourteen, and Britain four. The Supreme Commander, Europe (SACEUR) was given increased powers of control over NATO forces stationed on the European continent. This included the whole of the West German forces and provided an additional guarantee that they could not be used independently by Germany. In particular, SACEUR would control the logistical support of his armies. To quote Eden, "No modern army can, it seems, hope to operate without an exceedingly complicated system of supply . . . to take a simple example—without petrol supplies no modern army can move; and SACEUR can turn off the tap." The only way in which West Germany could be legally released from her obligations and obtain unfettered control over her armed forces would be by the reunion of the two Germanies. The arrangements described above were all made with West Germany. If the whole country were reunited it "would have the right to assume, or not to assume, the previous obligations of" West Germany.

The British government promised not to withdraw its army of four divisions and the tactical air force from Europe without the consent of the majority of its Western European Union allies. The only exception to this promise was "an acute overseas emergency." Since the duration of the alliance was fifty years, the pick of the British army was committed to Europe for half a century. The earlier refusal to give this promise had been one reason for France's rejection of the EDC. To make it was an important break with Great Britain's traditional policy that her obligations to the Commonwealth and Empire made it impossible for her to surrender control over the disposition of her armed forces. The British government came to the conclusion that unless it gave France and the other allies this power of veto over the movement of British troops, the urgent necessity of finding an agreed substitute for EDC would not be met. President Eisenhower reaffirmed the promise he had made with reference to EDC that NATO was regarded as of indefinite duration, and the United States would maintain in Europe such troops "as may be necessary and appropriate to contribute its fair share of the forces needed for the joint defence of the North Atlantic area." In 1955 the terms of the agreement were ratified and put into effect.

SELECTED READING

BLOCH, MARC, *Strange Defeat*. New York: Oxford Press, 1949.

BROGAN, D. W., *France under the Republic*. New York: Harper and Brothers, 1940.

EARLE, EDWARD MEADE, *Modern France: Problems of the Third and Fourth Republics*. Princeton: Princeton University Press, 1951.

EINAUDI, MARIO, *et al., Communism in Western Europe*. Ithaca: Cornell University Press, 1951.

GOGUEL, FRANÇOIS, *France under the Fourth Republic*. Ithaca: Cornell University Press, 1952.

PERTINAX, *The Gravediggers of France*. New York: Doubleday and Company, 1944.

RUSSELL, FRANK M., *The Saar Battleground and Pawn*. Stanford: Stanford University Press, 1951.

SIMON, YVES, *Road to Vichy, 1918–1938*. New York: Sheed and Ward, 1942.

WOLFERS, ARNOLD, *Britain and France between Two World Wars*. New York: Harcourt, Brace and Company, 1940.

CHAPTER 21

GERMANY

A French premier remarked that his problem was that there were 20 million too many Germans in Europe with whom France must live in peace. This emphasized a very important point, that Germany had a much larger population than any country in Europe except Russia. The people were industrious, highly skilled, well organized, very amenable to discipline, and excellent soldiers. A second and most important advantage was the great coal deposits of the Ruhr and the extensive industrialization which resulted from them. Add an excellent system of communications by railway, road, and canal, and good seaports on the North Sea and the Baltic. The combination of all these factors made modern Germany the strongest single great power in Europe. These advantages entered into the calculations of the government in 1914 and again in 1939. On both occasions Germany counted on a short war and believed that France would be knocked out before Great Britain could mobilize her resources or help could arrive from overseas.

THE PRUSSIANIZATION OF GERMANY

The most significant feature in modern German foreign policy has not been aggression, but the support which it received from the very large majority of the people in both world wars. By contrast the British and Americans were most unwilling to go to war, France was no longer the nation of Louis XIV and Napoleon, and the Italians were half-hearted. Only modern Germany had altered for the worse. This raises an important problem for the future of Europe and world peace. What brought about the change in the Germans, and what can be done about it? The answer is not a double dose of original sin but a century of pernicious education which ended in the Prussianization of Germany.

The beginnings of that story go back to the eighteenth century when Germany was divided into 360 states. The rulers accepted the conventions of their day, which held that war and not too scrupulous diplomacy were legitimate instruments of policy as long as they were not carried to extremes. There was a common code of conduct which decreed what a gentleman was and was not allowed to do in his relations with another gentleman of a foreign nation. The one exception was the kingdom of Prussia, which had its beginning as a German outpost on the eastern frontier. The Prussian rulers had gradually conquered the Slavic tribes who lived east of the Elbe River and in the seventeenth century extended control over East Prussia. The necessity of defense and the desire to increase Prussia's territory bred a strong military tradition. Early in the eighteenth century King Frederick William I built up a powerful army and accumulated a large treasure, both of which were used to the full by his son Frederick the Great (1740–1786). He made Prussia the most powerful state of Germany by taking territory from his brother princes and the Austrian Empire, and by his share in the partitions of Poland which united Prussia and East Prussia. Frederick's policy reads like a more civilized version of Hitler's. His aim was aggrandizement, and he subordinated everything to this aim. His principal weapon was his army, though on occasion treaty breaking and unscrupulous diplomacy were employed very effectively. The government was a despotism where the subject had no rights, but merely the duty to obey orders without question or criticism. The whole history of the state was a persistent attempt to repeat over and over again the conquest of ever greater territories. By 1871 Prussia comprised two thirds of Germany's territory and population.

After 1815 Germany was a loose confederation of thirty-nine states. German liberals and nationalists desired to unite them into a single powerful nation. They also wished to replace the autocratic rule of their princes by democratic government. In 1848, the year of revolution, it looked for a time as if unity and democracy would be attained. The princes were frightened: they promised democratic constitutions and allowed elections to a parliament at Frankfort. After long delays this body in 1849 drew up a constitution for a German federation. But by then it was too late: the revolution was defeated and many liberals fled from Germany, often to the United States. The liberals at Frankfort made serious blunders; but Prussia, Austria, and Russia were primarily responsible for their lack of success. Democracy was seriously weakened by the flight of so many of the leading liberals and by its failure to achieve its goals. This effect was intensified by Bismarck's success twelve years later, when he united the nation and made his king of Prussia Emperor of Germany. Bismarck's policy of Blood and Iron was the old Prussian recipe of Frederick the Great. Its principal weapons were a brilliantly Machiavellian diplomacy and three successful wars of aggression in 1864, 1866, and 1870 against Denmark, Austria, and France, respectively.

The combined effect of the liberal failure of 1848 and the autocratic success of 1870 was to discredit democracy. The majority of Germans were patriots first and democrats second. They wanted both unity and constitutional governments; but a united Germany came first. Nothing succeeds like success, and increasingly Germans came to believe that the old Prussian law of force was superior to the professions of justice and good will by "soft" idealists and liberals. Democracy was a beautiful theory, but militarism delivered the goods. More and more Germans who were not Prussians accepted the Prussian way of life. The process of conversion was considerably assisted by propaganda by professors, teachers, and editors.

The political docility of a majority of the German people is one of their outstanding characteristics. It is significant that their history has no figures comparable with Washington, Danton, or Pym, for example. French and English peasants liberated themselves from serfdom, but in Germany it lingered on into the nineteenth century until it was abolished by official edict. The practical effect was that the Germans had no training in popular government. The typical Western belief is that the state is merely an agency to promote the welfare of the people, who must carefully control it lest it abuse its power. This is in sharp contrast with the German belief that the state is a master which must be served. When taxed with Nazi atrocities, a large majority of Germans argued that they were in no way responsible since they could not be expected to oppose or even criticize their rulers. The government of the German Empire had the appearance of democracy but not the reality, and it did little to train the people in self-government. The liberals and other middle-class parties did not really want to challenge the supremacy of the governing group. These were the Kaiser, the Junkers, or landed aristocracy who supplied a large part of the 30,000 officers of the regular army, and the leading businessmen and manufacturers. Class distinctions between the nobility and the middle class were carefully maintained, but there was a working alliance between the two. Industry would support autocracy and imperialistic policies, and the government and the Junkers would keep the socialists in their place and guarantee the established order of society. Business accepted a degree of state control that was unknown in the United States or Great Britain. In principle the socialist trade unions wanted democratic reforms, but in practice the leaders of each union ran it autocratically. The Germans aspired to play a great role in the world, and felt envious and frustrated that for centuries their country had been of little account while Britain and France had molded history. They exulted in the thought that the German Empire was a great and powerful state which had humbled France, and that other nations courted and feared it. Blood and Iron was clearly the way to get results. The soldier was at the apex of the social pyramid, and his ideas and manners were imitated by lesser mortals. To wear a uniform was bliss unalloyed, and there was an idolization of force and war. The nation lived in vague expectation of fresh military triumphs. This was the background of the foreign policy of the empire.

THE LEGACY OF BISMARCK

* The essence of Bismarck's policy from 1871 to 1890 was to isolate France and link all the other great powers with Germany, and in this he succeeded. The keystone of his system was the Austrian alliance of 1879, and his particular nightmare was a Franco-Russian coalition. Bismarck's success in gaining the support of both Austria and Russia was especially noteworthy, since their interests in the Balkans conflicted with one another. His methods were a continuation of the policy of Blood and Iron. In the background there was always the threat of force, and this was reinforced by clever and unscrupulous diplomacy. Bismarck believed that might is right, and looked upon armaments and alliances as the sole means of security. He knew that power created the German Empire, and he was certain that power alone could maintain it. He realized that Germany was not invincible, and he had a fine sense of the possible which saved him from overplaying his hand. A good illustration was his refusal to alienate Great Britain by building a large navy. Bismarck was dismissed from office in 1890. He left a dangerous legacy to the lesser men who succeeded him, and the glamor of his success partially blinded them to the risks involved in imitating his methods. His successors lacked the wisdom and the ability to apply his methods successfully. They accepted his gospel that German power was based on force and that everything was justified if it were in the national interests. Unlike him, they forgot that force has its limitations. They retained his methods of diplomacy, but their clumsiness was a travesty of his skill. In the end they destroyed Germany's unchallenged predominance in Europe and they brought together an opposing coalition.

POPULAR CHAUVINISM

The dismissal of Bismarck in 1890 roughly coincided with a fundamental change in Germany's policy. She ceased to be a satiated state content with dominance in Europe. She intended to keep what Bismarck had gained, but in addition she aspired to be a world power with colonies and a large navy. These ambitions were increasingly supported by the people, and their imperialism was heightened by the propaganda conducted by the government to win public support for the heavy cost of its naval building program. The people were filled with a sense of Germany's power and triumph. They had been brought up to believe that war was a romantic and pleasantly dangerous sport fought in someone else's country. It was argued that the world should belong to the strong, and that states too small or too weak to defend their independence had no right to it. With the exception of a tiny minority the liberals and socialists wholeheartedly supported the government's policy in World War I. The invasion of Belgium and unrestricted submarine warfare were generally approved.

After 1890 individuals and patriotic societies published books that glorified war and sketched ambitious plans of conquest. They helped to heighten the warmindedness of the German public. There is no evidence that the government sponsored them, but it did nothing to discourage them or counteract their influence. The Pan-German League was the most influential of the societies. During World War I unofficial but influential groups drawn from all classes of the population urged a variety of annexations. The programs included the following: the empire of middle Europe (central Europe and the Balkans) and the Turkish Empire; Belgium, the coal mining and industrial area of northeastern France, and the fortifications and iron mines bordering on Alsace Lorraine in order to "have done with the French menace once and for all"; the Baltic provinces of Russia, for settlement by German colonists; Egypt and the Suez Canal; an empire in middle Africa; and as large an indemnity as possible to cover the costs of the war.

It is impossible to say how far the German government would have accepted these unofficial programs since it lost the war in the west. In 1918, however, Germany imposed a conqueror's peace on Russia and Rumania, and the annexations went even further than the programs outlined above. On March 3, 1918, the Soviet government signed the German-imposed Treaty of Brest Litovsk, which ceded to Germany and Austria Russian Poland, Lithuania, and the Baltic provinces which later became Estonia and Latvia. In addition, Russia was compelled to recognize the independence of Finland, Georgia, and the Ukraine. This last had signed a treaty which made it virtually a German-Austrian protectorate. Russia lost 34 percent of her population, 32 percent of her agricultural land, 54 percent of her factories, and 89 percent of her coal mines. She was cut off from the Black Sea and very nearly from the Baltic also. The area left was immense, but the bulk of it was undeveloped and sparsely inhabited. If the Treaty of Brest Litovsk had stood, Russia would never again have dared oppose Germany to the point of war. On May 7, 1918, the Treaty of Bucharest was imposed upon Rumania. Apart from territorial losses, the oil wells were leased to Germany for ninety-nine years, and Rumania undertook to provide food for Germany at fixed prices. It is improbable that a victorious Germany would have been more merciful in the west than she was in the east. Finally, it should be noted that these plans of conquest did not end with Imperial Germany. They were revived with additions in the interwar period and found many supporters.

GERMANY'S PLACE IN THE SUN

Kaiser William II and his advisers abandoned Bismarck's policy of maintaining the status quo and aimed at expansion. They did not wish war: they merely wanted the spoils of victory. They could choose one of two courses with reasonable prospects of success. Germany could control and develop the Turkish Empire, thereby turning Russia into an enemy. Alternatively Germany could build a great fleet as an instrument of world power and so alienate Great Britain. Her blunder was that she followed both policies at once, and gradually drove both Britain and Russia over to the side of France.

The government began to build a large navy in 1898 and frankly admitted that this was in direct competition with the British fleet. Germany realized that without a strong navy she could not enforce her will outside Europe. There was no clear understanding as to the exact purposes for which it was wanted, or how it would be used. In 1904 Britain and France formed the Anglo-French Entente Cordiale. The German government was surprised and discomfited: it was determined to seize a favorable opportunity to break up the Entente. The occasion was France's penetration of the independent and anarchic state of Morocco, which was clearly meant to end in a protectorate. Germany would have been within her rights in demanding diplomatic negotiations, but her tactics gave the impression that she was trying to force war on France. In fact, Germany did not want war and was acting on the theory that the threat of it would drive Britain back into isolation. This blundering imitation of the Bismarckian technique heightened British distrust of Germany's aims and frightened her closer to France. In 1906 the European powers and the United States tacitly authorized France to continue her Moroccan policy. The Anglo-Russian Entente of 1907 led Germany to feel that she must at all costs support Austria Hungary, her only loyal ally. In 1908 the rival ambitions of Russia and Austria in the Balkans caused a serious crisis, and the former was compelled by a German ultimatum to give way in 1909. The Russian government was bitterly humiliated and determined never again to submit to such an experience. By 1911 it was evident that French control of Morocco would soon be complete. Germany could not prevent it, but she could demand a cession of territory as compensation. To put France into a more amenable frame of mind, Germany decided to make her thoroughly frightened by a bluff of war. She got her compensation in French Equatorial Africa, but she also drove France and Britain closer together. In both countries the belief spread that eventually war would be unavoidable.

The Triple Entente was inferior in strength to the German-Austrian alliance; but the period of Germany's unchallenged supremacy in Europe was ended. This she regarded as intolerable, but she refused to moderate her policy or her technique of forceful diplomacy. The Austrian government was growing pessimistic about its prospects of survival, owing to the increasing unrest among its subject races. In particular, Serbia with Russian support was encouraging a secession movement among the Croats, Slovenes, and other southern Slav subjects of the empire. The German and Austrian general staffs began to urge a preventive war to destroy Serbia and break up the Triple Entente while the preponderance of power was still in their favor. The murder of the Archduke Franz Ferdinand, the heir to the throne of the empire, provided the pretext for attacking Serbia in 1914. The Austrian and German governments hoped it would be a small local war. An attack on Russia's protégé Serbia, however, was reasonably certain to lead to a head-on collision between the German-Austrian drive to the south and the Russian drive to the west. France wished only to be left in peace, but she felt her only salvation against Germany was to fight alongside her Russian ally. The British government and people were so torn between isolation and pacifism on the one hand and fear and suspicion of Germany on the other that until the last moment they themselves did not know what they would do. All of which meant that a local war against Serbia was likely to develop into a general war. Germany realized the danger of this, but she preferred to fight if she must before the Russian army reforms were completed. She feared that otherwise the ultimate result would be the collapse of the Austrian Empire and Russian hegemony in the Balkans. Germany believed that she could win a war against Russia and France, and she gambled on the chance that Great Britain would remain neutral. The German government gave the green light to Austria. At the last moment, when it realized that Britain might come in, it made a feeble and unsuccessful attempt to restrain its ally.

THE WEIMAR REPUBLIC

The German army was completely defeated in the last three months of the war, and the government's representatives were compelled to accept the armistice terms laid down by the victorious Allies. On November 9, 1918, the monarchy was overthrown, and Ebert, the Socialist leader, became president of the Weimar Republic. The general enthusiasm with which the Germans had welcomed the war in 1914 had vanished by 1918 as the result of privations, Communist influence, and defeat. The military leaders and the Kaiser bore the brunt of popular disfavor, and the demand for his abdication was widespread. The middle class and the peasants wanted little change in the existing order of society. The Socialists were determined above everything else to prevent the Communist minority from seizing power. They were as anxious as the generals themselves to evade the disarmament clauses of the Versailles Treaty. The only people who could help them to attain both aims were the officers of the old army; therefore, they formed an alliance with their enemies. Nominally parliamentary control of the army was introduced; but the ordinance of August 11, 1920, which transferred the functions of command to the commander in chief (General von Seeckt) made him almost independent of the minister for defense, and turned the latter into a virtual puppet. The power of the army was shown as early as 1920, when Dr. von Kapp seized Berlin with a force of irregulars. The regular army refused to support him, judging his action to be premature; but from a feeling of trade union solidarity it declined to suppress the rebel troops, who were trying to overthrow the government of which the army was the nominal servant. The revolt was defeated by a general strike of the workmen, the rebels were mildly reproved, and nobody was punished. The Socialists likewise made no attempt to weaken the position of the Junkers, who despised the republic and held a key position in the army and the administration. As Scheidemann, the Socialist chancellor, said: "There has been no revolution in Germany at all. We prepared no revolution. We wanted no revolution."

The Weimar Republic tried to carry out the terms of the Versailles Treaty, hoping that thus they would be modified more quickly than in any other way. The Germans chose to forget that the government had some considerable success in this policy. It ended reparations; it secured the military evacuation of the Rhineland in 1930; and it won membership in the League of Nations. Until the onset of the great depression in the 'thirties German industry was rapidly expanding its production, and Hitler was regarded as a spent force. There were many reasons for the fall of the republic besides the Treaty of Versailles. The widespread unemployment caused by the great depression won Hitler many recruits since he promised work. An exaggerated fear of communism led the industrialists to finance him in the belief that he would protect them and break the trade unions. Members of the middle class, ruined by the inflation, found themselves being forced down to the level of the workmen. Resenting this intensely they blamed the republic for their loss of position and turned to Nazism. The army, the only organized force in the state, was no friend of the republic and eventually joined Hitler in his conspiracy to overthrow it. The multiple party system meant a succession of weak and short-lived governments, and this discredited democracy. The principal reason, however, was that the majority of the people never accepted the republic because they did not appreciate the democratic freedoms. They preferred that someone else do their political thinking for them, and they did not undergo any fundamental change because a president had been substituted for a kaiser.

THE TREATY OF VERSAILLES

The peace treaty of Versailles, which was signed at Versailles on June 28, 1919, was largely the work of President Wilson, Prime Minister Lloyd George, and Premier Clemenceau, and to a lesser extent the Italian and Japanese representatives. By its terms Alsace Lorraine was returned to France, thereby righting an ancient wrong and also—it was falsely hoped—weakening Germany's ability to wage war by depriving her of her principal source of iron ore. Provisions were made for a plebiscite in Northern Schleswig, which had been taken from Denmark in 1866, to determine to whom it should belong. In accordance with the voting part of the area was returned to Denmark. Two small districts, Eupen and Malmédy, were added to Belgium to strengthen the frontier. France was given ownership of the Saar coal mines, while the district was separated from Germany and placed under the control of the League of Nations for fifteen years. The eighteenth-century partitions of Poland were reversed, and the republic of Poland was created.

Another group of clauses were intended to prevent Germany from again waging a world war. Conscription was abolished, and the army was limited to 100,000 volunteers serving for twelve years. Germany was forbidden to manufacture heavy artillery, tanks, poison gas, military aircraft, and submarines. The General Staff, the brains of the army, was dissolved, and the navy was drastically reduced. German territory west of the Rhine and for fifty kilometers east of it was demilitarized. All fortifications were destroyed in this region, and no troops could be stationed there. The area was to be occupied by Allied troops, which would be withdrawn in stages over fifteen years if Germany carried out the terms of the treaty. Germany was deprived of her colonies, all of which had been conquered during the war. Their economic value was small, but their strategic importance was considerable. Germans who had violated the laws of war were to be tried by Allied tribunals. Ultimately the trials were transferred to German courts, and of the 900 named in the Allied lists six received very light sentences for serious offenses. Germany was to deliver ships, coal, timber, and livestock and to pay heavy reparations, the amount of which would be fixed by an Allied commission.

THE POLISH-GERMAN FRONTIER

In German eyes loss of territory to Poland was perhaps the worst offense of the treaty, and the nation was determined to reverse it. On the flat plain of eastern Europe there was no clear-cut division but instead an intermingling of peoples. The Allies restricted as far as possible the transfer of Germans to Poland, but even so a minority (about 600,000 in 1939) was included in the new state, scattered here and there through the western part of the country.

The Germans had always looked down upon the Poles, and they felt it intolerable that members of the "superior race" should be placed under the rule of their inferiors. In addition, they had several specific grievances. Upper Silesia had a mixed population, and had been developed by Germany as a miniature Ruhr. It was divided in accordance with the results of a plebiscite, and Poland obtained about two thirds of the coal and the iron and steel industry. Poland was almost entirely an inland state, and there was only one point at which a thin finger of Polish population reached the Baltic. This was the ancient Polish province of Pomorze, better known by its German name of the Corridor. The Poles claimed free access to the sea, since otherwise the whole of their foreign trade would have to pass through the hands of their hereditary enemy Germany. It would seem reasonably certain that the Poles were still the majority of the settled inhabitants of the Corridor in 1919, despite Germany's efforts to force them out and bring in German settlers. Finally, there was the seaport of Danzig at the mouth of the Vistula River, which traditionally had handled the whole of Poland's foreign trade. In 1919 it had a population of about 300,000, 90 percent of whom were Germans. The Poles wanted to annex it for economic reasons; while the Germans claimed that it should remain part of Germany on grounds of nationalism. The Allied decision was that the Corridor should be annexed to Poland, but that Danzig and the surrounding district should become an independent city state under the ultimate control of the League of Nations. The German majority ensured that it would control the government of the city. The Poles were to control the harbor facilities, and Poland and Danzig were to form a customs union, so that the Danzigers could not hamper Polish trade.

The Germans never relinquished their claim that Danzig should return to Germany and take Poland's foreign trade with it. A few years after the treaty the Poles converted the tiny fishing village of Gdynia, a few miles from Danzig, into a well-equipped seaport, and divided their foreign trade between the two. This gave them a city that was indisputably Polish in origin, ownership, and population, but it gave the Danzigers the fresh grievance that their vested interest in monopolizing the foreign trade of Poland had been infringed. The Corridor was the principal bone of contention. The roads and railways connecting Germany with East Prussia crossed it, and the Germans complained that its existence hampered their trade. This grievance was removed by a treaty which provided that trains en route from Germany to East Prussia or vice versa would cross the Corridor without customs inspection.

The removal of concrete complaints merely made the existence of the Corridor more serious, since it came to be a purely emotional grievance. East Prussia was separated from Germany, and the fatherland was cut in two. The Poles pointed out with perfect accuracy that Pomorze had always interposed between Germany and East Prussia, from the time when the Knights of the Teutonic Order established it in the thirteenth century as a German colony in Slavic territory. The two had never been united until Frederick the Great annexed Pomorze in 1772. What the Treaty of Versailles did was to make the political and the racial boundaries coincide, and restore the situation as of 1772. This explanation left the Germans cold: they were determined to reunite the fatherland and the Poles were equally determined to defend their outlet to the Baltic. No compromise was possible: either there was a Corridor or there was not. It was the irresistible force and the immovable obstacle.

REPARATIONS AND WAR DEBTS

The principle that the loser pays the stakes is almost as old as war itself. Down the ages the victor collected his costs from the conquered. This practice was perfectly feasible in old-style war, which means until about a hundred years ago. For centuries the average army did not exceed 40,000. The flintlock musket and the muzzle-loading cannon were comparatively simple and inexpensive to make, and pay and equipment for so small a force were only a moderate burden. War was a select and comparatively inexpensive affair between professionals, and the defeated state was able to pay reparations. The last time that this was possible was in 1871, when Germany collected an indemnity of $1 billion from France. The principle broke down because of the total alteration in the character of war. Scientific invention enormously increased the effectiveness of weapons—and their cost. Compare the price of a tank and its predecessor the cavalryman mounted on a horse and armed with lance and saber. Railways and trucks made it possible to feed and supply several million instead of several score thousand men. The number engaged, the complexity of the weapons, and the immense amount of ammunition needed because of their rapidity of fire, all these required the services of a very great number of war plants and an army of civilian labor. The result was to raise the cost of war to astronomic figures.

World War I cost the Allies at least $120 billion, and in 1921 the amount of reparations which Germany was to pay was fixed by the Reparations Commission at $33 billion in gold. To make this huge payment was impossible; and, besides, Germany had no desire to pay. The result was moderate payments, and an increasing belief on the part of France that only force would compel Germany to pay. This led her to occupy the Ruhr in 1923 in an attempt to extract reparations. The Germans organized passive resistance, and the occupation proved fruitless. The German government had financed the resistance by printing paper money, and a runaway inflation developed which completed the collapse of the mark. All those whose savings were invested in anything but tangible property lost everything. The domestic debt both of the government and of private corporations was wiped out.

Both Germany and France were now ready to compromise, and in 1924 the Dawes Commission was appointed to work out a plan for reparations payments. It provided for the evacuation of the Ruhr, for foreign control over German finances, and for reduced annual payments. The amount demanded, $33 billion, could not be paid in actual gold: it did not exist. Neither could it be met by transferring marks to the Allied creditors, for marks were legal currency only in Germany. The creditors demanded payment in pounds sterling, francs, etc., or else in some foreign currency, such as dollars, which could easily be converted into their own national currencies. Reparations could only be paid if Germany had a favorable balance of trade of sufficient magnitude to meet the payments. This favorable balance could only be attained if Germany's creditors bought so much more goods from her than she imported from them, that they owed to her an amount in marks equal to the amount in foreign currencies which the German government needed to obtain in order to meet its reparations payments. Germany could then transfer these balances to the creditor governments.

The problem of Allied war debts was connected with reparations. During the latter part of the war and after the armistice the purchase of munitions and food by the European Allies was paid for by credits extended by the American government. Most of this money was spent in the United States. By 1922 the European Allies owed the United States in principal and accumulated interest $11,657,000,000, the chief debtors being Italy, France, and Great Britain. Great Britain's European Allies owed her about one and a half times as much as she owed the United States. The problem of transferring these huge sums to the United States was exactly the same as that which faced Germany in making her reparations payments to the European Allies. Between 1923 and 1926 the debtors agreed to pay America in principal and interest $22.2 billion dollars over a period of sixty-two years. With the addition of German reparations the grand total of international debts was about $61 billion. The debtor states could pay their debts only by a tremendous expansion of exports. The creditors, however, were not prepared to allow such an influx of imports owing to the opposition of their own producers. This was especially true of the United States, the greatest creditor of all, for in 1922 the Fordney-McCumber Tariff heightened import duties. The payment of war debts and reparations became practically impossible.

The United States always insisted that no connection existed between reparations and war debts. Technically this was correct, but the two were linked together in practice since about 65 percent of reparations would ultimately be sent to the United States in payment of war debts. From 1924 to 1929 reparations and war debt payments were met because the United States and Great Britain were priming the pump. Several billion dollars were borrowed by German governments and private corporations, over half of it from the

United States. Americans lent dollars to Germany, who forwarded part of the amount to, say, France labeled "This Year's Reparations." France relabeled it "This Year's War Debt" and sent it back to Washington. On this basis the payment of reparations and war debts could continue indefinitely. In 1928 American loans largely ceased, and Germany announced that she could no longer meet her payments under the Dawes Plan. In 1929 the Young Plan reduced the total amount of reparations with payments to continue until 1988. Soon afterward came the onset of the great depression. In 1931 the Hoover moratorium halted all inter-governmental payments for a year to save the German banking system from collapse. It was clear that no more reparations could be collected, and in June, 1932, the Lausanne Conference abolished them. The United States insisted that war debts must continue to be paid. In December, 1932, Britain, Italy, and some of the other European governments met their payments, while France and others did not. Token payments were made by some of the debtors in 1933. In 1934 Congress passed the Johnson Act, which forbade private American loans to defaulting governments, and the token payments ceased. Only Finland continued to meet its obligation. The intergovernmental debt structure had collapsed.

The German people believed that the reparations payments imposed by the Treaty of Versailles and the French occupation of the Ruhr were the causes of their inflation and bankruptcy. Actually, the inflation began during the war, as a result of the methods adopted to defray its cost, and increased after 1918 because of the government's financial policy. Reparations and the occupation of the Ruhr completed the collapse of the mark. As to the burden of reparations, the more conservative estimates consider that the amount of the foreign loans to Germany, on most of which she defaulted, was greater than the payments made to the Allies. Other estimates consider that Germany borrowed, mainly in the United States, more than double the amount which she paid in reparations. The reparations clause of the Versailles Treaty was a blunder, and in the end the victorious Allies literally paid for it.

THE DISARMAMENT OF GERMANY

An Inter-Allied Military Commission of Control was sent to Germany to carry out the disarmament imposed by the Treaty of Versailles. From the very beginning the government of the republic worked closely with the army and the foreign office to obstruct and deceive the commission, which was finally withdrawn in 1927. Lack of support from the Allied governments caused the commission's failure. The Weimar Republic persuaded them and particularly the British government that if the treaty were rigidly enforced Germany would go communist. Churchill's verdict was that "the strict enforcement at any time till 1934 of the disarmament clauses of the Peace Treaty would have guarded indefinitely, without violence or bloodshed, the peace and safety of mankind. But this was neglected while the infringements remained petty, and shunned as they assumed serious proportions."

The General Staff changed into civilian clothes, christened itself the Departments of Reconstruction, Research, and Culture, and worked out the plans which it believed would give success in the next war. The training of the small regular army was conducted in such a way that practically every private was a potential officer or at least a sergeant. The trained nucleus was provided for a very rapid expansion in numbers when it would become possible to reintroduce conscription. Meanwhile a beginning was made by militarizing the police (who had the unusual equipment of artillery and airplanes) and by encouraging the training of various illegal formations. In one way the restriction in size of the army was an advantage, since it enabled the commanders to handpick the recruits and prevent the intrusion of any republican influence. The Officers Corps of Imperial Germany had been a kind of guild with its own laws and customs. Each unit had the right to reject every candidate for a commission, irrespective of his technical qualifications, unless his brother officers were certain that he shared all their prejudices. Good birth and social position were esssential, and no liberals, socialists, or ex-privates need apply. The officer was feared and looked up to by civilians, including the cabinet ministers of the Weimar Republic. The Officers Corps under the republic continued to be what it had been under the kaiser—militarist and antidemocratic.

The Allied governments decided not to destroy war factories if they were converted to peaceful uses, since they were convinced that Germany would never again dream of going to war. One result was that she was left with every lathe that ever turned a shell. Krupp later boasted of how he manufactured illegal matériel. Submarines were illicitly built and their crews trained in other countries. Civil aviation was permitted by the treaty, and a government civil aviation department largely staffed by ex-flying officers created the nucleus of an air arm. Beginning in 1919 Rathenau, the minister of reconstruction, began to rebuild German war industry. All the new factories, many of them established with American and British loans for reconstruction, were designed from the outset for speedy conversion to war purposes. The work continued throughout the years of the Weimar Republic. If the republican ministers had not carried out all the preliminary preparations, Hitler could never in a few years have created the most powerful army the world had yet seen.

GERMANY AND RUSSIA

There was nothing new about the Russo-German Neutrality Pact of 1939. Bismarck performed some of his most spectacular diplomatic gymnastics to maintain German friendship with Russia, and the policy did not begin with him. Viewed dispassionately, there was much to be said in favor of a Russo-German combination. Soviet Russia never allowed ideology to stand in the way of expediency, and the Weimar Republic like the Nazis later on was equally broad-minded. Both governments were outcasts in the Europe of the early 'twenties, and both had designs on Polish territory. Russia needed technical experts, machinery, and foreign loans, and in return she offered concessions for the development of her natural resources. Germany had technical experts to spare, and her industrialists saw visions of great economic gains. The first sign of the rapproachement was the Treaty of Rapallo of 1922, which provided for trade facilities and the resumption of diplomatic relations. German officers helped to drill the new Red army, and in return German air force cadets were sent to Russia for training. The friendly relations were broken by Hitler, whose intense hostility to communism was deplored by many of his own Nazis as well as by an influential group in the General Staff. Ultimately their attitude was one factor in the negotiation of the Russo-German Neutrality Pact of 1939.

ANSCHLUSS

The Empire of Austria Hungary collapsed in 1918 because of the revolt of the Czechs and other subject peoples. In its stead emerged the five succession states of Austria, Hungary, Czechoslovakia, Yugoslavia, and Rumania. The peace conference of 1919 ratified the accomplished fact, and laid upon Austria the obligation to do nothing that might directly or indirectly compromise her independence. She was an empire shrunk to a province. Formerly the center of a state of 51 million, she was reduced to a country of 6 million, cut off from her former trading area by the high tariffs of the new states that had thrown off her control. Austrians found it so difficult to maintain a tolerable degree of prosperity that the desire became widespread for *Anschluss* or union with Germany. There were also the links of common language, racial descent, and culture. In 1931 the German and Austrian governments arranged to form a customs union. On grounds of pure economics there was much to be said for it since it would open to Austria the German domestic market, from which she was shut out by the tariff. France, Italy, and the new succession states successfully opposed the proposal. They feared that in the end the greater would draw the less, and Austria would become merely a province of her larger and wealthier neighbor.

The underlying reason for the opposition becomes plain when one studies a physical map of Europe. Geographically, Austria is the upper valley of the Danube, and its capital city Vienna is the road and railway center of central Europe. Hungary is the middle valley; Czechoslovakia is the barrier of mountains between the Danube valley and the plain of eastern Europe; and

Yugoslavia is the mountain country between the valley and the Adriatic. Austria is the strategic key to the control of the Danubian countries, and once the Germans occupied the upper valley they would have no great difficulty in extending their power. It was no accident that Hitler's annexation of Austria in 1938 preceded his assault on Czechoslovakia. German annexation of Austria meant so great a shift in power that it would seriously weaken the position of the French bloc.

HITLER'S GRAND DESIGN

Hitler's aims were an exaggeration of those of Imperial Germany. The chief difference perhaps was that the Kaiser's government hoped to annex territory retail, while Hitler planned to take it wholesale. The astounding successes which he achieved were a great source of emotional gratification to the Germans. He was speaking the truth when he said during the war that he had the support of the immense majority of the people. Even after Germany's total defeat many condemned Hitler for his technique but not for his aims. Their attitude was that he was a fool to invade Russia before he had finished off the West, but that there was much to be said for his policy of conquest. Hitler's promise to free Germany from the injustices, whether actual or alleged, of the Versailles Treaty also had a very wide appeal.

The Nordic theory dated from the nineteenth century, and had had wide popular currency long before Hitler's time. Its doctrine that the Nordic race was superior to all others and that the Germans were its finest flower was very flattering to a people with aspirations to world leadership. In reality after several milleniums of fine mixed fighting, migration, and intermarriage all races are mongrels. All good Nordics looked upon Slavs as a very inferior breed; but the Prussians were a cross between Teuton and Slav, and Bismarck himself had Slav blood in him. An ironical phase of the propaganda was that its leading exponents were notably unlike the Wagnerian heroes, who were the ideal Nordic supermen. The Germans themselves had a word for it—"as blond as Hitler, as slim as Goering and as tall as Goebbels." The theory required that all Germans in Europe must be liberated whether they wished it or not and added to the fatherland. There were fragments of the lost tribes in practically every country from France to Russia and from Scandinavia to Rumania. Very often their liberation would involve the conquest of large numbers of the inferior races, and after the process was completed the surviving remnants of these states would be so weakened that they would become German satellites. A final advantage of the Nordic theory was that Britain and France were deluded by Hitler's protestations that he merely wished to join Austrians and Sudeten Germans to their fatherland, until his annexation of the Czechs in 1939 exposed his real purpose.

Haushofer, the leading geopolitician, and his followers were not Hitler's source of inspiration, although he borrowed some ideas from them and they were a powerful tool of Nazi propaganda. The geopoliticians and Hitler alike were manifestations of the spirit of aggression and the desire for power that were so widespread in Germany. Their doctrines read like Frederick the Great modernized with geographic and philosophic embellishments. Control of Europe and Africa and alliance with Italy and Japan summed up the program, and thus far it tallied with that of Hitler. In one very important point it differed however. Borrowing an idea from Sir Halford MacKinder, the Scots geographer, Haushofer strongly urged an alliance with Russia as well as with Japan, and it was a bitter disappointment to him when Hitler invaded Russia in 1941.

In November, 1940, Hitler and Molotov held conversations in Berlin which revealed a good deal of Germany's war aims. Assuming that the war was almost over, Hitler suggested a friendly division of the loot. Italy, Germany's satellite, would be given North Africa (presumably French North Africa and Egypt). Germany herself wanted only Europe and tropical Africa. (This would bring her into contact with the Union of South Africa, which contained a strong pro-Nazi element among the Boer Nationalists.) Hitler admitted that he would need a century fully to develop this living space. Germany's only interests in Asia were economic and commercial, so he proposed that Japan take eastern Asia to the south of her, and that Russia expand to the south toward the Persian Gulf and the Indian Ocean. Turkey might remain independent but properly submissive to the Axis and Russia. Molotov replied that Russia was willing to cooperate politically with Germany, Italy, and Japan if the price were high enough. More concretely Russia wanted control of Turkey, Bulgaria, Finland, and the Rumanian province of Southern Bukovina, as well as gains in Asia. Hitler was shocked by such immoderate greed, and some weeks later he decided to invade Russia.

HITLER'S POLICY

When Hitler assumed power, he saw that before he could carry out his program of conquests the German army must be recreated and the demilitarized Rhineland refortified. The German General Staff believed that it would take until about 1943 to build up an army of several millions. The German navy, apart from U-boats, could not be expanded to its pre-1914 size in less than a dozen years. The airplane, however, could change the relative war power of states much more rapidly. Hitler believed that if Germany threw all her energies into the task she could in four or five years forge a weapon that would overcome the superiority in armed strength of the Western powers, especially if France and Britain neglected to counterarm. The skeleton of an air force had been created under the Weimar Republic, and Hitler seized the one chance which offered him a short cut to success. The army was also to be expanded as rapidly as possible; but a powerful battle fleet was not to be built. Construction was to concentrate on submarines and fast, heavily armed commerce raiders. The first few years of the new policy would be fraught with peril to Germany. Rearmament was or should have been an obvious threat to France and Britain, and their superiority in arms was so great that they could have forced a change of policy. Hitler possessed, however, an apparently intuitive capacity for the accurate measuring of risks, and an uncanny perception of the psychological moment for action. Each of his preliminary steps were gambles, but he felt certain that neither France nor Britain nor still less isolationist America would call his bluff. Hitler knew that ultimately success involved the use of force. In 1937 he secretly informed his chief lieutenants that it was "his irrevocable decision to solve the German space problem not later than 1943–1945," because his superiority in armed strength would then be at its height.

A ten-year pact of nonaggression with Poland was signed in 1934. Hitler had no intention of keeping it longer than suited his convenience, but temporarily it was expedient. It weakened the French-Polish alliance, and a Polish attack on him was now less likely when he moved against Austria. A few months later Hitler made a premature attempt to seize Austria through a revolt of the Nazi fifth column. On March 16, 1935, he reintroduced conscription and greatly increased the strength of the German army. In June, 1935, Hitler offered a naval pact that would limit his navy to 35 percent of that of the British. He promised that his U-boats would never be used against merchant ships! The Baldwin government accepted without consulting France or Italy, although the German shipbuilding program was a threat to all three. This indefensible action aroused justifiable hostility and suspicion in France and Italy. Italy's invasion of Ethiopia destroyed the growing cooperation between her, France, and Britain, and on March 7, 1936, Hitler took advantage of the disunity to reoccupy and refortify the demilitarized Rhineland. In 1936 he created the Rome-Berlin Axis, and the partners cooperated in making their protégé, Franco, dictator of Spain.

In May, 1935, a Law for the Defense of the Reich was enacted. It ordered total economic mobilization of the country, and was described by one of the generals as "the cornerstone of our preparations for war." At the same time Hitler strove to make Germany as economically self-sufficient as possible by inventing substitutes for imported raw materials. He realized that complete autarky was impossible, and he regarded it as a military and not an economic measure. It was a temporary expedient intended to safeguard Germany if she should have to undergo another British naval blockade before she had won her living space. The economic penetration of the countries of southeastern Europe proceeded apace. They were predominantly agricultural and their chief exports were foodstuffs, some oil (Rumania), minerals, and timber, which Germany needed. They imported most of their manufactures and armaments. After 1933 Germany negotiated a series of barter agreements with these states, paying in blocked marks which had to be spent inside Germany. The only way in which the creditors could use their credit balances was to buy German manufactures. The percentage of their imports from Germany rose from 19 percent in 1933 to 42 percent in 1938, and the percentage of the exports going to Germany increased from 16 percent to 45 percent. Control of so high a proportion of the trade gave Germany an economic stranglehold over these countries; and this was used to promote the establishment of political control.

In 1938 Hitler felt that his preparations were far enough advanced to move from strength and not by bluffing. He annexed Austria and stripped Czechoslovakia of its only possible defensive frontier by "liberating" the Sudeten Germans. Once more he had calculated correctly that France and Britain would not fight, and his influence in Germany was more firmly established than ever. The German people approved wholeheartedly of a ruler who had proved that he could win the spoils of victory without having to fight for them. The old guard of militarists entrenched in the General Staff originally supported Hitler, but they became increasingly alarmed at the risks of war he ran in his foreign policy. They approved of some of his aims, including control of Austria, Czechoslovakia, and Poland and an eventual war with France. What they objected to was that he was doing too many things too quickly, at the risk of a general war which they were certain Germany could not win. The generals were powerless against Hitler's astounding successes, and in the end he dominated the army as much as all the other elements in Germany. In 1938 during the Munich crisis a group of officers under Halder, chief of the General Staff, was "very nearly determined" to remove Hitler. Before they could make up their minds, the Western powers gave in, and Hitler had won a triumph that made him unassailable.

Opposition revived during World War II, particularly in the higher command of the army. Hitler imposed his views increasingly on the detailed conduct of campaigns, a field which demanded a professional skill that he did not possess. The generals gradually began to fear that he was leading the nation to military disaster. Other small centers of opposition also existed, including a few diplomats, some former members of conservative parties, government officials, and moderate socialists. The sole unifying force was the desire to overthrow Hitler and end the war. All recognized that the army was the only power capable of challenging his authority. If the plot to assassinate him had succeeded, the new government would not have been democratic, but a small group of conservative politicians and generals. On July 20, 1944, Colonel Count Klaus von Stauffenberg placed a brief case containing a time bomb near Hitler's chair during a staff conference. The explosion killed or wounded a number of officers, but Hitler was only slightly injured. The failure of the plot was followed by widespread executions.

THE RUSSO-GERMAN TREATY

The General Staff and the foreign office were divided in 1939 between the advocates of two conflicting policies. One group wanted to annex western Russia and destroy her power, while the other continued Bismarck's tradition that friendship and alliance with her were essential. Hitler hated communism but did not want a simultaneous war on two fronts. Consequently, he decided to buy Russia's neutrality by giving her the territory she wanted. The Russo-German Pact of August 23, 1939, promised that neither would attack the other, and that if either were at war with a third power, the other would give the latter no support. Poland was to be partitioned, and Finland, Estonia, Latvia, and a month later Lithuania were assigned to the Soviet sphere of influence. Both took note that Russia was deeply interested in the Rumanian province of Bessarabia while Germany was not. The trade treaty of August 19 guaranteed Germany stipulated quantities of food, oil, and strategic raw materials, which to a considerable extent nullified the effects of the British naval blockade. Russia agreed to buy metals and other raw materials for Germany in the United States and other neutral countries. Hitler was now free to fight a war in the west with an easy mind.

GERMANY'S NEW ORDER IN EUROPE

By the summer of 1941 most of the European states had either been conquered or had joined the Axis as satellites. In 1941 Hitler drove the U.S.S.R. into the war on the side of Great Britain, and in the first eighteen months of his campaign overran vast areas of her territory. Before 1939 it was a commonplace that modern war does not pay, and the standard proof was the failure of the victors of 1919 to collect even a fraction of their war costs in reparations. Germany was determined to disprove this judgment, and plans for exploitation were drawn up in advance. In general, there were two phases of economic policy, of which the first was short-term spoliation. Raw materials, machinery, manufactured articles, railway rolling stock, foodstuffs, and anything else of immediate value were sent to Germany or used by the armies of occupation. Factories were compelled to manufacture for the German army. Everything was done with all the forms of legality, and usually the Germans paid for what they took in worthless paper currency which the conquered were forced to accept. The policy of wholesale deportation for slave labor in Germany was followed in the conquered countries, the total number being estimated at 4,795,000. The principle governing the treatment of slave labor was "exploitation to the highest possible extent at the lowest conceivable degree of expenditure." Very heavy reparations were imposed on conquered territories. In two years France paid as much as Germany in ten years after World War I.

The long-term policy was the creation of a united and integrated Europe under permanent German domination. Greater Germany was to be "the steely core . . . a block of 100,000,000, indestructible, without flaw, without an alien element, the firm foundation of our power." Surrounding her would be her vassal states. Germany would control government, finance, and the bulk of the manufacturing, especially in potential war industries. The vassal states would largely be producers of food and raw materials as well as markets. The plans for France illustrate the projected policy. Alsace Lorraine was reannexed, and there were indications that Hitler was planning to separate from France the coal-mining and industrial area of the northeast and combine it with Belgium in a separate satellite state. The effect would be, in the remark attributed to General von Stülpnagel, the military governor of France, to make the country "half vegetable patch and half brothel." Agriculture would become the principal industry, along with luxury trades and Paris as a super Coney Island. France could never again equip an army or oppose Germany. Germans obtained a controlling interest in the most profitable enterprises, usually by compelling the French owners to sell them stock.

THE ALLIED OCCUPATION

Germany surrendered in May, 1945, and the Allies took over control of a country where all government had collapsed. Four zones of occupation were set up in accordance with agreements already made. Russia occupied about 40,000 square miles in the east, and the west was divided so that the United States and Great Britain each controlled about 40,000 square miles and France 20,000. Berlin in the heart of the Russian zone was placed under joint four-power government, and endless troubles were to develop since the roads and railways leading to it were in practice controlled by Russia. Supreme authority was to be exercised, on instructions from their governments, by the American, British, Russian, and French commanders in chief, each in his own zone and also jointly in matters affecting Germany as a whole. The four commanders would constitute the Control Commission whose decisions must be unanimous. Alsace Lorraine returned to France, the Sudeten German territory to Czechoslovakia, and Austria became again an independent state under four-power occupation.

In July, 1945, President Truman, Stalin, and Churchill (replaced by

Attlee when he won the British election) met and drew up the Potsdam Agreement. It set forth the political and economic principles which were to govern the treatment of Germany in the initial control period. These were demilitarization, denazification, deindustrialization, decentralization, and democratization. All German armed forces of every description including the General Staff were to be abolished, and all factories that could be used for military production were to be dismantled. Nazism and all its institutions were to be extirpated, and war criminals brought to trial. Education and law were to be democratized and democratic principles introduced into government. The plan of Henry Morgenthau that industry be destroyed and Germany reduced to an agricultural country was partially accepted although later it was abandoned. Germany was to be treated as a single economic unit. Reparations should be paid not in cash as after World War I but from external assets and in kind, e.g., in coal and machinery. Finally, it was agreed that the German population in Poland, Czechoslovakia, and Hungary would have to be transferred to Germany, but not until the Control Commission had considered how they could be distributed.

The Potsdam Agreement was never fully carried out, and divergences between the Allies began to develop. Demilitarization was quite thoroughly enforced, war criminals were tried, and Nazi organizations prohibited. The trouble was that for thirteen years a German who wanted to be successful was practically compelled to join the Nazi party. The difficulty lay in distinguishing between nominal Nazis who had merely paid lip service to party doctrines and fanatical adherents. Practice varied in the different zones and denazification, nowhere complete or thorough, ended in 1949. In the Russian zone, large numbers of ex-Nazis were recruited into the Communist party and advanced to fairly important positions.

The attitude toward the level of industry program was not uniform. Moscow removed some of the factories to Russia, but the majority were nationalized and linked with similar Soviet factories into great combines under the control of Soviet government officials. The aim was to obtain as much reparations as possible from current production. In the three western zones the United States had the major voice in shaping policy, since it was finding most of the money for the imports of food and raw materials. The emphasis was placed increasingly on the rebuilding of German industry and enlarging production, and finally the Morgenthau plan was dropped. When Secretary of State Marshall launched the European Recovery Program in 1947, Western Germany became one of the participants. One reason for this policy was that the safeguarding of Europe's peace had to be balanced against the necessity of retaining a very substantial degree of industrialization in order to provide employment in Germany and also to manufacture commodities which were needed for European reconstruction. A new reason for not pushing deindustrialization too far soon emerged, and this was to lessen the financial burden on the victors, particularly the United States and Great Britain. They found themselves spending about $1 billion a year in supplying foods and other essentials to their zones—a far larger amount than they were receiving in reparations. To end the drain both governments were anxious to preserve and where necessary rebuild enough of Germany's industry so that exports of manufactures could pay for imports. The economic problem was further complicated by the agreement to deliver reparations. They were drastically reduced in the Western zones in August, 1947, and were finally brought to an end in the interests of German economic recovery. The one Allied country which collected a substantial amount was Russia. A stable currency was introduced by the Western powers in 1948, and by 1949 the economy was beginning to recover from the effects of the war.

Democratization was the most difficult of the tasks the Western allies had set themselves. Democracy was discredited because it had failed twice, in 1848 and under the Weimar Republic. Following upon that the Nazis had systematically weeded out liberal-minded Germans by death or the concentration camp. Others had escaped abroad like Brüning, and did not return after 1945. The Prussianization of Germany had been going on since the latter part of the nineteenth century, and as a climax there came an intensive Nazification throughout Hitler's regime. Every agency of propaganda— school, press, pulpit, film, radio, party organization and military service— was used to create contempt for democracy and veneration for the Leader. The campaign was aimed especially at the rising generation, and on the whole it seems to have created in them an intense loyalty to Nazi ideas. The system was based on the old principle that the beliefs instilled into a child in its formative years usually remain with it throughout life. The Western powers did what they could in rewriting text books and removing the more blatant Nazis from among the teachers. Small neo-Nazi parties appeared about 1949, but so far their support is small. An unknown factor is the 9 million deportees, who have not been welcomed by the West Germans. They might support an extremist party which promised to recover their former homes.

In 1947 the state of Prussia was abolished, and the Allies agreed that Germany should be made into a genuinely federal state, as it had been from 1871 to 1918. The Germans themselves greatly preferred a unitary state, that is, one governed by a single central government. This meant a stronger Germany, and this was precisely the reason why the Allies were opposed to it. In 1946 the four powers created fifteen states or *Länder* (five in the Russian and ten in the Western zones). Each had a democratic constitution and an elected Diet, though still subject to the veto of the allied military commander of the zone. The formation of non-Nazi political parties was encouraged. In

1948 a German Constituent Assembly met at Bonn to draw up a provisional constitution, in accordance with a decision of the three Western powers. In 1949 the constitution was approved, and the Federal Republic of Western Germany was proclaimed. An Occupation Statute reserved to the three occupying powers the fields of disarmament, reparations, foreign affairs, and displaced persons, but otherwise gave the Federal Republic full powers. Military government by the occupying powers was replaced by civilian control, exercised by three high commissioners.

EAST PRUSSIA AND THE ODER-NEISSE FRONTIER

The pretext though not the cause of World War II had been the creation by the Versailles Treaty of Danzig and the Corridor which cut off East Prussia from Germany. President Roosevelt, Stalin, and Churchill agreed at the Yalta Conference that these territorial arrangements must be altered by assigning part of East Prussia to Russia and adding the rest of it and Danzig to Poland. To avoid the creation of another Alsace Lorraine they decided that the German inhabitants must be deported to Germany. Poland was to receive part of Germany east of the Oder River, but the final settlement of her western frontier was to be postponed till the peace settlement. Until then Germany east of the Oder and Neisse Rivers, from the Baltic Sea to the Czech frontier, was to be placed under Polish administration. The Yalta Conference also decided that Poland east of the Curzon Line, the provisional frontier fixed by the Western powers in 1919, should be annexed to Russia. It had a mixed population of Poles, Ukrainians, Lithuanians, and White Russians, and gave Russia almost as much territory as she obtained by the partition of 1939. At the end of the war Polish administration was established east of the Oder-Neisse line, and the German inhabitants deported to Germany. Poland with Russia's support treated the provisional occupation as virtual annexation, and American and British protests were ignored. When Russian control was established in eastern Poland a very large number of Poles abandoned their property and moved westward looking for a home. There was no room for them in what was left of prewar Poland, and they were settled on the vacant farms of the deported Germans. What the war has really done is to move Polish territory westward about 100 miles.

The new Polish-German frontier is a potential cause of trouble. The Germans, and especially several million deportees, are determined to recover the lost provinces. Since the real guarantor of this boundary is the Kremlin, it can be changed only by war or diplomatic negotiations with Russia. One reason the French were afraid of the inclusion of a German army in the European Defense Community was that they feared that Germany might try to drag her partners into a war with Russia. Alternatively the Kremlin

From Samuel F. Bemis, A Diplomatic History of the United States,
4th ed., New York, Henry Holt & Co., 1955, p. 892

Germany and Poland, 1945

might hold out the bait that it would take the territory away from Poland
and restore it to Germany if the latter would cooperate with the Soviet Union
instead of the West. This gives the Soviet government a strong advantage
over Washington and London in the competitive courtship for Germany's
favors in which East and West are engaged. Chancellor Adenauer places

alignment with the West ahead of the reunion of the country, but this might not be the policy of all future governments. Incidentally if ever Germany recovers the territory, the problem will at once arise of what to do with the roughly 4 million Poles who now live there. To put them under German rule would be to create another Alsace Lorraine. Yet they cannot return to their former home, for that is now part of Russia. It will not be easy to unscramble these eggs. The effect on the Poles is to drive them to the side of Russia, since it is only with her help that they can defend their new western frontier. To them Germany is permanent public enemy number one, while the Russian government—but not the Russian people—is runner up for the title. The distinction arises from the different treatment meted out to the Poles by Germany and Russia after the partitions of the eighteenth century. The former not only tried to destroy the Poles' nationalism but also did her best to take their land from them and give it to German colonists. The Russian government attacked Polish nationalism, but did not interfere with ownership of the land. As individuals, Poles and Russians were friendly, and there was none of the attitude of racial superiority that embittered relations with the Germans. The Poles make a distinction between the Russian people for whom they have friendly feelings, and the government which they regard as imperialistic. With their intense patriotism they want above everything to be independent, but with their geographic position they feel that they are between two fires. As a choice of evils many of them tend to believe that Russia is preferable. At the same time they are hostile to the Communist dictatorship she has imposed on them.

The Oder-Neisse frontier should be regarded as a Soviet precaution against another German invasion. In 1941 the Russian frontier stretched across a flat plain from the Baltic to the Black Sea, and it was impossible to prevent German armies from crossing at several points. The new frontier runs for 300 miles from the mountains of the Bohemian plateau to the Baltic, and it cannot be outflanked. A German army advancing into the Czech mountains would get a hot reception, and since 1945 the Baltic is a Russian lake. Therefore, the Germans would have to break out to the east by a direct frontal attack, and the rivers though narrow would be a temporary barrier. Moreover, Berlin is now practically a frontier town. It is the railway center of Germany and a vitally important point in troop movements toward the east. The next army that mobilizes there will not be as free from attack as its predecessor in 1941.

Several reasons explain the Yalta decision to give Poland Danzig and part of East Prussia. After the German atrocities in Poland it was impossible to reward Germany by letting it keep the Corridor and so reuniting the fatherland. Merely to re-establish the 1939 frontiers was to re-create the 1939 problem, and the only way out of the dilemma was to cede most of East

Prussia and Danzig to Poland and the rest to Russia. Two other reasons supported this decision. When Hitler invaded Poland in 1939, one German army mobilized in East Prussia and struck south behind the main Polish forces. It was felt that this must be made impossible in the future. Finally, East Prussia was a land of large estates, the property of the Prussian Junkers, the high priests of German militarism. To deprive them of their landed wealth would weaken the power of militarism in Germany.

SOVIET POLICY IN EASTERN GERMANY

The object of Moscow was to turn its zone into a satellite state, and if possible extend its authority over the western part of the country. One of the first moves was to break the power of the Prussian Junkers. Their large estates were expropriated, and 5 million acres were divided into over 500,000 small farms of two to twenty acres, and given to the peasants. Thus, the economic basis of the Junkers' power was destroyed. For a few years the new owners were left in possession, but in 1952 an intensive program began of combining the small holdings into large state farms on the Russian model. The Russians allowed the formation of four political parties, but early in 1946 the Socialists were compelled to join the Communists in the new SED (Socialist Unity Party). In the three western zones the Socialists decisively voted against a similar fusion. The Communists realized that they could not win a majority in a free election, and a struggle for control began between them and the anticommunist parties. The climax came in the elections of May, 1949. The method of counting the votes was wrapped in mystery, but it was officially announced that the SED had gained a two-thirds majority. The Communists then passed the necessary laws to ensure that they had complete and permanent control of the German Democratic Republic, and the anticommunist parties were reduced to insignificance. The usual secret police composed of reliable Communists was organized, and concentration camps were reopened for opponents of the regime. Russia, realizing that few adult Germans could be converted to communism, aimed to capture the German youth to ensure that the next generation would be reliable Communists. Membership in the youth organizations was virtually compulsory, and 2 million were enrolled between the ages of six and twenty-four. There was a judicious combination of indoctrination and propaganda, sports, and marching in colored shirts to waving banners and rousing tunes. There is a real danger that an ideological gulf may open between eastern and western Germans of the next generation.

In 1948 the first units of the People's Police were created, and by 1955 it numbered about 85,000 trained men. An army corps of three divisions with tank and artillery units was in existence, and it was proposed to raise two additional army corps. The nucleus of an air force and a navy was established. The percentage of Communist officers and privates has been increasing, and careful attention is paid to Marxist indoctrination. In 1948 Russia tried to oust the three Western powers from their zones in Berlin by blockading them and preventing the arrival of supplies by road, railroad and canal. The Western powers supplied their troops and the 2 million Germans in their sectors of Berlin by air, flying in three to four thousand tons of necessities each day. After all attempts to negotiate a settlement had failed, the Americans and British established a counterblockade from their zones of Eastern Germany in February 1949, and in May the Soviet blockade of Berlin was lifted.

The strikes and riots of 1953 revealed the hostility of the East German workmen to the Communist dictatorship. Their suppression with the assistance of the Red army showed their inability to overthrow the regime, and the determination of Russia to maintain her control. Further evidence of this was provided by Molotov's refusal at the Berlin Conference in 1954 to allow free elections for an all-German government that would unite the two zones. It is clear that such an election would sweep the Communist dictatorship from power. In March, 1954, Russia announced that East Germany was a sovereign state controlling its own domestic and foreign affairs, with the Red army "temporarily stationed" there.

GERMANY IN THE COLD WAR

The expectation in 1945 was that peace would be preserved by a continuation of the wartime collaboration of the United States, Great Britain, and Russia. As long as they worked together, no other state had the strength to challenge their decisions, and Germany would be powerless to carry out any ambitions which she might come to entertain. If antagonism developed between East and West, the beneficiary would be Germany. Her industrial capacity and her large and warlike population made her support of great value to each side. This gave her a very strong bargaining position. Precisely this situation developed, and Chancellor Adenauer took full advantage of it. He was the leader of the Christian Democrats, the largest political party. He believed that Germany's place was with the West, but he was able to point out that not only the small Communist minority but also the Social Democrats, the second largest party, advocated coming to terms with Russia. One argument in favor of this was that it gave the best hope of reuniting the country. To do this would also restore the former trade between the eastern and western zones and might open the markets of Russia and her satellite states. The tradition that Germany and Russia should work together was powerful. Then too there was the feeling that Soviet armaments were so immeasurably superior that the Western powers could not possibly defend

Germany against an invasion. The only result of attempting it would be a repetition of the destruction of World War II. It was argued that Germany should be neutral in the struggle between East and West. A national determination developed to recover complete sovereignty and assert a position of absolute equality with the Western powers.

The Korean war revealed the military weakness of the Western powers, and in September, 1950, the United States proposed the re-creation of the German army. France countered with the scheme for the six-nation European Defense Community. Russia made strenuous efforts to prevent the formation of an army, holding out the bait of a reunited and neutral Germany and the withdrawal of all occupation forces. Chancellor Adenauer was in a strong position to drive a bargain, and he negotiated treaties with the Western powers in which they made over 100 concessions to his demands. By the Bonn Conventions the occupation would come to an end, and the West German Republic would virtually regain its sovereignty and independence. Western troops would remain, but as allies for the protection of Germany and not as an army of occupation. The sentences on war criminals would be reviewed to placate German public opinion. NATO obligations were extended to the West German Republic. If it were attacked, each of the NATO members would at once assist by taking such action as it deemed necessary including the use of armed force.

Adenauer negotiated a treaty by which Germany was to join the EDC. He announced that the German contingent would consist of 500,000 men comprising six tank, four motorized and two mechanized infantry divisions, supplemented by artillery and other supporting units. The tactical air force of 86,000 men would have the most modern jet aircraft, and there would be a navy for coastal defense. The army would be a small but very powerful force. The training cadre would be 100,000 volunteers recruited from the officers and men of the old army, and conscription would be restored to provide the rest. Civil aviation would be re-established, and most of the restrictions on Germany's complete freedom to manufacture munitions would be abolished. It was announced that steel production could be increased at short notice from 14 million to 16.5 million tons. There were plans to modernize and expand the entire steel industry at a cost of $450 million, most of which was expected to come from the United States.

Chancellor Adenauer was committed to the EDC program but was strongly opposed by the Social Democrats. They argued that to join the West would destroy the hope of reuniting the two Germanies through negotiations with Russia. Opposition to rearmament was widespread for various reasons. There was a strong revulsion against militarism and the army owing to the complete defeat of World War II and the destruction it brought upon Germany. For the first time the civilian population had had personal experience of what war was like. From 1943 onward, first by air and then on land, Germans experienced the full force of modern war in their own country. Adenauer believed that this was a temporary psychological effect of the war, and was confident that he could bring the people round to his support. Opposition to an army was strengthened by the previous Western policies of demilitarization, democratic re-education, and the trial of war criminals. First of all the Allies lectured the Germans on their addiction to militarism, stated that they would not allow them to have any armed forces, and effectively disarmed them. Then suddenly in 1950 the West announced that it wished Germany to raise an army. Germans were rather bewildered at the reversal of policy, and many wished to be neutral in the cold war. The war crimes trials were increasingly resented, particularly in military and conservative circles, as unjust and a besmirching of German honor. They considered that the majority of those convicted were guiltless, and alternatively they had merely obeyed the orders of Hitler and a handful of deceased Nazis who alone were to blame for everything. Germans seemed to be unable to understand why fear and distrust of them should be so widespread in Europe. There was a strong demand that before Germany rearmed she must be given a position of absolute equality with the victors in every respect. She must be subject to no restrictions whatever which did not apply also to other nations. Some Germans opposed the re-creation of the army from the fear that this would reproduce the events of the 'twenties, restore the militarists to power, and destroy the possibility of firmly establishing a democratic government. They were afraid that given the German political tradition and the place of the German army in politics, German democracy might be unable to survive side by side with a revived German army. In 1954 the indications seemed to be that the majority of the public was veering in favor of Adenauer's policy. He was able to point out that the outcome of the Berlin Conference made it clear that Russia would not agree to the reunion of the country except on terms which were "a well thought out means for the Sovietization of all Germany." In March the federal legislature authorized the reintroduction of conscription and ratified the EDC treaty. In 1955 the legislature approved the treaties the chancellor had negotiated which restored German sovereignty and agreed to her rearmament and admission to NATO, and arranged for the Europeanization of the Saar. Adenauer himself seemed to take seriously the risk that the army might turn out to be a threat to democracy. It was reported that he wished to take five years for its creation instead of two. The first three would be spent in recruiting the 100,000 volunteers, ex-officers and sergeants, who would form the training cadre. His defense ministry believed that if it were given time to make a careful selection it could choose men who would be loyal to the civil authority and so prevent a return to the spirit of Nazi and Prussian days. Once the cadre was raised, conscription would be reintroduced and in two years more the army would be created.

Moscow's opposition to the formation of the German army and her union with the West remained unaltered, but the failure of the earlier attempts to prevent it seemed to be forcing a change of tactics. Chancellor Adenauer placed integration with the West ahead of reunion of the two Germanies. The Social Democrats put reunion first, and opposed the chancellor's whole policy as making its achievement impossible. The Soviet proposals of 1955 were designed to rally German support to the Social Democrats. When Molotov signed the Austrian peace treaty, he made it clear that the price for Germany's reunification was her neutrality. The stipulation in the treaty that Austria must be neutralized and must not join any defensive alliance was designed to show the German people that the same formula could be applied to them. Incidentally, it might be pointed out that the neutrality which was possible for a small and weak country like Austria was inapplicable to what was potentially one of the most powerful states in Europe. Furthermore, the Soviet proposals for the reduction of armed forces stipulated that their strength must be frozen as of December 31, 1954. This would prevent the creation of a West German army, but not affect the existing People's Police in East Germany. Altogether the Soviet proposals provided ammunition for Adenauer's opponents. They encouraged the belief that national reunification could be achieved by compromise with Russia, provided Germany did not link herself with the West. Adenauer was determined to continue his policy of working closely with the West, though he was emphatic that every effort must be made by the Western powers as well as by his own government to persuade Russia to agree to reunion. Probably Moscow did not expect to change Adenauer's policy, but hoped that it would undermine his support among the voters or that, the chancellor being eighty, he would soon be succeeded by a more pliable successor.

SELECTED READING

BIDWELL, PERCY W., *Germany's Contribution to European Economic Life*. New York: Royal Institute of International Affairs, 1949.

BUELL, R. L., *Poland: Key to Europe*. New York: Oxford Press, 1940.

CARR, EDWARD H., *German Soviet Relations between the Two World Wars, 1919–1939*. Baltimore: Johns Hopkins Press, 1951.

EBENSTEIN, WILLIAM, *The German Record: A Political Portrait*. New York: Farrar and Rinehart, 1945.

GOERLITZ, WALTER, *History of the German General Staff*. New York: Praeger, 1953.

MC GOVERN, W. M., *From Luther to Hitler: The History of Fascist-Nazi Political Philosophy*. Boston: Houghton Mifflin Company, 1941.

MORGAN, GENERAL J. H., *Assize of Arms: the Disarmament of Germany and her Rearmament.* New York: Oxford Press, 1946.

POUNDS, NORMAN J. G., *The Ruhr: A Study in Historical and Economic Geography.* London: Faber and Faber, Ltd., 1952.

ROSSI, A., *The Russo-German Alliance, August 1939–June 1941.* London: Chapman and Hall, 1950.

SNYDER, LOUIS L., *German Nationalism: The Tragedy of a People.* Harrisburg, Pa.: Stackpole Company, 1952.

TREVOR-ROPER, H. R., *The Last Days of Hitler.* New York: The Macmillan Company, 1947.

WHEELER-BENNETT, JOHN W., *The Nemesis of Power: the German Army in Politics, 1918–1945.* London: Macmillan and Company, 1953.

CHAPTER 22

ITALY

POPULATION, RESOURCES, AND FINANCE

Before World War II Italy was given the courtesy rank of a great power. In reality she was a middle power, that is, a nation such as Canada which lacks the material strength of the leading states yet is not in the same class as a small country such as Denmark. Among the nation's principal products are sulfur and mercury, minerals of considerable minor importance, but not in the first rank like coal, iron, and oil. Italy also possesses fine marbles, but great power cannot be built on a foundation of tombstones and sulfur matches. Three quarters of the iron ore, practically all the coal, and virtually all the oil are imported. The imports of most of the other minerals and vegetable raw materials, such as cotton, are as high and sometimes higher. With the exception of Japan, no country of importance is so badly provided with natural resources. The additional cost of importing raw materials has hampered the development of manufacturing, and steel production lags far behind that of France, Germany, or Great Britain.

The population is 48,433,000, and is increasing at the rate of 425,000 a year. Since industry cannot give it a livelihood, the alternatives are emigration or agriculture. Earlier in the century hundreds of thousands went abroad every year, particularly to the United States, South America, and France. The American Immigration Act of 1924 drastically reduced the number, and the great depression led to the same result in South America and France. Since 1945 there has been much discussion of facilitating the transfer of Italians to countries which like France have a shortage of labor, but little has come of it. So with this outlet closed the population banked up at home, and was forced back on agriculture.

Here again nature has been niggardly. Italy's area covers 119,700 square miles, but due to the mountainous character of the country less than three quarters is cultivable. On the whole the soil is poor, and part of it is only suitable for pastoral farming, which requires less labor than arable farming. The area planted with cereals cannot be greatly expanded. As a result too many people try to make a living off too little land. The system of land tenures does not help the situation. Roughly speaking in the north, e.g., in the Po valley, there is peasant ownership, but most of the holdings are so small that there is strong land hunger. There are many sharecroppers. Throughout the country, but especially in the south, absentee landowners interested only in their rents own *latifundia* or great estates, cultivated by badly paid day laborers. About 23 million people live on the land, but nearly half of it is owned by 1 percent of the landowners. Rural Italy is an ideal breeding ground for communism, and it is difficult to see how reforms can be much more than palliatives.

The result of the overpopulation is a low standard of living, widespread poverty, and frequently heavy unemployment. Discontent is heightened because the national wealth is unevenly divided between the wealthy few and the masses of the poor. Since World War II communism and socialism have been widespread among the factory workmen and peasants, and the Communist party with about 2.6 million members in 1951 is the largest in Western Europe. The average taxable capacity is low, and inadequate revenue does not permit Italy to play the part of a great power. Mussolini could never find the money to finance his grandiose plans, and heavy deficits in the budget were chronic.

THE PRISONER OF THE MEDITERRANEAN

The distance from the Straits of Gibraltar to the Suez Canal is 1920 miles, and Italy is about halfway from either exit. Great Britain controls both Gibraltar and the Canal, and France too has a strong position in the western Mediterranean. Both, moreover, have been far superior to Italy in sea power and wealth. The weakness of Italy's geographic position was intensified because 75 percent of her imports of vital raw materials could only be obtained from outside the Mediterranean. She was particularly vulnerable to a British long-range blockade. As soon as Mussolini declared war on France and Britain in 1940, he became a prisoner in the Mediterranean and dependent on Germany for coal, iron, oil, and a host of other necessities. Italy's strategic position has been worsened by her losses following World War II. The Greek annexation of Rhodes and the Dodecanese deprived her of an important base in the eastern Mediterranean. The former colony of Libya in North Africa, which she took from Turkey in 1912, is now an independent kingdom acting in close concert with Great Britain. Italy has lost the control of the Adriatic Sea, which she held between the world wars. Albania is a Soviet satellite and Yugoslavia has taken most of the Balkan seaports given to Italy by the peace settlement of 1919.

ITALY'S TRUMP CARD

Italy's greatest strategic weakness—her central position in the Mediterranean—is curiously enough her greatest asset. All shipping traversing the Mediterranean from end to end must follow a well-defined route. At one point—the passage between western Sicily and Cape Bon in French Tunisia —the Mediterranean is only ninety-five miles wide, and right in the middle of the passage was the Italian naval and air base on the island of Pantelleria. In addition there was a chain of naval and air bases on the west and south coasts of Italy, Sicily, and Sardinia. Mussolini built quite a powerful navy, a large number of submarines, and a strong air force. They covered the whole central Mediterranean, and largely closed it to hostile shipping from 1940 to the fall of Mussolini in 1943. What is surprising is that they were not even more successful. Out of one convoy of thirty-two store ships which left Gibraltar bound for Malta, only six got through. Losses on this scale were prohibitive; and, apart from provisioning, Malta shipping was diverted from the Mediterranean to the old route around the Cape of Good Hope. Italy's position as an unsinkable aircraft carrier in the center of the Mediterranean made her alliance worth buying, if the price were not too high. It should be noted that it is not necessary that Italian submarines and aircraft do the work, for many of the ships sunk were bombed by the Luftwaffe. It suffices that Italy lend her facilities to a great power.

FOREIGN POLICY

Bismarck made a very apt remark when he said that Italy was like a small boy in an apple orchard, a greedy little boy whose eyes were larger than his stomach. From the time a century ago when the Kingdom of Savoy began to unite the whole of Italy under its rule, the national ambitions were greater than the power to carry them out. This meant that Italy must find an ally who would do most of the fighting. This was impossible when Europe was at peace, but her opportunity came when war threatened. At such times she could win part at least of her objectives by bargaining for her alliance. Mussolini could cite many precedents for joining Germany as the only way to fulfill his Mediterranean ambitions.

By 1870 the whole of Italy had been united and freed from Austrian rule apart from a small Italian population on the Alpine frontier and in some of the seaports on the Balkan side of the Adriatic. Italy wished to liberate them and also advance her borders to the watershed of the Alps in order to control the Brenner Pass, the traditional road of invasion for Austrian and German armies. To do this would involve the annexation of about 230,000

Austrians, who lived in the valleys on the southern slope of the Alps. Italy wanted to create an African empire and eventually obtained three colonies of little value—Eritrea and Somaliland on the Red Sea and Libya in North Africa. This aim brought her into conflict with France, since both wanted Tunisia and France seized it in 1881. This led Italy in 1882 to form the Triple Alliance with Austria and Germany. Gradually the resentment against France faded, while the desire to recover the irredentas in Austria grew. From 1902 onward she had a foot both in the French and German camps, and in 1914 she proclaimed her neutrality. She then bargained with both sides for her support and entered the war on the side of the Triple Entente in 1915, since it was more generous than Austria in its offers of Austrian territory. At the peace settlement of 1919 Italy obtained the Austrian territory promised to her, and in addition seized the seaport of Fiume which the Allies had destined for Yugoslavia. She had been promised an extension of her colonies if France and Britain should increase their possessions in Africa, but the area added to Italian Somaliland and Libya was of little value. Italy felt that she had won the war and lost the peace, and was disposed to sympathize with Germany and oppose France.

Mussolini came to power in 1922 and preached an exaggerated version of the previous urge for expansion. He appealed to the strong nationalism which was influential among the educated groups of the population. The official justification was that Italy must have colonies since she was a "have-not" nation, with territory and resources too limited to sustain her population. Mussolini's picture of the pressure of overpopulation would have been more convincing if he had not done his best to make a bad situation worse by stimulating the birth rate. He wanted to establish his influence over the countries of central Europe and the Balkans, and the temporary powerlessness of Germany favored his designs. Yugoslavia was hostile because of the seizure of Fiume. When an Italian general was assassinated near the Greek frontier, Italy in 1923 bombarded the Greek island of Corfu and extracted an indemnity and an apology. The island, however, was evacuated under British pressure, and Mussolini gained no territory. Hungary had never reconciled herself to the liberation of her Slav and Rumanian subjects in 1918, and was bent on recreating the kingdom of Hungary with its 1913 boundaries. This could only be accomplished by wars with Yugoslavia, Czechoslovakia, and Rumania, which had banded together in the Little Entente and taken the further precaution of allying themselves with France. Hungary's success was contingent on finding a powerful patron, and Mussolini discreetly encouraged her ambitions. In May, 1934, he formed an Italian bloc by negotiating political and economic treaties with Hungary and Austria. For a few years his influence was strong; but as Germany recovered her strength and ambitions, his satellites gradually passed into Hitler's orbit. All that Mussolini salvaged from his central European and Balkan ambitions was the consolation prize of Albania, which he conquered in 1939.

AUSTRIA

Through Austria ran the old road of invasion along which many German armies had marched to the Brenner Pass and the invasion of Italy. The very last thing the Italians wanted to see was the Germans on the Brenner Pass. From their point of view post-1918 Austria was an ideal neighbor. A third-rate little state that suffered from chronic economic anaemia was no danger. For this reason Italy sided with France to oppose the proposed Austro-German customs union in 1931. It was forbidden by the International Court of Justice in 1931 on the ground that it might impair Austria's independence and so break her treaty obligations.

In 1933 the Austrian democratic republic was replaced by a fascist-style dictatorship under Dollfuss. In foreign policy the new regime was hostile to union with Germany and friendly to Italy, on which it leaned for support. Hitler put the union of the two countries at the head of his program, and there was a strong Austrian Nazi Party which acted as his fifth column. In February, 1934, the Austrian Socialists and their party army were crushed in bloody street fighting by the fascist private army and the government forces. It seemed that Dollfuss' ascendancy was complete, but in July, 1934, the Nazi army murdered him and made a premature attempt to seize control of the state. The government suppressed the uprising, and von Schuschnigg succeeded Dollfuss as dictator. Hitler was privy to the plot, but he had overestimated the strength of the Austrian Nazis. Mussolini mobilized his army at the Brenner Pass, and it was clear that if the Germans entered Austria from the north the Italians would come in from the south. In 1934 the German army was in no condition to fight Italy; and Britain and France, horrified at the brutal murder of Dollfuss, gave full diplomatic support to Mussolini. Hitler assured the world that he would not dream of interfering with Austria.

Mussolini had won a notable triumph, but there were ominous implications. The small state of Austria had split into three hostile factions of about equal strength each with its own private army. The Fascists had seized the government and alienated the Socialists, who like them were the enemies of the Nazis. They now had to oppose the Austrian Nazi party which received full support from Germany. Even if the country had remained united, it would have been difficult to maintain its independence against Hitler. By tearing herself to pieces Austria was becoming an accomplice in her own destruction. Even in 1934 it was fairly clear that France and Britain were unlikely to take any effective steps in her defense. Her only protector was Mussolini, and if ever he withdrew his help, Hitler would win.

THE ETHIOPIAN AFFAIR

For over fifty years Italy had contended that the possession of colonies was a great power's hallmark of respectability, but her three African dependencies ranked high amongst the most valueless parts of the continent. An attempt to conquer the kingdom of Ethiopia had ended in disaster and humiliation in 1896, when an Italian army was almost annihilated at the battle of Adowa. For ten years Mussolini had most eloquently announced his unalterable resolve to restore the Roman Empire. In 1932 he decided that his domestic prestige required him to take action and that Ethiopia was the place to begin. For economic reasons France and Britain were moderately interested in the country; but, on the whole, it made little difference to them whether it were independent or an Italian colony. Mussolini's advisers told him that three years were necessary to prepare Eritrea and Somaliland as bases for the invasion, and the actual attack was timed for the autumn of 1935. The movement of troops and supplies through the Suez Canal could mean only one thing, and Mussolini's intentions were an open secret to the governments of Europe. In 1923 Ethiopia had been admitted to membership in the League of Nations on the insistence of Italy and despite the objections of Great Britain, who argued that the country was too barbarous to understand its responsibilities. Ethiopia formally appealed to the League on January 3, 1935. The latter urged the two states to arrange a peaceful settlement, but otherwise refrained from active intervention until July.

The League's failure to take effective action against the Japanese invasion of Manchuria encouraged Mussolini to believe that history would repeat itself. He assumed that if any state gave him trouble it would be France, which had been the leader in every attempt to make the League an effective weapon against an aggressor. It was expedient to guard against this possibility. Furthermore, Hitler's attempt to seize Austria in 1934 had alienated Italy and led to a rapprochement with France. The latter genuinely supported collective security, but with the mental reservation that its main purpose was to protect her and her allies in Europe against Germany. Now that Italy showed every sign of siding with France both government and people felt it would be sheer imbecility to alienate this promising recruit because he was contemplating a private aggression of his own. Laval, the French foreign minister, hoped to convert the rapprochement into a military alliance that would strengthen his country against Germany. In January, 1935, he and Mussolini made an agreement in which, among other matters, they settled their colonial disputes in Africa. Despite Laval's denial it would seem that he must have given Mussolini some assurance that if he took action in Ethiopia, France would remain a disinterested spectator. The British government was unwilling seriously to involve itself in a dispute with Italy, lest Hitler should take advantage of the situation to bring off some coup. Additional reasons for avoiding war were the prevalent popular pacifism and the weakness of British armaments. The Admiralty estimated that in a naval war with Italy Britain might lose half of her twelve battleships. The one and only British division with modern equipment had to be sent to Egypt to counter a strong mechanized Italian army in Libya. Moreover, neither Britain nor France wanted to break the Stresa Front, which they formed with Italy in March, 1935. Hitler had repudiated the disarmament clause of the Versailles Treaty and reintroduced conscription. The three powers jointly warned him that the breach of another treaty might lead to unpleasant but unspecified consequences. Mussolini was justified in feeling that he need not expect any serious opposition.

This expectation was falsified by the British Peace Ballot of June 1935. For fifteen years the British public had been taught that peace would be preserved by the collective security of fifty-six nations united at Lake Geneva. They had no clear understanding that the League's economic and military sanctions, the instruments of collective security, could mean war. Rather there was the feeling that in some mysterious fashion the sanctions could suppress an aggressor without the British having to do much about it. They had no idea that the invasion of Ethiopia was timed to begin in October, 1935. In June, 1935, the League of Nations Union conducted the Peace Ballot, a questionnaire designed to arouse public support for the League. The fifth question asked whether in the event of aggression the other nations should combine to stop it by economic and if necessary military sanctions. The problem was presented as academic and abstract, no mention being made of Ethiopia. The question had to be answered "Yes" or "No" without qualifications. The propaganda accompanying the ballot emphasized that "Yes" meant a vote for peace and "No" a vote for war. Of 11,500,000 who voted, 10,033,000 supported the economic and 6,748,000 the military sanction against an aggressor. No government could ignore a mandate from half the electorate, especially when a general election was to be held the following November. It would seem reasonable to conclude that the voters in the Peace Ballot were telling the government to go as far as it could in combination with other League members to resist aggression, but to do its utmost to keep out of war. There was no suggestion whatever that Britain should apply the military sanction single handed.

There were two possible courses of action, and the British government followed neither of them. The first was to point out that when the League was founded it was assumed the United States would be a member, so that if sanctions were employed overwhelming pressure would be applied to an aggressor. But the League of 1935 was not the League conceived by President Wilson with the aggressor opposed by all the other great powers. The coercion of Italy would have to be undertaken by Britain and a lukewarm France. The moral of this would be that Britain would go as far in support of the League as France, and that probably would not be very far. The alternative was to accept the loss of Italy to the Stresa Front, and if the League members were willing to use sanctions to the utmost, for Britain to take her full share. The one thing to avoid was for Britain to take the lead and stop with half measures, and this was exactly what the government did. In Churchill's words "The Prime Minister had declared that sanctions meant war; secondly he was resolved there must be no war; and thirdly he decided upon sanctions. It was evidently impossible to reconcile these three conditions."

In September the League met to discuss the Ethiopian crisis. On September 10 Laval had a preliminary meeting with Sir Samuel Hoare, the British foreign secretary. Neither was willing to use the military sanction, and it was also clear that if it were employed, Britain would have to undertake practically the whole burden of the war. On October 3, 1935, the invasion of Ethiopia began, and in November fifty-two out of the fifty-six League members prohibited loans to Italy, placed an embargo on all Italian imports, and forbade the export to Italy of armaments and certain raw materials the supply of which was substantially controlled by League members. In August, 1935, the United States Congress passed a Neutrality Act which forbade the export of munitions but not of military raw materials to either belligerent. On October 5 President Roosevelt issued a proclamation which brought the embargo into force against both Italy and Ethiopia. He urged strongly that Americans refrain from selling military raw materials to both sides. American exporters were well aware that the President had no legal power to stop their business, and exports to Italy particularly of oil increased from 200 to 300 percent. Congress refused to restrict the sale of military raw materials, and on February 29, 1936, it re-enacted the previous law with the addition of a clause that forbade financial transactions with belligerents.

Both Washington and Geneva realized that to prevent the shipment of oil would paralyze the movements of the Italian army. For the League members to do so without parallel American action would merely divert the supply of oil from them to the United States, without in the least affecting the Italian campaign. In November the League began to discuss the possibility of putting an embargo on the sale of oil. Mussolini countered with the threat that the oil sanction meant war. Eventually in February, 1936, the League's oil committee reported that a ban on the sale of oil would be ineffective without similar American action. The attempt to impose the sanction failed in large measure because the League members did not control the American source of supply. The only way to stop American oil from reaching Italy and her colonies would have been by a naval blockade in the Mediterranean and the Red Sea. This involved the risk of war which the League members were not prepared to face. An economic sanction cannot be effective unless the members of the international organization control the supply of the commodities placed on the embargo list, and are prepared fully to cooperate. A naval blockade of China to enforce a trade embargo during the Korean war could not have prevented Russian goods from coming in over the land frontier.

Long before this Laval had decided that enough had now been done to vindicate the authority of the League and placate the British urge to help Ethiopia. The time had come to entice the Italian prodigal back to Geneva and the Stresa Front by the generous provision of an Ethiopian fatted calf. Italy should stop the war and in return receive a considerably larger part of Ethiopia than she had yet conquered. On December 7 Laval laid his proposals before Sir Samuel Hoare. The latter was convinced that if the oil sanction were imposed, Italy would attack and that Britain would have to fight the League's battle practically singlehanded. Collective security would be exposed as a sham, and this "would, it seemed to me, almost inevitably lead to the dissolution of the League." Hoare and the British cabinet agreed to the plan, but the disclosure of the terms aroused a storm of indignant protest from the British public and the rank and file of the Conservative government's supporters in the House of Commons. On December 18 the cabinet gave way to the outburst of public indignation, the plan was dropped, and Hoare was succeeded by Anthony Eden as foreign secretary.

Hitler's reoccupation of the Rhineland on March 7 made France and Britain more determined than ever to do nothing that could lead to war with Italy, and there was no further talk of an oil sanction. Ethiopian resistance began to crack, and on May 9, 1936, Mussolini was able to proclaim the annexation of Ethiopia to Italy. On July 4 the League voted for the abandonment of sanctions. The Ethiopian fiasco killed the League of Nations; henceforth no nation could trust its safety to collective security. The half-hearted application of sanctions was enough to anger Mussolini and destroy the Stresa Front. The rapprochement of Italy and Germany developed rapidly, and a new alignment of the European powers began to emerge. The League's failure helped to convince Hitler and Mussolini that they could follow a policy of aggression without fear of serious interference from the democratic powers.

THE SPANISH CIVIL WAR

During the nineteenth century Spain had had thirteen different constitutions, varying from absolute monarchy to republic, and every one had not only failed but ended in force. In the twentieth century constitutional monarchy and a corrupt travesty of parliamentary democracy became discredited, and in 1931 a republic was established. To understand what followed it is necessary to study the conflicting elements in Spain. Agriculture is the principal industry, but the soil is mostly poor and over much of the country the rainfall is insufficient. Northern Spain has adequate rainfall, and the peasants who either own their farms or hold them on long lease, are on the whole moderately prosperous and contented. They are devout Roman Catholics, and many of them fought for Franco. Roughly speaking, central and southern Spain has inadequate rain and has to support too large a farming population. It is divided into large estates owned by absentee landowners. They exploit the peasants to make as high a profit as possible from their estates, and for a century they have defeated all attempts at agrarian reforms. The cultivators, small tenants, and landless laborers are very poor and filled with bitter hatred of the landowners. The Roman Catholic Church was regarded as an enemy by the intellectuals, the town workmen, and many of the peasants, but it retained the devout loyalty of a considerable part of the population. The army was badly trained and equipped, and hostile to democratic government. The nineteenth century had established the tradition that it was not the servant but the savior of the state, and that the officers and not the government decided when the state needed to be saved. The military conspiracy which led to the civil war in 1936 had ample precedents. The traditionalists were ultra conservatives who looked back wistfully to the good old days of the seventeenth century when Spain was governed by the king, the nobility, and the church. They disapproved of the Falange, which wished to remodel the government according to the pattern of Fascist Italy. There were serious differences between Franco's supporters, but the cement which held them together was their still greater hostility to the leftist republic.

The Republicans were made up of as many conflicting elements as the party that supported Franco. Some were orthodox liberals of the nineteenth century pattern who wanted a political democracy but were lukewarm toward economic changes. The Socialists aimed at the nationalization of private property. The Communists were the enemies of the other parties and wanted a state on the Russian model. From their point of view a revolution in 1936 was premature, since they were strengthening their party by capturing control of the Socialist trade unions. The Anarchist Syndicalists were as hostile to a republic as to a monarchy. Their plan was that each village should own and cultivate its land and elect its own government, and each factory should be owned and operated by its workmen. There would be no central government, but instead the nation would be a loose union of the rural and industrial units, where each local authority would freely decide whether or not it would cooperate with the majority. The strongholds of the party were the factories in

Barcelona and other industrial cities, and the landless laborers and small tenant farmers on the big estates. The Anarchist Syndicalists fought for the republican government in 1936 as the lesser of two evils. Provincial patriotisms were strong especially in Catalonia and the Basque provinces. In the twentieth century Spanish conservative parties opposed local autonomy in the name of a strong Spain, while leftist parties favored it. For this reason the Catalonian and part of the Basque peasants fought for the government in the civil war.

The election of 1931 gave the Socialist and left-wing Republican parties an overwhelming majority in the Cortes or legislature. Owing to the multiple party system every government had to be a coalition. Since each party regarded compromise and cooperation with intense dislike, there were thirty-three ministries during the ninety-six months of the life of the republic. Both conservatives and leftists showed a willingness to use violence to gain their ends. The leftist government of 1931 introduced reforms which antagonized the landowners and the clergy. In the election of 1933 the conservative and moderate parties won a majority, and as far as possible postponed carrying out the reforms of 1931–1933 or allowed them to lapse. This stimulated the campaign of strikes and church burnings by extremist elements, and in 1934 led to abortive revolts in Barcelona, Madrid, and the mining region of the Asturias. The uprisings were crushed, but this appeal to force by parties that had lost the election of 1933 gave a useful precedent to Franco. Seven leftist parties formed a Popular Front coalition and won a majority in the election of 1936. The leftists were impatient of delay after their years in opposition, and the Socialists preached the necessity of a revolution to carry out their policy. Apparently they were overconfident and talked while the conservatives plotted. There was an epidemic of church burning, riots, strikes, forcible seizure of land by the peasants, and political murders by extremists of both right and left; and the government proved unable to maintain order.

On July 17 the army revolted and the civil war began. Army officers and perhaps other groups had been plotting for some time, and had received promises of help from Italy and Germany. Franco was supported by the conservative groups described above, and they seem to have numbered about half the population. The Popular Front government had on its side the leftist parties and part of the navy. To each side the war was a conflict of right against wrong. On the religious side one party regarded it as a struggle against clerical tyranny; the other as a war against anti-Christ. Economically it was the property owners against the enemies of private property. Politically it was Monarchists and Fascists against Republicans, Communists, and the Anarchist opponents of organized government. The different issues combined to intensify the peculiar bitterness inseparable from any civil war. Out of 22 million Spaniards, 1 million were killed or crippled and 500,000 were exiled. The destruction of property was so widespread that Spain has not yet recovered. The Falangists gained increasing influence on Franco's side and dominated his government after the war. In the Popular Front the Communists considerably increased their authority at the expense of the other parties. Their aim was to win control of the government, and by 1939 they dominated many trade unions, the best divisions of the army and the secret police. Dictatorship was inevitable, whichever side won. The one thing which could never have come out of the struggle was a democracy. The moderates on both sides were submerged by the extremists.

Italy and Germany sent troops, technical experts, and equipment to Franco. Russia helped the government with arms and technicians, and it largely inspired the recruitment of the International Brigades which reinforced the government troops. Presumably Russia hoped that the war would end in a Communist dictatorship. Italy wished to extend her naval and air power into the western Mediterranean, and may well have hoped that Franco would reward her with the Balearic Islands or Ceuta. The former would threaten the sea route between France and North Africa, and Ceuta in Spanish Morocco would neutralize the British base at Gibraltar. Both Italy and Germany hoped that when the time came Franco would take Gibraltar or perhaps aid one of them to do so. They expected that Spain and the Canary Islands would be available as bases for U-boats and long-range airplanes in the future battle of the Atlantic. Hitler intended to encircle France, by which he meant that in the next war part of the French army would have to be diverted to guard the Pyrenees Mountains in case Franco should attack. This would still further increase the numerical superiority of the German over the French army. Spain could also supply important amounts of tungsten and iron ore to Germany.

Public opinion in the United States was pro-republican but was even more determined to keep out of war, and the government enforced the Neutrality Act against the export of munitions to Spain. French sympathies were sharply divided between Franco and the republicans. Blum's Popular Front government sympathized with its Spanish opposite number, but decided not to intervene. A small minority in Britain urged aid to Franco, while a larger minority wished to help the government. The majority of the public did not wish to intervene on either side. Apart from their pacifism and isolationism they did not believe the war was between fascism and democracy. They regarded it as a struggle between rival dictatorships of left and right. The government was sensitive to public opinion, and in addition its principal aim was, as stated by Eden the foreign minister in 1937, "to neutralize and localize the war, and prevent its spreading to Europe as a whole." The policy of the American, British, French, and Russian governments was in accordance with international law. In a civil war the lawful authority, in this case the Spanish government, may request help from foreign governments, but cannot demand it as of right. The decision to give assistance or withhold it lies entirely with the foreign states. On the other hand, it is strictly forbidden to help the rebels, so that Italy and Germany were guilty of breaking international law.

In August the French proposal that all powers refrain from assisting Franco or the government was accepted, and a Nonintervention Committee was set up composed of France, Britain, Russia, Germany, Italy, and Portugal. All agreed in principle that no help should be sent to either side, but Germany and Italy continued to help Franco and Russia the Popular Front government. Each side protested its willingness to desist if only the other would do the same. The Nonintervention Committee was a solemn farce which dragged out its life until Franco's victory in 1939 led to its dissolution.

An honest man has been defined as one who when he has been bought will stay bought. Judged by this standard, Franco did not qualify. Axis help was probably the decisive factor in his victory, and Hitler and Mussolini were justified in feeling that one good turn deserved another. When Great Britain was fighting alone after the fall of France, Franco could have taken Gibraltar either with his own army or by allowing German troops free passage through Spain. The fortifications had been neglected as part of the British disarmament policy, and if the base had been attacked in 1940, it would have been captured. Full use of Spain by Axis submarines and airplanes would materially have increased losses in the Battle of the Atlantic. Strong diplomatic pressure was put on Franco, and this was reinforced by the threatening presence on his frontier from 1940 to 1942 of a powerful German army.

Franco's sympathies were with the Axis, and he had no love for democracies like the United States and Great Britain. He was obsessed with fear of communism and Russia, and he would have liked Gibraltar and Morocco. On the other hand, the majority of the Spanish people including the bulk of Franco's supporters wanted no more fighting of any description, and there was a growing dislike of the Germans and Italians. What would make the war even more unpopular was that it would bring starvation. Spain was dependent on imports of American wheat to feed her people, and these would cease the moment war was declared. At best Spain could stand the strain of only a short war, provided there was a guarantee that it was virtually over. Franco was not as confident as Hitler that Britain was practically finished, and with his cautious temperament he would only bet on a certainty. Franco made his decision purely and solely in terms of Spanish interests. Gratitude to the Axis for its help never entered his head. In a most crafty manner he played for time until the Anglo-American invasion of North Africa made him more doubtful than ever that Hitler would win. Then slowly and cautiously he began to move from pro-Axis to pro-Allied neutrality. Churchill summed up Franco's policy as "a monumental example of blazing ingratitude" which was "to the inestimable advantage of Britain when she was all alone."

THE ROME-BERLIN AXIS AND AUSTRIA

Hitler was determined to re-establish the empire of middle Europe which Germany had created during World War I. This required the annexation of Austria and the substitution of German for Italian influence in the Danubian countries. Mussolini was to be reconciled to this defeat by finding compensation in the Mediterranean. The Ethiopian affair played into Hitler's hands because it alienated Italy from Britain and France. In 1936, moreover, Mussolini intended to intervene in the impending Spanish civil war, which might rouse opposition from Britain and France. Hitler for his part was anxious for an alliance with Italy, which he felt was necessary for Germany's success. The result was that on July 11, 1936, an Austro-German Agreement was made with Mussolini's approval. Each state promised not to interfere in the domestic affairs of the other, and Hitler recognized Austria's full sovereignty. In October, 1936, Mussolini and Hitler signed an agreement for cooperation in Spain and against communism. The promise to respect the independence of Austria was repeated. Hitler never had the least intention of keeping it, and Mussolini was well aware of this. So, after a fashion, there was a frank understanding between the high contracting parties. In November, 1937, Italy joined the German-Japanese Anti-Communist Pact. Hitler wasted no time in boring from within until by 1938 the structure of the Austrian government was undermined. Mussolini was unable to give Austria any help since the war in Spain continued and made it impossible to engage in any other adventures. He refused to intervene in March, 1938, when Hitler forced von Schusnigg to resign in favor of a Nazi chancellor, Seyss-Inquart, and then invaded and annexed the country.

In proportion as Mussolini lost ground in central Europe, he was compelled to fall back on the Mediterranean. This was the one place where he might still hope to justify his boastings about reviving the Roman Empire. Conquests in the Mediterranean could only be made at the expense of Britain and France, and Italy was too weak to face either one of them, let alone both. So Mussolini's Mediterranean ambitions forced him more and more into the German camp, until eventually the Rome-Berlin Axis was changed from a diplomatic into a military alliance.

During the Munich crisis Hitler did not consult his partner and informed him of his intentions only at the last moment. In September, 1938, Mussolini discovered that Hitler meant war if his terms were not accepted. Mussolini was very unwilling to fight since the Italian army was completely unprepared, and at Munich he came out strongly in favor of a peaceful settlement. He felt that he was being treated as a mere satellite, but he also believed that Germany was invincible and that he had better join the winning side. Hitler was pressing him to form an alliance and eventually Mussolini agreed, while making it clear that Italy would be in no condition to go to war until 1943. The German-Italian Alliance of May 22, 1939, required that if one state became involved in hostilities, the other would enter the war on its side. As far as possible, Hitler kept Mussolini in ignorance of his preparations for war with Poland. When the latter learned of them, he strongly urged a peaceful settlement after the Munich pattern, for the excellent reason that his army was in poor condition. At the same time he wanted a share of the loot, and he knew he would not get it unless he fought for it. Mussolini always intended to enter the war on Germany's side at what seemed to him the right moment, but to decide exactly when this had arrived involved delicate calculations. It must not be too early since Italy could not stand the strain of a long war. Equally it must not be too late, or Hitler might remark that those who did nothing got nothing. By June 11, 1940, it was evident that the Battle of France would soon be over, and Mussolini declared war. The Italian armies met with disaster in Greece, Libya, and Ethiopia, and Germany felt compelled to step in to salvage the wreckage. From December, 1940, onward Italy became increasingly a German satellite. German troops, Gestapo, and economic experts took over the control of the country, and Rommel assumed command of the army in Libya. By the end of the war Italy's status was not materially better than that of the conquered countries.

ITALY SINCE 1945

Italy emerged from the war in a worse position than before it. Property damage was heavy, since the war had been fought from one end of the country to the other. Ethiopia regained its independence, and the three Italian colonies were all conquered by the British. Italian national pride demanded their restoration, and in 1950 the United Nations made Somaliland an Italian trusteeship. By a U.N. decision Libya became an independent kingdom in 1951, and in 1952 Eritrea became an autonomous unit federated with Ethiopia. Libya is strategically important because of its position in the central Mediterranean, and Britain vetoed Russia's demand that it be given to her as a strategic trusteeship.

The Communists had a large following among the peasants, they controlled the bulk of the trade unions with a membership of around 4 million, and they were loyally supported by Nenni's left-wing Socialists. As in France, they hoped that the discontent which sprang from economic distress would give them control of the country. Their expectations might well have been realized if it had not been for the substantial and continuous American aid which Italy received after 1943 in loans and grants of various kinds. In the election of 1948 Premier de Gasperi and his Christian Democrats won over half of the seats, and the Communists and their allies about 31 percent. The issue was not finally decided, however, for the unemployed continued to number nearly 2 million, and large numbers of land hungry peasants supported the Communists. In the 1953 elections the Communists and their allies increased their vote to 35 percent, and the right-wing monarchist and neo-Fascist parties had a considerable revival in strength. Both extremes are hostile to the Christian Democrats, whose electoral support fell to 40 percent. Under the multiple party system the Christian Democratic government retained a precarious hold on office by the uncertain support of several small middle-of-the-road parties. The prospects seemed to point to a period of weak and unstable governments.

The Christian Democratic government tried with some success to introduce agricultural reforms. It was strongly opposed by the great landowners who were wealthy and powerful, and also by the Communists. The former saw in land reform an attempt to undermine their most cherished privileges, and transferred their support from the Christian Democrats to the right-wing parties. The Communists did their best to sabotage measures which threatened to lessen their support among the peasants. Another formidable obstacle to reform was its heavy cost combined with limited revenue. Apart from compensation to the landowners for the expropriation of their estates, there was the expense of combatting soil erosion, flood control and irrigation, and loans to the new peasant owners to help them get established. By the land law of 1950 the government proposed to take over 1,750,000 acres and distribute it to small holders. This measure was on too small a scale adequately to deal with the problem; but considering the number who wanted land and the limited area available, it was easier to state the problem than to find a solution to it.

Italy is an important factor in the defense of Western Europe both by land and sea. She retains her commanding strategic position in the central Mediterranean. Substitute the Red for the German air force and submarine fleet, and the sea passage could again be closed as it was in 1940–1943. This is the principal strategic reason why the Communists have tried to make Italy a Soviet satellite: it would advance the Russian frontier to the middle of the Mediterranean and immensely increase the difficulty of helping Yugoslavia, Greece and Turkey. Trieste was for a decade the cause of strained relations between Italy and Yugoslavia. Italy claimed it because the city and a small surrounding area had a predominantly Italian population. It was also the natural outlet for the foreign trade of northern Yugoslavia as well as of Austria, and Tito's demand for it was based on economic grounds as well as on the presence of a Slav minority. By the Italian peace treaty of

1947 Trieste was to become a small independent city state. Temporarily it was divided into two zones, one of which was put under Yugoslav control, while the other (including the city of Trieste) was placed under Anglo-American military administration, supported by a small garrison of American and British troops. This stop-gap arrangement lasted for nearly a decade, for chronic deadlocks made it impossible to set up the projected government of the city state. Both Italy and Yugoslavia were determined to annex the whole area, and neither was willing to abate its claim. Such strong patriotic emotion was aroused on each side that it became difficult for the governments to arrange a compromise. In 1948 the Western powers declared themselves in favor of returning the whole territory to Italy, since they wished to strengthen the Christian Democratic government in its domestic struggle against communism. On the other hand, when Tito broke with Russia and moved toward the West, it became inexpedient to weaken his position. Eventually Washington and London arranged a compromise in 1954, by which the projected free state was abolished, Anglo-American control was withdrawn, and the territory was divided. Yugoslavia retained the zone it had held since 1945, and received a small additional area. Italy took over control of the former Anglo-American zone, and agreed to maintain Trieste as a free port. The settlement of this dispute aroused the hope that it might now become possible to arrange military cooperation between Italy and Yugoslavia, for their inability to work together had been a strategic liability to both in the event of a Russian attack.

SELECTED READING

BRENAN, GERALD, *The Face of Spain*. London: Turnstile Press, 1950.

————, *The Spanish Labyrinth*. New York: The Macmillan Company, 1943.

EBENSTEIN, WILLIAM, *Fascist Italy*. New York: American Book Company, 1939.

HAYES, CARLTON, *Wartime Mission in Spain, 1942–1945*. New York: The Macmillan Company, 1945.

HODGSON, SIR ROBERT, *Spain Resurgent*. London: Hutchinson and Company, Ltd., 1953.

HUGHES, H. STUART, *The United States and Italy*. Cambridge: Harvard University Press, 1953.

MACARTNEY, M. H. H., and CREMONA, P. *Italy's Foreign and Colonial Policy 1914–1937*. New York: Oxford Press, 1938.

MATTHEWS, HERBERT L., *The Fruits of Fascism*. New York: Harcourt, Brace and Company, 1943.

WISKEMANN, ELIZABETH, *The Rome-Berlin Axis, A History of the Relations between Hitler and Mussolini*. New York: Oxford Press, 1949.

CHAPTER 23

JAPAN

China's semicolonial status arose largely because she failed to modernize her civilization sufficiently to meet the West on equal terms. Japan faced the same problem, and at first had to grant similar rights of extraterritoriality to the United States and other Western powers. At the end of the nineteenth century they were abolished by agreement, and the Japanese government was freed from all restrictions on its authority. This raises the question of why Japan and China reacted so differently to the same situation. It was not that the Japanese were predisposed to welcome the foreigners, any more than the Chinese.

IDEAS AND INSTITUTIONS

The Chinese were convinced of their immeasurable superiority, and they believed for a long time that the Western barbarians could teach them nothing. The little group of soldier aristocrats who made modern Japan were far shrewder and abler than any leaders whom contemporary China was able to produce. They realized that the United States and Europe were determined to trade with Japan, and that if she merely resisted blindly and unintelligently as China had done, she would suffer the same fate of gradual subjection to foreign control. Therefore, the obvious remedy was to learn from the West the secrets of its superior power, and so maintain their independence. Several times in their history the Japanese showed the same marked ability to borrow or more accurately to adapt from foreign countries the things that would be useful to them. They never copied blindly, and they never altered the essential characteristics of their own civilization. Rather they chose those phases of the foreign culture which they thought would be serviceable, and fitted them into the general pattern of their national life. In carrying out their policy the leaders had the advantage that they were dealing with a well-disciplined people, trained for centuries to obey the orders of their superiors. In China, on the other hand, authority was decentralized, and even if the emperor had been an ardent reformer, it would have been exceedingly difficult for him to enforce his orders if the provincial officials were not in agreement with them.

What really interested the makers of modern Japan was the material achievement of the West in war, industry, and science. Outwardly Japan was Westernized at least in the cities. In ways of thought, code of behavior, and attitude toward authority it remained very largely the traditional Japan. A good illustration was the form of government prior to 1945, which had a specious resemblance to a European constitutional monarchy. There was an elected Diet or lower house, a House of Peers, a premier and cabinet, and a Mikado or emperor who seemed usually to remain aloof from politics. The reality was that elections had no necessary effect upon the composition and policy of the government, since the cabinet was not responsible to the Diet. The army and navy habitually exerted a very strong—in the end a dominating—influence without arousing popular opposition. The ministers of war and the navy must be a general and admiral on the active list, whose appointments were approved by their respective services. Therefore, the army or navy could unseat a cabinet by the simple expedient of forbidding any general or admiral to be a member. Legally the emperor was supreme and divine, but his counsellors worked the oracle. In a grave crisis he would be advised to issue an edict, and the awe with which his subjects had been taught to regard him ensured popular submission to the advisers who sheltered behind his name.

Japanese institutions were based on a foundation of habits of thought and traditions of conduct that had the compelling force which comes from centuries of usage. This was a hierarchical society where the individual was trained to suppress his own desires and obey his elders and betters—his parents, his superiors, and above all the emperor. Traditionally, as in Germany, the soldier had been looked up to as at the pinnacle of society, and it was felt that his profession gave him the right to take a prominent part in government. War and the military virtues were glorified, and as members of a superior race the Japanese believed that they had the mission to spread the benefits of their emperor's paternal rule over lesser peoples. These traditional ideas, reiterated in the home, the school, the Shinto religious cult, and the armed forces in which every Japanese served, were well calculated to create a race of superpatriots and brave, obedient soldiers, but they were not likely to produce democrats.

FOUNDATIONS OF THE EMPIRE

Chauvinistic ideas of conquest had been current among the samurai, the hereditary military aristocracy, even before the period of seclusion ended in 1867. They were held in check by the oligarchy of aristocrats who controlled the government because they appreciated that Japan was not ready for war, and for twenty-seven years they devoted themselves with great success to the modernization of the country. In 1894 the government went to war with China, nominally to assert the independence of Korea, and demonstrated to an astonished world that Japan and not China was the most powerful nation in the Far East. By the treaty of peace in 1895 she obtained Formosa and the Liaotung Peninsula (including the harbor of Port Arthur) in southern Manchuria. Japan had taken the first step in a policy of expansion on the mainland. She was compelled to return the Liaotung Peninsula to China under pressure from Russia, Germany, and France, and three years later Russia took it for herself. Russia also won virtual control of Manchuria and established a strong influence at Peking.

Japan agreed with the United States and Britain in opposing European encroachments on China's territorial integrity and especially those of Russia, since they threatened her own long-term plans. At this time Japan was particularly interested in advancing her interests in Korea, into which Russia was beginning to penetrate. An alliance with Britain was signed on January 30, 1902, by which she recognized Japan's special interests in Korea. Each signatory promised to remain neutral if the other were at war. But if either were attacked by more than one power, the other would come to its assistance. Japan still tried to negotiate a compromise with Russia, but when this failed she went to war in February, 1904. Russia was driven out of Port Arthur and south Manchuria, and by the Treaty of Portsmouth in 1905 her treaty rights there were transferred to Japan, while she retained her position in northern Manchuria. China's sovereignty over the province was recognized by both powers, and the Open-Door policy was reaffirmed.

During the war the United States as well as Great Britain had been favorable to Japan, since they felt that she was checking the most dangerous enemy of the Open-Door policy and the territorial integrity of China. They soon had reason to revise their estimate. In 1905 Japan established a protectorate over Korea and in 1910 annexed it. It became evident in south Manchuria that while the door might be open, it was so blocked with Japanese that it was difficult for any foreigner to pass through. Japan and Russia agreed not to poach on one another's preserves and to take common action if their spheres of influence were threatened. The United States began to protest against the infractions of the Open Door, and hostility toward Japan replaced the former friendship.

Japan entered World War I in August, 1914, as the ally of Great Britain and promptly destroyed Germany's position in the Far East. Besides capturing her sphere in Shantung, Japan also occupied the German islands north of the equator, the Marianas (excepting Guam), the Carolines, and the Marshalls. The Japanese government fully realized the possibilities opened to it in China as the result of the war. The situation in the Far East was very similar to what it was in 1937. The European powers were in no position to interfere until the war in Europe was over. The one nation that was free to take action on behalf of China was the United States, and Japan judged correctly that it would not use force. In 1915 Japan presented to China the Twenty-One Demands. One group extended and strengthened her position in south Manchuria. Others were for rights in China proper which would have established Japanese paramountcy over the whole country. Ultimately most of the demands were withdrawn. One principal result of Japan's wartime policy was further to strain relations with the United States.

Japan's delegates at the peace conference of 1919 asked that the draft covenant of the League of Nations contain a clause establishing the principle of racial equality. In principle President Wilson approved of the proposal, but he ruled against it because it was made clear to him that its adoption would raise intense opposition in California, British Columbia, and Australia. Five years later, in 1924, Congress embodied in an immigration act a clause aimed against the Japanese that aliens ineligible to citizenship should be denied entry. These two actions left a feeling of deep resentment in the Japanese popular mind.

THE WASHINGTON CONFERENCE

In July, 1921, President Harding invited the powers to an international conference at Washington. Those invited were Great Britain, France, Italy, Japan, China, Belgium, Holland, and Portugal, but not Russia. The agenda dealt partly with the Far East and also with naval disarmament. Washington wished to protect American interests, strengthen the position of China, and put a stop to Japanese aggression. These purposes merged into another, the limitation of fleet strengths. During the war the United States, Great Britain, and Japan had launched very large naval building programs, and these were continued after the war was over. A triangular naval race was developing which was very expensive and might have serious effects in creating international tension. There was also the problem of the Anglo-Japanese alliance. Many Americans believed that it was aimed against the United States and would eventually involve her in war against Japan and Britain. This was impossible, for when the alliance was renewed in 1911 the British inserted a clause which was designed to prevent them from being involved in a war between the United States and Japan. The British Commonwealth as a whole wished to continue the alliance, but at the Imperial Conference of 1921 Canada insisted successfully that it must be abrogated.

The naval limitation treaty was restricted to capital ships or battleships, battle cruisers and aircraft carriers. It established a ratio of naval strengths of 5-5-3-1.67-1.67. The United States and Great Britain would have a tonnage of 500,000 tons apiece, Japan 300,000 tons, and France and Italy each 167,000 tons. The limitation of fleet strengths was intimately connected with the status quo agreement on fortifications in the western Pacific. Within the designated area existing fortifications could be kept in repair but not strengthened, and no new ones could be built. The principal islands covered were: for the United States, the Aleutians, Guam, and the Philippines; for Great Britain, Hong Kong and islands in the south Pacific; and for Japan, the Kuriles, Ryukyus, Bonins, and Formosa. The Anglo-Japanese alliance was replaced by the Four-Power Treaty signed by the United States, Britain, France, and Japan. They agreed to respect one another's Pacific insular possessions and to settle in joint conference any dispute which might arise. All the delegates to the conference signed the Nine-Power Treaty, which guaranteed the Open-Door policy and the sovereignty, territorial integrity, and independence of China. The principal powers had bound themselves to accept the historic principles of American policy in the Far East. Further violations of them were forbidden, but rights already acquired were not surrendered.

Japan played her cards very cleverly at Washington, and while she gave substantial concessions, e.g., the return of Shantung to China, she also made important gains. The 5-5-3 naval ratio, combined with the status quo agreement on fortifications, gave her an impregnable position in the northwest Pacific. In case of conflict neither the American nor the British fleet had a sufficient margin of superiority to compensate for the disadvantages of a naval war fought so far from its bases and in Japan's home waters. Invasion would be impossible and also a blockade that would cut off Japan from her colonies. By 1922 both the American naval base in the Philippines and the British base at Hong Kong had become second-class. The fortifications were obsolescent, and the dry docks could not accommodate the battleship of 35,000 tons. Guam was a potential base, but had to remain unfortified because of the status quo agreement. This meant that in the event of war the nearest American first-class base was at Pearl Harbor, 3400 miles away. The future British base at Singapore was 3000 miles distant. Each was too far away to serve as the base of a navy engaged in the northwest Pacific. To coin a word, Japan was practically ungetatable. She had naval security and with it supremacy. It would be impossible for the United States to send effective aid to the Philippines, since they were 4800 miles from the Hawaian Islands, and were cut off by the barrier of the former German islands which Japan held as a League mandate. Effective help to China and to protect American interests there would be equally impossible. Their security depended upon the good faith with which the Nine-Power Treaty was observed.

During the 'twenties the Japanese liberals were generally in power and the Washington Conference treaties were observed. There was a reaction against the aggressive foreign policy of the previous governments. It had not succeeded and had aroused Western and particularly American hostility. The policy of the liberals differed from that of the conservatives and militarists in methods rather than aims. Both agreed that Japanese industry needed China as a market and a source of raw materials, and that above all the special position in south Manchuria must be preserved. The liberals, however, believed that Japan could gain her ends by conciliation rather than by force. They supported limitation of naval armaments, and in 1930 Japan signed the London Naval Treaty. It extended the 5-5-3 ratio of the Washington Conference to heavy cruisers, but granted a 10-10-7 ratio for light cruisers and auxiliary ships, and equality in submarines.

THE MANCHURIAN CRISIS

For some time the army and conservative elements in Japan generally had been growing more and more hostile to the liberal policy of sympathetic cooperation with China. They were alarmed at the growth of Chinese nationalism, and the efforts that were being made to dislodge Japan from south Manchuria. They believed that the only way to meet this situation was by force. The officers of the Kwantung army in Manchuria had decided to act independently of their government, and on September 18, 1931, their troops attacked the Chinese army of Marshal Chang Hsueh-liang. By 1932 his troops had been expelled from south Manchuria, and hostilities had spread to Shanghai.

China appealed to the League and also to the United States, as a signatory of the Briand-Kellogg Peace Pact. Secretary of State Henry L. Stimson assured the League of American cooperation, and on September 21 it requested China and Japan to seek a peaceful settlement by withdrawing their troops. Stimson deprecated any action which might arouse Japanese nationalism in support of the military and so make it harder for the liberal Shidehara cabinet to gain control of the situation. When the League powers cautiously sounded him out as to his attitude toward sanctions, he gave them no encouragement. He was opposed to the United States taking part in either the economic or the military sanction, "although we would not probably in any way allow our government to interfere through the fleet with any embargo by any one else." The only sanctions involving the United States which the secretary of state approved were the world moral condemnation of Japanese aggression and the refusal to recognize conquests made by force. Stimson miscalculated the effect of moral disapproval upon the Japanese, for its principal result was to encourage the militarists. The Kwantung army continued to advance, and the Shidehara government fell in December amid a rising tide of popular nationalism.

American opinion was strongly influenced by pacifism and isolationism, and there was no willingness to carry support of China's integrity and the Open Door policy to the point of war. There was a real possibility that if an economic boycott were imposed on Japan she might retaliate by going to war. She would be able to attack the Philippines, Hong Kong, and the international settlements in China, and because of the Washington Conference treaties these were potential hostages in her hands. Moreover, 1931 was the depth of the depression, and there was no enthusiasm for a policy which would still further damage foreign trade and burden the country with a heavy war debt. The British were pacifist, and had recently achieved another "gesture for peace" by scrapping some more of their navy. They had virtually no interests in Manchuria, and on September 21 the depression forced Britain off the gold standard. There was a section of pro-Japanese opinion, but it had little influence. The upshot was that she was not prepared to impose sanctions unless fully assured of complete American participation, and no such promise was forthcoming.

On January 7, 1932, Stimson informed Japan and China that the United States would refuse to recognize any situation brought about by force, or which impaired American treaty rights. On January 29 the League Council, and on March 12 the Assembly, passed resolutions adopting the policy of non-recognition. Japan turned Manchuria into the puppet state of Manchukuo. She established a foothold in northern China and resigned from the League. She also invaded the Soviet zone of northern Manchuria, and in 1935 Russia sold her railway interests to Japan. The League of Nations had failed in its first big test, and from that time it was uncertain how much reliance could be placed upon collective security.

The aim of the militarists was not merely to make conquests on the mainland, but also to seize power within Japan. Their success in Manchuria did not give them immediate victory, but during the decade of the 'thirties power passed increasingly from the civilian politicians and the moderates to the extreme militarists. The outcome was a uniquely Japanese version of the totalitarian state. There was no individual dictator like Hitler, but instead the dictatorship of a group or coalition of groups. The nominal head and when necessary the controlled mouthpiece of the government was the emperor. Between 1931 and 1936 a series of assassinations removed prominent politicians, bankers, industrialists, and moderate militarists, whose patriotism fell short of the exacting standard of their self-appointed liquidators. A propaganda campaign taught that Japan's mission was to spread the beneficent rule of the emperor to the benighted Chinese and others who suffered under corrupt or Communist leaders, or who had fallen prey to Western imperialism. This propaganda won the extremists a large popular following.

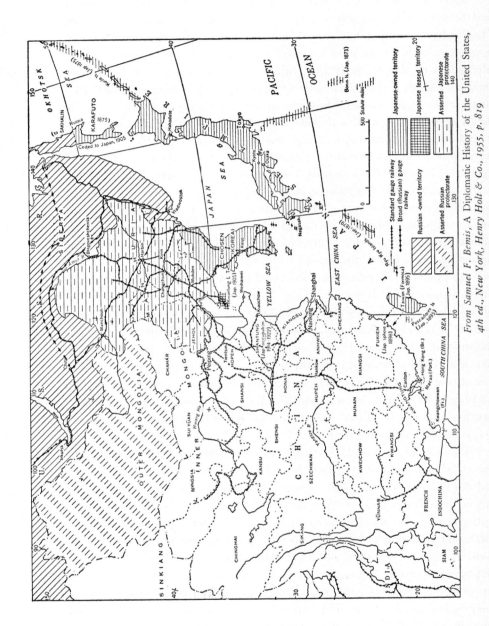

From Samuel F. Bemis, A Diplomatic History of the United States, 4th ed., New York, Henry Holt & Co., 1955. p. 819

The Far East, 1936

Gradually too the great Zaibatsu houses which controlled so much of the wealth and industry of Japan began to give their support to the militarists, for expansion abroad meant large orders for armaments.

MOTIVES FOR EXPANSION

The policy of conquest was the result of a combination of motives. Even before the modernization of Japan began, many of the governing class had had dreams of empire building. Temporarily they were shelved as impracticable, but they grew in influence from the late nineteenth century onward as the new Japan accomplished her astoundingly rapid rise to the rank of a great power. The sense of strength and the intoxication of success combined with traditional ideas to produce the conviction that Japan had the power and the right to impose her New Order in Greater East Asia.

More material considerations contributed to the growth of imperialism, and provided useful arguments to justify it. The population grew from perhaps 30 million in 1867 to 73,114,000 in 1940. By the 'thirties the annual increase was about 900,000. Assuming that not all of these would come on the labor market and that others would fill existing jobs as older people retired, there would remain a net annual increase of 500,000 for whom employment did not exist. The economy would have continually to expand so as to create half a million new positions every year. The alternative would be increasing unemployment and economic distress—and the growth of communism. The surplus population could not be drawn off by emigration, since the areas which the Japanese favored were closed to them, i.e., the United States, Canada, New Zealand, and Australia. Only about 600,000 settled in Manchuria, principally because they could not compete against the Chinese who formed the bulk of the population and had a lower standard of living. The annual increase could not be provided for by the expansion of agriculture in Japan since there was a lack of cultivable land. The area of the islands was only 142,300 square miles, smaller than California, and owing to the mountainous character of the country only 17 percent was cultivable. Perhaps another million acres could be farmed, but this would do little to provide for the yearly increase in population.

The only remedy was industrialization, and for this raw materials and an assured market were essential. The only raw materials of which Japan produced all or most of her requirements were silk, copper, sulfur, and coal. Domestic iron ore supplied only 12 percent of the demand. It was necessary to import a large part and frequently the whole of practically all the other raw materials, as well as 20 percent of the food. An assured market could not be adequately provided by domestic consumption. Between 1914 and 1938 about 20 percent of the total value of Japanese production had to be sold abroad. The chief characteristic of foreign markets after World War I was the likelihood of losing them through the raising of trade barriers. Japan had to look to foreign countries for her raw materials and a market for the sale of the manufactures which provided her with the foreign exchange needed to pay for her imports. This applied equally to peacetime needs and the purchase of military raw materials. Both in peace and war Japan was dependent upon foreign states and particularly upon the United States and the British Empire, which were at the same time her best markets and her principal sources of supply. They were in a position to make or break her by their trade policies. Japan's militarists were gravely perturbed by this situation, and their ambition was to make her economically independent. Manchuria was fairly rich in some of Japan's necessities, and her economic position was much improved by the conquest of 1931. North China, however, had the largest coal reserves in the Far East, as well as iron and other products that Japan needed. China too was an obvious market for Japanese manufactures, but Chiang Kai-shek was encouraging the development of industry by tariffs which reduced imports from Japan. The solution from the militarists' point of view was to bring China and particularly north China under Japan's control.

Strategic considerations played a part in shaping policy. The bases for the invasion of Japan are Korea, Manchuria, and north China. By 1937 Korea and Manchuria were no longer a potential danger, but China was another matter. Chiang Kai-shek himself was too weak to dream of attacking, but Russia's record of predatory expansion in the Far East was as noteworthy as Japan's. If ever she won control of China, she might use it as a base for attack. Moreover, Russia had the weapon of communism, of which the Japanese leaders of all shades of thought were intensely afraid. It was decided that the best way to avert this potential danger was to bring north China under Japanese control.

THE SINO-JAPANESE WAR

The militarists judged correctly that they need not fear foreign intervention if they attacked China in 1937. Germany and Italy would not interfere with their associate in the Anti-Comintern Pact, and France had her hands full with domestic dissension and the growing threat from Germany. Great Britain would be hostile because of her trade and investments in China, but their safety was a minor matter compared with the threat to the British Isles. The growing menace of Nazi Germany made it essential to avoid a war with Japan at all costs. "When the house is on fire, no one troubles about the barn." This left the United States as the one great power which was free to act in the Far East, but the America of the Neutrality Acts was in no mood to go to war on behalf of China.

The Japanese had hoped to confine hostilities to north China, but Chiang Kai-shek refused to cooperate by giving in. The war spread further and further, and when Chiang lost the richest parts of China, he retreated to Chungking and held out there. The Japanese set up a puppet Chinese government in the occupied areas—over 500,000 square miles with a population of nearly 200 million—and began their economic exploitation. The United States and Great Britain gave such help to Chiang Kai-shek, e.g., by loans, as they could without involving themselves in war with Japan. Japan missed no opportunity of injuring American and particularly British interests and prestige. Especially after the outbreak of World War II it became more essential than ever for Britain to avoid war with Japan, which several times seemed imminent.

JAPAN AND SOUTHEAST ASIA

In September, 1940, the militarists won a conclusive victory over the moderates. An alliance was signed with Germany and Italy, which recognized Japan's leadership in Greater East Asia. The cabinet agreed that the war in China must be brought to an early and victorious conclusion and that Japan must take advantage of the situation in Europe to secure control of Southeast Asia even at the risk of war. Apparently it was agreed that to ignore the United States and attack the British and Dutch empires alone would be strategically unsound, since this would leave the American fleet at Pearl Harbor on the flank of the Japanese line of communications. War with the United States should be avoided if it accepted Japan's demands. In January, 1941, approval was given to the plans for an attack on the American fleet before war was declared, if this should prove necessary. On April 13, 1941, Japan and Russia signed a treaty of neutrality which temporarily freed each of them from the fear of immediate attack by the other. This left them at liberty to concentrate on more pressing matters.

Manchuria and north China supplied part but not all of Japan's needs in raw materials. The requirements still lacking could be obtained from Southeast Asia. In addition Japan would control about 66 percent of the world's tin and 90 percent of its natural rubber, and she would have a valuable and growing market of 147 million customers. The strategic key to Southeast Asia was the British naval base at Singapore, but it was 3000 miles from Japan. This was too far for a direct attack, and it was necessary to shorten the distance by taking French Indochina. It was weakly defended, it was valuable in itself, and in the south it had the large modern seaport of Saigon, only 647 miles from Singapore. This could be used as the advanced base where troops and stores could be collected for the invasion of Malaya. By the summer of 1941 the whole of Indochina was in Japanese hands. After the fall of Holland Japan put heavy pressure on the government of Indonesia to cooperate politically and economically, but the Dutch firmly refused the sweeping Japanese demands. Putting everything together it became increasingly clear that the Co-Prosperity Sphere was about to receive a big southward extension.

There was grave reason to fear that attack would be successful, since everywhere defenses were weak. Britain's rearmament had reached the point where she was fairly strong in actual combat areas such as Egypt, but she did not have the ships, aircraft, and equipment adequately to garrison Burma and Malaya. Their loss would mean that British sea communications would be cut with Australia and New Zealand and that these two dominions as well as India would be in danger of invasion. If Hitler succeeded in breaking through into the Middle East, as he was trying to do in 1941, there was the possibility that the German and Japanese armies might meet somewhere in India. Great Britain would be gravely weakened in her struggle against Germany, and it was not in American interest that this should happen. A Department of State memorandum stated that the advance into Southeast Asia "created a situation in which the risk of war became so great that the United States and other countries were confronted no longer with the question of avoiding such risk, but from then on with the problem of preventing a complete undermining of their security."

In 1941 American hostility to Japan's policy in China was reinforced by growing apprehension in the State Department as her designs on Southeast Asia became clearer. Japan was feeling the lack of an increasing number of military raw materials, for which since 1940 the United States had been refusing export licenses. Chiang Kai-shek was refusing to make peace, and American help was strengthening his determination to resist. During the greater part of 1941 negotiations for a peaceful settlement were carried on between the American and Japanese governments. Secretary of State Cordell Hull laid down certain principles from which the United States refused to depart. These were (1) respect for the territorial integrity and independence of China and all other nations, (2) the Open-Door policy, (3) no forcible disturbance of the status quo in the Pacific, and (4) withdrawal of troops from Indochina. In other words, Japan must abandon her whole China policy and her ambitions in Southeast Asia. Japan proposed that the United States cease giving help to Chiang Kai-shek, Indonesia and Malaya, and supply Japan with the war materials she needed. The United States must also suspend its defensive preparations in the Philippines and induce Chiang to make peace. It was clear that Japan intended to control north China and refused to respect the Open Door and American rights. Japanese troops would be withdrawn from Indochina after Chiang made peace, but assurances were evaded that Japan would not conquer other territories in the southwest Pacific. In short, the United States was to assist Japan to control China and Southeast

Asia, and in return she would merely guarantee the neutrality of the Philippines. The United States had only two choices—either to yield to the Japanese demands and sacrifice principles and security, or decline to yield and take the consequences. Neither government was willing to recede from its position, and it became increasingly clear that the only hope of averting war was the unlikely chance that Japan would abandon her policy of aggression. On November 26 a Japanese squadron sailed from the Kurile Islands for Pearl Harbor.

Japan's policy was of her own devising and was not dictated by Germany. When the alliance was first made in 1940, Hitler did his best to persuade her to attack the British and Dutch colonies and, after his invasion of Russia, Siberia, but to avoid bringing the United States into the war. During 1941 Japan's determination hardened to attack the United States if she failed to get her own way in the negotiations. In November, 1941, the Nazis realized that Japan was moving toward war with the United States and that Germany must either break her alliance or else support her. The Germans were far from pleased at the prospect of being pulled into war against America, but they considered the Japanese alliance essential to their victory. On the eve of Pearl Harbor Hitler promised to assist Japan against the United States, and on December 11 he declared war.

THE OCCUPATION OF JAPAN 1945-1947

The United States had played the dominant part in the Pacific war, and it controlled postwar policy. A Far Eastern Commission representing the powers with Pacific interests was set up in Washington to formulate policies, and an Allied Council was established in Japan as a consultative and advisory body. The final decision remained with the American government or with General Douglas MacArthur, who was both commander of the predominantly American army of occupation and the executive authority to direct the political, economic and social policies of the occupation. He and his staff (SCAP) did not administer Japan directly but issued their orders to the emperor's government, which was responsible for executing them.

One purpose was to punish Japan for her offenses and to insure that she would not again become a danger to the peace of the world. She was deprived of all her colonies and most of her outlying islands. The United States retained the Mariana, Marshall, and Caroline Islands as a strategic trusteeship, and also the Bonins and Ryukyus. Chiang Kai-shek occupied Formosa, Korea was destined for independence, and Russia took southern Sakhalin and the Kurile Islands. The army, navy, and air force were disbanded, naval bases were destroyed, and over 5 million Japanese, soldiers and civilians, who were living abroad were returned to Japan. The major war criminals were brought to trial and some of them executed. Some 1300 ultra nationalistic or terroristic societies were dissolved, and nearly 200,000 persons were banned from public office and industry. In the new constitution of 1947 SCAP inserted a clause that renounced war and forbade Japan to have armed forces. If Japan were to be effectively demilitarized, it was essential drastically to reduce potential war industries to the extent needed for peacetime production. The aircraft, synthetic oil, and synthetic rubber industries were liquidated. Steel, chemical, and machine tool industries were limited, and originally it was intended that the machinery should be distributed to the states which had suffered from the Japanese invasion. Many of them, like the Philippines, were depending upon the deliveries to carry out their own programs of industrialization. In the end there was little actual transfer owing to a change in American policy, and in 1949 reparations were ended.

An important part of the policy of industrial demilitarization was the dissolution of the Zaibatsu or family combines such as the Mitsui family. An essential part of the nineteenth-century program of modernization was to industrialize as rapidly as possible. The government itself started many factories, but later it turned some of them over to the Zaibatsu so that industrial as well as financial capital came to be concentrated in the same hands. The government deliberately promoted this concentration of economic power, and supported industry with generous subsidies. The Zaibatsu established close working relations with members of the bureaucracy, which occupied a powerful position in the Japanese system of government. From 1897 onward large-scale enterprises expanded enormously and the Zaibatsu acquired great wealth.

Each family operated as a vertical trust consisting of a holding company, and subsidiaries specialized according to the field of enterprise. This was one reason why Japanese manufactures were able to undersell those of the West, though low wages and factory efficiency were also important factors. To cite a typical instance—cotton cloth—every firm engaged in the process from the buying of the raw cotton in the United States to the marketing of the finished product in, say, the Philippines, were subsidiaries of one Zaibatsu, including the shipping company which transported the cotton, the bank which financed transactions, the insurance companies which insured cargoes, the importers, the exporters, the cotton factories, and sometimes the dry goods stores which sold the cloth. The family combines monopolized so much of the wealth and productive capacity of Japan that they became a political power. In the interwar period they at first opposed the foreign policy of the militarists because they doubted the efficacy of their recipe that force alone would solve all problems. Gradually in the 'thirties they swung over in support of the New Order in Greater East Asia. The Zaibatsu were no bulwark of peace and democracy, and one aim of SCAP was to break them up and encourage the sale of their assets as widely as possible. The principal members of the Zaibatsu were barred from politics and business. This removed from the business world many of its ablest executives and hampered production, thus running counter to the later American policy of rebuilding industry and trade. It is uncertain how completely the Zaibatsu have been eliminated from Japanese economic life.

General MacArthur introduced agrarian reforms that were long overdue. Since the late nineteenth century, at least, the peasants had been losing the ownership of their farms, and an increasing number had become tenants paying exorbitant rents (often 50 percent of the crop) and sinking deeper and deeper into poverty. By 1945 about 50 percent of all farm families owned only 9 percent of the land and 7.5 percent of the families owned half of it. Land hunger was strong, and the tenants were seething with discontent. The landowners had immense prestige and influence in every village and dominated local politics. They supplied many of the officers of the army and navy, supported ultra conservative political parties, and were a serious obstacle to the establishment of democracy. General MacArthur required the Japanese government to buy 5 million acres—about a third of the cultivated area—at prewar values and resell it to the tenants at a reasonable price. By 1952 the program had been carried out, and 90 percent of all cultivated land had been acquired by those who worked it. Tenantry was not extinguished, but rents were reduced by 50 percent. Experience in other countries has shown that mere ownership is not enough: unless loans are provided at low rates of interest, the farmer is forced to borrow from the moneylender and often loses his land through mortgage and foreclosure. It is a hopeful sign that rural cooperative societies now provide 71 percent of the farm loans. Even so the agrarian problem is not solved, for there are too many people trying to earn a living from the land, and farming methods need to be improved.

The instructions issued to General MacArthur in 1945 directed him to establish a government that should conform as closely as might be to principles of democracy. The new constitution, largely dictated by SCAP, was adopted in 1947. Sovereignty was vested in the people and not the emperor, who became merely a figurehead. Political power was transferred from the executive to the elected Diet, to which the cabinet was made responsible. The Diet was given the power to direct the all powerful bureaucracy through its control of the executive and the budget. The former system of education had been well designed to manufacture ultra nationalists and obedient servants of the state. Textbooks were rewritten, and where possible nationalistic and militaristic teachers were dismissed. For the first time trade unions were free to organize. As far as it was possible to make a people democratic by an act of parliament, the work was done. Whether the attempt will succeed in the long run depends on how successfully the new ideas and institutions acclimatize themselves. They are a revolutionary break with the past, and it is a formidable task to change the immemorial political thinking of a whole people and overcome the resistance of the old guard, which has been weakened but not eliminated. Perhaps one prediction might be risked. If democratic government is permanently accepted, it will not be a replica of its Western models, but something uniquely Japanese.

AMERICAN POLICY SINCE 1947

During the earlier part of the occupation policy was a combination of punitive peace and reform, but after 1947 the emphasis began to shift to reconstruction. There were several reasons why the hostility toward Japan that had been created by the war changed. One was the unexpectedly cooperative attitude of the Japanese toward Americans. Another reason was the heavy financial burden which the occupation placed upon the United States. Immense damage had been done to the islands by air bombing, and the loss of the empire had deprived Japan of 20 percent of its food and an important part of its raw materials. The population had grown from 73,114,000 in 1940 to 88,200,000 in 1954, with an annual increase of over a million, and may quite possibly rise to 100 million. Between September 1945 and 1954 shipments of food and raw materials to Japan cost the United States $2,490,-000,000. The only way to end the drain was to rebuild Japan's economy and make her self-supporting. A third reason for the change of policy was political. At the end of the war the United States assumed that China under Chiang Kai-shek would become the leading power in the Far East and that the two nations would work together in foreign policy. A weak Japan would play only a minor role. The victory of the Chinese Communists combined with the development of the cold war with Russia altered the whole situation. The attitude toward Japan changed in the same way as that toward Germany. Japan came to be viewed in American policy as an essential strong point in the first line of defense across the Pacific. If she were to play this role, it was necessary that she be allowed to develop into a power factor in the Far East, aligned with the United States in interest and sympathy.

The emphasis was placed on the reconstruction of industry and the restoration of foreign trade. The attack on the Zaibatsu was abandoned in 1949, and they seem to be re-emerging. SCAP, troubled by the growth of communism, tended to join forces with Japan's conservatives in taking a less sympathetic view of trade unions and strikes. Trade treaties were negotiated, and the aim was to encourage Japan to become the principal industrial center of noncommunist Asia. The trend in manufacturing was away from the prewar staple of consumer goods toward the production of rolling stock, ships, machinery, and capital equipment generally. A five-year plan was drawn up that called for a great expansion of electric power, coal, and steel, and a vigorous trade offensive was launched. With internal recovery Japan's imports of raw materials increased, but her exports of manufactures were hampered by tariffs, quotas, and high costs of production, especially in the engineering and shipbuilding industries. One great handicap was that Japan bought half her raw materials and food from the United States and other North American countries and had to pay for them in dollars. Since import duties kept down her exports to the United States to 18 percent of the total, she was compelled to sell mainly in the soft currency countries which could not meet her demand for payment in dollars. Their trade with Japan tended to be on a basis of barter, equalizing purchases and sales. Energetic attempts have been made to obtain raw materials from India and Southeast Asia and to increase sales there. Japan offered to help these countries to carry out their plans for industrialization by supplying technical help and capital equipment. Apart from the problem of payment, Japanese prices since the war have been higher than those of her major competitors. Another obstacle has been the hostility which continues in many countries, because of the memory of the brutality and oppression of the armies of occupation during the war. There has been a reluctance to promote the recovery of Japanese economic strength. In 1954 there was a heavy adverse balance of trade of about $1 billion, nearly half of which was with the United States, and much of the remainder with the sterling area.

Prior to 1945 China (including Manchuria) was of great importance as a market and source of raw materials. There was no direct trade after the Communists came to power, though some indirect trade was carried on through Hong Kong. The Chinese government has held out hopes of a revival of trade on a large scale if Japan became "truly independent," or in other words, ceased to align herself with the United States. Even today Japan is the strongest and most heavily industrialized anticommunist state in Asia, and the local power position would be radically altered if she could be brought over to the side of Russia and China. The United States strongly opposed the resumption of trade with China, but the government of Japan was under strong pressure to bring it about. In some quarters exaggerated hopes were entertained of a great expansion of trade. Part of the business community took a less optimistic and more realistic view of the possibilities. But they believed they could get a fair share of the orders for capital equipment which China imported from the Soviet bloc, and that they could buy raw materials more cheaply from China than from the United States and elsewhere. With her economic health so unsound Japan could not risk forfeiting American aid, but in 1955 there were indications that she was moving cautiously in the direction of re-establishing economic and possibly diplomatic relations with China and Russia.

THE TREATY OF PEACE

The peace treaty was drawn up largely by the United States and was signed by most of the countries against whom Japan had fought on September 8, 1951. Russia and China took no part in the negotiations, and India disapproved of the refusal to cede Formosa to China and the retention of American forces in Japan. The treaty ended the occupation and restored full sovereignty to Japan, including the right to maintain armed forces and develop industries. No reparations were imposed, but Japan was deprived of her colonies and of the islands already mentioned. An agreement between the United States and Japan authorized the retention of American forces in Japan and the Ryukyu Islands. A beginning was made in the re-creation of a small Japanese army, navy, and air force. The re-establishment of the armed forces would require the repeal of the clause in the constitution renouncing war and the maintenance of an army. There is fairly strong opposition to the American urgings that they do this, and in 1955 the size of the force was considerably smaller than Washington had hoped that it would be.

Russia is regarded with a mixture of fear, suspicion, and admiration for its growing strength and industrial expansion. Japan is conscious of the fact that she is within easy bombing range of Russia and China, that Russia is on her doorstep, and that the Korean war ended in a draw. There is a good deal of neutralism, particularly among the trade unionists and the students. Evoking memories of Hiroshima, they argue that it is a useless expense to build up conventional armaments, since Japan is completely vulnerable to nuclear attack. There has been a resurgence of Japanese national feeling, and with it a considerable amount of anti-American sentiment has arisen. This is found not only among the left-wing parties, but also among the conservatives who make up the government. Some of them resent their former exclusion from politics and the dissolution of the Zaibatsu by General MacArthur. They want to revise the constitution of 1947 to give themselves more power. They also wish to abolish or modify the article forbidding war and the creation of armed forces, so that Japan can rearm openly. While anticommunist, they would like Japan to follow an independent policy between the two camps into which the world is divided. What they want is a rearmed Japan with bargaining power between the two sides in the cold war, and with more freedom of action than she has had since 1945. At the same time there is a realization that Japan cannot dispense with help from the United States.

SELECTED READING

BALL, W. MACMAHON, *Japan, Enemy or Ally?* New York: The John Day Company, 1949.

BISSON, T. A., *Zaibatsu Dissolution in Japan.* Berkeley and Los Angeles: University of California Press, 1954.

BORTON, HUGH (ed.), *Japan.* Ithaca: Cornell University Press, 1951.

CLYDE, PAUL H., *The Far East: A History of the Impact of the West on Eastern Asia,* 2d ed. New York: Prentice-Hall, 1952.

FEIS, HERBERT, *The Road to Pearl Harbor.* Princeton: Princeton University Press, 1950.

GREW, JOSEPH, *Ten Years in Japan.* New York: Simon and Schuster, 1944.

LATOURETTE, K. S., *The History of Japan.* New York: The Macmillan Company, 1947.

MAC NAIR, HARTLEY F., and LACH, DONALD F., *Modern Far Eastern International Relations.* New York: D. Van Nostrand Company, 1950.

MAKI, JOHN M., *Japanese Militarism.* New York: Alfred A. Knopf, 1945.

QUIGLEY, HAROLD S., and TURNER, JOHN E., *The New Japan.* Minneapolis: The University of Minnesota Press, 1956.

SANSON, SIR GEORGE B., *The Western World and Japan.* New York: Alfred A. Knopf, 1950.

CHAPTER 24

THE SOVIET UNION

THE DRIVE TO THE SEA

The Soviet Union in Europe is a part of the vast plain which stretches from the Baltic Sea and the Arctic Ocean to the Black Sea, and from the Ural Mountains far beyond the western frontier to the Carpathian Mountains on the border of Czechoslovakia. The Urals are not a serious barrier to the penetration of Siberia and central Asia, for they can be by-passed to the north or the south. Great rivers traverse the European plain, some flowing into the Gulf of Finland and the Baltic and others into the Black and Caspian Seas. Until modern times roads were few and bad, and merchants and soldiers alike depended on the waterways. The headwaters of the rivers flowing to the north were not far removed from those running to the south, and they were linked by portages. By using the intricate system of rivers with their tributaries and the connecting portages, it was possible to journey from the Baltic to the Black and Caspian Seas. Along them the exports of northern Europe reached Russia, to be sold for furs and other products. By working eastward along the rivers and portages of northern Russia, it was possible to exploit the rich fur trade of Siberia. The southern rivers were used by merchants to exchange Russian goods for the manufactures of Asia and the Eastern Roman Empire at Constantinople. The great cities of Russia, such as Moscow, became rich and powerful because they were on the rivers or the portages joining them.

Another geographic factor of basic importance in the country's history was the grasslands which begin in central Asia, pass south of the Urals, and stretch across southern Russia and beyond it. They were used as the road of invasion by nomadic tribes of horsemen, such as the Mongols of the Golden Horde, who conquered Russia in the thirteenth century and penetrated as far west as Hungary and Germany. Russia was Europe's eastern breakwater against Asiatic invaders. For centuries the primary duty of a Russian prince was to protect his people against their devastating raids. The rivers and the southern grasslands were of great importance in shaping the foreign policy of Russia.

The original Slav kingdom, the Kievan monarchy, had its capital at Kiev on the Dnieper River, and its wealth and strength were based on trade along the rivers with Constantinople and northern Europe. The kingdom fought the nomads for several hundred years, but was finally conquered and comprehensively laid waste by the Golden Horde in the thirteenth century. When the resurrection of Russia took place, the leadership did not come from Kiev but from a hitherto obscure town named Moscow in a backward northern province. It was conquered like most of the rest of the Kievan kingdom, and the province was divided into a large number of states, the princes of which held their thrones as tributaries of the Khan of the Golden Horde. Moscow had its beginning in the twelfth century as an insignificant fort on a minor river. Its position was very central, since from it all the river systems of the vast territory that became the Russian empire could be reached by portage. Its rulers gradually enlarged their little kingdom by winning control of the lands of other Russian princes, while at the same time they kept on good terms with their Mongol overlords. When they decided the time was ripe, they broke away from the declining Mongol power and re-established an independent state.

Ivan the Great, the tsar of Moscow in the latter part of the fifteenth century, controlled a kingdom of substantial size, and he judged correctly that his resources were great enough to enable him to extend his frontiers. Working along the rivers, he conquered the remaining independent Russian states, and for the first time obtained a seaport at Archangel on the White Sea. Its value for foreign trade was limited, since the Arctic was frozen for the greater part of the year. Russia was still a landlocked state, and her rulers were determined to continue their expansion along the rivers and win commercial harbors and naval bases that were free from ice the year round. The road to the Baltic was blocked by the territories ruled over by the German Knights of the Sword, the Swedes, and the large kingdom of Poland-Lithuania. To the south the lower courses of the rivers giving access to the Black Sea and the Caspian ran through the territories of various Tartar (i.e., Mongol) khanates. An additional reason for attacking the Tartars was that they continued their traditional practice of making destructive raids into Russia for plunder and slaves.

Three hundred years of war were needed to accomplish these ambitions, and by the late eighteenth century Russia controlled the plain from the Baltic to the Black Sea, and the latter and the Caspian were Russian lakes. Sweden had lost her territories overseas, Lithuania had been annexed, Poland had been partitioned, the khanates had been conquered, and Turkey had been driven back. In the sixteenth and seventeenth centuries the Russians had made their way along the rivers of Siberia and conquered it as far as the Pacific. In the nineteenth century the finishing touches were added. Finland was annexed in 1809, rounding off Russian control of the Gulf of Finland and the upper Baltic. The tsars tried to set up their rule over the Balkans. In the south the Caucasus Mountains were conquered, and approximately the present Russo-Turkish frontier was established. Iran lost her northern provinces, and Russian central Asia was annexed.

The pattern was consistent throughout. Starting from the inland strategic center of Moscow, the tsars extended their dominion in all directions over the vast plain, wherever possible moving their armies along the rivers. Weaker kingdoms were annexed, and the advance was halted only when it reached the ocean or collided with some state too strong to defeat. The expansion did not stop when Russia had attained what might perhaps be described as her natural frontiers. It continued during the nineteenth and twentieth centuries, reaching out after still more seaports and territories to exploit. This brought Russia into conflict with the old Austrian Empire, Germany, Great Britain, Japan, and ultimately the United States.

TWO WORLDS

It is a commonplace that the way of life in Soviet Russia differs in many essentials from that in the Western world. The most obvious examples are the form of government and the lack of freedom for the individual. These differences did not originate in 1917: in many respects the same situation prevailed in tsarist Russia, though to a lesser degree. In 1839 a Frenchman, the Marquis de Custine, visited Russia. He was no lover of democracy and expected to find in autocratic Russia his spiritual home, but he returned to France disillusioned. Perhaps the most interesting thing about the book he wrote on his return is that time and again his descriptions of life a century and a quarter ago still apply to the Soviet Union. De Custine described the government as an all powerful despotism to which even the highest in the land were completely subject. Control of the citizen was so rigorous that it reminded the Frenchman of the discipline of an army rather than the ordered legality of France. The government was feared, and Russians did not dare to speak frankly. When one of the tsar's ministers was in disgrace, even his best friends were afraid to acknowledge acquaintance with him. There was a plague of secret police and informers, and the administration was extremely afraid of criticism and freedom of speech. Russians were forbidden to travel abroad lest they bring back what the Japanese police were later to describe as dangerous thoughts, and foreigners in Russia were automatically suspected of being spies. De Custine's account was not unique: as far back as the sixteenth century ambassadors from western Europe wrote that the tsar was more like an Asiatic despot than the absolute monarchs of Spain and France. Their contemporary Tsar Ivan the Terrible fully agreed with them. He wrote that "The rulers of Russia have not been accountable to anyone, but have been free to reward or to chastise their subjects."

Tsarism used as its instruments the landowning nobility, the army and police, the bureaucracy, and the church. The citizen had only such rights as the tsar chose to allow. When expedient, the government was above the law, and terror—exercised through the secret police and the Siberian prison camps—was a normal process of government. Few changes are necessary to adapt this description to the present government of Russia. The Communist party has taken the place of the landowning nobility. The secret police and the bureaucracy are more all pervasive than ever. Religion is attacked, but the Orthodox Greek Church is tolerated so long as it serves the purposes of the dictatorship. One principal difference between the two regimes is that tsarism was rather more humane, though the principle was the same. Its prison camps probably never had more than 60,000 inmates, while under the Soviet government the number is estimated to be about 12 million. Moreover, communications and organization have improved so vastly in the last thirty years that the present dictatorship is able to exercise a degree of control which the tsar might have wished he had, but could not realize in practice.

THE WESTERN AND RUSSIAN WAYS OF LIFE

There is a consistent pattern of government stretching back to the fifteenth century, and this raises the question why the development of Russia has been so different from that of the West. The answer seems to be that while the bases of their civilizations overlap, they are not identical. The American and the West European way of life are both subdivisions of the Western way of life, for they are fundamentally the same. The difference—that in material progress America is more advanced—is superficial. If the test of civilization were such useful but nonessential gadgets as say indoor plumbing, then many American farmers would have to be classified as totalitarians. As a rough but reliable test, consider what happens to a citizen if he stands up in public and eloquently damns the head of his government. If he is allowed to continue his damnations—if the police are prepared to protect him in doing so—then he is in a state which follows the Western way of life. If, however, he is removed from circulation and winds up in a prison camp, he is on the other side of the iron curtain.

The Western way of life had its origins 2000 years ago in Greece, Rome, and Palestine. Greece was the first to evolve the idea that government should be democratic and not despotic, and to create the first model of a working democracy. From Greece also came the claim to freedom of speech and the other rights of the individual. Rome gave what is implied in the phrase "law and order." The duly constituted authorities of the state had the right to demand the obedience of the citizens as long as they did not overstep their lawful authority, and if they were challenged by illegal means they were entitled to use force to maintain their position. Rome too was the first to build up a code of law which should be the same for all free men and under which all were equal. From Palestine came Christianity, and in the political field that brought the conception of what the New Testament calls charity. Perhaps a better translation of the Greek word would be brotherly love, in the sense that one should behave toward one's neighbors exactly as one would wish to be treated oneself. Christianity also taught the infinite value of the individual soul, and hence by inference of the individual in whom it dwelt. These were new and humanizing ideas in the Greco-Roman world of the first centuries of the Christian era. It knew equal justice for all free men but not for the slaves who made up the bulk of the population. For the underdog there was neither equality nor mercy.

The basic ideas of classical civilization were gradually accepted by the barbarian tribes which destroyed the Roman Empire of the West in the fourth century A.D. Many agents took part in the slow process. To name but a few, the Roman Catholic Church did the pioneer work of Christianizing and partially civilizing the barbarian conquerors of France, England, and the other provinces of the Western empire. The Renaissance, the rediscovery of the books of the classical world, had revolutionary effects. The Reformation was another great influence. Expansion overseas carried the West European way of life to the Western Hemisphere and the British dominions. It is a startling thought that Gandhi's demand for self-government arose in part because the city republic of Athens worked out the theory and practice of democracy 2400 years ago.

The Russians were the easternmost of the peoples of Europe, and their contact with it was limited. The Renaissance and the Reformation did not affect them at all. The principal westernizing influence came from the Eastern Roman Empire. It was economic, cultural, and above all religious, but the semi-Asiatic form of absolute monarchy at Constantinople does not seem greatly to have affected the political development of contemporary Russia. In the fifteenth and sixteenth centuries, when the tsar's power had already taken shape, he borrowed from the political theories of the Byzantine monarchy to justify his autocracy. Byzantine Christianity replaced heathenism in A.D. 989 during the reign of King Vladimir I. He had toyed with the idea of turning Muslim, but decided against it because it forbade alcohol. The king explained that it was quite impossible to be happy in Russia without strong drink. The Russians thus became members of the Orthodox Greek Church, while most of the other peoples of Europe accepted the Western form of

Christianity, Roman Catholicism. The rivalry between the two branches of Christianity led in 1053 to a final rupture between the churches of the East and the West. Henceforth religious hostility reinforced geography in cutting off Russia from the main stream of European development.

The Russian church supported the creation of the absolute monarchy in the fifteenth and sixteenth centuries because it taught that the prince was appointed by God and was responsible only to Him. Even a tyrant must be obeyed, and there was at least the implication that he was not bound to follow the laws which he had established. The church did not claim to be an equal or independent power, but tended strongly to be the obedient servant of the state. This attitude of the Orthodox Greek Church was the legacy of the relations which had existed between it and the emperor in Constantinople. It was in marked contrast to the policy of the papacy, which claimed an authority equal to and independent from that of temporal rulers, and on occasion even compelled them to obey its commands. The Orthodox Greek Church supported autocracy to a degree that was never true of the Roman Catholic Church in Western Europe.

The Mongols had an important influence from the thirteenth to the fifteenth century, the formative period during which tsarist Russia was taking shape. Mongol civilization was a half barbaric copy of that of China, and was completely different from that of Europe. Officials of the Great Khan lived in Russia to collect his taxes, and their princes often visited his court. During the period of decline of the Mongol power quite a number of men of high rank accepted Christianity and took service under the grand duke (later tsar) of Moscow. They and their retainers settled in his territory and intermarried with the Russians.

The Mongol khanate might be described as an absolute monarchy tempered by assassination, and the same description could be applied with a good deal of accuracy to the Russian tsardom. The personal power of the khan was paramount so long as he was feared, and his subjects were well accustomed to arbitrary caprice and despotic subjection. The old Kievan kingdom had been a blend of monarchy, aristocracy, and urban democracy, and the people had a voice in the government. The new Muscovite tsardom which emerged in the fifteenth century was an autocracy. The Mongol invasions had destroyed many of the cities and greatly weakened their power to hold their king in check. The Russian princes cooperated with the Mongol khans, and with their support completed the work of crushing the independence of the cities and also of the nobility. The Mongols imposed unprecedentedly heavy taxes and the conscription of men for their armies, and used the princes as their agents in enforcing their orders. The ultimate result was that the grand duke of Moscow became an absolute sovereign. All classes of the nation from top to bottom were made servants of the state. Service in the army and the administration became the main duty of the nobility and gentry, while the townspeople and peasants paid for all by heavy taxes and forced labor. The peasants were deprived of their freedom and the ownership of their lands and were made serfs. After freedom from the Tartars was achieved, there came three centuries of hard fighting to reach the Baltic and Black Seas and conquer the Mongol khanates. More and not less taxes and soldiers were needed, and this strengthened and perpetuated the absolute monarchy which had begun under the Mongols.

The material side of European civilization began to affect Russia in the sixteenth and seventeenth centuries in the form of better firearms and more effective organization of the army. European ideas did not reach Russia until the eighteenth century, when there was a vogue in aristocratic and court circles for such liberal French writers as Voltaire and Rousseau. The Tsarina Catherine the Great toyed with the idea of agrarian reforms, but finally decided to let bad enough alone. The full force of European ideas reached Russia in the nineteenth century. In the political field they ranged all the way from orthodox liberal democracy to communism. Their adherents were found chiefly among the reformist members of the aristocracy, the business and professional men, the intelligentsia, and the factory workmen. The final upshot was that the Communist minority was able to seize power in 1917; and during the next decade it virtually exterminated the liberals and socialists, along with the supporters of the former tsarist regime. So the end of the whole matter is that the only European ideas which flourish in Russia are those of Karl Marx.

TSARIST FOREIGN POLICY

The aims of tsarist foreign policy extended further than access to the Baltic and the Black Seas. Naval control of the Baltic was sought, but this was blocked by the superior sea power first of Denmark and later of Germany. The Black Sea is a glorified lake, the only exit through the Straits being controlled by Turkey. The tsardom was determined to win possession of this passage, and if possible of sea ports and naval bases in the eastern Mediterranean. Turkey must, therefore, be eliminated as an independent power. This could be achieved by outright annexation, or by compelling it to become a satellite state; and both methods were tried during the nineteenth century.

The policy had widespread ramifications since the Arab world and the Balkans formed part of the Turkish Empire until the early twentieth century. In the Middle East the tsar fished diligently in troubled waters, asserting his claim to be the protector of all members of the Orthodox Greek Church whenever trouble arose between the Christians and the Muslim Turkish government. Every effort was made to strengthen Russia's position in Turkey's Asiatic provinces. The greater part of the Sultan's Balkan subjects belonged to the Orthodox Greek Church, and the majority of them were Slavs. Turkish rule had become unbelievably oppressive and corrupt, and the growth of Balkan nationalisms led to a series of revolts. These were suppressed with great brutality, and the Balkan peoples turned to Russia as their natural protector on grounds of religion and racial kinship. Russia for her part saw the opportunity to kill two birds with one stone. There was genuine sympathy with the Balkan Slavs. At the same time assistance to them in winning their independence could be expected to evoke a decent sense of gratitude, which would lead to the establishment of some sort of Russian control. Russia's sphere of influence would be extended westwards to the Adriatic, which led into the Mediterranean. The power of Turkey would be greatly weakened, and "the road to Constantinople led through the Balkans."

Russia's imperialism roused the opposition of several of the great powers. Britain vastly preferred to see her safely locked up in the Black Sea with Turkey as the independent guardian of the Straits. Austria-Hungary had Balkan ambitions, and she became more and more alarmed at the growth of nationalism among her own subject races, most of whom were Slavs. If the Balkan Slavs became independent under the patronage of Russia, it would encourage her own subjects to redouble their efforts to end Austrian or Hungarian control. Germany came increasingly to feel that her Dual Alliance of 1879 with Austria was vital to her own security. In addition, from the late nineteenth century onward Germany had her own plans for the control and exploitation of Turkey, and did not propose to allow Russia to go off with the prize. Eventually this led to the growth of the conviction in influential Russian circles that the road to Constantinople lay through Berlin. By one combination or another tsarist Russia was always balked in her attempts to subjugate Turkey and establish herself in the Balkans. She played an important part in helping the Balkan peoples to win their independence; but so far as her own ambitions went, her only gain by 1914 was that Serbia was her particular protégé, and was carrying on a vigorous irredentist campaign among the southern Slavs of the Austrian Empire. In the final years before 1914 its government decided that the only remedy was to destroy Serbia, and this was the immediate cause of World War I. Tsarist Russia also failed in her attempt to control navigation on the Danube. This was of importance to many European states besides the Danubian powers. As a result of Russia's defeat in the Crimean War, she was compelled in 1856 to agree that its navigation should be placed under international control.

Control of Iran was included in tsarist aims from about the beginning of the nineteenth century. The attraction was not oil, for that was not discovered until 1908. What Russia sought was commercial ports and naval bases on the Persian Gulf. They would not only serve as trade outlets, but in addition a Russian fleet based on the Gulf would threaten the British sea route to India. Britain countered the move by bolstering Iranian independence, to the extent that southern Iran with its sea ports was kept out of Russia's hands. The nomads of central Asia were conquered between 1864 and 1885, and Russia reached the northern frontier of the unstable state of Afghanistan. Every army which had attacked India for 4000 years had followed the invasian routes that led from the new Russian province of central Asia through the mountains of Afghanistan to the plains of northern India. The British felt that it was essential that Afghanistan should be independent of Russia and if possible in friendly dependence on Great Britain. They became alarmed when attempts were made to establish Russian influence over the Afghan government and suspected that the ultimate purpose was the invasion of India. Until 1919 the British succeeded in keeping Afghanistan as a dependent ally. In 1860 the Chinese dependency of maritime Siberia was added to the Russian empire, and Vladivostok was founded. A lull followed until military communications were improved by the building of the Trans-Siberian Railway in the eighteen nineties. Within a few years Manchuria was brought under Russian control, a strong influence was established over the government of China, and the penetration of Korea began. This advance was checked by defeat in 1905 in the Russo-Japanese War.

Every aim of tsarist foreign policy has been carried over into that of the Soviet government. To a considerable extent the one is a continuation of the other. Communist Russia has attained almost every objective of the tsars except in Turkey and Iran, and its failure here has not been for want of trying. To some extent too Soviet policy since World War II has had as one motive the determination to obtain security against another German invasion. Twice in a single generation Russia was invaded and immense damage done. The government is determined that this must never happen again. This was one reason for making the Baltic a Russian lake, completely dominated by the Red navy and air force. It also explains the Oder-Neisse frontier which, as already pointed out, would make a future German attack on Russia far more costly and dangerous than in 1941. The third element in the Soviet government's policy is the Marxist contribution, and it is this which differentiates it from that of its predecessor.

MARXISM AND SOVIET POLICY

To understand communism it is necessary to remember that having abolished God it replaced Him by Karl Marx. To a devout Communist *Das Kapital* has the same authority as the *New Testament* to a sincere Christian. The meaning of many verses of the Bible is open to diverse interpretations, and the fathers of the church laid down the authoritative significance. The same doubt exists as to the exact meaning of many of Marx's writings, and to deal with this problem the Communists have an equivalent to the Christian theologians. This is Lenin and Stalin, and their pronouncements are binding upon all the faithful. The Marxist-Leninist theory of international relations has a profound influence upon Russian foreign policy. It is based to a large extent upon an ideological analysis of history. Communists believe that when it is applied to current events by the leaders of the party it is an infallible guide to the future. To question their statement of the party line is heresy, and Communists have the strengthening assurance that they cannot possibly be mistaken. Communism is a religion, and its devotees believe in it with a fanatical conviction which cannot be shaken. This fanaticism means that the mind of the convinced Communist is quite different from that of the ordinary man. He has no national loyalty and does not recognize the accepted standards of morality. An action is good if it advances the fulfillment of the Communist dream of world revolution, and bad if it retards it.

The Marxist-Leninist theory of international relations assumes that communism and capitalism are irreconcilable enemies, and that conflict between them is inevitable. Capitalism cannot possibly restrain itself from the exploitation of the toiling masses, and therefore carries the seeds of its own destruction. Its shortsighted greed and robbery arouse increasing hostility, and the result is revolution and the transfer of power to the workers. The role of the Communists is to intensify class hatred, capture the leadership of the discontented masses, and launch the revolution which will overthrow capitalism. Victory in this struggle is absolutely assured. Then will follow the dictatorship of the proletariat under Communist control. "Dictatorship means . . . unlimited power, based on force and not on law." After a necessary interlude devoted to liquidating capitalists, bourgeois, fascists, and other undesirables, the millennium will be established.

Lenin added to Marxism the theory that capitalism reaches its final and decaying stage in imperialism, when it is inevitably driven to conquer the underdeveloped areas of the world in order to control their raw materials and markets. One result of this is increasing rivalry between the capitalist powers and periodical wars between them for the ownership of colonies. They thereby weaken one another and play into the hands of communism. The second result is that capitalist-imperialist exploitation ultimately provokes a struggle of the colonial peoples for freedom from their oppressors. Their success will appreciably weaken the Western centers of capitalism. Communists must therefore do their utmost to help the colonial peoples to win their independence. Since they are not ready to accept communism, the appeal to them cannot be made in Marxist terms. Instead the Communists must exploit local grievances, e.g., against the moneylender and the landowner, and above all pose as nationalists working for freedom. They must collaborate with nationalist parties, and gradually bring them under Communist control. Ho Chi-minh's career in Vietnam is a good example of these tactics. The ultimate aim is the creation of a Communist state on the Russian model. Mao Tse-tung has entered upon this stage. In this way capitalism is weakened and communism strengthened by the transfer of a territory from Western to Communist control.

The local agents for bringing about revolts in the capitalist countries and the colonies are the national Communist parties. Russia is the headquarters of world communism, its brains and directing force, and also the basis of its power. She represents the first stage of the world revolution and a mighty base for its further development. The national parties must obey unquestioningly all orders from Moscow, and not the slightest deviation from them can be tolerated. At the appropriate moment Russia will intervene decisively to bring about the global triumph of communism. Until then the primary duty is to defend Russia and increase her power. Inside Russia this takes the form of the Five Year Plans and the strengthening of the armed forces. In the world outside it means that the Communist parties support every policy approved by their Russian masters and oppose those which they condemn. When France joined NATO, Thorez, the French Communist leader, announced that if the Red army invaded France, his party would work for its victory.

Communists believe that all capitalist states are filled with fear and hatred of the Soviet government, and that they are incessantly scheming to destroy it. Hence, there has been an abiding dread that in spite of their rivalries the capitalist powers might combine against it. The ideology of the Communists taught them that it was their duty to destroy the capitalist world, and their fear persuaded them that their self-preservation required it. It was true that in 1918–1920 the Western powers assisted the Russian enemies of the Communists in their attempts to overthrow the regime, but after the final failure in 1920 the policy was abandoned. After that date no state during the interwar period except Germany and Japan contemplated war against Russia. The cooperation of the Western powers with Russia during World War II was powerless to shake the illusion of their implacable hostility. Both before and after World War II Moscow did its best to bring about the overthrow of the capitalist governments. Thereby it gradually aroused the foreign hostility that it feared. Since 1945 suspicion has been directed primarily against the United States and only secondarily against Britain, because Moscow believes that the former is the rising and the latter the declining power. Its ideology teaches it that the United States will find herself becoming increasingly imperialist and driven to look for overseas markets and sources of raw materials. Moscow realizes too that the

United States and the British Empire in combination are the only power group on earth capable of meeting Russia on equal terms. It fears the combination of strength and independence, and for this reason it never loses an opportunity of trying to create distrust and ill will between the two.

Lenin once said that "the existence of the Soviet Republic side by side with imperialistic [i.e., capitalist] states for a long time is unthinkable. One or the other must triumph in the end. And before that end supervenes a series of frightful collisions between the Soviet Republic and the bourgeois states will be inevitable." Stalin quoted this statement with approval and underlined it by adding that "A peaceful victory over capitalism is not to be expected." By the statements of their leaders the Communists believe in the inevitability of conflict. Yet occasionally in interviews with Western foreign correspondents they have held out the possibility of the peaceful coexistence of the Communist and capitalist worlds, and have denied that they ever had plans for a world revolution.

The seeming contradiction disappears when one grasps the distinction which the Communists make between strategy and tactics, and also their conception of truth. Strategy is the general plan of campaign to win victory for Soviet foreign policy, while tactics are the maneuvers in detail by which the general plan is brought nearer to success. The strategic aims are to strengthen Russia at home, to aggravate the class conflict between the proletariat and the bourgeoisie in the capitalist states, to separate the capitalist powers from one another, and to arouse revolts against them in their colonies. The final objective of the strategy is to bring about the triumph of communism on a global scale by the destruction of capitalism. This is ultimately to be attained by revolutions and "a series of frightful collisions." Ideology teaches that the fall of capitalism is inevitable, and that time is on the side of the Communists. Therefore, no need exists to force the pace and strive for quick results. If one maneuver fails, others can be tried, for the end is sure. There is no reason to believe that the Communists have ever departed from their grand strategy.

Tactics are a totally different matter, and must be "highly flexible." They are determined by "a continual assessment of the status of forces in both the capitalist and the socialist systems." According to Stalin, they must be adjusted to the ebb and flow of the forces favoring revolution. Aggressive tactics should be timed with a rising tide; tactics of defense and even retreat go with an ebbing tide. So from 1941 to 1945 there was a rapprochement with the Western powers and the Communist parties supported the war effort because Russia urgently needed Anglo-American help against Germany. Germany's defeat and that of Japan combined with the weakening of Britain and France created a unique opportunity for establishing new positions of power in Europe and Asia. So the cold war replaced collaboration, and the

Communists abroad obediently toed the party line. There is no reason to think that the periodical references to the possibility of peaceful coexistence are anything more than tactics, intended to delude the Western powers into believing that Moscow has changed its strategy.

The Communist conception of truth must also be borne in mind. Truth is not absolute and immutable, but is created by the Kremlin to suit its own purposes. This causes no difficulty to the party members since they have been trained as rigorously as soldiers to accept without questioning whatever their leaders say. "Faith is the faculty by which we are able to believe that which we know is not true." This explains the gymnastic ability of the faithful to turn back somersaults and reverse themselves whenever a new party line goes out from Moscow. As regards foreign states, it is not necessary to keep faith with capitalists. The purposes of communism are so good that it is exempt from the petty restrictions of "bourgeois morality." The end justifies the means, and no Communist has any qualms of conscience because of the record of Soviet Russia for broken promises and treaties.

COMMUNIST ORGANIZATION

The guiding principle of recruitment to the Communist party is that the members are carefully selected after long and thorough investigation. They are required to be thoroughly trained in Marxist-Leninist theory, and they are centrally controlled from Moscow under rigid discipline. Periodical purges are held to weed out weaklings, for the purpose is to build up an elite and not the mass parties of the democratic nations. All other parties must be destroyed save when tactics make a temporary alliance with them expedient, like the Popular Fronts of the 'thirties. Inside Russia a single party which has ruthlessly crushed all opposition controls the whole power of the state. The real center of authority is not the Soviet government but an executive core within the central committee which controls the party. Until 1952 it was known as the Politburo and since then as the Presidium. It would seem that this was a change in name much more than in realities. The Presidium makes all the important decisions of domestic and foreign policy, and transmits its orders to the appropriate organ of government for execution. The complicated structure of the Soviet government is not the real seat of authority, but merely the machinery through which the Presidium carries out some of its decisions.

The Third or Communist International, also known as the Comintern, was founded in Moscow in 1919 as the headquarters and center of control for Communist parties throughout the world. Nominally, it was an international body independent of the government. Actually, the Politburo dominated its policy, tactics and personnel. The Comintern was the Politburo's general staff for the promotion of world revolution, while more orthodox activities were handled by the Soviet ministry for foreign affairs. By this dualism in machinery Russia was able to combine diplomatic correctness with flagrant interference in the domestic affairs of foreign nations. The Soviet government negotiated many treaties in which it promised not to promote sedition. When a government protested that the agreement was being broken, the Soviet foreign ministry would reply that its conduct was above reproach, but that it could not possibly interfere with the revolutionary activities of an independent organization like the Comintern. Since it was known that the Politburo controlled both the ministry and the Third International, the effect upon foreign governments was to create an intense distrust of Russian good faith. The Comintern was officially dissolved in 1943, as a conciliatory gesture toward the Western powers, but the staff apparently remained in Moscow and carried on its work. Moreover, there were other ways, public and secret, by which orders could be sent out. In 1947 the Comintern was reborn as the Cominform or Communist Information Bureau of some of the European Communist parties.

THE SOVIETS AND THE WEST: THE FIRST PHASE

The Bolsheviks, the Russian Communist party, seized power in 1917 and established their dictatorship. In 1918 they were forced to accept the harsh terms of the Treaty of Brest Litovsk dictated by a victorious Germany. The new dictatorship soon became involved in a series of nationalist and counterrevolutionary wars. Russia's subject races in Europe, the Caucasus, and central Asia seized the opportunity to revolt. The White Russians, a mixture of supporters of the tsar, socialists, and other opponents of the regime, attacked the Communists in various parts of Russia and Siberia, and received some help from the Western powers. By 1920 the uprisings had been crushed, and the West abandoned its attempts to overthrow the Communist regime. The nationalist revolts in the Caucasus and central Asia were defeated, and Russian rule re-established. In Europe Finland, Estonia, Latvia, Lithuania, and Poland won their freedom. Russia had lost most of the territory conquered by Peter the Great and his successors, and was almost cut off from the Baltic. The Russians were too exhausted after six years of war to continue the struggle, but in the long run the precarious independence of the new states would depend upon whether collective security under the League of Nations became a reality.

The Comintern was established in 1919, and a vigorous campaign was carried on to promote revolutions abroad. There were uprisings in Germany, and short-lived dictatorships were set up in Bavaria and Hungary. Financial assistance was given to the British trade unions in the general strike of

1926, but the Kremlin was disgusted and disillusioned when the strikers played football with the police guarding private property. The League of Nations was bitterly denounced as a capitalist conspiracy. In China Russian advisers helped the Kuomintang party to conquer the country, and lost no opportunity of injuring Western and particularly British economic interests. The outcome of all this effort was that not a single country outside Russia had gone permanently Communist. Gradually formal diplomatic relations were established with foreign states. The capitalist countries wanted to regain their pre-1914 trade with Russia, and the Communist dictatorship badly needed loans for reconstruction and development. Both sides were disappointed in their expectations.

The death of Lenin in 1924 was followed by a struggle for power between Trotsky and Stalin, in which the former was finally defeated in 1929. Stalin's triumph was more than a personal victory: it meant also a change of policy. Trotsky emphasized the necessity of vigorous support for revolutionary action in the capitalist states. Stalin objected that for the time being the attempt had failed. He considered that subversive activity abroad should be toned down and continued only on a minor scale. Stalin emphasized a national policy, the strengthening of communism in Russia. Its practical embodiment was the successive Five Year Plans, the first of which was launched in 1928. The U.S.S.R. was to be transformed from an overwhelmingly agricultural into an industrial state. The rudimentary network of roads and railways was to be immensely extended, and large state farms were to replace the small individual holdings of the peasants. Particular emphasis was given to the development of heavy industry: the purpose of the Five Year Plans was as much military as economic.

THE RAPPROCHEMENT WITH THE WEST

The outside world as a whole had no intention of attacking Russia; but there were two exceptions, Japan and Nazi Germany. When Japan took over control of Manchuria, she virtually eliminated Russia from the province, and there was constant and increasingly dangerous friction between them. Russia was anxious to avoid war in the Far East as long as the threat from Hitler continued. He had an intense hatred of communism, and his program for Russia had been frankly stated in his book *Mein Kampf*. "When we talk of more ground and room in Europe [for German settlement] we can in the first place think only of Russia and the border states depending on her [the territory lost to Russia in World War I]. . . . The gigantic empire in the East is ripe for collapse." When Hitler became dictator of Germany and began to rearm, the threat assumed concrete form, and the collaboration with the U.S.S.R. which had existed since 1922 was broken off. Obviously it was highly desirable for the Soviet Union to make friends in the capitalist world, and the Kremlin decided to build an antifascist front.

In 1934 Russia joined the League of Nations, which she had previously condemned as a "Holy Alliance of the bourgeoisie for the suppression of the proletarian revolution." Her representatives were the foremost champions of peace, disarmament, and collective security. The other League members were arraigned for failing to take effective action against Mussolini's conquest of Ethiopia, although there was no suggestion of active Soviet participation and sales of oil to Italy were increased. When the Spanish civil war broke out, Stalin gave moderate help to the government and roundly denounced France and Britain for their refusal to take concerted action to assist it. In 1935 mutual defensive alliances were signed with France and Czechoslovakia. The latter contained the clause that the treaty obligation to give assistance should be binding only if France had already gone to the aid of the country attacked.

Stalin's policy during the Munich crisis is obscure. Soviet propaganda gave the impression that Russia was ready to help Czechoslovakia, but that nothing came of this because France failed to carry out her treaty obligation and Britain refused to support France. The statement is true insofar as France and Britain are concerned, but it does not explain some remarkable omissions on Moscow's part. For one thing, Czechoslovakia was cut off from Russia by Poland and Rumania, and if the Red army were to take part in the war, it would have to cross their territory. Both states were afraid of Russia, and if they could have been persuaded to grant rights of passage, they would have insisted on guarantees that the Soviet troops would withdraw at the end of the war. Only Moscow could give these assurances, but it never discussed the question with the Polish and Rumanian governments. Instead it asked France to do so, and as could have been foreseen, the French request was rejected. Russia may have been prepared to help Czechoslovakia, but it does look as if she were no more anxious than France and Britain to precipitate a war. When the Munich Conference took place, Russia was excluded from it, and this aroused her resentment. The policy of France and Britain throughout the whole affair increased Stalin's distrust of their intentions and reliability and was one stage on the road toward his agreement with Germany in August 1939.

THE RUSSO-GERMAN PACT

From the time when Russia joined the League until the Munich Agreement, at any rate, Stalin had believed that an alliance between East and West would stop Hitler. After Munich he scathingly criticized France and Britain for their policy of appeasement and accused them of encouraging Germany to attack Russia. Yet just when Chamberlain and Daladier slowly and reluctantly abandoned appeasement and began to move in the direction of war on behalf of Poland, Stalin himself adopted an appeasement policy and encouraged Hitler to go to war in the West. Stalin's motives for this change of policy are in part at least conjectural. He himself said that his action was the result of the British and French appeasement of Hitler at Munich. This cannot be reconciled with the Soviet proposal of a military alliance with them in April, 1939, months after Munich. Alternatively it has been said that the explanation lay in Stalin's fear that France and Britain were pretending to negotiate with him, while at the same time they were trying to come to terms with Hitler and give him a free hand in eastern Europe. It is true that Stalin distrusted Chamberlain and Daladier as much as he did Hitler, but the question has still to be answered why he preferred one set of "capitalist imperialists" to the other. It has been suggested that Stalin's motive was to gain time to strengthen his armed forces. As against this the Soviet economy was not mobilized for large-scale armament production until after the fall of France in 1940. So Stalin cannot have felt it essential to buy time for intensive armament in August, 1939.

Soviet demands for territory were certainly one reason for Stalin's decision. He was determined to recover the provinces which Russia had lost after World War I. Britain and France refused to agree to his terms, while Hitler was prepared to pay this price for his support. Their determination to partition Poland gave them a community of interests which tended to bring them together. Furthermore, it seems likely that the Soviet leaders believed they would benefit from a war between Germany and the Western powers. They realized that if Hitler were assured of their neutrality, he would invade Poland, and that then war would break out in the West. Stalin seems to have overestimated the strength of the French army and to have believed the war would be long and exhausting. France, Britain, and Germany would all be enfeebled, and according to Communist theory domestic Communist revolts would break out. Until then the U.S.S.R. would remain at peace and grow stronger, and she would emerge as the dominant state in Europe. She could then use her power to ensure the victory of communism in a number of European states. As one Russian put it, "The Russia of the Soviets emerged from the last war; the Europe of the Soviets will emerge from the next."

SOVIET CONQUESTS 1939–1940

In 1939 Poland was partitioned for the fourth time between Russia and Germany. In 1939–1940 Estonia, Latvia, and Lithuania were forced to accept Soviet control. The Balts, the German landowning and ruling class who had dominated these countries for 700 years, were deported to Germany.

This ended the story of German colonization of the upper Baltic which had begun with the conquests of the Knights of the Teutonic Order. Finland refused to make cessions of territory which would have made her incapable of defending herself against Russia, and in November, 1939, the Red army attacked. The Finns defended themselves with great skill and tenacity, but were defeated in March, 1940, and forced to cede more territory than had originally been demanded. When Hitler invaded Russia, Finland entered the war on the German side. Russia had now recovered the territory in northeastern Europe which she had lost after World War I, and with it the access to the Baltic which had been won in the eighteenth century.

In 1940 Rumania was forced to cede the provinces of Bessarabia and northern Bukovina. The former was a very fertile agricultural area, with a mixed population of some 3 million. The Rumanians comprised about 56 percent, Ukrainians and Russians 23 percent, and Jews 12 percent. Russia conquered Bessarabia from the Turks in 1812, was forced to cede part of it to Rumania in 1856, recovered it in 1878, and lost the whole province in 1918. The Soviet government never accepted the Rumanian occupation, and fear of a possible future attack was a principal reason for Rumania's alliance with France. By retaking the province in 1940 Stalin recovered the last of the territories lost after World War I and a valuable addition to the wheat lands of southern Russia. He also advanced his frontier to the lower course of the Danube river and so laid the foundation for the revival of the old tsarist claim that the Danube should be controlled solely by the Danubian states, headed by Russia. Bukovina had never been part of Russia, but had been a province of the former Austrian empire until it passed to Rumania after World War I. The mixed population included Rumanians and Ukrainians. Strategically Bukovina was important since its railways linked together the Soviet annexations of Bessarabia, Ruthenia (later taken from Czechoslovakia), and the Polish province of Galicia acquired in 1939.

SOVIET-GERMAN COLLABORATION

At first the cooperation of the two dictatorships seemed to work very satisfactorily for both. Hitler was able to devote his full attention to the war in the west, and the supplies he received from the Soviet Union were an important help to him. Stalin could reflect that he had gained valuable territory without any fighting except in Finland. In the autumn of 1940 Molotov went to Berlin, and Hitler suggested an amicable division of territory. Molotov replied that the proposals were good as far as they went, but that they did not go far enough. Russia wanted more, but Hitler declined to increase his offer. The conversations are significant since they give further evidence of the similarity between Soviet and tsarist policy. Russia made it clear that her price for cooperation included Iran, a military and naval base at the Dardanelles, and a further strengthening of her position in Turkey by an alliance with Bulgaria. The failure of the negotiations left both sides dissatisfied, and in June, 1941, Hitler invaded the U.S.S.R. So in the end Stalin was pushed into the alliance which he had rejected two years earlier. On his part, it was strictly a marriage of convenience.

POSTWAR SOVIET FOREIGN POLICY

The outcome of the war gave Russia an unprecedented opportunity of realizing ambitions which the tsars had dreamed of but never been able to attain, owing to the opposition of the great powers of Europe. That obstacle was now largely removed in Europe and the Far East. Moscow was also determined to take such measures of security as would make impossible another German invasion. Finally there was the contribution of Marxist-Leninist ideology, which led the Kremlin to regard the noncommunist states as irreconcilable enemies. The wartime alliance was dismissed as a strictly temporary change of tactics. The American and British idea of a permanent collaboration of the Big Three to win the peace evoked no response. Moscow's ideology taught it that a world war would be followed by a widespread extension of communism. Perhaps this might not be universal—the United States in particular, the citadel of capitalism, would be hard to overthrow—but Europe and Asia offered a most promising field of exploitation. The first stage was to create a Soviet bloc of satellite states in eastern and central Europe. The course of the war had brought these countries under the sole control of the Red army. The only restraint upon Stalin was the agreement he had signed at Yalta with President Roosevelt and Churchill that their three countries would cooperate in assisting the peoples of central and eastern Europe to create democratic governments of their own choice. American and British commissioners were sent to several countries so that they could discharge this assignment in collaboration with a Soviet colleague. They found themselves completely ignored and their protests disregarded, while the Russian carried out his instructions to set up dictatorships in collaboration with the local Communists.

THE TECHNIQUE OF THE INSIDE JOB

Tsarist imperialism followed the traditional pattern. A Russian army invaded the country, defeated the defending forces, and established Russian government. This smash and grab raid had at least the merit that everyone concerned was fully aware of the exact situation. It was a frank and open war of conquest. The Politburo devised a far more subtle form of imperialism in which the people to be conquered to a large extent brought about their

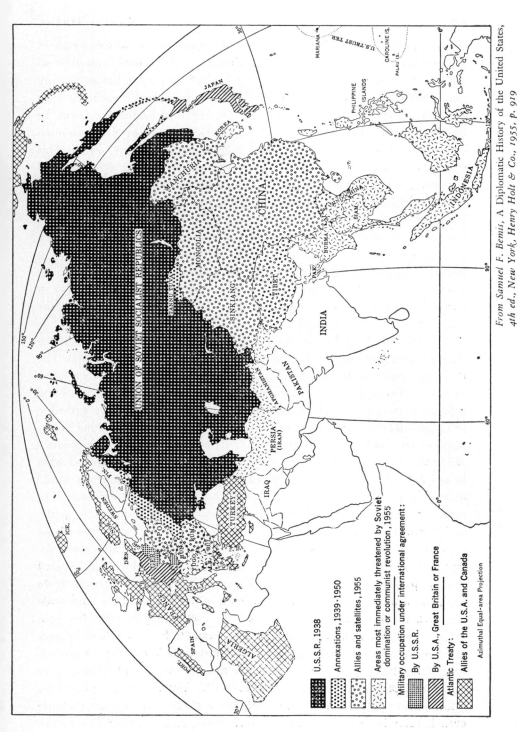

From Samuel F. Bemis, A Diplomatic History of the United States, 4th ed., New York, Henry Holt & Co., 1955, p. 919

Expansion of Soviet Power in Eurasia, 1939–1955

Legend:

U.S.S.R., 1938

Annexations, 1939-1950

Allies and satellites, 1955

Areas most immediately threatened by Soviet domination or communist revolution, 1955

Military occupation under international agreement:

By U.S.S.R.

By U.S.A., Great Britain or France

Atlantic Treaty:

Allies of the U.S.A. and Canada

Azimuthal Equal-area Projection

own conquest. Usually the Red army of occupation took no overt part in proceedings. In Rumania and Poland, though, it did actively intervene to crush a too obstinate opposition. Usually it played a passive but paralyzing role in the transition to the police state. Opponents of the Communists were afraid to campaign vigorously against them lest they be too successful. In Czechoslovakia it was argued that unless a satisfactory number of Communists were elected to the legislature, the Red army might impose its control. This method of indirect aggression had the merit of confusing the defenders and weakening their resistance. It also made interference by the Western powers far more difficult, for they could not say that they were intervening to prevent a foreign invasion. Far from that the *coup d'état* was always carried out by citizens of the state itself. Moreover they always called themselves the voice of the people, and asserted that they were establishing democracy by removing fascists from power. Especially in the early postwar years the uncritical admiration for Russia in the Western democracies was so strong that it would have been difficult to persuade their peoples that the exact opposite was true.

Stalin could have had the voluntary cooperation of at least most of the states of central and eastern Europe without making them into satellites. The majority looked to Russia, the great Slav power, as their natural protector against Germany, and they were prepared to collaborate in foreign policy and defense. At the same time they were strongly nationalistic, and they wished to be independent and to control their own domestic affairs. Stalin did not understand or tolerate freedom of action inside Russia: the alternatives were total obedience or oblivion. Being a logical man, he would not allow abroad what he did not permit at home. The problem was to find a party which would invariably sacrifice the interests of its own country to those of Russia. The only one which satisfied this requirement was the local Communist party, and except in Czechoslovakia it was never more than a few percent of the population. This was understandable, for all the present satellite states except Czechoslovakia were overwhelmingly agricultural. The typical citizen was the peasant who owned or rented a small farm. He might want more land, and if he were a tenant, he might wish to rid himself of the landowner and own his own farm. In other words he might support what has been called "green communism," but first and foremost he was a firm believer in private property and opposed to the Communist policy of the nationalization of the land. In these peasant states manufacturing and mining were underdeveloped, and the urban workmen—the best recruiting ground for Communists—proportionately few. Only in Czechoslovakia was there a fairly even balance between industry and agriculture, and a sizable Communist party.

The typical state of central and eastern Europe had the multiple party system. The first step of the Communists was to form a Popular Front with the Socialist and other parties which could be induced to work with them. In these coalitions the allies provided the necessary mass following, while the Communists furnished the direction and control. Frequently their leaders were brought home in the baggage carts of the Red army, after it had occupied the country. Often they had been living in Moscow so long that they had become thoroughly Russianized, and sometimes they had taken out Soviet citizenship. They were regarded as more reliable than local Communists who had not been exposed to long indoctrination in Moscow. The Communists thoughtfully allotted to their allies all the governmental positions which were of lesser importance, and themselves took those which enabled them to dominate the state. The president of a European republic for instance was merely a dignified figurehead—for example, a Socialist in this position made excellent window dressing. The uninitiated were convinced that the Communists were not trying to grasp power. The minister of the interior on the contrary held a key position, and was invariably a Communist. He controlled domestic administration and also the government officials. This term has a wider significance than in the United States, for many officials who are elected in America are under the orders of the minister of the interior in Europe. He also controlled the police and the secret police, the latter recruited as far as possible from Communists. They were carefully trained in the most effective methods of the Gestapo and the Russian secret police and were an essential part of the democratic process Soviet style.

The Communists captured the leadership of the trade unions, and often won popular support by posing as champions of needed economic and political reforms. In Hungary they broke up the large estates and divided them among the land-hungry peasants—with the mental reservation that later they would nationalize the farms. Hand in hand with this went the destruction of the anticommunist parties. Censorship of the press enabled the Communists to suppress editorials and news unfavorable to them, and through their control of the supply of newsprint they drastically reduced the circulation of anticommunist while expanding that of Communist papers. Control of the national broadcasting systems made it possible to prevent anticommunist speakers from having much time to give their views. Voluntary-compulsory parades of factory workmen were used to intimidate opponents. Meetings of the opposition were broken up by Communist strong-arm squads and the facts misrepresented in the controlled press. The secret police were not idle: there were arbitrary arrests, forced confessions of plotting against the government, and appropriate sentences. The old German concentration camps were reopened under entirely new management, and soon contained a mixed population of Nazi collaborators and democrats who had opposed both the Nazis and the Communists. Even more than the arrests the fear of arrest caused a reign of terror. Gradually the anticommunist parties became disorganized and discouraged, and the time approached when the people might freely elect their government as per the Yalta Conference Agreement.

Unkind observers have pointed out that the Communists never won an election when they themselves did not count the votes. This was sometimes true, for in the Rumanian election the Communist candidate in many districts was officially declared to have received more ballots than the total number of voters on the register. Complete reliance was not placed upon this method however. In the Polish general election of January, 1948, the secret police began arresting candidates and prominent supporters of anticommunist parties some weeks before the election. The purpose was twofold, to paralyze the party organizations as far as possible, and to terrorize the voters. The secret ballot was abolished so that on election day the Communist in each polling booth could see how every one voted, after noting the name and address. The result was that the Polish Communists and their fellow travelers received about 80 percent of the votes, while in prewar elections the Communists never polled more than 5 percent. The final destruction of the anticommunist parties soon followed. Their leaders either fled the country or were arrested and executed for treason.

The last stage was to disband the Popular Front, which had outlived its usefulness. The members of the other parties were invited to dissolve their organizations and join the Communist party, which would henceforth be the sole representative of the people. Some of the leaders were so unwise as to protest that this was ungenerous. They had done yeoman service in putting the Communists in power, and their only reward was to be eaten last of all. This explains why some leaders of the Socialist and other Popular Front parties went to swell the heterogeneous population of the prison camps. The survivors soon saw the light, and so the government became a single-party Communist dictatorship, naked and unashamed. Russia required not only cooperation on general lines, but one identical policy for the satellite countries down to the smallest detail, dictated by the interests of the Soviet Union alone. Whenever the two conflicted, the interests of the satellite must be sacrificed. This was achieved by creating Communist dictatorships. As in Russia the real authority did not lie with the nominal governments but with the party which controlled them. The local Communist parties themselves were closely controlled by the Politburo in Moscow. The satellite states had no real independence or sovereignty.

Next to the anticommunist political parties the most serious opposition in the satellite states came from the churches, especially those which had links with the West. Traditionally the Orthodox Greek churches were obedient to the state, and they were brought under control without difficulty. Protestant and Jewish church leaders strongly opposed communism, but except in Eastern Germany they were not very numerous. Recalcitrant leaders were removed, the churches were confined to purely spiritual duties, and they were cut off from any close connection with coreligionists in the West. The same policy was followed toward the Roman Catholic Church, which the Communists regarded as their most dangerous opponent. Outstanding incidents in this persecution were the trial and imprisonment of Archbishop Stepinac in Yugoslavia and of Cardinal Mindszenty in Hungary.

By 1948 the Communists had gained complete control in Poland, Rumania, Bulgaria, Yugoslavia, Albania, and Hungary. Finland managed to retain its domestic independence, and the government was anticommunist. In foreign policy, however, the Finns had scrupulously to avoid any action which might arouse Soviet suspicions. Militarily the country was at Russia's mercy, for the peace which was imposed after World War II left it indefensible. The loss of the seaport at Petsamo on the Arctic cut off Finland from direct contact with the American and British fleets; the Soviet naval base at Porkkala (given up in 1955) was close to the capital Helsinki; and the annexation of the province of Karelia deprived her of the frontier which the Finns defended so stubbornly in 1940. The three Baltic states of Lithuania, Latvia, and Estonia were annexed outright to Russia. Part of their population was deported and replaced by reliable Russians, thereby removing any risk of future nationalist revolts. The former German province of East Prussia was divided between Russia and Poland. The Soviet zone of Eastern Germany was well on the way to becoming a satellite state, though from motives of expediency the anticommunist parties were permitted to exist as anaemic and frustrated ghosts. The international control of the Danube was replaced by control by the Danubian states—most of them Soviet satellites—and Moscow successfully restored the tsarist policy of Russian control of navigation on the river. In the whole of eastern and central Europe and the Balkans only Greece, Turkey, and part of Austria remained free. The United States and Great Britain made a number of protests. The Kremlin ignored them since it realized that possession was nine points of the law, and that Washington and London were not prepared to challenge its position by force.

CZECHOSLOVAKIA

Ever since World War I Czechoslovakia had been the only genuine democracy in central and eastern Europe, and its president Beneš had been an international figure for thirty years. In 1943 he made a treaty of alliance with Russia, and after the war he collaborated loyally with her, refusing to believe that she would destroy the Czech democracy. His confidence was shaken when Russia annexed Ruthenia, the Czech province in the Carpathian Mountains which was inhabited by Ukrainians. (This carried Russia across the mountains and enabled her to dominate Hungary. The Carpathians were the defensive barrier that protected Hungary, the middle valley of the Danube, from invaders coming from the plains of Russia. The mountains in Ruthenia were crossed by passes which were traditional roads of invasion, and these were now in Russian hands.) Beneš acquiesced in the annexation, and continued his support of Moscow. In the election of 1946 the Czech Communists won 38 percent of the votes, and gradually they wormed their way into a position of power by methods similar to those already described. In 1948 they seized control by a *coup d'état* and set up their dictatorship. Until it was too late, the other Czech parties which collaborated with them believed that the Communists supported parliamentary democracy. The *coup d'état* of 1948 was probably one of the worst blunders of Soviet foreign policy. Russia had all that she needed, a faithful ally that would cooperate in everything essential. Czechoslovakia, more than any other state in the Russian sphere of influence, had a unique position in the regard of the Western world. The overthrow of its democracy was a profound shock, and hastened the awakening of the West to the purposes of Soviet foreign policy.

MILITARY ALLIANCES

The members of the Soviet bloc are knit together by military alliances far more tightly and efficiently than the Western nations in NATO. The NATO allies have to make decisions in a council where each member has a vote, and agreement must be reached through persuasion and compromise. In the Soviet bloc policy is settled in Moscow, and orders are transmitted to the satellites. Between 1943 and 1948 military alliances were negotiated between Russia and Czechoslovakia, Yugoslavia, Poland, Rumania, Hungary, Bulgaria, and Finland. The European satellites also have defensive alliances with one another. Gradually the satellite armed forces are being provided with Russian equipment, and Soviet military missions have supervised training. Often Russian officers have been appointed to high commands, thereby strengthening Soviet control. The standardization of equipment and training adds greatly to the effectiveness of the Soviet bloc armed forces. In 1955 a mutual defensive alliance was made at Warsaw between Russia and seven satellites—Poland, Czechoslovakia, Hungary, Rumania, Bulgaria, Albania, and East Germany. Marshal Koniev, the commander in chief of the Soviet army, was appointed commander in chief of the allied armies, with the satellite commanders as his deputies. The new arrangements did little more than give formal expression to the existing military situation in the Soviet bloc.

ECONOMIC LINKS

Before World War II the European satellite states apart from Czechoslovakia were predominantly producers of food and raw materials and importers of manufactures. Foreign trade was largely with Germany and Western Europe, which imported food and raw materials and exported manufactures. Trade with Russia was limited, for she could not supply her own domestic needs for manufactures and had little to offer. Since World War II trade with Russia has been very greatly increased, while with the West it has proportionately diminished. This reorientation has been far more to the benefit of Russia than of her satellites. Their products have been an important help in carrying out her Five Year Plans, but she has not been able to provide them with adequate quantities of manufactures. This policy has been enforced upon the satellites by their Communist dictatorships. It has aroused a good deal of discontent even in Communist circles, and the continuance of the trade is one of the evidences of the tightness of Russian control. The ultimate aim seems to be to make the Soviet bloc a self-contained economic unit. Close trade relations are being developed with China, which supplies food and raw materials in return for manufactures from Russia and her satellites.

The Soviet government has become the owner of a vast number of enterprises in the satellite states. In Eastern Germany most of the factories were nationalized, and many of them were linked with similar Russian plants in great combines controlled from Moscow. Outside Germany many properties were acquired under the guise of reparations for war damages. It was agreed at the Potsdam Conference that all German assets in the countries occupied by the Red army might be taken as Russian war reparations. No definition was made of what constituted a German asset, so Stalin obligingly supplied one and acted on it. A German asset was anything which had been acquired by purchase, theft, or any other means at all. Since the Germans had done a remarkably thorough job of looting in the countries they occupied, Russia became the owner of a wide variety of valuable properties. Another device was to suggest to the government of a satellite state that it and Russia should form a joint company to monopolize the development of the national resources of oil, bauxite, coal, etc. The managing director would be a Russian, and he need not consult the directors appointed by the satellite government. Communists are fond of talking about the exactions of Western imperialism, but the most grasping of Western exploiters would find it hard to come up to the standard set by the Russians.

An industrial revolution is developing in the satellite states and Eastern Germany. The Soviet zone of Germany was already quite heavily industrialized in 1945, as was Czechoslovakia. The other countries had in the aggregate a considerable supply of raw materials, largely undeveloped. There was little local capital, but their 90 million people provided an abundant labor supply. In some of the countries chronic rural underemployment existed since there were too many peasants and farm laborers trying to win a living from the land. Soviet policy has been to develop as quickly as possible a program of forced industrial expansion, which would supplement production in Russia herself. The emphasis has been placed on fuel and power, steel and chemicals, heavy engineering and precision tools. The consumer goods so badly needed by the inhabitants were slighted. The output is already considerably larger than before the war, and it is reported that the satellite countries produce half as much coal and electric power, about one third as much steel, and more than one quarter as much oil as the U.S.S.R.

THE EXCOMMUNICATION OF TITO

Tito, a Croat who had been a Communist agent for a generation, had risen in 1937 to the rank of head of the party in Yugoslavia. He ruthlessly purged it and made it a disciplined and effective body completely under his control. When Russia was invaded in June, 1941, he raised an army of guerillas known as Partisans and began to fight the Germans who had conquered Yugoslavia earlier that year. They were already being opposed by another guerila force called Chetniks under the command of a Serbian, Colonel Mihailovich of the Yugoslav army. The colonel was loyal to King Peter, and was hostile to communism and to Soviet control of the country. Tito, on the contrary, was a convinced Communist who was determined to abolish the king's government and establish his own dictatorship. The result was that the guerillas fought one another as well as the foreign invader. Mihailovich was badly equipped and increasingly avoided active operations against the Germans to save the civilian population from the wholesale executions carried out in reprisal whenever the enemy was attacked. Tito increased his assaults despite the suffering they brought upon the people. Churchill's policy was that he would supply arms to whoever would fight the Germans irrespective of ideology, and he was persuaded that to help Tito would give the best results. After 1943 British supplies were given only to him. By the end of the war he had largely freed Yugoslavia from the Germans and reduced his rival to insignificance. The Red army had little to do with his victory, and as far as he owed his success to foreign assistance, it was to Churchill. In 1945 Tito established a Communist republic with himself as dictator, and in 1946 Mihailovich was captured and shot. Yugoslavia became a Soviet satellite state, and in domestic and foreign affairs alike Tito modeled his policy on that of Russia.

In 1948 the Cominform excommunicated him for deviations from the pure Marxist-Leninist gospel, and called upon the Yugoslav comrades to overthrow the heretic. The results were startling: instead of the abject recantation which erring Communists usually made, Tito protested that he was at least as good a Communist as Stalin and complained of Soviet interference in Yugoslavia. He was supported in this appalling blasphemy by the bulk of the party in Yugoslavia, and the few who tried to carry out Russia's orders were dealt with in the orthodox Communist fashion. So to heresy Tito added the crimes of open defiance and obstinate refusal to cooperate by allowing himself to be liquidated. Gradually he realized that Moscow's hostility was implacable, and then he began slowly to draw nearer to the West because he could not help himself. Tito had ambitious plans for industrialization, but they could only be carried out if machinery, etc., were supplied from outside. The Soviet bloc established an economic blockade, and Tito's program was heading for a smash. Beginning in 1950 the United States and later Britain and France provided funds for the purchase of food, raw materials, and capital equipment, thus enabling Tito to continue his plans for industrialization. The danger of an invasion from the adjacent satellite states seemed to be a real possibility, for Stalin began to strengthen their armies while he refused to replace the Russian equipment of the Yugoslav troops. Their combat efficiency declined, but since 1951 the United States has supplied matériel.

This assistance was given for reasons of expediency. One principal source of strength of the Communist rebels in Greece was the aid given them by Tito. He ceased to do so when he broke with the Kremlin, and this was in considerable measure the cause of their defeat. It was clear too that if Tito would work with the West it would strengthen the defensive position of the NATO powers in the Balkans. On the ideological side Tito compelled Stalin to show the true aims of his policy. For in trying to destroy a loyal supporter he was admitting that his real aim was not the spread of communism but the expansion of Russian control. Forcing him to take off his mask of hypocrisy might perhaps have a salutary effect on Communists in other countries.

Tito was not willing to form a military alliance with the West, but in 1951 he announced that he would fight alongside it if Russia attacked. A rapprochement took place between Yugoslavia, Greece, and Turkey and in 1954 they signed an alliance providing for concerted action in the event of a Russian attack. The German invasion of 1941 showed that an attack launched from the present satellite states in the Danube valley threatens all three countries, and the coordination of their defensive measures improves the prospects of a successful resistance. It is hoped that the settlement of the Trieste question in 1954 will be followed by military collaboration between Italy and Yugoslavia. This would close a loophole in the Western defenses that has troubled military leaders. There is a road of invasion which leads from the Hungarian plain through Yugoslavia, across the mountains at the Ljubljana Gap, and debouches on the Italian plain at the head of the Adriatic. It is to the interest of both countries that the Gap be strongly defended, but cooperation was impossible as long as they were at daggers drawn over Trieste.

The inner significance of this curious episode is not clear. To anyone who is not skilled in the theological niceties of the Marxist-Leninist religion Tito seems to be justified in his assertion that he is a Communist. The general character of his government and domestic policy has all the hallmarks of the single-party Communist dictatorship. One difference is that he is moving more slowly than in Russia toward his goal of a completely communistic society, and opponents of his regime are punished less harshly. There are only 500,000 Yugoslav Communists, and Tito needs the support of the peasants particularly, who are 65 percent of the population and are anticommunist. His real offense was that he was determined to be the master of Yugoslavia and that he was not willing slavishly to imitate every Soviet policy, even though it was not suited to local conditions. Furthermore, Tito was not prepared always to sacrifice his country's interests to those of Russia. Stalin grafted onto communism the doctrine that the first duty of Communists everywhere was to work for the advancement of Soviet interests, no matter what the cost might be to their own countries. This came fairly close to decreeing that every Communist must be a Russian patriot. Stalin would not tolerate a loyal but independent collaborator: he insisted that a satellite dictator must be a rubber stamp. Tito was a man of ruthless determination and great personal ambition, and he looked upon himself as an independent leader and not merely as Stalin's servant. Moreover, he had a strong Yugoslav national pride, and he saw no reason why he should not be a nationalist as well as a Communist. Tito was challenging the supreme authority of the Kremlin, and for this he was condemned.

Stalin overlooked the fact that alone among the satellite dictators Tito was a self-made man. The others sat out the war in Moscow until the Red army defeated the Germans and opened the way for their return. Tito created his own party and force of guerillas, and won their loyalty because he fought alongside them and shared their dangers. His postwar army was built around a nucleus of devoted ex-partisans, and his secret police consisted of hand-picked Communists. Moreover, Tito was a veteran Communist leader who had nothing to learn about underground plotting. A minority of the Yugoslav Communists were pro-Russian, and Moscow created a fifth column in Yugoslavia, but Tito dealt with them efficiently. Finally, the Yugoslavs resented strongly the attempt of any foreign power whatever to interfere in their affairs, and Tito's championship of national independence rallied to his support the very same elements which attacked his domestic policies.

The reasons that enabled Tito to win his struggle against Stalin make it improbable that he will have successful imitators. Some of the Communist leaders in other satellites were nationalists and tried to oppose the "decisive role" of the Soviet Union, but Stalin disgraced or executed all of them. The power that had set them up could cast them down. None had made themselves by forging their own instruments of victory as Tito had. The satellite Communist parties and secret police obeyed the men in authority because Stalin had put them there; but their loyalty was to Moscow rather than to the local leaders. When Stalin condemned them, the Communist parties transferred their support to the new favorites, and the old leaders fell. The Kremlin seems to have learned its lesson. In 1954 and 1955 it made overtures for "sincere friendship" between Russia and Yugoslavia and pointed out that their quarrel had benefited only the West, the enemy of both. It can safely be predicted that Tito's response will be dictated solely by a completely realistic and shrewd appraisal of what is most advantageous for himself and Yugoslavia.

AUSTRIA

The allies agreed during the war that Austria should be re-established as an independent, sovereign state. Until a treaty of peace was signed it was to be occupied by American, French, British, and Russian troops, each in a separate zone of occupation. The Russian zone was the richest part of Austria, and included most of the factories, the small oil field, and the capital of Vienna, which was occupied jointly by all four powers. Apart from a minority of Nazis the principal political parties were the Socialists and the conservatives, the latter basing their power on the large peasant element of the population. The Soviet attempt to turn Austria into a satellite state was thwarted partly by the presence of Western troops and also by the refusal of the large majority of Austrians to vote for the Communist party which the Russians fostered. The government was controlled by the anticommunist parties, which showed much courage in resisting the Soviet attempts to intimidate them. The Russians exploited their zone and for ten years refused to agree to a peace treaty which would end the military occupation and restore political independence. The reason was probably that the Danube River was the invasion route into Germany from the south and that Vienna was the most important railway junction in central Europe. With one Russian army on the Danube and another on the Polish German frontier near Berlin, Germany was at a very serious strategic disadvantage.

In May, 1955, Russia suddenly agreed to a peace treaty. The four Allied armies evacuated Austria, and she became an independent, sovereign state with the same frontiers as when Hitler annexed her. She was forced to pay heavy reparations to Russia to redeem the German properties which the Potsdam Agreement had authorized the Soviet Union to take over as compensation for war damage by Hitler's armies. Most stringent and detailed stipulations were laid down which forbade any form of *Anschluss* or economic or political union with Germany. Austria was required to become a perpetually neutral state, joining no alliances and allowing no nation to maintain military bases on her territory. The most likely explanation of Russia's change of policy was that it was a hint to Western Germany that she too could win independence and reunion if she adopted neutrality and abrogated the treaties linking her with NATO.

Austria is a poor country which manufactures more than her population can buy. Without foreign trade prosperity is impossible. The Danubian countries which formerly composed the old Austrian Empire are the natural and obvious market for her factories. The loss of that outlet after World War I and the high tariffs erected by the new states had caused great economic distress and led to the demand for *Anschluss* with Germany. Today all of these states except Yugoslavia are Soviet satellites with the same policy of excluding Austrian trade, and thus the interwar problem survives under a new label. One solution would be for Austria to join Italy, but Italians are not popular enough with Austrians to make that a practicable solution. Germany too would be sure to oppose it. An alternative would be for Austria to join Germany, but this is forbidden by the peace treaty. Moreover, Russia as well as France and Italy would refuse to agree for the same strategic reasons that they opposed it between the world wars. Trieste at the head of the Adriatic was enlarged by the Austrian Empire as an outlet for Austria's trade as well as for that of other parts of the empire. If it is maintained as a free port this should help, providing Tito does not impede the movement of freight, since the railways linking Austria with the seaport run through Yugoslavia. Unimpeded passage to the sea, however, will not be enough unless Austria can also establish herself in foreign markets.

SOVIET POLICY IN GERMANY

Moscow showed a curious dualism in treating Germany as a defeated enemy and at the same time wooing her as a potential ally. Heavy reparations, forced labor, and the establishment of a Communist dictatorship in East Germany were combined with delusive offers of German unity and independence, free elections for an all-German national assembly, and the withdrawal of all foreign troops (thereby leaving the East German Communist "people's police" as the only army in Germany). The unstated postulate in Russian proposals was that Germany should be reunited on terms of such a nature that the Communist dictatorship in East Germany would have a good chance of extending its power over the whole country. Russia stipulated that the East German dictatorship and the freely elected government of West Germany must have equal authority in making arrangements for the elections. When it is remembered that East German elections are conducted according to the orthodox police state pattern, it is not hard to prophesy what sort of elections Moscow had in mind for its proposed national assembly. If the Soviet policy succeeded, the industrial center of the Rhineland would be joined to the expanding industries of the European satellites and Russia. A large and warlike population would be added to the Soviet bloc's manpower, and its frontier would be thrust forward to the Rhine. So great a victory would be a deadly menace to the whole of the Western world. If Moscow's proposals were refused as they have been to date, it was determined to retain Soviet control over East Germany, and the reunification of the whole country would be indefinitely postponed. Russia also tried her utmost to prevent the West German Republic from joining NATO and re-creating an army. One motive was clearly to prevent such an access of strength to the West. It was also quite possible that Russia was genuinely afraid of the prospect of a reborn German army, remembering what happened during the two world wars.

The Soviet Union had some advantages in the struggle for control of Germany. Neutralism was strengthened by the belief that the Red army was irresistible. The fear of an atomic war and the realization that Germany was in the front line reinforced this attitude. This was a diminishing asset which grew less as Western armaments were strengthened. Then too the West Germans wanted above everything else the reunification of their country. They realized that the only way in which this could be accomplished without war was by Russian consent. This explained much of the opposition to Adenauer's policy, for Russia emphasized that rearmament and union with the West would destroy the chance of uniting the two Germanies. Moscow also held out the hope that refusal to work with the West would be rewarded by throwing open the markets of the Soviet bloc to German manufactures. This made as strong an appeal as it did thirty years ago to the industrialists, who were an important element in the coalition that supported Chancellor Adenauer. On the other hand, Russia had to struggle against certain disadvantages in her courtship of West Germany. Most Germans were anti-Russian and anticommunist. They had vivid memories of the outrages committed by the Red army in 1945, and they tended to say that Hitler was right when he preached a crusade against communism. This attitude was reinforced by resentment at the annexation of German territory, the heavy reparations, and the retention of thousands of German prisoners of war in Russia. The steady stream of refugees from the Soviet zone made the West Germans well aware of what life was like under the Communist dictatorship.

SOVIET POLICY IN ASIA

The continuity of Soviet and tsarist foreign policy is nowhere more clearly exemplified than in Asia. There is no question here of defense against Germany. In the Middle East communism as such does not play much of a role, for no sizable Communist parties exist there, though the widespread poverty might some day provide a good recruiting ground for them. Moscow uses Communist support wherever it is available, particularly in Iran. In Turkey a Communist is so rare as to be almost a museum specimen. The Turks regard the struggle with the Soviets as a continuation of the one against the tsars, and they oppose the new imperialism as stoutly as they did the old. In the Arab world and Iran the Russians pose as the champions of freedom against the Western imperialists. They combine this with threats, particularly against Iran, that the acceptance of military aid would be tantamount to becoming an agent of the Western powers, and so threatening the security of peace loving Russia. This technique of making the flesh creep has been fairly effective.

Tsarist imperialism in general and the conquest of central Asia in particular convinced the British government of the nineteenth century that the ultimate aim was the conquest of India. Distrust was heightened by the methods of tsarist foreign policy. The promise would be made that no further expansion was intended, and then a few years later more territory would be annexed in central Asia. The tsar's government would express regrets, and explain that the conquest was the unauthorized act of local officers. Since the Russian flag had been hoisted, however, national honor made a withdrawal impossible. The effect upon the British was to create a feeling of suspicion and hostility that somewhat resembles the contemporary attitude toward the Soviet government. The truth seems to be that the British government exaggerated the Russian threat. There were influential circles at court which pressed for expansion in central Asia and entertained the hope that in the long run this might make possible an attack on India. In 1878, when war in Europe seemed imminent between Russia and Britain over the Turkish question, a Russian army was sent from central Asia to attack India. The threat of war ended at the Congress of Berlin, and the troops were recalled. There does not seem to have been an unchanging but rather an intermittent policy of aggression in this part of the world. India had on the whole a low priority, and as a rule tsarist Russia was much more interested in Turkey and the Balkans, or in the Far East. The Soviet attitude seems to be similar, though the pot is kept gently boiling through the activity of the Communist parties in India and Pakistan. They have made some progress among intellectuals, the peasants and the factory workmen. Nehru wages vigorous war against them at home, however neutral he may be in the international field.

Tsarist Russia was not interested in Southeast Asia, and the Communist activity there is a new departure. It arises from the enhanced importance of the area in a time of global cold war. In Southeast Asia the initiative is being taken by China rather than by Russia, though the latter is supporting its ally. The victory of Ho Chi-minh in Vietnam and the unsatisfactory situation in several other countries shows that the outcome in this part of the world is far from settled.

In the Far East both tsarist and Soviet Russia hoped to control Korea and Manchuria and bring the government of China under their influence. Tsarist Russia was checked by the Russo-Japanese War. The tsars also coveted the huge Chinese dependency of Outer Mongolia. It was valuable economically, and it could be a buffer protecting the vital and vulnerable Trans-Siberian Railway. Soviet Russia succeeded in converting Outer Mongolia into a nominally independent Soviet republic, which was a subject ally of Russia. The Soviet government also established itself in the far western Chinese province of Sinkiang. The initial attempt of the 'twenties to establish a Communist dictatorship in China was defeated by Chiang Kai-shek, but in the end it succeeded because of the favorable chain of events that followed World War II. Japan had been totally defeated, Great Britain politically speaking had retreated to Singapore, and the American protégé Chiang Kai-shek lost the war against the Chinese Communists. They received some help from Russia, though less than the Americans gave Chiang Kai-shek. On the whole, they won through their own efforts: it was the story of Tito over again. It is impossible to say exactly what the relations are between Moscow and Peking, but they are not the same as those with the dictator of a European satellite state. The rulers of China have power in their own right, and are treated more as equals. China is dependent on Russia for much of its military equipment and for economic help in carrying out its plans for industrialization. Russia gains by having a fairly strong ally which can divert a good deal of Western strength to secondary theaters of war like Korea, Indochina and Formosa, and which will grow more powerful as time goes on. Both benefit from their alliance, and in the near future, at least, there is no reason to expect it to break down.

SOVIET POLICY IN RETROSPECT

A survey of Soviet foreign policy shows that it is fundamentally aggressive, but that its tactics vary in accordance with the rulers' judgment of the world situation. The first decade of the Soviet republic was one of crusading zeal, when the chief aim was to promote world revolution. This was followed by a period when the principal object was to cultivate friendly relations with the West. There were two reasons here—to build up the U.S.S.R. by the Five Year Plans and to gain support against the mounting threat from Germany and Japan. This was followed by cooperation with Hitler, until his attack forced Stalin to make common cause with the Western powers. After World War II the Russian rulers decided that the time was ripe for a return to the policy of expansion.

The fulfillment of tsarist aims explains postwar policy in the Baltic countries, the Balkans, Turkey, Iran, and the Far East. At their most expansionist, however, the tsars were comparatively moderate. They never attempted to make Germany, France, and Italy into satellite states, or to assist say a pro-Communist government in Guatemala by shipping arms to it, as the Soviets did in 1954. The most that the tsars ever did in this field was to give discreet encouragement to the desire for freedom of the little Slav peoples who were subjects of the former empire of Austria Hungary. This method was feasible only in those few states which included Slav minorities. The Tsars were far too much afraid of revolt at home to dream of encouraging revolutions and proletarian dictatorships abroad. More than anything else it is the universal range of Soviet ambitions and its technique of the inside job that has aroused Western fear and hostility. The Soviet method is independent of appeals to race: it is not even completely dependent upon ideology. It requires a minority of Communists to seize the leadership, but the majority of their followers are not Communists. They are urban workmen who are discontented with their pay or conditions of work, land-hungry peasants, colonial nationalists who want independence, or groups who for some reason are opposed to the existing state of affairs. More often than not the local Communists do not preach communism, for to do that would defeat their purpose. To recruit a following they exploit existing grievances, and on occasion invent them. Other tactics used are the attempt to create popular distrust of anticommunist governments, espionage, sabotage, and the capture of the trade unions. Great importance is attached to fomenting strikes which would cripple the production of armaments—an obvious advantage to Russia when there is a global arms race—or which would damage the national economy. Making mischief by all methods short of war involving Russia in open hostilities, or the cold war, has been the order of the day.

The policy has included local wars not involving Russia like those in Korea and Indochina, but open attack by the Soviet armed forces is the only form of aggression which has not been used in the postwar period. There is no reason to believe that this limitation has been based on anything except a careful evaluation of the risks. The Kremlin has as much respect for strength as it has contempt for weakness. With the vast superiority in ground troops and airplanes it could have won the first round, if it had gone to war with the

West during the 'forties or early 'fifties. Western Europe could have been conquered as far as the English Channel and the Pyrenees, but the final outcome would have been uncertain. This was due to the immense superiority of the United States in industrial production and in its stock of atom bombs. There were also internal weaknesses though it is impossible to evaluate them exactly. Many Russians had little enthusiasm for the regime especially among the peasants, who resented the nationalization of their farms. In the invasion of 1941 a large number of troops surrendered to the Germans and civilians welcomed the invaders, either from economic discontent or because like the Ukrainians they wanted national self-government. The results for the dictatorship might have been serious if Hitler had had sense enough to welcome the collaborators instead of treating them with brutality. It is significant that to arouse the fighting spirit the Kremlin did not appeal to loyalty to the Communist party, but to Russian patriotism. There is also reason to believe that at the present time many soldiers from the satellite states would have no enthusiasm for fighting to retain their loss of independence. Altogether war with the West would have been a gamble, and the Kremlin does not take unnecessary chances. Its ideology teaches it that capitalism is irrevocably doomed to destruction. Since the end is predetermined, time does not matter, and it is foolish to run needless risks.

PEACEFUL COEXISTENCE

A Communist party congress was held in Moscow in October, 1952, shortly before Stalin's death, and pronouncements were made of future policy. They appeared to mean that Stalin and his successor Malenkov admitted that the postwar expansion of Communist power had gone as far as it could in the West. The Communist victory could be achieved over a longer period through relaxing immediate pressures in Europe, promoting disunity in the noncommunist world and encouraging weakness there, while at the same time developing the industrial and military strength of Russia. After 1952 international tensions lessened, and in small ways Moscow followed a less aggressive policy. Restrictions were relaxed on foreign travel in the U.S.S.R. Soviet football teams and ballet dancers visited Western Europe, and Soviet delegates to the U.N. went some way to cooperate with the West instead of opposing it. The Kremlin began to talk of peaceful coexistence in Europe, while at the same time it continued to assist China to press forward in Asia. This apparent change of policy raised three questions. Why this thusness? What did peaceful coexistence mean? Was it a change of strategy, or merely of tactics?

In trying to answer the first question it should be kept in mind that peaceful coexistence has a long history, dating from 1917 onward. It was put forward at various times by Lenin, Trotsky, Stalin, and Litvinov, but it was

always a tactical maneuver and not a change in the grand strategy of hostility
to capitalism. A stage of equilibrium seems to have been reached in Europe.
Barring unforeseen catastrophes, it is improbable that the Communists will be
able to establish control over any more European states through the technique
of the inside job. Moreover, the West has considerably strengthened its defenses. The Red army and air force are still markedly superior, but if they invaded Western Europe, they would not win as easily as in 1950. To quote Field
Marshal Montgomery, "Now we could give them a run for their money."
The United States retains its overwhelming industrial superiority, though the
atom bomb is less of a deterrent than it was because of Russia's progress in
that field. By and large the outcome of a war with the West is even more
uncertain than it would have been a few years ago—and Moscow will only
gamble on a certainty. On the other side, the West has no intention of fighting
a preventive war against Russia. Washington has officially denied that this is
its policy, and America's European allies would refuse to support her if she
did so. Evidence of peaceful intentions was given by President Eisenhower's
announcement that the strength of the American army would be reduced by a
quarter in two years without any corresponding reduction in the size of the
Soviet forces. Then too the Russians know as well as the West that an atomic
war might destroy the human race. Presumably the prospect has as little attraction for them as for the West. Altogether the times do not seem propitious for
more conquests in Europe. On the other hand, Asia is in a state of flux, and
the possibility exists of further expansion there. Surveying the global situation,
the Kremlin apparently decided that a truce was desirable in Europe but not
necessarily in Asia.

This leads to the second question: What did Moscow mean by peaceful
coexistence? Definitions were given in 1954 by leading members of the Kremlin hierarchy. The status quo in Europe must be preserved, which meant that
the West must make no attempt to interfere with Russian control over the
satellite states, including the Soviet zone of Eastern Germany. Moscow opposed as strenuously as ever the rearmament of the West German Republic
and its joining NATO. If this took place, "Germany will remain divided for
long years to come." The bait was held out that if West Germany remained
disarmed and neutral in the cold war, the reunion of the two Germanies might
be arranged. At the same time there was the hint that Moscow regretfully
accepted the fact that West Germany would probably rearm and link herself
with the West and that it would not oppose this by force. In addition, the
U.S.S.R. wanted the abolition of atomic weapons and the dissolution of
NATO. As a substitute for the latter, "collective security in Europe" was
proposed. Apparently this meant a league composed of a heavily armed Soviet
bloc controlled by Russia and of western European states which were no longer
linked in an alliance. Whether the United States would be unwillingly ac-

cepted as a member of the proposed league was not clear. This proposal would mean collective insecurity for everyone except Russia, and was rejected by the Western powers in 1954. Peaceful coexistence in Europe seemed to come down to this. The West should accept the postwar expansion of Russian power, and neither side should invade the other. This would give the Communists time to consolidate their power in their zone of control. Preferably, too, the West should weaken itself by dissolving its alliances, agreeing to German neutrality, and reducing its armaments. In Asia the government of Mao Tse-tung must be recognized, and the advance of communism would continue.

In addition to actual hostilities, there was political war, and under peaceful coexistence this would continue. Moscow would continue to interfere in the affairs of the noncommunist states, e.g., by working through the national Communist parties as it had hitherto. When a delegation of the British Labour party visited Russia in 1954, it tried to obtain the promise that the Communists would abandon their attempts to destroy the socialist parties in the West. "The answer indicated that there can be trade, and increased diplomatic intercourse. But no positive cooperation. Coexistence seems to mean peace from the shooting war but no change in ideology, and therefore no respite from political warfare." The attitude of the Chinese Communist leaders was much the same.

There was no reason to believe that peaceful coexistence was anything but a temporary change of tactics, made because of an alteration in world conditions. It did not appear that Moscow had abandoned its ultimate aim of world communism, nor did it think that coexistence was possible indefinitely. The fall of Malenkov in 1955 appeared to bear this out. Malenkov supported peaceful coexistence, and also a half-hearted attempt to allay popular discontent in the Soviet bloc by increasing the supply of consumer goods at the expense of heavy industry. The rise of his opponents to power coincided with a reversion to the former policy of giving first place to heavy industry. The meeting of the four heads of state—American, Russian, British, and French—at Geneva in 1955 was unwontedly cordial, and the communiqué signed by the participants contained such reassuring but vague diplomatic clichés as "desirous . . . convinced . . . recognizing . . . agree." When the four foreign ministers met in the autumn of 1955, the disagreement on every issue was so complete that they could not even agree on the terms of the communiqué which announced their failure. The one gain was the confirmation of the suspicion that Russia was as afraid of a nuclear war as the West.

The Communists believe that in the years ahead the free world will not be able to maintain a rate of economic growth comparable with that which will be forced in the Soviet bloc. The West's margin of industrial and economic superiority will decline, and along with this its ability to defend itself. It is undeniable that the Soviet bloc has important advantages over the free world.

It has a higher rate of savings because the dictatorship exacts large forced savings and invests them in industry. In a free state each individual decides for himself how much he will spend, and what proportion he will save. In a democracy too the government cannot ignore the consumers' demand for such items as refrigerators and automobiles. In a dictatorship very little attention is paid to their wants, and the standard of living is held down or even lowered so that more resources are available for the purposes of the state. Then again there is no feather bedding, no strikes, and no respect for vested interests. The single Soviet goal is overfulfillment of the current Five Year Plan, never mind at what cost in lives and freedom. "There are three types of economy in the modern world: laissez faire, welfare, and unfair. In the first progress is gradual, as the profit motive and the free supply of savings dictate. In the second progress is usually inhibited, lest some one get hurt in the short run. In the third progress is a Moloch to which all present values are sacrificed." The Soviet bloc is a formidable competitor, and the capitalist world will have to make strenuous efforts to prevent itself from being overhauled. Assuming that this is done, it is probable that the Soviet bloc will not be able to outproduce the United States and Western Europe in the foreseeable future, though it will probably outproduce Western Europe by itself.

SELECTED READING

BELOFF, MAX, *Soviet Policy in the Far East, 1944–1951*. New York: Oxford Press, 1953.

——, *The Foreign Policy of Soviet Russia, 1929–1941*. 2 vols. London: Oxford Press, 1947–1949.

CRESSEY, GEORGE B., *The Basis of Soviet Strength*. New York: Whittlesey, 1945.

DALLIN, DAVID J., *The New Soviet Empire*. New Haven: Yale University Press, 1951.

——, *The Rise of Russia in Asia*. New Haven: Yale University Press, 1950.

——, *Soviet Russia and the Far East*. New Haven: Yale University Press, 1948.

DEWAR, MARGARET, *Soviet Trade with Eastern Europe 1945–9*. New York: Royal Institute of International Affairs, 1951.

FISCHER, GEORGE, *Soviet Opposition to Stalin*. Cambridge: Harvard University Press, 1952.

FISCHER, LOUIS, *The Soviets in World Affairs*, 2d. ed., 2 vols. Princeton: Princeton University Press, 1951.

HAINES, CHARLES G. (ed.), *The Threat of Soviet Imperialism*. Baltimore: Johns Hopkins University Press, 1954.

HUNT, R. N. C., *The Theory and Practice of Communism. An Introduction*. New York: The Macmillan Company, 1950.

KERNER, ROBERT J., *The Urge to the Sea: the Course of Russian History*. Berkeley: University of California Press, 1942.

MAYNARD, SIR JOHN, *Russia in Flux*. New York: The Macmillan Company, 1948.

PARES, SIR BERNARD, *A History of Russia*. New York: Alfred A. Knopf, 1953.

SETON-WATSON, HUGH, *The East European Revolution*. New York: Praeger, 1951.

SHEPHERD, GORDON, *Russia's Danubian Empire*. London: Heinemann, 1954.

SMITH, WALTER BEDELL, *My Three Years in Moscow*. Philadelphia: J. B. Lippincott Company, 1950.

CHAPTER 25

CHINA

The revolution which brought the Communists to power in China began nearly a hundred and fifty years ago. The two primary causes, one domestic and the other external, were the decay of the Manchu dynasty and the impact of the West. Early in the nineteenth century there were indications that the Manchu emperors were beginning to lose their control over the country. All this had happened before, and the traditional remedy was a change of dynasty which brought to the throne a vigorous and capable line of rulers. If China had been left unmolested, history would probably have repeated itself. This time, however, the pressure from without was different from any that China had previously encountered.

CHINA AND THE WEST

Earlier invaders like the Manchus or the Mongols had been less civilized than the native Chinese, and after settling amongst their new subjects they had gradually adopted their customs and been absorbed by them. The West had a developed civilization which its holders considered vastly superior to that of China. It was fundamentally different from the Chinese way of life in its ideas, and on the material side it was incontestably more powerful. It was the greater power of the West which first impressed the Chinese; but in the long run it was the ideas of the West, e.g., democracy and communism, which had the more disturbing effects. The immediate neighbors of the Chinese were weaker and less civilized, and in varying degrees they had been brought under the political and cultural domination of China. The Chinese became convinced that their Middle Kingdom was effortlessly superior to all others, and that the rest of the world was inhabited by barbarians. It would be preposterous to treat them as equals or imitate any of their primitive practices. The shock and humiliation were profound when these barbarians imposed their will on China. This helped to bring about the fall of the dynasty, since the Manchus were plainly unable to protect their empire.

Eventually the Chinese felt that they must study and imitate the West, since in no other way could they get rid of its control. In the process the Chinese were influenced not only by the outward trappings of Western civilization—its factories, inventions and military organization—but also by its ideas. Communism for instance is a European idea which reached China by way of Russia. Today China is going through the most profound and comprehensive upheaval that it has known for over 2000 years.

A century and a quarter ago trade with the West was confined to Canton, and while it was profitable, the conditions under which it was carried on were regarded by the foreign merchants as onerous and humiliating. There was also the tantalizing feeling that if only they had free access to the empire of 400 million customers the profits would be immense. The government refused to modify its conditions. The Canton trade was a clash between essentially different commercial, legal and political systems. Ultimately war was inevitable since neither side was willing to compromise. Great Britain held the lion's share of the trade, and she was also the leading naval power. Government and merchants were determined to force open the China trade and compel the emperor to treat foreigners on terms of equality. While opium was the immediate occasion of the first Anglo-Chinese war of 1839, it was by no means the real cause. The two wars of 1839 and 1856 showed that the emperor was powerless to maintain his policy against Western navies and armies. The island of Hong Kong and a strip on the adjacent mainland were ceded to Great Britain in 1842. Various cities known as treaty ports were thrown open to British merchants; they were given the right of travel in the interior; missionaries were allowed to carry on their work; and a British ambassador was to reside at Peking. The Westerners in the treaty ports were to live in the foreign concessions set apart for their residence. Here they were to be governed by their own nationals in accordance with their own laws, without being subject to Chinese laws and taxes. In the twentieth century the rights of extraterritoriality embodied in the "unequal treaties" were to be fiercely resented as a humiliating infringement on China's sovereign rights.

The aim of Great Britain was trade and later investment, and there was no desire to annex territory. Hong Kong was taken in order to have a seaport where trade could be carried on free from the difficulties and occasionally dangers which hampered it at Canton. Being an island, it could easily be protected by the British navy. No attempt was made to monopolize the trade, and Britain was quite content that other nations should obtain by treaties the same rights that she had won for her own subjects. From considerations of self-interest she favored an open-door policy because she felt very sure of her ability to defeat all rivals provided only that the conditions were such as to permit of fair and open competition. Hong Kong, for instance, was a free-trade port, and the citizens of all nations were given equal rights with the British. The colony might be described as an international convenience administered by Britain for the benefit of world trade. It became the principal center for the foreign trade of southern China. The other Western states were content to let Britain take the lead in obtaining and enlarging the privileges which were then extended to them under the terms of most-favored nation treaties.

THE SCRAMBLE FOR CONCESSIONS

During the later nineteenth century China failed to strengthen herself by modernization as Japan was doing. She was in no condition to grapple with the threats to her territory which arose. In 1894–1895 Japan defeated China and annexed Formosa. In the next few years France obtained a naval base at Kuang-chou Wan in south China, Germany got the port of Tsingtao and extensive rights in Shantung province, and Russia established herself in Manchuria. By the end of the century Manchuria was in process of becoming a Russian province. Russia gained a naval base, Port Arthur, and a commercial port, Dalny, later known as Dairen, which were free from ice the year round. There was a Russo-Chinese defensive alliance, and Russian influence was beginning to penetrate Korea. Russia and France were concerting plans for an economic invasion of the Yangtze valley, the center of British trade interest.

The principles of equality of commercial opportunity and the territorial integrity of China were threatened to the obvious detriment of the United States and Great Britain. In March, 1898, and again in January, 1899, the British government appealed to Washington for some form of joint action to maintain the Open Door, but President McKinley refused. The British strongly preferred a free and open market, but as a second best they would try to safeguard their trade in the Yangtze valley. So between February and July, 1898, Britain secured from China a series of agreements which among other things promised never to alienate any territory in the Yangtze valley, and gave Britain a naval station at Wei-hai-wei as long as Russia should hold Port Arthur. Wei-hai-wei was a possible summer resort but so useless as a naval base that it was known in the British foreign office as "Why-oh-why." In the late summer of 1899 Secretary of State John Hay sent his Open-Door notes to the European powers and Japan, asking specifically for equal commercial opportunity within the spheres of influence. Most of the powers assented in principle with qualifications, but Russia virtually rejected the idea of equal opportunity. Professor Clyde's judgment on the episode is worth quoting. The United States

had failed to get unqualified acceptance of the principle [of the open door], and it had failed to attack the basic problem—the spheres of influence. . . . the Amer-

THE KUOMINTANG AND JAPAN

Domestic reforms were urgently needed and undeniable advances were made in this field, but less emphasis was placed upon them than on the attempt to destroy the Communists and recover Manchuria. In 1929 Chiang Kai-shek tried to oust the U.S.S.R. from its position in northern Manchuria. The result was an undeclared war: a Soviet army invaded Manchuria and continued its advance until China agreed to Russian demands. Incidentally, this was the first illustration of the ineffectiveness of the Briand-Kellogg Peace Pact of 1928.

Manchuria was the preserve of the young Marshal Chang Hsueh-liang, who succeeded as war lord when his father was murdered in 1928. His troops and officials controlled the province, so long as he did not unduly obstruct the Japanese and Russians who held the effective power. Chang Hseuh-liang was an ardent nationalist, and he and the National government tried with some success to whittle down Japan's political and economic rights. Their ultimate aim was the restoration of full Chinese sovereignty. The Japanese, liberals as well as ultra nationalists, had no intention of allowing their position to be undermined, and the officers of the Kwantung army in Manchuria were nursing ambitions to extend it. By 1931 it was doubtful whether either side was willing to compromise. In September, 1931, the Kwantung army took the law into its own hands. Marshal Chang Hsueh-liang's troops were driven out of Manchuria, and by 1935 it became clear that the aim was to extend Japan's control over Inner Mongolia and the northeastern provinces of China Proper. Roughly speaking, this was the part of the country which lay north of the Hwang Ho or Yellow River. After the failure of the League of Nations' attempt to intervene in Manchuria, the policy of the National government was to avoid war with Japan, in part because of its military weakness. In addition, the Kuomintang conservatives felt it was more important to crush the Communists, who had established themselves in northwestern China with their capital at Yenan. The government's policy became increasingly unpopular, and a growing and widespread demand developed for resistance to Japanese aggression. In 1936 Chiang Kai-shek was seized by his own generals and held prisoner until he agreed to stop the war against the Communists and form a united front with them to oppose the Japanese.

The following year the war broke out and gradually spread further and further over China. The Japanese occupied the richest, most developed, and most densely populated provinces, and set up a puppet government under Wang Ching-wei. Far from conciliating the conquered Chinese the brutality and spoliation of the Japanese aroused bitter hatred and stimulated the growth of Chinese nationalism. Chiang Kai-shek was forced to retreat to the mountainous and undeveloped part of western China, and he set up his capital at Chungking on the upper Yangtze River. His forces and those of the Communists were not strong enough to expel the Japanese. The latter hoped to wear down resistance by prolonged military stalemate. In 1945 1,300,000 Japanese troops were in China and Formosa and 700,000 in Manchuria. Gradually the Kuomintang's resistance grew feebler, and it was still further lessened by the breakdown of the alliance between it and the Communists. The final defeat of Japan was brought about with only limited help from China.

DECLINE AND FALL OF THE KUOMINTANG

Sun Yat-sen had laid down the principle that for a time there must be a period of political tutelage during which the Kuomintang would control the government while the people were taught how to use their new political powers, as a preliminary to the establishment of democracy. From the beginning the National government had been a single-party dictatorship which became more and more conservative. The Kuomintang, however, was never a united and well-disciplined party with an all powerful leader like the Nazi party. It was made up of various factions competing for control of the party machine, and Chiang Kai-shek retained the leadership by his ability to enlist the support of one or another of them. He was afraid to dismiss corrupt or reactionary followers lest he lose the support of a clique the help of which he needed to retain power. Prior to the Japanese invasion he had relied mainly upon the modern-minded businessmen and bankers of Shanghai and the other treaty ports which were captured by the Japanese. They were relatively progressive in their attitude toward social and economic change. When Chiang Kai-shek retreated to Chungking, he was forced to depend on the ultra conservative landowners and ex-*tuchuns* commanding armies, who opposed any reforms that would lessen their own wealth and power. The pre-1937 achievements of the National government should not be underrated. When in 1943 the Western powers gave up their rights of extraterritoriality, the Kuomintang had completed its task of liberating China from the unequal treaties. Nationalism and the sense of national unity were strengthened. Textile and other light industries were fostered, education was expanded, and something was done to help the peasants.

When the Sino-Japanese War began in 1937, the Kuomintang was still moderately progressive, the economy was expanding and the revenue growing, and the government was obeyed in most of China. By 1945 control over the country was greatly weakened, the economy was rapidly degenerating, and there was a very serious inflation. Tradition permitted officials to levy a moderate "squeeze": to make a reasonable financial profit was a legitimate perquisite of office. At Chungking, however, the civil and military structure became permeated with gross profiteering and official corruption. The peasants, poverty-stricken at best, suffered grievously from the wars and the conscription of the young men for military service. In addition to the land tax and the exactions of local officials, they were heavily in debt to the money-lenders, whose interest rates were very high. About a quarter of the peasants were tenant farmers. Their rents varied greatly, being much too high in some areas and low in others. It has been estimated that owing to the excessive agricultural population 80 percent of the farms were too small to enable the cultivator to make a decent living. The peasants were discontented and land hungry, and they felt no loyalty to a government which imposed burdens on them and gave them nothing in return. Chiang's dependence on the landowners for support and the land tax for revenue made it hard for him to introduce reforms, but his failure to do so played into the hands of the Communists. The salaried classes and the intellectuals became increasingly discontented. They contrasted their own poverty due to the inflation with the self-enrichment of those in power. Moreover, Chiang refused their demands that the dictatorship be democratized, and gradually many of them went over to the Communists. After 1945 the expansion of government-operated enterprises and the numerous corruptly and inefficiently administered economic controls so obstructed the opportunities for profitable business operations, that merchants decided that conditions could not be worse under the Communists. The climax came in 1948 when because of inflation the currency became worthless.

The Kuomintang lost to the Communists its position as the champion of Chinese nationalism. As the war went on, the government relied more and more openly on American aid. This became particularly marked after 1945, when the country was moving toward civil war. The Communists owed much to the indirect help given to them in Manchuria by the Russians, but few Chinese knew of this. From 1946 to 1949 the Communists unceasingly denounced Chiang Kai-shek as the "running dog" of the American capitalist imperialists. The propaganda fell on fertile soil. When to the above causes there were added the military blunders of Chiang's armies, it seems evident that the Kuomintang collapsed from its own weakness more than from the strength of its enemies.

The Communists emerged from the war much stronger than they entered it. Their army was larger, though far inferior to the National troops in numbers and equipment. The party itself grew from 100,000 to 1,200,000, and was a thoroughly purged and disciplined instrument in the hands of its leader. The territory and population controlled by it had increased manyfold. The Communists developed a program of land and local administrative reform which won the support of the peasants. At times they reduced the farmers' rent and their debt, and at others they liquidated the landowners and divided their land among their tenants. Either way the peasants gained, and they had something to defend which they feared the Kuomintang, the land-owners' party, would take from them.

AMERICAN POLICY

The policy of Washington was to support the National government, but at the same time it became increasingly critical of its efficiency, integrity, and its war effort against the Japanese. Initially, too, there seems to have been the belief that the Communists were agrarian reformers, willing to cooperate with other parties in a democratic government. When Japan surrendered, the Nationalist armies were in south and west China. With American help they were able to occupy part of the northeastern provinces between Shanghai and Manchuria, while the other provinces were taken over by the Communists. The question then arose who was to control Manchuria. The Nationalists did not completely control any of the major railways running from north to south. If Chiang pressed ahead with the occupation of Manchuria, he would be putting his armies at the end of a 1000-mile long supply line which he could not effectively protect. By overextending his forces he risked a disastrous defeat, and it was against American military advice that he decided to run the risk. Moreover, the danger he was running was increased by the action of the Russian armies in Manchuria.

When the Yalta Conference was held in February, 1945, the American government was very anxious to secure Russian help in the anticipated invasion of the Japanese home islands. In return for his aid Stalin bargained that the U.S.S.R. must regain practically all that she had lost in Manchuria as a result of the Russo-Japanese War of 1904, including control of Port Arthur and Dairen, and also southern Sakhalin. In addition, Russia was to receive the Kurile Islands north of Japan, which she had never owned, and the status quo in Outer Mongolia was to be preserved. (This former Chinese dependency had been a Soviet satellite state since 1921.) President Roosevelt undertook to inform Chiang Kai-shek and secure his compliance. In August, 1945, Chiang Kai-shek made a treaty with Russia confirming the arrangements made at Yalta. Russia promised to give military aid only to Chiang's government and to recognize its sovereignty over Manchuria. When Russia declared war, she quickly occupied Manchuria and removed much of the Japanese-owned machinery as war booty. She also impeded the entry of Chiang's armies, and while refusing admittance to Communist troops, she allowed large numbers of unarmed "civilians" to come in. They were permitted to arm themselves from the matériel taken from the well-equipped Japanese Kwantung army of 700,000 men. When the Russians withdrew in

1946, the Communists were left in control of Manchuria and were far better armed than they had ever been before.

In an attempt to avert civil war General Marshall was sent to China in November, 1945. He tried to arrange a coalition government of Kuomintang, Communists, and middle-of-the-road liberal groups. By January, 1947, General Marshall's mission had failed as a result of the mutual distrust of the Kuomintang and the Communists, and Chiang Kai-shek decided to wage war. The bulk of the American troops were withdrawn from China, but military assistance to Chiang was continued in the form of a relatively modest military training program and the sale or loan of surplus army supplies. The total aid given to the National government was estimated to be $1,727,000,000.

At the beginning Chiang Kai-shek's army was much larger and better equipped than that of the Communists. He was, however, unable to keep his troops in Manchuria supplied and reinforced, the military leadership was incompetent, and the morale of many of the soldiers seems to have been poor. Eventually they surrendered without a fight or deserted in droves, including the divisions which had been armed and trained by Americans. Meanwhile on the civilian front the Chinese were very weary of war and the National government was losing popular support. Having secured Manchuria, the Communists captured Peking and Tientsin, and in the spring of 1949 they crossed the Yangtze without effective resistance and occupied Shanghai. From there they moved steadily south and west, and by June, 1950, Formosa was all that was left to Chiang Kai-shek. The Communists received material help in Manchuria at a decisive moment. Nevertheless, their triumph was largely a product of forces within China itself, and its roots extend back to the revolution in Chinese thought and institutions which began early in the nineteenth century.

THE COMMUNIST DICTATORSHIP

The government of the People's Republic of China contains noncommunist elements, but the real control lies with the Communist party, which claimed to have over 5 million members in 1950. This regime is a dictatorship more effective and comprehensive than anything in China's past. The government bases its strength on the support of the workmen, and it has seen to it that they are on the whole much better off than they used to be. The landowners have been deprived of their estates, which have been distributed among the poor peasants and landless laborers. They have to pay a heavy graduated grain tax. The small businessman continues to exist, though he has been roughly handled and his profits severely limited. State ownership of banks, factories, and large-scale trade has greatly expanded. Terror has been extensively used as a method of government. By its own admission the government has executed 2 million, and many more have been imprisoned.

In the long run private ownership of the farms will not solve the problem of overpopulation, in a country where the agricultural population is estimated to be 1500 for each square mile of cultivated land. Much can be done by extension of irrigation and drainage systems, improved farming methods, road and railway construction, and expansion of cultivation in such outlying areas as Manchuria and Mongolia. The government believes that the real remedy lies in a program of rapid and comprehensive industrialization, which would drain off the surplus farm population into the new factory towns. Among the obstacles are the lack of domestic capital and technical experts, and the need to import the bulk of the steel, machinery, etc. Only the United States, Great Britain, and perhaps Germany are in a position to supply China's needs. Soviet Russia and her satellites have not a great deal to spare because of their own ambitious plans for industrialization. For this reason it was hoped that the People's Republic would feel it expedient to maintain friendly relations with the West, but the government preferred to turn to the Soviet bloc for help. In 1952 the Communists drew up plans for a program of industrialization modeled on that of the U.S.S.R., and dependent largely on the Soviet bloc for technicians and capital equipment. Emphasis was on the establishment of heavy and not light industry. The Manchurian plants which the Russians stripped in 1945–1946 were largely rehabilitated, and Manchuria was intended to play an important part in the plan. Because of Japanese development, it was the only industrialized part of China.

Before Mao Tse-tung came to power he said that he was a Communist, that Russia was his source of inspiration and the hope of the world, and that the United States was the incarnation of capitalism and imperialism. He was perfectly consistent when in 1949 he declared that China belonged to the anti-imperialist front headed by the Soviet Union and could look only to Russia for genuine and friendly assistance. Moscow recognized the People's Republic on October 2, 1949, and on February 14, 1950, the Chinese and Russian governments signed a thirty-year treaty of friendship and alliance. If either were attacked by Japan, or a state allied with Japan, the other would at once give all possible military aid. This clause was in part directed against the United States. The two allies would consult on all important international problems affecting their common interests and would give one another economic assistance. Moscow is careful not to treat the Chinese government as it does those of the European satellites, and behaves toward it with the most scrupulous consideration. The Soviet bloc supplied much of the equipment of the Chinese armies in the Korean war and also the arms which China sent to Ho Chi-minh. In 1954 Russia agreed to restore Port Arthur and increased moderately the amount of economic aid China was to receive in her industrialization program. The Sino-Soviet partnership has brought substantial gains to China, and at present there is no evidence to support the hope that Mao Tse-tung will become another Tito.

RELATIONS WITH THE WEST

British foreign policy in the twentieth century is ultimately based on a scale of priorities which sets Europe first, the Middle East and the Indian Ocean area second, and the Far East by a long way third. To the British, as to the other peoples of Western Europe, the Far East is exceedingly remote. If in a crisis certain interests have to be sacrificed, those which are located beyond Singapore must be the first to go, but security in Europe can never be jeopardized because the very existence of Britain as a nation depends on it. So in the 'thirties Britain kept out of conflict with Japan because war in the Far East must be avoided at all costs as long as the German threat continued. Apart from the Burma campaign in World War II, the British military effort was largely confined to the Middle East and Western Europe. After the war Britain virtually retired to Singapore, and left the primacy in the Far East to the United States. Americans attached much more importance than the British to the Far East, and they bore the brunt of the war in the Pacific. They felt that they were entitled to mold the conditions of the peace, and it was they who determined occupation policies in Japan and supported Chiang Kai-shek. The British rebuilt their colony of Hong Kong and tried to restore their China trade, but apart from this they viewed events in the Far East with the detachment of a spectator who felt himself quite outside the game. The Communist victory in China, therefore, aroused much stronger feeling in the United States than in Great Britain. The British did not like the new regime, but they thought it had come to stay and must be accepted as an unpalatable but accomplished fact.

The United States declined to grant diplomatic recognition to the People's Republic, but the British did so on January 6, 1950. Apart from their belief that Chiang Kai-shek was finished, they thought that to refuse to have diplomatic relations with the Communists would make them feel that Russia was their only friend. But if the West made friendly overtures, it could be hoped that trade relations would gradually weaken the links with Russia. Furthermore the British hoped to save their trade and their investments in China. The latter, possibly between $560 million and $700 million after World War II, were much larger than those of any other Western power. The fact that India had recognized the Communist government in December, 1949, also exerted some influence. It might have regrettable consequences if the Asian dominions recognized a fellow Asian state and the Western dominions ignored it. The Chinese government declined to establish diplomatic relations with the British chargé d'affaires in Peking, and made it practically impossible for British firms to continue operations. In 1952 most of them decided that the only course was to wind up their businesses and leave. In 1954 the British government agreed with Lord Vansittart that the value of their assets might have been reduced to something over $100 million.

The suspension of operations by most of the British firms inside China does not extend to Hong Kong. It continues to be, as it has been since 1945, the one place near China where merchants and bankers can operate. After World War II many Chinese and Western firms migrated there from Shanghai, owing to the impossibility of conducting business under Chinese governments. Hundreds of thousands of Chinese refugees came in, and the population was estimated to be about 2.5 million in 1950, of whom 98 percent were Chinese. The trade of Hong Kong was seriously affected by the lengthening list of articles, the export of which to China was prohibited after her entry into the Korean war. In 1952 exports to China were only 17 percent of the total compared with an average of 50 percent in the 'thirties, and imports from China were 21 percent compared with a prewar average of 32 percent. Largely cut off from their normal market, the merchants of Hong Kong were busily developing trade with other countries. Hong Kong exercises a restraining influence upon Britain's policy toward China. The colony is indefensible since the hills on British territory are dominated by a higher range on the Chinese side of the frontier. The British are most anxious to avoid being drawn into war with China, and more especially since the United States would be unlikely to give any help in the defense of Hong Kong. Short of actual hostilities, China could cut off the supply of food, most of which comes from the adjoining mainland. All in all it is the British policy to let sleeping dogs lie.

KOREA

China's motives for intervention in Korea were probably mixed. The Communist government regarded the United States with hostility for several reasons. It had helped Chiang Kai-shek; it was the leading capitalist power; and it was building up the strength of Japan. This was reinforced by the suspicion that the United States and the European states harbored designs of imperialistic exploitation. A powerful element also was nationalism. Since Korea had such an important position strategically, the presence of a Western army there could be interpreted as a veiled attempt to establish a base for the later invasion of China. Mao Tse-Tung's propaganda portrayed the United States as the enemy of China, while his government was presented as the defender of freedom. The purpose may have been to strengthen the Communist regime by enlisting Chinese nationalism in its support. Possibly Chinese imperialism was a partial explanation. Until Japan's conquest Korea had been a Chinese dependency for centuries, and the government might have seized the opportunity to re-establish its control. The reconquest of Tibet seemed to corroborate this.

The Korean war showed that the People's Republic was a major political factor in Asia. A generation ago the armies of the *tuchuns* were in most cases comic opera forces. They won their battles by intrigue and bribery more than by fighting. Chiang Kai-shek's troops were better, but they were incapable of holding their own against the Japanese. The story in Korea was different. There was a marked improvement in morale, leadership, training, and equipment, and the Chinese soldier demonstrated his will to fight. This did not mean that China had become a major military power. Her infantry, partially supplied with Soviet equipment, might be able to dominate by sheer force of numbers areas adjacent to China. But for a long time to come she would be handicapped by the major military deficiencies of lack of industry, inadequate communications, and limited air power.

The result of the war was in one way a stalemate. The original purpose, the preservation of the independence of South Korea, succeeded. General MacArthur's attempt late in 1950 to reunite the two parts of the country by carrying the war into North Korea was defeated by the Chinese intervention. The attempt failed to bring about a union by diplomatic negotiations in 1954 after an armistice had been arranged. The indications were that as in East Germany the Communists intended to hold on to what they had and that Chinese influence would be strong in the satellite state.

FORMOSA

American intervention in Korea was undertaken with the full participation of the United Nations; but the action affecting Formosa was decided on independently. On June 27, 1950, President Truman ordered the American Seventh Fleet not to allow any attack on Formosa by the Communists and to prevent Chiang's forces from carrying on any sea and air operations against the mainland. The determination of the future status of Formosa was left unsettled. The President's action was apparently taken to localize the Korean war by neutralizing Formosa, and also in deference to what seems to have been the view of the Joint Chiefs of Staff that Formosa was an essential part of the outer island perimeter security zone of the United States. After that date the United States was active in equipping and training the approximately 600,000 troops whom Chiang had with him on Formosa. Apparently the plan was to select the 300,000 judged to be potential combat effectives and organize them into a modern fighting force. Peking and Moscow demanded that Formosa be given back to China since the population was Chinese, and the Cairo Conference of 1943 at which Chiang Kai-shek was present had promised to return it. The United States did not receive the same full support from the U.N. members in regard to Formosa as to Korea. The states which believed that Chiang Kai-shek was finished were lukewarm toward a move whose effect would be to prolong his existence. President Eisenhower's action in 1953 in leaving Chiang free to attack the mainland was also disapproved. Great Britain, for instance, was skeptical whether Chiang had enough troops seriously to embarrass the Communist army of 5 million.

Intermittent hostilities continued between the Communist and Nationalist forces. Peking announced that it intended to conquer Formosa, and demanded that the United States cease to intervene in what it described as a Chinese civil war. In 1954 a defensive alliance was made between the United States and Chiang Kai-shek, and Secretary of State Dulles said that if the Communists attacked the "probable result" would be that the United States would go to war. At the same time Chiang Kai-shek promised in an exchange of letters that he would start no aggressive action against the mainland without the consent of the United States. With the approval of Washington the U.N. invited Peking to send representatives to the Security Council in order to discuss a cease fire, but the offer was rejected unless conditions were agreed to which were unacceptable to the Western powers. In January, 1955, Congress by an overwhelming majority voted approval of the President's policy of defending Formosa and the neighboring Pescadores Islands. It also authorized him if he felt it necessary to defend Quemoy and the Matsu Islands, which were held by Nationalist garrisons. Formosa itself lies about a hundred miles off the China coast. Quemoy and the Matsus are outposts within easy gunshot of the coast. Both in the United States and abroad there was sharp difference of opinion whether their retention was necessary for the defense of Formosa. It was also clear that the Communist troops had a much better chance of taking them than of capturing Formosa, which lay so much farther out to sea. Chiang Kai-shek was most unwilling to give up the offshore islands, for to retire to Formosa would be a tacit abandonment of his reiterated claim that eventually he would invade the mainland and reestablish himself in power.

The inference seems clear that President Eisenhower had tacitly abandoned any intention of helping Chiang Kai-shek to return to the mainland, and without this assistance the Nationalists had no hope of regaining control of the country. This was in harmony with the President's action in restraining Syngman Rhee, who had threatened to liberate North Korea with his South Korean army. The reason was that the President wished to extricate the United States from the danger of being involved in a war on the Chinese mainland. On the other hand, it was impossible to withdraw all support from Chiang Kai-shek, for this would mean that ultimately the Communists would capture Formosa. American public opinion would not permit it, and the effect upon the morale of Japan and Southeast Asia might be serious. Following upon the drawn battle in Korea and the French defeat in Vietnam, it could be interpreted that Communist China was winning the cold war. Chiang Kai-shek could not be required to renounce his ambition to regain China, any more than Mao Tse-tung could be expected formally to give up his claim to Formosa. But if a cease fire could be arranged, each side could refrain from attacking the other. After all, this would not be the first undeclared peace that the world has known since 1945, and sometimes a stopgap arrangement can be very long lived. The Communists would be tacitly assured that their control of the mainland would not be challenged; the Nationalists would have their haven of refuge on Formosa; and the danger of a local conflict which might develop into a general war would be avoided. The unknown factor was whether the Communist government of China was willing to accept this arrangement.

The Communists had always done their best to separate America from her allies, and from that point of view the situation had possibilities. If war broke out over Formosa and the United States became involved, would the allies give armed help as they had in Korea or would they remain neutral? The protection of Formosa was an American policy, and the allies were particularly apprehensive lest a large-scale Communist attempt to capture the offshore islands might lead the United States to intervene. Washington was carefully vague about whether an attack on the Nationalist garrisons of Quemoy and the Matsus would be regarded as a *casus belli* under the alliance with Chiang Kai-shek. In March, 1955, Eden, then British foreign minister, said in the House of Commons that the government would like to see the Nationalists withdraw from Quemoy and the Matsus. He did not define Britain's attitude if Formosa were attacked, though the guess might be hazarded that before any commitment was made there would be inquiries about what the United States would do if British involvement led to an attack on Hong Kong. Canada had always been unwilling to adopt a policy that ran counter to that of the United States. It was therefore significant that Pearson, the foreign minister, said in March, 1955, that Canada would not take part if the United States went to war because of a Communist attack on Quemoy and the Matsus. He described them as "islands which are in effect part of the Chinese mainland and the strategic role of which would seem to be more important in the defense of that mainland against attack than in offensive action against Formosa and the Pescadores."

Chou En-lai, the Chinese foreign minister, attended the Asian-African Conference at Bandung in April, 1955, and he offered to negotiate with the United States to relax tension in the Far East, particularly over Formosa. He coupled this with a reiteration of China's claim to "liberate" the island, and in a later speech he stated that China was willing to seek the liberation by peaceful means. He hinted that part of the bargain would be the withdrawal of American forces from Formosa and the admission of Communist China to the United Nations. Dulles replied that he was willing to negotiate a cease fire. With American approval, Britain and India through their representatives in Peking tried to ascertain whether a *modus vivendi* could be arranged. The probability was that China wished to avoid a major war, which, at the least, would delay her plans for industrialization. She did not have the military capability to carry out an amphibious operation across a hundred miles of ocean when opposed by American naval and air forces, unless she received very substantial supplies of matériel from Russia. On the other hand, the Communist government was sensitive about its prestige at home. It had publicized to the Chinese people its determination to conquer Formosa, and tacitly to abandon this policy might be difficult unless some substantial concession were made so that the whole negotiation could be presented in China as a resounding success.

SELECTED READING

CLYDE, PAUL H., *The Far East: A History of the Impact of the West on Eastern Asia,* 2d ed. New York: Prentice-Hall, 1952.

COHEN, JEROME B., *Japan's Economy in War and Reconstruction.* Minneapolis: University of Minnesota Press, 1949.

DALLIN, DAVID J., *Soviet Russia and the Far East.* New Haven: Yale University Press, 1948.

FAIRBANK, JOHN K., *The United States and China.* Cambridge: Harvard University Press, 1948.

INGRAMS, HAROLD, *Hong Kong.* London: H. M. Stationery Office, 1953.

LINEBARGER, PAUL M., *The China of Chiang Kai-shek.* Boston: World Peace Foundation, 1942.

MC CUNE, G. M., and GREY, A. L., *Korea Today.* Cambridge: Harvard University Press, 1950.

PRATT, SIR JOHN T., *War and Politics in China.* London: Cape, 1943.

SCHWARTZ, BENJAMIN, *Chinese Communism and the Rise of Mao.* Cambridge: Harvard University Press, 1951.

STEINER, H. ARTHUR (ed.), "Report on China," in *Annals* of the American Academy of Political and Social Science, 277 (September 1951), Philadelphia.

VINACKE, H. M., *The United States and the Far East, 1945-1951.* Stanford: Stanford University Press, 1952.

PART 5

MAJOR PROBLEMS OF INTERNATIONAL RELATIONS

CHAPTER 26

THE PROBLEM OF FORCE

POSTWAR HOPES AND REALITIES

Events since 1945 show that in essentials international relations are much the same as they were before World War II. Imperialism has changed its home but not its nature: and as always the policy of the aggressor forces the opposing states to adapt their methods to his. One point that emerges clearly is that power politics is inescapable in the world of states. Just as in the days of the Kellogg Pact there is the use of war or the threat of war as an instrument of national policy. This has brought with it an armaments race which throws into the shade those that preceded both world wars. There has been the same search for disarmament, and the same lack of success. Alliances and the balance of power have reappeared, this time on a global scale. The sovereign state still refuses to create an authority which shall be indisputably superior to itself at all times. To offset all this there are some signs of improvement. The Western powers have developed a degree of cooperation which would have seemed improbable in 1945, and inconceivable a generation ago. It is true that the chief credit for this change belongs by rights to Hitler and Stalin: they proved clearly that disunity meant weakness and peril. The moralist may object that cooperation based on fear does not proceed from a high motive. Looking at the matter from the practical point of view, however, the bond of common fear is a powerful one, and what began from necessity as a military alliance may spread into the political and economic fields.

The hope in 1945 was that the conquered states would be kept in a powerless condition for an indefinite period and that the Allies would continue to remain united to ensure peace. Under the leadership of the Big Three —the United States, Russia and Great Britain—they would form a concert of power so overwhelming that no nation would dare to challenge it. The principal organ through which they would operate was to be the United Nations. If war broke out, its weapon would be collective security. It was purposed that the member states would bind themselves to provide contingents of their national armed forces if the Security Council should call upon them to enforce its decisions. The U.N. was not intended to be a superstate: the ultimate authority did not lie with it, but with the sovereign states of which it was composed. Its effectiveness would depend upon the relations between its principal members. The interests and aims of the Communist and the noncommunist powers were widely divergent, and a struggle for power developed between them. The U.N. inevitably became one of their arenas of conflict and was unable to carry out its most important functions. Gradually it was realized that the high hopes which had been aroused by its creation could not be achieved as long as the division between East and West persisted. Both blocs in their dealings with one another relied on the traditional safeguards of power politics.

DISARMAMENT

In 1946 Soviet Foreign Minister Molotov introduced a disarmament resolution in the U.N. Assembly. The U.N. created two disarmament commissions, one to consider nuclear (atomic and hydrogen) and the other conventional armaments. Russia proposed the total prohibition of nuclear weapons (of which at that time the United States had a monopoly) and the reduction of other armaments by one third. The Soviet armed forces were so much larger than those of the Western powers that this flat reduction would have retained their immense superiority, while the abolition of the atom bomb would have deprived the West of the one weapon of which Russia was afraid. Russia discovered the bomb's secret in 1949, but the United States continued to have the advantage of a larger stock. Britain began to make the bomb in 1952. With the invention of the hydrogen bomb by all three nations, the arms race was extended to this infinitely more deadly weapon.

The United States in 1946 put forward the Baruch Plan. It proposed that an International Atomic Energy Authority should be created, with control of "all phases of the development and use of atomic energy, starting with raw materials." It would have control or ownership of all activities potentially dangerous to world security: it would have power to control, inspect, and license all other atomic activities: and it would carry out research and foster the beneficial uses of atomic energy. The American plan insisted on the paramount importance of an effective system of international inspection and control operated exclusively by the United Nations, since otherwise no nation would take the risk of reducing its armaments. When the U.N. Council was considering action against states engaged in illegal production, the veto must not be used to paralyze it. Once this scheme had been set up and operated successfully, the United States would disclose her secrets for manufacturing atom bombs and would destroy her existing stock, and the production of atom bombs would cease. The American proposals to give powers of inspection and control to the international authority made serious inroads into the traditional rights of the sovereign state. But to quote the third report of the U.N. Atomic Energy Commission in 1948, "Unless effective international control is established, there can be no lasting security against atomic weapons for any nation."

The Russian proposals were fundamentally different from the American. They pressed for the immediate outlawry of the production and use of atom bombs and the destruction of all existing stocks, without waiting to find out whether the measures of control and inspection were effective. In place of the International Authority states could own and operate atomic plants subject to the regulations of a control commission. International inspection was emasculated so that its effectiveness was doubtful. Russia proposed that when the U.N. Council was considering action against a state that had broken the regulations its proceedings would be subject to the veto. Russia, in short, insisted on national ownership and control, with international safeguards of very doubtful efficacy, and the immediate abolition of the weapon in which she was at a serious disadvantage. She was supported by the states of the Soviet bloc, while the large majority of the members of the U.N. sided with the United States. The battle lines were drawn, and through the countless meetings of the following years neither side receded appreciably from its position. A similar stalemate developed over the attempt to reduce nonatomic armaments. Proceedings were enlivened by an undiplomatic speaking of minds. Vishinsky testified in 1951 that the American proposals kept him awake all night laughing. Churchill, echoed by a French delegate, stated that the American lead in atomic weapons was perhaps the strongest deterrent to a Russian attack.

In 1953 Britain and India attempted to break the deadlock by moving that disarmament talks be transferred from the U.N. to a secret conference of the leading powers. In June, 1954, Britain and France brought forward a plan. The essentials of the proposal were that an effective international authority for inspection and control must be created before disarmament could begin. After this disarmament would be carried out in stages, the final step being the total abolition of nuclear (atom and hydrogen) and other forbidden weapons and a ban on their production. The Western powers agreed, and in September, 1954, the U.S.S.R. at last accepted the plan as a basis for discussion. Meanwhile a fresh issue had arisen, owing to President Eisenhower's proposal that the nations having nuclear secrets work together to give the world the benefit of their knowledge insofar as the peaceful uses of nuclear energy were concerned, e.g., medical research and power production for industry. Russia indicated that she might cooperate, but insisted that the international agency which would be in charge of the project must be controlled by the U.N. Council. This would enable Russia to use her veto, and for this reason the United States and Britain opposed the proposal.

In 1955 the disarmament conference met in London, the states represented being the United States, Britain, Russia, France, and Canada. Russia pressed for the destruction of all stocks of nuclear weapons without providing a ban on their production. She rejected the Anglo-French proposal for reducing the size of the armed forces, and instead revived her former demand for a one-third reduction all around. The Soviet delegate refused to disclose what the effect of the reduction would be upon his country's strength, until after the disarmament treaty had been signed. The Russian proposals for international inspection and control were carefully vague, and insisted that nuclear weapons must be destroyed before any other phases of disarmament were carried out. In essentials this was the same old formula—immediate ban on nuclear weapons, maintenance of Soviet predominance in conventional weapons, and complete vagueness on methods of enforcing the treaty.

Russia's disarmament proposals of May, 1955, partly reversed her previous position. She suddenly offered to accept the Anglo-French figures for the strength of the armed forces. These were a maximum of 1.5 million men for the United States, Russia, and China, and 650,000 apiece for Britain and France. She also agreed that the elimination of nuclear weapons should only begin after 75 percent of the reduction of conventional armaments had taken place. The proposals for international inspection and control of disarmament seemed to come closer to the Western requirements than ever before. They were vaguely worded, however, and it was far from clear whether the inspectors would be allowed the complete freedom to go anywhere and inspect everything which was essential if the system were to be reliable. A quantity of plutonium no greater than would fill one small suitcase could give world dominion to any power which was the only one to possess it.

Moreover, the disarmament proposals appeared to be linked with stipulations which would go a long way toward realizing Russian aims in Europe. Foreign troops in Germany must be removed, and all bases on foreign soil must be dismantled. One result of this would be that all American and British troops would be withdrawn from Europe. By contrast the Soviet troops in East Germany need only withdraw to one of the satellite states, e.g., Poland, as a result of the military alliance concluded in 1955 between Russia and her satellites. Moreover, so long as the United States had air bases in Britain, France, Germany, Greece, Turkey, North Africa, Canada, and Japan, its striking power was closer to the vital industrial and political centers of the Communist world than Communist air power was to American targets. Without the American air force in Europe and its bases NATO could not offer effective resistance to a Russian attack. As this came to be realized, it would lead to a revival of neutralism in Europe. There was the further consideration that altogether apart from Russia's own strength one reason for her position of dominance was her postwar advance to the center of Europe. Even if all Soviet forces were withdrawn to Russia, this lack of balance would continue as long as the satellite Communist dictatorships remained in power. The strength of armed forces must be stabilized as of December 31, 1954, or in other words West Germany could not create an army while Communist East Germany already possessed one. The Soviet disarmament proposals did not specifically state that a reunited Germany must be neutralized and must not join NATO. The manner in which Soviet leaders harped on this point, however, seemed to indicate that this was part of the Soviet disarmament proposals. The danger that "the Stone Age might return on the gleaming wings of science" was so great that no opportunity of lessening the peril could be foregone. The Western powers welcomed the disarmament proposals as giving "a new lease of life" to the discussions. At the same time the American and British governments were acutely aware that if the plan formed an inseparable whole the general result would be to eliminate most of Russia's fears, while their effect on the security of the West —even given the reduced Communist armies—would be exactly the opposite. The West wondered whether there had been a change of tactics but not of strategy.

Meanwhile American official opinion was beginning to veer from disarmament to deterrents. Disillusioned by a decade of abortive negotiations and losing faith in the possibility of finding an absolutely reliable system of international inspection and control, it had ceased to think about security through disarmament—that is, a system under which the states would disarm to the point where none of them had sufficient power to wage a major war. Instead security would be sought through a system of mutual surveillance which would give the Western and the Communist states the opportunity of protecting themselves against a surprise attack. This would be combined with the retention of overwhelming air and atomic power. "The free world must be sure that this deterrent capability is of such strength and flexibility that, even if it suffers a sudden atomic attack, it can still react with devastating power." The hope was that once the U.S.S.R. realized that an attack would be met by atomic retaliation, she would be willing to negotiate an agreement that would limit the amount of armaments on each side. In September, 1955, Secretary of the Air Force Quarles called his policy "peace through effective deterrence," while Churchill more bluntly described it as "a peace of mutual terror."

U.N. COLLECTIVE SECURITY

Collective security is effective on condition that the armed forces supporting the U.N. are overwhelmingly stronger than those of any single state or probable league of states. This prerequisite does not exist, for in conventional armaments the Communist states are more heavily armed than the West. This means that collective security might stop a war between two small states, provided that neither of them was supported by either of the two rival blocs. But in a major war between the Soviet and the Western blocs collective security would be inoperative, owing to the division of power and the Soviet veto in the U.N. Council. A war against aggression could not receive the official support of the U.N. as contemplated in the Charter.

The reaction to the invasion of South Korea in 1950 was a sharp contrast to the prewar fiascoes over Manchuria and Ethiopia. All three were long-term threats to peace and security, since if the international organization were successfully flouted it would be an encouragement to further acts of aggression. It is said that forty or more members offered assistance in the Korean war. In many cases offers were declined because it did not seem feasible to equip or transport and supply many small units which used equipment different from that of the American forces. The dispatch of armed forces by seventeen nations to Korea showed that many states took their U.N. obligations more seriously than they had their earlier commitments to the League. At the same time it would be wishful thinking to believe that their motives were entirely disinterested. None of the seventeen had any immediate stake in South Korea, but with all of them a long range appraisal of their national interests showed the advisability of participation. The Korean War however was not a genuine instance of universal collective security, for its supporters were far from having an overwhelming superiority in armed forces. The eight Communist countries helped North Korea, only seventeen states assisted South Korea, and the other U.N. members gave little more than moral support, or sometimes tried to mediate between the combatants. To date the verdict on the efficacy of collective security must be not proven. Until the day when the Western and Communist worlds cease to consider one another as enemies, collective security as envisaged in the U.N. Charter will remain a limited possibility.

ALLIANCES

The growing realization that the United Nations could not fulfill its original expectations compelled the states which feared Soviet aggression to find other means of security. They recognized that the U.N. was useful within limits, e.g., as a meeting place where views could be exchanged and even perhaps reconciled, and they continued to support it. But increasingly they relied for their safety upon armaments and alliances. Groups of states with similar interests formed regional alliances, the element common to all being the presence of the United States in each of them. Chapter VIII, Article 52 (1) of the U.N. Charter authorizes "the existence of regional arrangements or agencies for dealing with such matters relating to the maintenance of international peace and security as are appropriate for regional action." Chapter VII, Article 51, says that "nothing in the present charter shall impair the inherent right of individual or collective self-defence if an armed attack occurs against a Member of the United Nations, until the Security Council has taken the measures necessary to maintain international peace and security." The original intention was that a state or group of states would exercise the inherent right of self-defense until the Council took enforcement action to restore peace. It now appears that in any serious war the Council will be paralyzed by the use of the veto and unable to act. States must, therefore, fall back upon their inherent right of self-defense, and it seems likely that the period during which they will exercise it will be the whole duration of the war.

The Pact of Rio de Janeiro of 1947 is a regional alliance of the United States and the Latin American republics. The United States and Canada have arrangements for joint security purposes. The North Atlantic Treaty Organization of 1949 is a regional defensive alliance between the United States, Canada, and thirteen of the states of Western Europe from Norway to Turkey. Yugoslavia and Spain are not members of NATO, but are linked with it for defensive purposes. Incidentally, the inclusion of a communist and a fascist dictatorship in an anticommunist league of democratic states is a good example of the inevitability of power politics. What matters in a turbulent age is not the capitalist, fascist, or communist nature of a state's economy, or the dictatorial or democratic character of its government, but its strategic position and the reliability of its support in case of war. This last will continue as long as there is a community of national interests. In the Pacific there are the Anzus Pact between the United States, Australia, and New Zealand; the American alliances with the Philippines, Formosa, and Japan; and the Manila Pact of 1954 for the defense of Southeast Asia. In the Middle East there is the alliance between Turkey, Iraq, Iran, Pakistan, and Britain, the American military aid to them, and the attempts to persuade other states of the area to form an effective regional alliance. Apart from the chiefly Asian states which are trying to avoid joining either bloc, the noncommunist world is linked in a series of regional alliances. On the other side of the iron curtain, Russia had already established military and political control over her European satellites before the West came together in a counterbloc. A Sino-Soviet defensive alliance was made in 1950. This is the most comprehensive network of alliances in the whole of human history.

THE GLOBAL BALANCE OF POWER

The breakdown of the wartime cooperation of the Big Three combined with the single-handed disarmament of the Western states, created a dangerous lack of balance in power relations. U.N. collective security was unable

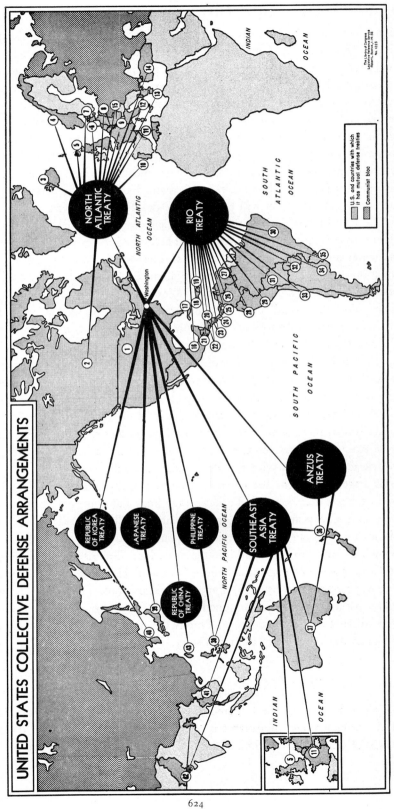

UNITED STATES COLLECTIVE DEFENSE ARRANGEMENTS

NORTH ATLANTIC TREATY

RIO TREATY

ANZUS TREATY

REPUBLIC OF KOREA TREATY

JAPANESE TREATY

PHILIPPINE TREATY

SOUTHEAST ASIA TREATY

REPUBLIC OF CHINA TREATY

Washington

NORTH ATLANTIC OCEAN

SOUTH ATLANTIC OCEAN

SOUTH PACIFIC OCEAN

NORTH PACIFIC OCEAN

INDIAN OCEAN

INDIAN OCEAN

U.S. and countries with which it has mutual defense treaties

Communist bloc

The U.S. Library of Congress
Legislative Reference Service
Robert L. Burns, 1-14-59
No. 1223

NORTH ATLANTIC TREATY (15 NATIONS)

A treaty signed April 4, 1949, by which "the parties agree that an armed attack against one or more of them in Europe or North America shall be considered an attack against them all; and . . . each of them . . . will assist the . . . attacked by taking forthwith, individually and in concert with the other Parties, such action as it deems necessary including the use of armed force . . ."

1 United States	9 Luxembourg
2 Canada	10 Portugal
3 Iceland	11 France
4 Norway	12 Italy
5 United Kingdom	13 Greece
6 Netherlands	14 Turkey
7 Denmark	15 Federal Republic
8 Belgium	of Germany

RIO TREATY (21 NATIONS)

A treaty signed September 2, 1947, which provides that an armed attack against any American State "shall be considered as an attack against all the American States and . . . each one . . . undertakes to assist in meeting the attack . . ."

1 United States	29 Peru
16 Mexico	30 Brazil
17 Cuba	31 Bolivia
18 Haiti	32 Paraguay
19 Dominican	33 Chile
Republic	34 Argentina
20 Honduras	35 Uruguay
21 Guatemala	
22 El Salvador	
23 Nicaragua	
24 Costa Rica	
25 Panama	
26 Colombia	
27 Venezuela	
28 Ecuador	

SOUTHEAST ASIA TREATY (8 NATIONS)

A treaty signed September 8, 1954, whereby each Party "recognizes that aggression by means of armed attack in the treaty area against any of the Parties . . . would endanger its own peace and safety," and each will "in that event act to meet the common danger in accordance with its constitutional processes."

1 United States
5 United Kingdom
11 France
36 New Zealand
37 Australia
38 Philippines
41 Thailand
42 Pakistan

JAPANESE TREATY (BILATERAL)

A treaty signed September 8, 1951, whereby Japan on a provisional basis requests, and the United States agrees, to "maintain certain of its armed forces in and about Japan . . . so as to deter armed attack upon Japan."

1 United States
39 Japan

REPUBLIC OF CHINA (Formosa) TREATY (BILATERAL)

A treaty signed December 2, 1954, whereby each of the parties "recognizes that an armed attack in the West Pacific Area directed against the territories of either of the Parties would be dangerous to its own peace and safety," and that each "would act to meet the common danger in accordance with its constitutional processes." The territory of the Republic of China is defined as "Taiwan (Formosa) and the Pescadores."

1 United States
43 Republic of China (Formosa)

PHILIPPINE TREATY (BILATERAL)

A treaty signed August 30, 1951, by which the parties recognize "that an armed attack in the Pacific Area on either of the Parties would be dangerous to its own peace and safety," and each party agrees that it will act "to meet the common dangers in accordance with its constitutional processes."

1 United States
38 Philippines

ANZUS (Australia–New Zealand–United States) TREATY (3 NATIONS)

A treaty signed September 1, 1951, whereby each of the parties "recognizes that an armed attack in the Pacific Area on any of the Parties would be dangerous to its own peace and safety and declares that it would act to meet the common danger in accordance with its constitutional processes."

1 United States
36 New Zealand
37 Australia

REPUBLIC OF KOREA (South Korea) TREATY (BILATERAL)

A treaty signed October 1, 1953, whereby each party "recognizes that an armed attack in the Pacific area on either of the Parties . . . would be dangerous to its own peace and safety," and that each Party "would act to meet the common danger in accordance with its constitutional processes."

1 United States
40 Republic of Korea

to guarantee independence, and the world fell back upon the only known alternative, the balance of power policy. The nations which feared and distrusted Russia drew together and created a counterweight to the Soviet bloc. An uneasy balance of power has been set up, which differs in two respects from the eighteenth- and nineteenth-century type. It no longer operates in Europe but on a global scale. It is not multiple but simple, and there is no longer a holder of the balance. The two leading powers, the United States and the U.S.S.R., are so much more powerful than their allies that they themselves largely determine the balance through their own preponderant weight.

Great Britain is no longer able to fulfill her traditional role of the holder of the balance. Nor can this be carried on by Britain together with her Empire and Commonwealth, for the looseness of the ties holding it together make its actual much less than its potential strength. The hope was expressed that Western Europe as a whole might take over the position of the balancer. The states of Europe, however, are so weakened by the war and also so divided that they cannot resist a Soviet attack without outside help. Western Europe cannot be the holder of the balance. Germany and Japan are beginning to recover their strength, and it is clear that each intends to follow its own independent policy and not be a docile satellite of the West. Neither of them could fill the role of holder of the balance, but they are sufficiently powerful for each of the blocs to be anxious to win their support. This gives them a bargaining power which will grow as their strength increases. To retain them on the side of the West will require a growing consideration of their national interests. India at present is not a leading power because of inadequate industrial development, limited wealth, and the smallness of her armed forces. She has considerable influence with the Asian neutral bloc, which is made up of weak and underdeveloped states. If they came under communist control, it would be a serious blow to the West owing to their combined resources and strategic position. So there are two blocs and in each of them the lesser allies are grouped around the predominant state. This is not a desirable situation, for a simple balance makes for increased tension and crises. As long, however, as international society is made up of sovereign states, the balance of power policy is unavoidable. The United Nations itself cannot operate successfully if there is no balance, because an omnipotent state can disregard it. The prospect of peaceful coexistence based on an armed peace, a balance of power, and a mutual fear of the consequences of a nuclear war is not entrancing. It reminds one of Bairnsfather's cartoon of World War I. Two soldiers had taken refuge in a shell hole during a heavy bombardment and one said to the other, "If you know of a better hole, go to it."

SELECTED READING

BALDWIN, HANSON W., *Power and Politics: the Price of Security in the Atomic Age.* California: Claremont College, 1950.

————, *The Price of Power.* New York: Harper and Brothers, 1947.

BECKETT, SIR W. ERIC, *The North Atlantic Treaty, the Brussels Treaty and the Charter of the United Nations.* London: Stevens & Sons, 1950.

BUSH, VANNEVAR, *Modern Arms and Free Men.* New York: Simon and Schuster, 1949.

LIDDELL-HART, B. H., *The Revolution in Warfare.* New Haven: Yale University Press, 1947.

LINCOLN, G. A. and ASSOCIATES, *Economics of National Security,* 2d ed. New York: Prentice-Hall, 1954.

POSSONY, STEFAN T., *Strategic Air Power: Pattern of Dynamic Security.* Washington: Infantry Journal Press, 1949.

ROYAL INSTITUTE OF INTERNATIONAL AFFAIRS, *Atlantic Alliance: Nato's Role in the Free World.* New York: Royal Institute, 1952.

————, *Defense in the Cold War, the Task for the Free World.* New York: Royal Institute, 1950.

CHAPTER 27

CONTEMPORARY ECONOMIC PROBLEMS

THE AFTERMATH OF WAR

The economic consequences of World War II were far more severe than those of World War I. The material damage in Europe and Asia was much greater and extended over a wider area, though even in the worst bombed areas the actual destruction was by no means complete. Even so, an immense amount of reconstruction was necessary to rebuild factories, mines, dwellings, bridges, railways, canals, harbor works, etc. Another cost of war was that the Germans had looted on a large and systematic scale, stripping the occupied countries of much of their movable property. Maintenance too had been postponed unless it were essential to the war effort. Everywhere machinery worked badly because it needed repairs or replacement. Stocks of raw materials had been used up, and heavy inroads made on mineral deposits, forests, soil fertility, flocks, and herds. The workshop of Western Europe was badly run down, and money was lacking to pay for the vast amount of material needed to restore it to productivity.

Two world wars had immensely impoverished the European peoples, who before 1914 had been the investing and controlling center of world trade. In addition to the heavy losses suffered at home, Britain, France, and Holland, in particular, found their invisible exports heavily depleted. Much of their merchant shipping had been sunk, and this together with the nearly fivefold increase in the number of American merchantmen deprived them of an important source of income from freight and passenger services. The dividends from foreign investments had fallen heavily. Some had been sold to buy munitions, others had been destroyed during the Japanese invasions of Southeast Asia, and still others were giving no returns because of the loss of European control in Indonesia, Burma, and Indochina. Owing to the great rise in prices after 1945, the income from the remaining foreign investments paid for fewer imports than in 1938. The marked decline in the triangular trade with Southeast Asia was an important cause of Europe's economic weakness. In 1938, for example, the United States sold to Europe $1,450,000,000 more than it bought from there. On the other hand, American purchases from Southeast Asia, especially tin and rubber, were far larger than sales to it, thus providing the area with a surplus of dollars. Southeast Asia used this money to buy from Europe much more than it sold to it or to pay interest on European capital invested there, and Europe in turn used these dollars to help pay its annual debt to the United States. After the war Europe was selling less to Southeast Asia, and the latter's exports to the United States had also fallen. This last was partly due to the development of the American synthetic rubber industry. Prewar Europe had had an important intercontinental trade. The industrialized nations of the west had sold manufactures to eastern Europe and the Balkans, receiving in return the food and raw materials which were their principal exports. After the war these countries were Communist satellites, and a large part of their production was diverted to Russia. Western Europe was compelled to obtain an increased part of its raw materials and food from the Western Hemisphere.

While Europe's economy had been shaken to its foundations, the United States had escaped the devastation of war, and as the arsenal of democracy had doubled its productive capacity and enormously increased its wealth. It accounted for 50 percent of the total production of noncommunist countries, and had 40 percent of the world's income. The United States everywhere sold more than it bought; while Western Europe had to buy greatly increased quantities but had far fewer dollars than before the war with which to pay. Canada, the other British dominions, and Argentina had taken great strides in industrial development, while increasing their agricultural output. To a much larger extent than before the war, they supplied their own needs in manufactures which they had formerly imported. The new independent countries of Asia, such as India and Indonesia, all had ambitious plans for industrialization. Everywhere Europe's prewar markets were contracting. Another minor blow was the very sharp decrease in trade with China after the Communist victory there. European production was loaded with heavy fixed charges that could not be reduced. Taxes were very high: in Britain they took about 45 percent of the national income. This was due in part to the domestic loans that had been floated as one method of financing the war, but also to the great extension of social services, e.g., the medical and hospital service provided in Great Britain mainly at the cost of the taxpayer. Wages had been raised and continued to rise sharply as postwar inflation set in, and the strength of the trade union precluded any idea of lowering them. Everywhere too it was recognized that full employment must be maintained, since large-scale unemployment would entail the danger of political revolution. The effect on international trade was that there was little possibility of exchange controls being removed until national reconstruction had been achieved, and until effective safeguards had been devised against sudden strains on the balances of payments.

POSTWAR BRITAIN

The position of Great Britain was crucial, since without her cooperation American plans for the restoration of multilateral trade could not succeed. Weakened and impoverished though she was, she was still the center of the sterling bloc, and the second largest trading and manufacturing nation. Forty percent of the total trade of the world was still financed in pounds sterling. Before the war her imports had exceeded her exports, and in 1936–1938 Britain had paid for them as follows: 55 percent from the sale of exports, 12 percent from shipping and 5 percent from banking and insurance services, and 23 percent from the income from foreign investments. This left a deficit of 5 percent, which was met by the sale of overseas holdings. During the war $4.5 billion of investments were sold to buy war supplies, of which $2,270,000,000 came from the sterling area and $1,725,000,000 from the United States and Canada. The Indian government paid off virtually all of the pre-war loans of $1,395,000,000 which it had floated in Great Britain, and other dominions did the same. Indians also bought some of the British enterprises in India, and toward the end of the war it was estimated that the British business investments there were reduced to $800 million. The British word for it was that to win the war they had had to spend most of their grandfathers' savings. The postwar result was that the income from foreign investments was greatly reduced. Further sales were made for some years after the war, e.g., in India, and by 1953 British business investments there were believed to be something less than $500 million. The extensive sinkings of merchant ships sharply curtailed the revenue from shipping services. Invisible exports could no longer fill most of the gap between imports and exports. Another result of the war was that Britain became a debtor nation. She owed over $4 billion to India partly in payment for supplies bought there for use in various theaters of war, and also for the cost of defending the country. When Indian troops fought outside India, e.g., in Burma against the Japanese, the whole expenditure was borne by Great Britain. She also incurred a heavy debt to Egypt for the purchase of supplies there for the British army which was defending the country against the Axis. These sterling debts totaled about $12 billion. Since the war they are gradually being repaid by the export of machinery and other manufactures to the creditor countries. This has been a heavy additional strain on Britain's balance of payments, since of course she receives no return for these unrequited exports. Frequently they require the use of imported raw materials, and it has been estimated that a sizable part of the Marshall aid granted to Britain was passed on to her creditors.

Britain's position came down to this that henceforth the great bulk of the imports must be paid for by exports. It was estimated that the exports must be 65 percent larger in volume than in 1938 in order to pay for the same quantity of imports as in that year, if the prewar standard of living were to be maintained. This must be achieved in spite of strong competition from the United States and, when they recovered, from Germany and Japan. In 1953 it was estimated that owing to the rise in prices since 1945 the increase in volume would have to be 75 percent over 1938. To make success more difficult a quarter of the national wealth was lost during the war. The alternative to this phenomenal expansion of exports would be a restriction of imports and a resultant fall in the standard of living. Distrust of the gold standard and laissez faire was widespread, and all political parties were determined to maintain full employment. The Labour party to a decidedly greater degree than the Conservatives believed that this could be done by planning and the maintenance of an elaborate system of controls over economic life. There was general agreement that imperial preference could only be given up in return for concessions of equal value. Influential groups went further and urged that in preference to multilateral trade Britain should concentrate on development and commerce within the sterling area.

The outbreak of war completely transformed the sterling bloc by creating the dollar pool. In spite of Lend Lease many goods had still to be paid for in dollars, and United Kingdom exports which would have earned them had been reduced to 31 percent of their 1938 volume. All parts of the empire except Canada mobilized and combined their resources in gold and dollars, by selling them to Britain and maintaining all or most of their currency reserves in the form of sterling assets. A unified system of exchange control was placed about the entire area. The dollar pool was managed from Great Britain, which supplied from it the foreign exchange that the member countries needed for imports. It was agreed that each would limit its demands to essentials. Sterling was nonconvertible: it could not, as before the war, be changed into dollars. No formal authority controlled the sterling bloc. Coordination of its operations was attained by constant discussion between the central banks and occasional meetings of the finance ministers, and not by dictation from London. Some members earned more dollars than they used, while others were allotted more to spend than they contributed. The arrangement was necessitated by the severe shortage of dollars, and it has been continued since the war for the same reason. In 1954 United Kingdom imports from the United States exceeded exports to it by $345 million, primarily because of the height of the American tariff. In addition there was the annual payment of principal and interest on the American loan of $3,750,000,000 made in 1946. Within the sterling area there were no exchange controls and no restrictions on trade (apart from tariffs) or the movement of capital. In this way a large area has freedom to trade, to travel, and to invest, far greater than could be achieved by its various parts acting independently.

MULTILATERAL *VS.* RESTRICTED TRADE

The position of the United States in 1945 was rather similar to that of Great Britain in 1815. Productive capacity and wealth had been immensely increased, while the European belligerents had been impoverished and their manufacturing, agriculture, and systems of transportation severely damaged. Americans like the British after the Napoleonic wars were not afraid of competition, and had a robust confidence in their ability to expand their trade if they could win free access to foreign markets. They, therefore, pressed for the restoration of multilateral trade in order to restore competitive world markets. The American proposal was that import quotas, exchange controls, and all forms of discriminatory trade regulation should be abolished. Tariffs should be reduced, and the new lower rates extended to all nations with which there was a most-favored nation treaty. The Americans were convinced that multilateral trade would create prosperity for the rest of the world as well as enhance their own. For one thing, the prosperity of the American farmers requires that they sell abroad from a quarter to a half of their wheat, tobacco, cotton and some other crops. Then again mass production is only possible if there is a very large market. For some American industries even the domestic market is not sufficient, and they need large foreign sales if they are to make full use of their productive capacity.

The countries of Europe doubted their ability to hold their own in free competition, particularly against the United States. It is easier to rely upon competitive efficiency when there is no doubt of one's own strength. Any sudden abolition of the controls on trade might impose an insupportable strain on the balance of international payments, with most serious effects upon the domestic economy. Suppose that Great Britain, for example, had suddenly abolished controls, domestic demand would have led to an inflow of imports which would have greatly exceeded the exports which the country was in a position to produce. Since the British demand for dollars would have been larger than the American demand for pounds, the foreign exchange value of the pound would have fallen. Gold and dollars would have been drained out of the reserves of the Bank of England. Importers would have had to pay more pounds to obtain the dollars with which to buy American goods. Inside Britain the price of imports would have risen. At the same time the lowered value of the pound would have increased the foreign demand for British goods, and many articles which would otherwise have been sold at home would have been diverted to export. The combined effect would have been inflation, from too much money chasing too few goods. Supposing the inflation did not become uncontrollable, eventually a new equilibrium would have been established with much higher domestic price levels, and the exchange value of the pound much lower in terms of dollars. This would have lessened the inflow of imports because of their en- hanced price while exports increased. The process of attaining the new equilibrium would have inflicted great hardships on large sections of the population. Nation-wide strikes would have won the wage earners higher pay, but the increase would have lagged behind the rise in prices. Even if distress and discontent did not lead to revolution, it is unlikely that free private enter- prise would have survived intact. Very probably the government would have hastily ended the experiment of a pound freely convertible into foreign cur- rencies by reimposing exchange controls.

While Great Britain was given as an example, the other nations of West- ern Europe were in the same situation. All of them experienced the problem of the dollar gap. There was a fundamental disequilibrium in world trade, inherent in the run down condition of Europe's manufacturing, its dependence on American imports, the lack of necessity for the United States to import heavily and its possession of the most extensive and most efficient industrial organization in the world. There was also grave doubt in Europe whether in the free enterprise system of the United States the government would be able to adopt the measures necessary to control the booms and slumps of the busi- ness cycle. If the nations of Europe abolished the controls which partially in- sulated them from outside influences, they feared that the economic fluctua- tions in the United States would react upon them with intensified effect. Dur- ing 1954, for example, the prediction was freely made that a 5-percent recession in American economic activity would mean a 25-percent recession in Euro- pean trade, since the United States would at once reduce its imports of raw materials and manufactures. In actuality, the effect of the American recession was much less serious than had been anticipated.

Western Europe was willing to agree to the abolition of controls and the restoration of multilateral trade, but it insisted that the change be made slowly and gradually. The governments also reserved the right to intervene in the system of free competition if national interests required it. That seemed to be about as close as any multilateral trading system would be allowed to come to the vanished world of pre-1914. A prerequisite to the establishment of multi- lateral trade by Europe was the increase of its exports in order to pay for imports. This in turn meant the repair of the damage caused by the war and the restoration and improvement of prewar productivity. Another matter which troubled Europe greatly was the limited market open to its products in the United States. Tariffs against its exports were frequently still high in spite of the reductions in import duties made by the Reciprocal Trade Act. Even before the war the United States had a favorable balance of trade with practically all its best customers. After the war the gap was filled by the United States lending or giving Europe the credit necessary to buy its necessities through the British loan, the European Recovery Program, and other aid programs. This could only be a stopgap solution, and in the long run there must be either a diminished demand for American exports or an increased import of European goods into the American market, or possibly both. The former solution would be disastrous for Europe and serious for some segments of the American economy, while lowered tariffs would encounter strong opposition in the United States.

THE INTERNATIONAL MONETARY FUND

One measure which the United States proposed to restore multilateral trade was the creation of a fund which would make it possible to re-establish an international monetary system. The International Monetary Fund was agreed upon at a conference of forty-four governments at Bretton Woods in July, 1944, and was formally inaugurated in March, 1946. The world was divided into countries with hard or dollar currencies and those with soft currencies such as Western Europe and the sterling bloc. The soft currencies were inconvertible, that is they could not be freely sold for foreign currencies without the consent of the national governments. As long as this continued, foreign international trade could not be freed from the fetters of exchange controls, for to do so would have the devastating effects on the domestic economy already described.

The Bretton Woods Agreement accepted the ultimate goals of stable exchanges and convertibility of currencies. A pool of currencies of $8,046,000,000 was created to which each member state subscribed an agreed quota, partly in gold and the rest in its own currency. The members promised that after a transitional period they would abolish exchange controls and make their currencies freely convertible. If temporarily there were an adverse balance of trade and the value of a state's currency fell, it could buy from the Fund foreign exchange with its own currency. This would avoid the need to reimpose exchange controls. No government might depreciate the exchange value of its currency except with the consent of the Fund. The exchange stability aimed at was not a revival of the gold standard. Perhaps because the Bretton Woods conference underestimated the extent to which the world's economic life had been dislocated by the war, the Fund has not succeeded in making currencies freely convertible.

THE INTERNATIONAL BANK FOR RECONSTRUCTION AND DEVELOPMENT

The International Bank was established in 1945 with a capital of $8,348,-500,000 provided by the member states. Of this only 20 percent was paid in, and the rest was held in reserve as a guarantee fund against any losses the bank might incur. In addition to the funds subscribed, the bank was authorized to borrow from private investors. Foreign private loans had been one principal cause of the great trade expansion of the laissez-faire period, and the need for them after World War II was obviously going to be greater than ever. It was also clear that in the abnormal conditions prevailing private investors would often refuse to take the risk unless special protection were granted them. The two types of investment contemplated were the reconstruction of war-damaged countries and the development of economically backward areas. In some cases the bank would give its guarantee to private investors and in others it would lend itself. The bank, however, was not to be a philanthropic institution: every project was to be most carefully scrutinized, and a loan would only be granted if it could be expected to be serviced and repaid. At first loans were made chiefly to Europe, but of recent years increased attention has been paid to underdeveloped countries.

THE INTERNATIONAL TRADE ORGANIZATION

The wartime agreements signed by all countries receiving Lend Lease from the United States contained a clause that action should be taken for "the elimination of all forms of discriminatory treatment in international commerce and the reduction of tariffs and other trade barriers." This attack on obstacles to trade was continued in the Anglo-American Loan Agreement of December 6, 1945, by which $3,750,000,000 was lent to Great Britain. Britain agreed not to impose quotas which discriminated in favor of any country. She also undertook to make the pound freely convertible and abolish the exchange controls over the dollar pool of the sterling bloc. The result of making the pound freely convertible in 1947 was that countries with which Great Britain had adverse balances of payment hastened to convert their pounds into dollars. In a few weeks most of what was left of the American loan was used up, and in self-defense the pound was again made an inconvertible currency. This premature attempt to achieve convertibility showed that the economic position of Great Britain would have to be greatly strengthened before it could venture to abolish exchange controls.

The United States in 1945 drew up its Proposals for the Expansion of World Trade and Employment, which embodied its ideas on multilateral trade. They were accepted in principle by the British delegates who arranged the Anglo-American loan in that year. Negotiations were continued through 1946, and in 1947 the United Nations called a meeting at Geneva to consider the plan and a second conference at Havana to draw up the final form of the agreement. At Geneva twenty-three nations negotiated a series of bilateral treaties which reduced the barriers against international trade on over 45,000 items, representing about half the total of world imports. The signatories included the United States, the British Empire, and some of the leading states of Western Europe and South America. The Soviet Union did not participate, just as it stayed outside the International Bank and Monetary Fund. The lowered duties, which went into force in 1948, were extended to all countries with which there were most-favored-nation treaties. The twenty-three states signed a General Agreement on Trade and Tariffs (GATT), which was a charter for the conduct of international trade. At Havana fifty-two nations ratified it with modifications and drafted the charter of the International Trade Organization (ITO), intended to be a specialized agency of the United Nations, to supervise its execution. In practice the ITO would have no power to compel obedience, since sovereignty remained in the hands of the member states. The United States found it necessary to make some concessions to the views of the other nations, but the final agreements were a substantial acceptance of the American position. This was qualified by a series of exceptions and escape clauses, which permitted the signatories under certain conditions not to carry out the principles accepted. It was agreed that quotas and import and export licenses should be abolished, with the exception that a state might impose them to safeguard its balance of payments. This compromise was inevitable because of Western Europe's dollar shortage. The United States itself has imposed quotas principally on foodstuffs, in order to maintain its agricultural policy, which has raised the domestic price of many farm products above that of the world market. India and a strong group of Asian and Latin American states insisted successfully on the right of an underdeveloped country to establish infant industries by imposing not only tariffs but quotas and other import controls.

The United States strongly insisted that there must be no discrimination and that most-favored-nation treatment must be applied to all signatories without exception. The signatories agreed that in the matter of imports they would avoid bilateralism and allow the products of every country to compete within their markets on equal terms, so that the determining factors in making purchases should be price and quality and not national origin. The nations that have a dollar shortage have not found it possible to carry out this undertaking. The signatories bound themselves to negotiate a substantial reduction of tariffs, but at the American request it was agreed that tariff concessions could be abrogated if the result was that increased imports threatened serious injury to domestic producers. The United States also succeeded in its opposition to the established rule that when preferential arrangements were made between the parts of an empire, e.g., British imperial preference, foreign states could not claim the benefits under the most-favored nation clause. The increase of existing preferences and the establishment of new ones was disallowed. Existing preferences were gradually to be reduced or eliminated in the course of negotiating tariff reduction treaties under the most-favored nation clause. Owing to protectionist opposition the United States has not ratified the ITO charter, and the agency has not come into being. Much of the intended program however has been carried out within the framework of GATT by a series of multilateral tariff conferences.

EUROPEAN RECONSTRUCTION

It was realized during World War II that relief would be urgently needed in the war devastated areas. The United Nations Relief and Rehabilitation Agency (UNRRA) was established in 1943 and ended its major activities in 1947. The greater part of its fund of $4 billion, the bulk of which was provided by the United States, was spent in Western Europe. This was succeeded by a series of loans and gifts, most of which came from the United States, though Great Britain and Canada provided comparatively large amounts. Assistance came also from the International Bank and the International Monetary Fund. The loans were soon exhausted, and still the problem remained unsolved. Gradually it was realized that the injury sustained by Western Europe was far more serious and extensive than had at first been thought. By this time too the cold war was well under way, and the strong political consideration had arisen that it was not in American interests to allow Western Europe to fall under Communist control. The result was the European Recovery Program and the creation of the Economic Cooperation Administration in 1948. An extensive program of rehabilitation was carried out in Japan, and in 1949 the Point-Four program was inaugurated for raising the standard of living in the underdeveloped countries.

The reconstruction of Western Europe had a remarkable measure of success. By 1954 industrial production was 50 percent and agricultural production 20 percent above prewar. Steel production was about 58 million tons a year, compared with Russia's 38 million tons. In Great Britain production was about 50 percent and exports averaged 60 percent in volume above prewar. By 1954 western Germany completed a remarkable recovery, and was again becoming a formidable competitor in world markets. Trade between ERP countries was greater than in 1938, and about 83 percent of it was freed from the crippling effects of quotas. By means of The European Payments Union their currencies were made more freely convertible than they had been for a quarter of a century with one another and with the pound sterling, though not into dollars. Western Europe's overseas trade was larger than it had been before the war. Yet despite all this the recovery was precarious, and its chronic symptom was the dollar gap.

The program of intensive rearmament which began after the invasion of Korea seriously complicated the restoration of Western Europe's economic viability. Broadly speaking, it had reached the stage of recovery where it could manufacture most of its necessities and had a growing surplus for export. It was not in a position, however, to divert a large part of its factories to the production of military equipment. The provision of American matériel lessened the difficulty to an important degree, but did not do away with it. It was still necessary for Europe to import very large quantities of raw materials, and their price rose precipitately. To some extent this was the result of the world-wide competition for them, and especially the very large orders from the United States. There was, however, a more fundamental cause, which was brought to a head by the armaments boom. Industrial production in the Western world was much higher than in 1938, and it was estimated that the demand for raw materials was at least 60 percent larger than it was then. During the same period the production of raw materials increased only 34 percent. Their price rose sharply to the detriment of the countries which were heavy importers of them.

EUROPEAN CUSTOMS UNION

The United States pressed hard for an economic union of the countries of Western Europe. One reason for America's phenomenal expansion was the size of the domestic market, which made mass production possible. By contrast the European market was divided into many semi-watertight compartments. This seriously hampered the development of large-scale industry. It also led to a great deal of uneconomic duplication, since the trend was for each country to supply its own requirements as far as possible. If Western Europe could form a customs union, its prosperity would be considerably increased, and it would become more self-sufficient and stronger. Economic union would not be a panacea however. Insofar as the dollar gap was caused by inability to sell enough European exports in the United States, a customs union provided no solution whatever. A customs union is formed when two or more countries abolish virtually all trade barriers against one another's goods and levy substantially the same rate of duties on imports from outside. GATT exempted customs unions from the obligation to extend the benefit of lowered trade barriers to other states under the most-favored-nation clause.

The obstacles to a customs union are formidable, and if success is achieved, it will be gradual rather than sudden. Great Britain will not join, partly because to do so is incompatible with imperial preference. The dominions are strongly protectionist, and they would refuse to enter a customs union which would freely admit European manufactures that would compete with their own industries. If Britain alone joined the free entrance of European goods would deprive the dominions of the preferred position in the United Kingdom market which they now enjoy under imperial preference. The likely result would be that they would abolish their imperial preference for Britain's manufactures. In 1954, 48.5 percent of her exports went to the sterling bloc and only 28.1 percent to Western Europe. Britain will not endanger her empire trade for the sake of her far less important European market.

A customs union confined to Western Europe only would be dominated by Germany, since economically she is by far the most powerful state. In this age of nationalism no country will allow such a thing to happen, and more especially so when the fear and distrust of Germany, stimulated by World War II, are so strong. Another important stumbling block is that each government is determined to maintain full employment and the existing wage and price level and system of social security. These differ widely, and the countries with a higher standard of living are afraid that they would fall if free entrance were allowed to the products of states with a lower standard. No government dare take the risk of letting this occur. It would also be dangerous to arouse the opposition of the powerful vested interests of the trade unions, industrialists and farmers which have grown up during the long evolution of separate national economies. This is the obstacle that has stood in the way of forming a Franco-Italian customs union. The French wine makers are afraid that they will be drowned in a flood of cheaper Italian wines. Benelux, the postwar customs union between Belgium, Holland, and Luxembourg, removed tariffs but retained quotas and placed much reliance on cartel arrangements to limit competition between rival industries, at least for a lengthy transition period. It seems that the most likely line of advance is by carefully measured reciprocal reductions of trade barriers which do not expose the negotiating countries to the risk of having an adverse balance of trade. This might take the form of a partial customs union or preferential agreements between countries in what is vaguely described as the same economic region, and is sanctioned by GATT.

EAST-WEST TRADE

The intention of the U.S.S.R. is to make the Soviet bloc into an economic unit which as far as possible shall be self-sufficient. Imports and exports are entirely controlled by the state and are allowed only so far as they serve economic, military, or political purposes. The economic life of the satellite states is being integrated into that of the Soviet Union, and great emphasis has been placed upon the development of manufacturing, particularly of iron and steel goods. Before World War II the exports of the satellite states to Western Europe amounted to over $1 billion, the principal items being food, lumber, and Polish coal. Trade with Russia was negligible, because the two areas were competitive and not complementary. Broadly speaking both were exporters of food and raw materials, and Russia could not supply Eastern Europe and the Balkans with the manufactures they had to import since she did not have enough to fill her own needs. It is a triumph of political compulsion over economics that since 1945 the trade with Western Europe has withered away and a large part of it has been diverted to Russia. This has been to the benefit of the Soviet Union but not of the satellites.

Western trade with the Soviet bloc is confined to what the government decides that it requires, and the quantity sold to the West is limited to the amount necessary to pay for the desired imports. The market for any particular commodity is likely to be closed whenever the Russian government changes its plans. A further limitation is that since 1949 the United States and the states of Western Europe have drawn up a list of strategic articles —both manufactures and raw materials—the export of which is forbidden to the Soviet bloc. The items on the prohibited list are of military importance, and many of them are commodities which Russia is anxious to obtain. At the present time the volume of East-West trade is less than half what it was before the war. The imports that the Soviet bloc desires are largely capital goods for its industry and certain minerals in which it is deficient. The principal exports to Western Europe are coal, timber, and grain.

The dollar gap strongly affects the position. It compels Western Europe to limit its imports from the dollar bloc, often below the quantity that is required. Europe cannot afford to ignore a source of essential commodities which will reduce its adverse balance of trade. To obtain them Europe must agree to supply something that the Soviet bloc wants, and sometimes articles of minor strategic importance have to be included. Norway for instance supplied a limited amount of aluminum in return for manganese and the Soviet purchase of the bulk of her salted herrings, a staple export not easily salable in the West. No responsible person has any extravagant hopes of the volume or dependability of future East-West trade, but there is the determination to develop it for what it is worth. This involves minor relaxations of the list of prohibited strategic goods, but no fundamental change in existing trade relations.

THE DOLLAR GAP

The *Economic Survey of Europe* in 1948 stated that "there are only three possible lines of solution to the balance of payments problems of Europe and the United States; Europe can expand exports, curtail imports or go on borrowing. The United States can expand imports, curtail exports, or go on lending." To some extent European exports to the dollar area have been increased; but in 1953 the dollar gap was still running at the rate of between $2 and $3 billion a year. The principal means of filling it since the war has been American aid, but that policy is coming to an end. When it does, Europe will suffer severely, and the present level of American exports will fall abruptly. One remedy adopted by Europe has been to restrict as far as possible American imports. Essentials, e.g., raw materials for industry, may be admitted in larger quantities than before the war, but this is done at the expense of commodities which can be dispensed with. A good example of this is the restoration of European agriculture with virtually the same crops as before 1939, e.g., cereals. This is done by means of tariffs and subsidies. It is not pretended that European wheat is as cheap as that of the United States, Canada or Argentina: Europeans merely say that they have no dollars to pay for it. It is for this reason that Great Britain, which before the war produced only about 31 percent of her food, is now providing 50 percent of it.

The unique position of the United States in the world economy is an important cause of the dollar gap. At one and the same time it is a leading exporter of raw materials, foodstuffs, and certain types of manufactures; it is also the greatest industrial and creditor nation; and it has a highly protective tariff. The richness and variety of its natural resources enable it to produce almost anything, and necessary imports are mostly raw materials. There are many foreign products which would add to the amenities of life, but few which are essential. The United States is under little compulsion to buy from Europe, while foreign nations are compelled to buy heavily from the United States. This situation already existed before the war, but has become much more pronounced since 1945. In 1954 American imports were $10,207,000,000, while exports were $15,073,000,000. This brings in the problem of the balance of payments.

If American exporters and investors are to receive payment, this can only be done by enabling the foreign debtors to earn enough dollars to discharge their obligations. The policy of nineteenth-century Britain is apposite. The establishment of free trade enabled foreign states so to increase their sales in the United Kingdom that they were able to buy large quantities of British merchandise and also repay the heavy loans floated there. The American tariff, however, is still a formidable barrier despite the reductions made under the Reciprocal Trade Act. This is the implication of the demand voiced by the nations of Western Europe for "trade not aid." Tariff rates need not be prohibitively high to curtail imports. It suffices if fairly heavy duties are placed upon the commodities which foreign states are in a position to supply. This puts them in the semiluxury class and effectively reduces their sale. The tariff of the United States is designed like most others to do this, and an added obstacle is the complexity of the customs regulations and the delays and uncertainties arising out of their administration. Moreover, when an import increases to such an extent as to conflict with any American product, there is likely to be pressure to increase the duty against it. This took place for felt hats, bicycles, tobacco pipes, Swiss watches, etc., and in some instances the tariff was raised. Lower duties granted under the Reciprocal Trade Act may be withdrawn if it is decided that the imports resulting from the new tariff threaten serious injury to domestic production. The effect on European exporters is to create the feeling that it is not worth while to incur the heavy expense necessary to win a place in the American market, since any marked success may be countered by excluding them from it.

This protectionist policy incidentally penalizes the branches of American agriculture and manufacturing which must sell part of their product abroad in order to have full production. When the entry of Dutch cheese was restricted under the Defence Production Act, Holland was compelled to reduce her imports of American wheat. Imports must pay for exports unless loans or grants are given to solve the problem of payments for the time being. Failing that, the effect of protecting high-cost industries is to reduce the sales abroad of the more efficient branches of American production. To quote Sir Arthur Salter, a prominent British economist:

> [Since] the logic of the balance of payments is inexorable, it follows necessarily that . . . America's exports will be determined to a dollar by her foreign customers' dollar resources. . . . If a tariff prevents foreigners from earning X dollars which they would otherwise have earned, the total value of American exports will be X dollars less than it would otherwise have been. If a subsidy is given to shipping or shipbuilding which reduces foreigners' earnings by Y dollars, other American exports will suffer to the extent of exactly Y dollars. If insistence on "non discrimination" prevents two deficit countries from making preferential arrangements with each other which are not extended to surplus countries, the effect must be that the advantage to some American exporters is offset by exactly equal disadvantages to others. "Non discrimination" is not beneficial to a surplus country, so long as there is a dollar disequilibrium. Insistence on it merely impedes the removal of the disequilibrium. And the removal of that disequilibrium is the prior condition of fruitful "non discrimination," genuinely multilateral trade and convertibility.

In clarification of the final point, the United States protested successfully against the discrimination in favor of empire fruit in Britain. This increased the sale of American fruit, but caused a reduction in the orders for other American products owing to the shortage of dollars.

THE STERLING BLOC

The dollar gap is one of the principal reasons for the continuance of the sterling bloc. So far as possible all the members reduce their purchases from the dollar countries and trade with one another. In 1954 Great Britain received 44.4 percent of her imports from the sterling area and sold to it 48.5 percent of her exports. The United States supplied 8.3 percent of the imports and took 5.8 percent of the exports, while the figures for Canada were 8 percent and 5 percent. Comparison with the years preceding World War II shows a marked increase in trade between the United Kingdom and the sterling area and a sharp fall in imports from the United States. Sterling imports into the United Kingdom rose from about 30 percent of the total to 44.4 percent, while those from the United States fell from 11 percent to 8.3 percent. Britain's exports to the sterling area rose from about 44 percent to 48.5 percent. In 1954 the finance ministers of the Commonwealth met in Australia in a mood of qualified optimism. Thanks to a favorable year, the trade accounts of the sterling with the dollar bloc were in precarious balance, but there was as yet no certainty that this could continue. The Conservative government of Great Britain had made progress in the abolition of controls over private enterprise. The bulk of the imports from Western Europe had been freed from quotas, and foreign owners of approved investments were free to withdraw their dividends and capital. There was no desire to turn the Commonwealth into a customs union. It was not and could not be self-sufficient. The finance ministers agreed that the ultimate aim of their governments was the establishment of a freely convertible pound sterling and multilateral trade.

The rate of progress toward the goal depended in part upon the success of the Commonwealth nations in controlling inflation and balancing their external payments, especially with the dollar bloc. It was also essential that the United States adopt "good creditor policies" by lowering import duties, and that the International Monetary Fund make loans more readily available to maintain the exchange value of currencies. As one means of expanding the Empire's exports the finance ministers agreed to hasten the development of its large latent resources. Preference was to be given to projects which would produce goods the sale of which would help to balance payments rather than schemes for social welfare. It has been estimated that a program of rapid development would require a capital investment of at least $1.4 billion a year, most of which would have to come from Great Britain. The prospect of private investors finding this amount seems uncertain in view of the very heavy burden of taxation. In 1951–1953 the net overseas investment averaged only $504 million a year. Taking everything into consideration, it would appear that convertibility and free multilateral trade are not in the immediate future. First of all the sterling bloc must solve the problem of getting a balance with North America.

A difference of opinion is developing on the continuance of imperial preference. The Canadian finance minister admitted that while Canada was influential in introducing it and benefited from it before the war, she was now in favor of abolishing it. "As a trading nation with dollar currency we find that preference now works in reverse with Canada. A British preferential tariff gives Australia and other countries a big edge in trading, but does not help us much." Before the war Canada bought the bulk of her imports from the United States and found her best markets there and in Britain. She owed money to the United States and was owed it by Britain. As long as the pound was freely convertible, Canada sold the pounds she earned to obtain the dollars she needed to settle her adverse balance of payments. During these years imperial preference enabled Canadian foodstuffs largely to replace American in the United Kingdom market. This triangular trade was a war casualty, since the Canadian dollar was linked with the American dollar and not with the pound. After the war Britain was compelled to reduce her purchases from Canada owing to her lack of dollars. Imperial preference ceased to be of great benefit to Canada, while multilateral trade and a freely convertible pound held out alluring prospects. Canada, therefore, became a strong supporter of GATT. Australia, however, and the other sterling bloc dominions found that imperial preference plus an inconvertible pound strengthened their position in the United Kingdom market. Therefore, they supported GATT in principle, but were in no hurry to dispense with imperial preference. One final change in Canada's trade position should be noted. She continues to buy most of her imports from the United States, but since the war this is also her best market. Sales to America far exceed those to Great Britain. The explanation is that the expansion of American production has forced manufacturers to turn increasingly to Canada for raw materials, particularly wood products and minerals.

THE PROSPECTS FOR MULTILATERAL TRADE

In 1953 the Randall Commission on American foreign economic policy emphasized the particular desirability of making the pound freely convertible. The dollar gap was at the root of the trouble, and to remove it the commission advised President Eisenhower that somewhat greater opportunities should be afforded foreign countries to earn dollars by increasing their sales in the United States. The Reciprocal Trade Agreement Act should be continued for three years and import duties moderately lowered. Customs regulations should be simplified, and the International Monetary Fund should use its resources more actively in assisting foreign governments to make their currencies freely convertible. President Eisenhower recommended the program to Congress in 1954, but supporters of high tariffs strongly disagreed with the proposals. In 1955 Congress passed a fairly liberal measure. The President's power to negotiate trade treaties with foreign countries was extended to

1958, and he was authorized to reduce American import duties by 15 percent in return for equivalent concessions.

It seems unlikely that European countries will ever be able to sell enough in the United States to pay for what they want to buy. The hope has been expressed that the gap might be filled by developing a triangular trade between the United States, Europe, and the underdeveloped areas. Industrial expansion in the United States and the depletion of natural resources will require a growing import of raw materials. The Paley Report estimated that by 1975 the United States would use 60 percent more raw materials than in 1950, and that most of the increased demand would have to be met by imports. Many of them could be obtained by developing the resources of the underdeveloped areas. Before the war the latter obtained the bulk of their imports from Europe, as they still do to some extent. If their purchases were increased and if currencies became freely convertible, Western Europe could use its favorable balance of trade with the rest of the nondollar world to pay its trade deficit with the United States. To some extent in the British Empire and certainly in the rest of the world, the bulk of the money for development would have to be found by the United States. The Randall Commission considered that most of it must come from private investors, and it diplomatically suggested that many foreign governments must create conditions more attractive to Americans before their funds would be forthcoming. The growth of strong nationalism in many parts of Asia and South America has created a hostility toward foreign investors, that leads them to keep their money at home.

SELECTED READING

BROWN, WILLIAM A., *The United States and the Restoration of World Trade.* Washington: Brookings Institution, 1950.

CASSEL, G., *The Downfall of the Gold Standard.* New York: Oxford Press, 1936.

CASSELS, JOHN M., *The Sterling Area: An American Analysis.* Washington: U.S. Government Printing Office, 1952.

CONAN, A. R., *The Sterling Area.* London: Macmillan and Company, Ltd., 1952.

CONDLIFFE, J. B., *The Commerce of Nations.* New York: W. W. Norton and Company, 1950.

ELLIS, HOWARD S., *The Economics of Freedom. The Progress and Future of Aid to Europe.* New York: Harper and Brothers, 1950.

HARRIS, SEYMOUR E., *The European Recovery Program.* Cambridge: Harvard University Press, 1948.

HEILPERIN, MICHAEL A., *The Trade of Nations.* New York: Alfred A. Knopf, 1947.

MEADE, J. E., *The Balance of Payments.* New York: Oxford Press, 1951.

VINER, JACOB, *The Customs Union Issue.* New York: Carnegie Endowment for International Peace, 1950.

CHAPTER 28

POWER VACUUMS

"Power vacuum" is a phrase used to describe an area which is too weak to defend its independence and which if it obtained it, would be in danger of coming under the control of a strong state. The only new aspect of this situation is the term used to describe it. Throughout history certain peoples have been more powerful than others because they surpassed them in degree of civilization, resources, or numbers. They took advantage of their greater strength to establish their rule over the weaker races. For the better part of two centuries Poland has been dominated by Germany or Russia or by both together. The twenty years of the Czech republic were a brief interlude between several centuries of control first by Austria and today by Russia. Korea for centuries was a dependency either of China or Japan. The retreat of Western imperialism is creating a number of power vacuums, and the simultaneous growth of Communist aggression has raised the problem whether these areas will exchange one control for another.

THE MIDDLE EAST

The term Middle East is used in the contemporary though technically incorrect sense to include everything from Egypt to Iran. Strategically it is of very great importance since it contains the crossroads of the routes of invasion between Europe, Asia, and Africa. Geographically these three form one single continent, and whatever nation holds the Middle East can move from one to the other by land. It can thus avoid interference from the powers which control the sea. This was of fundamental strategic importance in both world wars between Germany, primarily a land power, and Britain and the United States, which were first and foremost sea powers. The route which Germany used in the first and tried to use in the second world war led through central Europe and the Balkans to Istanbul or Constantinople and onward through Asiatic Turkey. From there one branch continued through Iraq, Iran, and Afghanistan into India. The African road diverged from Turkey

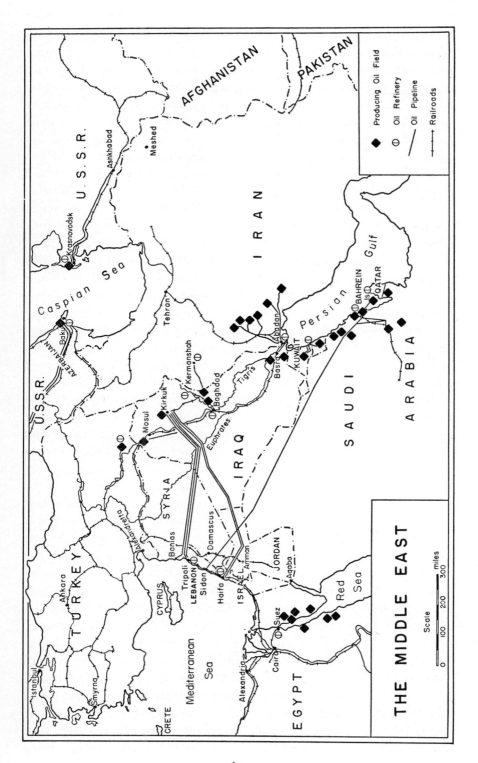

THE MIDDLE EAST

Producing Oil Field
Oil Refinery
Oil Pipeline
Railroads

Scale

miles
0   100   200   300

647

through Syria, Lebanon, and Palestine to the Suez Canal and Egypt. One route from Russia goes through Iran and Afghanistan into India. The other leads from Russia into Iran and Iraq, and from there through Syria into Egypt. For at least 4500 years invading armies have followed these roads.

The building of the Suez Canal increased the strategic importance of the Middle East, since the shortest sea route from Western Europe to India and the Far East passed through it. Whoever controlled the land would also control the canal. In the present century it was discovered that the Middle East had the largest untouched oil reserves in the world. After World War I came the development of the global air routes from America and Western Europe to the Far East and Australasia. All of them have to be routed through the Middle East, since foreign aircraft are not allowed to fly over Communist states. From the point of view of the Western powers and Russia, the Middle East is of importance less for itself than as a means of reaching the countries to the east and west of it. Transportation and oil explain why the United States and Great Britain are deeply concerned to keep Russia out of the area.

The traditional policy of Great Britain since the early nineteenth century has been to prevent any great power from gaining control of the Middle East. By preference Britain did not annex territory herself, but tried to block the attempts of first Russia and later Germany to do so. The favorite British method was to support the independence of the Middle Eastern states. During the nineteenth century this meant Turkey, which ruled over the whole Middle East except Iran and Egypt. After World War I the Arabs were liberated and divided into mandates, Syria and Lebanon going to France, and Iraq, Jordan, and Palestine to Britain. Britain's policy was to prepare her mandates for self-government and to assist Arabs and Turks alike in the maintenance of their independence. American interest in the Middle East prior to World War II was virtually confined to supporting the oil companies in their efforts to obtain concessions. After 1945 the United States became increasingly involved as opposition developed to Russian imperialism. In the global cold war the Middle East was too important to allow it to fall under Soviet control. The postwar weakness of Great Britain led the United States to take the lead in Turkey and Iran. American interests were the same as British, and the two followed a similar though not a co-ordinated policy.

Turkey is an essential part of the land route from Europe and also controls the sea passage from the Black to the Aegean Sea. Aircraft and warships based on Turkey could close the eastern Mediterranean to Western shipping. Its mountainous topography makes it the most defensible part of the Middle East. It has by far the best army, and its prestige stands high amongst the Arabs. They and Iran would be unlikely to resist for long once Turkey were conquered. Turkey has a population of 22,949,000, the large majority being peasant farmers of whom three quarters own their own land. The government established by Kemal Pasha was a dictatorship based on the support of the only political party allowed to exist. In 1946 it allowed the creation of an opposition party, and when the latter won a majority in the free election of 1950 it took over control of the government. Kemal and his successors worked with vigor and fair success to modernize and reform the country and improve the condition of the peasants. Turkey is almost free from the grave agrarian problem which exists in many Arab states. The Turks reject communism as merely the latest device of their hereditary enemy Russia, and therefore to be dismissed on general principles. They are resolved to keep their independence, and realize that they need foreign help to maintain it. They have satisfied themselves that neither the United States nor Great Britain wants to subjugate them, and therefore they are firmly on their side in the cold war.

The Arabs had been under Turkish rule for four centuries when they were liberated by the British during World War I. The strongest bond uniting them was the Arabic language and the Muslim religion and institutions; and the small minority of educated nationalists wished to establish a single, independent Arab state. There was no Middle Eastern Arab patriotism but rather a collection of local loyalties making for disunion. Arabs were loyal to Baghdad or Mosul or Damascus, but the conception of a Pan-Arab union was too big for their comprehension. Moreover, the Arabs lacked experience in self-government and in administration. The creation of a state including the whole Arab world would probably have been premature and a failure; and also it was ruled out by the wartime agreements between Britain and France. The French mandates of Syria and Lebanon won their independence in 1946. The British mandate of Iraq became independent in 1932 and Jordan in 1948. A Jewish National Home was established by the British in Palestine despite mounting Arab hostility, and after fighting a successful war it became an independent state in 1948. The kingdom of Saudi Arabia was completely independent from the start and included most of the Arabian peninsula. Britain overshadowed the Arab world during the interwar period, even after she conferred independence upon Egypt and Iraq. The explanation was that legally sovereign but weak states which have to rely on the help and protection of a strong power are not completely independent. When in difficulties, they turn to the advice and assistance of the dominant state.

Today the Arab countries have made some progress in developing national patriotisms, but the dream of union in a single state seems as far away as ever. The half Christian state of Lebanon is suspicious of its Muslim neighbor Syria, which in turn has no love for Jordan. The king of Saudi Arabia has a feud against the kings of Jordan and Iraq. Egypt wants the hegemony of the Arab world and looks with hostility on any Arab state which opposes it. If any state proposes a union, the others oppose it, lest their rival's power be increased. The principal policy on which all Arabs can unite is vehement hostility to the Jewish state of Israel. They can also combine in opposition to the West, apart from Jordan which is on the whole pro-British. The inability to work together is reflected in the Arab League, which was established in 1944 to promote unity in diplomatic, military and economic questions. Unanimity is achieved when it is a matter of opposing Israel or the West, but apart from this the League's meetings have reflected the disunity which is one of the chief causes of Arab weakness. Close cooperation with Turkey, e.g., a Middle Eastern defensive alliance, would be difficult to bring about. Turkey refused to join in the war against Israel, and its foreign policy has a Western orientation; while the attitude of the Arab states is strongly colored by suspicion and unfriendliness toward the West. Egypt, the principal Arab country, is jealous of Turkey's strength and prestige because of the former's ambition to be the leading Middle Eastern power. It will oppose any proposal such as the Turkish-Iraqi alliance which might weaken its own pretensions.

The Arab world and Iran are predominantly agricultural, but owing to the lack of rain only 6.15 percent of the area is cultivable. This varies from 2 percent in Egypt to 32 percent in Palestine. Apart from oil there are few industries, and the possibilities of future industrialization seem to be largely limited to the processing of local raw materials such as cotton. The population is about 64 million and rapidly increasing, and in 1950 the annual income per head for the whole population was around $100. A reasonably accurate estimate is that 10 percent of the population receive more than half the total amount, while the other 90 percent have an average income of about $50 per head. There are a small number of very wealthy landowners, most of whom are absentees and interested only in how much rent they can squeeze from their tenants. The bulk of the peasants own too little land to make a living on it or else are landless laborers or sharecroppers. Their normal rent is 50 percent of the crop, but sometimes the landowner takes as much as 80 percent. In addition, the peasants are heavily taxed and have a large burden of debt with excessive rates of interest to the moneylenders. Egypt has a particularly serious problem since the population is growing rapidly. A mere .49 percent of the population own 37 percent of the land, while 81 percent of the peasants are dwarf owners who hold only 13 percent of the area or landless laborers. Wages are very low since supply exceeds demand. The proposed Aswan Dam would increase the cultivable area by 30 percent; but the cost, estimated at about $600 million, is far beyond Egypt's resources, and she has been trying to obtain loans from the United States and Britain. They were hesitant about advancing so large a sum, but have agreed to finance the plan owing to the Russian offer of 1955 to build the dam. Throughout most of the Middle East there is a glaring contrast between the wealthy few and the poverty-stricken many. The peasants are beginning to lose their fatalistic acceptance of poverty as inevitable and want a better life. They might in time become fertile soil for communism, but they are still a long way from revolution. The small minority of poverty-stricken urban workmen are a more promising recruiting ground since they are less conservative in their outlook.

Egypt, Syria, Lebanon, Iraq, and Iran have been democratic in form and oligarchic in reality. They have been controlled by a small and corrupt governing class of landowners and wealthy merchants from the towns. They have done little to introduce agrarian reforms or improve the social services, which are very inadequate. To do this would lessen the income from their estates and compel them to tax themselves. Since they controlled the governments they have been in a position to block reforms. Eventually the armies led by their officers began to intervene in politics—in Iraq since 1936 and in Syria, Lebanon, and Egypt since World War II. They received a good deal of popular support, for democracy was discredited, and the opinion was prevalent among the Arabs that each state needed a Kemal Pasha to carry out reform with a strong hand. These military coups had as their avowed object the cleansing of democracy from the evil influences of the old-line politicians. The officers have wanted to introduce moderate agrarian reforms, but their success to date has been limited. It is possible that the sham democracies of the past will be replaced by military oligarchies. In 1956 Colonel Nasser, the ruler of Egypt, announced that he intended to establish a single-party elected legislature. It is understood that his followers will control the party and the election.

In foreign affairs the salient characteristic of the Middle East has been its intense nationalism, and except in Turkey and Jordan a hostility to foreigners which often comes close to xenophobia. This feeling has been growing for over a generation, and many of the politicians have intensified it. They discovered that a very good way to distract attention from their own shortcomings was to arouse patriotic indignation against the British and French as imperialist exploiters who denied the Arabs their freedom. The principal target has been Great Britain, since she was the country with which the Middle East came most into contact. Moreover, it was the British who established the Jewish National Home in Palestine despite mounting Arab protests and violence, and so made possible the ultimate creation of Israel. During the last few years hostility has also been aroused against the United States because of its strong support of the establishment of the Jewish state in Palestine. The Arabs consider that the United Nations has been pro-Jewish, and their suspicion and hostility extend to it, except insofar as they can use, e.g., the Trusteeship Council for their own purposes.

Hostility to Zionism has been the principal stimulant to the growth of Arab nationalism. It is largely responsible for holding together the loose confederacy of states that make up the Arab League. Jew and Arab represent two entirely different economies, religions, languages, mentalities, cultures, and civilizations. The Arabs fear that in the future Israel will try to conquer additional lands for its expanding population. Enmity is also kept alive by the presence in the Arab states of 800,000 refugees, the bulk of the Arab population of Israel, who either fled or were driven from their homes during the Palestine war of 1948. They have lost their property and livelihood, and are living in abject poverty and misery on a dole provided by the U.N. The Jews have the best army in the Arab world, the only comparable force being Jordan's small Arab legion created and led until 1956 by Glubb Pasha, a British officer. The Arabs were defeated and forced to accept an armistice, but they have refused to make peace. They have established a fairly effective boycott which prevents the Jews from selling their manufactures to the Arabs and buying from them in return the oil and food which they have to import. As long as the deadlock continues, any idea of cooperation in defense between Israel and the Arabs is out of the question, and an explosive situation will continue to exist along the armistice frontier. Arab-Jewish hostility will also continue to aggravate the ill will and suspicion which make the Arabs scrutinize with doubt any British or American proposal.

An undeclared guerilla war between Israel and the adjoining Arab states has been going on since 1948, and in 1955 the raids and counterraids became more serious. One principal reason why a full scale war was avoided was the military superiority of Israel. In 1955 Egypt bought large quantities of materiel from Czechoslovakia, and similar Communist offers were made to other Arab states. This increased the danger of war, besides strengthening the Arabs' feeling that Russia was their friend.

Any Middle Eastern state which has a quarrel with the West can count on the general support of the Arabs, e.g., Iran's nationalization of the Anglo-Iranian Oil Company's concession. They are determined to abolish any foreign "servitudes" such as the Anglo-Iraqi and Anglo-Egyptian alliances, since these are regarded as a lessening of their complete independence and equality. They are not impressed with the argument that American armed forces are stationed in Turkey, France, Japan, and Britain without these nations feeling that they have thereby become colonies of the United States. The leaders realize that owing to their poverty they need foreign capital to develop their resources and so raise the standard of living. At the same time foreign private enterprise is distrusted and disliked as exploitation, e.g., the popular agitation in Iraq to imitate Iran and nationalize the American, British, and French oil companies.

The attitude of the Arabs toward the cold war tends on the whole to neutrality. According to Hourani, an Arab authority:

For them it is unreal, an invention of Western propaganda, or else irrelevant, a quarrel between two groups of potential exploiters. . . . If forced to come down on the Western side they would do so with special reluctance because of their resentment of Western policy. Their immediate problem is still that of Western imperialism.

The Arabs have been in contact with France and Britain since the sixteenth century and recently with the United States, and their attitude is the outcome —to some extent a distorted reaction—of their experience. Unlike the Turks they have never had any contact with Russia, and therefore do not regard her as imperialistic. They refuse to face the danger of her military expansion along the invasion route from the East. The totalitarian character of Soviet rule does not repel a people whose own government has traditionally been autocratic. They have been somewhat influenced by Communist propaganda, which always presents the U.S.S.R. as the liberator of oppressed colonial peoples from their Western masters. There is also an element of fear of Soviet power. The Egyptians argued that when the British troops had withdrawn from the Suez Canal zone the Russians would have no reason to attack them, though the Iraqis who were nearest to Russia were in the end unable to persuade themselves of this. This was of course the argument of the European neutrals until Hitler attacked them in 1940. The Arabs have received very coldly the Anglo-American proposal for the creation of a Middle East Defense Pact. Their own suggestion was that the West put the Middle East on a sound economic footing and provide their troops with modern equipment. The Arabs would then defend themselves through the instrumentality of the Arab League, and Western troops might be permitted to return to the Suez Canal base if, but only if, an Arab state were directly attacked.

In 1955 Nuri es Said, the Iraqi prime minister, overcame domestic opposition and joined the alliance between Turkey and Pakistan. Britain and Iran also came in, and the government of Jordan declared its willingness to do the same. It was forced to abandon its intention owing to the serious riots that broke out in 1955 and 1956, and the adhesion of the other Arab states seems very unlikely.

Middle Eastern Oil

The oil of the Middle East could probably provide the whole world outside the Western Hemisphere and Russia with all it may want—and with enough left over to meet their demands. Europe has very little oil, and prior to 1939 its imports came partly from the Middle East and in part from the

United States and South America. At the present time 94 percent of its imports are from the Middle East. Not only is this the nearest source of supply, but much of it can be bought with sterling and to a modest extent francs, instead of spending the dollars which are so sorely lacking. The Marshall Plan took it for granted that Western Europe's oil would come from the Middle East. To a considerable extent the same situation holds good for southern Asia, Japan, and Australia. In Asia and Europe, just as in America, the consumption of oil has immensely increased since 1945, and there is every indication that it will continue to do so. The United States is also beginning to arrive at a stage where it will become increasingly dependent on imports of oil. The Middle East is on the whole a virgin field, for many of the companies only began production in the 'thirties, and their output is expanding very fast. Not only private American companies but also the government have been very much interested in acquiring a share of the Middle Eastern field as a reserve against future contingencies.

The cost of prospecting is high as is that of the refineries and other installations, and in addition, there is the expense of the fleets of oil tankers and marketing organizations. The result is that eight companies,—five American, two British and Dutch, and one French—control almost all Middle Eastern oil. Iran is believed to have very rich fields, and the Anglo-Iranian's (British and Dutch) concession was 15 percent of the total area. Production in 1950 was 242,475,000 barrels. Iraq's oil is controlled by the Iraq Petroleum Company, which is 47.5 percent British and Dutch, 23.75 percent American, and 23.75 percent French. The 1954 output was 252,722,000 barrels, or about five times what it was in 1950. Kuwait, a very rich field on the Persian Gulf, is 50 percent American and 50 percent British. Its 1954 production was 347,955,-000 barrels compared with 125,722,000 barrels in 1950. Saudi Arabia, the largest and probably the richest of all the fields, is an American monopoly operated by Aramco. The concession covers 440,000 square miles, and the production in 1954 was 347,845,000 barrels as compared with 199,547,000 in 1950. Minor but valuable and promising fields are the Bahrein Islands in the Persian Gulf (American monopoly) and Qatar in Arabia (owned by the Iraq Petroleum Company group). The companies' concessions expire about the year A.D. 2000. Total Middle Eastern production was 1,015,929,000 barrels in 1954 and 657,374,000 barrels in 1950.

Several of the companies have built pipelines to ports on the Levant coast, e.g., Aramco and Iraq Petroleum, and also refineries, to avoid the long voyage via the Suez Canal. Many of the companies have training programs for employees and provide them with social services similar to those of Anglo-Iranian. Profits are usually shared equally between the company and the Arab government. The very large sums now received—$500 million in 1952 —promise to revolutionize conditions of life in several states, e.g., Iraq hopes very greatly to develop its irrigation works. Other Middle Eastern countries have not shared in this prosperity since oil has not been found there.

Egypt and the Suez Canal Base

When the British government intervened in Egypt in 1882 it intended the occupation to be temporary. The troops were to be withdrawn as soon as the authority of the Khedive had been restored. Unrest was so serious, however, that it became clear that the disorders would start all over again as soon as the army left. The British government decided to remain until peace, order, and prosperity were firmly established, and for nearly forty years they were the power behind the throne in Egypt. They restored the government to solvency, lowered the taxes, increased the revenue by financial reforms, put down graft and illegal exactions levied on the peasants, improved the medical and education services, and greatly increased the cultivable area by building irrigation works. Egyptian nationalism gradually developed, especially among the middle class which grew up under British rule. In 1919 a revolt broke out under the leadership of the Wafd political party. It was suppressed, but in 1922 the British government granted part of the nationalists' demands. Egypt was recognized as an independent sovereign state, and a democratic constitution was established. Britain made several reservations including the right to protect the Suez Canal, and troops remained in the country for this purpose. By this British action Egypt obtained control of her own affairs for the first time since the Persian conquest in the sixth century B.C. During the 2400 years that followed she was ruled amongst others by Persians, Greeks, Romans, Arabs, Turks, and Mamelukes, but never by Egyptians. When the British came in in 1882, they did not overthrow a native government: the Khedive was an Albanian and the ruling class were Turks. Under the British the native Egyptians began a rise to power which culminated with the dethronement of King Farouk in 1952 and the seizure of power by the army.

The Egyptian nationalists never accepted the British reservations, but in 1936 the position was regularized by a defensive alliance. They were frightened lest Mussolini's conquest of Ethiopia should be followed by an attack on Egypt, and they realized that British help was needed. British troops were to be stationed in Egypt for its defense and that of the Suez Canal, and the alliance was to last until 1956. The treaty might be revised after ten years if both governments consented, but any revision would provide for the continuation of the alliance. During World War II the Egyptians gave the economic help called for by the treaty. The war ended the Axis threat, and Egyptian nationalism intensified. The alliance was regarded as out of date and a restriction on independence, and negotiations were begun for its revision in 1946. The troops were withdrawn from the Nile valley to the desert near the canal, and the British Labour government offered to remove them alto-

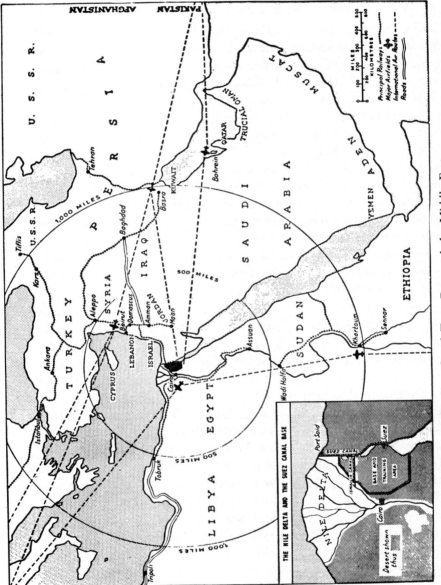

The Suez Canal Zone Base and the Middle East

Courtesy of the British Information Services

gether. It insisted however that they must return in the event of war or imminent threat of war, and that the base in the Canal Zone must be kept in a state of readiness by the Egyptians under an Anglo-Egyptian Control Board. Egypt rejected this offer and also the proposals on the future of the Sudan (the upper Nile valley which was under joint Anglo-Egyptian rule), and in 1951 she denounced the treaty. The British government pointed out that a treaty cannot be abrogated except with the consent of both signatories, and stated that the troops would remain as authorized by the alliance. It proposed that the single-handed British occupation of the Canal Zone base be terminated and replaced by an international army under a joint Middle East command. Egypt would be a full partner, along with Great Britain, the United States, France, and Turkey. In an emergency Australia, New Zealand, and South Africa would send troops if possible. Other Middle Eastern States were invited to join the common defense as partners. Egypt rejected the proposals, anti-British hostility mounted, and there were serious riots in Cairo and guerilla attacks on the troops in the Canal Zone, encouraged by the Wafd government.

The army revolted in 1952 under the leadership of a group of junior officers, who had as their nominal head General Neguib. They abolished the monarchy and drove the old guard of politicians from power. The government like its predecessors found it very difficult to agree to anything except complete surrender to its demands. For over thirty years Egyptian politicians acted on the principle that the best way to remain in office and distract public attention from their failure to introduce reforms was to blame everything on the presence of British troops. If any government showed a willingness to compromise, it was discredited by accusing it of being the servile tool of London. Gradually the propaganda created in the public an unreasoning emotional hostility to an oppressive and Machiavellian enemy which was holding them in servitude. To accept anything less than unconditional evacuation was high treason. The Egyptians insisted on regarding the question as purely a domestic one. They refused to admit that they had the geographic misfortune to live in a country which was as important strategically as, e.g., the republic of Panama, and that the outside world dared not allow them to settle the problem as they chose. Even a dictatorship like the military clique was to some extent the prisoner of the blind patriotism which had been worked up, and which it further intensified by inflammatory speeches. Any concessions would be seized upon by its enemies as a means of regaining power.

The Suez Canal Zone base was in both world wars the principal supply base for the campaigns in the Middle East and Libya. The total area was seventy miles by ninety, and in addition to three permanent army camps there were twelve airfields and one of the world's largest army, air force, and navy supply dumps. There were big repair shops, oil stores, power plants, military seaports, hospitals, railways, and all the other facilities needed for the maintenance of an army of a quarter of a million. The value of the installations was estimated at $1.3 billion. Several years would be needed to dismantle the base and rebuild it elsewhere, and no other site had the same strategic advantages. The base did more than protect the Suez Canal; no other site was so well placed for defending most of the Middle East, including the land invasion route into Africa which runs through Egypt. A thousand-mile radius of air action from the Canal Zone covers the southern Balkans, Turkey, the Iraq-Iran border, and nearly half the Arabian peninsula. The base was less open to attack than Basra or other Persian Gulf ports since it was further away from Russian territory.

The astronomical quantities of stores needed by a modern army in time of war would have to be sent by sea, for sufficient air transport does not exist. The possibility must be faced that the Mediterranean might be closed by enemy aircraft and submarines. This means that supplies might be cut off from any area with seaports only on the Mediterranean. In this list are Libya (where there is already an Anglo-American air base), Israel, and the British island of Cyprus. In addition, the last two are too small for the needs of a modern army. Jordan is large enough and has been a firm ally of Great Britain, but its only seaport, Aqaba on the Red Sea, can hardly accommodate anything larger than a fishing boat and has no road or rail communications with the interior. Iraqi ports on the Persian Gulf are dangerously close to Russia, apart from the heavy expense of building a new base. Egypt has seaports, such as Suez, which can be reached via the Red Sea. This was the route by which the British armies in Egypt were supplied in World War II. It is this back door on a fairly safe sea route that makes the Canal Zone uniquely suitable as a base.

The Egyptians believed their own army could defend the Suez Canal if provided with equipment. In 1948 however it was completely defeated by part of the Israeli army, although it was the best armed of all the Arab forces. What took place on that occasion was similar to what had happened to many other Egyptian armies in the past. Even the whole of the Arab League states could not build up an effective defense without the participation of troops from the Western powers. The British government was anxious to conciliate Egyptian and Arab opinion as far as possible. In 1953 it agreed in principle that the troops be withdrawn, and abandoned the demand that Egypt join a Middle East defense organization. Instead Egypt would maintain the base in readiness for use. The negotiations reached a deadlock over the conditions on which the troops might return. Britain contended that this was necessary in case of a direct attack on any Middle Eastern state, or if there were a clear threat of war in the area. The attitude of the American government was that the British troops should be withdrawn, but that the base should be kept in good working order and "be available for immediate use on behalf of the free world in the event of future hostilities." Egypt insisted that she would permit automatic return of the troops only if she or one of her partners in the Arab League were directly attacked. This would not cover an invasion of Iran or Turkey, which were the first line of defense in the Middle East. Egypt was also hostile to the Turkish-Pakistan treaty of 1954, which was intended to be the nucleus of a wider Middle Eastern defensive pact.

In October, 1954, Britain and Egypt signed an agreement by which the British troops were to evacuate the base within twenty months. It was to be greatly reduced in size and maintained in readiness for immediate use. For seven years the British forces could reoccupy it if an attack were made on Egypt, a member of the Arab League, or Turkey. In the event of a threat of an attack on any of these states Britain and Egypt would at once consult one another. The British right to use the base would end after seven years unless the two governments both decided to extend the agreement. Given the Egyptian desire for neutrality, it is impossible to predict what effect these last two clauses would have. One reason for the action of the British government was the desire to conciliate Egyptian and Arab nationalism and improve diplomatic relations with the Middle East. Eden defended the agreement against attack in the House of Commons on the ground that "The government had to adapt their minds to the conception that countries did not like to have foreign troops on their soil. Western nations tolerated it more easily than those where nationalism had recently been resurgent." The army made a strong case that with so many troops needed for overseas service in Germany, Malaya, Korea, etc., it was "overstretched and overstrained." If a sudden emergency arose, there was virtually no strategic reserve in Britain available for reinforcements, and there could be none as long as 65,000 soldiers were locked up in the Suez Canal base. The treasury stated that $140 million a year could be saved by withdrawing them. It was also pointed out that the destructive power of the hydrogen bomb had made the plans "which were founded and well knit together a year ago obsolete."

The government decided to bring back to Britain nearly two thirds of the troops. The remainder would be sent to Cyprus, Malta, and Libya. These were far from ideal, but apart from Jordan they were the only bases available. Jordan was unsuitable for the reasons already given, and in Iraq the nationalists were demanding that Britain give up the airfields which she held under the terms of the Anglo-Iraqi alliance. The only solution was to form a new system of alliances for the defense of the Middle East. Nuri es Said, the prime minister of Iraq, was a nationalist but not a fanatic, and despite opposition he was determined to replace the Anglo-Iraqi treaty by a regional alliance which would include Britain and Turkey and if possible some of the Arab states. In 1955 the Anglo-Iraqi treaty of defense was replaced by an alliance between Iraq, Turkey, and Britain. The former British airfields were handed over to Iraq, but were to be used by all three allies. Both Britain and the United States agreed to help in strengthening the Iraqi forces. Egypt tried hard to prevent the formation of the alliance, from jealousy of Turkey and because Iraq's refusal to give in to her objections weakened her leadership in the Arab world. She opposed the efforts of Turkey, Iraq, and the United States to persuade other Arab states to join the pact. Egypt succeeded in forming an opposition defensive league of herself, Syria, and Saudi Arabia in order to reassert her leadership. Syrian public opinion was sharply divided whether it should follow Egypt or Iraq.

The British position in Cyprus has been threatened by the Cypriot demand for Enosis or union with Greece. Cyprus is a small island forty miles off the coast of Turkey, and has a population of 514,000. It has never been part of Greece and the Cypriots are not Greek in race. About 80 percent of them however speak Greek, belong to the Orthodox Greek Church, and want to join Greece. Their leaders are the Orthodox Greek clergy and the local Communist party, which has a strong following and wishes to deprive the NATO powers of their Cypriot airfields. Enosis receives strong support from the Greek government and people. The remaining 20 percent of the Cypriots are Turks. They are content with British rule but are bitterly opposed to Enosis. Turkey strongly supports them partly from racial sympathy, and also because Cyprus in hostile hands would be a danger to her security. The Turks do not believe that Greece is strong enough to defend Cyprus in the event of war, and they are afraid that it might be captured by the Communists. Britain has more than once offered Cyprus domestic self-government; but it refuses to allow union with Greece as long as the struggle with Russia continues. Aircraft operating from Cyprus could reach almost any point in the Middle East, and the island is now the only base left to Britain in the eastern Mediterranean. The supporters of Enosis have replied by a terroristic campaign of sabotage and assassination of British and pro-British Cypriots, and so far all attempts to arrange a compromise have failed. In the international field Enosis has weakened NATO. It has estranged Greece from Britain, and has gravely damaged relations between Greece and Turkey. The intensity of Turkish feeling was shown by the very serious anti-Greek riots in Istanbul and Smyrna in 1955.

IRAN

Iran has the misfortune to be a weak state in a geographic key position. It forms part of the land roads of invasion to India and Africa, and its seaports on the Persian Gulf could be made into naval bases for attacks on the Indian Ocean sea route. The discovery of oil early in the twentieth century made it even more of a temptation. For about a century and a half Russia has been trying to annex it, and for much of that time Great Britain has been supporting its independence in order to keep Russia as far away as possible from India and the Indian Ocean. The concession granted to the Anglo-Iranian Oil Company in 1901 gave Britain an additional motive, since oil in the British Empire is limited. The British navy obtained much of its oil from Iran, and for this reason the British government holds 53 percent of the shares of the company. Politically and economically Iran follows the pattern of the Arab states already described. In constitutional theory the government is a parliamentary democracy and the shah or king has limited powers. In practice, Iran is controlled by an oligarchy of the landowners, wealthy merchants, and the small educated class. Apart from personal gain, the aim of the political parties has been to keep Iran safe for the wealthy few and avoid any agrarian reforms or expansion of the inadequate social services. The latter would require changes in the existing taxes which fall heavily on the poor and touch the rich lightly. The Tudeh or Communist party is almost the only one which is well organized. While it is always pro-Russian, it makes a parade of devotion to Iranian nationalism and freedom, and it is anti-American and anti-British. For tactical reasons it assisted Premier Mossadegh in his attempt to make himself a quasi dictator. Dr. Millspaugh, an American authority on Iran, considered that "a small organized minority with a definite aim and persistent activity can seize power from a majority that is divided, confused, cowardly, and corruptible."

Russia's attempt to create a puppet republic under her control in the province of Azerbaijan in 1945 and 1946 showed that the Kremlin had inherited the tsarist policy of aggression against Iran. After World War II it became clear that Great Britain no longer had the resources to continue her policy of single-handed support of Iranian independence. The United States therefore took over the main burden of bolstering up Iran. An American military mission was sent to train the troops, and army equipment was supplied. Small grants and technical assistance were given for economic development, but the request for a large loan of $250 million to assist in carrying out an ambitious development plan was refused. Russia strongly protested that Iran was becoming an accomplice of the United States in establishing a base that threatened Soviet territory. These veiled threats had their effect on a weak state, and much as Iran wished to preserve its independence, it felt itself obliged to steer a careful course between the two great opponents in the cold war.

In 1955 it joined the Bagdad Pact, the alliance between Turkey, Iraq, Pakistan, and Britain. On paper this closed the gap between Iraq and Pakistan, but the advantage will be more apparent than real until the training and equipment of the army have been improved and a stable government assured.

The Anglo-Iranian Oil Company

The company's concession covered 100,000 square miles, and was valid until 1993. Its refinery at Abadan was the largest in the world, and its 1950 production of 32 million metric tons supplied about 20 percent of Western Europe's requirements and over half of Asia's. The total value of the company's property was stated to be about $1.5 billion. Wages and working conditions were superior to those given by Iranian employers, as were the low-cost housing, free hospitals, etc., provided at company expense. The company also trained Iranians both in Abadan and Britain for skilled employment. E. A. Bayne, an American authority, estimated that the royalties and taxes paid to the Iranian government provided about 32 percent of the annual revenue. Iran has the same intense nationalism as the rest of the Middle East, and the same dislike of foreigners particularly the British. Gradually the Anglo-Iranian Oil Company became the focus of popular ill will. It was not merely that the company made a large profit, though this was resented. There was also the question of prestige: the largest oil refinery in the world was run by a board of foreigners sitting in London. This was resented as a symbol of Western predominance. Fanatical Muslim mullahs or priests such as Kashani, the holy terrorist who helped Mossadegh to power, aroused the latent hostility of the people to Christians and foreigners. The governing class found that to blame the company for exploitation was an excellent excuse for the wretched social conditions prevailing in the country, and their own failure to tax themselves in order to improve them.

Negotiations took place in 1948 and 1949 for an increase in the payments to Iran. The government rejected the company's offer of 50 percent of the profits from its holdings in Iran only, because it believed it would receive more by accepting a share of the receipts from the world-wide operations. The company had other oil fields besides those in Iran and sold oil in many countries. In 1949 a complicated agreement was drawn up by which the government was to receive a considerably larger royalty on the oil produced in Iran, and also a share of the profits from the company's activities in all parts of the world. General Razmara, the premier, delayed for a long time the submission of the agreement to the Majlis or parliament for ratification, owing to the growing nationalism and xenophobia which Mossadegh and the Mullah Kashani were fomenting. Eventually the Majlis rejected the agreement, and in February, 1951, the company reverted to its earlier proposal to share profits equally, but on Iranian oil alone. General Razmara accepted it, but he was murdered in March by a member of the Fadayan-I-Islam, a patriotic terrorist organization controlled by the Mullah Kashani. Mossadegh became premier, and the Majlis passed a law that nationalized the oil industry. Mossadegh, himself a wealthy landowner, assured the Majlis that the revenue from the oil industry would pay for all the social services and make it unnecessary to tax the ruling class.

The nationalization law created an Iranian company which was directed immediately to take over and operate the assets of the Anglo-Iranian Oil Company. Twenty-five percent of the current net income was to be deposited in an Iranian bank to pay compensation. This was to cover only the refinery and other physical assets of the company in Iran, and nothing would be given for, e.g., the abrogation of a contract which still had forty-two years to run. The government's "lawful and rightful claims" were to be deducted from the compensation, and Mossadegh stated that they included $137 million of royalties which would have been paid under the 1949 agreement if the Majlis had ratified it. The company and the British government accepted nationalization, but insisted on adequate compensation. They denied the claim to a royalty based on an agreement which Iran had rejected. The British also protested at Mossadegh's conception of negotiations, which was that he should dictate terms of settlement and the company should agree to them. This was in violation of a clause of the company's contract that its rights would never be changed by the single-handed action of the Iranian government, but only by agreement between them. Great Britain invoked another clause which stipulated that if Iran and the Company were unable to agree the dispute would be referred to arbitration. She took the case before the International Court of Justice, and asked it to rule that Iran was under a legal obligation to submit the dispute to arbitration. Mossadegh refused to agree to arbitration and denied the right of the International Court to adjudicate in what he claimed was a purely domestic matter. The British government appealed to the U.N. Council, but it voted to shelve the question until the International Court had given its decision. In 1952 the court decided by a vote of nine to five that it had no jurisdiction in the case and declined to pass judgment on the legality of Iran's attitude.

On October 4, 1951, all British oil technicians were expelled, and the whole of the company's plant was closed down, since no Iranians were capable of running it. The government's attempts to sell the oil in storage were a virtual failure, since the big oil companies refused to buy it. Mossadegh's seeming success had suggested to some of the Arabs that a similar policy might be profitable. The American and French oil companies had no desire to assist a policy which might lead to the nationalization of their own concessions. Temporarily the closing of the Iranian field reduced the Middle Eastern output of oil by 37 percent, but by the end of 1952 the loss had been made up by greatly expanded production in other parts of the area. Owing to the increase of production in Kuwait, the sheikh of that little state of 170,000 people suddenly found himself in receipt of an annual revenue from royalties of $159 million in 1953. To make up for the loss of Abadan, the building of refineries was accelerated in Western Europe and elsewhere. By 1954 Iranian oil could only be marketed by reducing production in other parts of the Middle East, though it could not be called superfluous in a world where consumption was continuing to grow.

Meanwhile in Iran the economic and political situation steadily worsened. The budget deficit mounted sharply, and there was hardly money to pay the police, officials and the 77,000 unemployed oil workers at Abadan. The failure of Mossadegh's oil policy roused increasing opposition among the politically conscious minority; but he dealt with this by intimidation, terrorism, and a rigged election. Eventually he became virtually a dictator and began to break down the authority of the Shah. Just when it seemed that Mossadegh had reached the pinnacle of success he was overthrown in 1953 by a *coup d'état* under the leadership of General Zahedi. The general found that Mossadegh's policy had cost Iran about $600 million, and that the country was on the verge of bankruptcy. He appealed to President Eisenhower for a large loan. The President made only a small grant, and replied that the American taxpayer could not be expected to carry an additional burden when Iran could find the necessary funds by settling the oil dispute. The general agreed with the logic of the suggestion, but Mossadegh had stirred up such intense xenophobia that he had to move cautiously.

By the end of Mossadegh's period in power it appeared inevitable that a ruined Iran would become a Red Iran. As this prospect grew more menacing, the economic consequences of the loss of Abadan to the outside world began to fade. To set Iran on her feet in the interests of world security became the dominant aim of Anglo-American policy. This enabled the Iranian government to drive a much harder bargain than would otherwise have been possible.

Mossadegh's nationalization was accepted, and the oil fields and refinery remained the property of the Iranian government. For the production and marketing of the oil Anglo-Iranian lost its monopoly and its place was taken by a consortium of eight of the principal oil companies—five American, one French, Anglo-Iranian, and Royal Dutch Shell (British and Dutch). Forty percent of the shares in the consortium were held by Anglo-Iranian, 14 percent by Royal Dutch Shell, 6 percent by the French, and 8 percent by each of the five American companies. The consortium set up two companies which had the exclusive right to prospect and operate the oil fields and refineries in the area covered by the concession. The consortium agreed that by the end of three years it would export about two thirds as much oil as Anglo-Iranian had been exporting each year before Mossadegh dispossessed it. Payments made to the Iranian government would amount to 50 percent of the value of the oil exported. The agreement was to run for forty years and might not be altered in any way by the Iranian government. In the event of disagree-

wars, but otherwise interfered little with the authority of the caïds. These chiefs realized that if Istiqlal and the sultan won their independence, they would impose their authority on the tribes, and therefore the majority side with the French. In 1953 El Glaoui, the pasha of Marrakech, mobilized the Berbers and with the support of French officials brought about the dethronement of the sultan. Ben Youssef was restored to his position in 1955 as one consequence of the serious revolt which forced a reversal of French policy.

France does not intend to relinquish North Africa and leave the French colonists without guarantees against discrimination. To do this would leave them at the mercy of a largely illiterate Arab majority. Since they have created much of the wealth of the country, they would be elected to pay the bulk of the taxes, without any prospect of sharing control of the government. A second reason for France's attitude is that the African airfields and naval bases combined with those of southern France are essential for the maintenance of French power in the western Mediterranean. The fear of war with Germany also exerts a strong influence. In North Africa, and especially among the Berbers, the French have some of the finest natural fighting men in the world. Like the Romans who ruled North Africa 2000 years ago, they have enlisted them in large numbers in the colonial army. In both world wars the North Africans were an important part of the French forces, and partly compensated for the numerical superiority of the German army.

The Arab League supports the nationalists' demand, and the Arab-Asian bloc has brought up the question several times in the U.N. The French supported by the British have strongly opposed all discussion on the ground that this is a domestic question which the U.N. is precluded from handling. The United States has been sympathetic toward the nationalists from traditional hostility to imperialism, and because it desires to establish closer and friendlier relations with the Asian states. On the other hand, it is not in American interests to weaken France or lessen French support for American policy in Europe. Moreover, the United States has built six large air fields in North Africa which play an important part in the plans for defense against Russia. They would be used as way stations on the route to the advanced bases in Saudi Arabia, Turkey, and Greece. North African nationalists resent the existence of these bases, and if they controlled the governments, they might well try to abolish them. Pulled both ways, America has followed an uncertain policy toward the nationalists' demands.

Serious disturbances occurred throughout North Africa in 1954–1955, marked by guerilla warfare and assassinations of French and North Africans who supported them. Over 300,000 troops, nearly half the French army, were used to cope with the outbreaks, thereby seriously weakening the NATO defense in case of a Russian attack. Negotiations were carried on between the French government and the Tunisian nationalists, and an agreement was reached in 1955. Tunisia was granted domestic autonomy, and guarantees were given that there would be no discrimination against the French minority. French officials and police would be replaced by Tunisians over a period of twenty years, and a constitutional monarchy would be established. France retained control of defense and foreign policy, and financial and economic relations with France remained unaltered. As a result of the widespread revolt of August, 1955, in Morocco the French government opened negotiations with the nationalists, with the intention of concluding an agreement similar to the one made with Tunisia. The French attitude was that complete autonomy was as impossible for Algeria as for Brittany, since it was an integral part of France unlike the protectorates of Tunisia and Morocco. The 1955 uprisings disclosed such prevalent discontent that the government announced its intention of introducing political reforms, as well as economic measures to improve living conditions. The great problem is to devise a compromise which will be accepted by the extreme Algerian nationalists who demand complete independence, and the French minority who have been terrified and embittered by the organized massacre of hundreds of French and pro-French Algerians during the revolt.

KENYA

The outbreak of Mau Mau terrorism in the British colony of Kenya drew attention to a situation which might develop into another power vacuum, not only here but in some other parts of Africa if the Negroes obtained their independence. The area is 224,690 square miles, about the size of Colorado and New Mexico, and the population is 5,842,000. Of these 5,640,000 are Africans, 130,000 Indians, 42,000 Europeans, mostly British, and 30,000 Arabs and half castes. The Indians, who emigrated to Kenya during the past sixty years, are townsmen who control the retail and part of the export trade. A large part of the Europeans are farmers who live in the White Highlands, an area of 16,700 square miles where only Europeans may own land. Of this, 4000 square miles are forest reserves, but the remainder is open to cultivation. The average elevation is between 3500 and 5000 feet, and at this altitude permanent settlement by Europeans is possible in the tropics. The settlers have come in during the past fifty years, and can claim to be permanent inhabitants as much as the Negroes and Indians. Most of the Africans are peasants tilling their own small holdings or employed on European farms, but an increasing minority live in the towns. Africans occupy 52,000 square miles of uplands of the same character as the White Highlands, and an additional 150,000 square miles of semiarid territory has a small population of pastoral nomads.

Kenya is a plural society and the situation resembles those in French

North Africa and South Africa. The colony is inhabited by races separated by different civilizations and standards of value, there is virtually no inter-marriage, and each seeks primarily to advance its own interests. The chief point of contact but not of union is economic. In other respects the different sections of the community live side by side, but separately, within the same political unit. The Europeans occupy the top stratum of society since they control the government and large-scale business and agriculture. Next come the Indians who dominate retail trade and money lending. At the bottom are the Africans as subsistence farmers, laborers, and office clerks. They have a minor role in the administration through their partial control of local gov-ernment. In all societies economic forces make for tension between groups with competing interests such as capital and labor. In a homogeneous society like the United States or Great Britain the conflict is lessened by common racial origin and citizenship, but in a plural society there is a corresponding cleavage along racial lines. The development of conflicting nationalisms, African and Indian as well as British, has begun to intensify the separation. Most Africans are still indifferent to politics, but the educated minority has begun to aspire to majority rule, which means African rule. The Indians dis-like the superior position of the Europeans, and they realize that if this could be overthrown and unrestricted Indian immigration allowed they would dominate the more primitive Africans. The leaders of the British settlers are willing to form an interracial partnership, but they do not intend to accept majority rule since they are far superior in knowledge, wealth, and political maturity, and it is they who have created the prosperity of Kenya. This pro-vides a possible opening for communism, which as yet hardly exists. One of its cardinal principles is to capture the leadership of colonial discontents by posing as the champion of nationalism and freedom. If Russian com-munism succeeded in enlisting the Africans on its side, so that the frontier between Western democracy and its enemies became racial as well as ideo-logical, then the danger to the West would be multiplied.

All this lurks behind the Mau Mau society, though it has no connection with communism so far as can be ascertained. The beginnings of the story go back sixty years, when Kenya was a congeries of warring tribes and the British were starting to establish their control. The Kikuyu were a some-what unwarlike tribe of cultivators who had the misfortune to be the nearest neighbors of the Masai, a particularly warlike tribe of nomadic cattle farmers. The Kikuyu abandoned part of their tribal lands in self-preservation, and Masai attacks together with an epidemic of disease reduced their numbers by somewhere between 20 and 50 percent. The result was that when the British arrived about 9000 out of the 12,700 square miles of cultivable land in the Highlands were unoccupied except for intermittent grazing by the Masai. The government bought most of the land from the Masai and the rest from the Kikuyu and other tribes and sold it to European settlers, largely between 1902 and 1915. The African tribes were given reservations which were more than sufficient for their numbers at the time.

During the first half of the twentieth century the African population more than doubled as the result of the British suppression of intertribal warfare and raiding for slaves, and the introduction of Western medical and health measures. While the death rate fell, the birth rate remained at the former level. Shifting cultivation increased the pressure of the population on the land. At any one moment a tribe cultivates only a small portion of its territory. Each family burns the forest on a few acres, farms it for several years until the fertility begins to decline, and then abandons it for a fresh tract of ground where the process is repeated. Anywhere from five to twenty years used to elapse before the family worked back to the original area, and meanwhile nature had restored its fertility. This form of arable farming requires a large stretch of territory and was feasible as long as the population was limited. It became progressively more unworkable as the population increased, cash instead of subsistence crops were grown, and part of Kenya was reserved for the White Highlands. Land was brought back into cultivation long before nature had restored its fertility. Joined with the primitive character of African farming methods, the result was erosion, which progressively reduced the fertility of the soil. The stock-raising tribes came to the same end by keeping larger herds than the size of their pastures warranted, thus leading to overgrazing and erosion. At present Kenya just manages to feed itself in a good year. The final result was that the reservations became overcrowded, and a growing number of Africans had to obtain employment in the towns or the White Highlands. The Europeans farmed their land scientifically, and today "through contrasting land use, the borders between native reserves and European areas, originally arbitrary, have become arresting features of the landscape."

The Kikuyu are a tribe of about 1 million adjoining the White Highlands and are more politically minded than the other Africans in Kenya. Suffering from overpopulation, the Kikuyu increasingly felt that the Europeans had taken their land from them and that their problems would be solved if they were allowed to take over the White Highlands. Secret societies and belief in magic are common in African tribes, along with oaths the binding force of which is based on black magic and ritual murders. By combining terrorization with appeals to discontent and age-old superstition a widespread and powerful secret society named Mau Mau was built up. The movement was antiwhite and anti-Christian, and the goal was to drive out the Europeans and re-establish Kikuyu control of the land. The method was the murder of isolated Europeans and of Kikuyu who were Christians or were loyal to their British employers or to the government. A guerilla war broke out, and by 1955 the Kenya government had greatly weakened the power of the society by means of British and African troops and a voluntary Kikuyu militia.

To allow the Kikuyu to settle in the White Highlands would be only a palliative. The growing population would soon require still more land, and African farming methods would create the erosion and falling fertility that are characteristic of the reserves. The plain fact is that in Kenya, as in a great part of Africa, traditional agriculture has become obsolete. Moreover, the Africans are beginning to want Western social services, and a subsistence farmer who eats most of what he produces cannot create a surplus large enough to pay the taxes necessary to support the social services of a modern state. African methods must be drastically modernized both in arable farming and stock raising. The government has been trying to do this, but at present only a minority of the peasants are willing to follow its advice. Far more strenuous efforts are needed to bring about reforms, and they will meet with much opposition. It is also necessary to draw off some of the surplus farm population by establishing industries to produce some of the articles which at present have to be imported. The colony is in the middle of a ten-year plan that calls for the spending of nearly $100 million on social services, over half of it on agriculture and the development of natural resources. Much of the money comes from Kenya's own revenue; but a substantial part is being provided by Great Britain under the Colonial Development and Welfare Act.

The Europeans will be essential for a long time to come. It is they who produce a great deal of the food on which the colony depends and 70 percent of the exports which pay for the necessary imports. They provide about two thirds of the taxes which pay for the Africans' social services. These are admittedly inadequate owing to insufficient revenue, but without the Europeans they would be very much more so. Only the Europeans can provide the capital necessary for future development, and they alone have the technical, administrative, and political knowledge that are essential. When the British first went to Kenya in the eighteen nineties, the Africans were in much the same stage of tribal development as the British themselves 2000 years ago. In two generations the Africans have gone a long way, but they could not be expected to progress from the iron age to the twentieth century. One evidence of this is the Mau Mau's use of witchcraft to spread its authority. Politically, the Africans are immature, and the immediate introduction of full parliamentary democracy and adult suffrage would be premature. If Kenya is to enjoy prosperity and racial harmony, it will have to be on the basis of a partnership between Africans, Indians, and Europeans. The Legislative Council, which controls legislation and finance, has a majority of unofficial or popular members representing the Europeans, Indians, Arabs, and Africans. In 1954 the

British government carried political education a stage further. It gave the population partial control over the executive by appointing six Europeans, Indians, and Africans to the sixteen-man Council of Ministers which decides policy for submission to the legislature.

UNDERDEVELOPED AREAS

The underdeveloped areas include the greater part of South America, Africa, the Middle East, South and Southeast Asia, and the Far East. Their population, including the 900 million who were recently and in some cases still are under colonial rule, is roughly 1,650,000,000 or two thirds of the world total. In most of Asia and part of South America the annual income per person was roughly estimated to be less than $100 a few years after World War II. It was believed to be about $60 in South Asia and $89 in the Middle East, compared with $473 in Western Europe, $560 in Great Britain, and $1680 in the United States. Sixty-six percent of the world's population has about 17 percent of its income, while 18 percent of the population has 67 percent.

Colonial governments during the past century tried to raise the standard of living, but their resources were completely inadequate. This was not because the metropolitan powers imposed a tribute: revenues raised in a dependency were spent there for the benefit of the local population. The general rule however was that each colony must live within its income: the ruling power refused to subsidize it. As a result, if a dependency were lucky enough to have valuable resources like Philippine sugar or Malayan tin and rubber, its standard of living was comparatively good and its social services fairly adequate. The poorest colonies had the worst social services because their taxable capacity was so low that nothing better could be afforded. In India, for example, in the nineteen thirties the average income was $30 and the tax per head was $1.75. India had the population of Europe without Russia, but to pay for all the expenses of government there was less than the revenue of New York City.

The first real break with the past came with the British Colonial Development and Welfare Act of 1940, which has been re-enacted in an enlarged form every five years. It laid down the revolutionary principle that it was the duty of the British taxpayer to provide, for a substantial period of years, money for development of resources or the improvement of public welfare in the colonies. Between 1945 and 1960 Great Britain will have contributed $616 million to supplement the funds raised by the colonial governments. A considerable part of the funds is allotted to education, medical and health services, low-cost housing, and nutrition. Part of the money is being spent on irrigation, soil conservation, hydroelectric projects, harbors, and other plans for economic development. Without that it would be impossible in the long run for colonies to maintain from their own resources the improved standard of living which the grants from Great Britain are temporarily providing. For the time being the taxpayer in Great Britain is taxing himself to give the peoples of the tropics better social services than they can afford to pay for themselves. This cannot continue indefinitely for in the long run the Britisher, who is protesting against the burden of taxation, will feel that it is impossible that he should be called upon for indefinite sacrifices for the benefit of the tropics. Ultimately a people will only have the social services for which they can afford to pay. It is essential therefore to expand the productivity of the tropics so that their taxable capacity will be adequate to support the social services that their peoples are beginning to want.

The changed attitude toward underdeveloped countries, heralded by the Colonial Development Act, comes in part from the humanitarian feeling that the Western nations have an obligation to assist the less prosperous countries. It is also considered that to raise their standard of living would greatly increase their value as markets for Western manufactures. Consumer goods, such as textiles, would of course be provided by their own factories; but there would still be a wide range of commodities, e.g., machinery which they would buy from the more developed industrial nations. Enhanced prosperity would also be a valuable means of combatting the spread of communism, which makes most headway amongst those who are poor and discontented. The masses in the underdeveloped areas are losing their traditional acceptance of poverty as inevitable, and are beginning to believe that it should and could be remedied. The Communist agents who galvanize these feelings into action are not so much the peasants themselves as the educated middle class. To a poor peasant there is a strong appeal in a program which promises to liquidate the landowner and the moneylender and give him the ownership of a farm free from debt. Admittedly this is not orthodox Marxism: it is more like an extreme form of free private enterprise. The Communists realize that the underdeveloped areas are not yet ripe for communism, and that to gain control they must camouflage their ultimate aims and exploit local grievances. In 1918 Lenin rallied the Russian peasants to his side by promising them ownership of the land. Communist agents also make great play with the material advances which they have introduced in the Soviet Union. The irrigation works, railways, and modern cities they have built in central Asia are intended to be a show window to impress the rest of Asia. Their effect on Asians should not be underestimated just because they do not awaken similar admiration among the peoples of the United States and Western Europe, who have a much higher standard of living than the Russians.

The United Nations has been giving technical assistance as far as its funds permit. In 1949 President Truman announced his Point-Four policy, and since that date economic and technical help has been given to Asia,

Africa, and South America. Apart from the Development Act, which applied to her dependencies, Great Britain contributed about $2 billion to South Asia between 1945 and 1950. In 1950 the Colombo Plan was adopted by the British Commonwealth to assist India, Pakistan, Ceylon, Malaya, and British Borneo. It illustrates so many of the problems and difficulties of aiding underdeveloped areas that it is worth analyzing in some detail. The Colombo Plan is concerned with projects which are beneficial but would never pay cash dividends and so do not appeal to private investors. If they are to be carried out, they must be financed by government grants and loans. They include the building of irrigation and hydroelectric works, roads, railways, and harbor works, and these account for over 70 percent of the expenditure. Industrial development amounts to another 10 percent, and the remainder is devoted to technical education, research, health, and housing programs. The completed plan is expected to bring 13 million acres more land under cultivation and increase food production by 6 billion tons. To date over 7 million acres have benefited by irrigation works in India alone, and the country has almost achieved self-sufficiency in food. Burma in 1952 reclaimed 633,000 acres of rice land which had gone out of cultivation since 1941. Part of the program calls for teaching the peasants better farming methods. Asians are to be trained partly in their own countries and in part abroad, and anywhere between 500 and 750 Western technical experts are being sent to South Asia. Seventy-four percent of the plan concerns India, 15 percent Pakistan and 5.5 percent apiece Ceylon and the British dependencies. It is expected to increase food production by 10 percent over the six-year period of the plan; but, on the other hand, the population seems to be growing at the rate of 1.5 percent per annum, and the projected health program will cause a further increase by lowering the death rate. National income is expected to rise by about 7.3 percent during the six years, and this again will hardly balance the population increase. The governments frankly admit that the plan will do little more than hold the present position, besides laying the foundation for subsequent improvement in the standard of living which will have to be financed by other Colombo Plans.

The question of finance deserves careful study, for it illustrates the problem inherent in all similar projects. The total cost of the Colombo Plan was estimated at $5,230,000,000 of which India and the other beneficiaries could provide only $2,195,000,000 from domestic capital. The reason was that "productivity and national income per head are so low that . . . the flow of savings is insufficient, for the great mass of the people have no margin above subsistence level." Income was low because productivity was low, and most of the former was spent on necessities so that far too little was saved to finance an ambitious development plan. Foreign capital to the amount of $3,035,000,000 was needed, and of this Great Britain promised to find $1,090,000,000 in grants and loans, and Canada, Australia and New Zealand about $224 million.

This left a gap of $1,721,000,000, which could be filled only by the United States. Her attitude, therefore, was crucial to the success of the plan. The United States became a member of the Consultative Committee of the Colombo Plan, but her grants have been given directly to the member countries through the Foreign Operations Administration. In 1951–1954 she made available in grants and loans for the whole of South and Southeast Asia about $867 million, of which $504 million went to India and Pakistan. Over half of this was special grants and loans for the shipment of wheat to relieve the emergency of a crop failure. In 1954–1955 India and Pakistan received about $145 million in economic aid. In 1955 the President's requests to Congress called for the expenditure of $1,451,000,000 in economic assistance to noncommunist Asia from Afghanistan to Japan. Only a small part of this was earmarked for the original Colombo Plan countries. Part of the deficit was filled by loans from the International Bank for Reconstruction and Development, but it could not be said that adequate funds were assured to carry out the plan. Altogether economic aid to India by 1956 was $325 million. It was clear that only a limited contribution could be made by Great Britain and the Commonwealth, and that not much could be expected from the impoverished countries of western Europe. The original membership of the Colombo Plan has gradually been expanded to include Burma, Indonesia, Vietnam, Laos, Cambodia, Thailand, the Philippines and Japan. The position of Japan will be that of a contributor rather than a recipient of development assistance. One way in which she can help is by giving training in improved techniques, e.g., of rice cultivation.

Little accurate data exists on the total cost of a program of aid to all underdeveloped areas. India's Bombay Plan, drawn up in 1945, partly depended upon obtaining $5 billion from the United States and Great Britain. Pakistan in 1953 suggested an American loan of $1 billion without interest. A group of experts appointed by the United Nations estimated that the capital required annually to extend industry and agriculture in order to raise the national income of the underdeveloped areas by 2 percent per capita was $19,134,000,000. Of this amount $10 billion a year would have to be provided by the West, including $3 billion as grants in aid which the recipients would not repay. The actual inflow including grants and loans about 1950 was estimated to be at most $1.5 billion and probably nearer $1 billion. When one considers the straitened finances of postwar Europe, it is clear that if this plan were ever carried out the bulk of the funds would have to come from the United States.

The money might be obtained either by private investment, the traditional method prior to 1939, or by government loans and grants as in the Mutual Security Program and the Colombo Plan. The former has become much less important since 1945 for several reasons. Taxation in many Western countries has become so high that corporations and individuals have far less to invest than they did a generation ago. In Great Britain not enough investment capital has been available even for the necessary expansion of domestic enterprises, and still less for the overseas empire. Furthermore, an investor looks for security as well as profit, and here as a general rule tropical colonies are less safe than the domestic field, and independent underdeveloped areas are the riskiest of all. Investment in the tropics has peculiar dangers which are not found in Western countries. Tropical diseases even today may play havoc with the labor force and require heavy expenditure for medical and health measures. Soil and climate are so different from those in the West, and so little research has been done on them, that as the British East African peanut fiasco showed, large amounts of capital can be lost while finding out how not to farm. From the Western point of view labor is often erratic and undependable, since in many countries it is drawn from peasants who prefer to work their own land instead of entering the employment of foreign enterprises. Some investors have done well, and others have lost every cent they put in. Rubber companies, for instance, made fortunes when rubber sold for $3 a pound in 1910, and they went bankrupt when the price was four cents in 1932. If both gains and losses are taken into account, the average profit has been much less than is frequently imagined. An analysis of the figures relating to some 200 Malayan rubber companies showed that on the total money invested the return was roughly 4.5 percent. The investors could have done as well if they had kept their money at home.

Political uncertainties have considerably increased the hazards, particularly in independent countries. Private buying of foreign government bonds, which was at one time the largest category of foreign investment, has virtually ceased. In 1946, 48 percent of all foreign government bonds sold in the United States were in default, as were 68 percent of the loans to Asia and Latin America. Many parts of Asia and Africa are suffering from a severe colonial hangover. It takes the form of an intense, and in our eyes unreasonable, suspicion of Western nations. Their actions are suspect as a veiled attempt to undermine the independence so recently won. The Western investor is under the additional handicap that he is regarded as an exploiter who drains the country of its wealth and is indifferent to its welfare. He establishes only those enterprises which are profitable to himself, and not those which would fit into a comprehensive and well rounded plan of development. The great bulk of American as of European investment in the underdeveloped areas is in the production of raw materials and not in manufacturing, which is what the governments of these countries want. Government policy in the former Asian colonies is semisocialist and involves more control of operations than is relished by foreign businesses. Many nationalists like Mossadegh demand nationalization of foreign enterprises. In some cases this has been carried out without adequate compensation as in Burma. In Indonesia pre-war companies are theoretically free to resume operations, but in practice they have often been unable to do so. Profits have been lessened by enhanced taxation, higher pay, and regulations about conditions of employment. Exchange controls often forbid the withdrawal of annual dividends. Sometimes governments are weak, and there is the fear that they may be overthrown by force.

The foreign investor insists on a stable government that can maintain law and order, reasonable taxes, and not too much interference with his operations. He wants what he considers a fair rate of return to compensate him for his risks, and in practice this means a higher rate than he would receive in his own country. He must be able to withdraw annual profits and exchange them into his own currency since otherwise he cannot enjoy the return from his investment; and if his enterprise is nationalized, there must be full compensation. If these demands are not met, the investor declines to invest. The governments of underdeveloped areas often realize the need for foreign private investment and would like to attract it, as in Egypt, Burma, and Indonesia. Nationalism is so strong, however, that if they give guarantees which satisfy the foreigner, they run the risk of being accused of betraying the national interests. In 1953 the Indonesian government was unable to carry out its policy of restoring the plantations on the east coast of Sumatra and the oil field in the northern part of the island to their foreign owners.

There has been little new private investment in underdeveloped areas since World War II, especially by Americans. The great bulk of it has been in Canada, Venezuela and the Middle East, about 70 percent being in oil. Of the $14.9 billion of American foreign investments in 1951, 37 percent was in Latin America, 29 percent in Canada and only about 11 percent in Asia. The Western investor would like to stop communism, but he is not prepared to risk his own capital to do this. Either he invests at home—about 99.5 percent of American private investment is domestic—or else he puts it where he thinks it is safe. Only $860 million was invested abroad in 1952, most of it in the Western Hemisphere and Middle Eastern oil. The United States has been trying to safeguard the interests of foreign investments by negotiating treaties which guarantee that dividends may be converted into dollars and withdrawn, and that adequate compensation will be paid in case of expropriation. Such treaties do not exist with many countries seriously in need of investment capital. The government also offers insurance protection to new American investments abroad against the risks of currency inconvertibility and expropriation, but few have taken advantage of it. Incidentally, if development of natural resources by foreigners and the draining away of the annual profits to the investing country is a sign of colonialism, then Canada has a colonial status toward the United States, just as the United States had toward Great

Britain in the nineteenth century. This is the price they had to pay for the rapid development of their resources, since they did not have enough native capital to finance their own exploitation. This situation is not a stigma of inferiority, but an economic phase through which an undeveloped country has to pass. Both the Point-Four policy and the Colombo Plan assumed that the bulk of the money needed to raise living standards in underdeveloped areas would come from private capital, but so far at least it has not been forthcoming. Lord Brand, a leading English banker, expressed strong disbelief that American and Canadian investors

with the strongest and safest investments at hand in their own safe countries . . . are going freely and widely to invest their savings in a world where, by and large, there is little political or currency stability, where the rights of private capital are much less regarded and where sometimes, as soon as the borrowing country has received the money, the charge of exploitation may be made against the lenders. I think we must put out of our heads the idea that there will be any very large amounts of private money directly available at present from creditor countries for underdeveloped countries.

The alternative method of financing development is by government to government loans and grants-in-aid as in the Colombo Plan, but here another set of difficulties presents itself. In many underdeveloped areas, e.g., the Middle East, the government is controlled by a wealthy oligarchy which follows the principle that there is no point in possessing authority unless one makes a financial profit out of it. In these cases there is danger that funds may be misapplied or dissipated through inefficiency and corruption, unless there is firm guidance from without. But if a Western nation insists on controlling the use of the money it provides, it will be accused of infringing national independence and will arouse against itself the hostility of the people. It might be easier to handle this delicate situation if the Western nations empowered the United Nations to control the disbursement of aid to underdeveloped countries instead of doing so themselves. The United Nations might be less likely to arouse suspicions of Western imperialism, since these countries have more confidence in the impartiality of an international organization in which they are themselves represented. American expenditure on economic assistance to underdeveloped Asian countries rose from under $100 million in 1948 to $1,451,000,000 in 1955. The latter figure included items which would strengthen defense as well as promote economic development. The avowed aim of the administration was to disprove "the spurious claim of Communist China to possess and be practicing the only effective formula for rapidly improving the material well being of underdeveloped and densely populated countries." They lacked the capital for their own development, and since private foreign investment was only "a trickle," it was necessary to provide government grants and long-term loans. Opposition came principally from the Republicans in Congress, and the President was supported by the Democratic majority. Much larger amounts than this would be needed substantially to improve the living standard of so many hundreds of millions. If they are forthcoming it seems pretty clear that they will have to be provided by government and not by business corporations, as originally proposed.

The Western powers alone had given help down to 1955, but in that year and 1956 the Russian government suddenly pressed offers of economic assistance on the countries of the Middle East, South and Southeast Asia, Liberia, and South America. The Kremlin offered, for instance, to build the Aswan Dam, steel mills, jet aircraft factories, and ordnance and tool plants, and to train technicians in its colleges. Asians were greatly impressed with this seeming generosity, and their self-respect was pleased since they thought they saw a way of escape from economic dependence on the West which had irked their pride. What they seemed to overlook was that their countries were to pay by sending their raw materials, and that this might make them increasingly dependent on the Russian market. Moreover, Soviet help meant the arrival of Russian technical advisers, who most certainly would not confine themselves to their economic functions. How far the Soviet bloc can fulfill its lavish promises is uncertain; but it has two advantages over the Western capitalist states. The direction of its foreign trade is influenced by considerations of political advantage as much as by the hope of profit. Moreover, a police state can divert commodities needed at home to foreign markets whereas it is difficult and often impossible for a democracy to do this. The meaning of the new Russian maneuver was clear. The Kremlin did not want an all out war with the West, so it was opening a new economic offensive. The purpose was to win the support of the underdeveloped countries, many of which had been neutral in the cold war. It was no answer to the challenge to point out that the United States and Britain had given as much help in the last five years as Russia was likely to be able to provide in the next ten. Given the temper of the underdeveloped countries, something much more cogent than the memory of past benefits was necessary.

SOUTHEAST ASIA

The future of Southeast Asia is being profoundly influenced by a vacuum in power. The conquests and defeat of Japan, the Communist victory in China, the withdrawal of imperial power from India, Burma, and Indonesia and its weakening in Indochina and Malaya,—all combined to create a zone of weakness throughout southern Asia. The postwar weakening of Europe has increased the insecurity of Southeast Asia as much as the growth of China's strength. Great Britain and France are no longer able to protect the area as they did before World War II. There is an important contrast here with

Western Europe. NATO defenses are sufficiently strong that it would be very risky for the U.S.S.R. to attempt to bring any more states under her control. An uneasy balance of power has been established, and for the time being Moscow's policy seems to be to strengthen its control over its satellites rather than to expand further. In Asia China has emerged as the strongest military power, and with 5 million troops it could overrun the countries on its borders by sheer weight of numbers. China knows too that the Western powers do not want to fight in Southeast Asia, and seems tempted to fill the vacuum that exists there. Southeast Asia is made up of the republics of Burma, Indonesia, and the Philippines, the constitutional monarchy of Thailand, the British dependency of Malaya, and the French dependency of Indochina. If the population of 177 million could be united, they could with Western help offer a fairly strong defense against aggression. Unfortunately about their only common interests are that they live in the same part of Asia and that they all want to be independent.

There is no common language or racial descent. In religion the Burmans, Thais, and the peoples of Indochina are predominantly Buddhists. The Indonesians and Malays are Muslims, and almost all the Filipinos are Christians. The Burmans, Indonesians, Malays, Thais, and Cambodians received their religion and much of their culture from India. The Vietnamese civilization has been deeply influenced by China, which ruled the country for a thousand years down to about A.D. 900. The culture of the Filipinos has been profoundly affected by nearly 400 years of Spanish and American rule. History too makes for disunity. Unlike China and India Southeast Asia never had a great empire which ruled over the whole area. Instead there were separate states which conquered the weaker peoples on their frontiers and sometimes fought one another. There is no memory of a united and prosperous past to which advocates of unity can appeal. In economics the different countries are competitive rather than complementary. Southeast Asia is in a way the debatable land between China and India. It never produced a genuinely native civilization, but grafted borrowings from its more advanced neighbors onto its own primitive cultures. There is a certain resemblance between Southeast Asia and the Balkans. Both are worth annexing for their economic and strategic importance; both are sandwiched in between far more powerful neighbors; and both are zones of weakness. The Balkans and Southeast Asia alike are inhabited by a number of small peoples who are divided by race, religion, and historical memories. Especially since World War II an intense nationalism has swept over Southeast Asia. On the whole this has had the same divisive effect as in the rest of the world. Each country prizes its independence above everything else, and is determined not to allow the slightest infringement of it. Any form of political union would require the separate governments to delegate some of their powers to a central authority, and this they are resolved not to do. A United States of Southeast Asia is not practical politics. Some of the governments, particularly Indonesia and Burma, follow Nehru's lead in his policy of neutrality in the cold war. In the background, however, is the fear that India may try to bring them under her economic control.

Adapted from Focus

About 80 percent of the people are subsistence farmers. Their chief crop is rice, and they eat most of what they grow. The postwar annual cash income is estimated to be $60 per person. Few enter business, and when they do, it is usually petty trade. They have little idea of the value of money, and they seem to lack what one might call a business sense. What money they earn, they spend about as fast as it comes, most of it on extravagances, and they have little thought of saving. Old-fashioned farming methods prevent the peasant from making as much as he should out of his land. Some areas are badly overpopulated since the introduction of Western medical and health services by the colonial governments lowered the death rate, while the birth rate remained high. The population of Java increased tenfold to over 50 million, and in the Red River delta of northern Vietnam an area of 6000 square miles tries to support over 7.5 million people. Farms became smaller and smaller as they were subdivided among heirs. A high percentage own less than two acres, which is too little to support a family even at the existing low standard. Since there is very little manufacturing, the swollen population is compelled to remain on the land. There are millions of surplus peasants trying to live by farming.

Farm debt is a heavy burden throughout the area, and most of the borrowing is for unproductive purposes such as giving a feast when the eldest son is born. The usual recourse of the peasant is to the moneylender, who often charges 100-percent compound interest or more. An unknown but high percentage of the people spend their lives hopelessly in debt. The existence of large estates cultivated by tenants is a serious problem in some areas, e.g., the Philippines and the delta of the Mekong River in French Cochin China. The landowner often takes half the crop, and the sharecropper cannot feed himself and his family from his share. He is therefore compelled to borrow, and when the landowner is also the moneylender, as in the Philippines, the sharecropper often sinks so deep into debt that he becomes a debt slave. Legally he is free, but he owes so much that he will spend the rest of his life vainly attempting to pay it off. In 1939, 35 percent of the Filipino peasants were tenants, mostly sharecroppers, and a growing number of small peasant owners were losing their land through debt to the large landowner *cum* moneylender. The depressed condition of the tenants and debtors caused a number of revolts before World War II, and was the basic reason for the Hukbalahap rebellion after 1945. Before World War II the peasants on the whole accepted poverty with resignation, as a situation that was inevitable and beyond remedy. Since the war a new spirit of unrest has begun to appear. The peasant is in revolt against his traditional way of life. This provides a heaven-sent opening for Communists, who pose as agrarian reformers and promise abolition of moneylenders and landowners. This has been part of Ho Chih-minh's policy in Vietnam, of the Hukbalahaps, and also of the Burmese Communists.

The Europeans in Southeast Asia

In the past there was little native capital or desire to exploit natural resources, and Europeans and Chinese filled the gap. The large firms which handled import and export trade were usually Western, with a minority of Chinese. This was also true of mines, plantations, oil fields, banks, and insurance and shipping companies. Before the war an estimated $4,370,000,000 of foreign capital was invested in the area. The rich natural resources remained practically untouched until they were developed, roughly during the past century, by foreigners. The only direct share in this wealth received by the local population was their wages as office workers or, when they were willing to accept regular employment, as manual laborers. They had been poor men in a poor country, and they became poor men in a rich country. With minor variations the same situation existed in the American, French, British, and Dutch dependencies. The ownership of so much of the wealth by foreigners explains why the new postwar governments are socialistic. Free private enterprise meant foreign ownership of business. Asian nationalists resented the economic power of foreigners as much as the political, and they were determined to bring both under their control. Only the government can command enough capital to operate large scale enterprises, and so the policy is either to nationalize them or at least bring them under strict regulation.

The Chinese

The Chinese to the number of 7,670,000 are found in every country of Southeast Asia except Burma, where before the war their place was taken by Indians. They comprise .5 percent of the population in the Philippines, 1.6 percent in Indochina, 2 percent in Indonesia, 16 percent in Thailand, and 44.9 percent in Malaya. They form the middle class, to the virtual exclusion of the natives. Everywhere they have an economic stranglehold over the people of the country through their triple monopoly of retail trade, produce buying, and usury. Especially in the villages, the same individual often is all three rolled into one, and he catches the villager three ways at once. Price rings with the Chinese in neighboring villages eliminate competition, and the peasant is overcharged for what he buys and underpaid for what he sells. The Chinese are among the most astute businessmen in the world, and from their point of view the unsophisticated native with his lack of money sense is the answer to prayer. The realization by the native that he is being exploited is one reason for the hostility to the Chinese. Increasingly too the men marry women of their own race, and there is no hope of assimilating the aliens by intermarriage. As long as they remain in the country, they are an undigested lump in the body politic. In Malaya and Indonesia the hostility of the Muslim for the heathen worshipper of many gods widens the gulf. Another ground for dislike in Malaya is the fear of the Malays that the more astute and mature Chinese will gain control of the country politically, as they already have economically.

The majority of the Chinese are immigrants, while a minority belong to families permanently domiciled overseas for one or more generations. The immigrants do not intend to live permanently overseas, and ultimately most of them return home when they have made enough money to retire in comfort. A minority remain permanently in the country to which they emigrate. The immigrants feel no loyalty to their temporary residence. Instead they regard it as a place of exile to which they have been driven by poverty. Some, but by no means all of those born abroad, are loyal to their adopted country, but an uncertain number regard themselves as citizens of China temporarily living abroad. The development of nationalism among the Chinese and the peoples of Southeast Asia has widened the gulf between them.

The majority of the Chinese were formerly supporters of Chiang Kai-shek, and only a small minority were Communists. His defeat led many of them to write him off as finished, but they have not yet become supporters of Mao Tse-tung. A high percentage of them are successful business or professional men, and those who do not yet own property are firmly resolved to acquire it. Their economic interests are opposed to communism, and from this point of view their sympathies are bound up with the success of the West in the cold war. On the other hand, they realize their unpopularity and fear for the safety of their wealth. They need a protector, and the only one to which they can look is Peking. The noncommunist Chinese could be a valuable fifth column, and they wonder whether in exchange for their help they could make a deal with Mao Tse-tung. Other motives enter into their calculations. They are not sure who is going to win the cold war in Southeast Asia, and they are determined to be on the winning side. Then too they have relatives in China, and threats have been made that these will suffer if the overseas Chinese do not support the Communist government. Furthermore, the Chinese are nationalists: they want China to be strong, and it is a source of gratification that Communist China prevented a complete Western victory in the Korean war. For all these reasons the Chinese as a whole are spiritually sitting on the fence, waiting to see on which side it will pay them best to come down.

The Stakes of the Game

Southeast Asia is of great strategic and economic importance, and the loss would be serious if it came under Communist control. It provides 59 percent of the world's tin and 92 percent of its natural rubber, mostly from Malaya and Indonesia. The tin smelter at Singapore is the largest in the world, and smelts 37 percent of the world's tin. The development of synthetic rubber in the United States and Canada has made natural rubber less essential, but has not replaced it. Two thirds of the world's coconut products and a third of its palm oil come from Southeast Asia, though other vegetable oils can be used as substitutes. The cinchona tree, still the main source of quinine, is grown on Javanese plantations. Among the minor but valuable products are Manila hemp, most of the world's kapok, much of the pepper, a tenth of the chromium, and before the war more than 17 percent of the tungsten (Burma). The oil fields of Indonesia and British Borneo produce about 2.7 percent of the world's output.

Rice is the staple food of southern and eastern Asia. Many countries are not self-sufficient including Japan, Malaya, India, and Ceylon. Before the war they made up their deficit from the three countries which had an export surplus. These were in order of importance Burma, Indochina, and Thailand, and between them they provided more than two thirds of the rice in international trade. At the present time exports have fallen very heavily because of the rebellions in Burma and Indochina. In 1952 exports were only about 2.9 million tons, compared with 5.7 million before the war, and the price had risen by 500 percent. If China were to gain control of Southeast Asia, it would have won an economic weapon of the first importance. Deficit countries with a total population of several hundred million would have to bargain with the Communists for their staple food.

The Strait of Malacca between Malaya and Sumatra is a sea route comparable in importance with the Panama and Suez Canals. It is used by the global shipping lines of all nations, and is one of the great trade routes of the world. The strait is vitally important to Europe, since it is the continent's principal sea link with the Pacific and the Far East. For Britain it is of special importance for communication with Australia and New Zealand. The island of Singapore dominates the Strait of Malacca and also the alternative passage through the Strait of Sunda between Sumatra and Java. All the round-the-world air lines must use Southeast Asia to avoid Communist territory. Whoever controls Southeast Asia can grant or withhold passage on the global air routes and sea lanes.

The mainland cannot be considered in isolation from the American naval and air bases in the western Pacific. The Philippines are only about a thousand miles from French Indochina. The whole area of Southeast Asia and the western Pacific including Australia is an interconnected strategic unit. It is to American interest that all of it be controlled by friendly governments. For India Southeast Asia is the first line of defense. A fleet steaming toward the Indian Ocean would pass through either the Strait of Malacca or the Strait of Sunda, and no admiral would risk an advance toward India without first capturing Singapore. This base cannot be held if the mainland of the Malay Peninsula is in enemy hands. The strategic importance of Indochina was shown by what happened in 1941–1942. By May, 1941, it had come under the control of the Japanese, and the port of Saigon

in the southern part of Vietnam was made their advanced base. Its possession brought them within 647 miles of Singapore. By the end of the year
their preparations were completed, and Japanese armies starting from Saigon
overran Malaya and Thailand. The latter became the base for the conquest
of Burma, and from there in turn India was attacked. Substitute the Chinese
for the Japanese in control of Vietnam, and there would be grave danger that
history would repeat itself. For the countries of Southeast Asia are in no
condition to resist a strong attack, supported by a domestic Communist revolt.

Indonesia

The Indonesian republic is a weak state grappling with civil wars and
social and economic problems which would puzzle Solomon himself. There
is a wide gap between the peasant 80 percent and the small minority of
Dutch-educated officials, schoolteachers, journalists, professional people, and
a few businessmen, from whom the leaders are drawn. There are nineteen
political parties in the legislature and while a few represent genuine differences of principle, the policy of most of them is similar. As in many
other parts of Asia, the majority are not parties in the American sense of the
term, but are groups supporting an individual leader. A struggle for power
has developed among the rival leaders. With this chaotic multiple party system every government has to be a weak and unstable coalition, which explains the rapid rise and fall of governments.

Because of the lack of trained officials, totally inexperienced men had to
be appointed to the government services. Consequently administration is inefficient. In addition, jobs had to be found for many young men who fought
against the Dutch. They felt that their country owed them a living, and many
of them have been lazy and corrupt as well as untrained. Lack of law and
order is serious, though conditions are better than a few years ago. One reason
is the failure of the government to control its troops and impose discipline
upon them. Many guerillas who were demobilized at the end of the war
took to banditry. In western Java, Sumatra, and Celebes revolts have broken
out and protracted guerilla wars are in progress.

The government has extensive plans to repair the roads and railways,
make good war damage, and raise the standard of living by such projects as
building factories, hydroelectric plants, and irrigation works. Owing to the
small amount of manufacturing in Indonesia, the necessary materials have to
be imported, and most of the cost must be met by the sale of exports. The
production of oil, tin, and rubber is greater than before the war, but the output of commodities such as palm oil and tea which come from Western-owned
plantations is only about half what it was in 1940 and seems unlikely to recover. The government has failed to protect European planters, and many
have been murdered. A large number of plantations have not been reoccu-

pied by their Western owners since the war. There have been many strikes fomented by the Communists. The laborers' demands have often been beyond the capacity of industries to support. Additional discouragements have been heavy taxes, inability to send profits out of Indonesia because of exchange controls, and the constant but ill-defined threat of nationalization hanging over a large part of the foreign investment. Some leaders realize the need of Western capital for development, but they hesitate to act because they know that many of their supporters would oppose the terms that must be offered if investors are to be attracted. Indonesians believe that foreign capital means exploitation and are afraid that its investment will lead to the loss of independence. As a result capital is not being invested in Indonesia, and there has been heavy disinvestment in foreign-owned properties.

The government is meeting serious difficulties in carrying out its plans for raising the standard of living since it lacks the money to pay for the necessary imports. The standard of living of the majority is estimated to be 10 to 15 percent lower than before 1941. During the revolt against the Dutch the leaders encouraged extravagant hopes that freedom would mean greater prosperity. But they have been unable to fulfill their promises, and there is the risk that the Indonesians might turn against them. Meanwhile the Communists are quietly strengthening their position. They pose as nationalists and economic reformers and hold a strong position through their control of the trade unions. Membership rose in two years from 8000 to 500,000, and the party was the best organized and one of the richest in Indonesia. The political diagnosis for Indonesia reads: "Condition serious but not grave. Some signs of improvement; but danger of relapse continues."

Burma

In 1947 the British government accepted the Burman decision to secede from the Empire, and the Burmese republic was established in 1948. A struggle for power developed between rival leaders. In July, 1947, ex-premier U Saw assassinated Premier Aung San and six of his cabinet. U Saw was hanged, and Aung San's lieutenant, U Nu, succeeded him as premier. In 1948 no less than four civil wars broke out. The Communists divided into two factions, Whites and Reds, and each independently attacked the government. One section of the party army which Aung San had created revolted. Then came the most dangerous rebellion of all, that of the Karens. They are a minority who, with good reason, regard the Burmans as their oppressors. Finally, there were the *dacoits* or gang robbers. For years gang robbery had vied with rice farming as the most popular rural occupation. After 1945 it reached spectacular proportions, and large and well-armed bands roamed the countryside. For several years an endless guerilla war kept Burma in a state of semi-anarchy, and a quarter of the rice lands went out of cultivation.

By the end of 1952 the government seemed to have recovered fairly effective control, and most of the rebel armies had degenerated into bands of gang robbers. Only the Karens were well organized, and some of them were willing to end the war in return for the degree of self-government offered by U Nu. Meanwhile a new danger developed: a fragment of Chiang Kai-shek's army, estimated at perhaps 12,000 troops, took refuge in Burma and sometimes made forays into China. The Burmese army was unable to defeat them, and the government was afraid that Peking might use the excuse of restoring order on the frontier to invade Burma. Previous Chinese governments claimed control over Burma because of temporary invasions during past centuries, and it is suspected that Mao Tse-tung may entertain the ambition to conquer the country. The United Nations has been trying to persuade the Chinese troops to leave Burma. Summing up the situation, the government is weak and has done as well as could be expected in partially restoring law and order. It has ambitious plans to repair the destruction caused by thirteen years of war, develop natural resources, extend the social services, and establish the welfare state. Improved conditions are necessary if the government is to compete successfully with the Communists for the allegiance of the peasants, but there is a lack of money, trained administrators, and technical experts. The government could not survive if its enemies inside Burma received help from the Vietminh Communists or China.

Thailand

Nominally Thailand has a democratic government; but the reality is that Field Marshal Phibun Songgram is virtual dictator so long as he can retain the support of the clique of junior officers who actually control the army. His other asset is his mastery of the devious methods of Thai politics. Phibun's principal opposition comes from the navy, but its various postwar attempts to seize power by force have been defeated by the superior strength of the army. The navy tends to side with what might be called the civilian clique of officials, lawyers, etc., which Phibun ousted from control of the government. The leader of this group is Pridi Banomyong, an able and ambitious man who has been in exile since 1947. In 1954 he broadcasted from Peking, urging the Thais to overthrow their pro-Western government. There have been other indications that China takes an unfriendly interest in Thailand. The air force usually remains neutral in the struggles between the factions, but occasionally intervenes with telling effect. Part of the profits from the record price of rice in world markets has been passed on to the peasants, the mass of the population, and they seem to be reasonably content with their government. The large Chinese minority of 2.5 million have grievances against the government because of the disabilities imposed on them. They resent the attempt to weaken their economic grip on the country by reserving various occupations to Thais only. The Chinese community includes a Communist party, and it has won some adherents among the Thais.

There are elements of opposition to the anticommunist dictatorship in the Thai navy, the civilian clique headed by Pridi and the Chinese. The army and military police have a strength of about 100,000 and are fairly well equipped. Phibun Songgram can control the situation so long as he has to cope only with domestic enemies. It would be a very different matter if he had to face an uprising supported by the Vietminh army.

Malaya

The fundamental problem of Malaya is that it is the home of three hostile and growing nationalisms of which only one, the Malay, is loyal to the country. Out of the population of 7,057,000, the Malays, the original inhabitants, are only 43.3 percent, the Chinese 44.9 percent, and the Indians 10.4 percent. The fear of domination by the Chinese is greater than anywhere else in Southeast Asia, for in Malaya alone they have a numerical superiority. The Indians are disliked for the same reasons as the Chinese, but their limited number makes them a much less serious problem. The Malays feel that as the people of the country and the only race which is loyal to it they have the right to rule.

The British have taken the first steps toward setting up parliamentary democracy, on the basis of equal rights of citizenship for all three races. Legislatures with elected majorities have been created, and Asian ministers have partial control of the executive. Attempts are being made to promote racial cooperation, but so far with limited success. If British policy is to succeed, the Chinese and Indians must transfer their loyalty from their countries of origin to Malaya, and they and the Malays must substitute racial harmony for mutual antagonism. If the three rival nationalisms continue to grow stronger, Malaya might become another Palestine. For the present the British are needed as the only impartial element which can exert a moderating influence. If they were to leave at present the Malays would probably have to fight to hold their position. Although the Chinese would be likely to win ultimately, most of their wealth would be destroyed.

The Communists are almost entirely immigrants from China, and seem never to have numbered more than about 7000 at any one time. Their principal object, in which they failed, was to paralyze tin and rubber production. The uprising was in no sense a nationalist revolt to win freedom, but an attempt by a small faction to seize power by methods of terrorism. A large majority of the several thousand whom they killed were their fellow countrymen. The Malays cooperated heartily with the British from the beginning of the revolt in 1948, and thousands volunteered for the armed police and troops.

Until recently most of the Chinese remained neutral since they were not sure the British were going to win, and any who helped them ran a serious risk of assassination. When it was clear that the war had swung in favor of the British, the Chinese began to support them.

Communist tactics were to avoid pitched battles by breaking up into small bands and making their headquarters in the jungle. From here they made hit and run attacks to murder isolated European and Chinese planters and miners or ambush small patrols of troops. The Communists were very hard to hunt down owing to the great difficulty of securing accurate information about their movements and also because of the character of jungle fighting. Malaya is roughly the size of Florida, and three quarters of it is covered with jungle so dense that visibility is only a few yards. To deal with the guerillas took 42,500 regular troops and 70,000 armed police. Since about 1952 the situation has greatly improved, and the risk of being ambushed is not serious. A hard core of several thousand Communist guerillas are still holding out in the depths of the jungle; owing to the great difficulty of finding them they are a potential danger which might continue for years, much as at present. The local situation is well in hand, but it would again become very serious if the Communists won control of Thailand and could send reinforcements and supplies to the terrorists in Malaya. The frontier between the two countries is largely jungle and sparsely inhabited, and it would be exceedingly difficult to prevent Malaya from being penetrated. In 1955 the Communists moved their headquarters across the border into southern Thailand.

French Indochina

Indochina consists of the three states of Cambodia, Laos, and Vietnam. The latter is composed of the three provinces of Tonkin in the north, Cochin China in the south, and linking them together the coastal plain of Annam. There are rich rice lands in the Red River delta in Tonkin and the delta of the Mekong River in Cochin China. Eighty percent of the population live in the two river deltas and the coastal plain, less than 14 percent of the total area. The remainder of Indochina is a sparsely inhabited area of mountains and plateaus, in great part covered with jungle. Laos has 1,260,000 inhabitants, Cambodia 3,860,000 and Vietnam 25,880,000. The Vietnamese have been the most aggressive as well as the most numerous, and the attitude of the other races toward them is not overly friendly. The Thai of Laos and the Cambodians want self-government, but they do not intend to exchange French rule for Vietnamese control. Hence, there are three separate nationalisms in Indochina. The Thai and the Cambodians did not join in the rebellion against France, which was confined to the Vietnamese.

Ho Chi-minh, the leader of the revolt, became a Communist in 1920 while studying in France, was trained in Russia, and worked for a time with the

Communists in China. During the Japanese occupation he organized the Communists and the prewar Vietnamese nationalist parties into the Vietminh party, and after the fall of Japan he established the independent republic of Vietnam and raised a guerilla army. Fighting began with the French on their return in 1945. In 1948 the French proclaimed Bao Dai, the former emperor of Vietnam, as chief of state, in the hope that he would win over a great part of the Vietminh to his support, but this expectation was not realized. In 1950 China and Russia gave diplomatic recognition to Ho Chi-minh's Vietminh government and supplied him increasingly with military assistance. The United States and Great Britain recognized Bao Dai's government, and American military equipment began to arrive in Vietnam.

The majority of the Vietminh party are nationalists who want independence, but they have become completely dominated by the Communist minority led by Ho Chi-minh. He has kept his communism in the background, knowing that it has no appeal for most of his followers, and has stressed nationalism and agrarian reform. All this convinced a large number in Vietnam and all over South Asia that Ho Chi-minh was merely a patriot fighting against French colonialism. He has seen to it that Communists have been appointed to key positions in the army and the party. He has also used terror and assassination to get rid of his enemies and of supporters of Bao Dai.

France underestimated the determination of the Vietnamese to have complete self-government, and thought that it would be enough to grant partial autonomy and retain a good deal of French control in military, judicial, and economic affairs. This played into the hands of the Communists and enabled them to win complete control over the nationalists by pointing out that it was impossible to come to terms with the French. The meager concessions were a prime cause of Bao Dai's failure to win over the nationalists in the Vietminh party. They dismissed him as a French puppet, and submitted to the increasing domination of Ho Chi-minh in order to win freedom. France, moreover, could not afford the cost of sending out enough troops, and until 1951 she was very slow to give Bao Dai's government an army of its own from fear of its reliability. Equally important, from lack of money the troops were starved of adequate and up-to-date equipment until the 'fifties. Even so, from 1946 to 1953 the war cost France $3,644,000,000, and the French treasury was in no condition to stand a heavier drain. From 1950 onward the United States gradually re-equipped the French army (180,000 in 1954) and also the Vietnamese army of Bao Dai (200,000 in 1953). It was estimated that if the war had continued through 1954 American aid would have amounted to $1,370,000,000, or 78 percent of the total cost. (The Cambodian and Laotian armies, which did not take part in the war in Vietnam, had a combined strength of about 30,000). Simultaneously China and the Soviet bloc sent increasing quantities of equipment as well as technicians and military advisers to Ho Chi-minh.

Part of his soldiers were transformed from guerillas into well-trained and formidable divisions of regular troops. His total force was somewhere between 300,000 and 400,000.

In July, 1953, Laniel, the conservative premier of France, informed the three states of Indochina that France was prepared to "perfect" their independence. Treaties were made in 1953 with Laos and Cambodia transferring to them the powers still held by France and stating that they were independent and sovereign states associated as members in the French Union or empire. Negotiations with Vietnam were very protracted, but in April, 1954, the French and Bao Dai governments signed an agreement that Vietnam was to receive total independence as soon as the terms of the treaties could be agreed upon. Vietnam and France would cooperate freely and on terms of equality in the French Union.

Dien Bien Phu and after. By the spring of 1954 the Vietminh held practically the whole northern province of Tonkin, with the exception of the delta of the Red River, which was garrisoned by the French. It included Hanoi the capital and Haiphong the seaport. From the military point of view this was the most important part of the province, since it was one of the two rice granaries of the country. Ho Chi-minh needed the grain badly to feed his troops. The delta was guarded by forts and 65,000 troops, but at least 15,000 Vietminh guerillas had infiltrated between them and established themselves between the French in the upper part of the delta and the port of Haiphong. The bulk of the French army was locked up in a number of not very strong forts, and mobile forces able to move to the defense of a threatened position were few. The French hold on the Red River delta was precarious. The Vietminh also occupied much of Annam, and there was minor guerilla activity in the delta of the Mekong, the other important rice-growing area. In 1952–1953 the Vietminh invaded Laos, which had taken no part in the war, and occupied part of it. The conquered territory was a sparsely inhabited region of mountains and jungles, defended by isolated French forts. In 1954 Cambodia was invaded. Both Laos and Cambodia had Issarak or "free" movements hostile to France. Neither had much popular support, and both were under Ho Chi-minh's control. When the Vietminh army invaded Laos in 1953 it set up a Free Thai government headed by the leader of the Laos Issarak movement at Samneua in the territory it occupied. The underlying motive may go further than an attempt to win the support of the Thai inhabitants of Laos. Other Thai live in Thailand, the Shan states of eastern Burma, Tonkin, and south China. It is possible that the ultimate purpose is to arouse the nationalism of these scattered branches of the Thai race in favor of a Thai state controlled by Communists. This would create a fifth column in Thailand and Burma.

General Navarre, the French commander, occupied and fortified the village of Dien Bien Phu in an attempt to force the Vietminh army to fight a pitched battle. The village was on one of the roads by which munitions were sent to the rebels from China, but its strategic importance was only moderate. Dien Bien Phu was in a valley buried in the mountains 185 miles from the main French army in the Red River delta, and once it was attacked it could be helped only from the air. What ruined General Navarre's plan was that when the Korean war was over, the Chinese were able to divert to the Vietminh troops much heavier artillery than they had previously had, and also radar directed antiaircraft guns which interfered seriously with air support of the defense. After a very gallant resistance of fifty-six days the fortress was taken by storm. The psychological effects of the disaster were more important than the military. The French lost perhaps 16,000 of their best troops out of 180,000, but the victory probably cost the enemy anywhere from 20,000 to 40,000. On the other hand, it must have made many of the Vietnamese wonder whether the Vietminh was winning the war, and so weakened their will to fight. In the past many of them did not support either Bao Dai or Ho Chi-minh, but waited to see who was winning. The victorious Vietminh army began to advance toward the Red River delta. It was doubtful whether the French could have held it in the face of strong assaults from without, combined with guerilla attacks from inside the delta. The French government asked for the assistance of American and British armed forces, but the request was refused.

The war had been unpopular in France, and opinion in the Assembly was very divided. Few Frenchmen were interested in Indochina, and there was widespread opposition to an endless war which seemed to produce nothing but losses. By the end of 1952 French casualties were over 90,000, of whom about 38,000 were killed, and though half the army was locked up indefinitely in Indochina, it was not large enough to defeat the enemy. The drain on the treasury was so heavy that more could not be sent. Meanwhile the defense of France herself was weak, and she was dissipating fruitlessly in Indochina the strength that was needed to counterbalance the reviving military power of Germany and to maintain French control over North Africa. France had spent over seven times as much as the prewar value of her investments in Indochina, and to continue was to throw good money after bad. The French felt too that they were fighting the Western world's battle against Communism as much as the Americans in Korea, and they asked why they were expected to provide all the troops. France was anxious to end the war by negotiations. Mendès-France became premier, and staked his political future on his ability to arrange an armistice at the Geneva Conference.

The Geneva Agreement. France had lost the war, and Mendès-France's bargaining position was weak. All things considered, the terms were the best that could have been contrived under the circumstances. On July 20, 1954, it was agreed that hostilities should end and that Vietnam should be temporarily partitioned. The armed forces of France and Bao Dai would evacuate the north including the Red River delta and would retire to South Vietnam. Ho Chi-minh would take over political control of North Vietnam and would withdraw his troops from the south. The usual democratic liberties were guaranteed, and any civilians living in territory under the rule of either government were to be free to move to the zone controlled by the opposite side. Neither party was to bring additional troops or equipment into its territory. An International Commission composed of an Indian, a Pole, and a Canadian would supervise and control the carrying out of the armistice. Both parts of Vietnam were forbidden to adhere to any military alliance, and the south was thus precluded from joining the proposed Southeast Asian defense pact. It was also agreed that the division of Vietnam would be merely temporary. A general election was to be held in 1956 which would reunite the whole country. Similar armistices were concluded for Cambodia and Laos, and it was stipulated that all Vietminh and French troops must withdraw, apart from a French military mission in Laos to train the Laotian army. Neither state was allowed to join any military alliance. The Free Cambodian forces (the Vietminh fifth column) were to be disbanded. The Free Laos guerillas on the contrary were to retain control of the two northern provinces which had been conquered by the Vietminh army. Ho Chi-minh kept a substantial base of operations in the weak state of Laos, and one which bordered on Burma as well as North Vietnam.

The most probable result of holding the election in 1956 as stipulated by the treaty would be that South Vietnam would lose its independence. Ho Chi-minh has an effective party organization and has extended his control over the territory evacuated by the French. The bulk of the population live in the north, and it can be taken for granted that they will give him one of those 99-percent majorities which are standard practice in dictatorships. In addition, he can count on part, and possibly a large part, of the vote of South Vietnam. This would give him a national mandate for uniting the whole country under Communist control. Various factors explain his influence in the south. Many of his guerillas did not retire to the north as the armistice required. Instead they put on civilian clothes and remained behind as party organizers. By a mixture of persuasion and intimidation they appear to have gained a large following. They are helped by the psychology of the band wagon. The desire of a very large number of Vietnamese is to back the winner, and thus far this means Ho Chi-minh. The argument that his victory means a Communist dictatorship counts for little with people whose tradition is autocratic rule and who believe Communists are nationalists and agrarian reformers.

The anticommunists of South Vietnam have not been an organized party, but a collection of influential individuals and factions, some with private armies, and motivated by conflicting ambitions for power. Bao Dai discredited himself by remaining in France during the crisis of his country's fate and exercising leadership by remote control. In 1955 a referendum deposed him and chose the premier, Ngo Dien Diem, as president of the republic of South Vietnam. Ngo Dien Diem is a strong nationalist who is hostile to Bao Dai and to French influence. He has shown great energy and determination in imposing his control on rival leaders, at times by armed force. His success is difficult to gauge, though it looks as if he were establishing his authority over the country. He would hardly have time to do so if the election were held in 1956; and it would seem that Ngo Dien Diem intends to postpone it. The Western powers are not in agreement over policy. The United States strongly supports Ngo Dien Diem, while France has no love for him. Moreover, she seems to feel that Ho Chi-minh will control the whole of Vietnam, and that the best course is to cultivate friendly relations with him in order to save as much as possible of her economic interests. The policy of the United States is based on the assumption that Ngo Dien Diem can save the south from communism if helped by American money and prestige. The United States is equipping the army and financing an economic program intended to raise the standard of living and blunt the appeal of Vietminh agents.

The danger to South Vietnam seems to lie not so much in armed invasion as in penetration and subversion from within, combined with the intimidating presence of the victorious Vietminh army on the other side of the frontier. This is the familiar technique of the inside job and is far more difficult to counter than open attack like the one on South Korea. If Ho Chi-minh wins control of South Vietnam, the weak states of Cambodia and Laos are unlikely to maintain their independence. The Vietminh invasions of neutral Laos and Cambodia showed that the Communists' aims were not limited to the control of Vietnam, and there is no reason to think that they end at the frontiers of Indochina. The strategic and economic importance of Southeast Asia is as great to the Communist bloc as to the West, and none of the countries are able to defend themselves unassisted. The French defense in Vietnam was like a road block, protecting Southeast Asia from Communist aggression. If the road block should collapse completely, Ho Chi-minh would have a common frontier with Thailand and Burma. Neither would last very long if the Communists gave help to the elements inside the country which are hostile to the present governments. The British would have their hands full defending Malaya, and Indonesia has a weak government and a strong fifth column.

The Southeast Asia Treaty Organization (SEATO)

Southeast Asia cannot defend itself, and it is too important to allow the Communists to eat it like an artichoke, leaf by leaf. An alliance of outside powers is the only way to guarantee its safety, and this might lead to war with China as it did over South Korea. If this should happen France would not bear the brunt of the struggle singlehanded. During 1955, 100,000 troops were withdrawn, and at the request of Ngo Dien Diem France agreed to evacuate the remainder and transfer all responsibility for defense to the South Vietnam army. The anti-French attitude of the government is no inducement to send them back. Britain would do what she could, but her own security forbids her to withdraw too many troops from Western Europe. Furthermore her primary interest in Southeast Asia is Malaya, and this applies also to Australia and New Zealand. The United States could not escape being very heavily involved. On the other hand, the mere fact that continued aggression might lead to a war with the West might moderate Communist imperialism, especially since the United States made it clear that in case of another war she would hold herself free to bomb China itself. A Western guarantee of the security of Southeast Asia is a calculated risk incurred for high stakes.

During the spring and summer of 1954 negotiations for a Southeast Asian defensive alliance were carried on between the United States, Britain, and France. Secretary of State Dulles wanted to hasten the conclusion of the pact, but Churchill insisted on delay. There was a fundamental difference in outlook between the two. Dulles contemplated a predominantly Western alliance with only two Asian members, the Philippines and Thailand. This combination had an unfamiliar appearance when looked at from the Asian point of view. The Philippines were dismissed as an American satellite, and Thailand as a minor state already aligned with the West. Asia regarded the proposed league as a Western alliance to bolster French colonialism. To prevent this Churchill insisted on delay, while he tried to persuade India, Pakistan, and Ceylon, and perhaps Burma and Indonesia as well to give their moral support to the alliance. They could contribute little in the way of troops, but their adhesion would be a guarantee of respectability that would counteract the Russian and Chinese propaganda that it was another attack by Western imperialism on Asian freedom. Pakistan, Ceylon, and Burma were suspicious of Communist imperialism, but India and Indonesia refused to recognize that China was any more of a threat to Asian independence than the West. In the end only Pakistan joined the alliance, partly because it was more alive to the Communist danger and in part because on principle it wished to do the opposite to India.

In September, 1954, a treaty was signed at Manila establishing the Southeast Asia Treaty Organization or Manila Pact. The signatories were the United States, Britain, France, Australia, New Zealand, Thailand, the Philippines, and Pakistan. The treaty area was the territory of the member states in Southeast Asia and the Southwestern Pacific. South Vietnam, Laos, and

Cambodia were included in the area covered by the treaty, although they were unable to join it because of the terms of the armistices. The allies would regard an armed attack in the treaty area as a threat to their own peace and security and would act to meet the common danger in accordance with their constitutional processes. It was realized that instead of open invasion the aggression might take the form of subversion from within. To meet this danger it was provided that if any signatory believed that the integrity of the treaty area was threatened by other than armed attack, the allies would consult immediately to decide what should be done. No action would be taken except with the consent of the government concerned. Unlike NATO no armed forces were earmarked specifically for the protection of the area. A council was created to consider military and other matters arising from the treaty. The signatories recognized that military action was only a partial answer to the danger of communism, and that financial and technical assistance to improve economic conditions was also essential such as the Point-Four policy and the Colombo Plan.

Nehru condemned SEATO as "diplomacy by threats" and an unwarranted intrusion by the Western powers into Asian affairs. China heartily agreed and worked hard to limit as far as possible Asian participation in the treaty. In 1954 Chou En-lai, her foreign minister, signed agreements with India and Burma which obligated them to conduct their foreign relations in accordance with five principles. These were mutual respect for one another's territorial integrity and sovereignty, mutual nonaggression, noninterference in each other's domestic affairs, equality and mutual benefit, and peaceful coexistence. The five principles were irreproachable generalities, but somewhat naïve when looked at in the light of Communist practice. Nehru took them at their face value and felt that they justified his policy of neutrality, or nonalignment as he preferred to describe it. He believed that the five principles made it unnecessary to join any defensive alliance such as SEATO and expounded this view at the Bandung Conference.

The Bandung Conference

This meeting of delegates from twenty-nine Asian and African nations was held in 1955 at Bandung in Java. They were at one in condemning imperialism and racial inequality, and demanding independence for all colonies and increased financial aid in improving their living standards. But when discussion moved from generalities to particulars, it became clear that the conference fell into two opposing groups. Fourteen nations including India, Communist China, Indonesia, Burma, and Egypt urged neutrality in the cold war and reliance upon the five principles. They opposed the formation of defensive alliances and condemned Western but not Communist imperialism. Fifteen nations including Turkey, Iraq, Pakistan, Japan, Thailand, the

Philippines, and Ceylon agreed that the five principles were fine, but insisted that so theoretical a declaration must be strengthened by defensive alliances. They insisted that Communist imperialism was as real and every bit as dangerous as Western colonialism. In the end the conference papered over the cracks by passing a carefully vague resolution which endorsed the five principles and defensive alliances, and another which condemned imperialism in general without specifying whether it referred to either or both varieties. So each side could claim that the conference endorsed its attitude.

Nehru seemed to hope that the conference would endorse his policy of neutrality and the five principles. His failure was a gain for the West, but Chou En-lai's personal success was another matter. He showed himself a most skillful diplomatist and made a very favorable impression. Chou En-lai assured Burma, Thailand, Laos, and Cambodia that China had no designs upon their independence and would not carry on subversive activities within their territories. Her sole aim was peaceful coexistence and the practice of the five principles. Chou En-lai sought to foster closer relations with Southeast Asia and encourage neutralism. He convinced many of the delegates that he was a sincere and moderate man of good will, and that he and his country would follow a policy of live and let live. The effect on weak neighbors like Cambodia and Laos was understandable. If one has to live near a Chinese dragon who is suspected of carnivorous tendencies, and the creature begins to purr or make whatever friendly noises a dragon makes, there is a temptation to take the overtures at their face value.

SELECTED READING

Arab World

ALLEN, H. E., *The Turkish Transformation*. Chicago: The University of Chicago Press, 1935.

CAROE, SIR OLAF, *Wells of Power: The Oilfields of Southwestern Asia*. London: Macmillan and Company, Ltd., 1951.

FRYE, RICHARD N. (ed.), *The Near East and the Great Powers*. Cambridge: Harvard University Press, 1951.

HOSKINS, HALFORD L., *The Middle East: Problem Area in World Politics*. New York: The Macmillan Company, 1954.

IRELAND, PHILIP W. (ed.), *The Near East, Problems and Prospects*. Chicago: The University of Chicago Press, 1942.

ISSAWI, CHARLES, *Egypt: An Economic and Social Analysis*. London: Oxford Press, 1947.

KHADDURI, MAJID, *Independent Iraq*. New York: Oxford Press, 1951.

LAMBTON, ANN K. S., *Landlord and Peasant in Persia*. New York: Oxford Press, 1953.

LENCZOWSKI, GEORGE, *Russia and the West in Iran, 1918–1948*. Ithaca: Cornell University Press, 1949.

LONGRIGG, STEPHEN H., *Oil in The Middle East: Its Discovery and Development*. New York: Oxford Press, 1954.

MIKESELL, RAYMOND, and CHENERY, HOLLIS B., *Arabian Oil: America's Stake in the Middle East*. Chapel Hill: University of North Carolina, 1949.

MILLSPAUGH, ARTHUR C., *Americans in Persia*. Washington: Brookings Institution, 1946.

NEWMAN, BERNARD, *Morocco Today*. London: Hale, 1953.

ROYAL INSTITUTE OF INTERNATIONAL AFFAIRS, *The Middle East: A Political and Economic Survey*. New York: Royal Institute, 1950.

SAKRAN, FRANK C., *Palestine Dilemma*. Washington: Public Affairs Press, 1948.

SPEISER, E. A., *The United States and the Near East*. Cambridge: Harvard University Press, 1947.

WARRINER, DOREEN, *Land and Poverty in the Middle East*. New York: Royal Institute of International Affairs, 1948.

Kenya

Africa South of the Sahara: An Assessment of Human and Material Resources. London and New York: Oxford Press, 1951.

HUXLEY, ELSPETH, *White Man's Country: Lord Delamere and the Making of Kenya*. London: Macmillan and Company, Ltd., 1935.

LEAKEY, L. S. B., *Mau Mau and the Kikuyu*. London: Methuen and Company, Ltd., 1952.

SMITH, EDWIN W., *The Golden Stool*. New York: Doubleday Doran, 1928.

Underdeveloped Areas

The Colombo Plan for Co-operative Economic Development in South and South East Asia. New York: British Information Service, 1950.

HOSKINS, HALFORD L., *Aiding Undeveloped Areas Abroad*. Philadelphia: *The Annals* of the American Academy of Political and Social Science, March 1950.

Measures for the Economic Development of Under-Developed Countries. New York: U.N. Department of Economic Affairs, 1951.

NURSKE, RAGNAR, *Problems of Capital Formation in Underdeveloped Countries*. New York: Oxford Press, 1953.

Southeast Asia

BALL, W. MACMAHON, *Nationalism and Communism in East Asia*. New York: Cambridge University Press, 1953.

FALL, BERNARD B., *The Viet Minh Regime: Government and Administration in The Democratic Republic of Vietnam*. Ithaca: Cornell University Southeast Asia Program, 1954.

GRUNDER, GAREL A., and LIVEZEY, WILLIAM E., *The Philippines and the United States*. Norman: University of Oklahoma Press, 1951.

HAMMER, ELLEN J., *The Struggle for Indochina*. Stanford: Stanford University Press, 1954.

HOLLAND, WILLIAM L. (ed.), *Asian Nationalism and the West*. New York: The Macmillan Company, 1953.

JONES, STANLEY W., *Public Administration in Malaya*. New York: Royal Institute of International Affairs, 1953.

MILLS, LENNOX A., and ASSOCIATES, *The New World of Southeast Asia*. Minneapolis: University of Minnesota Press, 1949.

MOOK, HUBERTUS J. VAN, *The Stakes of Democracy in Southeast Asia*. New York: W. W. Norton and Company, 1950.

PURCELL, VICTOR, *The Chinese in Southeast Asia*. New York: Oxford Press, 1951.

SPENCER, J. E., *Land and People in the Philippines: Geographic Problems in Rural Economy*. Berkeley: University of California Press, 1952.

ZINKIN, MAURICE, *Asia and the West*. New York: Institute of Pacific Relations, 1951.

CHAPTER 29

THE SHAPE OF THINGS
TO COME

TIMES OF TRANSITION

A time of transition seems to come ever so often in history. The existing form of civilization changes, and gradually there appears a new type which contains elements of the old but is different from it. The fifth century of the Christian era was such a period. The Roman Empire was a civilized world, such as men did not see again until the seventeenth century. The empire at last became too feeble to beat back the attacks from without, and its barbarian conquerors carved out kingdoms for themselves all over western Europe. Then came the dark ages, and it took more than a millennium to create a civilization comparable with that which had been lost. The fifteenth and early sixteenth centuries saw the breakdown of medieval civilization, and the slow emergence of the beginnings of the modern world. Elements of the old were carried forward into the new, but on the whole the way of life was markedly different. Both these epochs were times of transition. Both were times of troubles, and the people who lived through them were beset with fear and anxiety as to their future.

The twentieth century would seem to be another age of transition, when the comparatively settled world of the nineteenth century is changing into something different. Fifty years ago a man could plan his life with reasonable assurance. There were inevitable uncertainties, but he did not have to wonder whether aircraft flying over the Polar ice cap might blow him and his whole scheme of existence to bits. This assurance of a settled future began to disappear with World War I, and the full effect of the change became evident after World War II. If this seems exaggerated, would an American of 1910 have been glad to know that a chain of radar stations was being built in northern Canada? Would he have wondered whether he might be drafted for military service in Formosa or Germany, or might have to pay taxes to provide military equipment for Pakistan? If one considers the world outside America, the change is much more obvious. Europe which dominated the world for 400 years must have American economic and military help. The unchanging East is changing with bewildering rapidity. Who would have thought of a Chinese army winning a battle against Americans twenty years ago? Who would have dreamed that all the governments of the earth would be wondering what Russia was planning?

NUCLEAR WAR

Blaming the U.S.S.R. for the trouble is not the complete answer, for she is merely the latest in a long series of aggressors that extends from the beginning of recorded history. Until less than a century ago the harm that could be done was limited by the extent of scientific knowledge. A country might be laid waste and its people reduced to penury, but the damage was only local and civilization itself was not endangered. The discovery of nuclear energy and the promise of even deadlier weapons introduces the possibility that the planet itself might be destroyed. It is no consolation that nobody will do this deliberately. The desire for power and aggrandizement is much the same as when Alexander the Great or Ghenghis Khan set out to conquer the world. What has changed is that man's knowledge has outstripped his moral development, and so he is in danger of blowing himself up in the urge for self-expression.

A universal treaty promising not to use nuclear energy in war is a doubtful safeguard. Treaties can be broken, and even if all bombs were destroyed, the knowledge of how to make them would continue. The history of warfare shows that when a new weapon has been discovered, no appeal to humanity has prevented someone from using it. The medieval church made that discovery when it failed to ban the crossbow on the grounds that its bolt had such powers of penetration and made such an unpleasantly large hole. The only deterrent which has prevented the use of a new weapon has been the fear of retaliation or the uncertainty of satisfying results, e.g., the mutual forbearance from the use of poison gas in World War II. This is not a reliable safeguard against the use of nuclear energy in a future war. At the outbreak of hostilities both combatants might hold back from nuclear bombing from fear of retaliation. When one side was losing, however, it would be most unlikely to refrain from using every weapon at its command. The argument would be that to do this might win the war, and that if defeat came after all, the victor could do little by way of punishment. Once one side began using the bomb the other would have to follow suit. Nobody can predict with certainty what the consequences would be, especially when one remembers that war is the best of forcing houses for hastening the development of still deadlier weapons.

A WORLD EMPIRE

The problem has analogies with the situation in the middle ages, when domestic law and order were threatened by the overmighty subject, the feudal baron with his private army. The solution of the sixteenth century was to make the king so powerful that he broke the strength of the barons and forced them to keep the peace. The twentieth-century successor to the overmighty subject is the great power. The king has no successor, for there is no superstate which can enforce peace on the planet. Therefore, the question is, should the sovereign states be shorn of their powers and placed under the control of a world authority? One possibility is that one might impose its authority on all the rest. The Communist bloc would never peacefully submit to the capitalist way of life, and it is equally inconceivable that the Western powers would accept the Communist police state. The establishment of a world empire on this model would have to be preceded by a devastating war which would engulf the whole planet. It would be a fight to the death, and the victor might found his rule on the ruins of world civilization. This was the method by which Rome created her empire: all rival states were beaten down by force and the most dangerous of them, Carthage in Tunisia, was literally blotted off the face of the earth. The limited destructive powers of old-fashioned war made it possible to impose peace by conquest without serious consequences. In the areas where heavy fighting occurred the Romans "made a wilderness and called it peace"; but Western civilization continued undisturbed and indeed progressed in other parts of the classical world. In the twentieth century the power of destruction that science has given man makes this method out of date. To fight a nuclear war in order to liberate the world from the threat of a nuclear war does not make sense.

A WORLD UNION

An alternative is to establish a world state by general consent. This proposition has only to be stated to show its impracticability. The gulf between the Eastern and Western blocs is too deep for them to unite at the present time. One has only to remember the record of the United Nations. When it was created, its founders agreed that it was premature to establish a superstate, and they gave their organization limited powers. Even this proved to be asking too much, and the United Nations has become another arena where the conflict between the two great power blocs is fought out. In view of this, it is not feasible to set up a world government which would have the authority to compel the obedience of the present sovereign states. A political union can only succeed if the members trust one another and wish to unite. Each of the two blocs regards the other with the utmost distrust. Every proposal from the opposite camp is assumed to be made in bad faith, and is scrutinized with suspicion to determine where the trap lies.

Another insuperable obstacle is the form of government. How can a workable compromise be evolved between democracy and the police state? Also is economic life to be based on the principles of capitalism or communism? Furthermore, a world state would impose upon its citizens the strain of too large a loyalty. A nation cannot endure unless its citizens are devoted to its interests and are prepared to defend them—that is the secret of the power of the national state. The average man thinks in terms of his own country, and very few feel a patriotic devotion to the planet. To ask men to move from a national to a global loyalty is to demand too much of them. "The parliament of man, the federation of the world" must be relegated to some uncertain future.

UNION NOW

The proposal has been made, e.g., by Clarence Streit, that the superstate should be limited to the democracies of North America, the British Commonwealth, and Western Europe which accept the Western way of life. Each existing state would continue to manage its own domestic affairs under its present form of government, republican or monarchical. A federal government would control defense and foreign policy and have the power to tax, and there would be a customs union and a common citizenship. A less ambitious variant of this scheme was the constitution for a European Political Community which was drafted in 1953 at the suggestion of the foreign ministers of France, West Germany, Italy, Belgium, Holland, Luxembourg. These plans both have the advantage that they avoid an attempt to combine the incompatibles of democracy and dictatorship. They are also wise in excluding India and the other British Asian dominions. Assuming that their nationalism would allow them to join a Western federation—which is highly improbable—their presence would cause the most serious difficulties. If representation in the federal legislature were based upon population, the states of South Asia would elect about half the members, and with their rapidly growing populations they would soon have a majority. The United States and the European countries would refuse to be taxed and controlled in defense and foreign policy by an Asian majority, and it would not be long before there was a demand for tariff protection against the competition of Asian manufactures. Alternatively representation in the federal legislature might be based on wealth and economic development, which would give the

West a majority. The Asian states would not submit to this, with their suspicion of Western imperialism and capitalist exploitation.

A federation of the Western democracies would comprise a group of states in substantial agreement on the essentials of form of government, rights of the individual, and the rule of law. In economics some are capitalist and others semisocialist, and wide variations exist in costs of production and standards of living. The economic differences, however, are much less marked than those which divide them from the Communist states, or those of South Asia and the Middle East. Moreover, all of them are alive to the menace of Communist aggression, and no bond of union is stronger than the threat of a common danger.

THE EUROPEAN POLITICAL COMMUNITY

An argument in support of a purely European federation is often drawn from the success in federating the thirteen American colonies after the Revolution, and their expansion over half a continent. The analogy is misleading, however, for the majority of the Americans of the eighteenth century had a common racial origin, as well as the same ideas about government, and similar problems of foreign policy. There were no memories of traditional hostilities and wars between the states, and none of them feared that it would be completely dominated by another. It should be remembered, however, that a very bloody civil war was necessary to decide whether the federation was to endure. The Europeans who immigrated during the nineteenth century were absorbed into a homogeneous community, and furthermore they cooperated in the process. Most of them came to the United States because they decided to cut their links with Europe, and they wanted to be Americanized. South America gives a better analogy with Europe than the United States. Apart from Brazil the civilization and the governing class were Spanish, and it might have been expected that the liberated Spanish colonies would federate. Instead they set up over a score of separate republics, and while they have not fought one another since the war over the Gran Chaco ended in 1935, the development of separate patriotisms is an effective barrier to political union.

The peoples of Europe are not homogeneous, and there are important differences in race, national characteristics, and national interests. They have traditions of centuries of separateness, and some of them like France and Germany are divided by the memory of former wars and the fear of future aggression. Powerful vested interests have grown up behind each national frontier, and these often believe that union would be to their detriment. Conclusions cannot be drawn from the millions of Europeans who emigrated to the United States, for they were eager to change their nationality. Those who remained behind in Europe were equally well aware of the advantage of life in America, but for various reasons they preferred to forego this and retain their national identity. Another great obstacle to a European federation is that the Scandinavian states and Britain refuse to join it. The result is that France hesitates to become a member of a purely continental federation lest she be dominated by Germany. This distrust combined with the strength of nationalism was shown in the draft constitution for a European Political Community already referred to. The proposed federal executive was carefully weakened by the establishment of a Council of National Ministers, appointed by the states which might join the federation. This council was to have the right to veto many decisions of the federal executive, and usually was required itself to act unanimously. In other words, each member state could prevent action by the council, and this in turn would block the federal executive. The prospects for a United States of Europe are not bright, in the near future at least.

A WESTERN FEDERATION

The wider federation of the European democracies, the British Commonwealth, and the United States would be both easier and more difficult to create. It would be easier in that France and other European powers would not fear domination by Germany. Great Britain too would be more interested in the wider scheme, though she would be apprehensive lest membership might weaken the links between her and the Asian dominions of the Commonwealth. On the other hand, all the members would be rather afraid of entering a federation with the United States because of its vast superiority in power. Many would have visions of America dominating their foreign policies, invading their markets and perhaps threatening their full employment. France would wonder whether the United States would lay down the law in North Africa. South Africa would want to know if its racial policy would be affected. That all this is not imaginary is shown by the history of relations between the United States and Canada. The two countries work together closely in defense, foreign policy, and economics; but whenever a Congressman suggests that Canada should join the United States, Canadians *en masse* rally to the support of their independence. This is significant, for Canadians are closer to Americans than are the peoples of Europe. Finally, but by no means least, Americans show no signs that they would welcome with enthusiasm a federation in which they would be outnumbered by their European and Commonwealth co-citizens. There would be murmurs that the American milch cow would provide sustenance for Europeans who wanted more financial aid. American farmers and industrialists—cheese makers and textile manufacturers, for instance—would be up in arms at the prospect of unrestricted European competition. There would be a marked lack of enthusiasm for defending European tropical colonies, as the federation would have to do.

The great obstacle to a Western federation is the sovereign state, reinforced as it is by the strength of nationalism. There is no point in ignoring that the average citizen prefers his own country and supports its independence and its interests. He likes his foreign friends, but he does not want them always running in and out of his house, especially if he is half afraid they may take over the management of it. A very good example of this attitude is the refusal of the British dominions to form a federation with Great Britain for the joint conduct of foreign policy and defense. This is not from indifference or hostility to the Commonwealth connection. The acid test of whether one values something is one's willingness to fight for it, and in 1914 and 1939 the dominions voluntarily went to war in order to support Great Britain. The reason for the refusal is the strength of the dominions' nationalism: they are not willing to make the partial surrender of their sovereignty which would be necessary if they enter a federation. Yet Britain and the dominions have more in common than the United States has with Europe, or the European countries with one another.

All this is not to say that a Western federation will be forever impossible, but merely that it is too big a step to take all at once in an age of strong nationalism. After all, it is not so long ago that the United States was wedded to isolationism, Canada and South Africa were inclined in the same direction, and some of the European states were determined to remain neutral. They have come quite a long way in a short time, and it is not wise to force the pace too much. Federation can only succeed if the member states are determined to make it succeed, and a premature union may cause a reaction which will drive the Western nations further apart than they are at present. The French have a useful proverb that "The best is the enemy of the good." This can be freely translated as, "The perfect policy for an ideal world may make one refuse to accept the best attainable in the very imperfect world in which we live."

A REVISED UNITED NATIONS

It would be no advantage to break up the United Nations and reconstitute it without the Communist states. Their elimination would still further accentuate the division between the Eastern and Western blocs. In a time of crisis it is not wise to heighten the tension. It is doubtful whether the Asian states which follow a policy of neutrality would be willing to compromise themselves by remaining in the U.N. If so, the U.N. would be composed only of the countries joined in NATO and the Pacific alliances together with the Latin American republics, and could not call itself a world-wide organization. The principal advantage would be that the Security Council would be free from the paralyzing effect of the Russian veto, and would be able to take decisions. The paralysis of the present Council can be circumvented fairly successfully however by obtaining a favorable recommendation of the Assembly. The U.N. as at present constituted is a forum where the Communist and the Western representatives can discuss their problems, and sometimes even settle them. It is best to keep the U.N. as it is, working through it where this is practicable but not expecting too much from it. Obviously security must be sought outside it.

REGIONAL ALLIANCES

A world empire, a federation, and an effective United Nations are not feasible, and the anticommunist states have been falling back upon regional alliances. The United States and Latin America negotiated the Inter-American Treaty of Reciprocal Assistance in 1947. Western Europe and North America are joined in NATO. There are the alliances with Japan, South Korea, and Chiang Kai-shek, the Anzus Pact, the Manila Pact, and Turkey's alliances with Pakistan, Iraq, Iran, and Britain known as the Bagdad Pact. They are loosely interconnected, for the United States is a member of practically all and Britain is linked with several of them. A common characteristic is that the members of each are the states which have a particular interest in the part of the world to which the treaty applies. The weakness of a global organization like the former League of Nations and the United Nations is precisely that it is global. Probably the majority of those now alive acquired their ideas in an age when the citizen supported the interests of his own nation, but felt no compulsion to intervene in a dispute which did not seriously affect it. The further away the trouble was, the more detached was his attitude toward it. World War II partially changed this, but did not do away with it. This is a transitional age when states are beginning to feel that their obligations transcend their immediate national interests, but are not prepared to undertake universal responsibilities.

There is a great deal to be said in favor of making the security of each part of the free world the immediate responsibility of the states, the independence of which will be seriously affected by the result. Central and South America are of prime importance to the United States and the Latin American republics. The independence of Western Europe is equally essential to the European states and the United States. Norway for a time opposed the inclusion of Turkey in NATO on the ground that the obligation to defend it was so remote from Norwegian interests. Apart from the inhabitants of Southeast Asia, their future affects the United States, the European colonial powers, and Australia and New Zealand. South Africa, Canada, and the other NATO powers would not like to see a further expansion of Communist control; but their attitude is far more detached than if the danger were nearer them, and they did not join the Manila Pact. The Korean war and the Formosan question showed that America was more concerned about what happened in the Far East than her European allies.

One criticism which has been made of these alliances is their predominantly military character. In the short term this is natural, for they were called into existence to answer a military threat. Other forms of cooperation could be developed however which would strengthen the cohesion of the anticommunist powers. The members of NATO for instance are pledged to create an Atlantic Community. The statesmen who negotiated the treaty agreed that in addition to mutual defense its purpose was to bring about positive social, economic, and political achievements, and to encourage economic collaboration between the members. These phrases are vague, but they show an intention to make the treaty more than a purely defensive alliance. To some extent the economic aspect is being discharged through membership in GATT. It would be a gain, however, if some of the conferences of the NATO members were given over to a discussion of their mutual economic problems, such as markets, raw materials, and investments. Or again, the members have a common defense policy, but fifteen separate foreign policies. To some extent their foreign offices consult one another in an attempt to harmonize their policies. There have been some rather startling instances, however, where a leading member has acted first, and discussed the matter with its associates afterwards. Periodical NATO meetings on foreign policy could bring about closer co-ordination.

Similar arrangements would be beneficial for other parts of the world. There have been sharp disagreements over policy in the Far East and Indochina. One reason has been that the powers concerned have followed policies that were at times parallel and sometimes divergent, and that consultation to achieve co-ordination has seemed to occur after a disagreement has been well publicized in opposing national presses. Apart from the unwisdom of assisting the Kremlin's attempts to drive a wedge between the members of the anticommunist bloc, a closer collaboration would help to create a greater community of feeling between the allies. Granting that anything so rigid as a federation is ruled out, there is much to be gained by an informal but continuous cooperation in all fields of common interest.

ARMAMENTS AND POLICY

Alliances are useless without armed forces to support them, and until there is a radical improvement in international relations, the West cannot afford to abandon its program. To maintain the present high level of armaments will be difficult if there should seem to be a relaxation of tension. There is nothing that a democracy dislikes more than a heavy burden of expenditure on armaments, and its leaders are responsive to public opinion. A plausible argument could be made that a less openly hostile attitude on the part of Russia showed that the policy of aggression had been given up. Therefore, the Western nations could afford to reduce taxes, or else increase the expenditure on social services. This was what happened as the result of the temporary relaxation of tension which followed the meeting of the four heads of state at Geneva in 1955. Shifts in Soviet tactics have occurred in the past and will no doubt continue in the future, but there is no evidence whatever that there has been any change in the grand strategy of world revolution. Until there is clear proof of that, the West cannot afford to risk relaxing its precautions.

Armaments do not ensure peace, and when there is a conflict of policies, an armaments race heightens the tension. On the other hand, the interwar British policy of singlehanded disarmament disproved the thesis that weakness guaranteed peace: it merely encouraged Hitler to persevere in his aggression. There is more danger in a disparity of armed strength than in efforts to correct it. An armed peace based on a balance of power is not a situation that can be contemplated with equanimity. But when the greater part of the world is divided between two antagonistic blocs, there is no alternative as long as their policies continue to be opposed to one another. There is no reason to believe that this will continue forever, though it may last a considerable time.

A firm policy is not the same as a provocative one. No overtures should be rejected which Moscow may make for the discussion of world problems. There is always the possibility that they may be genuine, and the situation is too serious to neglect even the faintest chance of improving it. Moreover, refusal to discuss gives valuable ammunition to the Communists' propaganda, and can be used to support their argument that the danger to peace comes from the American warmongers. The West should also be scrupulously careful to avoid any action which would give the Communist states a legitimate grievance. It should avoid taking any position which it is not prepared to maintain if challenged, and it should consider very carefully before deciding what course to follow. Western nations sympathize deeply with the peoples of the Soviet satellite states, and such activities as sheltering refugees and Radio Free Europe should be continued. It would be a blunder, however, to enunciate an official policy of liberating these countries. Russia would not give up her control without fighting, and the West is not prepared to go to war on this issue. Such a proclamation would be provocative without accomplishing anything, and it might have the effect of encouraging the conquered peoples to acts of resistance which could not succeed except as part of a world war.

ECONOMIC POLICIES

Armed force by itself is not enough: the anticommunist world must also be strengthened economically. Moscow has waited hopefully for a repetition of the great depression; and if it took place, the tempo of aggression would accelerate. To a large extent Europe has recovered from the destruction caused by World War II. The economic outlook is on the whole encouraging; but the growing prosperity is based on precarious foundations, and a serious setback is possible. A solution to the economic ailments of the world is difficult but not impossible. It is to the interests of America that her allies should be prosperous. Not only does this lessen the attractiveness of communism, but also makes it easier for them to carry the heavy burden of armament. As allies, they become more powerful and more reliable.

Policy toward the underdeveloped countries is an important phase of the economic problem. Here are states most of which have not yet committed themselves to either side in the cold war. Collectively they represent an impressive amount of power in terms of natural resources, population, and strategic importance. Whichever side can gain their allegiance will have won an important round in the contest for world power. Even if the underdeveloped areas remain neutral, this would be far preferable to their joining the Communist bloc. No single policy can solve all the problems. Armed force has its place, e.g., the Korean war and the Manila Pact. Material betterment and social services by themselves will not stop an invading army. Force, however, is no answer to the technique of the inside job, and at the present time the Communists are posing, with a good deal of success, as nationalists and agrarian reformers.

The Western powers have been trying to counteract the Communist influence by helping the governments of the underdeveloped areas to raise the standard of living through grants and loans and the provision of technical experts. The causes of the widespread poverty are not easy to remove. They include overpopulation, agricultural underproduction caused by out-of-date farming methods, inequitable systems of land tenure, excessive rates of interest on loans, absence of industrialization, and widespread illiteracy. Western assistance can alleviate some of these causes, though success is bound to be slow. Others—e.g., land tenures and high birth rate—are domestic questions where change must be left to the local governments. The Western governments need to spend very large amounts to produce much of an effect, and hitherto their financial aid has been on a moderate scale. There is general agreement that the bulk of the money will have to be provided by private investors. Whether they will do so depends on whether they believe they can make what they consider a satisfactory profit. In some countries, e.g., Turkey and Saudi Arabia, their judgment is favorable, and investments have been made. In others, e.g., Indonesia, the investors decline to risk their money and are trying to withdraw it. There is not a great deal that the Western governments can do to increase the flow of investment. They cannot dictate to their own citizens what they are to do with their private property. They can urge the Asian governments to provide greater security and more liberal terms to foreign capitalists, but this must be done with great caution. Given the hypernationalism and the fear of Western exploitation, any move which could be construed as dictation would play into the hands of the Communists. There are indications that the amount of aid furnished by the Western governments may be increased, but it is impossible to predict whether the inflow of capital will be large enough to make a radical change in the standard of living. Improvement is bound to be a slow process, and the local Communist parties will do their best to win control before economic betterment jeopardizes their chances. In the bulk of the underdeveloped areas the issue of the cold war is still in doubt.

PROPAGANDA

One great difficulty with propaganda is to determine which appeal will be most effective with each country, and each group within the country. This requires very careful study of the particular circumstances in each individual case. Arguments that would convince a European who had had personal experience of Communist rule would be wasted on an Asian who believed that his Communist fellow countrymen were merely patriotic reformers. In order to be effective the propagandist must think himself under the skin of each people whom he is trying to influence, until he can see the world as they see it. To quote one example out of many, Professor Fifield has investigated why the United States is not generally popular in Southeast Asia. Some of his reasons will come as a shock, but they illustrate the problems which the propagandist must solve. Many Asians feel that the Communists won the Korean war, and that it is better to be on the winning side. The United States is considered imperialistic because it supported colonialism in Indochina. The financial and technical assistance given to raise the standard of living is intervention in domestic affairs. The McCarthy controversy showed there is no freedom in the United States. America considers that every country that is not allied with her is against her. The talk about massive retaliation combined with the atom and hydrogen bomb tests in the Pacific aroused fear that America would launch an atomic war in Asia. It is not enough to reply that these charges are not justified by the facts. They are made by people who know little of the world outside them. It is they whom the propagandist has to influence, and in order to do that he must first understand their point of view. Propaganda is an effective weapon, but it has to be used skillfully.

THE FUTURE

This chapter may seem about as comforting as a dirge; but as far as can be ascertained, it is a factual presentation of the existing situation. The first necessity in international affairs is to free oneself from illusions. Wishful thinking and good intentions are no substitute for a clear appreciation of the facts. These are dangerous times, and there is no gain in behaving like an ostrich. In the end a settled world will emerge as it has after every time of transition. Of course, it is possible that the evolution will be short-circuited by hydrogen bombs. As against this, both East and West know that neither could escape, and this is a powerful deterrent. It is possible that in fifty years historians will write that the present age was on the eve of the abolition of war and did not realize it. Perils lie ahead, but there is no need to be despondent about them. This is not the first time that man has lived through a period of turbulence. It is encouraging to remember that the Soviet Union does not hold all the advantages, for if she had been sure of victory, there would have been war before now. It is as dangerous to overestimate one's opponent as to undervalue him. The West has the support of scores of millions who know what they fight for and love what they know. Its armed forces are formidable and growing. It has the superiority in industrialization, natural resources, wealth, and technical skill.

There is no quick or easy solution to the problem of coexistence with the Communist states, as long as they refuse to abandon their long range strategy of world communism. The West must steel itself to what may be a protracted struggle in many fields—military, political, economic, and psychological. There is the encouragement that Moscow also has its troubles, e.g., oil and food, and that it has profound respect for material strength. Then, too, this is not the first time that free nations have had to struggle against an aggressor with a lust for power. Thirteen hundred years ago the Arabs, newly converted to Islam, swept over Europe and the Middle East. They were driven on by a fanatical zeal to make converts and to win territory and plunder. Their conquests and their power were immense, but they were stopped by France and the Byzantine Empire. Eventually their religious zeal and their imperialism died down, and that danger passed. Other outbursts of crusading fervor followed the same pattern—the Christian Crusades of the middle ages, the European religious wars of the sixteenth century, and the Turkish conquests of the sixteenth and seventeenth centuries. One can hope that in the end the Communists will lose their fanatical imperialism when they have been forced to realize that they can go no further. The hope of the West is that it will be able to create peace through strength, and so bring about an altogether easier relationship all over the world. Then, to quote

Churchill, "We might even find ourselves in a few years moving along a broad, smooth causeway of peace and plenty instead of roaming and peering around on the rim of Hell."

SELECTED READING

BAILEY, SYDNEY B., *United Europe, A Short History of the Idea*. London: National News Letter, 162 Buckingham Palace Road, 1947.

BONN, M. J., *Whither Europe, Union or Partnership?* London: Cohen & West, 1952.

BOYD, A. F., *Western Union*. London: Hutchinson and Company, Ltd., 1948.

BRINTON, CRANE, *From Many One*. Cambridge: Harvard University Press, 1948.

COUDENHOVE-KALERGI, RICHARD N., *Crusade for Pan-Europe*. New York: G. P. Putnam's Sons, 1943.

CURTIS, LIONEL, *The Open Road to Freedom*. Oxford: Blackwell, 1950.

HAWTREY, R. G., *Western European Union: Implications for the United Kingdom*. New York: Royal Institute of International Affairs, 1949.

KOHN, HANS, *World Order in Historical Perspective*. Cambridge: Harvard University Press. 1943.

REYNAUD, PAUL, *Unite or Perish*. New York: Simon & Schuster, 1951.

SCHUMAN, FREDERICK L., *The Commonwealth of Man: An Inquiry into Power Politics and World Government*. New York: Alfred A. Knopf, 1952.

STREIT, CLARENCE K., *Union Now*. New York: Harper and Brothers, 1939.

WARD, BARBARA, *Policy for the West*. New York: W. W. Norton and Company, 1951.

APPENDIX

CHARTER OF THE UNITED NATIONS

We the peoples of the United Nations determined to save succeeding generations from the scourge of war, which twice in our lifetime has brought untold sorrow to mankind, and

to reaffirm faith in fundamental human rights, in the dignity and worth of the human person, in the equal rights of men and women and of nations large and small, and

to establish conditions under which justice and respect for the obligations arising from treaties and other sources of international law can be maintained, and

to promote social progress and better standards of life in larger freedom,

And for these ends

to practice tolerance and live together in peace with one another as good neighbors, and

to unite our strength to maintain international peace and security, and to ensure, by the acceptance of principles and the institution of methods, that armed force shall not be used, save in the common interest, and

to employ international machinery for the promotion of the economic and social advancement of all peoples,

Have resolved to combine our efforts to accomplish these aims.

Accordingly, our respective Governments, through representatives assembled in the city of San Francisco, who have exhibited their full powers found to be in good and due form, have agreed to the present Charter of the United Nations and do hereby establish an international organization to be known as the United Nations.

Chapter I: PURPOSES AND PRINCIPLES

Article 1

The Purposes of the United Nations are:

1. To maintain international peace and security, and to that end: to take effective collective measures for the prevention and removal of threats to the peace, and for the suppression of acts of aggression or other breaches of the peace, and to bring about by peaceful means, and in conformity with the principles of justice and international law, adjustment or settlement of international disputes or situations which might lead to a breach of the peace;

2. To develop friendly relations among nations based on respect for the principle of equal rights and self-determination of peoples, and to take other appropriate measures to strengthen universal peace;

3. To achieve international co-operation in solving international problems of an economic, social, cultural, or humanitarian character, and in promoting and encouraging respect for human rights and for fundamental freedoms for all with-

out distinction as to race, sex, language, or religion; and

4. To be a center for harmonizing the actions of nations in the attainment of these common ends.

Article 2

The Organization and its Members, in pursuit of the Purposes stated in Article 1, shall act in accordance with the following Principles.

1. The Organization is based on the principle of the sovereign equality of all its Members.

2. All Members, in order to ensure to all of them the rights and benefits resulting from membership, shall fulfil in good faith the obligations assumed by them in accordance with the present Charter.

3. All Members shall settle their international disputes by peaceful means in such a manner that international peace and security, and justice, are not endangered.

4. All Members shall refrain in their international relations from the threat or use of force against the territorial integrity or political independence of any state, or in any other manner inconsistent with the Purposes of the United Nations.

5. All Members shall give the United Nations every assistance in any action it takes in accordance with the present Charter, and shall refrain from giving assistance to any state against which the United Nations is taking preventive or enforcement action.

6. The Organization shall ensure that states which are not Members of the United Nations act in accordance with these Principles so far as may be necessary for the maintenance of international peace and security.

7. Nothing contained in the present Charter shall authorize the United Nations to intervene in matters which are essentially within the domestic jurisdiction of any state or shall require the Members to submit such matters to settlement under the present Charter; but this principle shall not prejudice the application of enforcement measures under Chapter VII.

Chapter II: MEMBERSHIP

Article 3

The original Members of the United Nations shall be the states which, having participated in the United Nations Conference on International Organization at San Francisco, or having previously signed the Declaration by United Nations of January 1, 1942, sign the present Charter and ratify it in accordance with Article 110.

Article 4

1. Membership in the United Nations is open to all other peace-loving states which accept the obligations contained in the present Charter and, in the judgment of the Organization, are able and willing to carry out these obligations.

2. The admission of any such state to membership in the United Nations will be effected by a decision of the General Assembly upon the recommendation of the Security Council.

Article 5

A Member of the United Nations against which preventive or enforcement action has been taken by the Security Council may be suspended from the exercise of the rights and privileges of membership by the General Assembly upon the recommendation of the Security Council. The exercise of these rights and privileges may be restored by the Security Council.

Article 6

A Member of the United Nations which has persistently violated the Principles contained in the present Charter may be expelled from the Organization by the General Assembly upon the recommendation of the Security Council.

Chapter III: ORGANS

Article 7

1. There are established as the principal organs of the United Nations; a

General Assembly, a Security Council, an Economic and Social Council, a Trusteeship Council, an International Court of Justice, and a Secretariat.

2. Such subsidiary organs as may be found necessary may be established in accordance with the present Charter.

Article 8

The United Nations shall place no restrictions on the eligibility of men and women to participate in any capacity and under conditions of equality in its principal and subsidiary organs.

Chapter IV: THE GENERAL ASSEMBLY

Composition

Article 9

1. The General Assembly shall consist of all the Members of the United Nations.

2. Each Member shall have not more than five representatives in the General Assembly.

Functions and Powers

Article 10

The General Assembly may discuss any questions or any matters within the scope of the present Charter or relating to the powers and functions of any organs provided for in the present Charter, and, except as provided in Article 12, may make recommendations to the Members of the United Nations or to the Security Council or to both on any such questions or matters.

Article 11

1. The General Assembly may consider the general principles of cooperation in the maintenance of international peace and security, including the principles governing disarmament and the regulation of armaments, and may make recommendations with regard to such principles to the Members or to the Security Council or to both.

2. The General Assembly may discuss any questions relating to the maintenance of international peace and security

brought before it by any Member of the United Nations, or by the Security Council, or by a state which is not a Member of the United Nations in accordance with Article 35, paragraph 2, and, except as provided in Article 12, may make recommendations with regard to any such questions to the state or states concerned or to the Security Council or to both. Any such question on which action is necessary shall be referred to the Security Council by the General Assembly either before or after discussion.

3. The General Assembly may call the attention of the Security Council to situations which are likely to endanger international peace and security.

4. The powers of the General Assembly set forth in this Article shall not limit the general scope of Article 10.

Article 12

1. While the Security Council is exercising in respect of any dispute or situation the functions assigned to it in the present Charter, the General Assembly shall not make any recommendation with regard to that dispute or situation unless the Security Council so requests.

2. The Secretary-General, with the consent of the Security Council, shall notify the General Assembly at each session of any matters relative to the maintenance of international peace and security which are being dealt with by the Security Council and shall similarly notify the General Assembly, or the Members of the United Nations if the General Assembly is not in session, immediately the Security Council ceases to deal with such matters.

Article 13

1. The General Assembly shall initiate studies and make recommendations for the purpose of:

a. promoting international co-operation in the political field and encouraging the progressive development of international law and its codification;

b. promoting international co-operation in the economic, social, cultural, educational, and health fields, and assisting in the realization of human rights and fundamental freedoms for all without distinction as to race, sex, language, or religion.

2. The further responsibilities, functions, and powers of the General Assembly with respect to matters mentioned in paragraph 1 (b) above are set forth in Chapters IX and X.

Article 14

Subject to the provisions of Article 12, the General Assembly may recommend measures for the peaceful adjustment of any situation, regardless of origin, which it deems likely to impair the general welfare or friendly relations among nations, including situations resulting from a violation of the provisions of the present Charter setting forth the Purposes and Principles of the United Nations.

Article 15

1. The General Assembly shall receive and consider annual and special reports from the Security Council; these reports shall include an account of the measures that the Security Council has decided upon or taken to maintain international peace and security.

2. The General Assembly shall receive and consider reports from the other organs of the United Nations.

Article 16

The General Assembly shall perform such functions with respect to the international trusteeship system as are assigned to it under Chapter XII and XIII, including the approval of the trusteeship agreements for areas not designated as strategic.

Article 17

1. The General Assembly shall consider and approve the budget of the Organization.

2. The expenses of the Organization shall be borne by the Members as apportioned by the General Assembly.

3. The General Assembly shall consider and approve any financial and budgetary arrangements with specialized agencies referred to in Article 57 and shall

examine the administrative budgets of such specialized agencies with a view to making recommendations to the agencies concerned.

Voting
Article 18

1. Each member of the General Assembly shall have one vote.

2. Decisions of the General Assembly on important questions shall be made by a two-thirds majority of the members present and voting. These questions shall include: recommendations with respect to the maintenance of international peace and security, the election of the non-permanent members of the Security Council, the election of the members of the Economic and Social Council, the election of members of the Trusteeship Council in accordance with paragraph 1 (c) of Article 86, the admission of new Members to the United Nations, the suspension of the rights and privileges of membership, the expulsion of Members, questions relating to the operation of the trusteeship system, and budgetary questions.

3. Decisions on other questions, including the determination of additional categories of questions to be decided by a two-thirds majority, shall be made by a majority of the members present and voting.

Article 19

A Member of the United Nations which is in arrears in the payment of its financial contributions to the Organization shall have no vote in the General Assembly if the amount of its arrears equals or exceeds the amount of the contributions due from it for the preceding two full years. The General Assembly may, nevertheless, permit such a Member to vote if it is satisfied that the failure to pay is due to conditions beyond the control of the Member.

Procedure
Article 20

The General Assembly shall meet in regular annual sessions and in such special sessions as occasion may require. Special sessions shall be convoked by the Secretary-General at the request of the Security Council or of a majority of the Members of the United Nations.

Article 21

The General Assembly shall adopt its own rules of procedure. It shall elect its President for each session.

Article 22

The General Assembly may establish such subsidiary organs as it deems necessary for the performance of its functions.

Chapter V: THE SECURITY COUNCIL

Composition
Article 23

1. The Security Council shall consist of eleven Members of the United Nations. The Republic of China, France, the Union of Soviet Socialist Republics, the United Kingdom of Great Britain and Northern Ireland, and the United States of America shall be permanent members of the Security Council. The General Assembly shall elect six other Members of the United Nations to be non-permanent members of the Security Council, due regard being specially paid, in the first instance to the contribution of Members of the United Nations to the maintenance of international peace and security and to the other purposes of the Organization, and also to equitable geographical distribution.

2. The non-permanent members of the Security Council shall be elected for a term of two years. In the first election of the non-permanent members, however, three shall be chosen for a term of one year. A retiring member shall not be eligible for immediate re-election.

3. Each member of the Security Council shall have one representative.

Functions and Powers
Article 24

1. In order to ensure prompt and effective action by the United Nations, its Mem-

bers confer on the Security Council primary responsibility for the maintenance of international peace and security, and agree that in carrying out its duties under this responsibility the Security Council acts on their behalf.

2. In discharging these duties the Security Council shall act in accordance with the Purposes and Principles of the United Nations. The specific powers granted to the Security Council for the discharge of these duties are laid down in Chapters VI, VII, VIII, and XII.

3. The Security Council shall submit annual and, when necessary, special reports to the General Assembly for its consideration.

Article 25

The Members of the United Nations agree to accept and carry out the decisions of the Security Council in accordance with the present Charter.

Article 26

In order to promote the establishment and maintenance of international peace and security with the least diversion for armaments of the world's human and economic resources, the Security Council shall be responsible for formulating, with the assistance of the Military Staff Committee referred to in Article 47, plans to be submitted to the Members of the United Nations for the establishment of a system for the regulation of armaments.

Voting
Article 27

1. Each member of the Security Council shall have one vote.

2. Decisions of the Security Council on procedural matters shall be made by an affirmative vote of seven members.

3. Decisions of the Security Council on all other matters shall be made by an affirmative vote of seven members including the concurring votes of the permanent members; provided that, in decisions under Chapter VI, and under paragraph 3 of Article 52, a party to a dispute shall abstain from voting.

Procedure

Article 28

1. The Security Council shall be so organized as to be able to function continuously. Each member of the Security Council shall for this purpose be represented at all times at the seat of the Organization.

2. The Security Council shall hold periodic meetings at which each of its members may, if it so desires, be represented by a member of the government or by some other specially designated representative.

3. The Security Council may hold meetings at such places other than the seat of the Organization as in its judgment will best facilitate its work.

Article 29

The Security Council may establish such subsidiary organs as it deems necessary for the performance of its functions.

Article 30

The Security Council shall adopt its own rules of procedure, including the method of selecting its President.

Article 31

Any Member of the United Nations which is not a member of the Security Council may participate, without vote, in the discussion of any question brought before the Security Council whenever the latter considers that the interests of that Member are specially affected.

Article 32

Any Member of the United Nations which is not a member of the Security Council or any state which is not a Member of the United Nations, if it is a party to a dispute under consideration by the Security Council, shall be invited to participate, without vote, in the discussion relating to the dispute. The Security Council shall lay down such conditions as it deems just for the participation of a state which is not a Member of the United Nations.

Chapter VI: PACIFIC SETTLEMENT OF DISPUTES

Article 33

1. The parties to any dispute, the continuance of which is likely to endanger the maintenance of international peace and security, shall, first of all, seek a solution by negotiation, enquiry, mediation, conciliation, arbitration, judicial settlement, resort to regional agencies or arrangements, or other peaceful means of their own choice.

2. The Security Council shall, when it deems necessary, call upon the parties to settle their dispute by such means.

Article 34

The Security Council may investigate any dispute, or any situation which might lead to international friction or give rise to a dispute, in order to determine whether the continuance of the dispute or situation is likely to endanger the maintenance of international peace and security.

Article 35

1. Any Member of the United Nations may bring any dispute, or any situation of the nature referred to in Article 34, to the attention of the Security Council or of the General Assembly.

2. A state which is not a Member of the United Nations may bring to the attention of the Security Council or of the General Assembly any dispute to which it is a party if it accepts in advance, for the purposes of the dispute, the obligations of pacific settlement provided in the present Charter.

3. The proceedings of the General Assembly in respect of matters brought to its attention under this Article will be subject to the provisions of Articles 11 and 12.

Article 36

1. The Security Council may, at any stage of a dispute of the nature referred to in Article 33 or of a situation of like nature, recommend appropriate procedures or methods of adjustment.

2. The Security Council should take

into consideration any procedures for the settlement of the dispute which have already been adopted by the parties.

3. In making recommendations under this Article the Security Council should also take into consideration that legal disputes should as a general rule be referred by the parties to the International Court of Justice in accordance with the provisions of the Statute of the Court.

Article 37

1. Should the parties to a dispute of the nature referred to in Article 33 fail to settle it by the means indicated in that Article, they shall refer it to the Security Council.

2. If the Security Council deems that the continuance of the dispute is in fact likely to endanger the maintenance of international peace and security, it shall decide whether to take action under Article 36 or to recommend such terms of settlement as it may consider appropriate.

Article 38

Without prejudice to the provisions of Articles 33 to 37, the Security Council may, if all the parties to any dispute so request, make recommendations to the parties with a view to a pacific settlement of the dispute.

Chapter VII: ACTION WITH RESPECT TO THREATS TO THE PEACE, BREACHES OF THE PEACE, AND ACTS OF AGGRESSION

Article 39

The Security Council shall determine the existence of any threat to the peace, breach of the peace, or act of aggression and shall make recommendations, or decide what measures shall be taken in accordance with Articles 41 and 42, to maintain or restore international peace and security.

Article 40

In order to prevent an aggravation of the situation, the Security Council may, before making the recommendations or deciding upon the measures provided for in Article 39, call upon the parties concerned to comply with such provisional measures as it deems necessary or desirable. Such provisional measures shall be without prejudice to the rights, claims, or position of the parties concerned. The Security Council shall duly take account of failure to comply with such provisional measures.

Article 41

The Security Council may decide what measures not involving the use of armed force are to be employed to give effect to its decisions, and it may call upon the Members of the United Nations to apply such measures. These may include complete or partial interruption of economic relations and of rail, sea, air, postal, telegraphic, radio, and other means of communication, and the severance of diplomatic relations.

Article 42

Should the Security Council consider that measures provided for in Article 41 would be inadequate or have proved to be inadequate, it may take such action by air, sea, or land forces as may be necessary to maintain or restore international peace and security. Such action may include demonstrations, blockade, and other operations by air, sea, or land forces of Members of the United Nations.

Article 43

1. All Members of the United Nations, in order to contribute to the maintenance of international peace and security, undertake to make available to the Security Council, on its call and in accordance with a special agreement or agreements, armed forces, assistance, and facilities, including rights of passage, necessary for the purpose of maintaining international peace and security.

2. Such agreement or agreements shall govern the numbers and types of forces, their degree of readiness and general location, and the nature of the facilities and assistance to be provided.

3. The agreement or agreements shall be negotiated as soon as possible on the initiative of the Security Council. They

shall be concluded between the Security Council and Members or between the Security Council and groups of Members and shall be subject to ratification by the signatory states in accordance with their respective constitutional processes.

Article 44

When the Security Council has decided to use force it shall, before calling upon a Member not represented on it to provide armed forces in fulfilment of the obligations assumed under Article 43, invite that Member, if the Member so desires, to participate in the decisions of the Security Council concerning the employment of contingents of that Member's armed forces.

Article 45

In order to enable the United Nations to take urgent military measures, Members shall hold immediately available national air-force contingents for combined international enforcement action. The strength and degree of readiness of these contingents and plans for their combined action shall be determined, within the limits laid down in the special agreement or agreements referred to in Article 43, by the Security Council with the assistance of the Military Staff Committee.

Article 46

Plans for the application of armed force shall be made by the Security Council with the assistance of the Military Staff Committee.

Article 47

1. There shall be established a Military Staff Committee to advise and assist the Security Council on all questions relating to the Security Council's military requirements for the maintenance of international peace and security, the employment and command of forces placed at its disposal, the regulation of armaments, and possible disarmament.

2. The Military Staff Committee shall consist of the Chiefs of Staff of the permanent members of the Security Council or their representatives. Any Member of the United Nations not permanently represented on the Committee shall be invited by the Committee to be associated with it when the efficient discharge of the Committee's responsibilities requires the participation of that Member in its work.

3. The Military Staff Committee shall be responsible under the Security Council for the strategic direction of any armed forces placed at the disposal of the Security Council. Questions relating to the command of such forces shall be worked out subsequently.

4. The Military Staff Committee, with the authorization of the Security Council and after consultation with appropriate regional agencies, may establish regional subcommittees.

Article 48

1. The action required to carry out the decisions of the Security Council for the maintenance of international peace and security shall be taken by all the Members of the United Nations or by some of them, as the Security Council may determine.

2. Such decisions shall be carried out by the Members of the United Nations directly and through their action in the appropriate international agencies of which they are members.

Article 49

The Members of the United Nations shall join in affording mutual assistance in carrying out the measures decided upon by the Security Council.

Article 50

If preventive or enforcement measures against any state are taken by the Security Council, any other state, whether a Member of the United Nations or not, which finds itself confronted with special economic problems arising from the carrying out of those measures shall have the right to consult the Security Council with regard to a solution of those problems.

Article 51

Nothing in the present Charter shall impair the inherent right of individual or collective self-defence if an armed attack occurs against a Member of the United Nations, until the Security Council has taken the measures necessary to maintain international peace and security. Measures taken by Members in the exercise of this right of self-defence shall be immediately reported to the Security Council and shall not in any way affect the authority and responsibility of the Security Council under the present Charter to take at any time such action as it deems necessary in order to maintain or restore international peace and security.

Chapter VIII: REGIONAL ARRANGEMENTS

Article 52

1. Nothing in the present Charter precludes the existence of regional arrangements or agencies for dealing with such matters relating to the maintenance of international peace and security as are appropriate for regional action, provided that such arrangements or agencies and their activities are consistent with the Purposes and Principles of the United Nations.

2. The Members of the United Nations entering into such arrangements or constituting such agencies shall make every effort to achieve pacific settlement of local disputes through such regional arrangements or by such regional agencies before referring them to the Security Council.

3. The Security Council shall encourage the development of pacific settlement of local disputes through such regional arrangements or by such regional agencies either on the initiative of the states concerned or by reference from the Security Council.

4. This Article in no way impairs the application of Articles 34 and 35.

Article 53

1. The Security Council shall, where appropriate, utilize such regional arrangements or agencies for enforcement action under its authority. But no enforcement action shall be taken under regional arrangements or by regional agencies without the authorization of the Security Council, with the exception of measures against any enemy state, as defined in paragraph 2 of this Article, provided for pursuant to Article 107 or in regional arrangements directed against renewal of aggressive policy on the part of any such state, until such time as the Organization may, on request of the Governments concerned, be charged with the responsibility for preventing further aggression by such a state.

2. The term enemy state as used in paragraph 1 of this Article applies to any state which during the Second World War has been an enemy of any signatory of the present Charter.

Article 54

The Security Council shall at all times be kept fully informed of activities undertaken or in contemplation under regional arrangements or by regional agencies for the maintenance of international peace and security.

Chapter IX: INTERNATIONAL ECONOMIC AND SOCIAL CO-OPERATION

Article 55

With a view to the creation of conditions of stability and well-being which are necessary for peaceful and friendly relations among nations based on respect for the principle of equal rights and self-determination of peoples, the United Nations shall promote:

a. higher standards of living, full employment, and conditions of economic and social progress and development;

b. solutions of international economic, social, health, and related problems; and international cultural and educational co-operation; and

c. universal respect for, and observance of, human rights and fundamental freedoms for all without distinction as to race, sex, language, or religion.

Article 56

All Members pledge themselves to take joint and separate action in co-operation with the Organization for the achievement of the purposes set forth in Article 55.

Article 57

1. The various specialized agencies, established by intergovernmental agreement and having wide international responsibilities, as defined in their basic instruments in economic, social, cultural, educational, health, and related fields, shall be brought into relationship with the United Nations in accordance with the provisions of Article 63.

2. Such agencies thus brought into relationship with the United Nations are hereinafter referred to as specialized agencies.

Article 58

The Organization shall make recommendations for the co-ordination of the policies and activities of the specialized agencies.

Article 59

The Organization shall, where appropriate, initiate negotiations among the states concerned for the creation of any new specialized agencies required for the accomplishment of the purposes set forth in Article 55.

Article 60

Responsibility for the discharge of the functions of the Organization set forth in this Chapter shall be vested in the General Assembly and, under the authority of the General Assembly, in the Economic and Social Council, which shall have for this purpose the powers set forth in Chapter X.

Chapter X: THE ECONOMIC AND SOCIAL COUNCIL

Composition

Article 61

1. The Economic and Social Council shall consist of eighteen Members of the United Nations elected by the General Assembly.

2. Subject to the provisions of paragraph 3, six members of the Economic and Social Council shall be elected each year for a term of three years. A retiring member shall be eligible for immediate re-election.

3. At the first election, eighteen members of the Economic and Social Council shall be chosen. The term of office of six members so chosen shall expire at the end of one year, and of six other members at the end of two years, in accordance with arrangements made by the General Assembly.

4. Each member of the Economic and Social Council shall have one representative.

Functions and Powers

Article 62

1. The Economic and Social Council may make or initiate studies and reports with respect to international economic, social, cultural, educational, health, and related matters and may make recommendations with respect to any such matters to the General Assembly, to the Members of the United Nations, and to the specialized agencies concerned.

2. It may make recommendations for the purpose of promoting respect for, and observance of, human rights and fundamental freedoms for all.

3. It may prepare draft conventions for submission to the General Assembly, with respect to matters falling within its competence.

4. It may call, in accordance with the rules prescribed by the United Nations, international conferences on matters falling within its competence.

Article 63

1. The Economic and Social Council may enter into agreements with any of the agencies referred to in Article 57, defining the terms on which the agency concerned shall be brought into relationship with the United Nations. Such agreements shall be subject to approval by the General Assembly.

2. It may co-ordinate the activities of the specialized agencies through consultation with and recommendations to

such agencies and through recommendations to the General Assembly and to the Members of the United Nations.

Article 64

1. The Economic and Social Council may take appropriate steps to obtain regular reports from the specialized agencies. It may make arrangements with the Members of the United Nations and with the specialized agencies to obtain reports on the steps taken to give effect to its own recommendations and to recommendations on matters falling within its competence made by the General Assembly.

2. It may communicate its observations on these reports to the General Assembly.

Article 65

The Economic and Social Council may furnish information to the Security Council and shall assist the Security Council upon its request.

Article 66

1. The Economic and Social Council shall perform such functions as fall within its competence in connection with the carrying out of the recommendations of the General Assembly.

2. It may, with the approval of the General Assembly, perform services at the request of Members of the United Nations and at the request of specialized agencies.

3. It shall perform such other functions as are specified elsewhere in the present Charter or as may be assigned to it by the General Assembly.

Voting
Article 67

1. Each member of the Economic and Social Council shall have one vote.

2. Decisions of the Economic and Social Council shall be made by a majority of the members present and voting.

Procedure
Article 68

The Economic and Social Council shall set up commissions in economic and

social fields and for the promotion of human rights, and such other commissions as may be required for the performance of its functions.

Article 69

The Economic and Social Council shall invite any Member of the United Nations to participate, without vote, in its deliberations on any matter of particular concern to that Member.

Article 70

The Economic and Social Council may make arrangements for representatives of the specialized agencies to participate, without vote, in its deliberations and in those of the commissions established by it, and for its representatives to participate in the deliberations of the specialized agencies.

Article 71

The Economic and Social Council may make suitable arrangements for consultation with non-governmental organizations which are concerned with matters within its competence. Such arrangements may be made with international organizations and, where appropriate, with national organizations after consultation with the Member of the United Nations concerned.

Article 72

1. The Economic and Social Council shall adopt its own rules of procedure, including the method of selecting its President.

2. The Economic and Social Council shall meet as required in accordance with its rules, which shall include provision for the convening of meetings on the request of a majority of its members.

Chapter XI: DECLARATION REGARDING NON-SELF-GOVERNING TERRITORIES

Article 73

Members of the United Nations which have or assume responsibilities for the administration of territories whose peoples have not yet attained a full measure of self-government recognize the principle that the interests of the inhabitants of these territories are paramount, and accept as a sacred trust the obligation to promote to the utmost, within the system of international peace and security established by the present Charter, the well-being of the inhabitants of these territories, and, to this end:

a. to ensure, with due respect for the culture of the peoples concerned, their political, economic, social, and educational advancement, their just treatment, and their protection against abuses:
b. to develop self-government, to take due account of the political aspirations of the peoples, and to assist them in the progressive development of their free political institutions, according to the particular circumstances of each territory and its peoples and their varying stages of advancement;
c. to further international peace and security;
d. to promote constructive measures of development, to encourage research, and to co-operate with one another and, when and where appropriate, with specialized international bodies with a view to the practical achievement of the social, economic, and scientific purposes set forth in this Article; and
e. to transmit regularly to the Secretary-General for information purposes, subject to such limitation as security and constitutional considerations may require, statistical and other information of a technical nature relating to economic, social, and educational conditions in the territories for which they are respectively responsible other than those territories to which Chapters XII and XIII apply.

Article 74

Members of the United Nations also agree that their policy in respect of the territories to which this Chapter applies, no less than in respect of their metropolitan areas, must be based on the general principle of good-neighborliness, due account being taken of the interests and well-being of the rest of the world, in social, economic, and commercial matters.

Chapter XII: INTERNATIONAL TRUSTEESHIP SYSTEM

Article 75

The United Nations shall establish under its authority an international trusteeship system for the administration and supervision of such territories as may be placed thereunder by subsequent individual agreements. These territories are hereinafter referred to as trust territories.

Article 76

The basic objectives of the trusteeship system, in accordance with the Purposes of the United Nations laid down in Article 1 of the present Charter, shall be:

a. to further international peace and security.
b. to promote the political, economic, social, and educational advancement of the inhabitants of the trust territories, and their progressive development towards self-government or independence as may be appropriate to the particular circumstances of each territory and its peoples and the freely expressed wishes of the peoples concerned, and as may be provided by the terms of each trusteeship agreement;
c. to encourage respect for human rights and for fundamental freedoms for all without distinction as to race, sex, language, or religion, and to encourage recognition of the interdependence of the peoples of the world; and
d. to ensure equal treatment in social, economic, and commercial matters for all Members of the United Nations and their nationals, and also equal treatment for the latter in the administration of justice, without prejudice to the attainment of the foregoing objectives and subject to the provisions of Article 80.

Article 77

1. The trusteeship system shall apply to such territories in the following cate-

gories as may be placed thereunder by means of trusteeship agreements;

a. territories now held under mandate;
b. territories which may be detached from enemy states as a result of the Second World War; and
c. territories voluntarily placed under the system by states responsible for their administration.

2. It will be a matter for subsequent agreement as to which territories in the foregoing categories will be brought under the trusteeship system and upon what terms.

Article 78

The trusteeship system shall not apply to territories which have become Members of the United Nations, relationship among which shall be based on respect for the principle of sovereign equality.

Article 79

The terms of trusteeship for each territory to be placed under the trusteeship system, including any alteration or amendment, shall be agreed upon by the states directly concerned, including the mandatory power in the case of territories held under mandate by a Member of the United Nations, and shall be approved as provided for in Articles 83 and 85.

Article 80

1. Except as may be agreed upon in individual trusteeship agreements, made under Articles 77, 79, and 81, placing each territory under the trusteeship system, and until such agreements have been concluded, nothing in this Chapter shall be construed in or of itself to alter in any manner the rights whatsoever of any states or any peoples or the terms of existing international instruments to which Members of the United Nations may respectively be parties.

2. Paragraph 1 of this Article shall not be interpreted as giving grounds for delay or postponement of the negotiation and conclusion of agreements for placing mandated and other territories under the trusteeship system as provided for in Article 77.

Article 81

The trusteeship agreement shall in each case include the terms under which the trust territory will be administered and designate the authority which will exercise the administration of the trust territory. Such authority, hereinafter called the administering authority, may be one or more states or the Organization itself.

Article 82

There may be designated, in any trusteeship agreement, a strategic area or areas which may include part or all of the trust territory to which the agreement applies, without prejudice to any special agreement or agreements made under Article 43.

Article 83

1. All functions of the United Nations relating to strategic areas, including the approval of the terms of the trusteeship agreements and of their alteration or amendment, shall be exercised by the Security Council.

2. The basic objectives set forth in Article 76 shall be applicable to the people of each strategic area.

3. The Security Council shall, subject to the provisions of the trusteeship agreements and without prejudice to security considerations, avail itself of the assistance of the Trusteeship Council to perform those functions of the United Nations under the trusteeship system relating to political, economic, social, and educational matters in the strategic areas.

Article 84

It shall be the duty of the administering authority to ensure that the trust territory shall play its part in the maintenance of international peace and security. To this end the administering authority may make use of volunteer forces, facilities, and assistance from the trust territories in carrying out the obligations toward the Security Council undertaken in th regard by the administering authority, as well as for local defence and the maintenance of law and order within the trust territory.

Article 85

1. The functions of the United Nations with regard to trusteeship agreements for all areas not designated as strategic, including the approval of the terms of the trusteeship agreements and of their alteration or amendment, shall be exercised by the General Assembly.

2. The trusteeship Council, operating under the authority of the General Assembly, shall assist the General Assembly in carrying out these functions.

Chapter XIII: THE TRUSTEESHIP COUNCIL

Composition
Article 86

1. The Trusteeship Council shall consist of the following Members of the United Nations:

a. those Members administering trust territories;
b. such of those Members mentioned by name in Article 23 as are not administering trust territories; and
c. as many other Members elected for three-year terms by the General Assembly as may be necessary to ensure that the total number of members of the Trusteeship Council is equally divided between those Members of the United Nations which administer trust territories and those which do not.

2. Each member of the Trusteeship Council shall designate one specially qualified person to represent it therein.

Functions and Powers
Article 87

The General Assembly and, under its authority, the Trusteeship Council, in carrying out their functions, may:

a. consider reports submitted by the administering authority;
b. accept petitions and examine them in consultation with the administering authority;
c. provide for periodic visits to the respective trust territories at times agreed upon with the administering authority; and
d. take these and other actions in conformity with the terms of the trusteeship agreements.

Article 88

The Trusteeship Council shall formulate a questionnaire on the political, economic, social, and educational advancement of the inhabitants of each trust territory, and the administering authority for each trust territory within the competence of the General Assembly shall make an annual report to the General Assembly upon the basis of such questionnaire.

Voting
Article 89

1. Each member of the Trusteeship Council shall have one vote.

2. Decisions of the Trusteeship Council shall be made by a majority of the members present and voting.

Procedure
Article 90

1. The Trusteeship Council shall adopt its own rules of procedure, including the method of selecting its President.

2. The Trusteeship Council shall meet as required in accordance with its rules, which shall include provision for the convening of meetings on the request of a majority of its members.

Article 91

The Trusteeship Council shall, when appropriate, avail itself of the assistance of the Economic and Social Council and of the specialized agencies in regard to matters with which they are respectively concerned.

Chapter XIV: THE INTERNATIONAL COURT OF JUSTICE

Article 92

The International Court of Justice shall be the principal judicial organ of the United Nations. It shall function in accordance with the annexed Statute, which is based upon the Statute of the Permanent Court of International Justice and forms an integral part of the present Charter.

Article 93

1. All Members of the United Nations are *ipso facto* parties to the Statute of the International Court of Justice.

2. A state which is not a Member of the United Nations may become a party to the Statute of the International Court of Justice on conditions to be determined in each case by the General Assembly upon the recommendation of the Security Council.

Article 94

1. Each Member of the United Nations undertakes to comply with the decision of the International Court of Justice in any case to which it is a party.

2. If any party to a case fails to perform the obligations incumbent upon it under a judgment rendered by the Court, the other party may have recourse to the Security Council, which may, if it deems necessary, make recommendations or decide upon measures to be taken to give effect to the judgment.

Article 95

Nothing in the present Charter shall prevent Members of the United Nations from entrusting the solution of their differences to other tribunals by virtue of agreements already in existence or which may be concluded in the future.

Article 96

1. The General Assembly or the Security Council may request the Interna-tional Court of Justice to give an advisory opinion on any legal question.

2. Others organs of the United Nations and specialized agencies, which may at any time be so authorized by the General Assembly, may also request advisory opinions of the Court on legal questions arising within the scope of their activities.

Chapter XV: THE SECRETARIAT

Article 97

The Secretariat shall comprise a Secretary-General and such staff as the Organization may require. The Secretary-General shall be appointed by the General Assembly upon the recommendation of the Security Council. He shall be the chief administrative officer of the Organization.

Article 98

The Secretary-General shall act in that capacity in all meetings of the General Assembly, of the Security Council, of the Economic and Social Council, and of the Trusteeship Council, and shall perform such other functions as are entrusted to him by these organs. The Secretary-General shall make an annual report to the General Assembly on the work of the Organization.

Article 99

The Secretary-General may bring to the attention of the Security Council any matter which in his opinion may threaten the maintenance of international peace and security.

Article 100

1. In the performance of their duties the Secretary-General and the staff shall not seek or receive instructions from any government or from any other authority external to the Organization. They shall refrain from any action which might reflect on their position as international officials responsible only to the Organization.

2. Each Member of the United Na-

tions undertakes to respect the exclusively international character of the responsibilities of the Secretary-General and the staff and not to seek to influence them in the discharge of their responsibilities.

Article 101

1. The staff shall be appointed by the Secretary-General under regulations established by the General Assembly.

2. Appropriate staffs shall be permanently assigned to the Economic and Social Council, the Trusteeship Council, and, as required, to other organs of the United Nations. These staffs shall form a part of the Secretariat.

3. The paramount consideration in the employment of the staff and in the determination of the conditions of service shall be the necessity of securing the highest standards of efficiency, competence and integrity. Due regard shall be paid to the importance of recruiting the staff on as wide a geographical basis as possible.

Chapter XVI: MISCELLANEOUS PROVISIONS

Article 102

1. Every treaty and every international agreement entered into by any Member of the United Nations after the present Charter comes into force shall as soon as possible be registered with the Secretariat and published by it.

2. No party to any such treaty or international agreement which has not been registered in accordance with the provisions of paragraph 1 of this Article may invoke that treaty or agreement before any organ of the United Nations.

Article 103

In the event of a conflict between the obligations of the Members of the United Nations under the present Charter and their obligations under any other international agreement, their obligations under the present Charter shall prevail.

Article 104

The Organization shall enjoy in the territory of each of its Members such legal capacity as may be necessary for the exercise of its functions and the fulfilment of its purposes.

Article 105

1. The Organization shall enjoy in the territory of each of its Members such privileges and immunities as are necessary for the fulfilment of its purposes.

2. Representatives of the Members of the United Nations and officials of the Organization shall similarly enjoy such privileges and immunities as are necessary for the independent exercise of their functions in connection with the Organization.

3. The General Assembly may make recommendations with a view to determining the details of the application of paragraphs 1 and 2 of this Article or may propose conventions to the Members of the United Nations for this purpose.

Chapter XVII: TRANSITIONAL SECURITY ARRANGEMENTS

Article 106

Pending the coming into force of such special agreements referred to in Article 43 as in the opinion of the Security Council enable it to begin the exercise of its responsibilities under Article 42, the parties to the Four-Nation Declaration, signed at Moscow, October 30, 1943, and France, shall, in accordance with the provisions of paragraph 5 of that Declaration, consult with one another and as occasion requires with other Members of the United Nations with a view to such joint action on behalf of the Organization as may be necessary for the purpose of maintaining international peace and security.

Article 107

Nothing in the present Charter shall invalidate or preclude action, in relation to any state which during the Second World War has been an enemy of any signatory to the present Charter, taken or authorized as a result of that war by the Governments having responsibility for such action.

Chapter XVIII: AMENDMENTS

Article 108

Amendments to the present Charter shall come into force for all Members of the United Nations when they have been adopted by a vote of two-thirds of the members of the General Assembly and ratified in accordance with their respective constitutional processes by two-thirds of the Members of the United Nations, including all the permanent members of the Security Council.

Article 109

1. A General Conference of the Members of the United Nations for the purpose of reviewing the present Charter may be held at a date and place to be fixed by a two-thirds vote of the members of the General Assembly and by a vote of any seven members of the Security Council. Each Member of the United Nations shall have one vote in the conference.

2. Any alteration of the present Charter recommended by a two-thirds vote of the conference shall take effect when ratified in accordance with their respective constitutional processes by two-thirds of the Members of the United Nations including all the permanent members of the Security Council.

3. If such a conference has not been held before the tenth annual session of the General Assembly following the coming into force of the present Charter, the proposal to call such a conference shall be placed on the agenda of that session of the General Assembly, and the conference shall be held if so decided by a majority vote of the members of the General Assembly and by a vote of any seven members of the Security Council.

Chapter XIX: RATIFICATION AND SIGNATURE

Article 110

1. The present Charter shall be ratified by the signatory states in accordance with their respective constitutional processes.

2. The ratifications shall be deposited with the Government of the United States of America, which shall notify all the signatory states of each deposit as well as the Secretary-General of the Organization when he has been appointed.

3. The present Charter shall come into force upon the deposit of ratifications by the Republic of China, France, the Union of Soviet Socialist Republics, the United Kingdom of Great Britain and Northern Ireland, and the United States of America, and by a majority of the other signatory states. A protocol of the ratifications deposited shall thereupon be drawn up by the Government of the United States of America which shall communicate copies thereof to all the signatory states.

4. The states signatory to the present Charter which ratify it after it has come into force will become original Members of the United Nations on the date of the deposit of their respective ratifications.

Article 111

The present Charter, of which the Chinese, French, Russian, English, and Spanish texts are equally authentic, shall remain deposited in the archives of the Government of the United States of America. Duly certified copies thereof shall be transmitted by that Government to the Governments of the other signatory states.

In faith whereof the representatives of the Governments of the United Nations have signed the present Charter.

Done at the city of San Francisco the twenty-sixth day of June, one thousand nine hundred and forty-five.

NORTH ATLANTIC TREATY, APRIL 4, 1949

PREAMBLE

The Parties to this Treaty reaffirm their faith in the purposes and principles of the Charter of the United Nations and their desire to live in peace with all peoples and all governments.

They are determined to safeguard the freedom, common heritage and civilization of their peoples, founded on the principles of democracy, individual liberty and the rule of law.

They seek to promote stability and well-being in the North Atlantic area.

They are resolved to unite their efforts for collective defence and for the preservation of peace and security.

They therefore agree to this North Atlantic Treaty:

Article 1

The Parties undertake, as set forth in the Charter of the United Nations, to settle any international disputes in which they may be involved by peaceful means in such a manner that international peace and security, and justice, are not endangered, and to refrain in their international relations from the threat or use of force in any manner inconsistent with the purposes of the United Nations.

Article 2

The Parties will contribute toward the further development of peaceful and friendly international relations by strengthening their free institutions, by bringing about a better understanding of the principles upon which these institutions are founded, and by promoting conditions of stability and well-being. They will seek to eliminate conflict in their international economic policies and will encourage economic collaboration between any or all of them.

Article 3

In order more effectively to achieve the objectives of this Treaty, the Parties, separately and jointly, by means of continuous and effective self-help and mutual aid, will maintain and develop their individual and collective capacity to resist armed attack.

Article 4

The Parties will consult together whenever, in the opinion of any of them, the territorial integrity, political independence or security of any of the Parties is threatened.

Article 5

The Parties agree that an armed attack against one or more of them in Europe or North America shall be considered an attack against them all; and consequently they agree that, if such an armed attack occurs, each of them, in exercise of the right of individual or collective self-defence recognized by Article 51 of the Charter of the United Nations, will assist the Party or Parties so attacked by taking forthwith, individually and in concert with the other Parties, such action as it deems necessary, including the use of armed force, to restore and maintain the security of the North Atlantic area.

Any such armed attack and all measures taken as a result thereof shall immediately be reported to the Security Council. Such measures shall be terminated when the Security Council has taken the measures necessary to restore and maintain international peace and security.

Article 6

For the purpose of Article 5 an armed attack on one or more of the Parties is deemed to include an armed attack on the territory of any of the Parties in Europe or North America, on the Algerian departments of France, on the occupation forces of any Party in Europe, on the islands under the jurisdiction of any Party in the North Atlantic area north of the Tropic of Cancer or on the vessels or aircraft in this area of any of the Parties.

Article 7

This Treaty does not affect, and shall not be interpreted as affecting, in any way the rights and obligations under the Charter of the Parties which are members of the United Nations, or the primary responsibility of the Security Council for the maintenance of international peace and security.

Article 8

Each Party declares that none of the international engagements now in force between it and any other of the Parties or any third state is in conflict with the provisions of this Treaty, and undertakes not to enter into any international engagement in conflict with this Treaty.

Article 9

The Parties hereby establish a council, on which each of them shall be represented, to consider matters concerning the implementation of this Treaty. The council shall be so organized as to be able to meet promptly at any time. The Council shall set up such subsidiary bodies as may be necessary; in particular it shall establish immediately a defence committee which shall recommend measures for the implementation of Articles 3 and 5.

Article 10

The Parties may, by unanimous agreement, invite any other European state in a position to further the principles of this Treaty and to contribute to the security of the North Atlantic area to accede to this Treaty. Any state so invited may become a party to the Treaty by depositing its instrument of accession with the Government of the United States of America. The Government of the United States of America will inform each of the Parties of the deposit of each such instrument of accession.

Article 11

This Treaty shall be ratified and its provisions carried out by the Parties in accordance with their respective constitutional processes. The instruments of ratification shall be deposited as soon as possible with the Government of the United States of America, which will notify all the other signatories of each deposit. The Treaty shall enter into force between the states which have ratified it as soon as the ratifications of the majority of the signatories, including the ratifications of Belgium, Canada, France, Luxembourg, the Netherlands, the United Kingdom and the United States, have been deposited and shall come into effect with respect to other states on the date of the deposit of their ratifications.

Article 12

After the Treaty has been in force for ten years, or at any time thereafter, the Parties shall, if any of them so requests, consult together for the purpose of reviewing the Treaty, having regard for the factors then affecting peace and security in the North Atlantic area, including the development of universal as well as regional arrangements under the Charter of the United Nations for the maintenance of international peace and security.

Article 13

After the Treaty has been in force for twenty years, any Party may cease to be a Party one year after its notice of denunciation has been given to the Government of the United States of America, which will inform the Governments of other Parties of the deposit of each notice of denunciation.

Article 14

This Treaty, of which the English and French texts are equally authentic, shall be deposited in the archives of the Government of the United States of America. Duly certified copies thereof will be transmitted by that Government to the Governments of the other signatories.

In witness whereof, the undersigned plenipotentiaries have signed this Treaty.

Done at Washington, the fourth day of April, 1949.

INDEX